Advanced Praise for Inside LightWave 8

"Dan's been around for a long time and knows his LightWave inside and out. I've turned to his books for years to get answers and will continue to do so. Come to think of it, I've also been lending them for years. They're developing a nasty habit of not turning back up."

—**Aram Granger**, Emmy Award Winner, Zoic Studios

"I won't consider LightWave 8 officially released until Dan Ablan's *Inside LightWave 8* hits the shelves."

—**Dave Adams**, Digital Domain—Feature Division

"Within the walls of every studio where I have used LightWave on a commercial, feature film, television show or documentary, I have seen Dan Ablan's teaching materials scattered on desks or bookshelves. If seeing Dan's training material time after time and year after year being used by people who already have jobs doesn't speak for itself, then I don't know what does."

—**Peter D Hunt**, vfx artist

"Anything can be learned—even something as scary looking as LightWave. With Dan Ablan's *Inside LightWave*, it's not so scary. Just start with page one, and soon you'll be making models and animations with the best of 'em!"

—**Hunter Wolf**, CEO DIEHARD Studio (www.diehardstudio.com)

"When I was learning the software, Dan's books were a tremendous help in smoothing the learning curve. As LightWave has been rebuilt over the years, Dan Ablan's books are still a great resource for taking the mystery out of the new tools. Great for beginners and pros alike, you can't go wrong with a Dan Ablan release."

—**Kyle Toucher**, Senior Visual Effects Artist, Zoic Studios

"*Inside LightWave* is a must for any professional artist who uses LightWave 3D or any hobbyist who hopes to make it a profession. Dan's books helped me get to where I am now and get me where I want to go."

—**John McGinley**, Emmy-Nominated VFX Artist

"I am currently employed as a civilian for the U.S. Navy. My daily challenges would be so much greater if it weren't for Dan Ablan and his *Inside LightWave* books. Dan's books are always on hand in our multimedia department for quick reference, which results in immediate resolve to a lot of questions and problems that we experience daily. The *Inside LightWave* books are simply the best and save the U.S. Government time and money!"

—**Ted Domek**, CG Artist/Visual Information Specialist (www.teddomek.com)

"*Inside LightWave 8* takes Dan's series of *Inside LightWave* books to a new level, with all new, amazing, step-by-step instructions, written in an easy-to-read format. Dan really has a way of explaining even the most technical aspects of LightWave in a fun and easy-to-learn way. I always know I'll walk away a better 3D artist once I've been through one of Dan's books, and this is no exception."

—**William "Proton" Vaughan**, NewTek's LightWave 3D Evangelist

INSIDE LIGHTWAVE® 8

BY
Daniel M. Ablan

New Riders

1249 Eighth Street, Berkeley, CA 94710
An Imprint of Peachpit Press

Inside LightWave® 8

International Standard Book Number: 0-7357-1368-5

Library of Congress Catalog Card Number: 2004103766

Printed in the United States of America

First Printing: June 2004

07 06 05 04   7 6 5 4 3 2

Trademarks

All terms mentioned in this book that are known to be trademarks or service marks have been appropriately capitalized. New Riders Publishing cannot attest to the accuracy of this information. Use of a term in this book should not be regarded as affecting the validity of any trademark or service mark.

LightWave 3D is a registered trademark of NewTek.

Warning and Disclaimer

Every effort has been made to make this book as complete and as accurate as possible, but no warranty of fitness is implied. The information provided is on an "as is" basis. The authors and the publisher shall have neither liability nor responsibility to any person or entity with respect to any loss or damages arising from the information contained in this book or from the use of the DVD or programs accompanying it.

Publisher
Nancy Ruenzel

Production Manager
Gina Kanouse

Acquisitions Editor
Elise Walter

Development Editor
Chris Zahn

Senior Project Editor
Lori Lyons

Copy Editors
Kelli Brooks
Ben Lawson

Indexer
Brad Herriman

Composition
Amy Hassos

Proofreader
Sheri Cain

Manufacturing Coordinator
Dan Uhrig

Cover Designer
Aren Howell

Marketing
Scott Cowlin
Tammy Detrich

Publicity Manager
Susan Nixon

Media Developer
Jay Payne

Contents at a Glance

Table of Contents

About the Author

Dan Ablan is president of AGA Digital Studios, Inc., a 3D animation and visual effects company in the Chicago area. AGA Digital has produced 3D visuals for broadcast, corporate, and architectural clients since 1994, as well as offered post-production services in conjunction with Post Meridian, LLC. Dan is the author of five best-selling international LightWave 3D books from New Riders Publishing: *LightWave Power Guide* (v5.0), *Inside LightWave 3D* (v5.5), *Inside LightWave [6]*, *LightWave 6.5 Effects Magic, Inside LightWave 7,* and the co-author of *LightWave 8 Killer Tips*. He also is the author of *[digital] Cinematography & Directing,* and served as technical editor for *[digital] Lighting & Rendering*. Dan was a contributor to another New Riders book, *After Effects 5.5 Magic.*

Dan is also the founder of 3D Garage.com (www.3dgarage.com), a website dedicated to LightWave 3D learning and LightWave 3D sales. 3D Garage is owned and operated by AGA Digital Studios, Inc. and offers high-quality CD-ROM based LightWave courseware. AGA Digital Studios, Inc. is a NewTek-authorized LightWave training facility and reseller. Dan Ablan has released an ongoing series of training videos through *Class on Demand* (www.classondemand.net) and has written columns and articles for *LightWave Pro* magazine, *Video Toaster User* magazine, *3D Design* magazine, *3D World* magazine, and *NewTek Pro* magazine. Dan has been teaching LightWave seminars since 1995 across the country and at AGA Digital Studios, Inc. He also travels the country for personal training at television stations and corporations.

In addition to his daily duties at AGA Digital Studios, Inc., Dan Ablan is the Editor-in-Chief of *Keyframe Magazine* (www.keyframemag.com). *Keyframe* is a magazine dedicated to animation and digital imaging.

About the Contributors

Chris Golchert holds an Associate Applied Arts degree in Computer Art/Animation from The Art Institute of Dallas. He has worked as a Technical Director at DNA Productions, as Character Technical Director at Neutronium, and as Lead Animator/Technical Director at NT Media. His project credits include *Villisca: Living with a Mystery*, *BarnYard*, *Jingaroo*, and *Jimmy Neutron: Boy Genius*, which received an Oscar® nomination for best-animated feature. In addition to his technical review of this book, Chris also wrote Chapter 14, "Enhanced Textures and Environments."

William "Proton" Vaughan is a seasoned LightWave veteran, currently working for the makers of LightWave 3D, NewTek, Inc. in San Antonio, Texas. William is NewTek's LightWave 3D Evangelist. Not only does he love working in LightWave and promoting it around the globe for NewTek, he is also the recipient of several New Media Addy awards. William brings broad-based experience to his position at NewTek, having done 3D work for print, web, multimedia, games, and broadcast. Over the past ten years, Vaughan has established a strong reputation for his award-winning work for clients such as Compaq, New Line Cinema, Halliburton, and many others.

He has also worked in the LightWave community as an instructor at North Harris Community College. Vaughan's other activities in LightWave user education include training companies such as NASA, Fulbright & Jaworski, and KHOU Channel 11, the CBS affiliate in Houston. William contributed Chapter 10, "Modeling Quadrupedal Characters."

Matt Gorner is an industrial designer from the UK who started his design career in 1996 after graduating with an honors degree from the Consumer Product Design course at Coventry University. During that time he worked in many market sectors ranging from simple house-wares to high-speed train interiors, working for various clients in the UK as well as overseas in Japan, Hong Kong, and France.

Throughout his career Matt has been using LightWave to visualize and animate the products he designs. In more recent years Matt has also become an active community member, offering help and advice where he can; he praises the strong sense of community as one of LightWave's hidden features! Matt contributed the ScreamerNet information in Chapter 21, "Rendering and ScreamerNet." Contact Matt at matt@creactive-design.co.uk.

About the Technical Reviewers

These reviewers contributed their considerable hands-on expertise to the entire development process for *Inside LightWave 8*. As the book was being written, these dedicated professionals reviewed all the material for technical content, organization, and flow. Their feedback was critical to ensuring that *Inside LightWave 8* fits our readers' need for the highest-quality technical information.

Jack "Deuce" Bennett is a freelance CGI artist, whose background is in physical special effects for motion pictures and television, as well as military visualizations. Deuce has been working in the film industry his entire life and has such movies as *Robocop*, *Lonesome Dove*, and *Jimmy Neutron: Boy Genius* to his credit, as well as TV shows such as *Walker, Texas Ranger*. Deuce has been using computers since he was nine, and he started off writing his own graphic programs. He is a unique combination of physical knowledge and virtual know-how.

Chris Golchert holds an Associate Applied Arts degree in Computer Art/Animation from The Art Institute of Dallas. He has worked as a Technical Director at DNA Productions, as Character Technical Director at Neutronium, and as Lead Animator/Technical Director at NT Media. His project credits include *Villisca: Living with a Mystery*, *BarnYard*, *Jingaroo*, and *Jimmy Neutron: Boy Genius*, which received an Oscar® nomination for best-animated feature.

Dedication

For Amelia. You're the best little render an animator could ask for.

Acknowledgments

I cannot express my gratitude to my friend, Deuce. He, in many ways, has made this book possible. Without his help and sincere friendship, this book would be nothing more than a paperweight. Thanks, Deuce, for all of your help and direction.

Thank you to Chris Golchert and NewTek's William Vaughan for stepping in at the last minute to add their expertise and diversity to this book. Your additions helped keep us on schedule and gave the reader a wider viewpoint. Thanks guys!

Of course, I'd probably still be writing this tome at this very moment if it weren't for Elise Walter and Chris Zahn. My daily reminders of deadlines past kept me on my toes. Thanks to you both for your continued encouragement and nagging…uh, I mean… support, in getting this book written! To the New Riders team, thank you Associate Publisher Stephanie Wall for yet another great opportunity! The group at New Riders is the best around, and all you: Gina Kanouse, Lori Lyons, Kelli Brooks, Ben Lawson, Brad Herriman, Amy Hassos, Jennifer Eberhardt, Dan Uhrig, Aren Howell, Scott Cowlin, Tammy Detrich, Susan Nixon, and Jay Payne all deserve my gratitude for putting the polish on this book.

To the team at NewTek—Deuce, William, Donetta, Jim, and of course Chuck Baker— you guys have been a tremendous help to this book. Your efforts and support are sincerely appreciated. The LightWave 8 development team is often left in the shadows, but I know how hard you've worked getting this new, and clearly the best version of LightWave out the door. Congrats to all of you, and thanks!

To my wonderful wife, Maria. Your support while writing two books back to back has been amazing. I can't thank you enough for everything you do. You're the best.

Finally, to all LightWave users around the globe who read my books and use my training materials—thanks. Your feedback, on all levels, is greatly appreciated. All of you are the reason I lose sleep writing these books, so keep in touch and let me know what you'd like to see in future versions.

Tell Us What You Think

As the reader of this book, you are our most important critic and commentator. We value your opinion and want to know what we're doing right, what we could do better, in what areas you'd like to see us publish, and any other words of wisdom you're willing to pass our way.

When you contact us, please be sure to include this book's title, ISBN, and author, as well as your name and email address. We will carefully review your comments and share them with the authors and editors who worked on the book.

Email: errata@peachpit.com

Visit Our Website: www.peachpit.com

On our Web site, you'll find information about our other books, the authors we partner with, book updates and file downloads, promotions, discussion boards for online interaction with other users and with technology experts, and a calendar of trade shows and other professional events with which we'll be involved. We hope to see you around.

Email Us from Our Website

Go to www.peachpit.com and click on the Contact Us link if you

- Have comments or questions about this book.
- Want to report errors that you have found in this book.
- Have a book proposal or are interested in writing for New Riders.
- Would like us to send you one of our author kits.
- Are an expert in a computer topic or technology and are interested in being a reviewer or technical editor.
- Want to find a distributor for our titles in your area.
- Are an educator/instructor who wants to preview New Riders/Peachpit Press books for classroom use. In the body/comments area, include your name, school, department, address, phone number, office days/hours, text currently in use, and enrollment in your department, along with your request for either desk/examination copies or additional information.

Visit Dan Ablan's Websites

Dan Ablan keeps regular websites for book information at www.danablan.com. For continued LightWave learning courseware visit www.3dgarage.com. For up-to-date info on all of Dan's books, including Inside LightWave errata, please check these links.

Introduction

Welcome to the next installment of Inside LightWave. This book represents more than seven years of LightWave books written and published by myself, a few good friends, and New Riders Publishing. Inside books—a staple in the ever-growing digital image creation industry and your own personal library—are present in bookstores and online retailers around the globe. I personally want to thank you for your continued support, suggestions, and comments, which have helped make this new version of *Inside LightWave* the best the series has ever seen. To give you the most complete and up-to-date information, *Inside LightWave 8* was written in conjunction with the development of the LightWave 8 software from NewTek, Inc. No other book can offer you as much comprehensive information. With *Inside LightWave 8*, you will take your favorite 3D application to the next level. LightWave 8 is a major release for NewTek, Inc., and I've made this book as informative as possible while keeping it more organized and to the point. This is a completely new book, written from the ground up! Every tutorial and task you will create is better than before with straightforward explanations. Every project and tip will give you a clear and concise understanding of the powerhouse of tools LightWave 8 has to offer through simple and easy-to-follow tutorials.

Getting the Most from *Inside LightWave 8*

Although we have a set format for the *Inside* books, I had a situation while planning this book that forced me to change things a bit. I was at my favorite Borders bookstore in Chicago, looking for ideas to create a cool and modern website. Using my suite of tools from Macromedia and Adobe Photoshop 7, I had built a decent website but I still needed some excitement. Perhaps some of those cool animated Macromedia Flash header bars, some cool animated buttons, and a few little gizmos to spice up the site. But I found that there wasn't a book that just showed me how to do what I wanted. All the books I looked at were good, informative, well thought-out, and so on. But I just wanted to get going! I didn't want to sift through page after page of making curves and animating little clip art bumblebees and the like. This experience got me thinking! Afterward, I went back to the office and jotted down some notes on how I wanted to refocus the *Inside LightWave 8* book.

The formula for the *Inside* books has worked well for the past few years, and I don't want to change that. Many of the long-time readers look for this same format because of its proven track record. However, I did not want you to be in the situation I was in, especially when trying to learn a complex 3D application, not just a web-creation program. Therefore, I've put together the *Inside LightWave 8* "Quick-Start" for Chapter 1. This is a not-too-involved type of tutorial that will get you up and running with LightWave 8. It's at the beginning of this book, and I encourage you to run through these few pages to see what LightWave 8 is all about. This quick-start certainly doesn't inform you about all the tools and features in this new version, but it does help familiarize you with the software and its workflow. Then, you can move into the chapters and learn about the panels, modeling, texturing, layout, animation, and rendering.

About the Creation of This Book

Inside LightWave 8 was written entirely on Dell Inspiron 8500 and 9100 laptop computer. This is a testament to the performance of computer systems in today's marketplace, as many desktop systems couldn't support 3D applications a few years ago. The system used to write this book runs the Windows XP Professional operating system from Microsoft. It has a 2.5GHz (3.2Ghz on the 9100). Pentium 4 processor with 1GB of DDR Memory. The nVidia GeForce 64 MB mobile video card helped speed through the animation setup with blazing fast OpenGL graphics. For Macintosh users, tutorials written were tested on both an Apple iMac with 256MB of RAM and an Apple G4 733MHz with 1GB of RAM, both running the OS X 10.2 operating system (Jaguar). There are few differences between LightWave on the Mac and LightWave on Windows. The biggest difference is the use of a three-button mouse. If you are a Mac user, you should be aware that a Mac only comes with a one-button mouse. This is unfortunate because many programs, even the Mac operating system itself, employ right-mouse button functions. I highly recommend you get a two- or three-button mouse if you're working on the Mac—this will benefit you greatly working in LightWave 8 as well as other programs. The Logitech-brand optical mice work well from my experience. For you Mac users who cannot part with the one-button mouse, simply hold your Apple key in conjunction with the mouse button to achieve right-mouse button functions. We'll provide reminders to you throughout this book.

I used a Windows XP system to run LightWave and write this book simply because the PC systems at the time of writing had better video graphics and faster processors. Additionally, many of my purchased third-party plug-ins are Windows based. Your choice of using Mac or Windows is strictly up to you. There is no benefit or drawback from either. It's merely a matter of preference.

Using the LightWave 8 Software with This Book

LightWave 8 has many differences from LightWave 7 or 7.5. I recommend that you use the latest revision of LightWave with this book to maximize your learning. Many of the tutorials in this book use tools only available in version 8, and consequently those tutorials won't work with previous versions of LightWave. However, if you happen to have the *Inside LightWave 6* or *Inside LightWave 7* books, you can take advantage of the tutorials in those books with the LightWave 8 software. Although some buttons and panels may have changed, the core workflow and key functions of LightWave 8 work the same as with previous versions. Additionally, you can change LightWave's menus back to 7.5 mode through the Edit Menu Layout panel, found in the Edit drop-down lists in the program.

Always Use the LightWave 8 Manuals

People always criticize software manuals. I think it's almost a preconceived notion that these are not the best learning tools; and in some cases, they are not. However, they do serve a strong purpose: to introduce and offer reference material on the current version. The software manuals, either printed or electronic, present great reference information when you need to find out about a key function or tool. The current manuals from NewTek are the best they've been in years, so reference them often for specific technical information. For learning beyond what you find in the manual, use *Inside LightWave 8*. This book takes you to the next level by walking you through the toolset with projects and tasks. However, I've created this new *Inside LightWave* book as a manual replacement, and you can start learning LightWave with the quick-start tutorial in Chapter 1, then move on to learn about 3D animation basics in Chapter 2, and then explanations of the Modeler and Layout interfaces in Chapters 3 and 4. From there, learn about cameras, lights, texturing, and utilize that information in projects throughout this book.

Where Should You Start?

It kills me to buy a big new book on a software application and, as I mentioned earlier, be forced to sift through page after page of information that doesn't provide the answer I'm looking for. In the past, I've written the *Inside LightWave* books as "start to finish" guides. With this version, I've tried to make a collection of little books, so to speak—that is, you start with the tutorial in Chapter 1, "Quick-Start." With this, you get up to speed and familiarize yourself with LightWave 8. At this point, you can put the book down and start playing around with the software. When you're comfortable with the workflow of LightWave 8 and ready to go further, pick up this book and do one of two things. You can either start at the beginning with Chapter 2, learning about 3D basics, then move to Chapter 3 and learn about the panels, modeling functions, and so on. Or you can hop over to a chapter of your choice and start working through a project right away. The benefit of this is time efficiency—if you're short on time, you can get in, learn something and get out, then come back later for more. It's totally up to you. Some chapters will use projects from other chapters. For example, you might model in one chapter, and then animate that object in another. If you would like to just learn about animation, you can load the finished object from this book's DVD.

Explore the Software

Learning LightWave or any other software application often requires a technical skill. It requires keen insight, forethought, and clever deduction. There's a term for this we use in the industry—experimentation! Seriously, don't get hung up on being a mathematical wizard or a serious traditional artist. These skills help, but they are not necessary to create beautiful 3D animations and graphics. Explore software on your own terms. Experiment with buttons and tools, and don't be intimidated by the software. There is no substitute for practice, whether it's a musical instrument, athletic ability, or 3D animation. With any skill, the time and effort you put into learning only serves to better you. I've said it before, and I'll say it again: Don't wait until you have a paid project or assignment to work in LightWave! All the extra time you spend modeling and animating will help give you that extra edge.

No Method Is the Best Method

If you've ever read any of the 3D forums on the Internet, you might have seen some discussions about what is "the best" modeling method, or "the best" renderer, and so on. Do yourself a favor; read those posts and then forget them. They are nothing more than opinion. What matters is what works for you. Perhaps you like to model with splines? Great. Perhaps you would never like to see a spline curve for the rest of your life. That's great, too. Have you ever watched the Fox Television show *American Idol*? If you've ever listened to what the judges say, it can be applied to learning LightWave: "Make it your own." Young hopefuls sing their guts out on live television with their own renditions of popular songs. What makes their performance stand out is of course their delivery, but what puts them over the top is when they make the song their own by adding feeling, style, and creativity. Do this with 3D modeling and animation. Find what works for you and run with it.

Use Other Books with This Book

People often ask me how I write these books; sometimes, I ask myself the very same question! Whether I'm completing my daily animation work, editing *Keyframe* magazine, creating courseware for 3D Garage.com, or preparing for the next *Inside LightWave* book, I find that using other books in my daily work is a huge help. In other words, books on topics such as architectural design, photography, anatomy, and just about any other subject can be significant resources for 3D modeling, texturing, lighting, and animation. Don't limit yourself to only LightWave, computer, or 3D-related magazines. Go beyond the scope of what you're doing by referencing other books. You can find many resources for character study, sculpture, and even drawing that can help you understand foundations that 3D models and animations are based on, or they can simply inspire you to create.

The Organization of This Book

Inside LightWave 8 is organized differently than our previous versions. This book starts with the basics, then moves to intermediate projects, and then walks you through advanced concepts. At the end of this book, we've added bonus information such as plug-in information and a resource section for further learning.

The new LightWave quick-start chapter at the beginning of this book will get you up and running fast with LightWave's workflow and toolset. You'll also find a chapter overview on the new tools and enhancements available in LightWave 8 for both Modeler and Layout (Chapters 3 and 4). From here, you can learn about 3D basics, following that up with an overview of both working with cameras, lights, and textures.

In the next part of this book, you'll model with just about all possible methods, allowing you to decide which method is right for you. You'll start with simple modeling using text, then move to the intermediate with real-world objects, and then finish with the organic, such as characters, cartoon animals, and more. These chapters will instruct you in the process, tools, and organization needed to create literally anything you can think of.

After you have modeling mastered, along with some texturing and animation, you can educate yourself on more powerful texturing and lighting techniques, while explaining how to put everything in motion. You'll learn how to make LightWave's character tools bring your 3D models to life, while incorporating compositing.

Toward the end of this book, you'll learn to get your animations rendered and into a playable format. You'll learn about LightWave's powerful rendering engine, network rendering, and new render options. You'll also learn how to use LightWave to create cool effects with the system's new dynamics engine. You'll see how easy it is to use real-world physics to collide objects, push them around, and blow them up.

In the appendixes, you'll find an updated version of our popular plug-in list that first appeared in the *Inside LightWave 7* book. This list is your guide to installing plug-ins, assigning keyboard shortcuts to them, arranging them, and of course their functions. Another appendix details where you can go for further learning. The final appendix contains important information on using this book's DVD. Please read this appendix before you insert the DVD into your computer.

Identifying the Conventions Used in This Book

As you read this book, you'll find helpful notes and warnings. These will be noticeably marked with a small icon.

Control areas throughout the program will be referred to as a *panel*. Fields in which you enter values are called *requesters*, and buttons that have a downward-pointing triangle are *drop-down lists*. Be sure to go through Chapters 3 and 4 for clear overviews of Modeler and Layout control areas.

When working in LightWave, specifically Modeler (LightWave is comprised of two programs, Modeler and Layout), be sure the Caps Lock is off. Keyboard shortcuts are first programmed in lowercase keys, whereas more complex, less-used commands are programmed with uppercase keys. Should you be following a tutorial in this book and are instructed to press a keyboard function and do not see results, there's a good chance you've got your Caps Lock on.

Finally, you'll see two special notes throughout this book, one is labeled *Important* and the other *Tip*. These two notes will appear periodically to instruct you on any pertinent information appropriate to the lesson or topic at hand.

System Considerations

Inside LightWave 8 has had a boost in performance over previous versions. In addition, a good amount of display options have been added, which can be great for your animation setup but taxing on your system. Obviously, the better your video card, the better the performance that you'll see, and more memory is always good. But you don't need to have a multi-thousand dollar system to run LightWave efficiently. On the contrary, LightWave can run exceptionally well on systems costing just a few hundred dollars. Of course, this is all dependent on the type of work you're doing. Simply put, the more detail you put into a 3D model and animation, the more system resources you'll need. If there is one thing I cannot stress enough, it's memory. Do not go out and get the fastest processor and skimp on the memory. You are better off with a 1GHz processor and 1GB of RAM than a 3.0GHz processor and 256MB of RAM. You may render a little slower, but you'll be able to work faster. Many system crashes are attributed to lack of memory, so try to make your absolute minimum 256MB. Your NewTek manual can also instruct you on the optimal system requirements. You can also work directly with your LightWave dealer or computer dealer to assist you.

One thing to remember when working in a computer-based field: Don't wait. There will always be an upgrade, always a faster system and cheaper parts. But if you wait too long, you'll put aside valuable hours in which you could have been learning and creating, as well as earning! Buy a computer that is comfortably within your budget but as powerful as it can be, and get to work.

Video Memory

Don't think that because you have the latest processor on the market, or the fastest Mac available, you'll have the best computer for animation. Processing power is only one part of the computing process when it comes to creating with LightWave. Your system memory—in this case, 256MB of RAM or more—is important to a productive system. However, your video memory is just as important.

With LightWave 8's expansive interface enhancements, you should have a decent OpenGL-compatible video card with at least 32MB of RAM or more. Personally, I wouldn't go less than 64MB. LightWave's Modeler and Layout allow great control over viewports, shading, and interface color, and there are brand new OpenGL controls in Layout, all of which will rely heavily on your video memory.

You can view images projected through lights, fog, reflections, and multi-textures, and view them more directly in Layout. Because of the popular video-game market, graphic cards have become ridiculously fast and cheap. And, the Macintosh market finally has some powerful graphics cards. It's highly recommended that you get a decent video card, which by the way, shouldn't cost you more than $150 US.

Any video graphics card you use should be fully OpenGL compliant. Also, video cards change often, so be sure to check with NewTek about any new card recommendations the company may have.

Dual Monitors

Even though they are commonly seen these days, you might not be familiar with dual monitors. Essentially, many video cards now allow you to connect two, or even three, computer monitors to a single card. You can also add a secondary video card and put your monitors side-by-side for an expanded, wide desktop. This is a wonderful way to work with LightWave and many other graphics programs that require a great deal of onscreen real estate. With LightWave, you can keep panels open and move them to the secondary monitor, such as the Graph Editor, for constant control over your keyframes for timing and motion.

Installing LightWave 3D

Installing LightWave 3D is as easy as putting the software disc into your PC or Mac. Follow the instructions that NewTek, Inc. has provided in its software manual. If you have any LightWave 3D installation problems, please direct those questions to NewTek's Technical Support (www.newtek.com). However, it's often best to let the installer do its job—that is, don't be clever and try to install different parts of the application to different parts of your hard drive.

Using the Book's DVD

The DVD that comes with this book contains all the necessary project files for you to follow along with the examples. Additionally, you can load finished project scenes and dissect them for your interest and reference.

What's on the DVD?

In addition to the project files on the book's DVD, you'll find materials to take your LightWave 8 learning further unlike any other LigthWave book you'll find:

- Free video tutorials from 3D Garage.com, which will take you further with many of the book's chapters

- Full-sized color images of this book's figures

- Free textures

- Demo plug-ins for LightWave

- Free 3D objects

See Appendix C, "What's on the DVD," for more detailed information.

Installing the Practice Files

Too often, readers install a book's DVD into their drive and then try to open scenes. Sure enough, an error appears that LightWave "can't find" a necessary object or image. This is not a defective DVD, but rather has to do with LightWave's Content Directory. You'll learn more about this as the chapters progress. Basically, the Content Directory tells LightWave 3D where to look for files. If you press the o key (not zero) in LightWave Layout or Modeler, you'll get the General Options panel (see Figure I.1). At the top, you can click the Content Directory button. Set the Content Directory to point to *yourDVDdrive://*Projects. That's it!

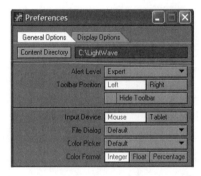

Figure I.1   The LightWave 3D 8 Content Directory button is located within the General Options panel (press o) in both Modeler and Layout. The Content Directory is where you tell LightWave where to look for files.

Tip

For your convenience, we've put the necessary project files from this book online, just in case you have trouble with your DVD. Go to www.danablan.com and click the Books page for download. Unzip or unstuff the file, and you'll find a Projects folder. Simply put this folder somewhere on your hard drive and point LightWave's Content Directory to that folder.

Within the Projects folder is an Images folder for necessary textures and images, an Objects folder containing LightWave 3D objects, and finally a Scenes folder that is home to this book's LightWave scenes. When you load a scene into LightWave Layout (you cannot load a scene into Modeler, only objects), the Scene file looks to the Content Directory for the necessary objects. The objects loaded look to the Content Directory for the necessary images. It sounds complicated, but it's not. All you're doing is telling LightWave where to find its files. By default, the Content Directory should point to *yourdrive*://LightWave.

Throughout these chapters, if you're called upon to "load an object," simply selecting the Load Object command in Layout or Modeler automatically opens the Objects folder within your set Content Directory. The same goes for images or scenes, so be sure to keep this set while working through the projects.

Words to Work By

The 3D market has changed since I got into this business. In the beginning, it was like a little club, and everyone got along. Anything we did, and I want to stress *anything*, was just cool as hell. In a small LightWave user group in Chicago that met monthly, each month's 3D creations were crude, generally poor quality, but great to look at nonetheless. Now, some 14 years later, it's a different world. 3D is everywhere—in movies, television, video games, even the Internet. Our likes and dislikes have changed, and the market has grown beyond belief. Not everything is cool to look at anymore, but that's OK. No matter what, it's always great to see someone's work because you can learn from it. The 3D world we live in is no longer a small club of enthusiasts, but rather a world full of 3D artists all working toward that ultimate render. It has become a competitive industry, but an industry created on passion and the love of 3D art. To this day, I've never met anyone that just "had" to do 3D. They "wanted" to, and I'm pretty sure you are one of those people. That hunger for 3D animation is what makes your digital creations better each time you sit down in front of the computer. You're striving to learn more and to make it better, perhaps convey a message and portray your artistic style. That is what it's all about, after all.

The tools you have at your fingertips were not conceivable 14 years ago, even 6 years ago. Some of you are students; some of you are professionals; and some just hobbyists, young and old. You have the ability to create anything you can imagine. Do not feel that you need additional plug-ins, or other four-lettered software applications to do "better" work. You don't. LightWave, like any other application, is nothing more than code. It is buttons and an interface. It is simply a machine that you are driving, and your job is to finish the race. Now, turn the page and start working through Chapter 1's quick-start tutorial as I help you steer down the course.

Chapter 1

Quick-Start

Inside LightWave 8 was designed to teach you how to use LightWave 3D, version 8. However, as with many books covering such a powerful program, it takes nearly a thousand pages to cover everything, and even then, there's always more to learn. With this fourth edition of *Inside LightWave*, this first chapter is an entirely new idea to help you get up to speed quickly. After you get through this chapter, you can read through each chapter to learn about the software changes, updates, and more specific topics. Do this in order from Chapter 2, "3D Animation Basics," onward, or skip around as you like. The choice is yours.

When planning this chapter, I tried to find the best way for you to really get your feet wet in LightWave quickly, without too much explanation, but with enough clarity for you to understand what you're doing. I thought back to 1990, when I was pretty new to LightWave 3D. Then, it was just version 1 and the coolest thing since cable television. How did I learn the program back then? There was no Internet and no email, and there wasn't a book like this to teach me. Heck, I didn't even have a cell phone to call someone to ask questions. NewTek had a few tutorials in the manual, which, by the way, simply consisted of photocopies in a great, big three-ring binder. It was the best!

One tutorial in particular was an animated butterfly. You'd laugh if you saw the final animation I created! It looked like the butterfly had a few too many at the local pub because one wing didn't work, and the body unnaturally flipped around the screen. Regardless of the fact that this animation was only a 320×240 low-resolution file and that it took three days to render just four seconds, it was the coolest thing we'd ever seen come out of our computers. I was hooked.

It's now 14 years later, and I thought that if I could learn how to create a drunken butterfly, then so could you! Maybe if it got me excited about learning and creating anything I could imagine in LightWave, then it would for you, too. With the tools and speed available in LightWave 8, I can imagine your eagerness to harness everything it has to offer. This chapter shows you how to model a butterfly, use 3D layers, apply textures, put the wings in motion, and then bring it all together to make a great-looking animation. And get this—it won't take three days to render, no matter what system you're using! Now, grab your mouse, fire up LightWave 8, and get ready to rock!

Specifically, this chapter teaches you about the following:

- LightWave 8's workflow
- Creating and managing 3D models
- Saving and loading files
- Applying surfaces
- Setting up an animation and keyframing
- Previewing and rendering your work

Quick-Start Project Overview

As we begin, I want to stress that this chapter is simply a quick-start to using *Inside LightWave 8*. Its design is clear and simple to get you creating and seeing results right away. With some slight liberties taken, I assume that you know a little bit about 3D space, and perhaps how to select and deselect both points and polygons in LightWave's Modeler. You can refer to Chapter 2, "3D Animation Basics," for more information or your NewTek LightWave 3D manual that came with your 3D software.

Each chapter from this point on has much more explanation of steps and procedures. You can use the tutorial in this chapter to flag topics you'd like to learn more about, such as keyframing or texturing. Additionally, LightWave 3D is actually two programs, Modeler and LightWave. From this point on, we'll refer to LightWave as Layout. Many projects start in Modeler, where you build or create your three-dimensional objects—basic primitive shapes, organic smooth shapes, or even text. Although many surfacing options are available in Modeler, complete surfacing can be done in Layout. The chapters ahead explain in detail the difference between applying surfaces in Modeler and applying surfaces in Layout. Surfacing is nothing more than the act of applying a color or texture to a surface of the 3D model you've created. What is crucial, however, is identifying surfaces. This is only done in Modeler. Identifying surfaces means that you are able to apply colors or textures on the appropriate areas of your 3D model. For example, perhaps you've created a bottle of water for a print ad. This bottle needs to have clear plastic for the main areas, a white cap, and a colored label. In Modeler, after the object is built, you select the specific areas and identify their surfaces so that later you can apply the appropriate surface colors and textures. You'll perform these steps in this chapter on the butterfly.

The LightWave workflow is as simple as this:

$$\text{Model} \rightarrow \text{Texture} \rightarrow \text{Light} \rightarrow \text{Animate} \rightarrow \text{Render}$$

Begin in Modeler

Begin in LightWave Modeler by running the application either from your program group icons, desktop shortcut, or dock. Figure 1.1 shows the LightWave 8 Modeler screen at startup.

Figure 1.1 The LightWave 3D 8 Modeler interface.

Important

Please be aware that throughout this book, we use a default LightWave installation. No third-party plug-ins have been added, and the menus have not been modified. For more information on customizing your LightWave programs, please see Chapter 3, "Modeler," and Chapter 4, "Layout."

Tip

Unless otherwise stated, always use the left mouse button. Macintosh users have only one mouse button, so just use that. Many right mouse button functions are touched on throughout the book, and you'll be instructed accordingly. Macintosh users: Hold the Apple key to simulate right mouse button functions in combination with the mouse.

Exercise 1.1   Creating the Butterfly Wing

To begin creating the butterfly, you'll first create just one wing. Because the wing is the same on both sides of the creature, you can use Modeler's mirror function to copy it. This saves the trouble of modeling two of the same thing. The top left quadrant of the interface is the Top viewport. If you create the wing in this view, when you bring it to Layout later for animating, it will be lying flat in the 3D workspace. If by chance you build the wing in the bottom-left quadrant, the Back viewport, your wing will be standing up later in Layout. For this project, you'll model the wing in the Top viewport.

1. Click the Create tab at the top of the screen, as shown in Figure 1.2. When you click the tabs across the top of the interface, the tools on the left side of the interface change.

Figure 1.2   The Create tab at the top of LightWave Modeler, where all object creation begins.

The Create tab contains many tools you can use to create 3D objects such as boxes, balls, discs, text, and even curves. For this project, select the Pen tool, as in Figure 1.3.

2. You'll see a dark crosshair in the viewport. This is the 0 axis, which we'll talk about more in Chapter 2. For now, start to the right of the vertical crosshair, near the center of the viewport. To use the Pen tool shown in Figure 1.3, just click on it to activate it. The tool is now ready to use, so in the Top viewport, click about 30 points in a clockwise motion, in a rough butterfly wing shape. Figure 1.4 shows the rough points.

Now, you'll need to adjust the points you've created to simply tweak the shape of the butterfly wing. To do this, you'll use another tool called Drag. Drag is located within the Modify tab. Drag works like most other tools, by simply selecting it and then working in one of the viewports. Drag enables you to click on a point with the left mouse button and move it around.

Figure 1.3
The Pen tool is located on the left side of the Modeler screen within the Create tab.

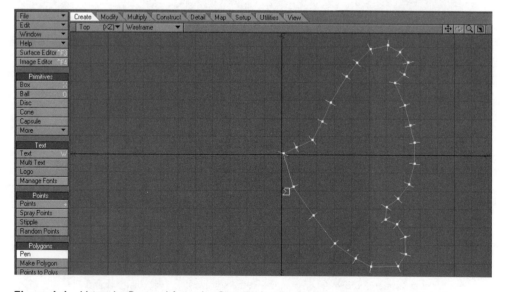

Figure 1.4   Using the Pen tool from the Create tab, you can click with the left mouse button to create shapes.

3. Select Drag, as shown in Figure 1.5, and then click on a point and drag it slightly in the Top view to shape the wing more accurately, as shown in Figure 1.6.

 Important

> Be careful using the Pen tool. Often, if you click to create a new point too close to the previous one, you might move the existing point instead of making a new one. One way to avoid this is to click far enough away from the previous point and then hold the mouse and move the point into place.

Figure 1.5
The Drag tool is located on the left side of the Modeler screen within the Modify tab.

Can you see how the workflow is starting? You begin with the first tab at the top of the Modeler screen, the Create tab. You create 3D objects with the various tools. Next, you move to the Modify tab to adjust what you've created. From there, you move on to making copies, using the tools within the Multiply tab.

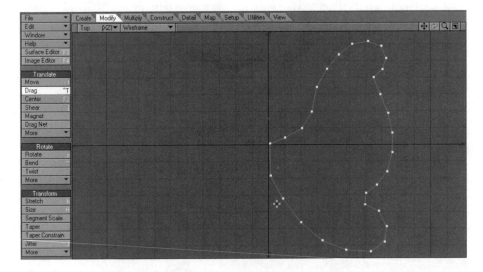

Figure 1.6   Using the Drag tool from the Modify tab, click and drag the points created to adjust their positions.

 Tip

> One of the mistakes many new LightWave users make is that they overbuild 3D objects—that is, they add too many points. In LightWave, it's always easier to add more geometry, more detail, than it is to take it away, so keep that in mind.

Now you should have a basic wing shape for the butterfly model. It's crude but is starting to resemble something. With the basic wing shape now in place, there's a very important step every LightWave user needs to learn—SAVE! Too often, users save only when they're finished, but there's a reason to save often. Of course the system may go down on you because of a power outage, software failure, or what have you. But more importantly, you may make some changes or additions to your model that you don't like. By saving often and saving different versions, you avoid the risk of wasting hours on a model you can't use because of a simple mistake.

4. From the File drop-down menu at the top left of the Modeler interface, select Save Object As. Find a place on your hard drive to save the model and call it BFlyWing1, or something similar. Be sure to add the number 1 after it, as this will serve as a reference. When you make changes later, you can save a new version. Figure 1.7 shows the operation.

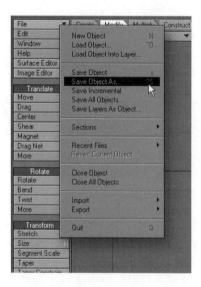

Figure 1.7   Be sure to use the Save Object As command from the file menu drop-down list at the top left of the Modeler interface. It's a good idea to save often and save versions of your model as you progress.

Tip

Although it's not crucial that you save your objects to a specific directory, bad habits
are hard to break! If you read about LightWave's Content Directory within the "What's
on the DVD" section of the Introduction, you'd know that LightWave has three main
file folders: Scenes, Objects, and Images. These three folders are located within your
installed LightWave directory. A smart way to work is to create a new folder within
each of LightWave's three main folders. For example, with this chapter's quick-start
tutorial, you would create a folder in Scenes named Butterfly, then a folder within the
Objects folder named Butterfly, and the same within the Images folder. If you keep this
method for all your projects, you'll be able to find and access files quickly and easily.
What's more, with your Content Directory set to yourdrive://LightWave, you'll never
have to change it (unless you're using this book's DVD!) Just as a reminder, press the o
key (not zero) in either Modeler or Layout to call up the General Options. You can set
your Content Directory at the top of this panel.

Working with Layers

Now that your butterfly wing is saved, you'll be able to see its saved name at the top right
of the Modeler interface. Figure 1.8 shows the current object list. As you load or create
more objects, they become visible and selectable from this list. Right now, we're creating
one object with multiple layers.

Figure 1.8   At the top right of the Modeler interface, you'll find the Modeler Object List.
Here, you can see the saved name of your object, as well as select from other
created or loaded objects.

If you've ever used Adobe Photoshop or a similar imaging program, you're familiar with
layers. Essentially, LightWave Modeler enables you to create a 3D object that has layers,
or multiple parts. The reason? For animation! For example, say you're modeling a car.
The car needs to move, each wheel needs to turn, and the doors need to rotate open. Yet
all these parts need to be separate objects for LightWave to be able to animate them. If a
door, for instance, is attached to a car, it moves as one piece. This is where the layers
come in. By having each piece that needs to be animated on its own layer, you can save
just one object, but it will have individual layers that can be animated.

Layers go much further for actual model creation, which we cover later in this book. For
now, continue with the butterfly quick-start tutorial and use LightWave Modeler's layers for yourself.

If you look closely at Figure 1.8, you'll see that there is a row of small buttons across the top right of the Modeler screen. These are the layers. You can have as many layers as you want within your model, yet only 10 are shown at a time. See that little number 1 right before the layer buttons? That's the first set of 10. If you click the right arrow next to the 1, it changes to the second set of 10 layers, and so on.

You'll notice that the first layer button is pressed. This means that you're working in that layer. Do you see the small dot in the layer in Figure 1.8? That means there is some geometry in the layer, such as points or polygons.

Important

Points and polygons are discussed in detail in Chapter 2. Simply put, points make up polygons. Points do not render in Layout (you can't see them in an animation), but polygons do. Think of points and polygons as "connect-the-dots," similar to the way you used the Pen tool at the beginning of this chapter. When you created points with the Pen tool, it automatically created lines between each—the polygon.

Exercise 1.2   Creating the Second Wing

You've now created just one half of the butterfly's wings. To fly properly, this little guy needs two wings, so follow the next few steps to make a duplicate copy of the wing and flip it over for the opposite side. Not only does this save you the time and trouble of building another wing, but also it helps keep a uniform look throughout the model.

1. With the first layer of the butterfly wing object still selected (like in Figure 1.8), copy it by pressing Ctrl+c on your keyboard. You won't see anything happen, but you've placed a copy of the wing in LightWave's buffers.

Figure 1.9
Copying and pasting the original wing into a second layer shows that geometry has been added by displaying a small dot in the layer button.

2. After you've copied the butterfly wing, click the second layer button at the top right of the interface. Then, back at the bottom of the Modeler interface, paste the copy of the wing by pressing Ctrl+v. You've copied what you created in one layer and pasted in the next. You should also see a small dot in the second layer button, which means you now have something there—some geometry, as in Figure 1.9.

3. Now you have two wings, but they are both on the same side! You need to create a wing on the other side so the butterfly can fly straight! Instead of rebuilding the entire wing, you can simply flip it over. You'll do this with the copied wing in Layer 2. Click the Multiply tab at the top of the Modeler interface. Then, click the Mirror tool on the left side of the screen, as in Figure 1.10.

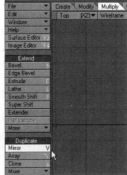

Figure 1.10
The Mirror tool is found within the Multiply tab.

Using the Mirror tool is as simple as a click and drag operation with the left mouse button. However, you're working in 3D, and there are three axes you need to be concerned with: X, Y, and Z. We cover the ways these axes work in LightWave 3D in Chapter 2, but for now, you want to mirror on the X-axis, or left and right. The Mirror tool also works based on where you click the mouse.

4. Before you click anywhere in the interface, press the n key. This calls up Modeler's Numeric panel, where every tool has options and controls. You can leave this open as you work, and it will update for each tool you use. Figure 1.11 shows the Numeric panel.

Important

When working with LightWave 3D, either in Modeler or Layout, always work with lowercase! That is, be sure your Caps Lock key is off on your keyboard. Many keyboard functions, such as Create New Object, work with the uppercase letters. For example, in step 4, you were instructed to push the n key for numeric. If your Caps Lock key was on, you would have actually told LightWave N, which is Create New Object. The result: a new blank Modeler interface appears! Don't worry if this happened. Go to the top right of Modeler and click the Object List button, next to the Layers. Here, you'll see the objects you've created, such as the butterfly wing. Just select it from this list, and your object will reappear.

Because the Numeric panel defaults to 0 on the X-axis, your butterfly wing should have automatically mirrored! Figure 1.11 shows the Modeler screen after the n key is pressed. You can see a small line in the middle of the wings—this is the Mirror tool. You'll also notice that the Center X field is highlighted in the Numeric panel, and Merge Points is checked. This tells Modeler to merge any duplicate points that are created from a mirror operation.

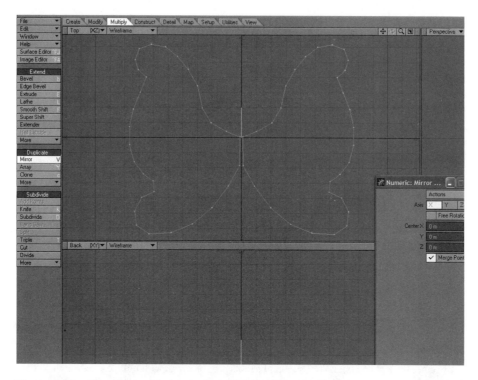

Figure 1.11   Pressing n in Modeler calls up the Numeric panel. You can also access this panel by clicking the button at the bottom of the Modeler interface.

Tip

Merge Points doesn't just merge along the mirror line; it merges all points in the current layer occupying the same space.

5. To keep this mirror operation, close the Numeric panel and then click on the Mirror tool button at the left of the interface to turn the tool off. Remember, all tools in Modeler work similarly, in that you click the tool to turn it on, work within the Modeler viewports, and then click the tool to turn it off.

But wait! Wasn't there a wing on the first layer? Now you have two right wings and one left! That's OK—you're just going to delete one of them.

Important

Although you could have mirrored the wing on the first layer, saving the copying and pasting step, you would limit your animation later. By having each wing on its own layer, they can be animated separately.

Finally, you should know that layers can be viewed in the foreground or background. This is helpful for aligning an object with other objects, such as the placement of a wheel on a car. Figure 1.12 shows the object layer buttons at the top right of the Modeler interface.

Figure 1.12
Pressing beneath the diagonal slash mark on an object layer makes that layer visible as a background layer.

6. With the second layer selected as shown, click beneath the slash mark on Layer 1. Notice how a diagonal line cuts across all the layer buttons? When you click beneath the slash, you make that layer a background layer.

By making an object layer a background layer, you'll see it in the Modeler viewports as a black wireframe. It's important to know that you can't move this object, adjust it, or modify it in any way. It's simply there as a reference. If you're familiar with Adobe Photoshop and have worked with image layers, this is similar in that you use layers for reference and control.

Tip

A layer can't be both a foreground and background at the same time. However, you can view multiple layers in the foreground simply by holding the Shift key while you select the desired layer. This is helpful for aligning or creating 3D objects to match other objects that exist on more than one layer.

You now have created a simple object, and using a few key tools, you have created a shape, edited that shape, and copied it. You've also applied the Mirror tool. These actions and the process you've used are good examples of the modeling workflow in LightWave. Read on now to go a step further!

Selection Modes

Down at the bottom of the Modeler interface are the selection commands Points and Polygons. Earlier in this chapter, it was mentioned that all 3D objects in LightWave are made up of points and polygons. Although some tools, like Drag and Mirror, don't require you to have any points or polygons selected to work, other tools often do. You may even want to apply a tool or function only to a specific area of a model. This is where selection comes into play. In this particular case, you simply need to delete one wing.

Exercise 1.3   Deleting One Wing

1. Click the Polygons button at the bottom of the Modeler interface. This tells Modeler that you want to work with polygons, the actual visible surface of the object, not the points between the lines. Figure 1.13 shows the selection.

Figure 1.13
The Polygons button.

 Tip

> Pressing the Spacebar in LightWave 8 Modeler quickly switches you between Points and Polygons selection modes.

2. Now that you're in Polygon mode, make sure that any tools you've used are off. Just click on the particular tool that might be on to turn it off. Then, click directly on the right wing in the Top viewport. Note that you need to click on the edge of the polygon because you're working in Wireframe mode. Figure 1.14 shows the selection, which is now highlighted yellow.

3. It's selected, right? Just press the delete (Del) key on your keyboard to remove the selected polygon. Or, press Cut at the bottom of the interface. You can also press the Ctrl and x key to cut away.

4. At this point, it's a good idea to save your object again. Because you've already saved it, you can just press the s key. Alternatively, if you want to save this as a new object, just press Shift and the s key at the same time. This is the Save Object As command. Give it a new name, and you're good to go.

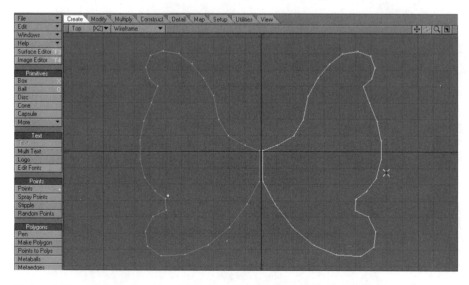

Figure 1.14   Click on the edge of the right wing to select it. Because your viewports are set to Wireframe mode, you need to click on the edge of the object.

Working with Primitives

At this point, you've created two wings for a butterfly in a couple steps. First, you drew one wing with the Pen tool. You then mirrored and copied it to a new layer so that you can animate it separately from the other wing later in Layout. Now, you need to build a body for the butterfly. You can do this with the primitive modeling tools found under the Create tab.

Exercise 1.4   Building the Body for the Butterfly

1. You should have the original butterfly wing on Layer 1 and the copy of it on layer two. Now, click the third object layer, which should be blank. You can tell that it's blank (meaning there are no objects in it) because the Modeler interface is empty and there is no small black dot in the object layer button.

2. After you've clicked the third layer, hold the Shift key and select Layer 1 and Layer 2 as a background layer. Remember, click beneath the diagonal slash on Layer 1 and Layer 2 to do this. Figure 1.15 shows the operation.

Figure 1.15   To create the body of the butterfly, start by going to a new object layer while making layers one and two background layers.

3. Click the Create tab at the top of the Modeler screen. Then, on the left side of the interface, click the Capsule tool.

4. Press the n key again to call up the Numeric panel. As soon as you do, a pill-like capsule suddenly appears right down the middle of the butterfly wings. Figure 1.16 shows the operation.

   The Capsule tool's default size is roughly 2 meters in length, and its default axis is Z. Because of this, the capsule was created in the proper orientation needed. If the default were Y, for example, the capsule would have been created more vertically, standing up rather than laying down. You can always select a primitive shape such as capsule, disc, box, or ball, and simply click and drag with the mouse in the viewports to create your own custom shape. Here, however, you're using the Numeric panel to set a more specific size.

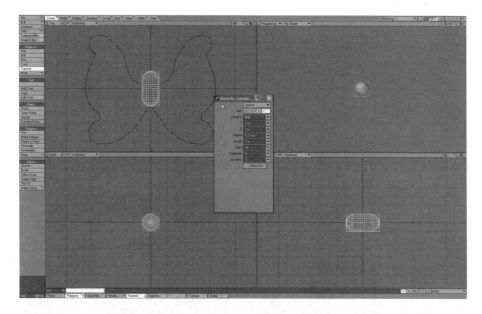

Figure 1.16   Using the Capsule tool from the Create tab and then pressing the n key to call up the Numeric panel instantly creates a capsule-like 3D shape.

5. In the Numeric panel, you can click and drag the tiny left and right arrows next to values such as Radius and Length to adjust the size of the capsule. When you do this, hold the left mouse button down while you drag these arrows. Change the Radius to about 270mm or so, and the Length to about 3m. Figure 1.17 shows the Numeric panel.

6. When you're finished, close the Numeric panel (or move it aside) and click the Capsule tool at the left side of the screen to turn it off and commit the object to your settings. Figure 1.18 shows the capsule in a foreground layer with the new settings, while each wing layer is set as a background layer.

7. Save your object by pressing s on the keyboard.

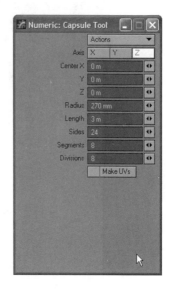

Figure 1.17
With the Numeric panel, you can click and drag the arrow buttons to the right of each value to change the object's shape and settings.

Tip

Although the Spacebar toggles between Points and Polygons selection mode at the bottom of the Modeler interface, it has another function as well. When a tool is selected, such as the Capsule tool, pressing the Spacebar is a quick way to turn off the tool. Be careful, however; if you have the Numeric panel open and your cursor is in an entry field, pressing the Spacebar will add a space to that numeric value rather than turn off the tool. A way to make sure this doesn't happen is to press the escape key (Esc) on your keyboard first to get out of the requester and then the Spacebar to turn off the tool.

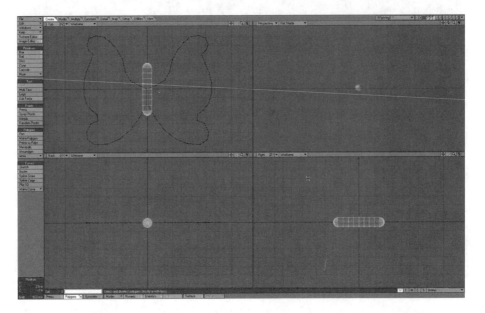

Figure 1.18   After the Capsule tool has been used to create a basic shape, its parameters are adjusted slightly to create this 3D object.

Important

There's something you should know about creating primitive shapes in LightWave Modeler. You'll see a light blue outline around the 3D object when it is created. In this state, you're still able to adjust its length, size, or level of detail through the Numeric panel. After you turn off a tool, you've committed to the settings. Turning on the tool again creates a new object—it does not adjust what you've just made. You can adjust any model by modifying points and polygons later.

Adjusting Shapes

Now that the basic shape of the butterfly body has been created, you can use Modeler's other key tools to change the shape into something that resembles a bug.

Exercise 1.5   Modifying the Body's Shape

1. At the bottom of the Modeler interface, click the Points button to change to Points selection mode. This tells Modeler that you want to work with the points of objects, rather than the polygons or surfaces. Figure 1.19 shows the selection.

Figure 1.19   Choosing Points selection mode at the bottom of the LightWave Modeler interface tells the program that you want to work with the points that make up the object.

2. Adjusting points is easy; simply select them and then modify them in some way. With Points selection mode on, from the bottom of the Modeler interface, click and drag your mouse across the top row of points, just beneath the rounded end, as shown in Figure 1.20.

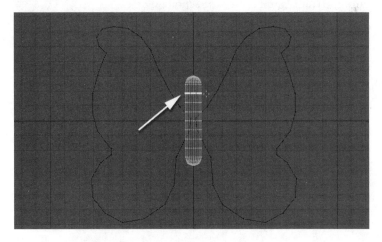

Figure 1.20   Select the points around one section of the capsule object by dragging the mouse across them.

3. With the points selected, click over to the Modify tab at the top of the Modeler interface.

4. On the left side toolbar, select the Size tool. Figure 1.21 shows the tool.

Tip

Here's a good rule of thumb: When nothing is selected, whatever you do applies to everything. For example, if you select Size and then click and dragged on an object, the entire object changes in size. If you have any number of points or polygons selected, and you use the Size tool, only those selected are affected. Be sure to keep that in mind while modeling.

5. In the Top viewport, click and drag the mouse button to the left. You might see the selected points move off of the capsule object, as in Figure 1.22.

   The reason these points move like this or anywhere else on the screen when you use the Size tool is because, by default, LightWave Modeler's Action Center is set to Mouse. This is helpful in many circumstances and troublesome as well. This means that any operation you perform under this mode happens based on where your mouse cursor is. For this project, you want those selected points to stay in place and size down accordingly. To change the Action Center, look at the center bottom of the Modeler interface, to the right of the Points and Polygons selection modes.

6. You'll see a button labeled Modes. Click this drop-down list and choose Action Center: Selection, as in Figure 1.23. This tells Modeler that when you use selected tools, they should be applied based on their selection, not on the mouse position.

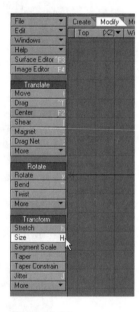

Figure 1.21
The Size tool is selected from within the Modify tab in LightWave Modeler.

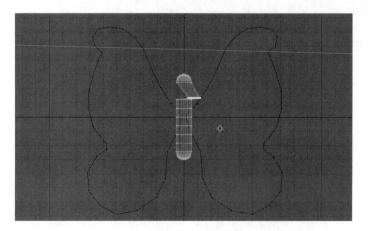

Figure 1.22
Using the Size tool on the selected points moves them toward your mouse cursor.

Figure 1.23   You can set the Action Center to Selection, rather than Mouse, from the Modes drop-down list at the bottom of the Modeler interface.

7. Press the u key to undo the size operation from step 5. Then, making sure the Size tool is still selected, click and drag the mouse again in any viewport, and the selected ring of points changes size in place. Figure 1.24 shows the change.

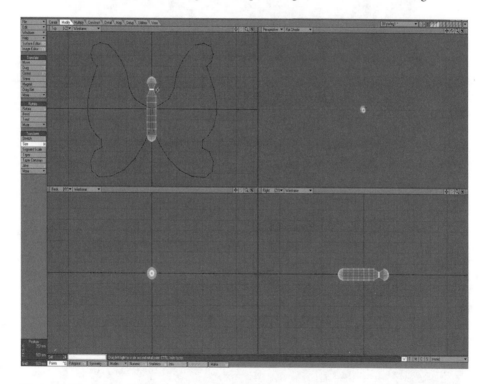

Figure 1.24   Using the Size tool with the mode set to Action Center: Selection keeps the selected points in place as they are sized.

8. Press the Spacebar to turn off the Size tool. Then, press the / key to deselect those points.

9. Still in Points selection mode, from the bottom of the Modeler interface, use your right mouse button to select the bottom end of the capsule by drawing around the points, as in Figure 1.25. If you're on a Macintosh, hold down the

Apple key while using the mouse to simulate right mouse button functions. This is called a lasso selection.

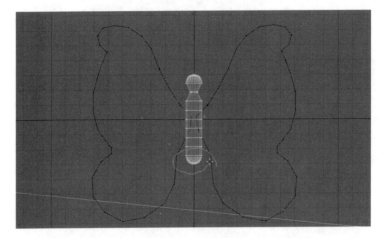

Figure 1.25   With the right mouse button, you can select points (or polygons) in a "lasso" mode.

10. With the tail-end points selected, use the Size tool to shrink them down.

11. Select Move from the Modify tab and then move the points out from the rest of the object to make a narrower end to the butterfly body, as in Figure 1.26.

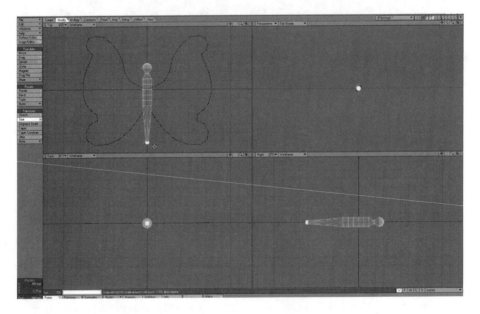

Figure 1.26   After lasso selecting the tail-end points of the capsule object, you can size them down to taper the object.

12. Press the Spacebar to turn off the Move tool and then press the / key to deselect the points.

13. Save your object.

Identifying Surfaces

Now that your crude butterfly model is coming together, you need to be able to put surfaces on it. Each part of any object should have its own unique surface name, such as the carpet in a room, the glass on windows, or the wood on the doors. For the butterfly you're creating, each wing needs its own unique name, as does the body. Because you last created the body in layer three, which is currently in the foreground, you can start identifying this surface first.

Exercise 1.6   Naming the Surfaces of the Body and Wings

1. While in Polygons mode, look down to the bottom of the Modeler interface, and you'll see a button labeled Surface. Click this, and the Change Surface panel appears. Note: Not Surface Editor, just Surface! Too often, people get confused by these two. Figure 1.27 shows the selection.

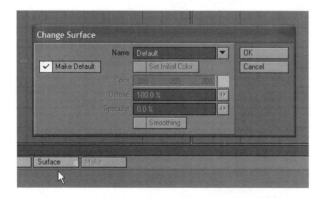

Figure 1.27   The Change Surface panel is accessed by pressing the Surface button, not Surface Editor, at the bottom of the Modeler interface. This enables you to assign unique surface names to polygons.

2. In the Change Surface panel that appears, you can give the current foreground object a unique surface name. Where it says Name, enter **ButterflyBody**, as in Figure 1.28.

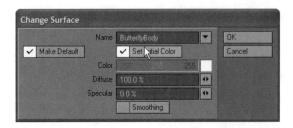

Figure 1.28   Using the Change Surface panel, you can give 3D objects their own unique surface names.

The rule stated earlier still applies here: *If nothing is selected, whatever you do applies to everything!* So in this case, you did not have any polygons selected in the butterfly body, which means using the Change Surface command identifies the entire object as ButterflyBody.

3. After you've set a name for the object, you can give it some color. Please note that this color setting here is merely a reference setting. Although it does apply a color to the surface, its purpose is to help you distinguish surfaces from each other.

You will be changing and applying different surface attributes later in Layout. Setting a color is not that important. Figure 1.29 shows the settings of the Change Surface panel for the butterfly body.

Figure 1.29   You can assign a generic color in the Change Surface panel to help you identify a newly created surface name.

4. Turn off Make Default in the panel. With this on, any newly created objects will have a surface name of ButterflyBody! Click OK to keep the settings.

5. To view your model a little closer, click and hold the upper-right rotation icon in the Perspective view. The Perspective view can really be any viewport; by default however, it's set to the top-right quad. Figure 1.30 shows the rotation control.

6. Save your object changes by pressing the s key, or Ctrl and the s key together to save the object with a new name. Pressing Shift and the s key together will save an incremental version.

7. Select layer one and press the q key to call up the Change Surface panel again. Identify this surface as RightWing or something similar, as shown in Figure 1.31.

8. Make layer two a foreground layer by selecting it from the upper right of the Modeler interface.

9. Press q to open the Change Surface panel and set the Name to LeftWing or something similar.

10. Save the object.

Figure 1.30
At the top right of each viewport are move, rotate, and zoom commands. Click, hold, and drag on these to interactively change a view.

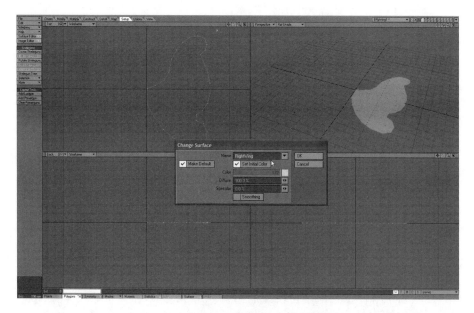

Figure 1.31   With layer one now selected as the foreground layer, you can identify the right wing surface.

Surfaces and Motions in Layout

Your modeling tasks are now complete! Congratulations! You've just modeled and created surfaces in 3D. For this project, the modeling portion is complete. You've created three layers, each with its own object. This means that each object can be animated independently, yet they all belong to the same 3D object. What's next is applying textures to the butterfly and putting the wings in motion. This section shows you how to do just that, but not in Modeler. Rather, you can make your object come to life in Layout.

Applying Surfaces to Objects

Now you need to get your model to LightWave's Layout, set up some colorful surfaces, and then put the little creature in motion.

Exercise 1.7   Surfacing the Butterfly Wings

1. At the top right of the Modeler interface, you'll find a small down arrow. Click and hold on this little arrow, and you'll see three options: Switch to Layout, Synchronize Layout, and Send Object to Layout. Figure 1.32 shows the selection.

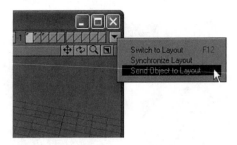

Figure 1.32   You can quickly send an object to Layout, LightWave's animation area, by using the drop-down selector at the top right of the Modeler interface.

2. Select the last option, Send Object to Layout. This takes the currently saved object and its layers and transports it to LightWave's animation program, Layout.

Important

Using the Send Object to Layout command from Modeler makes use of LightWave 3D's HUB. The HUB is discussed in more detail in Chapter 2. Essentially, the HUB links the two programs, Layout and Modeler. You can jump between the two programs, and LightWave will continually update your models as you work. If you can't select from the drop-down list, your HUB is not active. If you performed a normal installation of LightWave 3D, the HUB should be functioning normally. It runs when you start either Layout or Modeler. If not, simply save your object on your hard drive, and in Layout, select the File drop-down list from the top left of the Layout interface and choose Load, Load Object. Then, load your saved object into Layout.

3. When you selected Send Object to Layout, your object was sent through LightWave's HUB and placed into the Layout workspace. Additionally, the Layout window should have automatically popped up. If it didn't, simply hold the Alt key on your keyboard and press the Tab key to switch over to Layout. This works on a Mac or PC.

4. Figure 1.33 shows the default perspective view in Layout with the butterfly model. Press 2 on the keyboard to switch to a top view of the model.

Figure 1.33   Using the Send Object to Layout command from Modeler dumps your object into LightWave's animation section, Layout.

There are many facets to LightWave Layout, such as lighting, keyframing to make objects move, camera work, and of course, texturing. For this quick-start tutorial, we won't cover all those areas in too much detail. These areas are covered in detail throughout this book, specifically in Chapter 4. What we will cover, however, is how to get your butterfly wings surfaced and in motion.

5. At the left side of the interface is the Surface Editor button. Click this, and LightWave's robust surface control center appears. Slide this over to one side of your screen so you can see both your butterfly and the Surface Editor, as shown in Figure 1.34. Note that you can move your view as in Modeler by clicking and holding the viewport controls at the top right of the interface.

You'll notice that in the Surface Editor on the left side of the panel are three names: ButterflyBody, LeftWing, and RightWing. Remember those surface names you created in Modeler a few steps back? That's what these are! You identified each wing and the body of the butterfly in the Change Surface panel in Modeler. The point of that step was so that now when the Surface Editor is open, you can apply the appropriate surface to each part of the object.

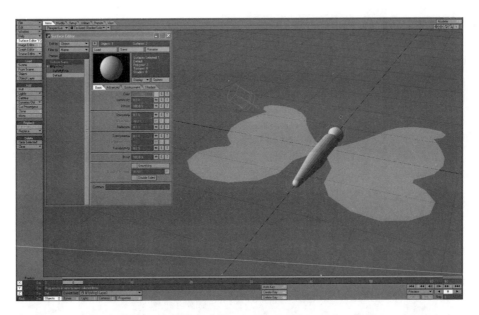

Figure 1.34 The LightWave 8 Surface Editor is a control center for applying textures and surface attributes to your models.

6. In the Surface Editor, make sure the ButterflyBody surface is selected. Then, to the right of that selection, you'll see the Color listing, underneath the Basic tab. You can click on the color swatch to call up your system's color selector. Do this and choose a soft brown color. Figure 1.34 shows the selection in the panel.

7. When surfacing objects, you simply work your way down the panel. Leave all the settings at their defaults after you've changed the color, and then set the Specularity to 30%. This is the shininess of the object.

8. Finally, click the Smoothing button at the bottom of the panel, which activates a Phong-type shading to make your object surface appear smooth. Figure 1.35 shows the panel with the changes.

   After you apply any surface, you should get into the habit of saving the object. Why? Simple—surface settings are saved with objects, not with scenes.

9. From the File drop-down menu at the top left of the Layout interface, select Save All Objects.

10. Back in the Surface Editor, select the next surface in the list, LeftWing. For this surface, you'll go one step further than applying a color; you'll apply a texture. Click the T button to the right of the Color settings. LightWave's Texture Editor opens, as in Figure 1.36.

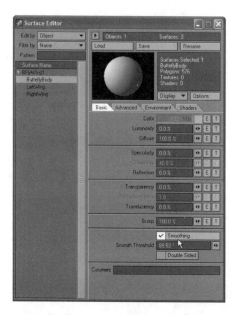

Figure 1.35   The process of surfacing objects ranges from simple to complex. For this tutorial, a simple surface is all you need, and all you need to do is select the ButterflyBody surface and choose a color.

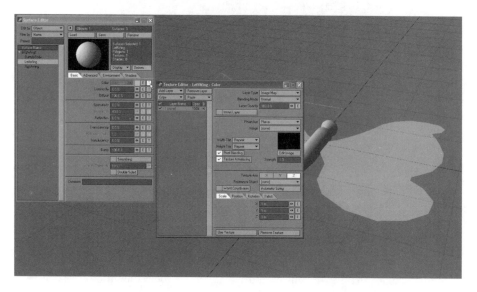

Figure 1.36   Clicking the small T button next to Color in the Surface Editor opens LightWave's Texture Editor.

11. The Texture Editor can get very complex, but don't be overwhelmed by it. On the simplest level, it's quick and easy to create an image-mapped surface. At the top of the panel, you'll see the Layer Type. By default, this is set to Image Map. Killer! One step already completed!

12. Move down the panel a bit to Projection. Its default setting is Planar. Great! That's done for you already! Planar means flat—you're going to apply an image map, flat onto a surface. Easy enough! What surface? The one you selected before you went into the Texture Editor. OK then, what image will be applied? Underneath the Projection setting is Image. Currently, it says (none). Click that and select (load image), as in Figure 1.37.

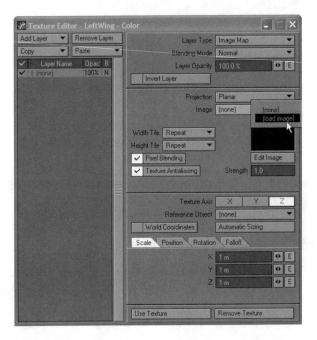

Figure 1.37   Adding an image map to a surface is as easy as point and click within the Texture Editor.

13. When you select (load image), your system's file requester will appear. Point to the Projects folder on this book's DVD, whether you have it in your disc drive or have copied the files to your hard drive. If you set your content directory properly, the Images folder should automatically open because you chose (load image). In there, choose Chapter 1, and load the Wing.jpg image.

14. Beneath the Image selection, you'll see Texture Axis. This tells LightWave which axis to apply the loaded image to. Because the butterfly is lying flat in Layout, you need to lay the image on the wing, sort of like a blanket. This would be the Y axis. Click Y for Texture Axis. Figure 1.38 shows the loaded image in the Texture Editor.

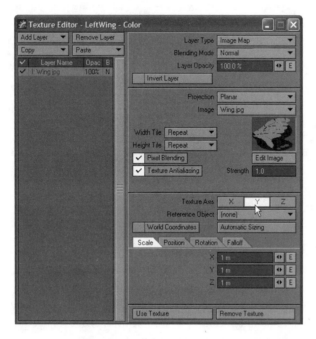

Figure 1.38   With an image of a butterfly wing loaded, it is applied flat (planar) on the Y axis, on the LeftWing surface.

15. If you look over to Layout, you might see the wing image sort of tiled across the wing! This is because the width and height repeat is on in the Texture Editor. This is great for tiles and carpets; but for now, simply click the Automatic Sizing in the Texture Editor. Figure 1.39 shows the Texture Editor to the side of the interface with Layout visible. You can see that the texture now fills the surface.

Tip

If you can't see your images directly applied in LightWave Layout, press the d key to call up Display Options. There, make sure OpenGL Textures is turned on.

Of course, the image is not quite aligned with the wing. This is typical with image mapping, and it's easy to adjust. Within the Texture Editor, you have full control over size and placement. The Automatic Sizing gave you a quick size that was pretty close to a good fit. You need to move and position the image slightly to get it perfect.

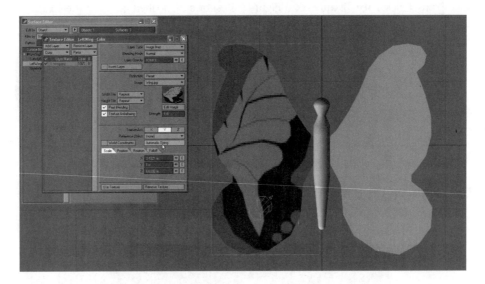

Figure 1.39   Applying an image and using Automatic Sizing instantly adjusts the image map to the current surface.

16. In the Texture Editor, the first thing you need to do is flip the image over. Because the initial image is more of a right wing image that you're placing on the left, you need to flip it horizontally. To do this, make sure the Scale tab is selected at the bottom of the Texture Editor panel, and where you see X, place a minus (−) before the value and press the Enter key. You'll see the image on the wing flip over. Figure 1.40 shows the change.

17. Click over to the Position tab, and click and drag the small arrows for the X position to move the image on the wing.

18. Click back to the Scale tab, and feel free to scale the image slightly on the Z. Your image should now be aligned on the wing, as in Figure 1.41.

19. In Layout, select Save All Objects from the File drop-down menu to keep your surface settings.

20. Back in the Texture Editor, from the top left of the panel, select Copy and choose Selected Layers. This copies all the image map settings you just created. Then, at the bottom of the panel, click Use Texture to close the panel and keep your settings.

21. Back in the Surface Editor, select the RightWing surface, and click the T button next to Color to enter the Texture Editor for the second wing.

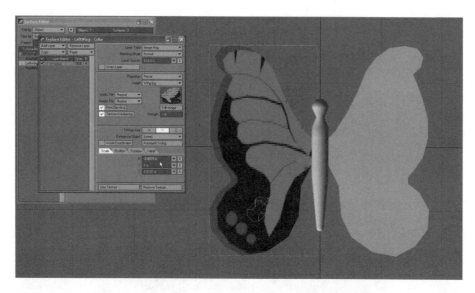

Figure 1.40   Flipping an image map horizontally is easy—simply place a negative value before the X axis setting.

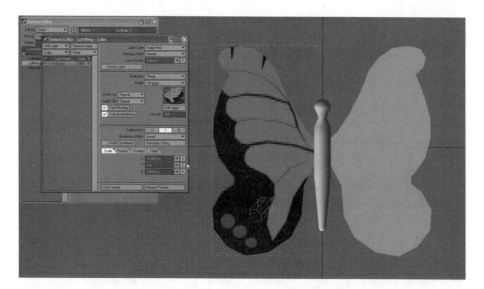

Figure 1.41   Adjusting the image's position and scale slightly makes it fit snugly on the wing.

22. This is easy now—just click Paste, and choose Replace All Layers as in Figure 1.42. You'll see that the image is now applied to the second wing, but it's not positioned properly, as in Figure 1.43.

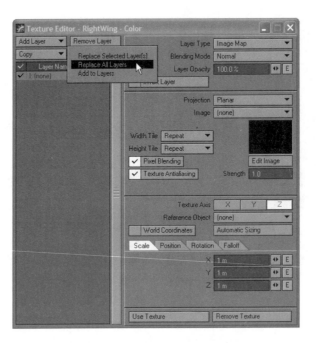

Figure 1.42   Pasting the image map layer down is done by selecting Paste and Replace All Layers.

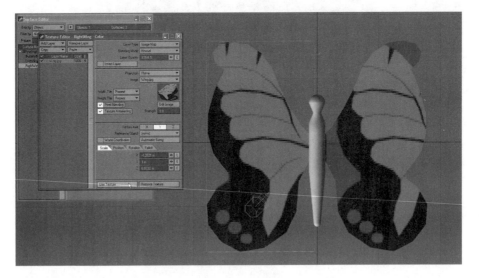

Figure 1.43   The image pasted down onto the second wing is not aligned properly.

23. If you remember, you added a negative value to the X scale to flip the image horizontally. So, go to the same setting (the X value for scale), but this time, remove the negative value. Figure 1.44 shows the image map now flipped.

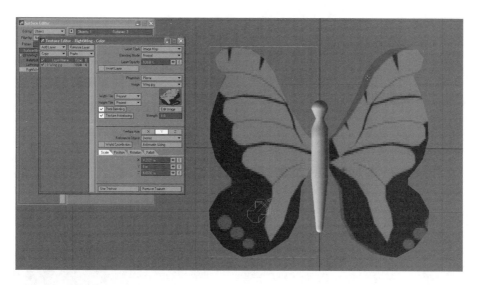

Figure 1.44   With a positive X value for scale, the image is now facing the right direction, but it needs a slight alignment.

24. Now, all you need to do is go to the Position tab within the Texture Editor and move the X position for the image slightly. Figure 1.45 shows the final mapped image. Click Use Texture to keep your settings.

25. Choose Save All Objects from the File drop-down menu.

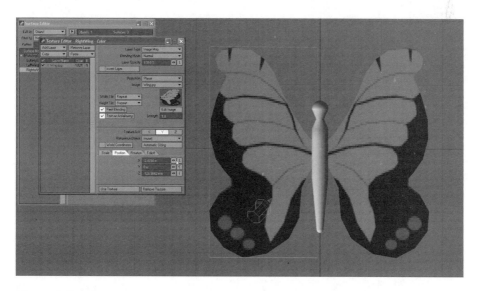

Figure 1.45   A slight adjustment to the position of the image, and the second wing is now textured.

The butterfly is now built and textured. The textures are simple, but you should now have a good idea of the process of working within LightWave up to this point. You saw how models are created in Modeler and how to work with points and polygons. You learned how to apply color as well as image maps to identified surfaces in Layout. Now, you need to make those wings fly!

Creating Motions

For this project, the modeling portion is complete. You've created the wings, the body, and applied surfaces. Congratulations! That's half the job of any project! Now, you need to put things in motion.

Exercise 1.8   Putting the Wings in Motion

1. Make sure you have your butterfly object loaded from the previous steps. Then, at the bottom of the Layout interface, select the Objects button as in Figure 1.46.

Figure 1.46
At the bottom of the Layout interface are Objects, Bones, Lights, and Camera. These are the various selection modes for LightWave Layout.

   Whenever you need to work with Layout's items, such as 3D objects like the butterfly, lights to brighten the scene, or cameras to view the animation, you'll tell LightWave what you want to work with by first choosing one of the item buttons, as shown in Figure 1.46. Then, above that selection is the Current Item option. Here, you select the item you want to work with. So in this case, you've first told LightWave Layout that you want to work with Objects by clicking the button at the bottom of Layout. Then, you click the Current Item list to select the desired object. The same method applies to Lights or any other item.

2. After you choose Objects as the items you want to work with, choose the right wing of your object as the Current Item. In this case, the current item shows as BFlyWing2 (which is the object name) and then Layer 1.

   If you remember, when you built the butterfly in Modeler, you created it on three different layers. The current item shows the object name, followed by the layer. Later in this book, you learn how to rename the layers when working with more complex objects.

3. With the right wing selected, press the m key on your keyboard. Remember, as with Modeler, always work in lowercase.

4. The Motion Options panel appears. Look closely at the title bar in the panel. It reads Motion Options for BFlyWing1:Layer1. Figure 1.47 shows the panel.

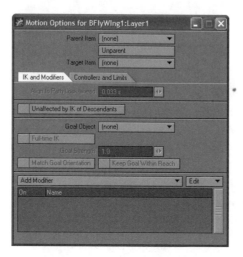

Figure 1.47   The Motion Options panel for the Current Item.

Tip

If you press the m key and nothing happens, make sure that your LightWave Layout is active. Click into Layout or the title bar of the program. If that still doesn't work, make sure your Caps Lock key is off. Remember to always work with lowercase keys!

This panel gives you control over various motions of the selected item. If you had selected a light in Layout and pressed the m key, the Motion Options for that selection would appear. This is why it's important to take a look at the title bar header of the panel from time to time if you're not sure.

5. At the top of the Motion Options panel, the first selection is Parent Item. Because this is the motion option for the wing, you can tell LightWave to parent this current item to another item. Select the drop-down list next to Parent Item and choose Layer 3. Figure 1.48 shows the selection.

If you remember, you built the body on Layer 3 in Modeler. What you're doing here is parenting the wing to the body. The result is that when the body moves, the wing stays attached.

Figure 1.48   The Motion Options panel gives you the ability to tell one object to belong, or be parented, to another. Here, the right wing object is parented to the body of the butterfly.

6. Now, you need to parent the other wing to the body. You can do this without closing the Motion Options panel. To change the current item, you have two options: either go down to the bottom of the Layout interface and change the Current Item to Layer 2 (the left wing), or simply use your keyboard's up arrow to change between items.

Because you have selected the Objects button at the bottom of the interface, using the up and down arrows cycles through those particular items. The same would apply to lights, bones, or cameras.

7. When the left wing, Layer2, is selected, parent this to Layer 3, as shown in Figure 1.49.

Figure 1.49   The left wing is now parented to the body of the butterfly.

8. Close the Motion Options panel and then save the scene. To do this, go to the File drop-down list at the top left of the LightWave Layout interface. Go to Save, Save Scene As, and save this scene as butterfly setup, or something similar. Figure 1.50 shows this operation.

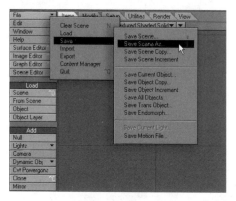

Figure 1.50   Be sure to save the scene from the File drop-down in Layout. This saves the parented items you've now set up.

 Important

Saving scenes in LightWave Layout ensures that all objects loaded, lights added, and any motions you've created are saved. Think of this as saving the project. It is not saving an animation—that comes later under Rendering. Additionally, you need to use Save All Objects, also found under the file drop-down menu to save any surface settings applied to your objects.

9. In Layout, select Layer 3 of the object from the current item list at the bottom of the interface. This should be your butterfly body. Then, make sure that the Modify tab is selected at the top of the interface, and on the left side, choose Move (if it's not already selected). Figure 1.51 shows the selection.

10. With the body selected, you need to get to a different view, other than above. So at the top of the Layout interface, you'll see a drop-down list that currently should say Top (XZ), which means you're viewing the 3D layout from above. In Chapter 2, we explain the XYZ in more detail, but for now, click this drop-down list and choose Camera view, as in Figure 1.52.

Figure 1.51
The Move command is found on the left side of the Layout interface within the Modify tab.

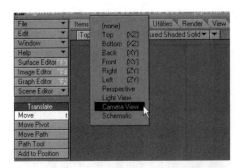

Figure 1.52   The Camera View selection from the top of the Layout interface.

Your view probably looks like nothing really. This is because the camera is pointing down the Z-axis (straight ahead), and the butterfly is lying flat. Figure 1.53 shows what the LightWave camera sees.

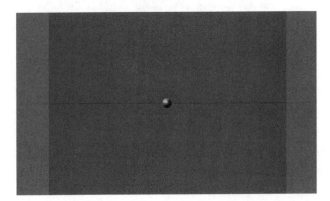

Figure 1.53   The camera view sees the tail end of the butterfly, which is lying flat in the 3D space.

You're looking at the tail end of the butterfly, but you need to be in the camera view because when you render the animation—when you process it to make an animated file—it will be seen only through the camera view. Too often, users get used to setting up an animation in a viewport such as the Side or Top view, and when it's time to render the animation, it looks nothing like what they've set up! LightWave renders from the currently selected camera.

11. At the bottom of the Layout interface, there is a button labeled Auto Key. This will serve well for this tutorial because it automatically creates keyframes. Make sure it's on.

Keyframes tell an item, such as the butterfly body, to be still or stay in place at a particular point in time. You probably have noticed the timeline along the bottom of the Layout interface. Here, you can begin creating moving animations!

12. Make sure the slider in the timeline is set to 0 on the left side of the interface, as in Figure 1.54. This is where your animation will start.

Figure 1.54   Using the timeline, make sure the time slider is set to 0. This is where you begin setting items in motion.

13. Move the butterfly around to see if the wings stay attached. They should because you parented them to the body in the Motion Options panel.

14. Select Rotate and rotate the butterfly up so you see the wings. The idea here is to get a feel for the LightWave tools, nothing more. Move and rotate as you see fit.

15. When you're comfortable with moving and rotating, move the butterfly body into a sort of side rotation, facing upwards, as in Figure 1.55.

Figure 1.55   Start the animation of the butterfly rotated upwards, as if it's flying.

16. Select the right wing object. Because you want to make these wings move, you need to select it first.

17. Choose the Rotate command from the Items tab in Layout.

You should see some round green, red, and blue outlines around the center area of the wing. This is the wing's pivot point, which will be covered more in detail throughout this book. The handles, as they are called, enable you to click and drag directly on them, constraining movements and rotations to a specific axis. If you don't see these handles, press the d key to call up the Display Options panel and turn on Show Handles.

18. Click and drag on the blue outline to rotate the wing up. Make sure you're still at frame 0 in your timeline at the bottom of the Layout interface, and make sure the Auto Key is still on beneath the timeline. Figure 1.56 shows the movement.

Figure 1.56   By grabbing just the blue outline handle on the right wing, you can rotate it up.

19. Because Auto Key is on, rotating (or moving) the wing at frame 0 automatically creates a new keyframe. Now, slide the timeline to frame 5. Rotate the wing down, as shown in Figure 1.57.

Tip

When you rotate the butterfly wings, you might see that the backside of the wing is invisible! This is because surfaces by default in LightWave are one-sided. To change this, click the double-sided check box at the bottom of the Surface Editor panel. You can do this for each wing.

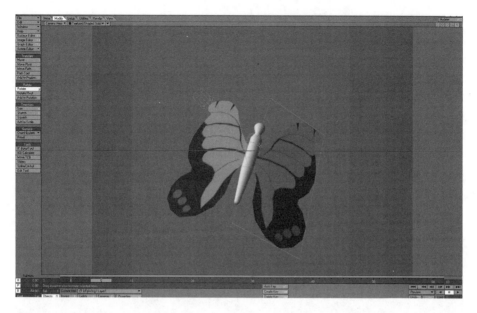

Figure 1.57   Clicking and dragging the blue outline for the right wing allows you to rotate it down at a new point in time.

20. Because you want the wing to repeat, you need to make the last keyframe the same as the first. Drag the timeline slider to frame 0, but then press the Create Key button located at the bottom of the Layout interface, just below Auto Key. In the panel that pops up, enter 10 and press OK, as in Figure 1.58.

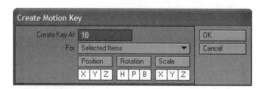

Figure 1.58   By creating a new keyframe from an existing keyframe position, you've success-fully copied a keyframe!

21. Save the scene, and then drag the timeline slider back and forth. You should see the wing flap!

22. The wing stops after frame 10, so how do you make it repeat? You don't need to continually keyframe the wing every five frames. Instead, you can use LightWave's Graph Editor to automatically do this for you. Click the Graph Editor button at the top-left side of the Layout interface. Figure 1.59 shows the Graph Editor.

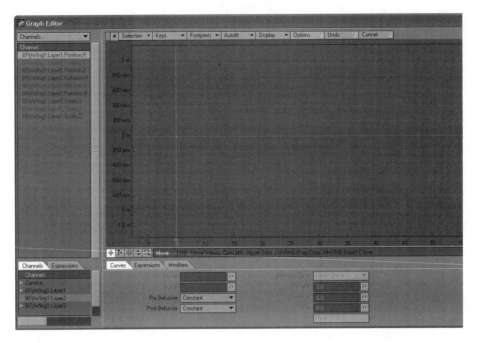

Figure I.59 LightWave's Graph Editor, where you can add more specific control to keyframes.

23. Because the left wing in which you were keyframing was selected when you opened the Graph Editor, the object's motion channels were automatically entered into the Graph Editor's channel bin. This appears in the top-left quadrant of the Graph Editor panel. In that area, select the blue Rotation B channel, as shown in Figure 1.60. You should also see a slight curve on the right side of the Graph Editor, representing the motion curve. Notice that it curves and then stops. This is the channel you keyframed in Layout, the Bank rotational channel.

24. At the bottom of the Graph Editor, you'll see an option for Post Behavior. Select this and choose Repeat, as in Figure 1.61.

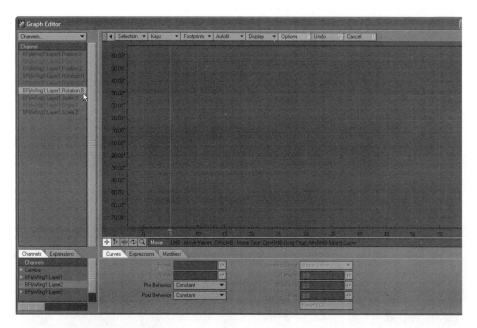

Figure 1.60 Select the Bank rotational channel in the Graph Editor, which is the channel you keyframed in Layout.

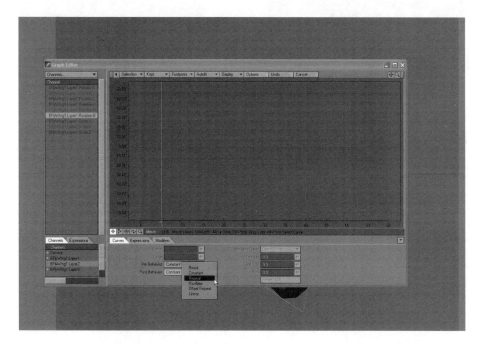

Figure 1.61 Changing Post Behavior to Repeat repeats the rotational movements of the butterfly wing.

25. You'll see the curve in the main Graph Editor window suddenly repeat, as in Figure 1.62. That's it! Close the Graph Editor, and at the bottom right side of the Layout interface, press the right-most triangle, which is the play button.

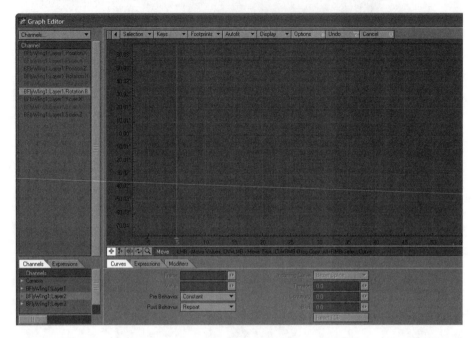

Figure 1.62 By setting the Bank rotational channel to repeat, the visible curve in the Graph Editor shows a repeating motion.

26. Select the left wing of the butterfly and repeat the previous steps to keyframe and repeat the motions on your own.

27. Select the body of the butterfly, and at frame 0 (move the timeline slider to 0), move the butterfly off to the left side of the screen, as in Figure 1.63. Note that you can use variations of rotation on the body of the butterfly to rotate the entire object. If you want to move the butterfly up and down, select Move, then drag the green arrow that appears in the center of the body.

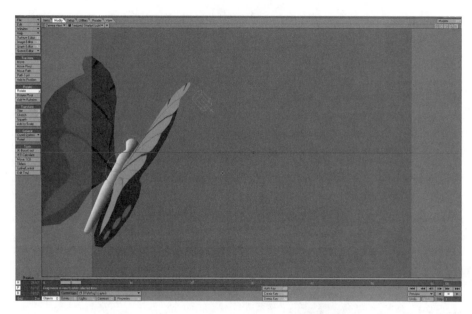

Figure 1.63 Move the butterfly body to the left side of the screen.

28. Go to frame 60 by dragging the timeline slider all the way to the right. Move the butterfly body across the screen to the right side. Figure 1.64 shows the second keyframe.

Figure 1.64 Moving the butterfly across the screen at frame 60, with Auto Key enabled, creates a second keyframe, the first being frame 0.

29. Press the play button at the bottom right of the Layout interface, and you'll see the butterfly move across the screen with its wings flapping.

30. Save your scene!

Tip

If you want to be creative, you can drag the timeline slider to see the movement of your butterfly. Then, say at frame 30, move the butterfly body up or down and then press the play button again. Your butterfly now has three keyframes, the start and the end, plus one in the middle. Your butterfly will not fly as straight as it had, but rather dips along the way. You should see a motion path drawn between each keyframe as well. If you don't, press the d key for Display Options, and enable Show Motion Paths.

Congratulations! You've now made your first LightWave 3D animation! But, take it just one step further by adding a sky and rendering it out as an AVI or QuickTime movie.

Backgrounds and Renders

If you rendered the animation at this point, it would look just fine, but the butterfly would be on a black background, which is LightWave's default. This section quickly shows you how to add a sky backdrop and then render the final animation.

Exercise 1.9   Adding a Sky and Rendering the Animation

1. Click over to the Window drop-down list at the top left of Layout. You can always find this selection at the top left of the Layout interface, regardless of what menu tab you're working in.

2. From there, click Backdrop Options on the left side of the screen.

3. When the Effect panel opens, you'll see four tabs across the top. Click the Compositing tab, as in Figure 1.65.

You should also note that you can go directly to the Compositing Options directly from the Window drop-down menu. The Backdrop Options panel you've chosen encompasses Backdrop, Volumetrics, Compositing, and Processing. These are all areas with tools you'll use throughout this book.

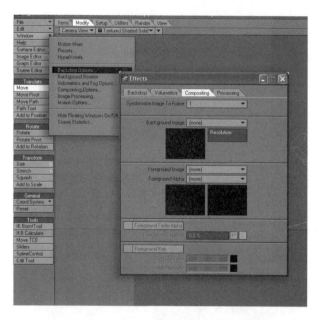

Figure 1.65   The Effects panel open, with access to background image controls.

4. At the top of the panel, you'll see a listing for Background Image. Click the drop-down list next to it that currently says (none), and select (load image). Figure 1.66 shows the operation.

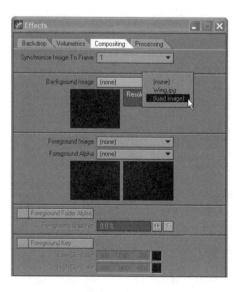

Figure 1.66   Select (load image) from the Compositing tab to put an image in LightWave's background.

5. Point to the images folder for Chapter 1 on this book's DVD. Load the
CityShot.jpg image. Figure 1.67 shows the image thumbnail that appears
when loaded.

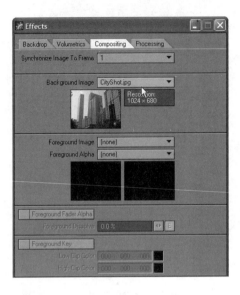

Figure 1.67   Loading an image into LightWave's background is as easy as selecting the image.
When loaded, a small thumbnail appears.

6. Close the Effect panel, and save the scene. Then, press the F9 key. This is
LightWave's Render Current Frame command. It's also found by going to the
Rendering drop-down list at the top left of the Layout interface, and choosing
Render Current Frame. Figure 1.68 shows the single frame render.

Tip

If you don't see a larger render pop-up, you might want to turn on your Render
Display. Do this by going to the Rendering drop-down list at the top left of Layout.
Go to Render Options, and where it says Render Display, click the selection and
choose Image Viewer.

7. To render the animation, go to the Render menu tab at the top of Layout and
choose Render Options on the left side of the interface. Figure 1.69 shows the
Render Options panel.

Figure 1.68   Pressing F9 renders the current frame, which in this case was frame 31. You can now see the butterfly rendered, or drawn, over the photo.

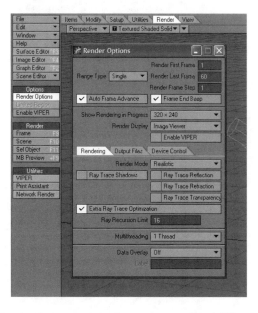

Figure 1.69   The Render Options panel, where you can tell LightWave how and where to save your animations.

8. Although there are a lot of variables in this panel, for now, you only need to worry about one area—output. Click the Output Files tab. There, click the Save Animation button.

9. A file requester will come up when you click Save Animation. Find a place on your hard drive where you'll save the animation. The desktop is a good place to start. Give it a name like "butterfly" and click Save.

10. You need to specify what type of animation you want to save, such as an AVI or MOV. Click the selection button next to Type and choose your preference. Figure 1.70 shows the panel with the setup.

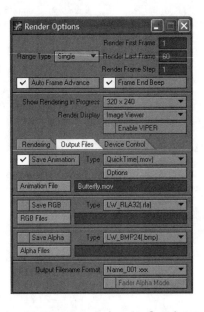

Figure I.70   Saving an animation is as easy as choosing Save Animation, giving it a name, and choosing the type of file. All this is done within the Render Options panel.

11. Guess what? One last step. Render! From the Rendering drop-down list at the top left of the Layout interface, choose Render Scene.

Depending on the speed of your system, your animation will be finished in a matter of minutes. Take a break, go grab a snack, and when you come back, you'll see your first LightWave animation! Just find the file where you saved it (which is why the desktop is a good place) and double-click it to play.

Conclusion

So there you have it! Your first LightWave animation. It's not as complicated as it looks, is it? You first modeled, then textured, set up motions, and rendered a scene, even including a composited background image. This, in a nutshell, is the LightWave 3D process. Although there are many more complex areas to be explored throughout the program, this quick-start tutorial provided enough information for you to now close this book and experiment on your own. When you're ready, continue to explore the more detailed chapters of *Inside LightWave 8*!

Chapter 2

3D Animation Basics

Learning a new software application can be daunting, to say the least. Adding a third dimension often takes the learning curve off the chart. Because of this, *Inside LightWave 8* includes a chapter to clearly explain 3D space and how it relates to the LightWave 3D applications, Modeler and Layout. In this chapter, you learn about:

- What the third dimension is
- Understanding the X-, Y-, and Z-axis
- Understanding the H-, P-, and B-axis
- 3D space with LightWave's grid
- Working with the HUB
- Proper working methods

Computing Technology

You know what 3D animation is, and you can visually see how it differs from 2D animation. The 2D animation many of you grew up watching on television is a classic art that should be cherished. Although many of the classic traditional artists feel that creating 3D animation is nothing more than pushing a few buttons, nothing could be further from the truth. It is an art all its own.

The technology you know today as 3D animation, or computer generated imagery (CGI), has evolved over the last 50 years. That's right, 50 years! Computer graphics technology began in the early 1950s, mostly as a visual aide to military and applied sciences. It had nothing to do with art as we know it today. As time progressed, computers became more accessible and user friendly, parts and chips decreased in price, and by the 1970s, computer technology was appearing in offices, laboratories, and other areas that needed computing. Computers then were the size of refrigerators (now those same computers can be outperformed by your tiny cellular phone). The evolution of computers from big machines to personal tools began in the 1970s. Granted, it took years before we saw them used on a daily basis in our lives, but this evolution of technology was as important to your history as the industrial revolution was in the early 1900s. In the 1980s, computers worked their way into our homes, primarily in the form of a Macintosh or the IBM PC. Anyone who was fortunate enough to get his or her hands on a Mac or PC knew that the future had arrived. In the early 1990s, computer manufacturing was booming. With these new, faster, cheaper computer systems, software began emerging that helped artists visualize their creativity. Artists began incorporating computers into their regular lives and soon began relying on computer technology not as an aide, but as a tool.

In the mid 1980s, a little California company called Pixar was creating mind-blowing computer-generated art. Although most people were used to seeing animation drawn by hand one frame at a time, Pixar used computer technology to generate images in 3D. Rather than seeing just a flat image drawn up and down and left and right, the computer-generated images now had depth—the Z-axis—or forward and back. As computers evolved and became faster, programmers could do more. Pixar introduced proprietary software called RenderMan in 1988 that enabled viewers to see more than just crude computer-generated 3D images, but rather lit and textured surfaces. Other companies in the 1980s started developing 3D technology, such as Alias, Wavefront (Alias and Wavefront eventually merged and created Maya), Side Effects Software, and another company out of Topeka, Kansas, named NewTek.

Tip

Check out an early pioneer of 3D, Professor Charles Csuri, at
`http://accad.osu.edu/main/history1.htm`.

There was a program in the mid to late 1980s called Aegis Videoscape 3D. The programmers who created it were eventually hired by NewTek, and LightWave was born. Figure 2.1 shows the original interfaces. In 1990, the Videoscape and Aegis programs became what we know today as LightWave 3D. Figure 2.2 shows the first-generation LightWave interface.

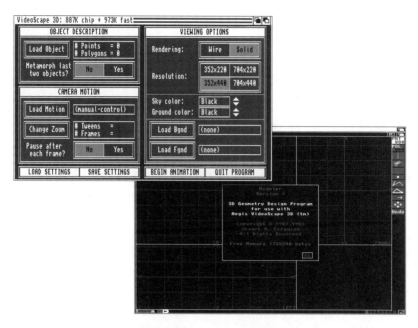

Figure 2.1 The first 3D programs from NewTek, Inc. appeared in 1988 as Videoscape 3D and Aegis Modeler.

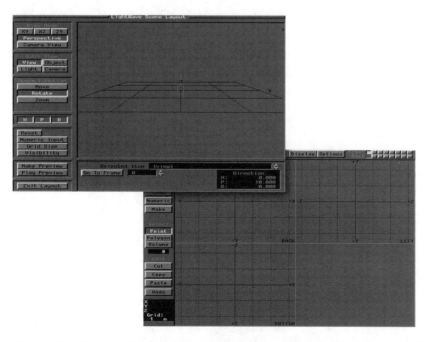

Figure 2.2 The year 1990 heralded the arrival of a new decade and the beginning of what we now know to be LightWave 3D.

The history of 3D animation, computer technology, and the ever-evolving digital world is a fascinating topic. The information here is simply a quick overview of how LightWave started. But to better understand how it works, this chapter will focus its attention on some basic three-dimensional principles that not only worked 15 years ago, but are the foundation for 3D today.

What Is 3D?

Simply put, 3D animation is computer-generated creations that involve not just the Y-axis (up and down) and X-axis (left and right), but also the Z-axis (forward and back). However, it is much more than that. 3D animation has become an entire art form all its own. It is now one of the most popular majors in art colleges, and is the fastest growing medium to hit television and movies since sound. 3D animation allows you to create whatever you can imagine. Although this is a LightWave book, you can create just about anything you can think of in just about any of the 3D modeling and animation packages out there. The software applications today are nothing more than tools for you to create stunning 3D models and animation.

With that in mind, take a look at how 3D animation differs from 2D animation. 2D, or two-dimensional animation, as I mentioned earlier, is what many of you might have grown up with. You know, the Saturday morning cartoons, drawn one frame at a time by hand? These hand drawn animations are fine art, and 3D animation is not intended to replace this medium. Often, 3D is used in conjunction with 2D animation to create an entirely new breed of eye candy. Figure 2.3 shows a hand-drawn 2D image, whereas Figure 2.4 shows a 3D image.

Figure 2.3   A 2D image is flat and lacks depth.

Figure 2.4   A 3D image has depth and picks up highlights of shading from light sources and more.

Notice how in Figure 2.3, the image is flat. It can be animated, but it lacks depth. Figure 2.4 shows how 3D animation has depth and also can incorporate shading from light sources, shadows, and more. The 3D animation you know today takes into consideration many real-world principles, such as lighting, depth of field, radiosity, and more, all of which we'll cover throughout this book.

Understanding Axis Movement

Perhaps one of the most important parts to understand in 3D animation is that you need to think in the third dimension—that is, whatever object you're looking at (be it a box, ball, or fire-breathing dragon) should have a top, back, bottom, front, and sides. Too often, artists forget this and only consider what's in front of them on their computer screens. You need to remember that the object you're modeling or animating, even if it is flat, has a top and a back!

Axes are often confusing at first, but pretty simple if you know how to think about them. Don't try to remember which axis is which; instead, associate the X, Y, and Z with something. For example, when thinking of X, crisscross your arms. When you do this, you position your arms to the left and right. There's your X-axis, left and right. Now, think about that stupid YMCA song you hear at weddings. What do you do when you sing out the "Y" of YMCA? You stand up, and put your arms up in the air representing Y. Guess what? There's the Y-axis, up and down. What's left? Z! Z-axis is easy to remember if you think about Zorro and his whip. When he throws it, it's forward, and then back. That's the Z-axis, in front of you and behind you. Figures 2.5, 2.6, and 2.7 show the X-, Y-, and Z-axis positions within the LightWave interface.

Understanding axes might not come easily at first, but it won't be difficult to understand once you begin working through projects in the book. Knowing about axes is crucial to everything you do in LightWave, but it's not hard to figure them out. Often, just remembering two axes helps you figure out the third. As you work through the tutorials in the book, you'll be reminded of which axis is which.

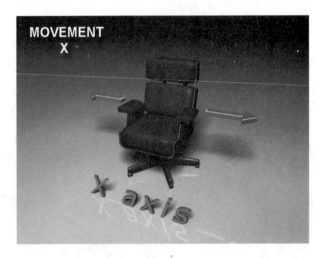

Figure 2.5   Sliding this chair to the left or right is movement on the X-axis.

Figure 2.6   Raising this chair up or down is movement on the Y-axis.

Figure 2.7   Rolling this chair forward or backward is movement on the Z-axis.

Understanding Axis Rotation

Alongside axis movement on the X-, Y-, and Z-axes are the rotational axis controls H, P, and B. H stands for heading, P stands for pitch, and B is bank. A good way to think of this is to imagine standing at a crossroad in the city or country. You stand in the middle of the road and wonder which way to go. If you turn your body, you're now heading in a new direction, right? It's the same thing in 3D. Heading is like sitting in a chair and turning around. Pitch, on the other hand, is like sitting in your chair and tilting back or forward. Now go one step further. You're sitting in your chair, and you've turned around (heading) to see who's coming in the door. You stop to talk to your friend and lean back in your chair (pitch). He asks you if you can borrow this book for a little while to brush up on LightWave 8. You hesitate, but agree. Then, you reach to your side to grab the book and your chair begins to tip to the side (bank). Figures 2.8, 2.9, and 2.10 show rotational axes.

There you have it! Not as hard as calculus, and definitely easier than engineering an aircraft! These six axis controls are important not only for how you model, but also how you work and move about in LightWave's 3D universe. We'll reference the X-, Y-, and Z-axes as well as the H-, P-, and B-axis controls throughout the book to help you understand this concept further.

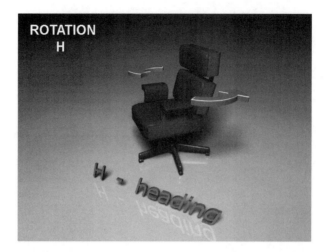

Figure 2.8   H, or heading, is the way your object, camera, or light is facing. Rotating this chair, such as spinning in it, is a heading rotation.

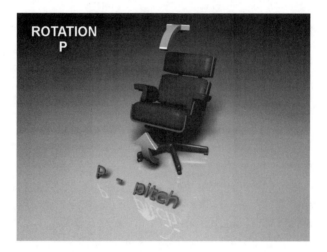

Figure 2.9   P, or pitch, is the way your object, camera, or light is tilted.

Important

If you look at the color version of the figures, located on this book's DVD, you'll notice that the arrows for movement and rotation are each different. X and H are red; Y and P are green; and Z and B are blue. The reason for this is to match LightWave's handle colors. These handles (turned on in the Display Options panel) in Layout represent both the movement and rotation axes while providing specific control. You'll learn more about these controls and others in Chapter 4, "Layout."

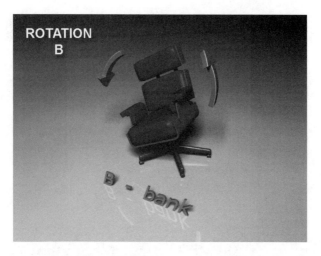

Figure 2.10   B, or bank, is the way your object, camera, or light is leaning.

LightWave's Unit of Measurement

The axis is first discussed in this chapter because it is crucial to every modeling and animation project you approach. In addition, the axis plays a key role when it comes to LightWave's texturing capabilities. Understanding proper axis rotation allows you to quickly apply necessary surface settings. Many of the values you apply throughout LightWave for texturing situations or movement are simply arbitrary. Other settings, however, are based on LightWave's unit of measurement. This measurement varies based on the size of your 3D models. When modeling is discussed in detail in later chapters, you'll see that 3D models can be any size you want, yet it's a good idea to try and model everything to scale.

LightWave's measurement system when creating 3D models can be set to English, Metric, or System International (SI). Throughout this book, we'll use LightWave's default measurement of SI. When it comes to animation in LightWave Layout, the unit of measurement varies based on the size of the grid. Figure 2.11 shows the grid as it is, by default, in Layout.

Figure 2.11 The LightWave Layout has a grid that measures 100 meters by default. This grid is a reference for both animating and texturing.

If you look closely at the bottom left of the Layout interface, you'll see a setting labeled Grid, with a value of one meter (1m), as in Figure 2.12.

This means that every square you see within the grid in Layout is 1m in size (see Figure 2.11). Given that, if you're trying to create a motion that needs to move 4m, simply move that item four grid spaces. This grid measurement can vary, and often does automatically, based on the scale of your 3D objects. When you read Chapter 4 about LightWave Layout, you'll see firsthand how this grid works and how it can be adjusted.

Modeler also has a default unit of measurement. Figure 2.13 shows the LightWave Modeler, and if you notice, there is also a grid pattern in the main views, similar to Layout.

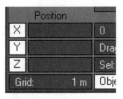

Figure 2.12
LightWave's default Grid size in Layout is one meter, or 1m.

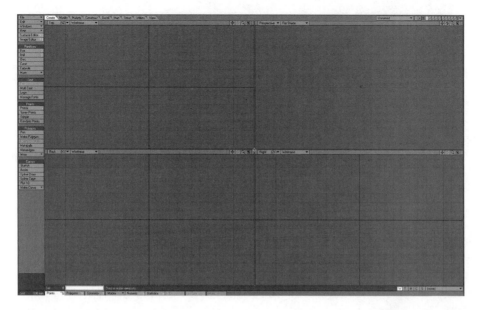

Figure 2.13   LightWave's default Grid size in Modeler is 500 millimeters, or 500mm.

If you look down to the bottom left of the Modeler interface, you'll see a numeric value of 500mm (see Figure 12.14). This is the default unit of measurement for Modeler, and similar to Layout, it means that every grid square you see is 500mm in size. If you create a 3D box that is the size of two grid squares, you'd have a box that is 1 meter in size.

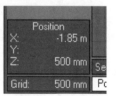

Figure 2.14
LightWave Modeler's default Grid size in Layout is one grid square equal to 500mm.

You'll be called upon to view this info area in the bottom-left corner of both Modeler and Layout throughout this book. When building models, setting up textures, applying motions with the Graph Editor, or even incorporating depth of field focus effects, this info area provides valuable information.

Working with LightWave's Grid

LightWave's grid is important. It's not often discussed, and it changes based on your 3D models. Understanding how the grid affects your working 3D space can be tricky, but the following fighter jet example will help illustrate. By default, the Grid Square Size in Layout is one meter (1m), and as stated earlier, every square you see is 1m in size. Figure 2.15 shows the default view in LightWave Layout with the default grid.

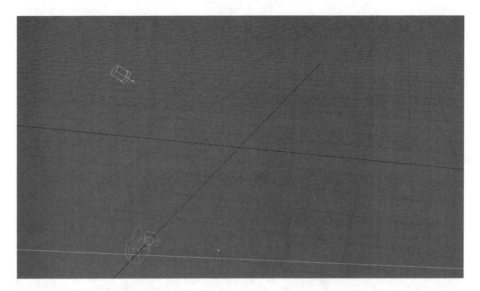

Figure 2.15   The LightWave Layout default grid, as seen from the default Perspective view.

Exercise 2.1   Working with the Grid

Let's say that you want to animate a cool F16 fighter jet 3D object.

1. Start LightWave Layout, and then load the object. Click the Items tab at the top of the screen. On the left side of the interface, you'll see various tools, some of which are the Load tools. Under Load, select Object. Your system's file requester appears, as in Figure 2.16.

   Based on how you set up LightWave's Content Directory, your system may or may not point to the right location to load the file. On the book's DVD, within the Projects folder, you'll find folders named Images, Objects, and Scenes. Go to the Objects folder, and select the Chapter02 folder. In there, you'll find the F16 object. If you accidentally select the Images or Scenes folder, it might appear that there is nothing there. Don't be fooled. Because you told LightWave to "Load Object," it looks specifically for files with the LWO extension, a LightWave object file. All other file types are hidden from view.

   Important

   The LightWave Content Directory is explained in the Introduction in the section, "Using the Book's DVD," and also in Appendix C, "What's on the DVD." Be sure to follow these steps to properly use the book's DVD so you can access all the project files.

Figure 2.16   When you select Load Object from the Item tab's tools, your system's file requester appears.

Notice that the size of Layout's grid has changed slightly. It was originally 1m by default (look at the bottom-left corner of Layout in the Info panel). Now, it's 5m! The grid size automatically adjusted because of the model you just loaded.

2. With the F16 object loaded into Layout, click the Object command under Load again and load the BumpyEarth object from the same Chapter02 folder.

   You'll see the grid size now change to 50km! That's 5000m! Huge! If you try to select and move the F16 object, you're going to have a difficult time because LightWave has adjusted the grid to match the new object, which is roughly 160km in size!

3. You can move this object around by pressing t on the keyboard or selecting Move from the Modify tab. Figure 2.17 shows Layout from the Perspective view with the earth object moved to the side. Notice that the original F16 model is nowhere to be found. Or is it?

4. Press d on the keyboard to call up the Display Options panel, as shown in Figure 2.18.

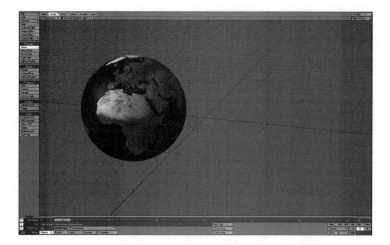

Figure 2.17   You can easily move the earth around, but the first object you loaded, the F16, seems to be missing.

Figure 2.18   The Display Options panel, where you can adjust many Layout settings.

5. Near the top of the Display Options panel, you'll see a setting for Grid Square Size. This is the LightWave Layout grid setting, which had automatically adjusted to accommodate the huge earth model you loaded. Change this to 5m. All you

need to do is select the 50km that's there now, type in 5, and press Enter on your keyboard. The value will default to meters and add the m to the 5. Figure 2.19 shows area to enter this value.

6. After you change the Grid Square Size in the Display Options panel (d key), you can close the panel and go back to Layout. Look! Your F16 has reappeared! Must have flown through the Bermuda Triangle or something!

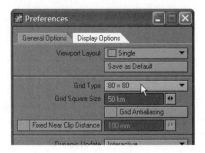

Figure 2.19   You can easily change Layout's Grid Square Size in the Display Options panel.

You don't always have to go into the Display Options panel every time you load an object. In fact, it's not often that you'll have scenes with such dramatic differences in size. When you do, you can simply adjust the Grid Square Size as needed, directly in Layout from the keyboard.

7. With the F16 object in view in Layout, you might have noticed that your BumpyEarth object is nowhere in sight. This is because we're actually inside it! It's so large, that it's surrounded the Layout. You can press the right bracket key (]) on your keyboard (two keys to the right of the p key). With this, you can interactively change the Grid Square Size a few meters at a time. Press it a couple of times and you'll see your BumpyEarth object come down into view. Conversely, you can use the left bracket key ([) (next to the p key) to decrease the Grid Square Size.

One final note on the grid size in Layout: Why would you use this? Just to view objects? Not exactly. Movements and rotations (discussed earlier in this chapter) are all based on the size of this grid measurement system. At times, you may need to precisely align or move or rotate a Layout item, such as a light, camera, or object. Often, you might find that you cannot get the alignment precise enough, and when this happens, you can adjust the Grid Square Size. By the same token, your Layout item might not be moving enough. Take the F16 and BumpyEarth models you just worked with. If you were to load the F16 model, and then load the BumpyEarth, your Grid Square Size becomes quite large. Then, if you select the F16 and zoom in your view to see it, moving it across the screen would seem to make it disappear—that is, you would find yourself moving the F16 out of view in one simple movement. It is moving, but with a small object moving in a 50km space, the relationship is so large, you see huge movements. It's very much like being in an airplane at 30,000 feet. Did you ever notice how slow the earth moves beneath you, even at 400mph? This is very much the same in LightWave with the Grid Square Size.

Important

When you adjust the Grid Square Size in Layout, it appears that the wireframe icons for lights and cameras tend to grow or shrink. They really don't. The grid is the only thing changing in size. Lights and cameras do not change size. Objects do change size, but only when you use the Size tool from the Modify tab. Adjusting the grid does not change an object's size, only its visible state.

Throughout the book, if needed, you'll be instructed to adjust the grid accordingly. But it's important for you to understand what's happening to your program when you load and work with objects of varying sizes.

Working with LightWave's HUB

Because LightWave 3D incorporates two programs, Modeler and Layout, NewTek has created the HUB. The HUB runs automatically when you start either Layout or Modeler. Its function is simple: keep a working copy of objects in a buffer and update each program accordingly. This means that if you create an object in Modeler, you can quickly send it to Layout for animation.

Exercise 2.2   Updating Objects with the HUB

Whoops! Forgot to attach wings to that plane? No problem! Jump back to Modeler, make the change, and your model is instantly updated in Layout. Check it out for yourself.

1. Make sure both Layout and Modeler are closed. Then, start LightWave Layout.

2. Load the same F16 object from this book's Chapter 02 folder on the DVD, as you did in the previous Grid Square exercise. Figure 2.20 shows the object loaded in Layout from the Perspective view.

   You should see a small button in the upper-right corner of Layout named Modeler, as in Figure 2.21.

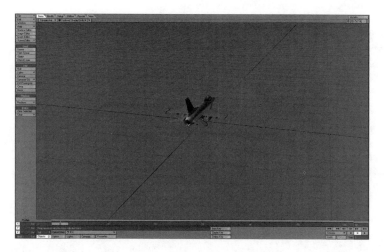

Figure 2.20 The F16 model loaded in Layout from this book's DVD.

 Important

If you don't see this Modeler button in the upper-right corner of Layout, your HUB has not started. This may be because another version of LightWave is running, or your HUB was never closed properly from a previous session. Make sure you close both Modeler and Layout if running, and also check to see if the HUB program is running. On the PC, you'll see a small LightWave logo icon in your task bar. On the Mac, simply Force Quit the HUB. Then, restart LightWave Layout and you should now see the Modeler button in the upper-right corner.

Figure 2.21
When you start LightWave Layout, the Modeler button in the upper-right corner connects you to Modeler via the HUB.

3. With the F16 fighter jet model loaded, click the Modeler button in the upper-right corner of Layout. After a moment, the LightWave Modeler starts. You'll see the Modeler screen appear with the F16! Figure 2.22 shows the view.

One thing you will notice is that the F16 fighter jet is not fully visible within the Modeler views because of Modeler's default grid size. Although LightWave Layout automatically adjusts its grid for different sized objects, Modeler does not.

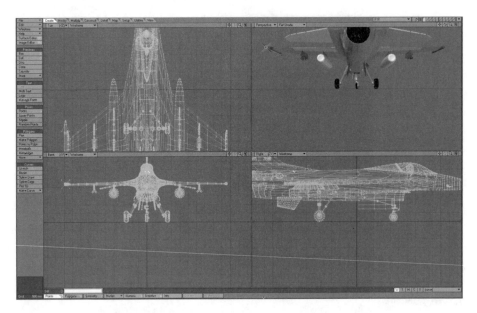

Figure 2.22   Clicking the Modeler button from within LightWave Layout opens the LightWave Modeler via the HUB and automatically brings in the currently selected object.

4. Press the a key on your keyboard. The F16 model will be "fit" to all views. This Fit All command can also be found under the Display tab in Modeler.

Important

Remember that when working in either Layout or Modeler, always use lowercase keys on your keyboard. Keep the Caps Lock off.

5. In Modeler, go to the top of the interface and select the Modify tab.

6. On the left side of the screen, select the Shear tool, as shown in Figure 2.23.

7. With the Shear tool selected, click and drag with the left mouse on the top of the F16 model in the top view. The top view is the upper-left quadrant in Modeler. It's the view that's looking down at the top of the 3D model. Figure 2.24 shows the operation.

Figure 2.23
The Shear tool selected from within the Modify tab in LightWave Modeler.

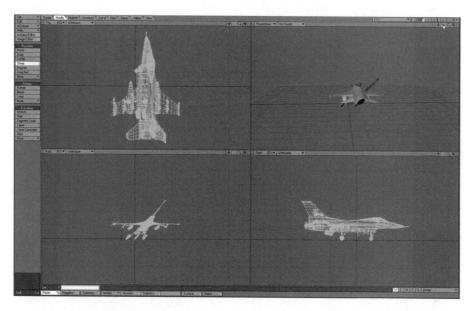

Figure 2.24 Using the Shear tool, click and drag with the left mouse button to modify the F16 3D model.

8. With your F16 fighter jet sheared a bit, press either the Alt+Tab key combination on your keyboard or the F12 key to jump back to Layout. Look what's happened! The operation in Modeler has updated the model in Layout. Figure 2.25 shows the change.

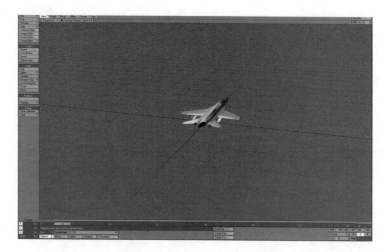

Figure 2.25 A change to a model in Modeler on an object that resides in Layout is updated in both programs, via the HUB.

9. If you press Ctrl+z for Undo in Modeler, and jump back to Layout, the change is also reflected. Play around with various tools to see the effects on the model and the HUB.

Now that you see how the HUB works, here's the bad news. It can really screw you up if you're not careful! Here's a good example. You've created a cool-looking 3D character. It's taken days to get it just right—perhaps even weeks! Of course, you've saved it in stages, but this latest version is just perfect. You make some final tweaks and send it to Layout for texturing and animation. With hours invested in texturing and getting it just right, you realize that you're missing a crucial wart on the character's oversized nose. So, you hop on into Modeler and make some changes to the model. You save it and jump back to Layout. Guess what!? Your textures are gone! ARGH! What the #$#%#@%!!*&!

What's happened is that the HUB keeps a copy of the model in a buffer. When you work with the model in Layout, applying textures and such, you are really working with a copy of the model that resides in Modeler. Jumping back and forth between Layout and Modeler doesn't bring the model back and forth with you, but rather, displays two copies.

Here are a few tips when working with the HUB:

- Try not to jump back and forth between Modeler and Layout during projects.
- Save purposefully—that is, using Save All Objects in Layout deliberately saves the textured version of your work.
- Saving from Modeler when there's a textured version of your model in Layout overrides that model. Be careful.
- Consider modeling and then saving the object.
- Send the object to Layout, then close the Modeler program entirely.

Finally, there are a few more commands that rely on the HUB to work. In the upper-right corner of the Modeler interface, there's a tiny downward-pointing arrow. Click this, and you'll see three options: Switch to Layout, Synchronize Layout, and Send Object to Layout. If these options are ghosted, your HUB is not active and your programs are not connected. If so, review this section on working with the HUB to get it going, or refer to your LightWave 3D user's manual. More simply though, just restart all programs, LightWave Layout, LightWave Modeler, and make sure that the HUB is closed from any previous session.

Proper Work Methods

As Chapter 2 wraps up, you're about to start discovering all the features available in LightWave 8. But before you turn to the next chapter, it's good to know a few basic principles that can help expedite your work in LightWave.

Proper Content Directory Setup

The Content Directory is a confusing issue for some, but it doesn't have to be. The Content Directory is where LightWave looks for files. Simple enough, right? Many studios use multiple Content Directories, and you can as well. But this requires you to change the Content Directory within LightWave and point it to a new location each time you work. Honestly, if you don't have to work this way, don't. Although LightWave offers a Recent Scenes option under the File menu in Layout, which can help you locate previously used files, you still need to change this each time you work.

LightWave has three basic elements you can load, in addition to various motion and data files. These basic elements are images, objects, and scenes. Scenes are the projects, so to speak, that you create in Layout. A scene includes objects you build in Modeler, and the objects hold images that you use for texturing, either in Modeler or Layout. When you tell LightWave to load a scene, it automatically points to your set Content Directory and looks for a Scenes folder. The same applies to images and objects. A smart way to work is to create project folders within each of the default Images, Objects, and Scenes folders that LightWave already has created on your hard drive during its installation. For example, pretend you're doing a job for MumbaJumba Hot Sauce, Co. With your default LightWave Content Directory normally set to *yourdrive*://LightWave, you can create a folder labeled MJHot (or something similar) within each of the Images, Objects, and Scenes folders that live in the LightWave folder. Save all images for this client in the MJHot Images folder. Save all objects in the MJHot Objects folder, and do the same for your scenes.

The benefit of doing this, other than being organized, is that you can instantly back up your projects. If you need to save the MJHot client projects, just burn those three folders to a CD. Or, if you want to back up all of your work, simply burn or copy your LightWave folder on your drive. Because everything you create is within this folder, it's all in one easy-to-locate place. And, you still only have one Content Directory.

Your Work Environment

Anyone working in the arts of any sort has, at one time or another, probably been hassled by someone not involved in his or her craft. Perhaps you have collectibles around your computer monitor or study the latest sci-fi epic until all hours of the night. Whatever your case, you're different from everyone else—you're a creative. You're not a corporate suit who likes to have meetings about meetings! You march to the beat of your own drum, and as it should be, your work environment should reflect that. It's not that you should go to work in your underwear or anything, but here are a few tips to help your creative juices flow:

- Lighting! Proper lighting is so critical to an animator's working environment; it's odd that we even need to mention it! Turn off fluorescent lights. Turn on desk lamps or dim any overhead can lights.

- Clean your desk! Not to sound like your mother, but a less cluttered workspace can help you organize your goals when tackling projects. The same goes for your computer's desktop. Organize your files and take an extra few seconds with each project and put things where they belong. Quickly saving anywhere only leads to wasted time later.

- If your computer monitor is bugging you, change it! Adjust the brightness and contrast for a pleasant balance. If your monitor flickers, perhaps you should crank up the refresh rate.

- Listening to music while you work is very good for the soul. That's right! With Internet radio available, or even just a collection of your favorite CDs, you'll find that you may be able to concentrate more on your work with a little noise in the background.

Someone once said that animators are not morning people. You might be one of them. Too often in the field, you're under the gun to meet a deadline or "be creative." Your boss comes in and tells you at 8 a.m. that he needs a "cool 3D character" by 1 p.m. for an emergency print ad. "Sure," you say and then start to panic. The panic is natural. Most animators do it at one point or another, so don't think you're the only one. Being creative under pressure is not easy. It's not as if you can turn on a switch and go. If you're like most, you need to be in the groove or mood to get that project done. The point here is that there will be good days and bad days when working with LightWave or any other

3D application. Some days, you'll be amazed at how fast you can create something. Other days, you'll spend hours and hours and it's still just "not right." That's OK! Every once in a while, you need to take a break, walk away from your computer, and get your thoughts together. Work to the best of your ability and have fun at it—everything else will fall into place.

The Next Step

If you've started at the beginning of this book, you've already modeled, textured, animated, and learned about 3D space. In addition, you've worked through the LightWave HUB and seen how LightWave's grid affects your models and work environment. When you're comfortable with these steps, move on to Chapters 3 and 4 and get to know LightWave Modeler and Layout. From there, Chapter 5, "Keyframing and Graph Editor," begins our in-depth tutorials—so get ready to create!

Chapter 3
Modeler

What is a 3D Modeler? Too often, people assume you know what this means. If you think about 3D animation, you have an unlimited number of variables to deal with. However, I want you not to think about the overall cluster of buttons in LightWave, but rather the tools. A Modeler is where your 3D animations begin. Although some animations can be created with animated textures or photographs, most animations include 3D models. These models are made up of points and polygons. This chapter guides you through the explanation of points and polygons and how to use them to create 3D objects, which you will eventually animate and render.

Even with so many improvements in LightWave over the years, version 8 includes some of the most complex changes to date. LightWave Modeler has been touted as one of the best 3D Modelers in the industry, and the latest update makes it a more efficient, powerful tool. This chapter introduces you to the LightWave Modeler and instructs you on the workflow and tool usage process. Some of the key areas discussed in this chapter are:

- LightWave 8 Modeler Interface Navigation
- Understanding Viewports
- Creating Simple Objects
- Working with Points and Polygons
- Selection and Deselection
- Splines and Subpatches

Modeling in 3D takes discipline, focus, and a keen sense of direction because to properly construct a 3D model, you need to fully understand the tools you're using. Just as if you're building a cabinet in your garage or redoing the tile in your own bathroom, you start with a plan or blueprint. The same can be said for both 3D models and animations. This is because you want your 3D models to be efficient. That is, the models need to be constructed properly so they can be animated correctly. When you know the tools and methods, the goal is not difficult to accomplish. Your focus should be clear, and as mentioned earlier in the book, your work environment should be comfortable. There's nothing worse than working on a complex model without a plan and in an uncomfortable workspace. Be prepared, both mentally and physically.

Understanding 3D Modeling

At this point, you should be well versed in the medium that is 3D animation. You should understand how the X-, Y-, and Z-axes relate to each other and your LightWave workspace. If you don't, please refer to Chapter 2, "3D Animation Basics," for a little refresher course.

Important

Too often when people work in 3D, either in modeling or animation, they only consider the flat screen in front of them. Do not make this mistake! That is to say, understand and remember that your 3D models are more than just what's in front of you—they have a side, a top, a bottom, and a back, even if you can't see it.

3D modeling is like interactive geometry. You can begin creating models with simple points and connect them with a curve or a straight line. LightWave gives you a slew of basic geometric shapes to work with, and you'll see throughout this book just how those basic shapes, like a box, can be used to create more complex 3D models. 3D modeling involves a good amount of math, but that does not mean you'll need to be calculating measurement and equations to create 3D models. LightWave is smart enough to do the math for you, as you'll see throughout this chapter. The system works in either metric or English measurements, so if you're in America, France, Japan or elsewhere, you can understand the values LightWave Modeler uses. Before you concern yourself with building complex 3D models, however, take a look at how the LightWave interface is laid out.

LightWave 8 Modeler Interface

LightWave 8 has brought some of the industry's most desired tools to the surface of an already powerful modeling application. Although much of this book focuses on the modeling tools in action, this section highlights the new features of LightWave 8 Modeler. You'll be able to try them out in just a few steps to gain a strong working knowledge of their functions. Both LightWave Layout and Modeler have been significantly streamlined, and navigation has never been easier.

If you're new to LightWave with version 8, the interface will obviously look unfamiliar to you. If you're an existing user of LightWave and have just upgraded to LightWave 8, you'll notice at first a similarity to previous versions. Upon closer inspection, however, you'll find that things are a good bit different. Initially, working through the interface will be frustrating, but rest assured that this new button arrangement will greatly help your workflow. Figure 3.1 shows the new LightWave 8 Modeler upon startup.

Figure 3.1   The LightWave 3D 8 Modeler Interface.

Modeler Viewports

Let's take a look at the viewports first. These are the areas that will be your work environment, and by default, they can show all sides of your 3D model. Figure 3.2 shows the same full Modeler interface as Figure 3.1, but this time with a 3D model loaded.

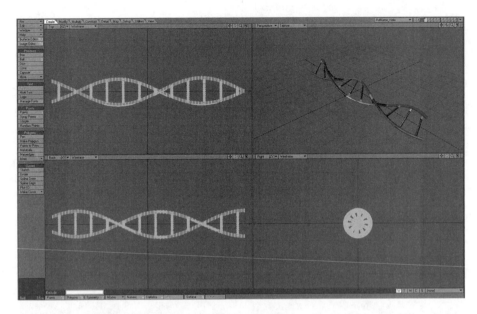

Figure 3.2 A 3D Model loaded into LightWave Modeler can be seen from all sides, and the default layout also shows a solid color version.

Don't let this layout of viewports fool you, however. You can change any viewport to look any way you like. Take a look at Figure 3.3, where a close-up of the top-left viewport is shown.

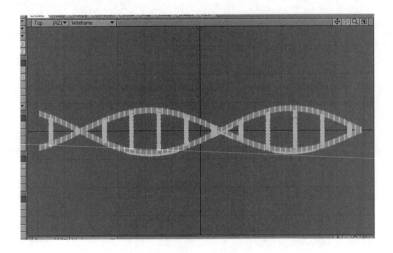

Figure 3.3 A close-up of the top-left viewport with some geometry loaded.

This top-left viewport is called Top by default, and it shows the 3D object from above—you're looking at the "top" of the object. Notice that, at the top of the viewport, there are some buttons labeled Top (XZ) and Wireframe. This tells you that the particular viewport is set to Top. The XZ means these are the two axes you have control over. Because you're looking down the Y-axis, you can't adjust your object for that axis in this view.

To the top right of the viewport, you'll see four small icons. These are your viewport position controls. Figure 3.4 shows the buttons up close.

Figure 3.4
The four small icons at the top right of each viewport enable you to move, rotate, zoom, and maximize the viewport.

 Important

You'll notice that, depending on the viewport, certain position control icons are ghosted, such as the Rotate icon in the Top viewport. This is because you can't rotate in an orthogonal (X, Y, Z) view.

Click, hold, and drag on one of these buttons, and you'll be able to use them. Too often, people click them and release, but that's not how they work. Click and hold to use! The first button is Move, the next is Rotate, the third is Zoom, and the last button is the Maximize viewport button. Click this one, and your viewport will become full screen. This is great for getting up close to your model for fine-tuning point position or measurements. To return from a full screen viewport, just click that icon again.

 Tip

If you don't want to click the Maximize viewport button in each view (very handy if you have a laptop since most laptops don't have a numeric keypad), you can also just press the 0 key on your numeric keypad. That's 0, as in zero. Press it again to return from full screen mode. Be sure your mouse cursor is in the particular viewport you want to maximize before pressing the 0 key.

Viewport Customization

Each of the four viewports in Modeler can have its appearance customized any way you like. By default, LightWave Modeler gives you a Top, Back, and Right view. Each is a little awkward at first, but try to remember this:

- Top view (XZ) controls the Y-axis. You are looking down at the top of your object.

- Back view (XY) controls the Z-axis. You are looking from the back of your object toward its front.

- Right view (ZY) controls the X-axis. You are looking at the left side of your object, toward its right.

Yes, this sounds extremely confusing, but after you get used to it, it will make more sense. You see, when you get to Layout later, the Back view you see in Modeler is the same default view that the LightWave camera sees. The LightWave camera looks toward the back of the object, forward in the scene.

With that out of the way, take a look at Figure 3.5. Here, you can see that each viewport can become a Back, Top, Side, or otherwise. You can make all four viewports Top views if you like, although it might not help your modeling process too much.

Something you might change more than the viewport view is the viewport style. Figure 3.6 shows the drop-down choices available, from a Wireframe style to full Smooth Shade to the new Textured Wire style. Figure 3.7 shows each viewport set to a different style so you can see how flexible the options are.

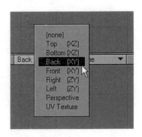

Figure 3.5
Each viewport can be set to any view you like.

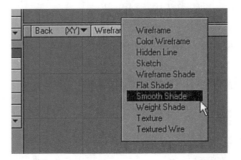

Figure 3.6   Each viewport can also have a unique viewport style, such as Wireframe or Textured Wire.

Tip

Your choice of viewport style will be based on the model you are creating. Often, a good way to work is with the default settings—wireframe style in the X, Y, and Z viewports, while a Smooth Shade, or Textured Wire style is used in a perspective view. It's totally up to you.

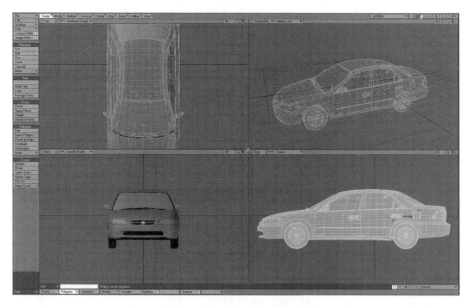

Figure 3.7   Here, each viewport is set to a different style. There are a total of ten viewport style choices.

Working with Objects and Layers

At this point, you're probably chomping at the bit to actually do something. Understood! But first, take a look at how LightWave works with objects. From there, you'll learn about points, polygons, selection, and deselection, which will require you to make a few simple objects.

LightWave objects are unique to the program, and if you've found any items on your hard drive with the .lwo extension, you've found a LightWave Object file. You can load existing objects from LightWave's content directory simply by pressing Ctrl and the o key for open (that's o as in OH!) But also take a look at the File drop-down menu at the top left of the Modeler interface. Click it, and you'll see all your common load and save functions, plus a few extras. Figure 3.8 shows the panel.

Each object can have its own set of layers. This means that if your car has four wheels (hopefully it does), each object needs to be animated separately. The wheels can't roll unless they live on their own layers. If a wheel is attached to the car within the car layer, you will end up animating the entire layer.

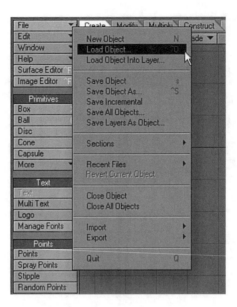

Figure 3.8 Using the File drop-down menu in Modeler, you can load, save, and perform other similar operations.

Think of this: If you're a Photoshop user, you are probably familiar with using layers. Let's say you build a billboard ad, and in the backdrop you put a gradient color. In a new layer, you add text, and in another, you add a picture, and so on. Why do you do all this in layers? So that each layer can have its own set of parameters, such as size, position, effects, and so on. If they all lived on the same layer, you'd have a tough time applying effects to any individual element, because everything is on one big layer. So along those lines, LightWave Modeler works the same way. Each item that you need to control individually should live on its own layer. That's it! You use layers later in the book to perform various modeling actions. So, take a look at the top right of the Modeler interface, and you'll find a set of ten little buttons, as in Figure 3.9.

Figure 3.9 At the top right of the Modeler interface are the Layer buttons.

Upon first glance, these look like they do nothing, but they are crucial to properly setting up and building certain types of models. Don't be fooled, however; you can have many more than ten layers. Layers are infinite in LightWave, and when you press F7, the Layers panel opens, as shown in Figure 3.10. You can also open this panel from the Window drop-down menu in Modeler, as shown in Figure 3.11.

Figure 3.10   Pressing F7 opens the Layers panel, which gives you access to Modeler layers.

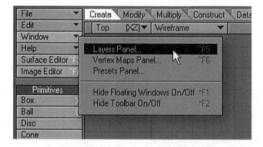

Figure 3.11   Use the Window drop-down menu to access the Layers panel if you don't like
the F7 key.

To demonstrate how LightWave Modeler works with existing 3D models, insert this
book's DVD into your computer. Be sure you have set up the content directory as
instructed in the beginning of this book, as well as read the read-me section of the disc
contents.

 Important

Although we included a DVD with this book to fit all the necessary support and
bonus files, we are aware that you might not have a DVD in your computer. If so, go
to www.danablan.com and point to the book's page to download the project files
for Inside LightWave 8.

Loading Objects and Naming Layers

Loading objects is the same, whether they contain layers or not. The LightWave object
file contains this data, and it's not something you need to worry about. LightWave
objects are smart and are saved with whatever data they have associated to them, such as
textures.

Exercise 3.1   Loading Objects and Naming Layers

1. Press Ctrl+o or Load Object from the File drop-down menu and load the SimpleRaceCar object from the Chapter03 folder from this book's DVD.

2. Figure 3.12 shows the model loaded into LightWave Modeler. You'll see that the first layer button is depressed by default, and small dots appear in the next four layer buttons.

Tip

You can load multiple objects at the same time into Modeler. However, unless you specifically cut and paste those objects together in some fashion, you can view only one object at a time. Figure 3.12 shows the layer buttons at the top right of the interface, and to the left of the layer buttons is the Current Object selection list. Any objects loaded into Modeler can be selected from this drop-down list.

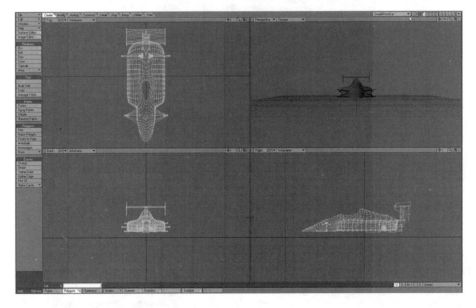

Figure 3.12   The simple racecar loaded into Modeler also shows that there are five layers of objects associated with this object.

These dots inform you that there is geometry in those layers, such as points or polygons. Open the Layers panel (Ctrl+F5) and look at what the listings show. You'll see the name of the object, and if you click the small white triangle to expand the object's layers, you'll see four listings that read "unnamed." Unnamed refers to the geometry in the layer, which you've yet to name.

3. Double-click the last "unnamed" listing, and two things will happen. You'll see the objects in Modeler change from the body of the car to the front passenger wheel. You'll also see a panel pop up that reads Layer Settings.

4. In the Layer Settings panel, enter **Front Passenger Wheel** as the Name. Then select Layer 1 as the Parent from the drop-down list. Figure 3.13 shows the operation.

Tip

Just to the left of the ten layer buttons at the top left of Modeler is a number with a left- and right-arrow button. Upon startup, you'll see the number 1. This means you're working with the first set of 10 layers. You can click the right arrow to get to another set of 10, and the number changes to 2. Click again, and you're in the third tier of layer buttons, and so on. However, this is cumbersome, and the Layers panel is often a better way to go. Open the panel and put it aside while you work! Unlimited layers, baby!

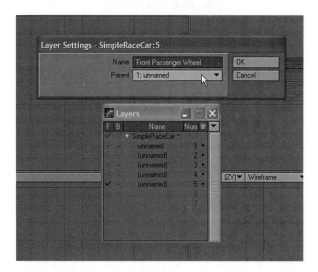

Figure 3.13   By double-clicking a chosen layer in the Layers panel, you can both rename and parent the layer to other layers.

Now, layer 1 is not yet named, but if you noticed when you loaded this object, you saw the body of the car, and the layer 1 button was selected. Layer 1 is the body of the car. You've now parented the front passenger wheel to the car. This means that later in Layout, if you animate the car, the wheels will stay attached when you move the body.

5. Click OK to close the Layer Settings panel.

6. Repeat the steps with the other layers by double-clicking each and naming them accordingly.

Layer 1 is the body, while layers 2, 3, 4, and 5 are the wheels. Parent the wheels to layer 1, the body, and you're all finished. Figure 3.14 shows the Layers panel with each layer named.

Figure 3.14   By double-clicking each individual layer, they are now named.

So, what's the point of all this, you ask? Even though this is a very simple object, all your 3D objects will be handled this way. The purpose of naming each layer is so that when animating later, you're not guessing which layer is which. You can quickly select the front passenger wheel, or the body, and so on. With that said, naming your object layers is not necessary, but it's an efficient way to work and organize. When you save your object, these layers are also saved with it. What's great about this is that you can send just this one single object to a co-worker or client, and all of its parts (such as the wheels) are contained within, as well as the parenting hierarchy.

Foreground and Background Layers

There are a few more things to note about the Layers panel. Looking at Figure 3.14, you can see some additional labels in the Layers panel. The F at the top left of the panel stands for Foreground, while the B stands for Background. As you get into more complex projects, you'll use these commands to place objects in both foreground and background. To try this out, follow these steps:

1. Select the body layer of the simple racecar object, as in Figure 3.15. This object is now in the foreground, and its wireframe is visible in a bright color in the viewports.

2. Don't click the layer itself, but click the check box beneath the B column (B for background) next to one of the other layers. Figure 3.16 shows the selection.

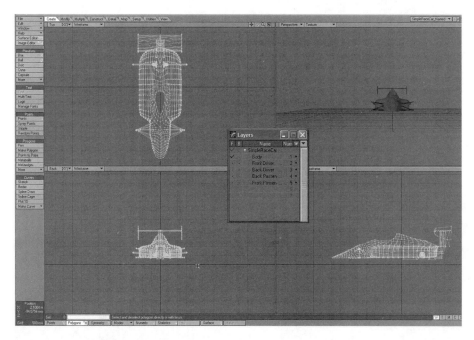

Figure 3.15 Selecting a layer in the Layers panel brings that layer to the foreground.

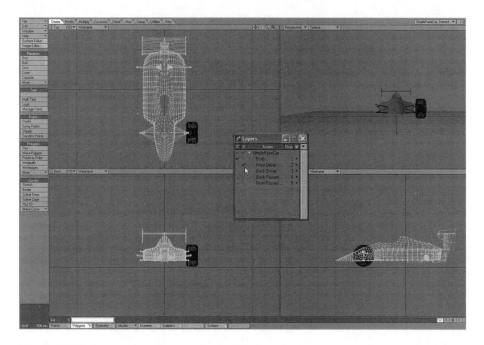

Figure 3.16 By selecting a layer under the B column in the Layers panel, you can put layers in the background for reference.

Take a close look at the Modeler interface, and you'll still see the body of the car, but in a dark outline, you'll see the wheel layer you selected. This layer is now in the background. Congratulations!

The reason for this is threefold, really. Objects in background layers are used for reference, separate animation elements, or as modeling tools.

You can hold the Shift key and select multiple background layers as well. On the right side of the Layers panel, you'll see numbers. These are the layer numbers for each layer, and unlike Photoshop layers, the order does not matter.

 Important

Layer order is not important in cases like this simple racecar object. Layer order is important, however, when using foreground and background layers as modeling tools. This will be done later in the book.

Layer Visibility

To the right side of the Layers panel, at the top, is a small eyeball icon. Beneath that, next to each layer is a little dot. Let's say you've placed an object in a background layer and used it as a reference to build a new object. If you save your LightWave object and load it into Layout, all layers will be visible. However, if you click that little dot in the Layers panel in Modeler, when the object is loaded into Layout, the unchecked layer will not be visible. Load it back into Modeler, and it will be there. This is great when you use objects as modeling tools, such as in Boolean operations.

Finally, there's one more area you should be aware of in the Layers panel, and that's the Hierarchy view option. It's easy to miss, but at the very right top corner of the Layers panel, there's a small drop-down arrow. Select it and you see the option for List or Hierarchy. So far, you've been seeing the Layers panel in List view. Figure 3.17 shows the Layers panel in Hierarchy view. You'll notice that the wheel layers are indented underneath the body of the car layer—hence, the hierarchy. This is really useful for more complex objects like characters or mechanical creations.

There are many more panels in LightWave 8 Modeler, but it's important to understand how to navigate before you get more involved. Working with the layers is essential to any model you create, which is why it's covered first in this chapter. Now, to the menus!

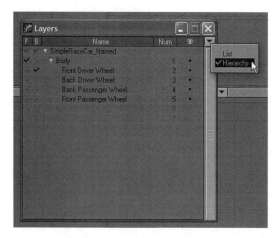

Figure 3.17   You can also choose to view your object layers as a List or Hierarchy.

Tabs and Menus

Across the top of the Modeler screen, you'll see nine tabs, each representing a different category of modeling tools. This section guides you through the different tabs and explains how they are organized. Figure 3.18 shows the tabs across the top of Modeler.

Figure 3.18   The LightWave 8 Menus are tabbed across the top of the interface. Selecting any of these brings up various tools on the left side of the screen.

When you select different tabs, different toolsets become available. The LightWave Modeler toolset works similarly throughout the program, with slight variations depending on which tool you are using. This next section guides you through the toolset categories within each of the Modeler tabs.

Important

On the top left of the Modeler interface, you'll find a set of drop-down menus that will always appear, no matter what tab you've clicked. These include File, Edit, Window, Help, Surface Editor, and Image Editor. These selections are the same in Layout and are covered in detail in Chapter 4, "Layout."

Create Tab

When working in LightWave Modeler, you must think about what you're doing. Really think about the process, and you'll have a much easier time locating the proper tool. For example, say you've just started up Modeler and want to build a 3D television set. You want to create something and need basic geometry to get started. OK, head on over to

the Create tab. Choose the box tool, and go. Then, let's say you want to change it in some way, perhaps rotate it or move it. What are you doing? You're modifying it, right? You'd go to the Modify tab to find the necessary tools. What if you need to add to this, perhaps by beveling it a bit? Think about a bevel, and you might realize that this operation will add to the geometry of your object, so look under the Multiply tab. Every tool in LightWave 8 has been rearranged so that it makes sense and is easy to find.

The Create tab calls up the basic tools you need to create geometric shapes such as boxes, balls, discs, and more. Additionally, you'll find tools to create points and curves. Figure 3.19 shows the tools under the Create tab.

The first thing you'll see when you click the Create tab is that the toolset starts at the top of the screen on the left side and pretty much fills up the entire interface! The first six buttons at the top will always be there, no matter what menu you're in (unless you customize your interface and change their location, which you'll do later in this chapter). These key tools are the File menu, Edit menu, Window menu, Help menu, Surface Editor, and Image Editor. These are important areas that you will access often, which is why they're always accessible.

Primitives

At the top of the toolset under the Create tab is the Primitives category, as shown in Figure 3.20. Here you'll find the tools to create basic geometric shapes such as a Disc, Box, Ball, Gemstone, Capsule, and more. These basic (and some not-so-basic) geometric shapes are key building blocks for just about anything you want

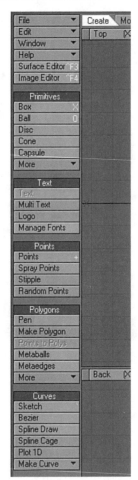

Figure 3.19
The Create tab is home to many basic tools that you'll need throughout the creation of most modeling projects.

to create. Think about it—everything around you is based on geometric shapes. A television, a couch, a kitchen sink! They all start out as a basic shape and are multiplied, cut, shaped, and formed into their final objects. The Primitives section of the Create tab gives you the tools to create a vast number of projects.

Figure 3.20
The Primitives category within the Create tab offers a wide range of basic (and some not-so-basic) shapes you can use to create 3D models.

Text

The Text category is a place you might find yourself quite often. Believe it or not, much of the LightWave work out there is not spaceships and animated characters, but rather 3D text. As you'll see in Chapter 5 of this book, you can make some pretty outstanding broadcast style animations and graphics with these tools. But what's more, text objects can also be used as building blocks. For example, you can take the letter C, turn it on its side, extrude it, and you have a slide you can put into a 3D playground. Or how about using the letter E as a building block for creating a 3D maze?

To use the text tools properly, you need to first select the Manage Fonts button, as shown in Figure 3.21. This tool enables you to load fonts into Modeler. Because many systems have enormous amounts of fonts these days, loading all of them could take a toll on your system's resources. Instead, just load the fonts you want for the current project. When loaded, the Text tool will be available. Be sure to go through the tutorials in Chapter 5, "Keyframing and Graph Editor," to see these tools in action and learn how to use them properly.

Figure 3.21
The Text tool category is where you'll find the Manage Fonts command, as well as the Text creation tool.

Points

Often you'll need to build an object from scratch, meaning that you do not start with a box or a ball, but rather a point. Later in this chapter, you'll read about points and polygons, but essentially, points make up polygons, sort of like connect the dots. The Points category gives you the tools to create points one at a time, in a cluster with the Spray Points tool, or with the Random Points generator. Figure 3.22 shows the category.

Figure 3.22
The Points category offers tools to create single points or clusters of points. Points, as you know, make up objects.

Polygons

Just because primitive shapes make basic objects and points create individual points doesn't mean that you can't create simpler polygonal objects. The Polygons category has a tool called Pen, which is very similar to the Points tool, except that as you create with this tool, polygonal lines are automatically generated between each point. You used this tool in Chapter 1, "Quick-Start." Additional Polygon tools include the Make Polygon command, which you can use after you've used the Points tool from the previous category. Additionally, you can create some organic objects with the MetaEdges and Metaballs tools. Figure 3.23 shows the category.

Figure 3.23
The Polygons category offers additional tools for building polygons from points with the Pen tool.

Curves

Last in the Create tab is the Curves category. Here, you can generate curves from points you've created. Curves are useful for many things, from motion paths to extrusion paths to actual models. The Sketch tool enables you to just click and draw, and when you release the mouse button, you have a 3D curve! You can use curves to build objects with splines. You'll do this later in the book, but splines are useful for building organic objects such as boats, curtains, or sometimes characters. Another key tool in this category is Spline Draw, with which you can precisely create curves, not only for models, but even text or custom shapes. Figure 3.24 shows the category.

Figure 3.24
You can use Curves for text, characters, motion paths, and more.

Modify Tab

The Modify tab. Sounds simple enough, right? Well, it is. Anytime you want to modify your object in some way that does not require adding or removing any points or polygons, you need to use a modify function. This tabbed area shows the same six menus at the top left (which will always be available through each menu tab) and then three toolset categories: Translate, Rotate, and Transform. Figure 3.25 shows the toolset.

Figure 3.25
The Modify tab is used when you need tools to move, rotate, or size your object.

Translate

No, this category doesn't contain tools to change your object into a foreign language, but rather to move it in 3D space. Typically, the 3D industry calls a move function a translation. The Translate category contains tools like Move, Drag, Magnet, and a few others. Each tool modifies your object in some way. Figure 3.26 shows the category.

Rotate

This category should be self-explanatory. Of course, you can rotate points or polygons with the Rotate tool, but there's much more! You can also bend, twist, and even use the cool Vortex tool. However, remember that no matter what the tool is called, it is a form of the category it lives in. In this case, the Vortex tool is a form of Rotate. Other tools like Rotate to Ground or Rotate to Normal provide extra control for precise rotations. Figure 3.27 shows the category.

Transform

Transform is a sizing function, so anytime you hear a seasoned animation veteran talk about "transforming the object," they're not talking about a Saturday morning cartoon. The Transform category includes modification tools such as Size, Stretch, Pole, and others. Every tool in this category is a form of sizing. For example, Size scales your object or selection equally on all sides. Stretch sizes your object or selection on a specific axis. Other tools, such as Smooth Scale, enable you to equally scale curved objects. Use the Transform tools when you want to size your objects or selections. Figure 3.28 shows the category.

Figure 3.26
The Translate category not only enables you to move your geometry around, be it points or polygons, but it also enables you to employ cool tools like the Rove tool.

Figure 3.27
The Rotate category contains your basic rotation tools, as well as some cool extras like Vortex.

Figure 3.28
The Transform category is the place to find Size/Scale tools.

Multiply Tab

Up to this point, the Create tab and the Modify tab tools are generally easy to wrap your brain around. When you get into the Multiply tab (see Figure 3.29), the tools become more complex. You'll use many of these throughout this book. For now, read on to find out what the categories in the Multiply tab can do for you.

Extend

The Extend category is the first category of the Multiply tab, and it contains some very common multiply-like tools. First, think about what Multiply means. It means to add onto your selection. OK, with that in mind, the Extend category contains the tools that take your existing selection and extend off of it, such as a the Bevel tool or Extrude tool. Figure 3.30 shows the category and its tools. There are more complex Extend tools, such as Rail Bevel, which enable you to build a bevel from a curve placed in a background layer. Remember earlier that when we were talking about layers, we mentioned that using foreground and background layers is not just for reference, but for modeling as well. Rail Bevel takes advantage of this.

Figure 3.29
The Multiply tab contains some complex tools that enable you to build up your object in a variety of ways.

Figure 3.30
The Extend category of tools within the Multiply menu tab offers tools to add to your objects or selections, such as bevel tools.

Duplicate

You might think that Duplicate tools would be under the Modify tab, but think again! Remember, creating more than one object by mirroring it, cloning it, or otherwise copying it is a form of multiplication. The Duplicate tools create copies of selections or objects in various ways, but these additions are not attached to your original object or selection like the Extend category tools are. Figure 3.31 shows the tools.

Subdivide

Ah, the Subdivide category. It's a deep, dark secret set of tools that can enhance your object or selection in a variety of ways. The Subdivide tools perform very cool operations to slice up your object or selection, add to it, or split it up in some way. Let's say you built a cool character and soon realize that you can't bend the character's leg because you've only made one long object. To make the leg bend at the knee, you would use the Knife tool to slice the leg and give it another segment so it's able to bend. Another cool set of tools in the Subdivide category is the QuickCut tools. These enable you to quickly slice up an object evenly, which helps you create additional detail for animation. Figure 3.32 shows the category.

Figure 3.31
Duplicate tools add to your object or selection by mirroring, cloning, or otherwise copying it.

Figure 3.32
The Subdivide tools enable you to break up your model for added detail and animation control.

Construct Tab

When you're building 3D models, it's easy to confuse the tools in the Construct tab with the tools in the Detail tab. If you take a closer look at the categories here, however, you'll see that there is a sharp difference between the two menus. Figure 3.33 shows the Construct tab tools.

Reduce

The Reduce category contains tools that enable you take away geometry from your model without being destructive. Why would you do this? You could be creating a model for a video game that requires a very low number of polygons. Or perhaps you realize you've overbuilt the model and don't need as much detail. Why not just leave it detailed? Simple—the more detail you have in an object, the longer it takes LightWave to calculate and render. Add that to other objects, lights, and shadows, and you're asking for longer renders. As mentioned at the very beginning of this chapter, you need to work efficiently from the ground up. Planning is key, and making models that are not too simple but not too complex is essential to 3D animation. The Reduce category enables you to reduce or remove points or polygons while keeping them intact with tools like Bandglue. Figure 3.34 shows the toolset.

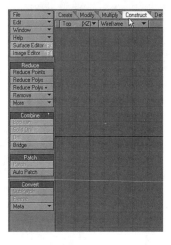

Figure 3.33
Using the Construct tab tools, you can add or subtract points and polygons to and from your models.

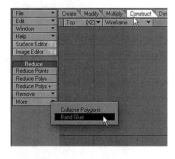

Figure 3.34
Often, you might need to reduce points or polygons within an object or selection. The Reduce category contains the necessary construction-type tools to do this.

Combine

From time to time, you'll need to use an object to cut holes into other objects. This is called a Boolean function, and it's found under the Combine category. This feature also requires you to use two layers to perform the operation, and the cutting object must be placed in a background layer. Another cool Combine tool is the Bridge tool, which enables you to select points and "bridge" or connect them together. Figure 3.35 shows the category.

Patch

The Patch category of tools is useful for splines. Splines are curves that can be put together in multiple fashions to build objects. After you have enough curves together, you can patch them to create a surface. Think of an umbrella and its wireframe mesh underneath as the curves. Patching would stitch the wireframes together to create the skin. Figure 3.36 shows the tools.

Convert

Using the Convert category of tools is helpful for more than you might think. Let's say you're building the ultimate 3D logo. You've created curves around the client's logo, and then you realize that you need to be able to render this out! Curves do not render, but polygons do. So, head on over to the Convert tools and use Freeze to convert your curves into polygons. Other tools in here include the very popular SubPatch command, which converts your three- or four-point polygons into curves, helping you create smooth organic objects. You'll use this feature extensively in the character modeling sections of this book. Figure 3.37 shows the tools.

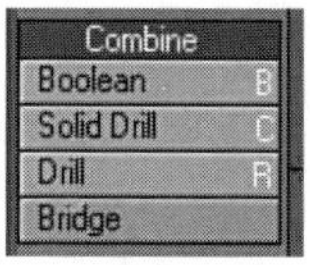

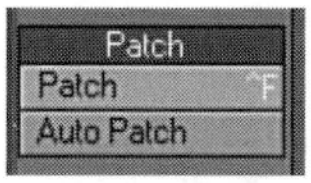

Figure 3.36
When working with curves, you need to use the Patch tools to build a skin over them.

Figure 3.35
The Combine category of tools offers ways to cut holes in objects, stencil objects, or bridge connections.

Figure 3.37
The Convert category of tools within the Construct tab gives you the freedom to change—change to SubPatch mode, change back, or change a curve to a polygon.

Detail Tab

It's all about the detail, isn't it? The Detail tab provides the tools that are very useful for, and sometimes essential to, creating decent 3D models. Figure 3.38 shows the panel.

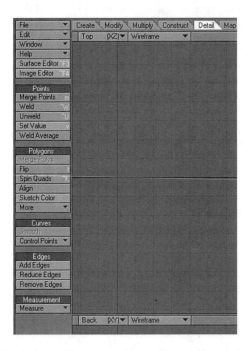

Figure 3.38   The Detail tab provides quite a few tools to make specific changes to points and polygons within your models.

The Detail tab of tools includes features such as the capability to move a selected point or group of points to one specific location or ways to add and remove edges of your models. Check out the categories!

Points

Not to be confused with the Points category in the Create tab, the Points category in the Detail tab gives you tools to make specific changes to point detail within your model. You can take a few points, for example, and choose the Weld tool to weld them together. You also can take those same points and use the Set Value command to move them to a specific location. Figure 3.39 shows the tools.

Figure 3.39
The Points category of tools gives you the power to control the detail of selected points within your models.

Polygons

The Detail tab's Polygon category enables you to merge polygons, flip them, or perhaps just align them! Again, these are detail controls that really help you fine-tune your models. So anytime you need to make detailed, specific polygon changes, this is the place to be. Figure 3.40 shows the category.

Curves

The Curves category offers just a few tools that enable you to quickly smooth out curves or control the start or end points of a curve. For example, if you're spline modeling, you may often use the Smooth function here to smooth out the curve. You'd do this because after you create splines, you must patch them, or create a skin. If you don't have the curves set properly from the start, they'll be uneven, or just not so clean. Using the Smooth function in the Curves category helps even out those curves. Figure 3.41 shows the category.

Edges

The Edges category helps you really control fine detail within your model or selection. Here, you can select the Add Edges tool, which enables you to take a selected polygon and precisely add to its edges. It's similar to the Knife feature in the Construct tab, but you use the Add Edges tool on a specific point-by-point basis. Click one edge, click another, and you've added an edge to your polygon. This is great for character modeling.

Figure 3.40
Polygon details such as Merge or Fix Poles enable you to really control those nasty polygons.

Figure 3.41
Tools for creating details for curves can be found in the Curves category of the Detail tab.

Figure 3.42
Creating detailed edges can be found in the Edges category of the Detail tab.

Measurement

Finally, the last item in the Detail tab is the Measurement category. Here, you can choose from a few different measurement tools, then click and drag across a selection for precise measurement readout in the lower left info panel. But wait, there's more! You can also find the center of an object or even calculate a bounding box representation of your object. Figure 3.43 shows the tools.

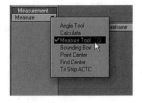

Figure 3.43
Often, you need various tools to measure your object, find its point center, or generate a bounding box representation. Do this with the Measurement tools.

Map Tab

The Map tab is home to all the tools you'll need for working with vertex and weight maps in Modeler. Here, you can see that there are a lot of tools, but don't worry, they're not all used all the time. These tools are easy to understand when you break them down into categories. LightWave employs various vertex maps for weights, morphs, and more. You'll learn about setting these later in this chapter. When you begin working with vertex maps, you can edit and control them through the tools in the Map tab. Figure 3.44 shows the Map tab tools.

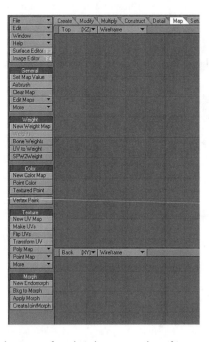

Figure 3.44   The Map tab group of tools is home to a lot of interesting commands, some of which are very powerful.

General

You'll find the General category of Map tab tools to be quite useful for things like setting vertex map values, creating vertex maps with the Airbrush tool, or just editing existing maps. Figure 3.45 shows the tools.

Weight

Weights are a big deal in LightWave. You gain weight sitting in front of the computer while adding weights to your 3D models. That's a joke. But you do work with weights throughout the modeling process because they help you control the flow of curves and can be used in Layout later during animations. The Weights category provides the tools to create new weight maps, apply weights to bones for character animation, or change specific UV maps to weights. You'll learn about UV maps in this book's Texturing sections. Figure 3.46 shows the category.

Color

Now don't confuse this category with the color of your object. Again, be aware of what you are doing and which panel and button you're working with. You're in the Map tab, not the Surface Editor, which means the Color category has different applications. These applications include creating color maps, which you can then use for specific surface control later in Layout. You can also access Vertex Paint, which enables you to paint color onto your model's vertices. This blends with any polygonal surface textures you apply later. This is great for skin, landscapes, or just about anything. Figure 3.47 highlights the tools.

Figure 3.45
The General category of the Map tab offers basic tools to edit and set values for vertex maps.

Figure 3.46
Working with weights in LightWave Modeler means you need to head on over to the Weights category of the Map tab to control them.

Figure 3.47
The Color category gives you access to tools that can help you manipulate the color of an object's vertices (or points).

Texture

The Texture category is an area you'll use often when creating and working with UV Maps. UV's represent the different axes of a surface. Using UV maps is like creating an unwrapped skin of your 3D model. UV's are often used in video games because one image can be used to surface an entire object. Later in this book, you'll learn about working with UV's and create them yourself. When you do, you'll be guided to this Texture category of the Map tab. Here, you can edit the UV's, create them, set UV values, and more. Figure 3.48 shows the category of tools.

Figure 3.48
The Texture category does not relate to the actual texture of a surface; instead, these tools give you control over any UV maps applied. Hence, the Map tab.

Morph

Morphs in LightWave are sort of misleading. People often think you can change one object into another by pushing a button. Well, not really. A morph, technically called an endomorph, is a change in point position, and because polygons are created based on points, you change the shape of an object. The Morph category within the Map tab gives you tools to control morphs, which is also a type of vertex map. You'll use morphs later in the book to make a character talk. Figure 3.49 shows the Morph category. You'll also see the M button down at the bottom right of the Modeler interface, which is where you can access morphs that your model might have.

Figure 3.49
The Map tab group of tools is home to a lot of interesting commands, some of which are very powerful like the Morph functions.

Setup Tab

This tab is where you'll find all the necessary tools to create Skelegons. What's a Skelegon? No, it is not an evil cartoon character (that's Skeletor), but rather it's a deformation tool. Skelegons are bone structures that you build in Modeler along with your model. Later, when animating, you convert these to bones, and they in turn enable you to deform and animate your object. Also, you can find setup tools to create Luxigons and Powergons. Luxigons enable you to select polygons and generate lights from them. This is a great tool for making a disco ball, stage lighting, or anything else you can think of. Powergons enable you to execute a tiny Layout command and attach it to a selected polygon. Perhaps you want to instantly add lights to a polygon for placement, like the headlights on a car. You can also define the properties for the light as well. Figure 3.50 shows the tab and its tools.

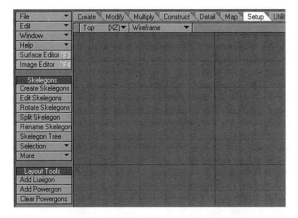

Figure 3.50   The Setup tab contains the tools you need for working with Skelegons as well as Luxigons and Powergons.

Skelegons

Easy enough, the Skelegons category is the area where you'll find all the Skelegon tools. Here, you can create Skelegons, edit them, rotate them, and so on. Figure 3.51 shows the tools.

Layout Tools

Because the end result of creating Luxigons and Powergons in Modeler happens in Layout, the Layout Tools category is where you'll find these commands. Figure 3.52 shows the category.

Figure 3.52
When creating Luxigons or Powergons, you access the tools from the Setup tab.

Figure 3.51
The Skelegons category houses all the tools you need to create and edit Skelegons, which later you'll convert to bones in Layout.

Utilities Tab

The Utilities tab contains useful categories for extended control within Modeler. Say you want to add a third party plug-in you bought, or perhaps you want to work with LightWave's custom scripting language, LScript. All these tools can be found here. Also, if you added a third party plug-in and don't know where it went, just look at the Additional drop-down list within this tab. Figure 3.53 shows the panel.

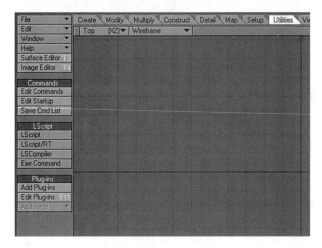

Figure 3.53   The Utilities tab is home to various commands, LScript tools, and plug-in controls.

Commands

The Commands category is where you'll find tools enabling you to edit various commands, or instructions, for LightWave Modeler. Say you want to always perform the same string of events on an object. You can create a custom command to do so with the Edit Command tool. Or perhaps upon startup, you like to have a Luxigon created from a ball. You can do this and much more with the Edit Startup tool. Figure 3.54 shows the category.

Figure 3.54
The Commands category gives you access to command operations to create your own custom actions.

LScript

LightWave's custom scripting language enables you to create your own plug-ins and scripts. Here, you can access the LScripts you've created with the various tools. You might also find various LScripts from friends or the hundreds available for free on the Internet at places like Flay.com. If you'd like to try them out, you can compile and load them with the tools in this category. Figure 3.55 shows the tools.

Figure 3.55
The LScript category gives you the tools to load and compile LScripts.

Plug-Ins

Finally, in the Utilities tab is the Plug-in category. Here, you can add a single plug-in or edit your existing plug-ins. You'll also find the Additional list, which is empty by default, but if you add third party plug-ins, you can find them here. Using LightWave's Edit Menu feature from the Edit drop-down list enables you to create custom buttons for those added plug-ins. You'll learn how to do that in this chapter. Figure 3.56 shows the Plug-ins category.

Figure 3.56
The Plug-ins category gives you the tools to manage your plug-ins.

View Tab

Earlier in this chapter, we discussed LightWave's viewports, but we have not yet talked about the other view options available to you. In the View tab, you can find many tools designed to help you maximize your modeling experience, including Magnify tools, various Layer tools, and cool selection tools. Figure 3.57 shows the panel.

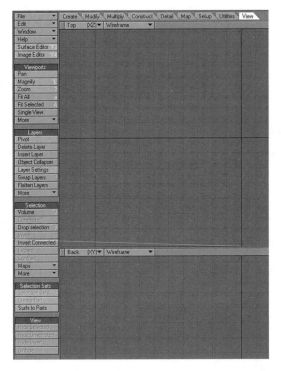

Figure 3.57 The View tab includes tools that help you effectively utilize the LightWave modeling environment.

Viewports

Much of the viewport control you'll access on a regular basis is done through the keyboard (like pressing 0 for maximize), or directly within each view. However, the Viewports category gives you all those controls and more, such as Fit and Fit All, as well as various zoom controls. So, anytime you want to adjust your viewports and what you're seeing, look here. Figure 3.58 shows the category.

Figure 3.58
Take control of what you see with the Viewport category tools.

Layers

We talked about layers and the Layers panel (Ctrl+F5) at the beginning of this chapter. However, here in the Layers category within the View tab, you can quickly add new layers, swap layers (foreground to background), or even flatten all layers into one. Look to this category for specific layer control in addition to the Layers panel. Figure 3.59 shows the tools.

Figure 3.59
Work with your layers effectively by employing the Layers category tools in the View tab.

Selection

The Selection category is where you can find various ways to select and deselect your points and polygons. Coming up right after this section, you'll learn about this key operation in Modeler. You'll also find in this category some very cool selection tools like Select Loop, Select Outline, and many more. You'll employ these tools throughout the modeling chapters in this book. Figure 3.60 shows the tools.

Figure 3.60
LightWave 8 Modeler offers a wide range of selection tools, all found under the View tab.

Selection Sets

Selection sets are often overlooked by animators, but they are really quite helpful. You can very easily select points or polygons together and group them as a selection set. The benefit of this is twofold—not only can you easily select those same points or polygons again whenever you need, you can also use them as specific controls in Layout. Figure 3.61 shows the tools.

Figure 3.61
LightWave 8 Modeler enables specific selection controls for groupings, small or large.

View

Finally, in the View tab is the View category. Here, you can hide or unhide selected items. You would do this on models in which you need to work on specific parts. Often, a wireframe mode can look cumbersome, and by hiding various selections, you'll be able to see what you're working on much easier. Just remember that if you hide some geometry, you'll need to unhide it again! Don't forget it's there! Figure 3.62 shows the category.

So, there you have it: all the LightWave 8 Modeler menus in a nutshell. When you break them down and understand how they are organized, it will be much easier not only to find them but also to understand what they do. This next section shows you how to work more specifically with geometry in Modeler through point and polygon selection and deselection processes.

Figure 3.62
The View category within the View tab enables you to hide selected or unselected geometry at the push of a button without destroying your object.

Points Versus Polygons

No matter what you create in Modeler, you'll need select or deselect points and polygons. As mentioned earlier, and as you saw throughout Chapter 1, you create points to make polygons. A polygon can't exist without a point. It's like connect-the-dots. With that said, take a look at Figure 3.63. Here, you can see the Point and Polygon modeling modes.

Figure 3.63   At the bottom of the Modeler interface are the Points and Polygons selection modes. Select the appropriate mode you want to work with.

These two selection modes can be either clicked on with the mouse, or you can toggle between them by simply pressing the Spacebar. Essentially, all you need to do is think about what you want to extend, move, rotate, and so on, and then choose the appropriate mode.

Selection Modes

Let's say you have a 3D logo you've created for your best client. They come to you and say it's great, but they would like you to just move the bottom of the letter g in the logo up a bit. For something like this, you would want to move the points that make up the bottom side of the letter. So, you select Points selection mode, click on the points of the letter, and move them. Now, in some cases, you may need to select the actual polygons. Perhaps the client tells you that now the bottom of the letter g is moved up, the entire letter g should be moved over slightly. In this case, you'll work in Polygon selection mode.

Exercise 3.2   Selecting and Deselecting Polygons

Follow these steps to get a feel for selection, deselection, and the various options available to you.

1. From this book's DVD, open the Logo object from the Chapter 3 project folder.

2. Figure 3.64 shows the object loaded into Modeler. Notice that the letter g's hook is a little too high. Select the Points mode at the bottom of the interface in the Back view. Note that you should be working with a wireframe viewport style. Doing so will select the points in the front and back of the object.

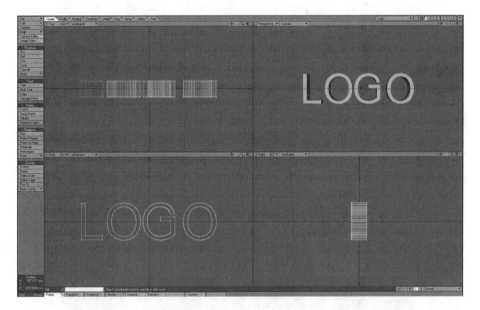

Figure 3.64   The simple logo object loaded into Modeler.

3. With Points selection mode enabled, you can select points of the object. Now, you have two ways to do this. You can use the left mouse to directly select a desired point. Click on any point in the g letter. Your point should become highlighted as in Figure 3.65.

   When you let go of the mouse, you automatically enter deselect mode. Click on the point again, and it will be deselected. This is exactly how the polygon selection mode works. Now that there is nothing selected, you can begin selecting points again. If you click on a point and then realize you want to select more, just hold the Shift key down and continue your selection.

Figure 3.65 Directly clicking on a point with the left mouse button selects it. Let go of the mouse, click again, and you deselect.

4. You can also use Lasso select mode. With the right mouse button held down, run your mouse around the points of the g that make up the end of the logo, as in Figure 3.66.

Figure 3.66 Use the right mouse to select a range of points in Lasso mode.

 Important

Mac users, if you're not working with a two-button mouse, even though you should be, hold the Ctrl key to accomplish right mouse button functions in LightWave 3D.

5. With the points of the g selected, press the t key to select the Move tool from the Modify tab. Click and drag the points down in the Back view.

   Congratulations! You just edited points. That's all there is to it! After the points are adjusted to your liking, you should deselect them.

6. To properly deselect points or polygons, first turn off any tool you're using, such as Move. You can either click directly on the Move tool, or simply press the Spacebar. Then, press the backslash key (/) to deselect.

Working with points and polygons is often a three-step process. First, choose a mode, either points or polygons, and then you take three actions: select, use a tool (like Move), and deselect. Then, move on to another action. That's all there is to it. Too often, people learning LightWave (or even those who already know it) jump the gun and forget to deselect their points or polygons and move on, only to accidentally get unwanted results in their model.

Volume Mode

Next to the Points and Polygons is Volume mode. This type of selection mode is not often used, but it can come in handy at times. It allows you to select a range you want to select in (or not) by dragging out a bounding region. From there, you can use the Statistics panel to select the points or polygons in or out of that region. See the information about the Statistics panel coming up in this chapter.

Modes: Action Center

To the right of the Points and Polygons selection modes is another button, a drop-down list called Modes. This is a pretty important aspect of modeling, which you'll find out as you build more complex objects. Figure 3.67 shows the Modes.

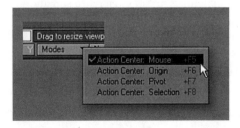

Figure 3.67   The Modes selection area enables you to change how tools react to the mouse.

The Modes options enable you to change how certain tools work with the mouse or how their "action" is centered. For example, by default, the mode is set to Action Center: Mouse. This means that if you select the Rotate tool from the Modify tab, you can click and rotate in any viewport, and where you do so is where your object or selection will rotate around. Now, if you change the Action Center to say, Selection, your rotation will happen around the selected object, polygon, or point.

You'll use these varying modes depending on what you're creating. If you're sizing an object within another object, it can be very difficult to size perfectly in place using the Action Center: Mouse. Instead, with Action Center set to Selection, the Size tool works perfectly, and the object or selection is sized without shifting toward the mouse location.

Modeler General Commands

Now take a look at the rest of the buttons along the bottom of the interface, as in Figure 3.68. Here you can see a series of buttons and tools. These are key to working in Modeler, which is why they are always visible on the interface.

Figure 3.68   The LightWave 3D 8 Modeler Interface contains key tools along the bottom of the screen.

At the bottom left of the interface is a small information area. This is the "info" area to which you'll be referred throughout this book. It shows you many properties, depending on the tool at hand, such as the size of objects, point position, and more. Figure 3.69 shows the panel.

You'll use the info area sometimes just as a reference and at other times as key information for movements and measuring.

Figure 3.69
The info area at the bottom left of the Modeler interface shows key information for your tools.

Numeric Panel

Vital to just about any modeling tool is the Numeric panel. Although many tools will be used just by turning them on and clicking and dragging, most tools have added control through the Numeric panel. Figure 3.70 shows the Numeric panel open with the Move tool selected. Although you might think the Move tool is pretty simple, it actually has a lot of unexpected controls, such as falloff and specific numeric values.

Figure 3.70 The Numeric panel, accessible by pressing n on the keyboard or by choosing it from the bottom of the interface, is useful for specific tool control.

Use the Numeric panel often, as both a reference and a control center for your tools.

Tip

The Numeric panel can stay open all the time. Adjust your interface to fit the Numeric panel into its own location on your screen. It's useful for determining whether a tool is on. If the Numeric panel is blank, no tool is on.

Statistics

The Statistics panel is another key panel you should keep open. Here, you can view information about your points, polygons, surfaces, and much more. You'll employ this panel through the book. Figure 3.71 shows the panel open. Note that it will change statistical information for both points and polygons based on which selection mode you're working in. You can also use this panel to select specific surfaces you've set up and even sub-patched polygons.

Figure 3.71   The Statistics panel, accessible from the bottom of the LightWave Modeler interface (also by pressing the w key), holds key information for points, polygons, surfaces, and more.

Info Panel

The Info panel was often a hidden and little-known feature in LightWave. Version 8 brings this panel out to the forefront, and an accessible button is available directly on the interface at the bottom of the screen. Figure 3.72 shows the Info panel open.

In this panel, you can gain access to specific point or polygon information, based on what has been selected. You can color wireframes with this panel, as well as view surface names, groupings, and more.

Surface

Another very important button in Modeler is the Surface button at the bottom of the interface. Now please, do not confuse this with the Surface Editor. This button should really be named Identify Surface, because that is what you are doing with it. When you build objects, you access the Change Surface requester by pressing the q key or the Surface button at the bottom of the interface. The panel that appears enables you to identify and set a surface name for a selected polygon. That's it! Even though you can assign a basic color, most of your actual surfacing and texturing is done in Layout. You use this panel to tell LightWave that the eyeballs on your character are white, that the polygons that make up the fingernails are green, and so on. Otherwise, without using this panel, your object will have one surface, meaning you can only apply a color or texture to the entire object. Figure 3.73 shows the Change Surface panel.

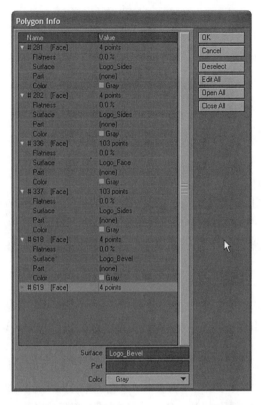

Figure 3.72   The Info panel allows you access to point and polygon information about your models. You can also color their visual representation as well.

Figure 3.73   The Change Surface panel, accessible from the bottom of the Modeler interface (or by pressing q), enables you to identify a polygonal surface.

Make

The Make button does not have a panel, but only the single button at the bottom of the Modeler interface. Say you created a few points to build an object. After your points are laid down, you can press the Make button (or the Enter key on your keyboard) to "make" the polygon.

Using and Understanding W, T, M, C, S

To the far right of the bottom of the interface is a set of tools that you'll use regularly, depending on the model you're creating. Figure 3.74 shows these tools.

Figure 3.74   The W, T, M, C, and S function controls.

Each tool is part of LightWave's vertex map system and works in a similar fashion. Of course, each has a different function. To use them, they require you to first select the tool and then select New from the drop-down list to the right. From there, the appropriate panel will appear. But what are these tools? They are simpler than you might think.

W, for Weights

Now typically, when you're first learning to create 3D models, you're not going to be using weights. Weights are a tool that LightWave lets you apply to points or polygons for specific control later in Layout. However, you can apply a SubPatch weight to sub-patched objects as well to change the shape of the curves. To do this, first select the W button for Weights. Then from the drop-down list to the right, choose SubPatch Weight. Go the Map menu tab at the top of the interface, and then on the left toolbar, select the Weights tool from the Weight category. Simply click and drag on a point of your sub-patched object, and you can sharpen or smooth the curve. You'll use this feature later during the modeling chapters.

T, for Texture

The Texture mode enables you to create a new UV Map for your objects. By first choosing the T button and then selecting New from the drop-down list, you can access the Create UV Map panel. UV Maps are great for texturing complex objects, especially those with curves. Later in the texturing tutorials in this book, you'll see this in action.

M, for Morph

Morph (or endomorph) is a powerful feature in LightWave that enables you to move a point or set of points from one position to another over time. By first selecting the M button and then New from the drop-down list to the right, you'll be able to create a new endomorph. This endomorph simply records the position of points or polygons. You can make multiple endomorphs and then use the Morph Mixer in Layout to access this data, which is saved with the object. You'll use this feature to change the shape of an object over time, such as a character talking or a car suddenly crashing and bending.

C, for Create Vertex

Create a new color vertex map with the C button. Performed similarly to the previous tools, creating a new vertex map color tells LightWave Modeler to label specific selections that you can then access in Layout for added surfacing and details. If you press Ctrl+F6 or go to the Edit drop-down menu, you can open the Vertex Map panel and see which vertex maps are applied to your objects.

S, for Selection Set

Finally, the last button in the row at the bottom of the Modeler interface is S, for Selection Set. This handy option enables you to take a group of points, for example, and create a selection set. It's like taking a bunch of points you've selected and giving them a group name. This group name can be accessed later in Layout for things like animated dynamics, cloth, and more. It's also very handy for creating selection sets around areas of your models to create endomorphs. For example, you can create a selection set of points around the eye area of a character. By opening the Statistics panel (w), you can quickly select this group anytime and adjust it, changing the shape of the eye for example, and then move on. This is a very handy feature.

Modeler Options

There's one final area you should be aware of in LightWave Modeler, and that's the options available to you. Press d on the keyboard, and you'll see the Display Options panel appear, as in Figure 3.75.

Here, you can tell Modeler to change the way the layout of the viewports looks or change what's visible in the views, or you can use this panel to hide all your tools from view. What's more, in this panel you can specify background images and place them in Modeler's backdrop. Doing this enables you to work over a template, helping you build 3D models to real world objects. You'll do this in the character modeling section of the book. Also in the Display Options panel, you can tell Modeler to work in English, Metric, or SI. SI is set by default, which is System International, a common unit of measurement. This book uses all default settings for tutorials.

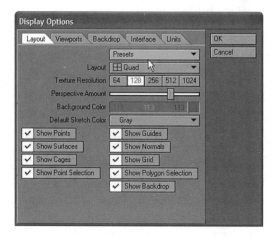

Figure 3.75   Pressing d calls up the Display Options panel, enabling you to change a number of display-type variables.

Now, if you press the o key on your keyboard (that's OH!), you get the General Options panel, as in Figure 3.76. Here, you can set LightWave's content directory as well as SubPatch level and the number of undo's you would like.

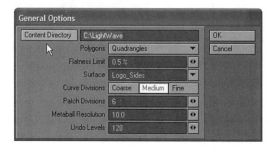

Figure 3.76   The General Options panel lets you set number of undo's, content directory location, and more.

Tip

The maximum number of undo's available is 128. It's a good idea to set this value to the max and leave it. The only reason it should be lower is if you have limited resources and are working with very large amounts of polygons. Undoing too many times on large objects can bring down even the best of systems.

The values you set in the General Options panel will become default after they've been set and after you've quit Modeler. Doing so writes the information to LightWave's configuration file.

The Next Step

This chapter has taken you on a tour through LightWave Modeler. And although it's not the most exciting chapter in this book, it is a chapter you can come back to often when you ask yourself, "What was that tool for?" Throughout this chapter, it was mentioned often that a certain tool is used later in the book. Be sure to go through every chapter when you can so that you can see how all these tools come together and so you can learn just why they are included with your 3D software. There are a few other customizable areas that you should be aware of, but these work the same way in LightWave Layout, so they'll be covered there. These include tools that enable you to edit your menus and set up custom keyboard shortcuts.

The next step is to take a tour of LightWave Layout in Chapter 4. When you get to Chapter 9, "Simple Modeling and Animation," you will begin creating simple objects, surfacing them, and animating them. From there, we'll ramp up the complexity and get you into even bigger and cooler projects.

Chapter 4

Layout

Installing LightWave 3D puts two programs onto your computer: the LightWave 3D Modeler and another application called LightWave. This book refers to LightWave as Layout. Layout is where all of your hard work in Modeler pays off! In Layout, you apply textures, lights, and motions, and it's where you see the final animated results!

Just about everything in Layout can be animated, from textures to lights to cameras and, of course, to objects. There are plenty of tools for you to harness; in fact, many people spend more time in Layout than they do in Modeler! This chapter guides you through a tour of the LightWave 3D Layout interface, its workflow, panels, and possibilities. You learn about such topics as the following:

- LightWave 8 Layout interface navigation
- Creating simple motions
- Understanding viewports
- The new Scene Editor
- The Dope Sheet
- Inverse kinematics enhancements
- Render overview

Understanding Layout

3D animation is about geometry and movement. Because you've created the 3D geometry in Modeler, Layout is where you'll put things in motion. LightWave's animation program is appropriately referred to as Layout, because that's where you lay out your scene. A scene is comprised of any 3D models, lights, and cameras. Think of Layout as your stage. The 3D models you generate in Modeler are your actors. You are the director. Oh, and if you haven't figured it out yet, you're also the gaffer, taking care of lighting, and the production designer. Keep this in mind as you learn about navigating the Layout interface.

LightWave 8 Layout Interface

When you first start up Layout, you see a large empty workspace. This workspace, however, is a three-dimensional space, rather than a flat grid like many programs. The view you're looking through is a Perspective view—sort of a bird's eye view of your virtual set. After all, Layout is your virtual television studio, and if you noticed, there is a camera and a light already in place for you. Figure 4.1 shows the Layout interface upon startup.

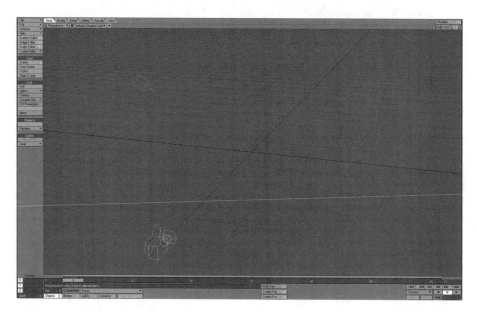

Figure 4.1   The LightWave 3D 8 Layout interface.

This view is the default, and there is always one light and one camera. You'll notice a familiarity about the interface, because it resembles LightWave Modeler in its organization and workflow.

To understand how the LightWave 3D world works, consider this: LightWave Layout is a big 3D space. Do not look at your interface and consider it a flat palette like that used in Photoshop or a simple paint program. When you're working in Layout, you're inside a big invisible sphere, and everything you do in that sphere can react in various ways with everything else, such as reflections, shadows, and even dynamics such as gravity.

Across the top of the interface are tabbed menus, each containing key tools for object editing, animating different items, compositing, and more. Before you learn about the different menus, take a look at the bottom of the Layout interface. Here, you'll find your timeline.

The Timeline

Animation is all about timing. It's about telling items such as lights, cameras, objects, or even textures to occupy a specific point in space at a specific time. Figure 4.2 shows the LightWave Layout timeline.

Figure 4.2 The LightWave 3D 8 Layout timeline.

By default, Layout works in frames rather than seconds or minutes. This is because 3D animation, and even 2D animation, is a frame-by-frame process. Although the computer automatically interpolates motions, it's still up to you to create the "key" frames. A keyframe is nothing more than a marker in time. At the left side of the timeline, the value is 0, representing the first frame of the animation.

Tip

Just because the front of the timeline defaults to 0, you are not locked into this value. You can start an animation at frame 6 or frame 40. You can also start an animation before 0 by entering a negative value. You would do this for certain animations that need a head start, for example. Let's say our object needs to already be in motion. If it starts at frame 0, then ramps up to speed, you could start the animation at the point of when it's in full motion. Similarly, you could keyframe the motion before frame 0, and then when your animation starts at 0, the item is already in full motion. It's all about control!

At the right side of the timeline is the ending frame number, which defaults to 60. Because LightWave works initially in NTSC video standard, 60 frames is 2 seconds, at a 30 frames per second rate. You can change this easily by pressing o (that's o as in oh!) and opening the General Options panel. Here, you can change the Frames Per Second to anything you like. Later in this chapter, you learn about all of LightWave Layout's preferences.

For example, the last frame of your animation can be changed just like the first frame. Most likely, many of your animations will go well beyond 60 frames, or 2 seconds. To change your current animation's overall time, it's just a matter of changing one value:

1. Double-click in the end frame window, which should read 60, by default. You can also just click and drag over the number.

2. Enter a new value—for example, 250—and be sure to press the Enter key on your keyboard.

After you enter the value, you'll see the timeline looks a little different—this one's busier because it's now displaying keys for 250 frames, rather than 60. If you need more frames for your animation, just change that value. You'll see that beneath the timeline on the left are four interesting buttons labeled Objects, Bones, Lights, and Cameras. Above the buttons is a drop-down list called Current Item. Figure 4.3 shows the item selection buttons.

Figure 4.3   The item selection buttons allow you to choose which type of item you want to work with.

Here's your goal: Do not be confused by the buttons. Think about what you're doing before you click. Too often, animators click the mouse, press the Spacebar, or press the Escape key until something happens. Usually, something does happen, but not what they intended. Do yourself a favor and think about your actions just as you do in Modeler. Select an item, turn on a tool, use it, and turn off the tool. Think about the process. Then, by paying attention to the buttons at the bottom of the interface, you'll know whether you are working with Layout's Objects, Bones, Lights, or its Cameras. After you've selected an item category, simply choose the Current Item from the drop-down list. Then, pick a tool, such as Move, and have at it!

Of course, there's more to animation than point, click, move! So much more, actually! What's great about LightWave's vast toolset is that some things stay the same no matter what you're doing, such as the timeline. Take a look at the bottom right. You see a set of VCR-like buttons. These are your playback buttons. Don't confuse these with a final animation or real-time reference. These give you a pretty good idea of how your animation will play back. Figure 4.4 shows the playback controls.

Figure 4.4   The LightWave 3D 8 playback controls in Layout.

Important

Never judge your animation entirely by the Layout playback buttons. This applies to motions, timing, shadows, textures, and so on. Always save judgment until the animation has been properly rendered out.

Keyframes

The best way to understand timing is to work with it, every day, all day. Timing is truly the hidden art of animation. Without it, nothing works. Sure, you can make pretty images, print ads, and the like. But if you're putting anything in motion, the timing needs to be dead on. It needs to "work." With that said, follow this next simple tutorial to set up some keyframes of your own, and see how LightWave handles the interpolation.

Exercise 4.1   Creating Keyframes

1. Open LightWave Layout and make sure that nothing is in the scene. The scene is like your current project, so if you've loaded any objects, or sample scenes, be sure to save your work, and then choose Clear Scene from the File drop-down menu (or press Shift+n).

2. With a nice new default blank scene, all you're going to do is animate the camera. Click Cameras at the bottom of the Layout interface, as shown in Figure 4.5.

Figure 4.5
Tell LightWave Layout that you want to work with cameras by selecting the Camera button at the bottom of Layout.

3. Because there is only one camera in the scene, it is automatically selected and highlighted after you choose to use Cameras. If you had multiple cameras in the scene, you would select which camera you want from the Current Item drop-down list, just above the Cameras button.

Tip

To add multiple cameras to a scene, go to the Items tab at the top of Layout; then from the tools on the left side of the interface, choose Camera from the Add category of tools. You can name this camera anything you like. Multiple cameras are great for scenes in which you need to show your client different views. Rather than always moving the camera, it's better to switch between multiple cameras.

4. Make sure that the Auto Key button is on, beneath the timeline.

5. You can grab the slider in the timeline to make sure it's at frame 0 all the way to the left. This is the start of your animation.

6. Make sure the camera is still selected (it should be highlighted in yellow) and press the t key on the keyboard. This calls up the Move tool from the Modify tab. Move the camera slightly to test.

7. Drag the timeline slider down to frame 60, and then click into the Layout and move the camera to a new position. Figure 4.6 shows the operation.

Tip

A good way to keep track of your keyframes is to simply look at the timeline. When a keyframe is created, LightWave puts a small yellow dash at that point in time, like a marker. If you're every wondering how many keyframes you've created, look to see how many markers are in the timeline.

8. Click the Rewind button at the bottom-right of the Layout, beneath the timeline, as shown in Figure 4.7. This quickly jumps your timeline slider back to 0.

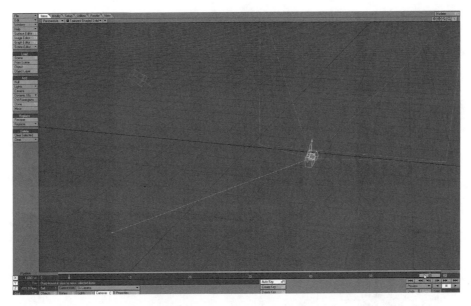

Figure 4.6   By using the Auto Key button beneath the timeline, and moving the frame slider to 60, a keyframe is automatically created for the new position of the camera.

Figure 4.7   The Rewind button in the timeline quickly brings your timeline slider back to 0.

9. Press the play button in the timeline, and you'll see your camera move from its 0 keyframe position to its 60 keyframe position.

   LightWave Layout calculates the rest, and you might notice that after a keyframe at 60 is created (automatically with Auto Key), a motion path appears. That's the white line you see connecting the first frame to the last. LightWave has interpolated the motion of the frames in between. Of course, this is just a straight line. So, try what is suggested in this next step.

10. Move your timeline slider to frame 30. Then, move the camera in some way, perhaps off to the side. You should see the motion path now curve, to accept the new keyframe. LightWave interactively updates the motion path, as shown in Figure 4.8.

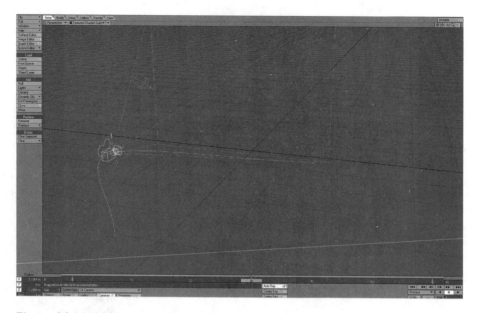

Figure 4.8   LightWave interactively updates motion paths with the Auto Key button active.

This example shows keyframing in the simplest form. Throughout this book, you'll be creating more advanced keyframing—and more precise keyframing. The Auto Key button you turned on to automatically create keyframes is on by default in LightWave; but as helpful as it is, it can be quite destructive too. There are times when you should use it—for example, when tweaking character animation. Other times, you shouldn't use it—for example, when doing precise mechanical animations. You'll see how this use (or non-use) of Auto Key plays a part in your keyframing in the animation chapters, such as Chapter 16, "Animating Characters."

The Dope Track

There's a hidden feature in the Layout timeline that you may or may not have found. If you move your mouse just above the timeline, right in the center, a small arrow appears, as shown in Figure 4.9.

When you see the arrow, click the bar that separates the Layout view and the timeline. The LightWave 8 Dope Track appears, offering additional control over your keyframes. See, it's all about control—the more you have, the better!

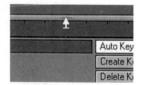

Figure 4.9
Just above the timeline in Layout, you can click to open the Dope Track.

A Dope Track is a short or mini version of a Dope Sheet. What's a Dope Sheet, you ask? It is a page that outlines all of your keyframes, motions, and timing. LightWave 8 has a Dope Sheet, which we'll get to later in this chapter. For now, the Dope Track is a simplified version of the Dope Sheet that offers you enhanced control over your keyframes. You'll use this during animation tutorials later in this book.

Exercise 4.2   Working with the Dope Track

To get an idea of how the Dope Track works, do the following:

1. Click the top center of the timeline to pop open the Dope Track.

2. If you still have your three-keyframe animation in Layout, you can use that. Otherwise, load it from the Chapter 4 projects directory on the book's DVD. This scene is nothing more than one camera with three keyframes applied at 0, 30, and 60.

3. You'll see what looks like a second timeline appear above the first timeline, as in Figure 4.10.

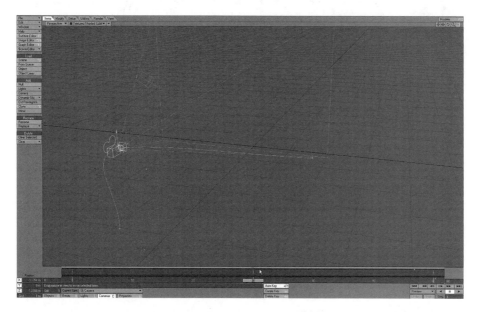

Figure 4.10   When the Dope Track is opened, you'll see what appears to be an additional timeline, above the standard timeline.

4. With just three keyframes applied to the camera, you can see their representations in the Dope Track.

5. If you right-click on one of the keyframes in the Dope Track, you get a list of commands available to you, as in Figure 4.11.

Tip

Mac users! Remember to hold down that Ctrl key to simulate right mouse button functions. Hey, did you go out and get a two-button mouse yet?

Figure 4.11
By right-clicking on one of the keyframes in the Dope Track, you are greeted by a list of tools.

Some of these commands are ghosted with such a simple scene. However, as you build more complex animations, you'll find these tools very useful. Here are some tips to demonstrate the power of the Dope Track:

- Keyframes in the Dope Track are shown on a per-channel and per-mode basis. In other words, if you create keyframes on the X-, Y-, or Z- axes and you change the Rotation tool, which controls the heading, pitch, and bank, you won't see the keyframes created on the X-, Y-, or Z-axes.

- The Dope Track enables you to work in individual Channel Edit mode.

- In the Dope Track, the left mouse button selects keyframes.

- If you hold the Alt key and drag keyframes in the Dope Track, you can make copies of those keyframes while leaving the originals untouched.

- You can hold down the Alt key and select a range in the Dope Track, which gives you a local zone. In this zone, you can bake keyframes for Move or Rotate. Baking is the process of freezing LightWave's interpolated frames into actual keyframes. Conversely, holding down both the Alt and Shift keys sets a zone allowing you to bake everything, including other objects.

- To delete a zone you might have created with the previous step, hold down the Ctrl and Alt keys and drag.

- You can grab the arrows on either end to allow the zone to become bigger or smaller. Or, grab in the center and move the zone.

- You can snap keyframes in the Dope Track. LightWave's general options (press O in Layout) allow you to turn on a feature called fractional keyframes. If this is on, you can snap the selected keyframe to the closest whole keyframe, such as 1, 2, or 5. A fractional keyframe is in between a whole keyframe, such as 1.3, or 2.7.

- A really cool feature of the Dope Track is that you can copy and paste keyframes. You can't do this in the timeline. However, when you paste keyframes, LightWave uses the timeline slider as a guide for where to paste.

You'll get to see the Dope Track in action later in the book. Hopefully, this gives you an idea of how this feature enhances LightWave's timeline and keyframing capabilities.

Layout Viewports

Like Modeler, Layout has multiple viewports. Look at Figure 4.12. Here, you can see the viewport controls at the top of the Layout window, as you did in Modeler.

Figure 4.12 The default Perspective view in Modeler can be changed to any other viewport style from the buttons at the top of the interface.

Figures 4.13 and 4.14 show the options available for which viewport you're working in, such as Light view or Camera view, as well as the viewport render style. The viewport render style allows you to view Layout items such as objects in a solid form, wireframe form, or even with textures applied.

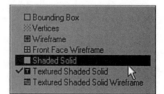

Figure 4.13 Click the list at the top of the Layout viewport to change which view you work in.

Figure 4.14 You can also choose how the objects in the viewport will be drawn.

You'll find that you change these views often, depending on the project at hand. Just to the right of the viewport styles drop-down at the top of the frame are additional view options. Figure 4.15 shows the additional options, such as Bone X-Ray mode. This mode enables you to see any bones applied to an object, even if the object is solid, hence the X-Ray title.

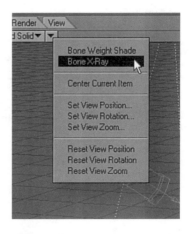

Multiple Viewports

You might be one of the select few that can work in multiple viewports while animating. If you're not sure whether that's your style, press the F3 key, and you see a quad view just like LightWave Modeler, as shown in Figure 4.16.

But wait, there's more! Press F3 again, and again. You cycle through all of LightWave Layout's available viewport arrangements. You can press F4 to go back. Let's say you have

Figure 4.15
Additional view options are available directly to the right of the viewport render styles drop-down, at the top of LightWave Layout.

a quad view in Layout set, as Figure 4.16 shows. You can set any view to any style you want—for example, you can make two views a Perspective view, one view a top view, and the other a camera view. Many animators like to make the Layout viewports match that of Modeler. However, you might find that working in a large single view, one at a time, is quite useful.

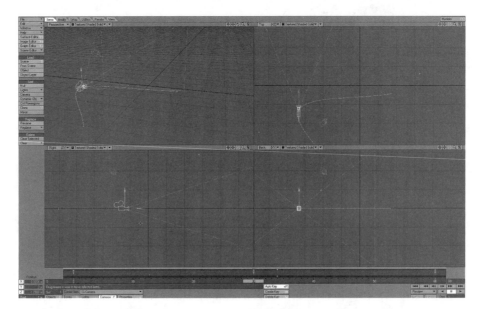

Figure 4.16   Pressing the F3 key cycles you through LightWave Layout's available viewport arrangements.

Tip

A great way to work in Layout is to employ your numeric keypad! Or, use the number keys across the top of your keyboard. Pressing the 1 key jumps you to the Back view looking down the Z-axis, whereas 2 is the Top view looking down the Y-axis. As you can guess, pressing 3 takes you to the Right view looking down the X-axis. Press 4 to get to a Perspective view, 5 for a Light view, and press 6 to switch to a Camera view. Do this as you work, and you'll be flipping back and forth between views without thinking about it.

Viewport Movement Control

To the top right of any Layout viewport are the viewport movement controls, just as you found in Modeler. Figure 4.17 shows a close-up of these tools.

Figure 4.17
At the upper-right side of the Layout interface are the viewport movement controls. Click and drag to use.

It's important to note that you cannot use these controls all the time, in every view. Their usage varies depending on which view you're working in. In Perspective view, the default viewport, these tools are all available. The five buttons are as follows:

- **Center Current Item**. This first button stays on when clicked. Click it again to turn it off. It keeps the currently selected item—be it a camera, light, or object—centered at all times.

- **Move**. The Move button enables you to move your view around in the Perspective, Top, Side, and Back/Front viewports.

- **Rotate**. Click, hold, and drag to rotate your viewport in the Perspective view only.

- **Zoom**. The Zoom viewport tool is useful for all views except Light view and Camera view.

- **Expand**. The Expand view control is great to quickly maximize any viewport. For example, let's say you're using LightWave Layout with a Quad viewport style like Modeler. Click this button in any viewport to maximize it to full screen. Click it again to return to your Quad view.

Use these viewport controls to properly take a look at your scene. They can help you stay aware of what's going on, and controls like the Center Current Item button can help you quickly find a missing item. Select the button at the top right of the viewport, then select the item you're looking to find, and it will instantly jump to view. Zoom out slightly, and you can see where this item is in relation to the rest of your scene.

Menus and Tabs

Across the top of the Layout interface are six tabbed menus. Like Modeler, each tab reveals a menu of tools. When you click on one of these tabs, the toolset on the left side of the interface changes accordingly. Figure 4.18 shows the tabs.

Figure 4.18 The LightWave Layout tab set across the top of the interface.

It's important to note that the eight buttons at the top left of the Layout (starting with the File drop-down) always appear, no matter what tab you've selected. These are key tools and commands you'll use throughout LightWave, both in Modeler and Layout. Figure 4.19 shows these buttons.

Tip

> Remember that we're using the default LightWave tabs and menus throughout this book. Although you can change the menus to look like anything you want, the default setup keeps these eight tool buttons at the top left of LightWave Layout.

Figure 4.19
The eight buttons at the top left of the LightWave Layout always appear, no matter what tab or menu you're working in.

File Menu

First, let's talk about the first of these buttons: the File drop-down menu. When we say *drop-down* menu, we're talking about a button that has a small tiny downward pointing arrow. Click this button to expand and you'll find additional tools. Figure 4.20 shows the File menu.

Figure 4.20 The File menu drop-down always appears at the top left of the Layout interface.

The File drop-down menu allows you to load scenes, save scenes, and use the new Save Scene Increment. Using this feature adds a 001, 002, and so on to the end of your scene name each time you save. You can also export scenes through LightWave's Content Manager.

Tip

Pressing Ctrl+s on your keyboard tells LightWave to Save Scene As, whereas pressing Shift+s automatically saves a scene in increments.

Clear Scene

As the name implies, you can select this, or press Shift+n, to clear your scene. After you perform this command, all that is left is a light and a camera. Be warned: You will not have an opportunity to save after you do this, and LightWave does not inform you that data might be lost. It asks you if you're sure you want to clear the scene, but that's it. So, save often!

Additionally, simply loading a new scene overrides your current scene. Therefore, using Clear Scene before you use Load Scene is a wasted step.

Load

The Load command from the File drop-down allows you to load scenes, load recent scenes, and load an item from a scene, which is a cool feature,. You can also load objects and revert the current scene to previously saved.

Load Items from Scene

This handy option is often used for character animation. It allows you to load one scene into your current scene. For example, let's say you create a cool looking giraffe and set up a workable bone structure for it. Of course, you've saved that scene so that you can work with it later. Then, you've built a huge safari scene with textures, landscapes, and lighting. Now, all you have to do is use Load Items from Scene and choose the giraffe scene. The giraffe and all of its motions and bones will be imported into your existing scene. This allows you to set up scenes on their own for both speed and productivity, but use them together for final results.

Export

Certain third-party applications still work very well with LightWave. However, Lightwave's core structure changed with version 6 in the year 2000, and many scenes were no longer compatible with third-party applications. Because of this, NewTek has added the ability to export your scene to LightWave version 5.6 with the Export command, which is also found under the File drop-down menu.

Content Manager

LightWave's Content Manager is extremely handy for backing up your scenes and sending them to co-workers or clients. You see, LightWave's scene file is comprised of objects or 3D models you create in Modeler. The objects in your scene hold surfacing data, whereas the scene file itself holds motion data. These data files can sometimes be located in various folders around your hard drive. By using the Content Manager, LightWave gathers all of the files associated with the current scene and makes a copy of it to a directory you specify.

Edit Menu

The Edit drop-down menu is home to quite a few useful tools that enable you to edit menu and keyboard layouts, change window configurations, and even choose your Content Directory. The main features you'll use in this drop-down list are the Edit Keyboard Shortcuts and Edit Menu Layout commands.

Undo and Redo

In most circumstances, you'll use Ctrl+Z and Z to undo and redo within LightWave. However, if you want, you can use the buttons directly; they are found under the Edit drop-down list. Remember that you can set unlimited undo's in LightWave Layout, by pressing o for General Options.

There are a few warnings to note about using undo: First, too many undos can kill your system resources! Also, remember that undos don't apply to everything—that is, if you accidentally turn off a texture editor layer on your surface, there's no going back. However, if you make some bad keyframes, undo is an easy way to set them up again.

Edit Keyboard Shortcuts

Everyone likes things customized to their liking, right? LightWave 3D gives you this freedom by allowing you to assign keyboard equivalents to commands throughout the program. This next exercise shows you how to use these Edit features. Figure 4.21 shows the Edit Keyboard Shortcuts selection.

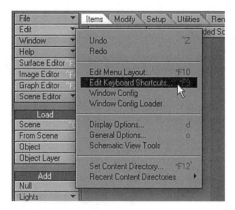

Figure 4.21   The Edit drop-down menu gives you access to key tools like Edit Menu Layout and Edit Keyboard Shortcuts.

Exercise 4.3   Editing Keyboard Shortcuts

1. Click the Edit drop-down menu and choose the Edit Keyboard Shortcuts command, or press Alt+F9.

2. A panel appears where you can choose any of LightWave's tools and apply your own keyboard shortcut. Figure 4.22 shows the panel.

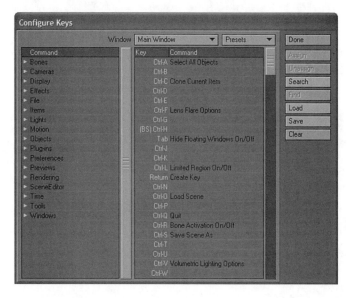

Figure 4.22   The Edit Keyboard Shortcuts panel enables you to rearrange existing keyboard shortcuts, as well as create new ones.

Tip

You can see any existing keyboard shortcut right on the Layout button. Any keyboard shortcut you apply will be visible on the buttons, as a helpful reminder.

3. On the left side of the panel are the various commands Layout offers. On the right are keyboard shortcut listings. Scroll down the left side and select the SceneEditor listing. Click it to expand.

4. Within the Scene Editor commands, you find Open. Select it, as shown in Figure 4.23.

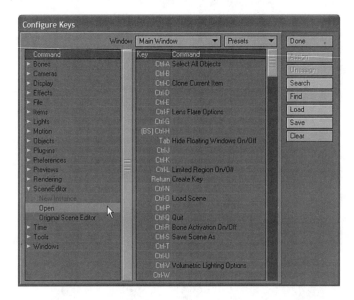

Figure 4.23 It's easy to select various commands from the categories. Here, the Open Scene Editor command is selected.

5. Scroll down the right column to choose a keyboard equivalent to assign the Open Scene Editor command to, perhaps F1.

6. Select the F1 keyboard shortcut in the window, and on the right, click the Assign button, as shown in Figure 4.24.

7. Assign more keys to your liking, and click Done.

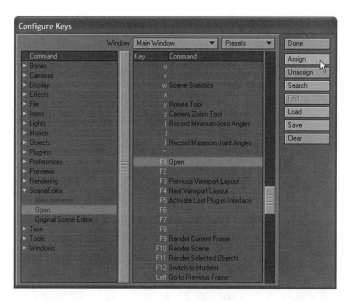

Figure 4.24   Assigning keyboard shortcuts is easy. Just pick a command, pick a key, and click Assign.

You can always go back to LightWave's default keyboard shortcuts by choosing the appropriate preset in the Configure Keys panel. Just click and select from the Presets drop-down at the top right of the panel. You can also set up keyboard shortcuts for the Graph Editor, by choosing the option from the Window drop-down.

Another thing to remember is that you can apply these keyboard shortcuts in LightWave's Modeler the same way. Just select the Edit drop-down in Modeler and repeat the preceding steps.

 Tip

Be sure to use the Save button within the Configure Keys panel to save your keyboard setups. Should you choose to select the default preset, your changes are gone forever.

Edit Menu Layout

Changing keyboard equivalents is great, no question. But if you want to go one step better and really make LightWave your own, try editing the menus!

Exercise 4.4   Editing Menus

1. From the Edit drop-down list, select Edit Menu Layout or press Alt+F10. You are greeted with a panel that looks very similar to the Configure Keys panel from the previous exercise. Figure 4.25 shows the panel.

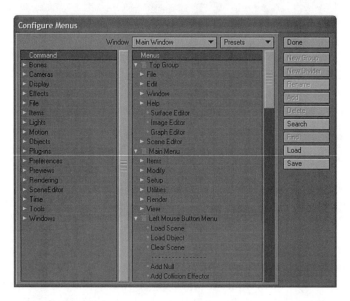

Figure 4.25   The Configure Menus panel, chosen from the Edit drop-down list's Edit Menu Layout command.

2. You'll use the panel the way you did editing keyboard shortcuts. Most tools are already out on the interface, but this panel is great for moving buttons, adding new menus, or creating buttons for your third-party plug-ins. Select the View listing from the Menus column on the right, as shown in Figure 4.26.

3. To the right of the panel, select the New Group button. You see a new tab on the Layout interface appear just after the View menu tab. You just made a new blank menu! Figure 4.27 shows the addition.

4. You can select various tools from the command window on the left and select your new group. Then, click the Add button. You've now added buttons for commands in your own custom group. Feel free to select your new group and choose the Rename button to customize it.

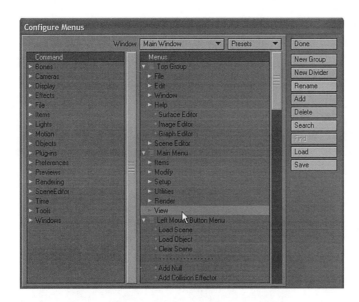

Figure 4.26   You can select and edit any existing menu in the Configure Menus panel.

Figure 4.27   Creating your own menu group is as easy as the push of a button.

You should know a few things about using these configuration panels. When a command is ghosted, that means it's already assigned. However, it does not mean that you can't assign it again. Also, if you ever dislike what menus you've created, you can always choose Default from the Presets drop-down menu in the panel.

Window Menu

Beneath the Edit menu drop-down list is the Window menu. Here, you can access various ous windows or panels throughout LightWave. These windows are controls for Motion Mixer, LightWave's non-linear animation controller, Backdrop Options, Compositing Options, as well as the Image Processing tab. Figure 4.28 shows the panel.

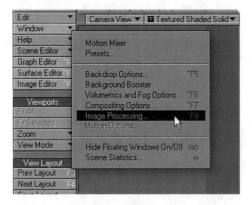

Figure 4.28   The Window drop-down menu gives you access to many key panels throughout LightWave Layout.

You'll be employing all of these windows throughout this book's tutorials. Note the keyboard shortcuts to the right of the listings for quicker access.

Help Menu

LightWave's Help menu can be found directly in Layout all the time. This is helpful (pun intended) for accessing LightWave's web-based help system. Figure 4.29 shows the menu.

Additionally, you can enter your valid license key in this panel, as well as access LightWave's About section to check your version number, including information about your system's graphic card.

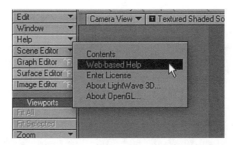

Figure 4.29   The LightWave 8 Help menu gives you quick access to online help and licensing.

Scene Editor

In the past, the Scene Editor was accessed by one button. Now, there is a drop-down menu for opening different versions of the Scene Editor—the killer version 8 Scene Editor or the classic version you've come to know and love. The Scene Editor menu is shown in Figure 4.30.

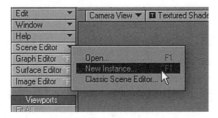

Figure 4.30   The Scene Editor menu gives you access to both the classic LightWave Scene Editor and the new LightWave 8 Scene Editor.

The LightWave 8 Scene Editor is quite powerful, incorporating spreadsheet capabilities, a Dope Sheet, and overall editing of various scene parameters. It does not allow control over every aspect of LightWave, but it can significantly improve workflow by allowing control of multiple items at once. There are five main areas within the Scene Editor: Items, Surfaces, Channels, Property, Dope Sheet. Exercise 4.5 guides you through a quick overview of the tool.

Exercise 4.5   Working with the Scene Editor

1. From the File drop-down menu, select Clear Scene.

2. From the Scene Editor drop-down menu, select New Instance. Because of the design of the Scene Editor, you can have multiple instances of the panel open at the same time. After you've created an instance, the Open command will be visible in the Scene Editor drop-down. Figure 4.31 shows the Scene Editor.

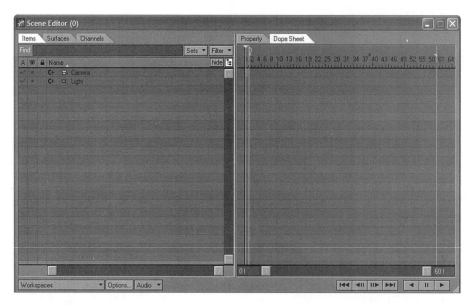

Figure 4.31   A new instance of the LightWave 8 Scene Editor is created, and the panel appears.

3. On the left of the panel are the items in your scene. Figure 4.32 shows that by clicking the small mark in front of an item, you can expand it to see its channels.

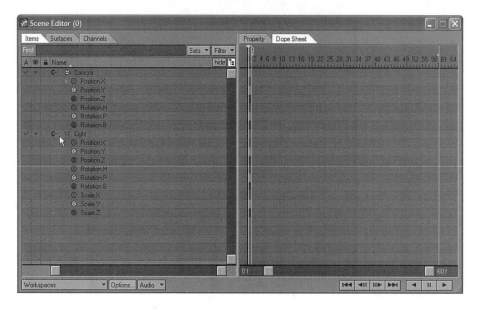

Figure 4.32   The left side of the Scene Editor contains the items you want to control.

4. At the top left of the Scene Editor are three tabs: Items, Surfaces, and Channels. Click the Surfaces tab, and the list changes, giving you access to any surfaces in your scene.

5. After you've selected certain surfaces to work with, you can select them on the right and make changes. This is useful for quickly seeing and editing all of your surfaces outside of LightWave Surface Editor. Figure 4.33 shows a simple scene loaded so you can see the surfaces.

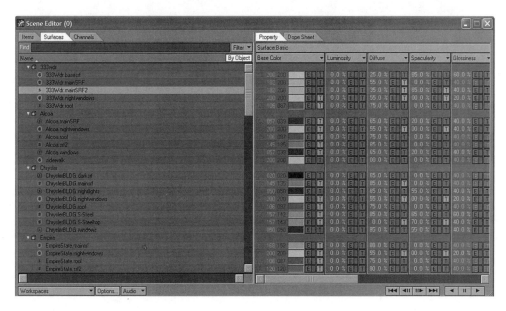

Figure 4.33   With a simple scene loaded, you can quickly see how powerful the new Scene Editor can be, enabling group editing of surfaces.

Dope Sheet

Within the Scene Editor is the Dope Sheet. You can find it to the right side of the panel. After you set up keyframes and complex motions, especially for characters, the Dope Sheet will be your best friend. The Dope Sheet allows you to see all of your keyframes for multiple items at once. You can set times and numeric offsets and even erase keyframes. You can select certain keyframes and change their values, as well as edit them in the Graph Editor. Figure 4.34 shows the Dope Sheet with a character scene loaded from the LightWave Content Directory.

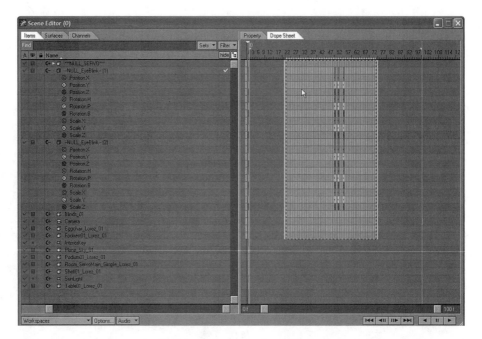

Figure 4.34   When a scene with keyframes is loaded, the Scene Editor's Dope Sheet gives you enhanced control over time, movement, and other parameters.

The Scene Editor is very powerful, and to show its uses, we're going to throw it right into the tutorials later in this book. This chapter's coverage should give you a quick overview of the power behind this cool new addition.

Graph Editor

Also part of the eight key menus in Layout is the LightWave Graph Editor. This panel gives you specific control over the motion channels of your Layout items. Each item, such as a light, camera, bone, or object, has nine motion channels. There is a specific channel of motion for the X-, Y-, and Z-axis for Movement, Scale, and motion on the H, P, and B, (heading, pitch, and bank) for Rotation. You can control all of these channels in the Graph Editor. Figure 4.35 shows the panel.

In the Graph Editor, you can adjust the timing of specific channels. For example, you've created a spinning top. You have rotated the top over 30 frames, but you need it to continue for 300. Rather than re-keyframing it, you can use the Graph Editor to "repeat" the post behavior of that specific motion channel. But you can do so much more, such as edit keyframes or create them. You can apply various motion plug-ins, such as a texture environment to the Y (up and down) motion channel to simulate an earthquake. As you work through tutorials in this book, you'll use the Graph Editor to perform these functions as well as learn how to navigate through the panel.

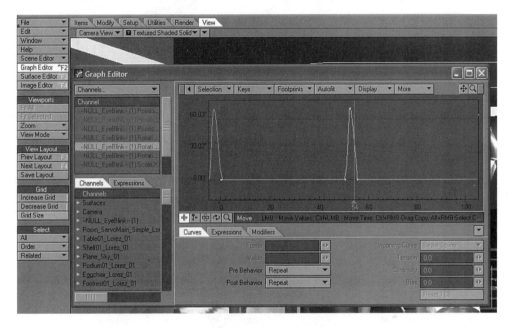

Figure 4.35   The LightWave 8 Graph Editor offers specific control over motion channels for your Layout items.

Surface Editor

Beneath the Graph Editor is the Surface Editor. Here, you can apply and perform all of the texturing to your objects. Figure 4.36 shows a scene loaded and the surface list in the Surface Editor.

The Surface Editor is easier to work with than you might think. Again, if you think about the process, you can easily navigate through the panel. First, you tell the Surface Editor which surface you want to work with. Where did you get that surface? You created it in Modeler with the Change Surface requester, accessed through the Surface button at the bottom of the Modeler interface. After a surface is chosen, you work your way down the panel from color to luminosity to transparency and more.

Of course, texturing is a time consuming aspect of 3D animation and art, but you'll see in the next chapter, applying basic surfaces and reflections is easier than you might think. Be sure to read Chapter 5, "Keyframing and Graph Editor," to learn about creating simple models with surfaces and how to apply them.

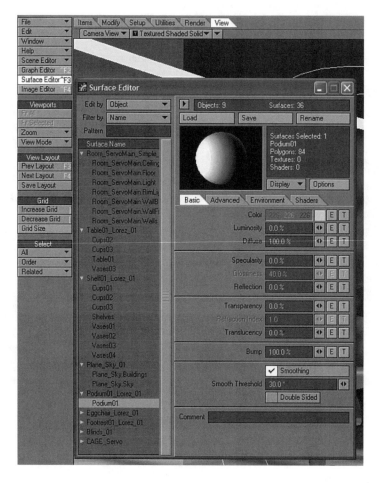

Figure 4.36 The Surface Editor in LightWave is your home for all surfacing.

 Important

Throughout the Surface Editor and LightWave, you'll see little E and T buttons. These are very important because the E allows you to create an Envelope for the given parameter. What's an envelope? It's a change in value. The E allows you to animate that value. The T buttons allow you to apply textures. Pressing a T button opens the Texture Editor.

 Tip

If you click on an E or a T accidentally, simply hold the Shift key and click the button again to release. Undo does not work for this.

Image Editor

The last of the eight menus at the top of LightWave Layout is the Image Editor. Here, you can load images or movie files into LightWave. Figure 4.37 shows the Image Editor.

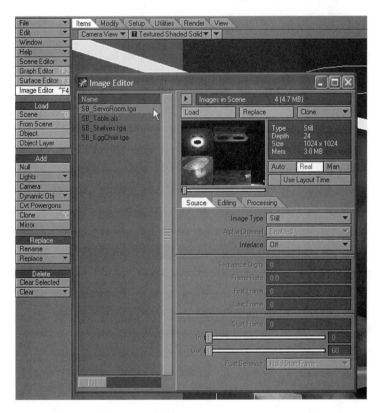

Figure 4.37   The Image Editor in LightWave 8 allows you to load images and movies, as well as edit them and apply effects.

You can do more than just load images in the Image Editor; you can edit them! A Processing tab allows you to create simple enhancements of your images and movies. Additionally, you can apply textures to your images with the T buttons! You'll be using the Image Editor in the next chapter to load reflection maps.

These key tabs and menus will be accessed and used often, which you'll see as you work your way through various tutorials in this book. First, read on to learn about the tool categories of the six main menu tabs in Layout.

Items Tab

Across the top of the Layout interface are the six key menu tabs you'll access quite often. The first is the Items tab (much like Modeler's Create menu tab), which is where you can find the simple item controls, as shown in Figure 4.38. Here, you find one-click load tools, replace, add, and delete functions. In previous versions of LightWave, it took a number of clicks to access these tools, and after a while, it became a bit annoying.

Load

The first category you see within the Items tab is labeled Load. You can load a scene, which is an entire project containing lights, motions, and objects. It overwrites whatever you have in your Layout, so be sure to save before you load. You can also just load an object into your scene with the Load Object button. Loading an object is the way to begin creating a scene. You'll also find a button for the previously discussed Load Items from Scene command, found under the File drop-down menu. Add to that the Object Layer button. This allows you to load just the layer of an object. Let's say you create a complex living room, with 12 layers. Layer 5 contains that awesome flat panel plasma television you modeled (because your wife won't let you buy it!).To select it, select Object Layer and choose the object, and then the layer in the requester that appears.

Figure 4.38
The Items menu tab in Layout, where you can load scenes and objects, as well as replace, add, and delete.

 Important

When you apply textures to your objects, you need to be sure to use the Save All Objects command from the File drop-down menu.This saves any textures or surface settings to your objects. Saving the scene alone does not save the surfaces on objects. Saving the scene only saves motion data, light data, and whatever elements you've added to the scene. Colors and textures are saved with objects.

Add

With the Add category of the Items tab, you can easily add items to your scene. These items include Null objects, which are very useful for parenting, grouping, and effects. These are single points that do not show up in the render, but rather help facilitate control throughout your animations. It's easy to add dynamic objects, such as particle emitters, wind, gravity, and collision items. Also within the Add category in the Items tab are tools with which you can mirror and clone selected items at the click of a button.

Replace

Replacing objects is easier now with the Replace category under the Items menu. Perhaps you need to replace a simple stand-in object with a high polygon model for final rendering. Not a problem; just select the item and choose Replace. Also, you can rename any item here, such as a light, camera, or object.

Delete

Not to be outdone, the Delete category lives within the Items tab and can be used to quickly delete a selected item, or group of items all at once. Use this category for quick-click deletions.

Modify Tab

You might find that you visit the Modify tab often while working in Layout. Of course, you'll see the same familiar eight menus at the top starting with the File menu. But if you look further down as in Figure 4.39, you'll see five categories of tools.

Translate

The first category, Translate, houses several Move tools. These are all translate-type functions, as in Modeler. Use them for any item in Layout from bones to objects to lights. It's best to learn their keyboard equivalents too, such as the t key for Move.

Rotate

You'll also find Rotation tools just below the Translate tools. You can rotate any item, as well as an item's pivot point. You learn about pivot points in Chapter 5 during the tutorials.

Transform

Not to be confused with Translate, the Transform category offers various sizing tools, Squash and Stretch.

Figure 4.39
The Modify tab in Layout, one of the more used menus.

General

This next category under the Modify tab is quite important to your workflow. Although the category title says General, the options within this category are anything but! They're more global than they are general. You'll find options for the Coordinate System, which determines how an item in Layout is controlled in relationship to the 3D world that is Layout. Earlier in the chapter, the LightWave Layout was characterized as a big invisible sphere in which you work. When you change the Coordinate System, you tell LightWave to adjust the relationship between the world's coordinates and the items. Figure 4.40 shows the Coordinate System selections. You'll also find the Reset button. This is handy for keeping track of your items.. Let's say you move your camera around, and then at some point, lose track of it. This can happen with any item, even a light. If you first select Rotate (also from the Modify tab) and then click Reset, the rotation resets to the 0,0,0, setting. The same applies for Move. Keep this in mind when you're ready to scrap what you've done and start again without redoing your entire scene.

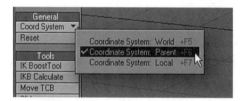

Figure 4.40   The Coordinate System category from the Modify tab offers key changes for animation.

To explain the Coordinate System further, look at Figure 4.41. This is the default LightWave Layout, where the X-axis is left and right, the Y-axis is up and down, and the Z-axis is forward and back. The object in the scene has default coordinates set to Parent from the Modify tab.

Notice the axis handles on the object (which you learn about in this chapter under Display Options) show the default coordinates as well. The axis handles have the Y handle standing vertically, the X handle is lying down to the side for left and right, and the Z handle points towards the back of the Layout interface. Now look at Figure 4.42.

In Figure 4.42, the Coordinate System is set to Local. When the shoe object is rotated, you can see that the coordinate control handles stick with the object. This means that if you move the object up on the Y-axis, it moves on the angle in which it is rotated, rather than straight up and down.

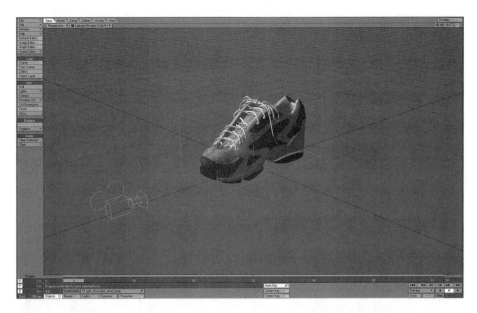

Figure 4.41   The default LightWave Layout, with the default Coordinate System set to Parent.

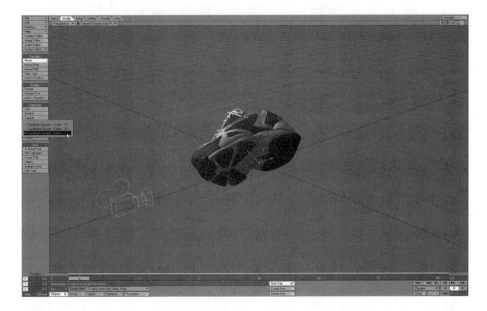

Figure 4.42   The object is rotated, and the Coordinate System is set to Local.

You'll use this feature often when working with bones for character animation, as well as mechanical animations. Many times, when setting up hierarchies of parented objects, you'll need to change between Parent, World, and Local. Parent and World coordinates are essentially the same thing, except that if your object is parented to another item, it takes on that item's coordinates.

As you work through the tutorials, you'll see how this all comes into play. But remember: As you're setting up your animations, if something does not rotate or move the way you want it to, look to the Coordinate System in the Modify tab.

Tools

Finally, the Tools category found under the Modify tab is the location of some very powerful tools. As you can see in Figure 4.43, these tools are not as obvious as the Translate or Rotate tools. Don't let the names fool you—these commands are some of LightWave 8's most important features.

Figure 4.43
The Tools category is home to the new IK Boost tool, as well as Move TCB and others.

IK Boost Tool

The IK Boost Tool stands for inverse kinematics. It is a powerful new system primarily used for, but not limited to, character animation. This intense new system gives you quick and fast setup of inverse kinematics. What is inverse kinematics? Inverse kinematics, or IK, in the simplest explanation, is like a puppet on strings. When you grab the string attached to the hand of a puppet, the arm follows. That's it! You'll be setting up your own IK in the upcoming character animation chapters.

The IK Boost Tool applies IK to a said hierarchy, and allows you to instantly set parameters, limits, and controls for every aspect of your hierarchy. You'll also use the IKB Calculate command found just beneath the IK Boost tool in the Tools category of the Modify tab.

IKB Calculate

After you've set up inverse kinematics and bone options, you can simply click the IKB Calculate button. This is used for bone dynamics especially. You'll see this in full action later in the dynamics chapters (Chapter 17, "Particle Dynamics," and Chapter 18, "Hard and Soft Body Dynamics") of this book.

MoveTCB Tool

The Move TCB command is sort of a new incarnation of an old feature. When you create a motion path with an object, LightWave creates a curve. Tension, Continuity, and Bias, or TCB, are ways you can control how one keyframe of a curve reacts. For example, a common setting is to apply a positive tension to an ending motion keyframe to have an item "ease into" place. What's the big deal about MoveTCB? Up until now, you had to open the Graph Editor, select the specific channel(s) you want to edit, and apply the appropriate T, C, or B. Now, you can use the MoveTCB tool directly in Layout. You can see your settings down at the bottom left of the Layout interface in the Info area.

Sliders

You'll also find key tools such as SplineControl and Sliders in the Tools category. You can apply sliders to your scene for specific control over various items. This is very helpful during character animation or precise movements where you only want an item to move between two specific ranges. Applying a slider allows you to set a minimum and maximum value for a specific item channel. Then, you can simply drag the slider to adjust the motion within that range.

The Sliders button enables you to apply various preset motions to items. For example, you can add the custom plug-in within an object's Properties panel, and then specify how much the item should rotate on the heading, or bank. Using the Sliders option, you can see a control directly in Layout that floats over the interface, allowing you to drag the slider between the minimum and maximum values you've specified. This works on move, rotate, size, and so on.

Spline Control

Spline Control is a tool that, when active, allows you to see a visible and controllable motion path for a specific item. You select the item to edit and turn on Spline Control. From there, click and drag on the control handles that appear in Layout to change the shape of the motion path.

Edit Tool

You may have clicked this little bugger and found that it seems to disable any movements in Layout. But wait! This is actually a very cool little tool. Let's say you added a particle emitter to Layout. Click this Edit Tool, and your particles are all identified numerically. Click any one of those particles and move or delete! This is great for those annoying particles that won't behave, or just don't belong. Get rid of them, we say!

Setup Tab

The Setup tab in Layout is your pit stop for all things skeletal—that is, this is where you find controls for bones. Figure 4.44 shows the menu with its tools.

General

Yes, there is another General category, this time it's under the Setup tab, and we're talking about deformation tools. The General category offers bone tools such as Bone Edit functions, and globally turning bones on or off. You can also make sure inverse kinematics is active within this category.

Important

Bones are deformation tools, meaning they deform your objects, such as a curtain blowing in the wind, the pages of a book curling, or animated characters. Throughout the character animation chapter, you'll find yourself guided to these tools for adding bones, editing bones, splitting them, and much more. If you remember the discussion in Chapter 3, "Modeler," Skelegons were introduced. When you create Skelegons in Modeler for an object, they are converted to bones in Layout. Controlling, editing, and adjusting those bones are done in the Setup menu.

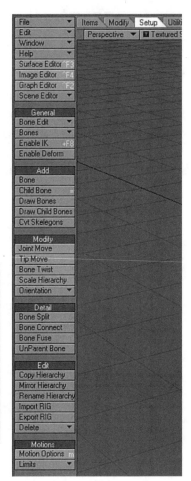

Figure 4.44
The Setup tab in Layout is where you find all the tools needed to work with bones, LightWave's deformation tools, and the Layout equivalent of Skelegons.

Add

Not unlike the Add category of the Items tab, the category here again relates to all things bones. You can add a bone, add a child bone, draw bones in Layout, or draw child bones. But another important tool is labeled Cvt Skelegons. This is the Convert Skelegons command that you'll use to change skelegons (created in Modeler) into bones for use in Layout. Without this, skelegons in Modeler are useless.

Modify

When talking about bones, at some point, you'll need to modify what you've added. The Modify category offers the necessary tools to adjust your bones. These tools are quite powerful because with them, you can move the joints of bones, move the tips of bones, twist them, and scale them. Pretty handy for properly setting up a perfect character rig, which you'll do later in the character animation chapter.

Detail

Modifications are great, but sometimes when working with bones, you need to control more specific details. The Detail tab offers tools to split bones, and not just once. You can take one bone, for example, and cut it into four without destroying the hierarchy of your setup. This is useful when you've put a bone into a foot, for example, and then realize you need another one so the foot can bend! You'll also find Bone Fuse, which allows you to put two split bones back together, just in case you didn't want to split them after all. And, you can use the UnParent Bone tool here to remove a bone from its hierarchy.

Edit

Again, all of the tools within the Setup tab relate to bones. Bones are not just for character animation, and you can use the Edit category tools to copy hierarchies, rename them, save them, and load them.

Motions

One small category within the Setup tab relates to bones, and every other item in your scene. You can use the Motion Options in the Motions category to access various motion tools and plug-ins. This can be for bones, lights, cameras, objects, or any effect item in your scene. Additionally, you can record minimum and maximum joint angles with the Limits drop-down selection.

Utilities Tab

Whenever you need to add plug-ins, edit them, or work with LightWave's LScript scripting language, you can click over to the Utilities tab. Figure 4.45 shows the menu tab and its tools.

Commands

The Commands category offers controls for looking up your command history or entering specific commands for LightWave to follow. Additionally, if you want to keep track of commands you've used, use the Save Cmd List option. Refer back to this for similar projects.

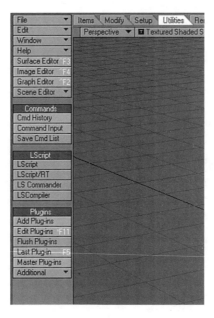

Figure 4.45   The Utilities tab is home to command tools, LScript programming tools, and plug-in tools.

LScript

The LScript category is home to LightWave's custom programming language. Here, you can load LScripts, use the LScript compiler to build your own, or use the LS Commander to quickly automate LightWave functions. The LS Commander creates plug-ins that perform the steps you specify within its interface. You can create your own plug-in that loads an object, saves it, and then saves the scene, all in one button!

Plug-Ins

The Plugins category is where you find the tools to add individual plug-ins, load multiple plug-ins with the Edit Plug-ins tool, and quickly find the last used plug-in. Within this category is the Master Plug-ins panel, which is where you can load Master class plug-ins, such as the LScript Commander. You also see the Additional list, where you can find additional plug-ins and any third-party plug-ins you might have added. Be sure to check out Appendix A, "Plug-In List." Here, you'll learn all about plug-ins, how to work with them, how to add them, and what each one does.

Render Tab

If you are a previous user of LightWave, you'll love the Render menu tab. In previous versions of LightWave, rendering was sort of hidden away. No one is certain why it was hidden, but that's not an issue now; you can focus on the tools right in front of you. Figure 4.46 shows the Render menu tools.

Figure 4.46   The Render menu tab encompasses all of your necessary render tools. Without these, you see nothing!

Rendering is the process of your 3D software drawing the final image. If you look at Figure 4.47, you see the Render Options panel. This is accessed by clicking the Render Options button under the Objects category within the Render menu.

Render Options

Within the Render Options category are the tools necessary to set up single frame renders, arbitrary renders, or full frame animations. You'll work through this panel and see how to render locally and over a network in Chapter 21, "Rendering and ScreamerNet." You'll also see the Enable VIPER button. This is sort of an on/off switch for VIPER, LightWave's virtual preview render system, discussed later in this chapter.

Render

The Render category of the Render tab might seem confusing because the names are awfully similar! Seriously though, this is where you can click a button to render a single frame, a scene, a selected object, or see a motion blur preview right in Layout. Click the MB Preview to see any motion blur your scene might be using.

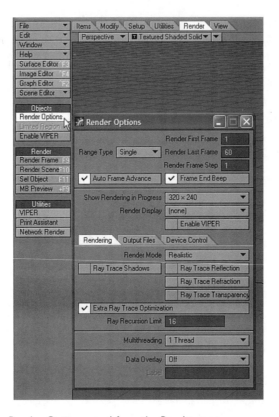

Figure 4.47   The Render Options panel from the Render menu.

Utilities

The Utilities category of the Render tab is where you find the tools needed for additional render options. First is VIPER.

VIPER

If you look further down the tool list in the Render menu tools, you see a button called VIPER. VIPER stands for Virtual Interactive Preview Renderer. You can use VIPER to instantly see changes to surfaces, particles, and volumetrics, without performing a formal render. This saves time! You'll use VIPER in the next chapter's tutorials.

Other Tools

Other tools within the Render menu tab allow you to push one button to render a single frame, render a scene, or render just a selected object. It's a good idea to take note of the keyboard shortcuts for these tools, such as F9 for a single, current frame render. You'll employ this continually throughout your LightWave career.

Print Assistant

Another utility within the Render menu is the Print Assistant. This fantastic little plug-in is great for all of you print people. As noted previously, you learn how to set up network rendering in Chapter 21. The Print Assistant will be used in Chapter 5's text tutorials. This great tool quickly sets up the proper pixel aspect ratio for high resolution renders. Because LightWave is made for video, its output settings are not designed for print—that is ay, they're not set up for 300dpi, or 200dpi, and so on. They are set up in video format such as 720×486. For example, you can use the Print Assistant tool in the Render menu to set up a 300dpi image that is 8×10 inches in size. It automatically creates a render setting to match this value. But be careful, these large renders can take some time to finish!

Network Render

Using LightWave's ScreamerNet control, this option enables you to tie other computers on your network into your rendering. This is especially good because you only need one copy of LightWave on your host or main computer system. Be sure to read up on how to set up your own network rendering system in Chapter 21.

View Tab

The last menu tab across the top of Layout is the View tab. Here, you can find necessary tools to control your Layout viewports. Figure 4.48 shows the tools.

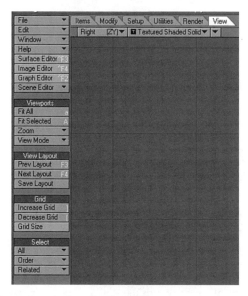

Figure 4.48   The View tab is the last one above Layout.

Viewports

The sets of tools available in this menu give you additional control when working in Layout. Earlier in this chapter, we discussed the viewports, as well as setting up multiple viewports. The Viewports category in the View tab gives access to buttons that control those views. You can also use the Fit All and Fit Selected commands to quickly bring your items to view. Note, however, that these tools only work in certain viewports, such as the Top or Side views.

View Layout

The View Layout category is a quick way to jump between preset layout views, such as single, quad, and so on. If you set up your own view, and perhaps click and drag the center of the windows to adjust, you can save that particular layout with the Save Layout button.

Grid

Also within the View menu, you can find the Grid Size control in the Grid category. If you recognize that LightWave is a big 3D universe that you work within, it should be easy to understand that the Grid Size is the default unit of measurement you work with. By default, this measurement is 1 meter in size, as you can see in Figure 4.49.

Figure 4.49   LightWave Layout's default unit of measurement, Grid Size, is 1 meter. The Grid Size can be increased or decreased as needed.

This means that every grid square you see in Layout, from any view, is 1 meter in size. Count three squares, and that's 3 meters, and so on. The reason you can increase and decrease the Grid Size in the View menu is because not all objects are created equally. For example, if you load in a Mars rover spacecraft, your unit of measurement automatically adjusts to the fit the size of the craft. You should be able to move and rotate the object just fine. If you load in the planet Mars, and it is built to scale, the Layout Grid Size might jump to 5 kilometers, and your rover will essentially disappear! This is because LightWave's grid adjusts itself to fit this large object. If you find your rover and move it, it will shoot off the screen with the slightest mouse movement. If this happens, you need to decrease the grid size.

Tip

Adjusting the grid appears to change the size of the camera and lights, but it really doesn't. It only changes the relationship of those items to LightWave's world.

Select

The last category in the View tab is the Select category. Here, you can choose from various ways to select objects, lights, and cameras. You can choose to select by name or search by name. You can also select related parent or child items here, in addition to selecting in order, from one item to the next. A quicker way to select, however, is to click directly on the item in Layout and then use the up or down arrows on your keyboard to select the next or previous item.

Preferences

LightWave, like many programs, has its own set of preferences. However, because LightWave is not native to particular operating systems and utilizes its own custom interface, accessing these options is not as easy as finding an Edit button at top of your computer screen. Instead, press the d key or the o key. The d key calls up Display Options, as in Figure 4.50.

If you had pressed the o key, the General Options tab would have appeared, but both panels are embedded in the Preferences panel. Within the Display Options tab, you have specific control over settings that pertain to what you see in Layout. These are options concerning grid size, overlay colors, and many OpenGL options. The OpenGL, or Graphics Library, is the color shaded and textured views you see in Layout. Your video card determines how many OpenGL options you can support, but these days, even the simplest gaming cards work tremendously with LightWave. You can tell LightWave to turn on many OpenGL options concerning lens flares, textures, reflections, and even transparency.

Figure 4.50
LightWave's Preferences panel is opened by pressing the d or the o key. Here, you can see the Display Options tab.

Bounding Box Threshold

An important value in the Display Options tab is the Bounding Box Threshold. You might have installed LightWave and hopped right into Modeler. The model you have created ended up being made up of 5,000 points and 5,200 polygons. When you send your object to Layout for animating, you see the object, but as soon as you move it, it turns into a wireframe box. What's going on? This is LightWave's way of saving system resources. If your object is made up of too many points and polygons, it can significantly slow down your system when you try to move or rotate it. This is because LightWave needs to redraw the object in real time on every frame. If it can't keep up, it stalls. The Bounding Box Threshold allows you to set a limit of when LightWave has enough, so to speak. A basic 64MB video card can have a bounding box threshold set to about 40,000. In other words, if your object is 35,000 polygons, it stays drawn all the time. If it's more than 40,000 polygons, it turns to a bounding box upon any movement. Set this one time, and you can leave it. Note that this does not affect rendering in any way.

General Options

If you press o for General Options, you see a tab with a few less variables, but no less important, than those shown in the Display Options. Figure 4.51 shows the General Options tab.

You see the Content Directory at the top of the panel. Earlier in the book, the Content Directory was discussed, and it is important for using this book's DVD. This setting tells LightWave where to look for files.

Other options in the General Options panel, such as Alert Level, are set based on your skills. You can set this to Beginner, Intermediate, or Expert. If you have the Alert Level set to Beginner, any warnings or errors will pop up on your interface. Set it to Expert, and any errors will appear beneath the timeline, without the need for clicking OK to close a panel. A small warning will appear, assuming you know what you're doing, and you can continue working.

You can change LightWave's Input Device from a mouse to a tablet, as well as set how your frame slider is viewed. By default, the LightWave timeline shows frames, but you can change this to show SMTP time code, film time code, or time in seconds. The most common setting is frames, as in frames per second.

LightWave also offers its own custom color picker, which you can turn on in this panel. When picking colors for backgrounds or surfaces, for example, LightWave calls up its own custom color picker rather than your Windows or Mac system color picker.

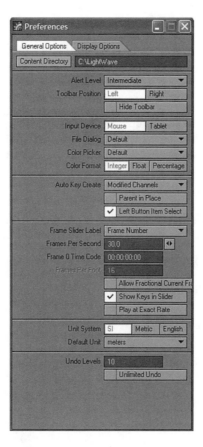

Figure 4.51   The General Options tab within the Preferences panel contains key settings for LightWave Layout.

In Chapter 3, the unit of measurement was discussed, and the same applies to Layout. Essentially, you can set LightWave's default measurement to System International (SI), Metric, or English. SI is the default and is what we'll be using throughout this book.

Finally, as mentioned previously, Layout offers multiple undo levels, which can be accessed in this category. Be careful with this. You can't undo everything; primarily, this is useful for undoing keyframe motions. Let's say you add a few keyframes to your animation and decide you don't like them. Press Ctrl+z a few times to undo. Again, if you accidentally click Remove Texture in the Surface Editor rather than Use Texture, there is no undo for that! So be cautious.

The Next Step

This chapter has taken you on a brief overview of Layout and how it's laid out. You have seen how the menus are arranged and how they work and were given a tour of the tools available to you.

There is more to learn, and it's about to get more exciting. Soon, you'll be working completely on tutorials, learning firsthand the tools and how they work. What's more, you'll learn why you're instructed to do what you're doing. Subsequent chapters guide you through the basics of lighting, textures, and motions. Then, you'll take this knowledge into longer, full-blown projects.

Too often, books just click you through, leaving the figuring out up to you. *Inside LightWave 8*'s tutorials are designed to ramp you up from beginner to intermediate to advanced tutorials, clearly explaining along the way.

We have a big journey ahead of us, so take a break, get some caffeine, and get ready to rumble!

Chapter 5

Keyframing and Graph Editor

There are so many facets to 3D animation, from modeling to texturing, lighting, and even scripting, that it's sometimes a real headache trying to figure out where to start. When you think about animation, you think about movement. Movement in animation is created with keyframes, so you might think that this is the first topic this book should have discussed. 3D image creation isn't always about movement, but regardless of whether you're dealing with still or moving images, understanding the environment in which you are working in is key to your success as an animator and 3D artist. Knowing how to create an effect or where to make the right adjustments saves you not only time but also aggravation. Understanding timing is a constant in an animator's career, and it's also the focus of this chapter.

LightWave 8 is uncluttered yet very functional. Many programs fill up the screen with useless icons—thankfully, LightWave names buttons clearly. This enables you to focus on your creative goals instead of having to figure out what a particular icon means. Going one step further, LightWave's powerful Graph Editor offers you complete control over a specific item's motion and timing. This item can be a camera, object, light, or any other type of parameter that can be enveloped or changed over time. It was mentioned in Chapter 4, "Layout," that you'll find those little E buttons throughout the LightWave interface. This chapter discusses what to do with those E's when you click on them.

The Graph Editor that opens when you click on an E button also gives you control over every channel of an item, such as the X position, heading rotation, dissolves, light color, and so on, all over time. Each channel can be controlled through the use of expressions, modifiers, or even keyframes, all from within the Graph Editor. The Graph Editor is used to edit any type of parameter that can be enveloped, or as the non-technical folk like to say, animated. In this chapter, you will learn about the following:

- Creating motion with keyframes
- Understanding splines
- Adjusting motions
- Working with the Graph Editor

Creating Motions with Keyframes

You might think that the title of this section is redundant. Creating motions with keyframes? Duh! How else would you do it? Actually, there are many ways in LightWave 8 to create motions, all without keyframes. These areas include procedural motions, expressions, and of course dynamics. Dynamics enable you to move one item and have it affect another item. Or, you can just add gravity to an object and watch it move without keyframing.

So why even use keyframes? Ah, there's the rub, my friend. Keyframes are essential! To create an animation that's really "in the pocket," you need to master the art of timing. That's right, the "art" of timing. It is an art, and either you get it, or you don't. Not to sound harsh, but timing is everything—in life, in comedy, and in animation.

Keyframing is the act of setting or marking an animatable attribute in time. For example, when you want a ball to move from point A to point B over two seconds, you need to set keyframes to tell the computer to "start here" at point A in time, and "end here" at point B. The more keyframes you set, the more quickly you will get a feel for timing. You can set keyframes yourself or let LightWave manage them for you. Everything in LightWave has at least one keyframe. This initial keyframe tells the item to "be here" at a certain point in time. The way it moves from that point is up to you. Keyframing goes beyond just animating position and rotation. It encompasses light intensity, color, various surface attributes, and virtually anything in Layout that has a value that can be changed.

Because the Layout interface was covered extensively in the previous chapter, as well as navigating the timeline, this chapter focuses on putting you to work. You'll start by first setting up some basic keyframes. From there, you'll use multiple objects and then learn how to set targets and parents and adjust the motions in a variety of ways. Ready? OK, go!

Automatic Keyframing

The Auto Key button is turned on by default in Layout at the bottom of the Layout interface. We discussed this briefly in Chapter 4, but the following is a hands-on tutorial to further explain when and why to use this feature. Auto Key adjusts the values of existing keyframes automatically. For the Auto Key feature to automatically create keys, you need to make sure the Auto Key Create option is on in the General Options tab (press the O key). Any commands such as Move, Rotate, Size, or Stretch are remembered for selected items at the current frame. Exercise 5.1 explains this feature further.

Exercise 5.1   Using the Auto Key Feature

1. Clear your scene in Layout by going to the File drop-down list and selecting Clear Scene and then clicking the Object button under the Load category of the Items tab. Load the gemstone object from the book's DVD (Chapter 5 directory). Figure 5.1 shows the object loaded into Layout.

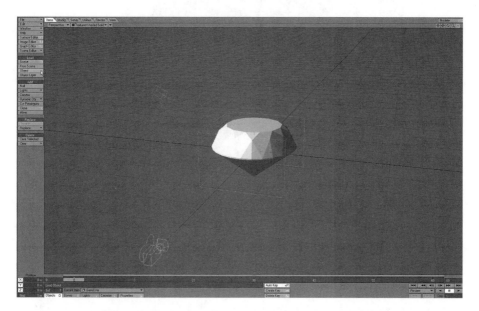

Figure 5.1   A gemstone object, created in Modeler from the primitive tools under the Create tab, is loaded into Layout.

2. With the gemstone object loaded, be sure the frame slider at the bottom of the Layout interface is at 0, be sure Auto Key is enabled, and activate Auto Key Create in the General Options tab within the Preferences panel (o) to have keyframes created automatically.

3. Select Modified Channels from the selection area of the Auto Key Create command, as in Figure 5.2. Modified Channels creates keyframes for those channels that have been changed, whereas setting Auto Key Create to All Motion Channels creates keyframes for everything in your scene.

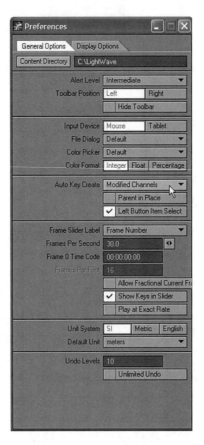

Figure 5.2 Be sure to set the Auto Key Create option to Modified Channels in the General Options tab.

In the Layout window, you'll notice that there is always a key at frame 0 by default. Thus, an object is locked in place even without Auto Key.

Tip

Auto Key merely lets you make an adjustment at frame 0 (or any other existing keyframe) without having to recreate the key.

4. Move and rotate the gemstone by selecting Rotate from the Rotate category under the Modify tab. It's fine to stay in Perspective mode to do this. You can also just press y on the keyboard to activate Rotate.

5. Move the timeline slider to frame 10.

6. Rotate the object to a different angle.

7. Click and drag the timeline slider forward a few frames.

   The object doesn't move! This is because Layout has automatically locked it in place at frame 10 (the point in time where your slider was), thanks to Auto Key.

8. Drag the timeline slider to frame 20.

9. Now use the Move tool by selecting it from the Modify tab (or by pressing the t key), move the object to a different position, and give it some rotation. Press y to jump to the rotation tool.

Tip

Some of the most common tools you'll use in Layout are the Move and Rotate commands. Although you can select them easily from the Modify tab or press t for Move and y for rotate, there's an easier way to jump back and forth. You can simply press the Spacebar on your keyboard to cycle through Move, Rotate, Size, and Stretch. Additionally, if your computer mouse has a wheel, you can use it to toggle between Move and Rotate.

Important

When setting up keyframes, LightWave automatically draws a motion path. When the keyframe is set at frame 20, you will see a line appear representing the object's path of motion if Show Motion Paths is enabled from the Display Options panel (d).

10. Move the timeline slider to frame 40, and then move and/or rotate the object again.

11. Press the Rewind button at the bottom of Layout, which has the two small arrows pointing to a line on the left, and then press the Play Forward button, which is the small right-pointing triangle above the Step value entry.

   The three buttons underneath the Rewind button are the Play Forward, Play Reverse, and Pause buttons. You should see the gemstone object move and rotate between keyframes 20 and 40. You can shuttle through the animation by grabbing the timeline slider and dragging.

Important

Often, Auto Key can make your animation work go smoother, especially during character animation. However, if you're not careful, this tool can also damage your work. There may be situations where your keyframing needs to be precise. Having Auto Key enabled and accidentally moving the wrong object or moving the right object the wrong way could potentially cause you more work. Although you can use the Undo key, always work with caution when using the Auto Key feature.

Manual Keyframing

Now that you've learned one way of keyframing, you most definitely need to learn another. Manual keyframing is often a more common way to work than using the Auto Key, but of course the choice is up to you. Manual keyframing requires that you develop a keen sense of timing, and although this can't be done overnight, a few practice animations can get you started.

Tip

A good way to work is to turn off the Auto Key Create option in the General Options tab (press the o key) and work only with Auto Key enabled. Auto Key adjusts existing keyframes without the need to create them again after any changes are made. This way, if you accidentally move the timeline, you won't create unwanted keyframes, destroying a precisely placed item.

Exercise 5.2   Manual Keyframing

1. Load the train car object from the Chapter 5 project directory on this book's DVD into a clear Layout scene. Be sure to turn off Auto Key. Figure 5.3 shows the train car loaded from the Perspective view.

2. Press 6 on the numeric keypad to switch to Camera view.

    If the train car object is not selected, click it with the left mouse button. A bounding box highlights around the object, and its control handles become visible, as in Figure 5.4.

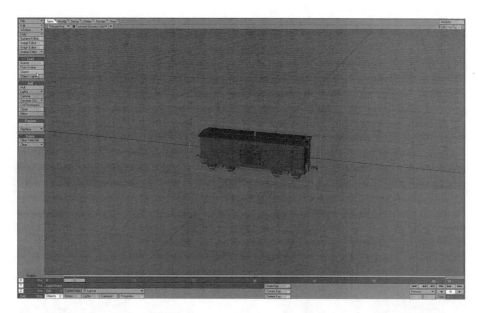

Figure 5.3   Making sure that the Auto Key button is off at the bottom of Layout under the timeline, load the train car object.

Figure 5.4   Selecting the object creates a bounding box around the object with control handles.

Important

A few things you should know here: When there's a blank scene and you load a single object into it, that object should automatically be selected. If you click with the left mouse button to select the item and it's not selecting, be sure you have Left Button Item Select turned on in the General Options panel (press o), as in Figure 5.5. If the control handles do not appear in the center of the object, make sure that the Show Handles option is turned on in the Display Options tab (press d), as in Figure 5.6.

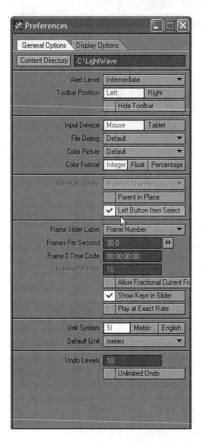

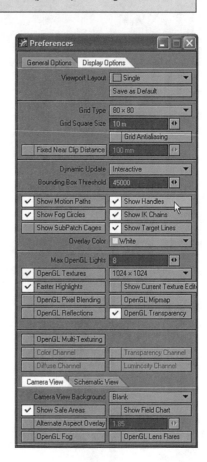

Figure 5.5 Pressing o opens the General Options panel, where you can turn the Left Button Item Selection option on or off.

Figure 5.6 Pressing d opens the Display Options panel, where you can turn the Show Handles option on or off. This setting is on by default.

3. With the left mouse button, click and drag the red arrow to the left of the view, which moves the train on the negative X-axis. Figure 5.7 shows the new position.

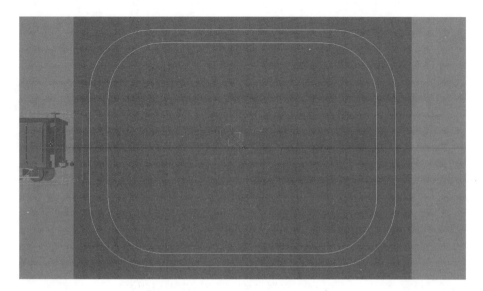

Figure 5.7   Using the control handles, you can move the train car just on the X-axis.

Move the train car until it just leaves the frame. This is where you want the object to start from in the animation. Now you need to tell LightWave to make the train car stay at this location.

4. Press the Enter key on your keyboard once to call up the Create Motion Key panel. You can also click the Create Key button at the bottom of Layout under the timeline.

The current frame will be highlighted when the panel appears, as in Figure 5.8. You also can select the Create Key button at the bottom of the interface.

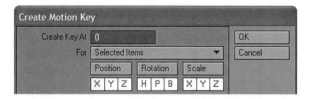

Figure 5.8   The Create Motion Key dialog always opens with the current timeline frame selected.

If the timeline slider was at frame zero, a 0 will appear in the Create Key At command window.

5. If the timeline slider is not at frame zero, enter 0 and press the Enter or Return key again.

The keyframe is now set.

Important

You should know a few things about the Create Motion Key panel. In it, you can specify that you want to create a keyframe for Selected Items (which you just did), Current Item Only, Current Item and Descendants for parented items, or for All Items. Additionally, you can set keyframes for specific channels of motion. For example, say you have a logo keyframed to make a continuous loop, and then you realize you need to move it to a new location without disturbing the rotation. You can create a keyframe for just the new position, not rotation. Try it out!

Tip

You might be in the habit of clicking in each numeric window, erasing the existing values, and then reentering them. This is not necessary. When you open the Create or Delete key panels, the existing value is already selected. All you need to do is enter the desired value. This saves time.

Tip

You do not need to move the timeline slider to set keyframes throughout an animation if you are manually setting keyframes. However, moving it helps keep you organized and aware of the current animation frame.

6. Now move the train car to the right side of the screen, past where it originally was, as shown in Figure 5.9.

Tip

If you can't see the object to grab it, you can switch to the Back view by pressing the number 1 on the keyboard. Mac users, remember to use the Apple key for right mouse button commands.

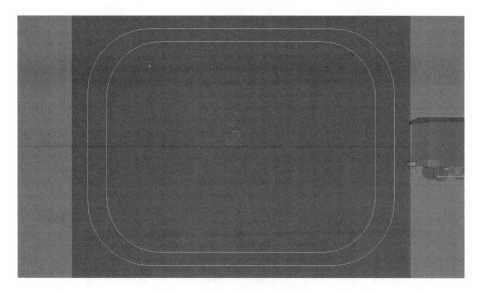

Figure 5.9   Click and drag on the red handle to move the train car over to the positive X-axis.

7. Press the Enter key to call up the Create Motion Key command.

8. Type 60 from the numeric keypad and press Enter, as in Figure 5.10.

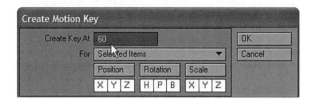

Figure 5.10   When the train car is in its new position, create a new keyframe for it at frame 60, which is 2 seconds.

Too often, users are in the habit of using the number keys across the top of the keyboard. Although this works just as well, you will save time by using the numeric keypad.

9. Press the Play button (right arrow icon) at the bottom right of the Layout interface.

The train car should move from left to right across the screen.

Important

LightWave Layout defaults to 60 frames for a 2 second animation. In most cases, you'll end up creating keyframes well beyond this value. Be sure to change the last frame number in the timeline to something a little higher than your last keyframe value. This ensures that you can see all of your animation when it's played back.

Because you want the train car to end at frame 60 where it originally was positioned, you could have created a keyframe when it was in that position. You can use a single position of an object to create various keyframes by entering the desired keyframe values in the Create Motion Key dialog. For example, you just created a keyframe for the train car at frame 60. If you want this train car to sit for one second, then return to its position at frame 0 and do the following:

1. With the train car at frame 60, to the right of the Layout screen, press the Create Key button (or press Enter on your keyboard).

2. When the Create Motion Key panel appears, enter a value of 90, which is 3 seconds, as in Figure 5.11.

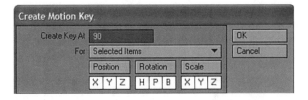

Figure 5.11 Create a new keyframe for the train car in the same position as frame 60.

You've just copied a keyframe. You took the position of the selected item, the train car, and told LightWave to make it "be here" at frame 90, as you did for it at frame 60.

When you play back the animation, it starts on the left side of the screen at frame 0, moves to the right side of the screen over 2 seconds, ending at frame 60, and then sits there for 30 more frames, to frame 90.

Now, you could grab the red handle and drag the train car back to 0. Instead, try this: Press the f key to call up the Go To Frame command. Enter the frame you want to go to, which is 0. Because the train car already has a keyframe at 0, and this is where you want it to also end up, just press the OK button (or Enter on your keyboard). Figure 5.12 shows the panel.

Figure 5.12   A super-quick way to jump your timeline to a specific keyframe is to use the
Go To Frame command by pressing f.

You'll now see the train car back in its original starting position at frame 0. Create a new
keyframe for this object's position by pressing the Create Key button (or Enter on your
keyboard) and enter the value of 150, as in Figure 5.13.

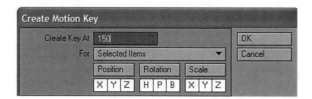

Figure 5.13   Create a new keyframe at 150 for the train car, using its position from frame 0.

Because the last frame you created was 90, and you want the train car to travel back to
its original position at frame 0 over 2 seconds, you needed to add 60 frames to 90–150.
Make sense? Just remember, you're working over time, so you're always adding up
frames.

Press the Play button at the bottom of the Layout screen, and you'll see the train car
move from left to right, sit for a moment, and then move back. You've done it!

You can call up the finished scene, called train_car_motion_1.lws, from this
book's DVD.

However, you might have noticed a problem or two with the motion. See how the train
car doesn't really stop? It sort of floats and drifts a bit before it begins its trip backward.
Because LightWave creates motion curves between keyframes, you need to control the
curve for each keyframe. You can do this with the Graph Editor. However, there is a
quicker way to change this motion right in Layout. Let's use that option first and then
use the Graph Editor to control specific motion channels so you can see both methods.

That tutorial was really basic and is the simplest thing in this book, but it's important for
you to get the hang of keyframing. You told the train car to be at a certain position
at frame 0, the beginning of the animation. Then, you moved the object to its resting
position at the end of the animation at frame 60. You then told LightWave to hold that

position of the train car at frame 90, creating a 3-second animation. LightWave interpolates the frames between 0 and 90. You then used the information from the train car's position at frame 0 to create an identical keyframe at frame 150. Like magic, you made an animation. The motion curve that the computer created is the in-betweening that traditional animators would have to draw by hand.

Important

You also can delete keyframes just as easily as you create them. Pressing the Delete key on the keyboard calls up the Delete Motion Key dialog, with the cursor set at the Delete Key At field and the current frame already selected, as shown in Figure 5.14.

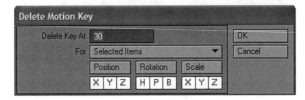

Figure 5.14   Deleting keyframes works the same way as creating them. Select an item to adjust, go to a specific point in time, and press the Delete Key button at the bottom of Layout.

As with creating keyframes, the timeline slider does not need to be on the specific keyframe to delete a key. Enter the key you want to delete when the Delete Motion Key window opens. Again, use your numeric keypad to save time! And remember, just as you can create keyframes for specific channels, you can delete them as well.

Controlling Curves with the Move TCB Tool

The Move TCB tool in Layout is perfect for quickly controlling the motion curve created from multiple keyframes. Coming up in the Graph Editor section, you'll see how to precisely change each motion channel. For now, learn how to use the Move TCB tool in Layout on the train car motion created in the previous exercise.

Exercise 5.3   Working with the Move TCB Tool

1. If you don't have your train car scene still in Layout with the multiple keyframes you created, load the train_car_motion_1.lws scene from this book's DVD.

   This is the keyframed object that should sit still between frames 60 and 90. The object should sit still because you created two keyframes in the exact same position. Due to the motion curve, the train car slides between the curves, ramping up for its trip back to its starting position for frame 150.

2. Press the f key to call up the Go To Frame window and go to frame 60.

3. From the Modify tab, select the Move TCB tool on the left, as in Figure 5.15.

Figure 5.15 The Move TCB tool can be found under the Modify tab in Layout.

4. Click and drag in Layout, but watch the info area on the bottom left of the Layout screen. You'll see that this area now lists T, C, and B, for Tension, Continuity, and Bias. Clicking and dragging with the left mouse button enables you to increase or decrease the tension for the current frame, which is 60.

5. Drag until the tension reads 1.0, as in Figure 5.16.

6. Go to frame 90 and set a tension of 1.0 as well. Repeat for frames 0 and 150.

7. Play back the animation, and you'll see that the train car starts out slower and ramps up to speed. It comes to rest at frame 60, holds for a second, and then backs up to frame 150, easing into place.

You can add frames to a resting position by simply creating another keyframe. For example, if you wanted the train car to stay at frame 150 for 3 seconds, you would create an additional keyframe in the same position at frame 240. Just think about your timeline process and what you're trying to accomplish. Be specific in what you want your object to do, and you'll have an easier time creating motions.

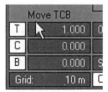

Figure 5.16 Click and drag with the left mouse button in Layout at frame 60 with the Move TCB tool active to apply tension.

Now, there are a few things to know about TCB and how to set them:

- **TCB** can be set to either negative or positive, with a range of values from -1.0 to 1.0.

- **Tension** is used to ease in or ease out of a keyframe. You would set a tension of 1.0 to make an item slow down before it came to its resting position. On the flip-side, you'd use a tension of -1.0 to make an object speed up coming into its resting position—perhaps for things like a ball bouncing.

- **Continuity** is used to break or enhance a change in a motion path. A positive continuity setting overcompensates for an item as it passes through a keyframe. A more common setting is a negative continuity, which enhances a keyframe. Use this for exaggerated character motions, for example.

- **Bias** is used for setting up anticipation. You can set a positive bias to create slack after a keyframe. Let's say your fire truck is speeding around a corner. Add bias to that keyframe, and it will slide around that corner. A negative bias creates slack before a keyframe. You could use this for, say, a race car before it goes into a sharp turn.

- **To set tension using the Move TCB** tool, just click and drag the left mouse button in Layout for an item's desired keyframe to change Tension.

- **To set continuity using the Move TCB** tool, hold the Ctrl key and click and drag the left mouse button in Layout for an item's desired keyframe to change Continuity.

- **To set bias using the Move TCB** tool, just click and drag with the right mouse button in Layout for an item's desired keyframe to change Bias.

Keyframe Rules for Thought

There are a few more things you should know about keyframing in LightWave. A common misunderstanding with keyframes is that the more you have, the more control there will be in a scene. Not so!

See, when you set up keyframes, you're creating a motion path. That motion path is a curve, controlled by the keyframes you set. A good rule of thumb to use when setting keyframes is to initially make two keyframes: your first keyframe and your last one, and then set your frames that fall in between. For example, say you want an object to move down a path and around an obstacle. The movement needs to be smooth, and trying to guess the timing might be tough to do. Set the beginning keyframe and then the ending keyframe to create the initial motion path. If you drag the timeline slider, the object moves between the two keyframes. If you move the timeline slider to the point where the object would move around the obstacle, you'll have the exact frame to set your next key. By creating the keyframe at this point, you've adjusted the motion path evenly.

In later chapters, you'll have many more opportunities to work with advanced keyframe techniques.

Navigating the Graph Editor

You've now worked through a series of basic keyframing steps. The process of creating keyframes is no different, even in large-scale animation projects. Overall, the increase in complexity results from the fact that there simply are more keyframes, and many more items to keyframe as well. However, you can alter those keyframes in various ways through LightWave's Graph Editor. From Layout's interface, you can access the Graph Editor by clicking the Graph Editor button at the top left of the screen while working under any menu tab. Conversely, you can press Ctrl+F2 to call up the panel. Figure 5.17 shows the Graph Editor at startup.

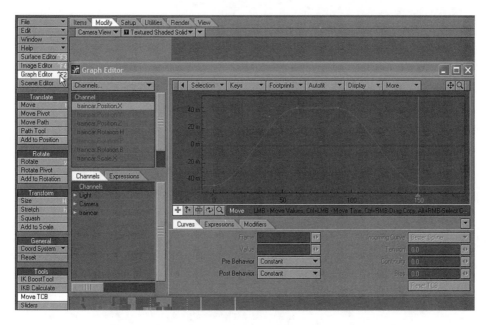

Figure 5.17   Opening the Graph Editor from the top left of the Layout interface gives you specific controls over your item's motions.

Tip

Any of the small buttons labeled E throughout LightWave Layout can also access the Graph Editor. You can find them next to the values of items that can be edited in the Graph Editor, such as Surface Color.

When you open the Graph Editor, you'll notice four general areas:

- The **Curve Bin zone** is in the top-left quadrant. You won't see the name Curve Bin, but just remember that this is the area of the Graph Editor where you select the specific channels (the curves) you want to edit (see Figure 5.18).

Figure 5.18   The Curve Bin zone of the Graph Editor is the area where you've put channels you want to edit.

- The **Curve Window zone** is in the largest area, the top-right quadrant. This is the area where you edit curves. You can adjust values, edit keyframes, and more (see Figure 5.19).

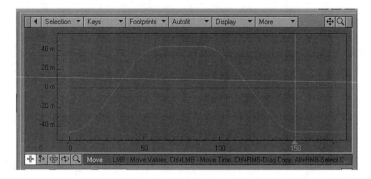

Figure 5.19   The Curve Window is the large main area of the Graph Editor, where all curve editing takes place. Here you can see your keyframes, motions, and more.

- The **Curve Controls zone** is in the bottom-right quadrant. Here you can set frames, values, behaviors for keys, and modifiers, as well as expression plug-ins, spline controls, and so on (see Figure 5.20).

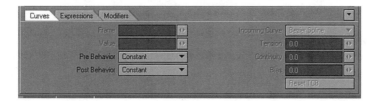

Figure 5.20   The Curve Controls zone at the bottom right quadrant of the Graph Editor is where you set specific controls such as expressions, modifiers, spline controls, and more.

- The **Scene zone** is in the bottom-left quadrant and shows your current scene elements. Lights, cameras, and objects are listed here, and you can select any or all of their channels, bring them into the Curve Bin, and begin editing. This area also shows you any expressions that might be applied (see Figure 5.21).

Figure 5.21   The Scene zone in the bottom left corner of the Graph Editor shows a list of items in your currently loaded scene in Layout. You can also access any expressions loaded by clicking the tabbed area.

You will work with each zone to adjust, modify, or create various motions, timing, and values for LightWave elements. Here you can control all Layout items, from the camera to lights to objects—including color, light intensities, morph envelopes, and more. You may be asking yourself where you should begin with the Graph Editor and wondering what it really does. Good questions! The Graph Editor is a complex part of Layout, one that is best explained through examples.

Tip

An envelope in LightWave is an animatable feature controlled through the Graph Editor. Many settings throughout Layout have a button labeled with an E. This E represents "envelope," which leads you into the Graph Editor. For example, suppose that you have set a Light Intensity value somewhere in your scene. Clicking the E button for Light Intensity (Lights panel) lets you envelope values—you can vary the value over time. This goes for any of the E buttons you see throughout LightWave.

The exercise in the following section provides an illustration of how to navigate through the Graph Editor interface.

Working with Channels

When you begin creating an animation, you will often need specific control over one keyframe or a group of keyframes. The Graph Editor gives you this control, but you first must understand how to set up the channels with which you want to work. This exercise introduces you to working with the Position and Rotation channels for a light and a camera.

Exercise 5.4   Working with the Position and Rotation Channels

1. In Layout, save any work you've been doing and select Clear Scene from the File drop-down menu. Then, select the default Camera.

2. Click the Graph Editor button on the toolbar (or press Ctrl+F2) to enter the Graph Editor.

   You don't need to load anything into Layout as you follow along here.

   Look at Figure 5.22, and you'll see that the attributes in the Scene list (lower-left quadrant) relate to the items in Layout, such as the Camera. Click the small white triangle next to the Camera listing under the Channels tab to expand, and you'll see all the appropriate motion channels for the selected item listed here.

Tip

You can maximize the Graph Editor window by clicking the standard system maximize button next to the X in the top right of the panel. Clicking this square opens the Graph Editor to full view. Mac users can resize the window as well. Also, you can rearrange the order of items in the Curve Bin by clicking and dragging them. This does not affect your scene.

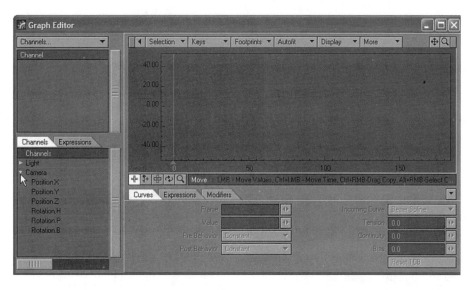

Figure 5.22   The Scene list in the lower left of the Graph Editor shows the items in your scene. Clicking the small white triangle next to an item expands to show all its channels.

3. Hold down the Shift key and double-click the Camera label in the Scene list area. This is in the lower-left corner of the Graph Editor interface.

Double-clicking the Camera item adds all its channels to the Curve area, overriding any channels already in the bin. Doing this now makes those channels available for editing.

You can also just click and drag a specific motion channel from the Scene list to the Curve area. This is great if you just want to add a selected channel or two. If you hold the Shift key, select a channel, and then select another channel, all channels in between will be selected. You can then drag those channels to the Curve area. And, like many areas within LightWave, such as the Surface Editor, holding the Ctrl key while selecting enables you to select noncontiguous channels.

4. Go back to the Scene list area at the bottom left of the Graph Editor and expand the Camera's channels if you haven't already by clicking the small white arrow to the left of the Camera label.

Tip

You can resize the individual quadrants in the Graph Editor by simply placing your mouse cursor on the line that separates the areas and then clicking and dragging (see Figure 5.23).

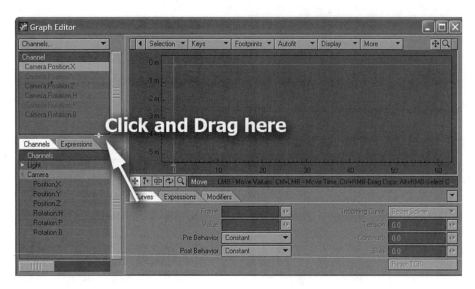

Figure 5.23   When you expand an item's channels, you can use the Scrollbar on the right of the Scene Display quadrant to access them, but it's better to resize the display area.

5. Double-click any of the Camera's channels in the bottom left zone.

The channel is now added to the Curve Bin and overrides any other channels. However, you can add more channels to the Curve Bin without overriding the existing channels by using the Shift key.

6. To add the Position.X and Rotation.H channels to the Curve Bin, hold down the Ctrl key and select the two channels. Then drag the selected channels up to the Curve Bin. You've now added channels instead of replacing them.

Tip

If you have noncontiguous channels (channels not in order) to select, use the Ctrl key rather than the Shift key to make your selections in the Scene list.

Now that you know how channels are added to the Curve Bin, the next thing you can do is modify or edit them in many different ways.

Working with the Graph Editor

Navigating through the Graph Editor is not as complicated as it might seem. You select the channels you want to edit from the Scene list and add them to the Curve Bin, as you did in the previous exercise. Then, from the Curve Bin at the top left of the Graph Editor, you select the desired channels and edit their curves in the Curve Window, the large main area of the Graph Editor.

Editing curves is one of the primary functions of the Graph Editor. Think of your workflow from bottom left, to top left, to top right, to bottom right to help understand the flow of editing curves.

Editing Curves

Editable curves are values that you've created in Layout to control lights, objects, cameras, and other animatable Layout attributes, such as textures or intensities. You can animate not only layout items, but also many values and properties throughout the program. Regardless of the property, working your way through the Graph Editor is the same. The preceding section talked about the Scene Display area and the Curve Bin. This section discusses the Curve Window.

Figure 5.24 shows the Graph Editor in full frame with the same train car scene from earlier in this chapter loaded (train_car_motion_2.lws). You can find this scene in the Projects/Scenes/Chapter 05 folder.

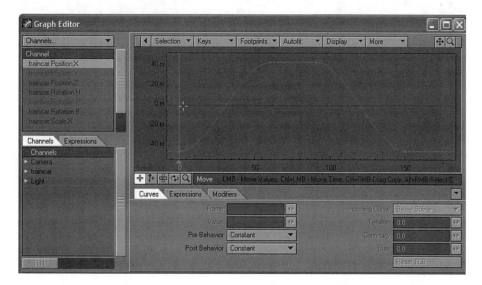

Figure 5.24   With a scene loaded into Layout and the train car object selected, opening the Graph Editor reveals all motion channels already in place for the selected train car object in the Curve Bin.

In Figure 5.24, the first channel (Position.X) in the Curve Bin is selected by default. In the Curve Window, the channel that represents the object's X position is highlighted. On your computer, you'll notice that each channel has a specific color in the Curve Bin: X is red, Y is green, and Z is blue. The same color represents the corresponding curve in the main Curve Window. If you move the mouse pointer over one of the small colored dots (which represent keyframes) on an active curve, which is also the item's motion path, numeric information appears, as shown in Figure 5.25.

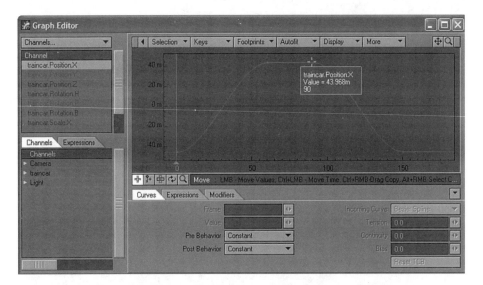

Figure 5.25　Moving the mouse pointer over a keyframe instantly displays the keyframe number, the value, and which channel (such as Position.X) you're working with.

Before you begin working with the Graph Editor, you should know that you can configure the window so that it is visible along with Layout. Figure 5.26 shows a possible interface configuration.

To resize the Graph Editor, do the following:

1. Drag the lower-right corner of the Graph Editor window. Make sure that the window is not maximized.

2. Click and drag the Layout window from the top of the panel, and move it to the upper-left portion of your screen.

3. Open the Graph Editor and resize it as well. Move it beneath the Layout window.

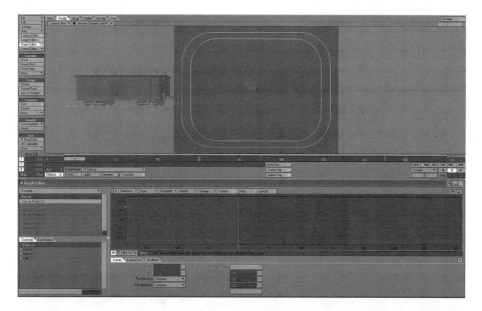

Figure 5.26   You can resize Layout and the Graph Editor, keeping both of them open while you work, thanks to LightWave's resizable non-modal panels.

Additionally, you can keep the Surface Editor and Preset Shelf (found under the Window drop-down) open while you're working in Layout if you like, perhaps also using the Dope Sheet. This is beneficial because you can make a change, see the result in Layout, and continue working. You do not have to continually open and close panels—simply leave them open. Either a large monitor or a dual-monitor setup is helpful for screen real estate when setting up configurations like this.

Adjusting Timing in the Graph Editor

The Graph Editor enables you to do many things, such as create, delete, or adjust keyframes for specific channels. You can also modify various entities within LightWave, such as surface color and light intensities. One of the more common uses for the Graph Editor is adjusting the timing of elements in your LightWave scenes. The Graph Editor has many uses, which you will inevitably take advantage of at some time during your career as an animator.

Exercise 5.5 Working with the Graph Editor

1. Load the ArrowSwoosh scene into Layout from the Chapter 5 projects directory on this book's DVD.

   This loads a simple logo animation that can be used for animated logo elements.

2. The G_3D object should already be chosen because the scene was saved with it selected. Open the Graph Editor.

   You'll see that all the object's channels are automatically loaded into the Curve Bin. However, in this tutorial, you are adjusting only the object's timing on the X-axis; therefore, the remaining channels are not needed. Figure 5.27 shows the Graph Editor with Position.X selected. If you have the Graph Editor open, the channels will have the same curves. If so, you can use the Selection > Get Layout Selected command (Shift+G) to update the Graph Editor.

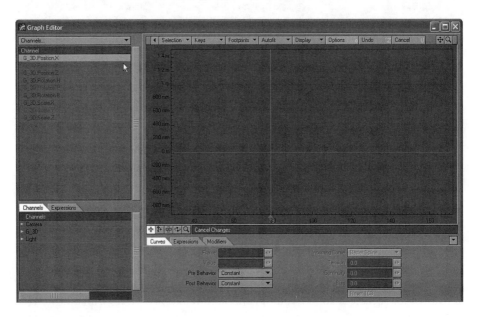

Figure 5.27 Opening the Graph Editor with a selected object in Layout reveals all its channels in the Curve Bin.

3. To remove the remaining channels, first select Position.Y in the Curve Bin. This is identified in green and should be the second channel in the list.

4. Holding down the Shift key, select the Scale.Z channel, the last channel in the list.

   This selects all the channels between Position.Y and Scale.Z, as shown in Figure 5.28.

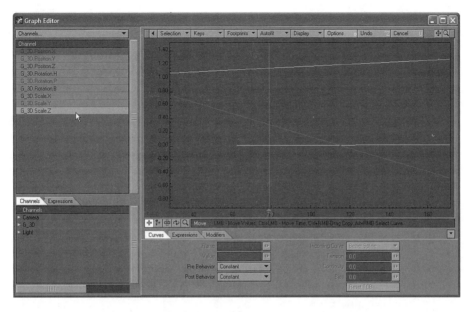

Figure 5.28   Selecting the Position.Y channel, holding the Shift key, and selecting the Scale.Z channel selects all the channels between Position.Y and Scale.Z.

5. To remove these selected channels, you can right-click the selections and choose Remove from Bin, as shown in Figure 5.29. Or, as an alternative, you can choose Remove Channel From Bin from the Selection drop-down list at the top of the Graph Editor panel. Figures 5.29 and 5.30 show the commands. As an option, you can use the Clear Unselected Channels option from the Selection drop-down.

Tip

If you take a close look at the functions available in the Selection drop-down list, you'll see that you can do much more than simply remove channels. You can clear the Channel Bin, reverse selections, select all curves, and more. Experiment with these options to get a feel for their usefulness.

Important

You don't need to remove channels if you're making changes to only one specific channel. However, it's a good idea to keep just the specific editable channel in the Channel Bin to help keep things uncluttered and organized. This is also a good idea because it keeps you from accidentally editing the wrong curve.

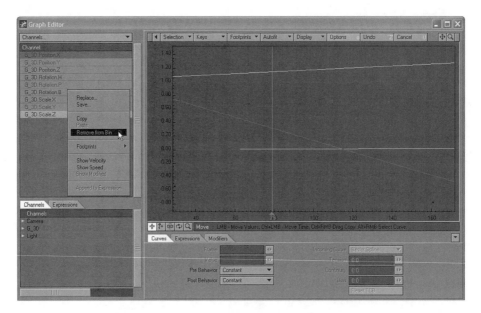

Figure 5.29   To remove selected channels, you can right-click the selections and choose Remove from Bin. Choosing Remove Channel from Bin from the Selection drop-down list removes selected channels from the Curve Bin.

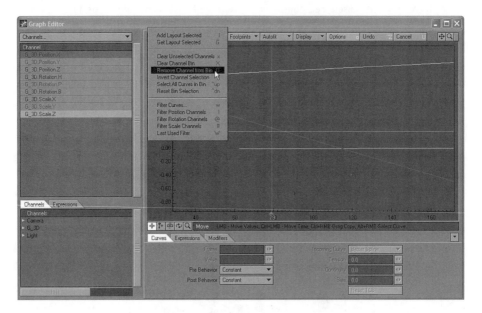

Figure 5.30   The Selection drop-down list at the top of the Graph Editor gives you access to a number of controls, including the ability to remove the channel from bin.

After removing the Position.Y to Scale.Z channels, you should now be left with only the Position.X channel in the Curve Bin.

6. Select the Position.X channel to highlight it in the Curve Window.

   This represents the motion of the X position for the object. The tall vertical line is the current frame.

7. Move your mouse over the first small dot (the first keyframe) on the curve for Position.X to see the information for that keyframe (see Figure 5.31).

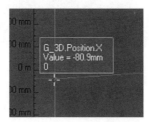

Figure 5.31   Move your mouse cursor over the first dot, which represents the first keyframe for the X position motion channel.

The information tells you what curve it is, which in this case is Position.X for the G_3D object. It also tells you the current frame and the value. The value is the object's position. For example, the value in Figure 5.31 reads –80.9mm. You are working with the Position.X channel, so this means the object is –80.9mm away from the 0 axis on the positive X axis. It is to the left of center in Layout, at frame 0.

It's probably hard to identify that first keyframe in the curve. To simplify this, you can use the Graph Editor's Custom Point Color function.

8. While still in the Graph Editor, press the d key to call up the Display tab of the Graph Editor Options panel. Click Custom Point Color at the bottom of the list, and the color selector will become active, as in Figure 5.32. The default color white is fine, so simply click OK to close the panel. Your keyframes in the Curve Window will now be easier to identify.

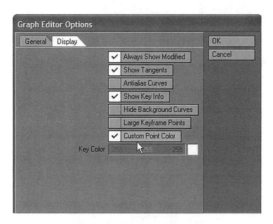

Figure 5.32   Setting the Custom Point Color in the Graph Editor Options panel helps make a curve's keyframes more visible.

 Tip

A number of other commands within the Options panel can help you when working with the Graph Editor. You can also access these commands and others easily by clicking the Display drop-down list from the top of the Graph Editor interface. Figure 5.33 shows the list of commands for Display.

Figure 5.33   The Display drop-down list atop the Graph Editor interface gives you controls for working in the Graph Editor Options panel.

9. In the Curve window, click the first keyframe to select it. Be sure that the Move edit mode button is selected. It is the first button located above the Curves tab, beneath the Curve Window, as shown in Figure 5.34. You can directly click the key to select it, or use the right mouse button to draw a region of selection. This second method is good for selecting multiple keyframes.

Figure 5.34   The Move edit button in the Graph Editor resides just below the Curve Window, along with Add, Stretch, Roll, and Zoom. Selecting a specific tool displays the appropriate keyboard legend. Here, the Move tool is selected, enabling you to move selected keyframes in the Curve Window.

You'll see the keyframe highlight slightly, and the values throughout the Curves tab will appear at the bottom of the screen, as shown in Figure 5.35.

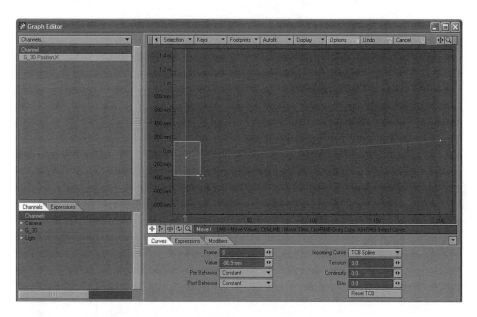

Figure 5.35   When a keyframe is selected, the commands in the Curves tab area become available. Here, a right mouse button click and drag lasso selects the key.

Tip

Too often, you may be clicking around too quickly in LightWave. It happens to the best of us! Doing so in the Graph Editor can really screw up your keyframes because it's easy to accidentally move the keyframe, adjusting its value unwillingly. Instead, use the right mouse button lasso select. Not only will you be sure you're getting the keyframe selected (they are pretty tiny), you also won't accidentally move it.

The middle of the Graph Editor interface offers five tools for you to choose from: Move, Add, Stretch, Roll, and Zoom. These are small icons. When you select them, information is displayed to the right, explaining what the function will do using a keyboard legend. Refer to Figure 5.34 to see the area.

The Move tool can be used to select and move single or multiple keyframes in the Curve Window.

10. Select the Move tool and click and drag the first keyframe in the Curve Window.

    Notice that you can move only its value. Doing this changes the position of the object in Layout.

11. Move the keyframe to set the value around 2m.

    Perhaps you do not want the G_3D object to move until frame 100, rather than starting its motion right at frame 0. This kind of delayed movement is easy to do in the Graph Editor.

12. Make sure that the Move tool is selected. While holding down the Ctrl key, click and move the 0 keyframe to the right. You'll see the frame number appear over the keyframe, as shown in Figure 5.36.

Tip

If you don't care to hold down the Ctrl key and use the mouse, you can numerically enter the specific keyframe. At the bottom of the screen in the Curves tab, you can enter the selected keyframe by clicking in the Frame field and typing the number. You also can set the value numerically by typing it in the Value field.

13. Adjust the value and keyframes of selected objects and return to Layout to see the effects. You can adjust values by dragging the keyframes in the Curve Window or by entering them numerically in the Curves tab area.

    Additionally, you have a number of key controls available from the Keys drop-down list atop the Graph Editor panel. Figure 5.37 shows the Move Keys selection, which enables you to numerically set offset values. You will soon get the hang of editing in the Graph Editor.

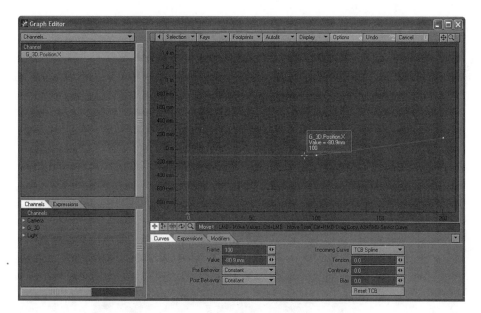

Figure 5.36   Holding the Ctrl key and moving selected keyframes adjusts timing. You didn't realize it was this easy, did you?

Figure 5.37   The Move Keys selection enables you to set a specific numeric value to move a key.

There's much more to the Graph Editor than this. One really good option to try out is the Lock Selected Keys from the Keys menu. This is really handy if you don't want to accidentally move a perfectly set keyframe. The first part of this chapter guided you through basic navigation and editing of channels and keyframes. Up next, you'll learn about the capability to move groups of keyframes, adjust curves, and add modifiers.

Copy Time Slice

Going beyond just basic keyframes, you can really control your animations with the Copy Time Slice command. Let's say that you have your scene all set up, and the timing of a motion is just right. However, you'd like to copy the object's position at a point where there is no keyframe. What do you do? You could do it numerically, by writing down the Move and Rotation values in Layout and then going to a new keyframe and entering them. A much easier way, though, is to use Copy Time Slice in the Graph Editor.

Exercise 5.6   Using the Copy Time Slice Feature

1. Select the curve you want to edit, such as the Position.X channel, using the previous exercise files. Drag the timeline bar to the desired frame of motion you want to copy (in the main Curve Window), as shown in Figure 5.38. You drag the timeline slider from the bottom.

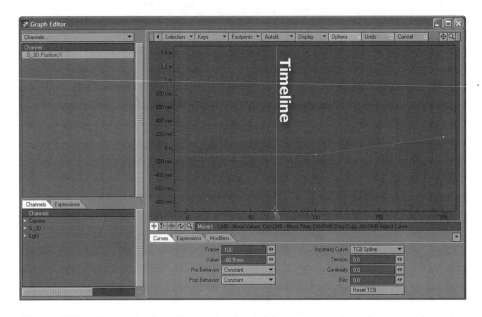

Figure 5.38   Use the timeline slider in the Graph Editor to move through your item's motion.

2. From the Keys drop-down list, select Copy Time Slice, as shown in Figure 5.39.

3. Drag the timeline slider to a new desired position.

4. From the Keys drop-down list, select Paste Time Slice, and a new keyframe will be created with the values from the previous position.

Tip

You can also use the keyboard shortcuts for Copy Time Slice: Ctrl+C for copy, and Ctrl+V for paste. This is the same for Macintosh and PC systems.

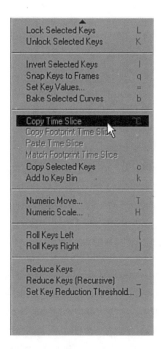

Figure 5.39   The Copy Time Slice command, accessed from the Keys drop-down list, records the current position of the timeline slider.

Copy Time Slice is an extremely handy function of the Graph Editor. If you set two keyframes in Layout for an item—at frames 0 and 90, for example—LightWave will interpret the motion for the frames in between those two keys. We talked about "in-betweening" earlier. Using Copy Time Slice enables you to copy the motion of any one of those interpreted keys and paste them somewhere else on that existing curve.

Multi-Curve Editing

But wait! There's more! You can also use multi-curve editing when you want to edit multiple curves simultaneously or use curves of different items as references. By selecting the desired curves in the Curve Bin (as demonstrated earlier in this chapter), you can edit them together as one in the Curve Window. You easily can drag and drop curves from the Scene Display window (bottom left zone of the Graph Editor) into the Curve Bin. For example, you might combine the Position.X of an object with the Rotation.Y of a light, and add in the Scale.Z of a camera. You can use any channel you want.

Tip

Here's a really quick way to instantly select all curves in the Curve Bin. Hold the Ctrl key and press the up arrow on your keyboard. Deselect all by holding the Ctrl key and pressing the down arrow.

Foreground and Background Curves

When you add selected curves to the Curve Bin, you can see them in the Curve Window and view them as either foreground or background curves. Curves that are selected in the Curve Bin will become editable foreground curves in the Curve Window. Conversely, the curves unselected won't be editable background curves in the Curve Window.

There are benefits to working with foreground and background curves. You can interactively cut and paste keyframes from one curve to another. You also can replace an entire curve with another, or lock areas of curves together. By having multiple curves selected when you create keys, the curves can be identical at those selected areas during an animation. Additionally, you have the capability to compare one curve to another, such as a light intensity to the H rotation of a camera. If you remember how Chapter 3, "Modeler," talked about using layers both for reference and as a tool, the same can be said for foreground and background curves in the Graph Editor. This next tutorial demonstrates some of these features.

Exercise 5.7   Working with Foreground and Background Curves

1. Clear Layout (you can press Shift+n) and open the Graph Editor. If the Graph Editor was already open, it will automatically be cleared with the Clear Scene command.

2. Move Camera Position.X and Light Position.Y to the Curve Bin. Do this by expanding the item in the Scene Display (bottom left) and then dragging the desired motion channel up into the Curve Bin.

3. When loaded, hold down the Shift key and select both channels in the Curve Bin. You'll see both curves highlight in the Curve Window. Right now there are only straight lines because the channels have no motions applied.

Important

Remember that you can click and drag on the bar between the Curve Bin and the Scene Display windows in the Graph Editor to quickly resize the two windows.

4. Select the Add Keys button beneath the Curve Window, as shown in Figure 5.40.

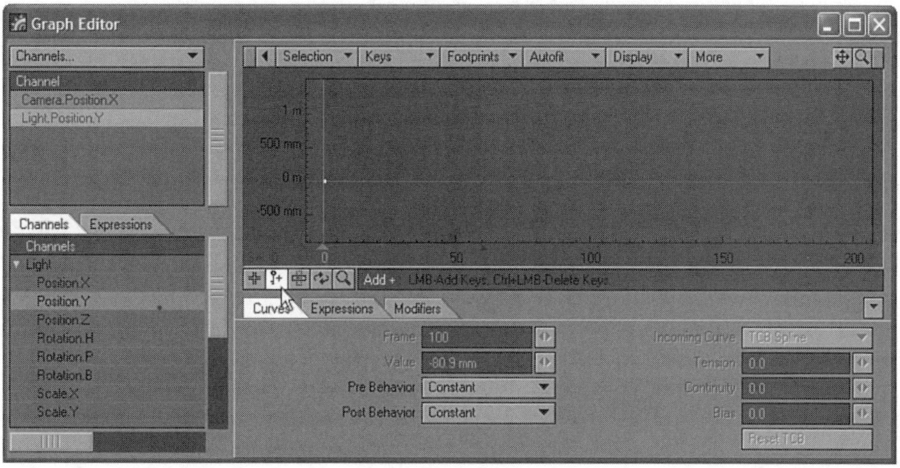

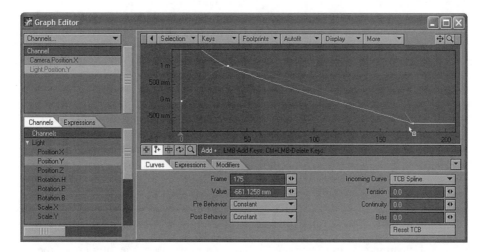

Figure 5.40   You can choose to add a key from the Graph Editor window, and you can also use the Move, Stretch, Roll, and Zoom commands.

5. Click once in the top area of the Curve Window and once near the bottom right, similar to Figure 5.41. You'll see the two curves adjust to the keys you just created.

Figure 5.41   You can create keyframes for the selected motion channels directly in the Curve Window.

> **Tip**
>
> At times, your curve may be out of view in the Curve window. As in Modeler and certain views in Layout, just press the a key to "fit all."

Navigating the Curve Window

When you select Multiple Curves, you can edit them together, create keyframes together, and so on. However, you also can adjust one of these curves based on the background curve: Simply select only the curve you want to adjust in the Curve Bin. The remaining curves in the Curve Bin appear slightly darkened in the background of the Curve Window. From there, you can select the Move tool and click and drag a keyframe to change its value. The following are just a few quick steps to remember when working in the Graph Editor:

- Select the Move keyframe button (in the center of the Graph Editor) and click and drag to adjust the selected key(s).

- Select the Move keyframe button and click and hold the Ctrl key to adjust the selected key's position in time—for example, to move a keyframe from frame 5 to 15.

- Hold the Alt key and click in the Curve Window to adjust the entire Curve Window view.

- Press the period (.) key to zoom into the Curve Window; press the comma (,) key to zoom out.

- Press the a key to fit the Curve Window to view—for example, if you zoom into the Curve Window, press the a key to instantly fit all keyframes of curves to the full window.

- You can import curves into the Graph Editor by pressing Shift+g. Many animators think you need to close the Graph Editor, select your next item in Layout, and then reopen the Graph Editor for the particular curve to be added. Instead, move the Graph Editor aside, select an item in Layout, and then use Shift+g back in the Graph Editor to update.

- Select Numeric Limits from the Display drop-down list at the top right of the Graph Editor window to set the minimum and maximum frame for the Curve Window. Holding Ctrl+Alt while moving the mouse left and right, and up and down, drags and zooms the Curve Window. You also can set a minimum and maximum value. Alt drag options are similar to their use in Layout's Perspective viewport. Figure 5.42 shows the Numeric Limits panel.

Figure 5.42   You can set Numeric Limits to control the frame and value settings in the Curve Window.

Exploring Additional Commands in the Graph Editor

In addition to the commands you'll use most often as you animate your scenes, you should know about the Graph Editor commands that can help you increase the speed of your workflow. As you've learned in other areas of LightWave, clicking the right mouse button in certain areas gives you access to additional tools that enable more control. The same goes for the Graph Editor.

Key Pop-Up Menus

In both the Curve Bin and Curve Window, you can access additional controls by using the right mouse button. Figure 5.43 shows the key pop-up menu in the Curve Bin. Figure 5.44 shows the pop-up menu in the Curve Window. All these controls are available in one location as well through the Keys drop-down list at the top of the interface. The right-click popup appears in the Curve Edit window only if your mouse cursor is positioned directly over a key.

Selecting a specific channel and right-clicking it in the Curve Bin gives you controls to perform a number of tasks. You can replace a channel with a pre-existing one. You can also save a specific channel's properties, which is useful when you want to save and reuse motions like a flickering light or a rotating globe. Instead of setting up new keyframes, you can save the channel motion and reload it later.

You also can copy and paste a specific channel's motion if you want to create a duplicate. Other controls include Show Velocity, which you can use to add a visual representation of the selected channel's velocity in the Curve Window; Show Speed, to make the speed of the selected channel visible in the Curve Window; and Remove From List, to delete a channel from the Curve Bin.

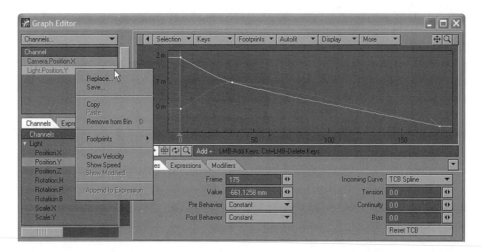

Figure 5.43 Right-clicking a selected channel opens the key pop-up menu for additional control.

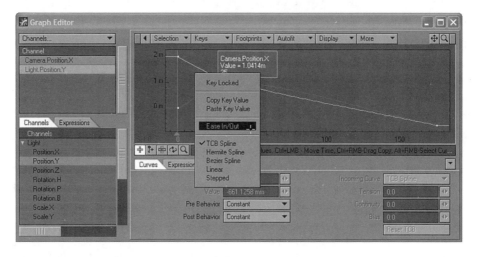

Figure 5.44 Right-clicking a selected keyframe opens the key pop-up menu for control in the Curve Window.

Footprints

Part of the charm of the LightWave Graph Editor is the capability to create footprints for a selected channel. Because you are not always sure of the adjustments you might make to a keyframe or curve, setting a footprint helps you visually remember the shape of your curve before it is adjusted. You can then return your curve to the footprint if you choose. Follow this next tutorial to learn more about footprints.

Exercise 5.8   Creating Footprints

1. Open Layout, clear the scene, and open the Graph Editor.

2. Select the light in the Scene window of the Graph Editor and drag it to the Curve Bin.

   All the motion channels for the light are added to the bin, as shown in Figure 5.45.

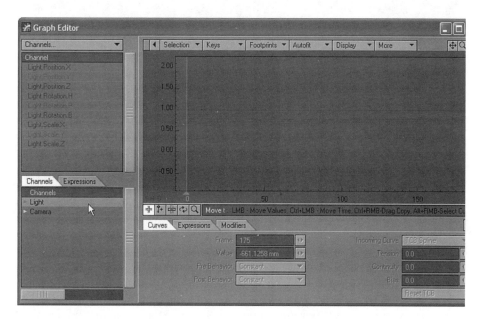

Figure 5.45   Selecting just the light from the Scene Display area and dragging it to the Curve Bin adds all its motion channels.

3. Select the light Rotation.P, which is the Pitch rotation for the light. Of course, any selected channel will do for this exercise.

   When a channel is selected, you'll see it highlighted in the Curve Window.

4. Select the Add Keys command, the second small icon beneath the Curve window, and then click throughout the Curve Window to create some keyframes for the selected channel. Figure 5.46 shows the channel with a few keys added.

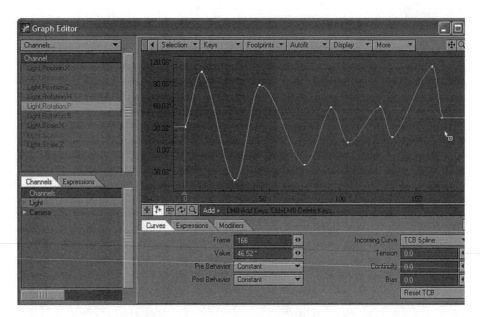

Figure 5.46   A few keyframes are added to the light's Rotation.P channel in the Curve
Window.

5. Go back to the Curve Bin, and with the Rotation.P channel still selected, right-
    click it to open the pop-up menu.

6. Choose the Footprints selection and then select Leave Footprints. You also can
    do this through the Footprints drop-down list at the top of the Graph Editor, as
    shown in Figure 5.47.

    It won't look like much has happened in the Curve Window, but wait.

7. With the right mouse button, click and drag to select a region over all your
    keyframes in the Curve Window.

    This selects all keys, as shown in Figure 5.48.

Tip

You also can hold the Shift key and double-click in the Curve Window to select all
keys. Move mode must be selected to do this. Clicking once in the blank area of the
Curve Window deselects keyframes.

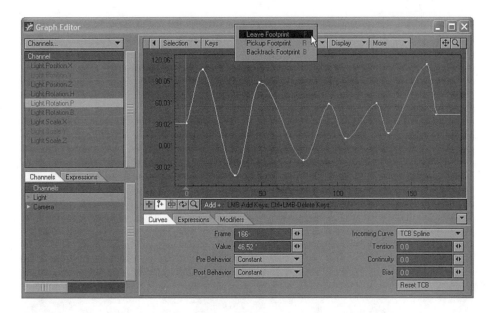

Figure 5.47   Right-click a selected channel to select the Footprints option, or select the Footprints drop-down menu at the top of the Graph Editor.

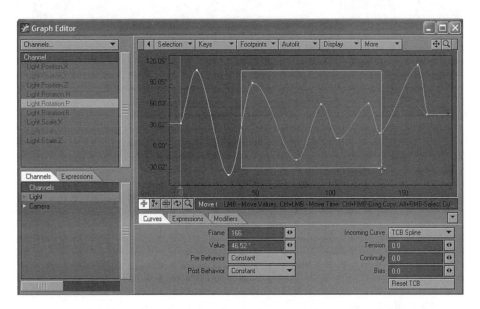

Figure 5.48   Right-clicking and dragging in the Curve Window lets you select multiple keyframes. Mac users, don't forget to hold the Apple key while clicking the mouse button to perform a right mouse button function in LightWave.

8. With all the keyframes selected, click and drag in the Curve Window to move the entire motion curve up, as shown in Figure 5.49.

You'll see a faint line underneath the curve you just moved. This is the footprint that tells you where your curve was.

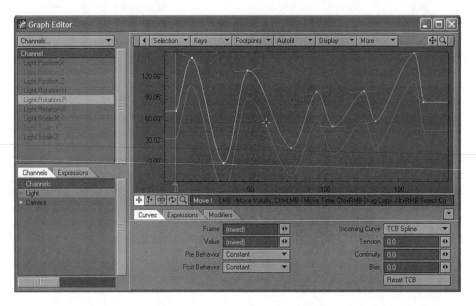

Figure 5.49   After a footprint is created, moving either single or multiple keyframes reveals the footprint.

9. Go back to the Curve Bin, right-click again on the Rotation.P channel, and choose Pick Up Footprint or Backtrack. You can also use the command from the Footprints drop-down list. Also note the keyboard shortcuts for each command on the respective buttons.

Picking up the footprint removes it from the Curve Window. Selecting Backtrack resets any channel adjustment to the original footprint position.

Footprints provide a simple way for you to keep track of what you're doing and where you've been while working in the Graph Editor. It is easy to make too many changes and lose your place when adjusting various channels. Using the Footprint option helps you organize your steps by enabling you to get back to your original curve if you need to.

Using the Curves Tab

At the bottom of the Graph Editor interface is the Curves tab. Here, you can adjust the value of a selected keyframe and its pre- and post-behaviors. This area is ghosted until a keyframe is selected. For example, suppose that you have created a spinning globe that takes 200 frames to make a full 360-degree revolution. Your total scene length is 600 frames, and the globe needs to rotate throughout the animation. Instead of setting additional keyframes for the globe, you can set the post-behavior to repeat. After the globe completes its 200 frames of motion, the Graph Editor's post-behavior takes over. You can also set pre-behaviors. A pre-behavior is what happens before the first keyframe. You can set either pre- or post-behaviors to the following settings:

- **Reset**, which resets the current value to 0.
- **Constant**, where values are equal to the first or last key's value.
- **Repeat**, which repeats the motion from the first to the last keyframe.
- **Oscillate**, which mirrors the channel repeatedly. For example, you can make a spotlight rotate from frame 0 to frame 30 on its heading rotation. Set post-behavior to Oscillate, and the motion sways back and forth between the two keyframes like a searchlight.
- **Offset Repeat**, which is similar to Repeat but offsets the difference between the first and last keyframe values.
- **Linear**, which keeps the curve angle linearly consistent with the starting or ending angle.

The Curves tab also is home to Spline controls. Earlier in the keyframing section of this chapter, we discussed how to use the Move TCB tool in Layout to adjust Tension, Continuity, and Bias (TCB). Remember, LightWave's motion paths (the channels that you're editing in the Graph Editor) are curves. Using TCB is one way to work with these curves, but LightWave offers more control than simple TCB splines.

Spline Controls

Spline controls come in many varieties, and they give you the control you need over your curves. When an item is put into motion in LightWave, it instantly has a curve. The Graph Editor gives you control over the individual channels of an item's motion as you've seen throughout this chapter. You can adjust the keyframes of the curve that is created with various types of splines. Figure 5.50 shows the Incoming Curve types. An Incoming Curve is the type of curve that precedes a keyframe.

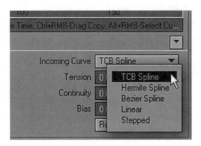

Figure 5.50 LightWave has numerous curve types from which to choose.

TCB Splines

To add a little more information about the TCB splines, they are easy to set and are useful for creating realistic motions. As mentioned earlier during the keyframing section, the values for each spline range from 1.0 to −1.0.

A tension with a value of 1.0 is often the most commonly used TCB spline because it enables items to ease in or out of a keyframe. For example, a 3D-animated car needs to accelerate. Setting it in motion without TCB splines makes the car move at a constant rate.

TCB Shortcuts

LightWave enables you to quickly and easily control Tension, Continuity, and Bias controls in the Graph Editor. You don't even need to select a key! Simply move your mouse over a particular keyframe. Press F1 and drag the mouse to the left to set a negative Tension, or drag to the right to set a positive Tension. Do the same for Continuity with F2 and Bias with F3. Cool stuff.

TCB splines are not the only spline controls you have when it comes to controlling keyframes. This version of the software employs Hermite and Bezier spline curves as well.

Hermite and Bezier Splines

Although TCB splines are often used for common, everyday animated elements, such as flying logos or animated cars, Hermite and Bezier splines offer a wider range of control. Hermite splines have tangent control handles that allow you to control the shape of a curve. Figure 5.51 shows three keyframes with Hermite splines added to the middle keyframe. Its handles are adjusted.

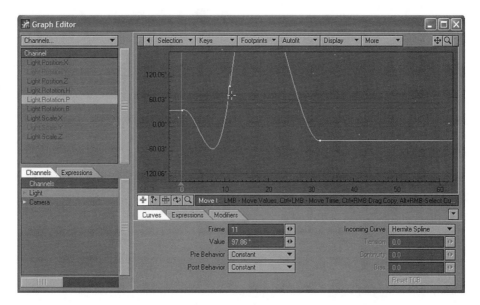

Figure 5.51   Hermite splines are added to the middle keyframe. These splines offer more control than regular TCB splines.

Figure 5.51 shows three keyframes—one low, one high, and one low again—in a sort of bell shape. However, the middle keyframe has a Hermite spline applied and the left handle of it has been pulled down quite a bit. The figure shows how an adjustment to one keyframe can have a drastic effect on the shape of a curve. You can do this by clicking and dragging on the small blue handles that appear on a selected keyframe after the spline is added.

If you apply a Bezier curve, you acquire a different type of control than for a Hermite spline. A Bezier spline is a variant of a Hermite spline and also shapes the curve. Figure 5.52 shows the same bell curve of three keyframes with one handle of the Bezier curve pulled down drastically.

Important

The biggest difference between Hermite and Bezier is that Bezier lets you change the length of the tangent, which also affects the curve shape.

Both Hermite and Bezier splines can help you control your curve. It's up to you to experiment and try both when working with the control of an item's motion. Knowing when to apply curve controls such as these is important. As you work through the tutorials in this book, the necessary controls are used so that you can see the direct effect. Keep an eye out for their use. You might find, however, that the majority of animations you create work best with simple TCB-adjusted curves.

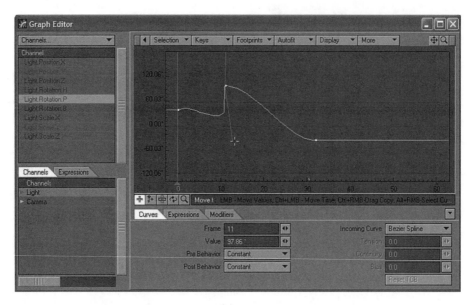

Figure 5.52   Bezier splines, although a variant of Hermite splines, work when the next key is also set to Bezier.

Stepped Transitions

Using a stepped transition for an incoming curve simply keeps a curve's value constant and abruptly jumps to the next keyframe. Figure 5.53 shows the same three keyframes with a stepped transition applied.

Stepped curves are usable when you want to make drastic value changes between keyframes for situations such as lightning, interference, or blinking lights. You might also find that applying stepped transitions works well for pose-to-pose character animation at times.

Whether you create motions in the Graph Editor or simply adjust pre-existing ones, you should understand the amount of control the Graph Editor gives you. The Graph Editor in LightWave 7 even enables you to mix and match spline types for individual channels. Follow along with this next exercise to make and adjust curves in the Graph Editor. Although you have many options for curve control in LightWave's Graph Editor, using the Tension, Continuity, and Bias (TCB) controls can provide the most natural motion for your animations.

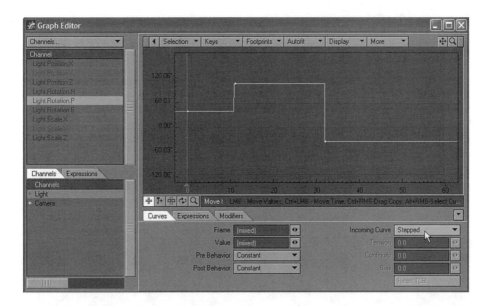

Figure 5.53   Stepped transitions for curves abruptly change your motion from one keyframe to the next.

   Tip

Pressing the o key in the Graph Editor opens the General Options tab of the Graph Editor Options panel. Here, you can set the Default Incoming Curve as well as other default parameters (Figure 5.54).

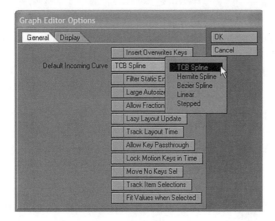

Figure 5.54   You can define the Default Incoming Curve in the General Options tab of the Graph Editor Options panel. Press o to access this tab.

Exercise 5.9 Creating and Adjusting Curves

Start by saving anything you've been working on in Layout and then clear the scene. These next few steps provide the information to create curves and adjust them so that certain areas match perfectly. These techniques can be used with any of your projects.

1. Open the Graph Editor, and in the Scene Display, double-click the Position.Z channel for the camera.

   The Camera's Z position is now added to the Curve Bin, and your Graph Editor interface should look like Figure 5.55.

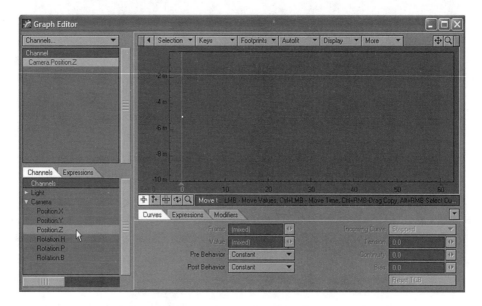

Figure 5.55 Double-clicking the camera's Z position channel adds it to the Curve Bin.

2. Expand the channels for the Light in the Scene Display by clicking the small white triangle.

3. Hold down the Shift key and double-click the Light's Position.Z channel to add it to the Curve Bin. If you don't hold the Shift key while double-clicking, the new selection overrides anything already added to the Curve Bin.

4. In the Curve Bin, hold down the Shift key and select both the Camera Position.Z and Light Position.Z channels. Or, hold Ctrl and push the up arrow on your keyboard.

5. Select Add mode, and in the Curve Window, create three keyframes to the right of the first keyframe at zero.

   Figure 5.56 shows the Graph Editor with the additional keyframes.

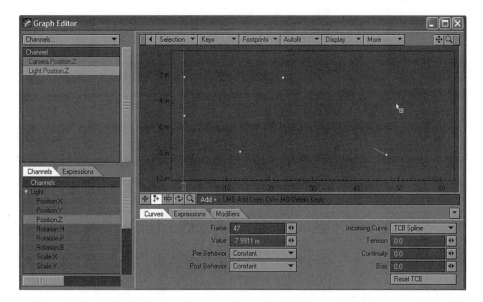

Figure 5.56 With multiple curves selected, you can create identical keyframes for both channels at once.

6. Select just the Camera Position.Z channel in the Curve Bin. This automatically deselects the Light Position.Z channel.

7. Select Move mode and move up the last keyframe.

   You'll see the Light Position.Z channel in the background. You've created similar motions on the Z-axis for both the camera and light, but toward the end of the motion, the value has changed. Figure 5.57 shows the adjusted channel.

Tip

When modifying identical channels on one keyframe, you need to compensate surrounding keyframes slightly. Because of the spline curves, one keyframe affects another.

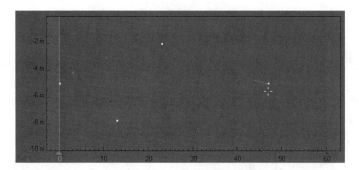

Figure 5.57   One keyframe of matching channels is adjusted.

A more realistic example of matching curves is a formation of flying jets. Each jet flies in unison, swooping, looping, and twisting in perfect sync. After the formation, one or two jets might need to fly off from the pack. Using the preceding example, you can easily select the appropriate channel and adjust the value at the desired keyframe.

It's easy to see where you would move the jet in Layout, but in the Graph Editor, translating the visual motion to a value might take a little more work. Don't worry; this next exercise helps you adjust values in the Graph Editor.

Exercise 5.10   Adjusting Values

1. Select Clear Scene from the File drop-down menu, or press Shift+n.

2. In the Graph Editor, click the small white triangle to expand the Camera channels in the Scene Display window.

3. Double-click the Camera Position.Y channel.

   Because only one channel is in the Curve Bin, it is automatically selected.

4. In the Curve Window, create a few keyframes. Figure 5.58 shows the additional keyframes.

5. With Move mode selected, hold the Shift key and double-click in the Curve Window to select all keyframes, as shown in Figure 5.59. When the keyframes are selected, you'll see small lines extending out from each. These are control handles for the particular incoming curve setting.

   Take a look at the Frame and Value areas under the Curves tab. Instead of values, they are highlighted with the word [mixed], as shown in Figure 5.60. This means that the currently selected keyframes have different values.

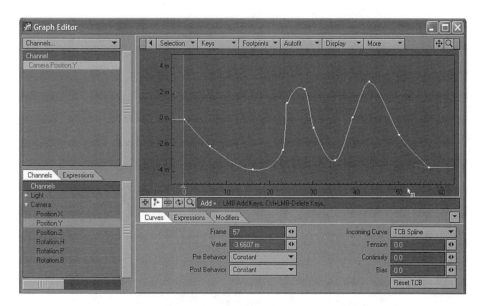

Figure 5.58   One channel is added to the Curve Bin, and additional keyframes are created in the Curve Window.

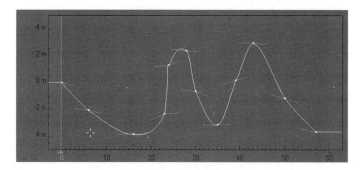

Figure 5.59   Hold the Shift key and double-click in the Curve Window to select all keyframes. Also, you can use the right mouse button to draw a bounding box to select multiple keyframes in the Curve Window.

Figure 5.60   Because multiple keyframes are selected, the word [mixed] represents different Frame and Value areas.

6. In the Value area, type the value 10 and press Enter.

All selected keyframes now jump to the same value, and perhaps even out of sight. Press the a key to make the curves fit back into view.

Setting one value to multiple selected keyframes is useful when you need to adjust many keyframe values, of course. Instead of selecting a keyframe and adjusting individual values, you can change values in one step as long as multiple keyframes are selected.

Important

By selecting multiple keyframes with the bounding box selection, you can also set all spline controls at once.

Editing Color Channels

Did you know that everything discussed in this chapter also applies to things like light intensities, objects dissolves, and much more? Sure you did. Well, a slick feature in LightWave's Graph Editor is the capability to animate color channels as well. This is really cool for animating colored lights for such things as stage lighting or a gradually changing sunset.

Exercise 5.11 Animating Color Channels

1. Close the Graph Editor, clear the LightWave scene, and then select the scene's default light. You can do this by first selecting the Lights button at the bottom of the LightWave Layout interface.

2. Press the p key to enter the light's Properties panel. You can also get to the properties by clicking the Properties button at the bottom of Layout.

You will see a series of small buttons labeled E. As mentioned earlier, these are accesses to envelopes, meaning their accompanying values are animatable. Anywhere you see them throughout LightWave, they will guide you right back to the Graph Editor. However, when you access the Graph Editor in this manner, you have control over only the specific area from which you have selected an envelope, such as Light Color.

It's important to note that entering the Graph Editor by using the E buttons tells LightWave that you want to perform a specific function. For example, if you click the E button next to Light Color, you are telling LightWave that you want to animate the Light Color, and the Graph Editor opens accordingly. Entering the Graph Editor on its own from the Layout interface would not enable you to animate the Light Color initially. After you have entered the Graph Editor using any E button, the value you enter remains there until you clear it. Therefore, you need to enter the Graph Editor from particular E buttons only once.

3. Click the E button next to Light Color, as shown in Figure 5.61.

After you've clicked on the E button, you'll be in the Graph Editor. It looks similar to the Graph Editor you've been reading about in this chapter, but there is a strip of color along the bottom. LightWave enables you to use the Graph Editor's capabilities on color channels as well as motion channels. Figure 5.61 shows the Graph Editor with the color channel.

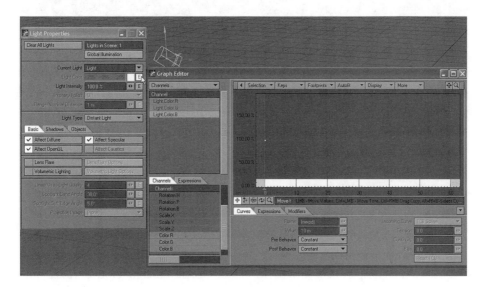

Figure 5.61   The E button (envelope) guides you to the Graph Editor for specific control over Light Color.

In Figure 5.61, the Curve Bin doesn't show position, rotation, or scale channels, but rather color channels.

4. Select a color channel, such as Light.Color.G, for the green color value. You can also select all color channels at once if you like. By default, though, they should all be selected as soon as you click the E button.

5. Create a few keyframes in the Curve Window, right-click over a key, and then choose Open Color Picker.

Change the color for a particular keyframe. Figure 5.62 shows what just one color channel looks like when it's been adjusted.

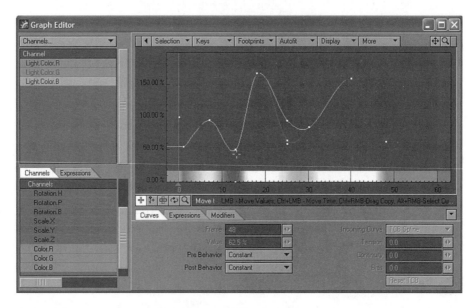

Figure 5.62   Scaling the value for a particular RGB color channel changes the color channel for a set keyframe.

6. You also can change the value of a key as well. From the Curves tab at the bottom of the Graph Editor, adjust the value and watch how the curve changes.

You'll see the color you've selected appear as a gradual change in the Curve Window.

7. Set colors for the other keyframes and adjust their values accordingly to set precise timing. Experiment with these values to see the different types of results you can achieve.

You can cycle colors like this for lights, backgrounds, textures, just about anything! And all this goes back to one thing—timing! Cycling lights is cool, but if you master the timing and keyframing aspects of animation, you can make your dancing lights look even cooler!

The Next Step

So there you have it—keyframing, timing, splines, curves, motions, and the Graph Editor. The Graph Editor is a home base for your animations and envelopes. Before long, you will be using it with most of your animations, and you might even consider keeping it open while you work. Try using the Selection drop-down list above the Curve Window to access more control over your keyframes. LightWave's panels are non-modal, which means that you don't have to be in a certain "mode" to keep them open. Additionally, you can shrink the size of Layout and configure your computer screen to show Layout, the Graph Editor, and even the Surface Editor all at once. Remember that you can collapse the left side and lower portion of the Graph Editor to reveal just the Curve Window, too.

Important

By default, the Graph Editor opens with your currently selected Layout item's channels already entered into the Channel Bin. You can leave the Graph Editor open while you work, but if you want to have additional item channels to edit, you need to manually bring them into the Channel Bin. However, if you press Shift and the g key at the same time, the Graph Editor is updated with the currently selected item in Layout. What's more, you can turn on Track Item Selections from the General Options panel of the Graph Editor.

Don't let the Graph Editor overwhelm you. Although much of this chapter introduced you to the many features and functions of the Graph Editor, you don't always need to use it for keyframing. A good way to work is to use traditional keyframing methods directly in Layout so that you can see what you're doing, and then use the Graph Editor for tweaking and adjustments. As with much of LightWave, you have multiple ways to achieve the same result. Refer to this chapter any time you need to control your keyframes with splines or specific modifiers or when you need specific control over individual channels. You'll find yourself using the Graph Editor for adjusting timing, clearing motions, saving motions, creating object dissolves, or animating color channels more often than you think. Practice creating, cutting, and adjusting keyframes and channels in the Graph Editor. Just remember one thing—save often! Save in increments so you can always take a step back! Now, when you're confident of your ability (you know you already are), read on to learn about the killer lights available to you in LightWave 8.

Chapter 6
Lighting

Working in 3D animation requires you to wear many hats. You're a draftsman, a 3D modeler, a producer, a painter, and even a gaffer. A gaffer is the person on a film set who takes care of the lighting. As a 3D animator, unless you're working in a big animation studio, you do your own lighting. And like many, you might consider lighting to be one of the less important aspects of your 3D animations, or perhaps it is an area you are just not comfortable with. Yet lighting is crucial to your success as an animator. Lighting can be used for so much more than simply brightening a scene. Lighting can completely change the look of a shot. It can convey a mood, a feeling, or even a reaction. Lighting is vital in film, photography, and of course, 3D animation. Basic lighting can make your renders hot or cold, in that the color of the light you choose, where the lights are placed, and so on all play a role in the final image. Lighting can improve your animations. But you need to be aware of some basic real-world principles before you can put it all together.

A close relation to lighting is texturing. This is probably one of the areas animators struggle with the most, and an area that can often make or break your project. However, don't worry; LightWave makes it very easy to apply complex surfaces and get instant feedback. The look of a texture can change significantly based on the lighting associated with it. The two go hand in hand. This chapter will focus on the LightWave lighting system, and the next chapter will demonstrate the powerful Surface Editor and what you can do within it. Are you ready? Let's go!

This chapter instructs you on the following:

- Basic lighting principles
- Using different light sources
- Lighting with gobos
- Creating soft shadows

 Tip

Lighting in 3D animation is an art all its own. Although we could dedicate this entire chapter and more to theory, design, and usage, we thought it better to demonstrate by doing. This chapter will focus on specifically using LightWave 3D's lighting system, so you can achieve results immediately. For an excellent lighting reference book, check out *Digital Lighting & Rendering* by Jeremy Birn from New Riders Publishing.

As you work through lighting setups in this chapter and throughout this book, look at the types of lights LightWave has to offer. If you look at the bottom of the LightWave Layout interface, you'll see the familiar item selection buttons—Objects, Bones, Lights, and Cameras. Click the Lights button at the bottom of the interface, and then click the Properties button to the right. Conversely, you can always press the p key to open any item's properties. You'll see the LightWave Light Properties panel, as shown in Figure 6.1.

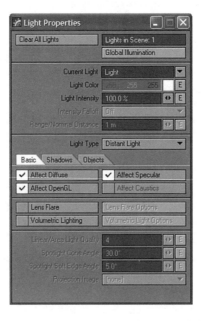

Figure 6.1   The Light Properties panel, as shown with a single default light.

Looking closely at Figure 6.1, you can work your way down the panel, using the following explanations as your guide. At the very top of the panel, you can quickly clear all lights by clicking the button. Be careful with this, as it clears all the lights in your scene, except for the single default distant light. If you've changed the default light, clicking this option resets it. Next to the Clear All Lights button, you'll see an information display called Lights in Scene.

Beneath the Lights in Scene information display is the Global Illumination option. This is an important area of your 3D lighting setups, which will be covered just after the basic lighting information, later in this chapter.

Working with Lights

For some reason, many animators using LightWave have come to this software after work in traditional fields, such as television production, film production, or perhaps set design. If this describes you, you have a great asset for working with LightWave's lighting system. The lights in LightWave work in a way that is similar to lights in the real world, making it easier to understand. They do not exactly mimic lights in the real world, but with a few settings and adjustments, you can make any light appear realistic.

Five lights are available in LightWave Layout. Each has a specific purpose, but each is not limited to that purpose:

- **Distant lights.** You can use a distant light for simulating bright sunlight, moonlight, or general lighting from a nonspecific source. Shadows from this light are hard. A distant light's position does not matter to your scene, only its rotation matters.

- **Point lights.** You can use a point light for creating sources of light that emit in all directions, such as a candle, light bulb, or spark. Unlike a distant light, a point light's rotation does not matter in your scene, only its position matters. It, too, has hard-edged shadows.

- **Spotlights.** The most commonly used lighting, spotlights can be used for directional lighting such as canister lighting, headlights on cars, studio simulation lighting, volumetric lighting, and more. Spotlight rotation and position play roles in your scene. A spotlight's shadows can be either hard or soft with shadow mapping.

- **Linear lights.** You can use a linear light to emit light in elongated situations, such as fluorescent tubes. Linear lights can have very realistic shadows but take additional rendering time.

- **Area lights.** The best light to use for creating true shadows, area lights create a brighter, more diffuse light than distant lights and therefore can create the most realism. They do, however, take longer to render than spotlights, distant lights, or point lights.

Important

> While you're working in LightWave's Modeler, you will not see a light source illuminating your shaded model in a Perspective viewport. Do not let that fool you because it has nothing to do with your final lighting setup. Lights are available only in Layout.

The environment in which your animation lives is crucial to the animation itself, which is why we dedicate a chapter to lighting and textures. You should consider color, intensity, and ambient light each time you set up a scene. Too often, tutorials overlook the power of light, but you know better! Using light, as well as shadows, as elements in your animation can be as important as the models and motions you create. As you work through setting up lights in your 3D scenes, you should get used to setting one variable in particular—light intensity, also called brightness.

Tip

> You'll see the Current Light drop-down list near the top of the panel. This includes the name of each light. The default single distant light is named, simply, Light. Select this listing directly in the panel and you can quickly rename it. You can do this for any light you add.

Light Color

The color of the light you use is important and useful in your images and animations because it can help set tone, mood, and feeling. No light is ever purely white, and it's up to you to change LightWave's default 255 RGB light color. The color selector works the same as the other color selectors in LightWave. You can also animate the RGB values with the Graph Editor. Be sure to read about this in Chapter 5, "Keyframing and Graph Editor."

In LightWave, you can even animate colored lights. If you read Chapter 5, a small example is given on how to set keyframes for things like light color. Clicking the E button takes you to the Graph Editor, allowing you to vary the light color over time. Very cool! You'll use this for all kinds of things, such as animating a rock concert where you need to have fast-moving lights shining on the stage. By animating the light color, you can change the colors over time at any speed you want.

Light Intensity

When you start LightWave Layout or choose Clear Scene, by default, there is always one light in your LightWave scene. It has a light intensity of 100% and is a distant light. Although you can use this one light and its preset intensity as your main source of light for images and animations, it's best to adjust the light intensity to more appropriately match the light and the scene at hand.

Did you know that light intensities can range from values in the negative range to values in the thousands? You can set a light intensity to 9000% (or higher) if you want, just by typing in the value. The results might not be that desirable and perhaps even unstable, but you never know what your scene might call for. In general, if you want to create a bright sunny day, a point light, which emits light in all directions, can be used with a light intensity of 150% or so for bright light everywhere. On the other hand, if you want to light an evening scene, perhaps on a city street, you can use spotlights with light intensities set to around 60%. As you build scenes throughout this book, you'll be asked to set up different light types, with varying intensities. This will also help you get a feel for setting the right intensity.

 Tip

> The slider (the left and right arrows) next to the Light Intensity setting in the Light Properties panel allows you to click and drag values ranging from 0 to 100. However, by manually entering values, you can set higher or even negative values!

Negative lights, or "dark lights," can also be handy depending on the scene you're working on. Whereas lights with a positive light intensity can brighten a scene, negative lights can darken a scene. You might be asking why you would darken a scene with a negative light instead of just turning the lights down. For example, you might have to add a lot of light to make areas appear properly lit. Depending on the surfaces you've set, the extra light might make one area look perfect, while making other areas too bright. This is where negative lights come into play. Adding a negative light (which is any light with a negative light intensity value) takes away light from a specific area.

Adding Lights

In most cases, you're going to use more than one single distant light in your 3D scenes. This section shows you how to add lights. Follow these simple steps to add lights to LightWave Layout to get a feel for how they work. And remember, unless you are working with Auto Key enabled, you'll need to create a keyframe to lock your lights into position after they're moved, just like objects.

Exercise 6.1   Adding Lights to Layout

1. Open Layout or select Clear Scene from the File drop-down menu.

   This sets Layout to its default of one distant light.

2. Make sure you are in Perspective view so that you have a full view of Layout. Under the Items tab, under the Add category, select Lights, and then Spotlight to add a spotlight to the scene. Figure 6.2 shows the menus.

   You have the choice to add any type of light you want.

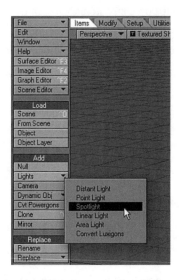

Figure 6.2   You can add lights directly in Layout under the Items tab.

3. Before the light is added to Layout, a Light Name panel appears, as shown in Figure 6.3.

Figure 6.3 After a light is added, the Light Name panel appears, enabling you to set a specific name for your light.

4. Type in the name you want to give the new spotlight, such as the name of your favorite breakfast cereal.

 Important

You don't have to change the name of a new light. Instead, you can accept LightWave's default light name by clicking OK when the Light Name panel appears. By default, LightWave names new lights Light (1), Light (2), Light (3), and so on.

The added light is placed at the 0 axis, or the origin, as shown in Figure 6.4.

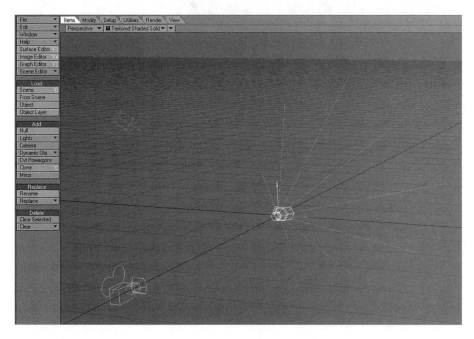

Figure 6.4 Added lights are placed at the 0-axis (the origin) in Layout pointing toward the back of the scene down the positive Z-axis.

Clone Lights

Besides adding lights, you can clone lights. Cloning a light creates an exact duplicate of a selected light. This includes the light's color, intensity, position, rotation, and so on. Any parameter you've set will be cloned. Cloning lights is just as easy as adding lights, but often good to do after you're sure of your existing light's settings. You don't want to clone a light 20 times, only to realize that you forgot to change the color! You'd need to make changes to 20 lights. However, should you need to make changes to many lights at once, you can quickly select the lights to change in the Scene Editor. Figure 6.5 show two lights in the Scene Editor edited once.

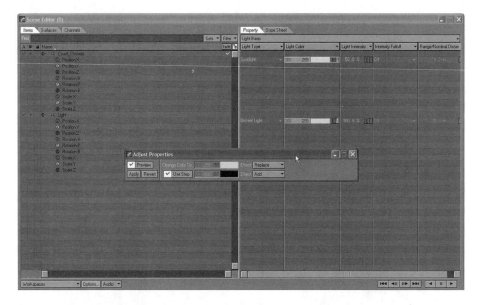

Figure 6.5 If you have one light, two, or twenty, you can use the Scene Editor to edit variables for those lights all at once.

Tip

> With LightWave 8, you can multiselect lights directly in Layout. Just hold the Shift key and select them. Then, rotate, move, and so on.

To clone a light, first select the light to be cloned in Layout, and then select the Clone button under the Items tab, Add category. Enter the number of clones (copies) of the light you want in the pop-up panel, and click OK or press Enter. Wiz bang! The selected light is cloned. You know what else? This operation works the same for cloning objects or cameras. Figure 6.6 shows the command.

Figure 6.6   You can clone lights (or any other item) directly in Layout from the Items tab.

Mirror Lights

You know what's cool? Mirroring your light! Let's say you move the light to a specific position. Use the Mirror button under the Add category in the Items tab. Select a light (or other item in Layout) and click the Mirror button. Choose the axis to mirror across, and go! Figure 6.7 shows the operation.

Figure 6.7   In addition to cloning lights, you can also mirror them.

Global Illumination Options

Have you ever stopped to look around you? Take your face out of this book or away from the computer for a moment, and just look around. Whether you're at your desk, in your living room, or outside, everything has global lighting properties. These global properties—global light intensity, global lens flare intensity, ambient intensity, ambient color, radiosity, and caustics—can be controlled in the Global Illumination panel. You can find the Global Illumination panel under the Light Properties panel in Layout. Figure 6.8 shows the panel.

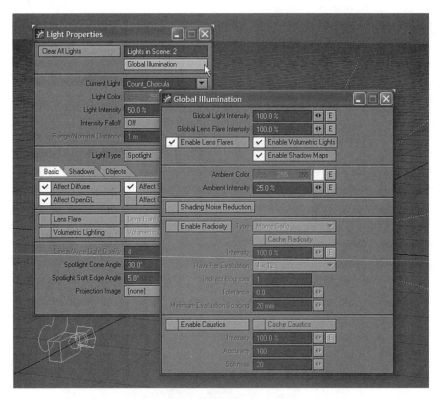

Figure 6.8   The Global Illumination panel, found under the Lights tab in Layout, is where you can control such properties as global light intensity, global lens flare intensity, ambient light, ambient color, radiosity, and caustics.

Global Light Intensity and Global Lens Flare Intensity

The Global Light Intensity setting, found at the top of the Global Illumination panel, is an overriding volume control for all lights in a scene. This can be very useful for scenes that have multiple lights that need to get brighter or dimmer over time. Let's say you're animating a stage play or musical concert, for example. You have 43 spotlights shining on the stage, the players, and the actors. All their intensities are randomly and quickly changing to the beat of the music, and perhaps focusing on key performs. At the end of the song, you want all the lights to fade out equally. Instead of setting the light intensity 43 times for each light, which you could do through the Scene Editor, it is better to ramp down the Global Light Intensity setting. Similarly, if you have lens flares applied to these lights, you can change the Global Lens Flare Intensity setting.

Ambient Light and Ambient Color

Did you know that the light around you is either direct or ambient? Direct light comes predominantly from a light source. Ambient light has no specific source or direction, such as the light underneath your desk, or behind a door.

Within the Global Illumination panel, you can set the intensity of your ambient light. A typical setting is around 5%. LightWave defaults to 25%, which is often too high a value for most situations. It is better to lower the value, sometimes to 0%, and use additional lights for more control. Don't rely on ambient light to brighten your scene. Instead, use more lights to make areas brighter.

 Tip

> The default Ambient Intensity setting of 25% is a carryover from the old Amiga version of LightWave 3D. Back then, there was no OpenGL—only wireframes when working in Layout—so users couldn't tell what their object looked like until rendered. This default ambient would allow the user to quickly render an object and see what it looked like before setting his lighting.

You also can set the color of your ambient light so that the areas not hit by light still have some color to them. Let's say you have a single, blue light shining on an actor on a stage, for example. You can make the side of the actor not hit by any light visible by using an Ambient Intensity setting; with the Ambient Color setting set to blue (like the light), the shot will look accurate. Remember, ambient light hits all surfaces, not just those that are unlit by actual lights, which is why knowing about ambient intensity is important.

Radiosity and Caustics

Also within the Global Illumination panel are the Enable Radiosity and Enable Caustics settings. These two features in LightWave enable you to take your 3D creations even further by adding more real-world lighting properties.

Radiosity is a rendering solution that calculates the diffused reflections of lights in a scene. It is the rate at which light energy leaves a surface. This also includes the color within all surfaces. In simpler terms, radiosity is bounced light. A single light coming through a window, for example, can light up an entire room. The light hits the surfaces of the objects and bounces, lighting up the rest of the room, in turn creating a realistic image. Ambient light is often considered a poor man's radiosity. *You can use it to brighten areas not directly lit by lights.*

You'll use radiosity and learn more about its settings in Chapter 14, "Enhanced Textures and Environments."

Caustics are created when light is reflected off a surface or through a refracted surface. A good example is the random pattern often seen at the bottom of a swimming pool when bright sunlight shines through the water. Another example of caustics is the ringlets of light that can appear on a table as light hits a reflective surface, such as a gold-plated statue. The light hits the surface and reflects. Chapter 14 steps you through an exercise explaining this technique further.

Lens Flares

The lens flare, often overused but needed, was introduced in LightWave 3.0. Lens flares are a popular addition to animated scenes, but too often when you add a light to a scene, such as a candlestick, the light source emits, but no generating source is visible. By adding a lens flare, you can create a small haze or glow around the candlelight. Other uses for lens flares are lights on a stage, sunlight, flashlights, and headlights on a car. Any time you have a light that is in view in a scene, you should add a lens flare so that the viewer understands the light has a source. Lens flares in LightWave can be viewed directly in Layout before rendering. You'll be setting up lens flares later in this chapter.

Volumetric Lights

You need to be aware of one more area when it comes to LightWave lighting before you start working through exercises. Volumetric lighting is a powerful and surprisingly fast render effect that can create beams of light. Have you ever seen how a light streaks when it shines through a window? The beam of light that emits from the light source can be replicated in LightWave with *volumetrics*. Volumetric settings add volume to a light source. Additionally, you can add textures to a volumetric light to create all sorts of interesting light beams.

Applying Lights in LightWave

You will encounter many types of lighting situations when creating your animation masterpiece. This next section steps you through a common lighting situation that you can use for character animation tests, product shots, or logo scenes. Chapter 11, "Modeling Electronics," will have you add lights to a model you create. Be sure to check it out.

Simulating Studio Lighting

One of the cool things about LightWave is that you don't have to be a numbers person to make things happen. You can see what's happening throughout the creation process from object construction to surfacing to lighting. This exercise 6.2 introduces you to basic three-point lighting often used in everyday video production. You can apply this lighting style to LightWave and create a photographer's backdrop (or cyc for cyclorama) to act as a set for your objects. Creating a set in LightWave is a good idea so that even simple render tests are not over a black background. By rendering objects on a set, you add more depth to your animation.

The goal of this project is to introduce you to a common lighting setup that can be useful in just about any type of render situation when simulating studio lighting. You'll use a pre-made scene from this book's DVD.

Exercise 6.2   Simulating Studio Lighting

1. In Layout, load the Bones_Start scene from this chapter's folder on the accompanying DVD.

   This loads the multilayered object, which includes two layers—the skeleton and a simple set. Figure 6.9 shows the loaded scene through the Camera view.

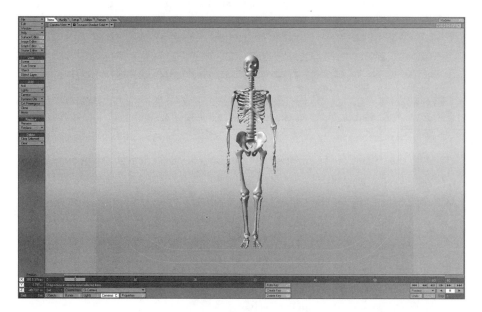

Figure 6.9   A pre-existing scene with one multilayered object, perfect for testing some lighting situations.

2. Select the default light that is already in the scene. This is a distant light and is not the most effective lighting. To see what this lighting setup looks like, press the F9 key on your keyboard for a single current frame render. Figure 6.10 shows the render.

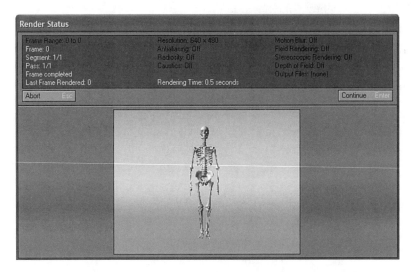

Figure 6.10   Pressing the F9 key performs a single current frame render. By default, the render really isn't any different from what you see in Layout.

Tip

Be sure that you have Show Rendering in Progress selected with a chosen resolution (such as 320 × 240) to see the render when you press the F9 key. Go to the Render tab at the top of Layout. On the left, under the Objects category, click Render Options, and then apply the option as shown in Figure 6.11.

3. With the default distant light selected in Layout, press the p key to open the Light Properties panel.

4. In the panel, change the Light Type to Spotlight.

   The spotlight you've just created will be the key light, or the main light in the scene setup. You'll be creating a three-point lighting situation in this scene.

5. Change the Light Intensity to 90%. You can do this by either clicking or dragging the value slider in the Light Properties panel, or simply entering the value. Figure 6.12 shows the panel with changes.

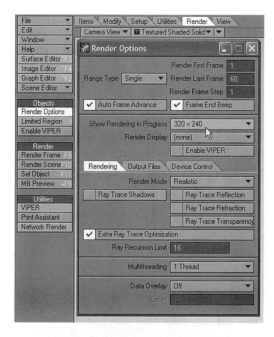

Figure 6.11   To see your render, make sure the Show Rendering in Progress option is on in the Render Options panel.

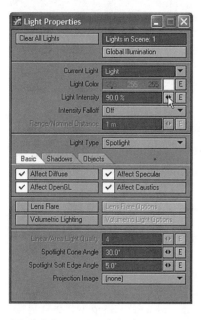

Figure 6.12   Change the default light to a spotlight for more accurate lighting, and set the Light Intensity to 90%.

Important

Three-point lighting is a common lighting setup used in most studios. It consists of a key light, which is the primary source of brightness; a fill light, which is less bright than the key and used opposite the key; and a backlight, sometimes referred to as a hair light, which is used to separate the subject from the background. You'll find a basic three-point lighting scene on this book's DVD, in this chapter's directory.

6. Set the Light Color to off-white (245, 245, 220 RGB). You can do this by clicking and dragging directly on the RGB values or by clicking the color swatch and using your computer's color picker to set the value.

You've set the Light Color to off-white because light is never purely white. In a studio setting, the key light burns with a slight off-white tint. At the bottom of the panel, set the Spotlight Cone Angle to 40 and the Spotlight Soft Edge Angle to 40. This creates a nice edge falloff for the key light. Figure 6.13 shows the changes in the panel.

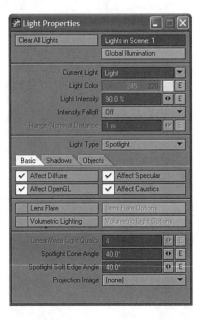

Figure 6.13 In the Light Properties panel, you can change the light color and the cone angle.

7. Click the Shadows tab and set the Shadow Type to Shadow Map, which creates softer shadows than ray-traced shadows.

8. Change the Shadow Map Size to 2000. This setting is the size of the pixels of the shadow map. Leave Shadow Fuzziness set to 1.0.

Tip

If you want to convert the Shadow Map Size to actual megabytes, square and multiply by 4. So, 2000 × 2000 × 4 = 16MB. That means a Shadow Map Size of 2000 will take an extra 16MB of memory for calculation.

9. Be sure the Fit Cone option is selected. This tells LightWave to make the shadow map match the cone angle of the light, which is what you'll most often do. Turning this off opens an option to set a custom shadow map angle. For example, the light can be wide and shine more light on a larger area, but the shadows will only happen within a smaller fixed area.

Important

You can use shadow maps only with spotlights. This is because LightWave uses the same procedure to calculate areas that are hidden from the Camera view by objects as it does for a spotlight. The result is a soft shadow.

The larger the Shadow Map Size, the more memory LightWave uses to calculate the shadow. Larger shadow map sizes produce cleaner shadows but increase render times. Choosing a value between 1000 and 2000 gives you a good size to work with. If you want to increase the Shadow Fuzziness setting to 8, for example, the Shadow Map Size setting should be increased to 3000 or higher. This is high, and you'll need decent memory just for this light, but the result will be cleaner shadows. That's not to say this is an unreasonable setting—just be prepared to have a lot of RAM if you have multiple spotlights with shadow map sizes this large. One or two lights are not a big deal.

10. In Layout, press 5 on your numeric keypad to switch to Light view. Looking through the light to set it in position is the quickest and most accurate way to set up lights.

11. With the current light selected, press the t key to select Move from the Modify tab, and then right-click directly in Layout view and move the light up on the Y axis about 30m (keep an eye on the info area at the bottom left of the Layout to see your movement values).

Mac users, don't forget that Apple key with the mouse button to access right mouse button functions.

When you load the scene, the Grid Size in Layout changes to 5m. You're now moving the light up six grid squares. LightWave shows the grid squares for the Y-axis when in the Side and Front views. You can lower the grid size to your liking for more control over your items from the General Options panel (press o).

12. On the numeric keypad, press 1 for Front view or 3 for Side view to see the light position. You might need to use the various view tools in the upper-right corner to move the Front or Side views around. Figure 6.14 shows the Front view of the scene.

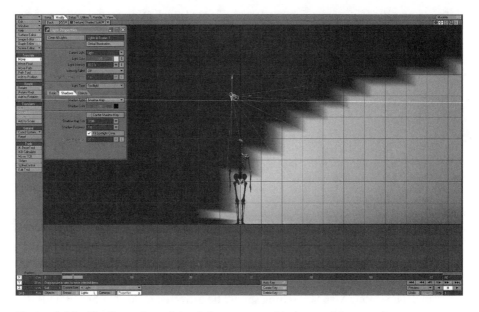

Figure 6.14 The Front view of the skeleton scene with the spotlight moved up.

13. Switch back to the Light view (press 5). With the left mouse button, move the light back away from the object so that it has a larger coverage area, as shown in Figure 6.15. Also, be sure to create a keyframe at frame 0 to lock the light into its new position.

Setting the position of the spotlight from the Light view is quick and easy. Because of the way the object is shaded, you can see that the light is in front and to the upper left of the set.

14. Save your scene as Bones_Lit or something similar.

Before you add the other lights, you need to rename this light to keep your scene organized.

15. From the Light Properties panel, select the default light name (which is just Light) and rename it to Key Light, as shown in Figure 6.16.

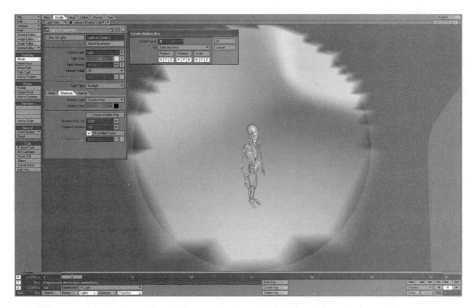

Figure 6.15   By adjusting a light from the Light view, you can easily and quickly place it into position.

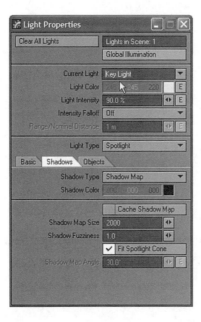

Figure 6.16   Rename a light from directly within the Light Properties panel.

You now need to add another light to create the fill light.

16. From the Items tab, under the Add category, select the Lights drop-down list and choose Spotlight. After you add the light, LightWave asks you to name it. Name this light Fill Light (or Phil Light if your name is Phil).

17. In the Light Properties panel (select the light and press the p key), change the Light Intensity setting to 75%. Change the light color to a soft blue (135, 170, 230 RGB).

    Adding a blue light as a fill light is often a nice touch when setting up lights, either in a studio or in outside situations. It helps create the feeling of distance while illuminating without notice. It's also great for illumination at night.

18. Change Shadow Type to Shadow Map for this spotlight, as you did with the Key Light; change the Spotlight Cone Angle to 40; and change the Spotlight Soft Edge Angle to 40. Do this from the Shadows tab of the Lights Properties panel.

19. Move the fill light to X: 40m, Y: 7m, Z: -18m, and rotate the light to H: –60, P: 0.0, B: 0.0. To do this, make sure the Fill Light is selected, press t to move and then n to access the numeric values at the bottom left of the interface. Enter the value and press Enter on the keyboard. Press y for rotate and then n for numeric again. Create a keyframe at 0 to lock the light in place. Figure 6.17 shows a view of the set from the fill light. Figure 6.18 shows a Perspective view of the entire scene so far.

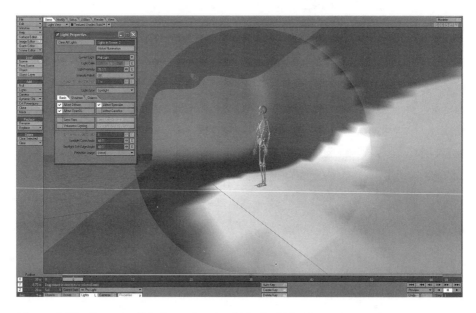

Figure 6.17   Rename a light from directly within the Light Properties panel.

Figure 6.18   In this overview of the scene, you can see the key light to the left and the fill light to the right.

You need to add one more light to the scene to set up the backlight. This also will be a spotlight.

20. Based on the settings for the Key Light and Fill Light, add another spotlight and set the values similar to the key light. Color it a rich orange and position it above and to the back of the room slightly, above the skeleton. Call this light Back Light, and be sure to create keyframes at 0 to lock the lights in place. Save the scene.

Tip

You also can clone a light in Layout by first selecting the particular light, and then selecting Clone from the Items tab under the Add category.

Tip

You can quickly choose different lights in the Light Properties panel by clicking the small drop-down arrow to the right of the Current Light drop-down list.

21. Press F9 to render, and you'll see a nicely lit, simple set, as shown in Figure 6.19. Note that the Render Display is set to Image Viewer from the Render Options panel under the Render tab.

You can load the Bones_Lit scene from this book's DVD to see everything to this point.

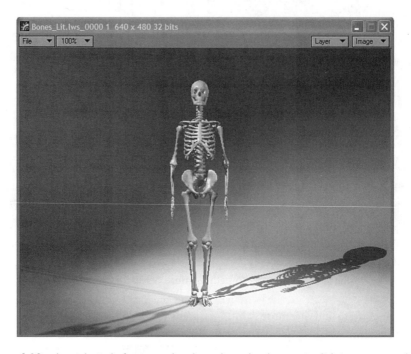

Figure 6.19   A quick single frame render shows how the three-point lighting setup works.

 Important

> The view shown earlier in Figure 6.9 shows the Camera view with Safe Areas
> enabled to help frame the shot for video. You can find out more about safe areas in
> Chapter 8, "Cinematic Tools." To turn on the safe areas, press the d key for the
> Display Options tab, choose the Camera View tab, and check Show Safe Areas.

Enhanced Studio Lighting

Now that you have some basic lighting set up, you need to create some drama and depth. You have a set and lights, but no textures, no life. Exercise 6.3 shows you how to adjust your lighting situation using ambient light and textures to enhance the lighting environment.

Exercise 6.3   Enhanced Lighting Setups

1. Be sure the scene you've been working on is loaded in Layout. If not, use the one from this book's DVD labeled Bones_Lit.

2. From the Light Properties panel, open the Global Illumination panel. Set the ambient intensity setting to 5%.

   The default Ambient Intensity is 25%. This is much too bright and can make your renders appear flat and washed out. Ambient is the general level of light in your scene. It is the area in your scene not affected directly by light sources. LightWave allows you to make this brighter or darker based on the Ambient Intensity setting. As a good rule of thumb, keep this setting low, often as low as 0. If you need more light, add it with a light—don't fake it with ambient intensity.

3. Press F9 to render the frame. The dark areas are darker, and the shot begins to take on depth. But you still need to do something about the set that the skeleton is on!

4. In LightWave, you can replace specific layers of objects. For now, the skeleton is fine, but the set needs a little something more. Select the set object by choosing the Objects button at the bottom of Layout, and then Layer 2 of the current item, as shown in Figure 6.20.

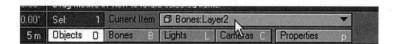

Figure 6.20   Select the Objects mode button at the bottom of Layout to tell LightWave you want to work with objects. Then, choose Bones:Layer2 as the current item.

5. After the correct object is selected, choose the Replace drop-down list from the Replace category in the Items tab, and choose the With Layer option. When you select an object with the Replace With Layer option and then select an object for replacement, a panel comes up asking you which layer (of the new object) you want to use as a replacement. Select Layer 1 of the Textured Set object as the replacement. Figure 6.21 shows the replacement options.

   The set change looks similar to what it looked like before, but it has a new color and procedural textures applied (which you'll soon learn about). At this point, you can finesse the scene with light adjustment.

6. Press the d key to enter the Display Options tab for Layout (which is part of the Preferences panel). Make sure the Max OpenGL Lights is set to 4 or higher.

This enables you to set up effects of lights directly in Layout. The maximum number of lights you can set for OpenGL visibility is 8.

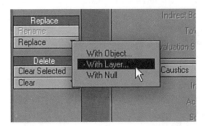

Figure 6.21   You can tell LightWave to replace just the layer of an object with the Replace option.

7. Close the Preferences panel.

8. To get a feel for how your lighting looks, press the F9 key to render a frame. You should see something similar to Figure 6.22. Although the three-point spotlights work great for studio-type lighting, you can create a softer, more natural look simply by changing the lights.

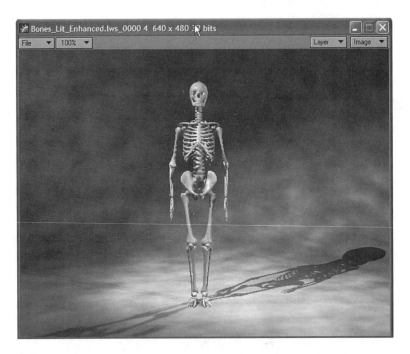

Figure 6.22   A new set replaces the flat dull original. Same shape and size, but new textures add a little dimension to the scene.

Using Projection Images on Lights

LightWave's Projection Image feature is a useful lighting tool that mimics real-world lighting situations where cookies or gobos are used to throw light onto a set. A *gobo,* also referred to as a *cookaloris,* is a cutout shape that is placed in front of a light, sort of like a cookie cutter. Certain areas of the gobo hold back light, whereas other areas let light through. In Exercise 6.4, you use a gobo that creates the look of light coming through a window.

Although the previous exercise was basic in design, it is the core lighting situation for many of your LightWave scenes. Perhaps with a slight variation, this basic three-point lighting scheme can be used for product shots, animated plays, logos, and much more. Things like simple stage sets, equipment, figures, generic objects, or any element can benefit from this type of lighting design. Of course, you are not limited to using just three lights for these types of situations. You can start with the basic three, and then add or remove lights to highlight certain areas, brighten dark areas, or use additional lights as projection lights.

Figure 6.23 shows the gobo you'll use to create the effect. This image is nothing more than white lines on a black background that are blurred in Adobe Photoshop. When this image is applied to a spotlight, the white areas allow light to shine through, whereas the black areas do not.

Figure 6.23   A simple black-and-white image can be used to cast light onto a set.

Tip

Gobo images can be created with a paint package such as Adobe Photoshop. The image should be 24 bits and the size should match your render resolution. However, if it's a tiny image that's not viewed close up, you can save memory and use 8-bit images. Video resolution gobo images should be a pixel size of 720 × 486.

Exercise 6.4   Creating Gobo Lights

1. Add a new spotlight to the scene and name it Gobo Light or something similar, perhaps Set Light. The idea is that you identify the lights properly as you set them up to keep organized. Select the new spotlight and press 5 on the keyboard to switch to Light view.

2. Move the gobo light up and to the upper-right or upper-left side of the scene, slightly behind the skeleton object. Point the light onto the back of the set, and be sure to create a keyframe for it at frame 0 to lock it in place.

   Remember, everything has a keyframe at the first frame of your animation even if it is not moving. In this case, the first frame is 0.

3. Make the new gobo light slightly off-white in color and set the Light Intensity to anywhere from 60% to 90%. Figure 6.24 shows the new light in place.

Figure 6.24   A new spotlight is added and focused on the set behind the skeleton.

4. Select the key light and change it to a point light. Also, change its light intensity (in the Lights tab) to 30%. This light will be a general soft light to fill up the set.

This will help the viewer focus a little more on the gobo in the backdrop. A bright key light would take away from it.

5. To project the image from the gobo light, select it and press the p key to open the Light Properties panel. You can also select the light from the Light Properties panel with the small drop-down arrow next to Current Light.

6. In the Light Properties panel for the gobo light, select the drop-down list next to Projection Image at the bottom and select (load image), as shown in Figure 6.25. Load the ZigZagGobo image from this book's DVD. You can find it under the Images folder within the Projects directory for this chapter.

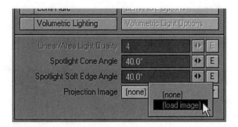

Figure 6.25 You can add a projection image to a spotlight, simulating a cool design projected on a set.

7. After the image has been loaded, press F9 to render. You'll see what appear to be windowpanes across the room. The light is now projected through the black-and-white image, which you can see from the Light view (see Figure 6.26). You can take a closer look at the gobo image in the Image Editor. Note that your image might appear slightly different to variances in light placements.

8. Press F9 to perform a single frame render to see how the gobo light looks projected on the back of the set. If you don't like it, move the light a little, press F9 again, and so on. Adjust to your liking. Moving the light farther away works well for creating a streaked gobo image too. Figure 6.27 show the render with the gobo light added.

Figure 6.26   LightWave 8 allows you to see your projection images through the Light view.

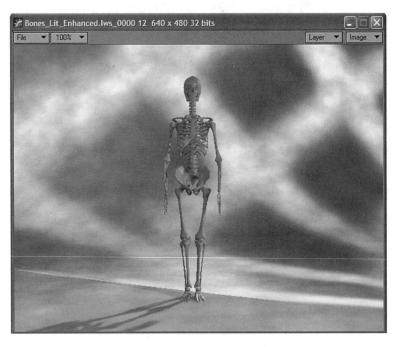

Figure 6.27   Just two lights in the scene and a gobo on a spotlight give the set a different look.

You can load this final scene into Layout from this book's DVD and look at the final settings if you want. The scene is called Bones_Lit_Enhanced. Take a look at it and modify it for your own scenes.

Adding gobos is easy. But it's probably a more powerful feature than you realize. Creating a simple pattern on a set is nice, but you can accomplish much more with gobos:

- Use a black-and-white image of tree branches to simulate shadows from a tree.
- Use color images for added dimension. Darker areas will hold back more light, and lighter areas will shine more light. For example, you can create the effects of light through a stained-glass window.
- Use softer, blurry images for added effects.
- Use animation sequences as projection images.
- Use imported movie files! Create real projected movies in your animation by projecting an AVI or QuickTime movie onto a movie screen in 3D.
- Create windowpanes and project them onto your set to create the look of light coming through a window.

You also can apply volumetric effects for projection images. Later in this book, you'll learn about volumetric lighting and the cool things you can create with this feature. Combine those techniques with these lighting techniques and you're ready to rock!

Using Area Lights

Distant lights and point lights produce hard-edged, ray-traced shadows. Ray-traced shadows take more time to calculate, which of course means more time to render. Spotlights also can produce ray-traced shadows, but with spotlights, you have the option to use shadow maps, which take less time to render than ray-traced shadows. Softer than ray-traced shadows, shadow maps use more memory to render than ray-traced shadows. Ray-traced shadows use more processing power.

Area lights also can produce realistic ray-traced shadows, but to do so they require more rendering time. For example, say a person is standing outside in bright sunlight. The shadow that the person casts has sharp edges around the area by the subject's foot, where the shadow begins. As the shadow falls off and away from the subject, it becomes softer. Ray-traced shadows from distant lights, point lights, and spotlights cannot produce this effect—neither can shadow maps. Area lights can produce these true shadows and create a softer overall appearance to animations.

Spotlights are the most common lights, and they are the most useful for your everyday animation needs. But on occasion, the added rendering time generated from area lights is worthwhile. An area light is represented in Layout by a flat square and emits light equally from all directions except for the edges, producing very realistic shadows.

Exercise 6.5   Working with Area Lights

1. Load the Area Setup scene file from this book's DVD. This scene includes a Lathed disc from Modeler, made into a spring. It sits on a single flat polygon made from a box. There is one area light in the scene.

2. Select the Light and press p to go to the Item Properties panel. Change the Light Intensity setting to 60%. Keeping the default 100% Light Intensity setting would be too bright, and the image would appear washed out.

3. Move the Light Properties panel aside and return to Layout.

4. If the new area light is not selected, select it and change your Layout view to Perspective to get an overall view of the scene. Figure 6.28 shows the Perspective view. The area light appears as a small box outline. This light is already positioned above and to the left of the spring object.

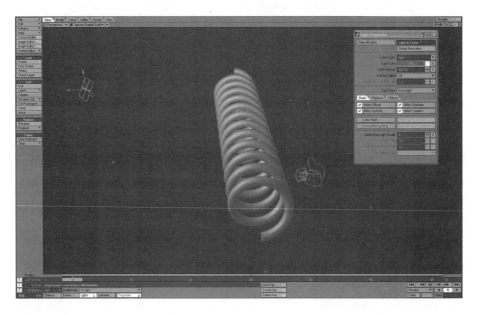

Figure 6.28   The single area light can create beautiful shadows, even on a simple object.

Tip

To help set up lights in Layout, change the Maximum Render Level to Textured Shaded Solid. You can find this setting by clicking the small drop-down arrow to the right of the viewport style buttons at the top of Layout. Make sure Max OpenGL Lights is set to at least 1 or above from the Display Options panel (press d). Also, always make sure that the Affect OpenGL option for the light in the Light properties panel is turned on. This makes the light source's effect visible in Layout, and helps you line up the direction of the light source.

You need to tell LightWave to calculate the shadows for this light; it doesn't know to do it on its own. The Light properties told the light what kind of shadow to use—Ray Trace by default—but now you need to actually turn on the feature.

5. Under the Render tab, select Render Options, and then check Ray Trace Shadows to have LightWave calculate shadows for the area light, as shown in Figure 6.29.

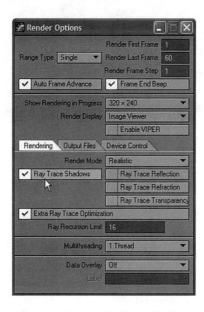

Figure 6.29 You tell LightWave to calculate Ray Trace Shadows while rendering from the Render Options panel.

Tip

While you're in the Render Options panel, make sure you choose a Show Rendering in Progress setting, such as 320 × 240. This enables you to see the render as its being drawn.

6. Press F9 to render the current frame. You'll see that the shadow has a hard, chunky edge, as shown in Figure 6.30.

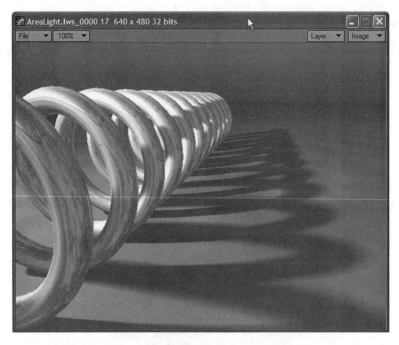

Figure 6.30   The default area light casts an okay shadow, but it's not very clean.

7. In Layout, select the area light, and then select Size from the Items tab. Size the light up (click and drag) to about 7.6m. Be sure to create a keyframe for this new size to keep it!

   To access the numeric values and directly enter the size change, you can also type in the numeric values by pressing n on the keyboard. Figure 6.31 shows the resized light.

8. Press F9 to perform another render. Figure 6.32 shows the render with softer shadows.

Tip

If you increase the size of the area light, the shadow softens. However, it might appear grainy or jagged. If so, simply increase the Area Light Quality setting in the Light Properties panel. The default is 4—good for most renderings. Often setting a value of 5 works slightly better but takes more render time. Isn't that always the case? Note that 5 is your maximum value.

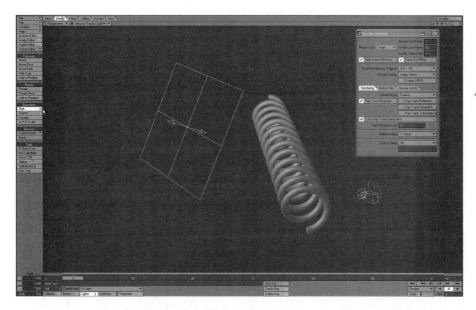

Figure 6.31 You can resize an area light for softer shadows.

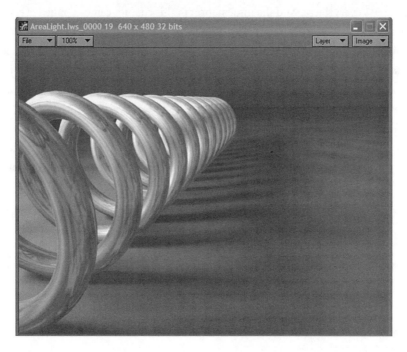

Figure 6.32 An area light that is sized up can create soft, long shadows that are true to form. They are sharper at the base of the object, and soften as they fall off.

Sizing a light might seem odd, but it helps spread the amount of light and thereby the shadow as well. If you notice in Figure 6.32, the shadow is soft and very realistic. Area lights take a long time to render, but they produce the best results.

Here are a few more things to remember when using area lights:

- Quality settings can be adjusted. The default Area Light Quality setting of 4 results in 16 samples per area light. Values of 2 and 3 result in 4 and 9 samples per area light, respectively.

- Linear lights perform like area lights but emit light from a two-point polygonal shape, similar to a fluorescent tube.

- You can mix spotlights, distant lights, point lights, and linear lights with area lights for added effects.

The Next Step

Lighting. It's everywhere. And the information in this chapter can be applied everywhere in LightWave. It can be applied to any of the exercises and projects in this book. These basic lighting setups and core functions will apply to all of your LightWave work in one way or another, either in simple form or complex. Use the information here to branch out on your own and create different lighting environments. Use lights to your advantage—remember, there are no wires or electric bills to worry about when creating virtual lighting situations. You don't need to worry about light bulbs burning out either! Experiment by adding more lights to your everyday scene or perhaps taking some away. Use negative lights, colored lights, dim lights, overly bright lights, and whatever else you can think of to make your animations stand out.

What makes your lighting work even better is proper surfacing. Read on to Chapter 7, "Textures," to learn about LightWave 8's surfacing capabilities.

Chapter 7
Textures

It's a never-ending battle. It's a constant struggle. But the results are worth every bit of sweat and frustration. We're not talking about watching what you eat, but rather the art form known as 3D texturing. The realism of 3D animation can be very eye-catching, and this realism is created by two key factors, lighting and surfacing. As mentioned in Chapter 6, "Lighting," both of these factors play an extremely important role in your 3D creations, and they help bring your animations to life. This chapter helps you take the next step with LightWave by introducing you to the powerful Texture Editor and teaching you how to navigate its interface and how to use it. You'll learn about:

- Using the Surface Editor
- Organizing surfaces
- Setting up surfaces
- Using the Image Editor
- Working with image map references on surfaces

Perhaps one of the best things about LightWave's Surface Editor is the fact that everything you need to set up simple to complex surfaces can be done in one location. The Surface Editor gives you control over everything you need to create a blue ball or an aged 3D human. If you are familiar with the Surface Editor in previous versions of LightWave, you'll find that the Surface Editor is not much different but is definitely improved. Figure 7.1 shows the Surface Editor interface at startup.

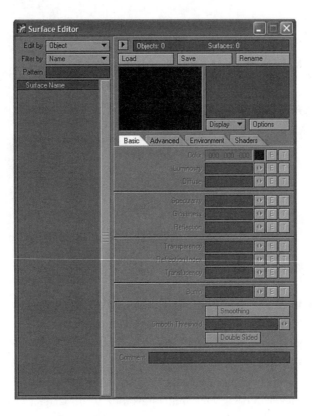

Figure 7.1   LightWave's Surface Editor at startup.

The Surface Editor is part of the software you probably use most often. In LightWave versions previous to 6.0, the process of setting up surfaces for your models began during model building in Modeler. However, you could only make basic surface changes in Modeler—essentially, you could only name selected polygons. From there, you needed to apply any image maps or procedural textures in Layout. However, in this newer version, you have the choice of using the Surface Editor in either Modeler or Layout. It's the same panel in both programs, so this chapter applies to both Modeler and Layout in most respects. You'll always find the Surface Editor in Modeler at the top-left side of the interface. The Surface Editor button is the third button from the top (see Figure 7.2).

The button that accesses the Surface Editor in Layout is also at the top-left side of the interface, but it's the sixth one from the top (see Figure 7.3). You can also use the Ctrl+F3 keyboard command in both Modeler and Layout to access the Surface Editor panel.

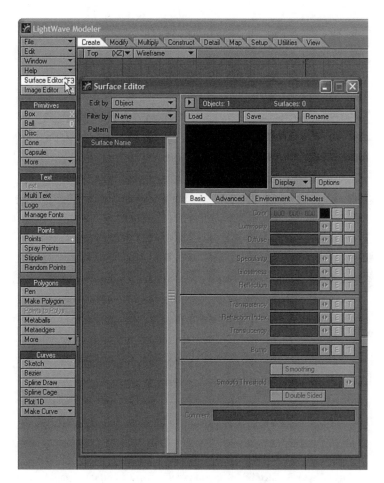

Figure 7.2 LightWave's Surface Editor can always be accessed at the top left in Modeler.

Important

Using the Surface Editor in Modeler does not give you access to LightWave's VIPER (Versatile Interactive Preview Render, discussed in detail later in this chapter), so for major surfacing projects, use the Surface Editor in Layout and take advantage of VIPER. VIPER requires rendered data to work, and you can only render in Layout. VIPER uses information stored in LightWave's internal buffers for instant feedback. It really works because it uses magic.

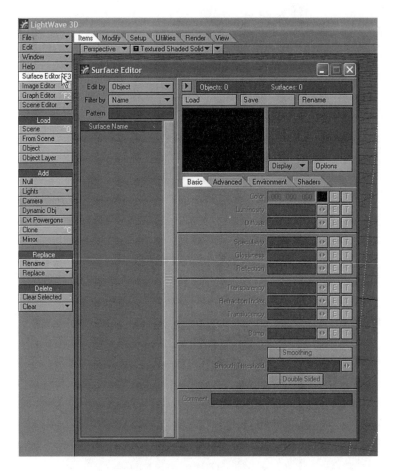

Figure 7.3 LightWave's Surface Editor is the same in Layout, and it's always accessed at the top left of the interface.

 Tip

Remember that LightWave enables you to completely customize the user interfaces in both Modeler and Layout. However, you should be working with the LightWave default Configure Keys (Alt+F9) and Menu Layout (Alt+F10) settings throughout this book.

Using the Surface Editor

As mentioned earlier, all of your surfacing needs can be accomplished within the Surface Editor, so you should be familiar with its features. This section guides you through its uses and helps you make sense of the panel. Believe it or not, it's much easier than you might think! As with any task, you start by getting organized.

Organizing Surfaces

Managing your 3D work, from models to keyframes to surfaces, will make you a better artist. The Surface Editor makes it easy for you to manage your surfaces. Figure 7.4 shows the Surface Editor with an object loaded that has multiple surfaces.

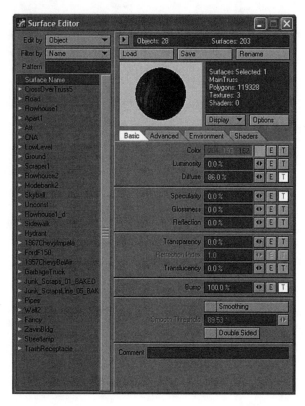

Figure 7.4   The Surface Editor enables you to manage your surfaces easily on an Object or Scene basis. You also can filter your surface names for organization.

If you enter the Surface Editor after a scene has been loaded, the scene's surface names are listed alphabetically, as you can see in Figure 7.4. The Surface Name list enables you to easily manage your surfaces by grouping individual surfaces as a drop-down list from each object. Clicking on the small triangle next to the object name expands the list, showing the surfaces associated with that object. Note that by default, if an object is selected in Layout, its first surface is selected in the Surface Editor. Figure 7.5 shows the same scene as in Figure 7.4, but with a surface of the first object selected. Note that this setup is using the Edit By Object selection from the top left of the Surface Editor, which lists the surfaces with their appropriate objects.

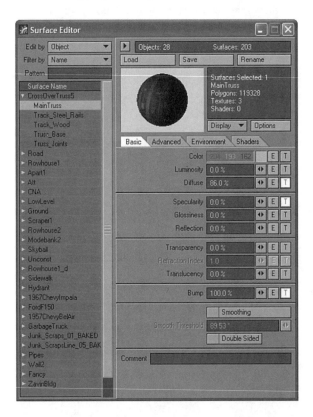

Figure 7.5   Surfaces are grouped with their respective objects if Edit By Object is selected.

When you click the small white triangle next to a surface name in the surface list, your surface settings, such as color, diffusion, or texture maps, won't be available until you click on a surface name. You must select one of the surfaces in the list before you can begin to work with it. When you select a surface, you see the surface properties change.

Working with a hierarchy like this is extremely productive, enabling you to quickly access any surface in your scene.

LightWave's Surface Editor enables you to collapse the Surface Name list, saving desktop real estate. Figure 7.6 shows the Surface Editor with the collapsed Surface Name list. When this happens, you can choose your selected surface through the drop-down selection at the top of the list, as in Figure 7.7.

Figure 7.6   The small triangle at the top of the Surface Editor panel is clicked to collapse the Surface Name list.

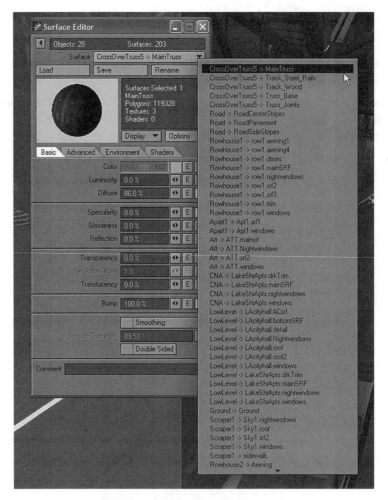

Figure 7.7   Selecting surface names in a collapsed view is done through the Surface drop-down list.

Selecting Existing Surfaces

Take control of your surfaces, and you'll have a better time navigating through the Surface Editor panel. You have three modes to assist you in quickly selecting the surface or surfaces you want:

- Edit By
- Filter By
- Pattern

Tip

> Did you know that the Edit By feature is less about how you select surfaces and more about whether they are global to the scene or local to the object? That's right! It just so happens that these two alternatives change what appears in the list. Users shouldn't get used to changing the Edit By mode just to change what is listed. Also, you won't have access to the Edit By, Filter By, and Pattern sorting commands with a collapsed Surface Name list. Expand the list to access these controls.

The Edit By mode, found at the top-left corner of the Surface Editor panel, has two selections: Object or Scene. Here, you tell the Surface Editor to control your surfaces according to just that, the Objects or the Scene. For example, say you have 20 buildings in a fantastic-looking skyscraper scene, and eight of those buildings have the same surface on their faces. If you choose to Edit By Object, you must apply all the necessary surface settings eight times.

The Edit By setting is saved from session to session in LightWave. You might accidentally overwrite previously saved surfaces by switching between Edit By Object and Edit By Scene settings. To avoid this, always make each surface name unique. However, you also can set the Edit By feature to Scene, and as a result, setting one surface affects all surfaces that share its name. So, in the case of the 20 buildings with eight identical surfaces, one setting takes care of all eight surfaces. The best way to work is to name your surfaces accordingly when building objects. This way, there is no confusion when using the Surface Editor. In addition, creating and naming surfaces properly in Modeler makes surfacing easier, and you end up using the Edit By feature as an organizational tool, not as a search engine.

Important

> As a reminder, any surface settings you apply to objects are saved with the object. Remember to select Save All Objects as well as Save Scene. Objects retain surfaces, image maps, color, and so on. Scenes retain motion, items, lighting, and so on. Both objects and scenes should always be saved before you render. This is a good habit to get into!

At the top-left corner of the Surface Editor panel, you'll see a Filter By listing. Here, you can choose to sort your surface list by Name, Texture, Shader, or Preview. Most often, you'll select your surfaces by using the Name filter. However, say for example, you have 100 surfaces, and out of those 100, only 2 have texture maps. Instead of sifting through a long list of surfaces, you can quickly select Filter By and choose Texture from the drop-down list. This displays only the surfaces that have textures applied. You also can select and display surfaces that use a Shader, or you can use Preview. Preview is useful when working with VIPER because it lists only the surfaces visible in the render buffer image.

In the space just beneath the Filter By setting, you have a space available to type in a Pattern. Pattern enables you to limit your surface list by a specific name, and it works in conjunction with Filter By. Think of this as an "include" filter. Any surface that does not "include" the Pattern won't show up in the surface list. Have you ever created an object with multiple surfaces and found yourself wasting time looking for one of those sur-faces? You may have spent quite a bit of time scrolling up and down a surface list in the past, where now you can type in a keyword. For example, say you created a scene with 200 different surfaces. You have six surfaces named carpet, and for some crazy reason you can't find them. By entering "carpet" into the Pattern panel, only the surfaces named tree will appear in the Surface Name list. Handy feature, isn't it? Just remember that if you don't see your surface names, check to see if you've left a word or phrase in the filter area!

Working with Surfaces

After you decide which surface you want to work with and then select it from the surface list, LightWave provides you with four commands at the top of the Surface Editor panel that are fairly common to software programs: Load, Save, Rename, and Display.

The first command, Load, does what its name implies. It loads surfaces. You can load a premade surface and quickly apply it to a new surface or even modify it. For example, say you've been working hard to surface a nice wood-planked wall, and it took hours of tweaking to make it look just right. You can reuse this surface on different objects. To do so, you first need to save the surface.

The second command, Save, tells the Surface Editor to save a file with all the settings you've set. This includes all texture maps, bump maps, image maps, and so on. Having the capability to save your surfaces is handy because you can create an archive of sur-faces. For example, assume you made a shiny silver surface for a client, and you know that this client comes in every quarter and wants a big animated silver building. The client tells you, "Make it just like last time!" and you suddenly draw a blank. By having that surface saved, you can load it and not have to worry about matching something you did three months earlier.

Tip

A visual representation is always a good choice for previewing surfaces. Because LightWave's Preset Shelf saves and organizes all of your surface samples, it might be more productive to use it instead of Save. The Preset Shelf is discussed in more detail later in this chapter, and it can be found under the Window drop-down list at the top left of Layout.

Too often, you'll create a complex object with dozens or even hundreds of surfaces. Stressed throughout this book is the importance of organization. With the third command, Rename, you can rename any of your surfaces. This helps keep things in order.

The fourth command is Display. While you're working with the Surface Editor, you'll often want to see how your surface and textures are coming along. Without going through the process of a full frame render, you can simply point your eye to the Display window at the top of the Surface Editor interface. Here, you can see your surface change instantly. This is especially useful for Luminosity and Specularity, as well as for procedural texture settings. However, you might need to look at these or other channels independently. The Display command enables you to choose what type of display you'll see. Figure 7.8 shows a sample surface in the Display window.

Figure 7.8   The Display window within the Surface Editor can show you your selected surface.

The drop-down list for the Display command offers many choices, the first of which is Render Output mode. This is the default display, and it is the most commonly used. The Render Output mode of Display shows what the rendered surface will look like. This includes color, texture, bump, and any other surface settings you've added. With a surfaced object loaded, Figure 7.9 shows the full surface sample, the Render Output in the Display window.

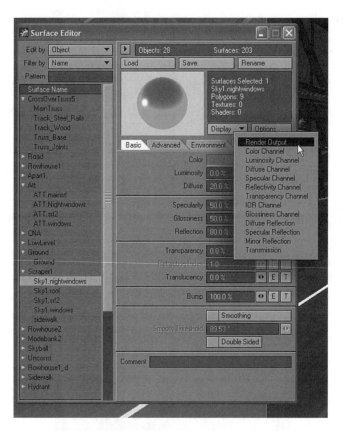

Figure 7.9   Choosing Render Output as the Display shows the current surface's attributes such as Color, Diffuse, Specularity, and Glossiness.

Sometimes, you might not want to preview the entire render output in the Surface Editor's Display window. Let's say you need to focus on a specific aspect of a certain surface, such as just the Color Channel. You can do this by selecting the Color Channel option from the drop-down list (see Figure 7.10). The Color Channel shows the color component of the surface. This component can be a texture image, a gradient, a procedural, or a combination. You'll see that color appear, rather than a complex surface with specularity, bumps, and more. You would do this to concentrate on a specific aspect of a surface.

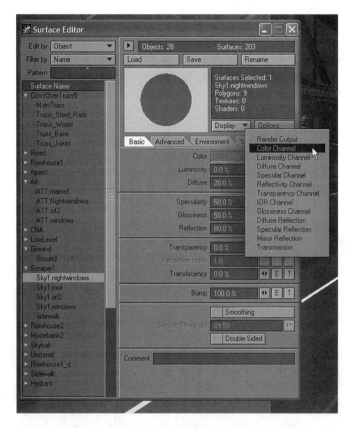

Figure 7.10   The same surface in the Display window with the Color Channel selected. Notice that the bump texture and specularity do not display as in Figure 7.9.

You can change this display to any surface aspect you want to concentrate on, such as the transparency of the surface, glossiness, reflection, and so on. If you are using a procedural texture for luminosity, for example, you might want to display just the Luminosity Channel. The choice is up to you. Most commonly, this value can stay at Render Output, but you have the control if needed.

Tip

> Except for Render Output and Color, all the channels are grayscale, with pure white representing 100% of that surface attribute and black being 0%.

Building surfaces is fun, no doubt. What's more fun is seeing results right away. Reusing those creations makes your time investment more worthwhile. You can use LightWave's Preset Shelf to save and load surfaces visually and instantly. From the top left of the

Layout interface, you can click the Presets command from the Window drop-down list to open the Surface Preset panel (see Figure 7.11). To save a surface to the Preset Shelf, double-click the Display window in the Surface Editor, and the currently selected surface is added. To copy a surface setting from the Surface Preset panel to another selected surface, first select the new surface name in the Surface Editor panel and then double-click in the preset surface in the Surface Preset panel. Also, double-click in the preview window to use the Save Surface Preset function. Be sure to have the Preset window open to see the saved surface. Double-click that surface preset to load it to a new surface. Similarly, you can right-click on the preview window for additional options such as Save Surface Preset.

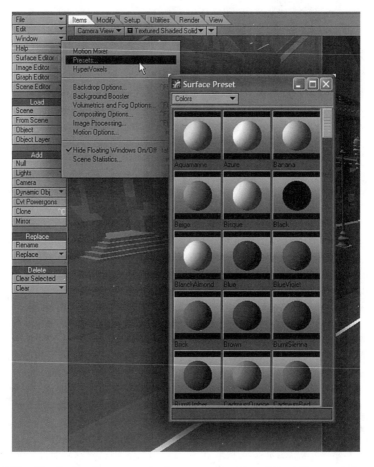

Figure 7.11 The Surface Preset panel is home to a number of NewTek-provided surfaces, as well as any you decide to add.

Important

OK, if you've opened the Preset Shelf and don't see anything, you've got a messed up install or something. People tend to move things around, not realizing that LightWave uses certain directories in a certain manner. The default presets should have been installed when you installed LightWave. This folder lives within the Programs folder, in your LightWave folder on your hard drive. You can visit www.3dgarage.com and download some additional free preset surfaces. After you download them, copy the folder into the LightWave/Programs/Presets folder on your drive.

If you right-click in the Surface Preset panel, you can create new libraries for organizing your surface settings. You also can copy, move, and change the parameters.

Setting Up Surfaces

So, we've jabbered on for nearly 10 pages now about the Surface Editor panel, but the main functions you use to set up and apply surfaces in the Surface Editor are located within four tabs: Basic, Advanced, Environment, and Shaders (see Figure 7.12). There is a method to this madness! You will soon be using these tools to fully understand them.

Tip

At this point, it's a good idea to assign LightWave's Content Directory to this book's DVD if you haven't already. Insert this book's disc into your computer. Either install the project files, or select the Cancel button if the DVD auto-starts to work from the DVD. Press the o key in Layout to access the General Options tab of the Preferences panel. At the top, click Content Directory and set it to the Projects folder on the DVD. Now, LightWave knows where to look for this book's tutorial files.

Figure 7.12   The Surface Editor consists of four primary tabbed areas of control.

Each tab controls varying aspects of the selected surface. This chapter introduces you to the most commonly used tab areas, the Basic and Environment tabs.

Aptly named, the Basic tab is home to all your basic surfacing needs. These are the most commonly used surface attributes, and they usually act as a basis for any advanced, environmental, or shaded surface (see Figure 7.13). It's here that you start most surfacing projects.

Figure 7.13   The Basic tab area in your Surface Editor is home to the most commonly used surface settings.

Within the Basic tab, you can assign the following:

- **Color.** Here, you can set the color of the selected surface in either RGB or HSV. HSV is hue, saturation, and value. Just right-click on the color values to change them.

- **Luminosity.** This is the brightness, or self-illumination, of a surface.

- **Diffuse.** Important to all surfaces, this is the amount of light the surface receives from the scene. You'll learn more about this shortly.

- **Specularity.** This value sets the amount of shine on a surface. Specularity is important for many surfaces, especially glass, water, metals, and more.

- **Glossiness.** Often confused with specularity, glossiness is the spread of the shine on a surface. A high glossiness setting keeps the specularity, or shine, to a tight hot-spot, similar to glass.

- **Reflection.** If you want an object to have reflection, you set the amount of reflection of a surface here, but you'll still need to tell a surface exactly what to reflect in the Environment tab. This value in the Basic tab is only "how much."

- **Transparency.** If you need to make a surface see through, it's here that you set the amount of transparency.

- **Refraction Index.** This is the amount that light bends through a surface, such as water or glass.

- **Translucency.** Add this value for the capability of light to pass through a surface, such as a thin leaf or piece of paper.

- **Bump.** This is a visual displacement based on procedural textures or image maps.

- **Smoothing.** This is a shading routine to make a surface appear smooth. LightWave employs Phong shading with this setting.

- **Double Sided.** This is the placement of a front or back on single-sided surfaces. Ideally, you don't want to use this unless you have to. All models created in LightWave Modeler have their surfaces facing in one direction. This option fakes it and forces the surface to face the opposite way as well.

- **Smooth Threshold.** This is how much smoothing will be applied to the surface. Generally, the default of 89.5 is too high. A typical beveled surface on a logo should be about 30.

- **Comment.** Make notes for particular surfaces as reminders or more detailed descriptions. This is great when sending objects to colleagues and clients.

Think about reflection for a minute. Reflect on reflection if you will, and you realize that a reflection is made up of its surrounding environment, right? When you set a surface's reflection in the Basic tab, you're only telling that surface how much to reflect, not what to reflect. When you click the Environment tab within the Surface Editor, you'll be able to set up the necessary reflection options, as in Figure 7.14. You can also set up refraction options in the Environment tab.

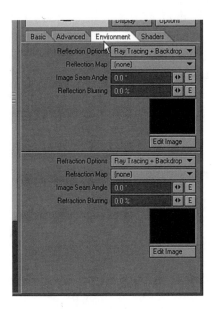

Figure 7.14   The Environment tab area gives you access to reflection and refraction controls.

Within the Environment tab, you can assign the following:

- **Reflection Options.** The type of reflection applied to a surface: spherical, ray trace, or backdrop.

- **Reflection Map.** What image will be reflected.

- **Refraction Options.** The type of refraction applied to a surface, either spherical or ray trace.

- **Refraction Map.** The image file used (if any) for refraction.

- **Image Seam Angle.** Where the seam of a reflected image will appear.

- **Reflection Blurring.** The amount of blur your reflections will have.

- **Refraction Blurring.** The amount of blur your refractions will have.

The best way for you to get a feel for using the Surface Editor and the Basic and Environment tabs is to try them out for yourself. An excellent way to observe the effect of the settings you choose is to use LightWave's VIPER feature.

Working with VIPER

VIPER stands for Versatile Interactive Preview Render, and it gives a preview of your scene within certain areas of adjustments in Layout, such as Volumetric settings or the Surface settings. It's important to point out that because VIPER does not do a full-scene evaluation, some aspects of your surfacing are not calculated, such as UV Mapping and shadows. This means that VIPER is limited in what it can show. However, it is very useful for most of your surfacing needs, such as color and texture. As you adjust your surfaces, you'll see what's happening and how the surface looks on the object in the scene you have set up without re-rendering. VIPER is available in Layout only.

 Important

VIPER is decoupled from plug-ins. It is a general server that has a controlling client (don't we all), which depends on the active plug-in. This setup enables more plug-ins to use VIPER. Some plug-ins are of course surface plug-ins, like HyperVoxels or Volumetrics. So what does this mean? It means you should be sure to have an appropriate panel open to see VIPER work, such as the Surface Editor.

Surfacing objects can be as simple or as complex as you want. A key role in how your surfaces appear when rendered has to do with the light and surroundings in the 3D environment. This chapter takes you through the key features in the Surface Editor. Later in this book, you will use these techniques, along with proper lighting, for ultimate images.

Exercise 7.1 Using VIPER with Basic Surfacing

For now, just to give you an example of how useful VIPER is, try this quick tutorial.

1. Start Layout, or if it's already running, from the File drop-down menu at the top left of the Layout screen, select Clear Scene (keyboard equivalent: Shift+n). Be sure to save any work you've completed thus far. You can also press Shift+n at the same time.

2. Load the Giraffe scene from the Chapter 07 folder within this book's DVD Projects directory.

You'll see a fun orange giraffe built by NewTek's own William "Proton" Vaughan.

Important

You can learn how to model this entire giraffe yourself in Chapter 11, "Modeling Electronics."

You don't always need to clear the scene before loading a scene. Simply loading a scene overrides your current scene. This two-step process here familiarizes you with the available tools and Layout's workflow.

3. Click over to the Render tab at the top of Layout, and then on the left side of the interface, click on the VIPER button (under Utilities) found at the top left third of the Layout window (Figure 7.15). When you do, the Enable VIPER button automatically becomes selected.

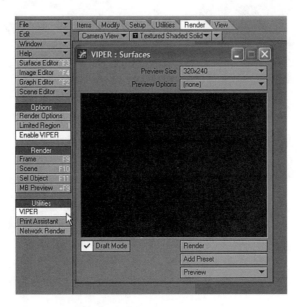

Figure 7.15   The VIPER command is found in Layout only, under the Render menu tab.

4. With the VIPER window now open, click the Render button at the bottom of the panel. An error appears stating that VIPER has no surface data to render. Click OK to close the error window.

This is normal. For VIPER to work, it needs you to render a frame so that it can store information from a buffer. Otherwise, VIPER has no idea what's in your scene.

5. Press F9 to render a single image of the current frame.

6. After the frame renders, press the Escape key (Esc) to close the Render Status window. Then, click the Render button again in the VIPER window. Do you see anything? Most likely not. This is because you need to have the appropriate panel open for VIPER to work.

7. Open the Surface Editor, and you'll see your last rendered frame appear.

Figure 7.16 shows the VIPER window, now with buffer information of the render, such as specularity, diffuse, color, and more.

Figure 7.16 Pressing F9 on the keyboard renders the current frame and stores the information in LightWave's internal buffer. Because of this, you can see your surface changes through VIPER.

8. Make sure the Surface Editor is still open, and from the Surface Name list, select the G_Skin surface. You may need to expand the NRGirfaffe_final object by clicking the small white triangle to the left. This is the main orange surface of the giraffe object.

9. To quickly see VIPER's interactivity, click and drag on the small slider to the right of the Diffuse listing within the Basic tab. Take the value down to 0 and let go of the mouse. You'll see VIPER update, and the giraffe appears black. What you really did was tell the specific surface not to receive any light, essentially turning off the lights for that surface.

10. Now, bring the value back to 100% and continue on.

    You'll see various surface settings appear throughout the commands on the right, on the Basic tab. The T button, for example, which stands for Texture, is available throughout LightWave. Here in the Surface Editor, you can apply a texture map to every surface property.

11. Click the T button to the right of the Color listing to open the Texture panel for the giraffe skin. Figure 7.17 shows the selection with the Texture Editor open.

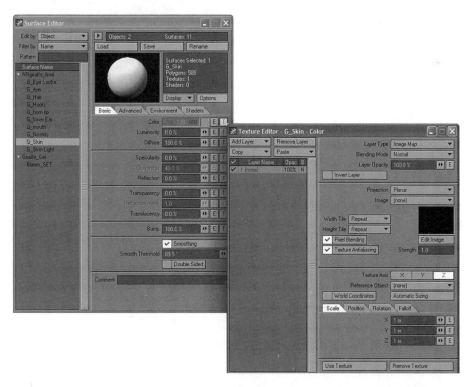

Figure 7.17   Clicking any of the T buttons throughout LightWave, including the Surface Editor, opens the Texture Editor.

You'll see that the Layer Type at the top of the commands is set to Image Map. You'll be able to apply images to a surface and much more with this setting. For now, change the Layer Type to Procedural Texture, as in Figure 7.18.

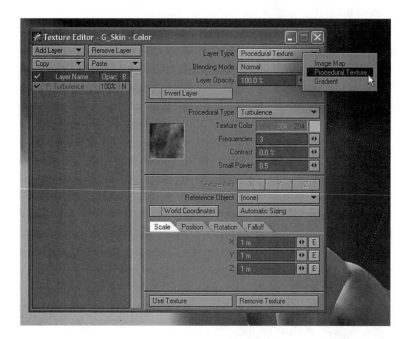

Figure 7.18   The default Texture Editor Layer Type is Image Map. Change this to Procedural Texture instead.

A procedural texture is computer-generated, meaning it has no end, no seams, and can often be just what the doctor ordered for organic-looking surfaces.

The Blending Mode is set to Normal, which tells LightWave to add this procedural texture to the selected surface.

The Layer Opacity is set to 100%, telling LightWave to use this procedural texture to the fullest extent.

The Procedural Type is set to Turbulence, a variation of fractal noise that has been used by LightWave animators for years.

Adding Turbulence as the Procedural Type to the current surface color of the giraffe, which is a bright orange, adds variances to the surface.

12. Make sure the VIPER window is open and visible to the side of the Texture Editor.

If VIPER is not open, click the VIPER button under the Render menu tab at the top of Layout. Then, on the left side of the Layout interface, click VIPER (not Enable VIPER). You rendered the scene in step 5, and LightWave remembers that by storing the data in its internal buffers.

13. With the Texture Editor and VIPER open, you can make changes to surface settings and see your changes in real time. Figure 7.19 shows the two panels open.

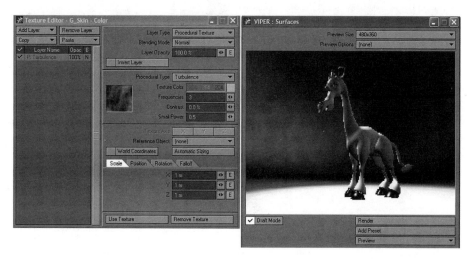

Figure 7.19   By having made a render of a frame (F9), VIPER can now display the render, and you can make surface changes in the Texture Editor (among other places) and see them in real time.

Tip

Remember that if you change the Preview Size resolution in the VIPER window, you'll need to re-render the image by pressing F9. Figure 7.19 shows a 480×360 size VIPER preview.

14. Make certain that the Texture Editor is still open (you got to the Texture Editor by clicking the T button next to Color in the Surface Editor).

You can see from the VIPER preview window that the nice orange giraffe skin surface is now sort of dusty-looking. This is because the basic default procedural texture was applied when you chose Procedural as the Layer Type.

15. Because the procedural turbulent noise texture was a little too heavy, change some of the parameters, such as the Size, found at the bottom of the Texture Editor panel under the Scale tab. Click and drag the X, Y, and Z values and watch VIPER redraw your image with the surface changes.

16. Experiment with the other procedural type settings such as Underwater or Crumple. From there, try to use other procedurals and adjust their properties as well. Figure 7.20 shows the Texture Editor and VIPER with a default Procedural Texture of Turbulence applied and the Scale made smaller.

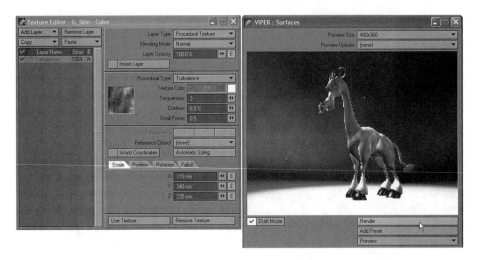

Figure 7.20   Changes to a few values like Color, Scale, and Contrast are easy to see with the VIPER window open.

 Tip

> To the left of the Texture Color setting in the Texture Editor window is a small square display. This area shows your procedural pattern. The base background color for the procedural is black. When combined with a dark Texture Color, this makes a hard-to-see swatch. To remedy this, right-click on the swatch and set a new background color. In addition, you can left-click on the Display window and drag the preview around. Doing this helps you see more of the procedural pattern. Figure 7.21 shows a close up. Mac users, remember to use the Apple key along with the mouse for right-mouse button commands.

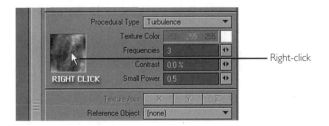

Figure 7.21   You can change the base background color for your procedural texture display by right-clicking in the display window.

VIPER will quickly become one of your best friends when working with LightWave Layout because it saves you time. Not only that, many of you may not be mathematical wizards and do not care to calculate every value within the surface settings. Using VIPER can answer many of your questions when it comes to surfacing because you can instantly see the results from changed values. It's guaranteed that during your practicing, you'll utter a loud "Oh, that's what that does" from time to time.

Final VIPER Tips

Here are a few more VIPER tips before you move on:

- Never trust VIPER as your final render. That is to say, if something looks odd, always make a true render (F9 or F10) for final surfacing.

- You can use VIPER to see animated textures by selecting Make Preview from the Preview drop-down list in the VIPER window.

- Pressing the Esc key aborts a VIPER preview in progress.

- Clicking Draft Mode on the VIPER window helps decrease redraw time.

- Clicking on a particular surface in the VIPER window instantly selects it in the Surface Editor's Surface Name list. This is a great feature in that it can save a lot of time on complex textured scenes.

- VIPER is available only in Layout, not Modeler.

- To move beyond VIPER, visit www.worley.com and check out the FPrime plug-in. This killer LightWave plug-in allows real-time previews of just about everything in Layout, including reflections, ray-tracing, transparency, and even radiosity.

Common Surface Settings

To take you even further into the LightWave Surface Editor, try Exercise 7.2.

Exercise 7.2   Applying a Reflection to a Surface

You may sometimes have a project that requires you to use a vehicle, machine, household item, or something completely different from what you're used to working with. This could be an object that you've created yourself, purchased, or downloaded from public archives on the Internet. Follow these steps to apply a simple reflection to a surface.

1. Be sure to save any work you've completed thus far. Start Layout, or if it's already running, choose File, Clear Scene.

2. From the DVD that accompanies this book, load the Watch_Basic scene from the Chapter 7 projects folder. To load the scene, go to the Items tab, and then on the left side of the interface, select the Scene button under the Load category, as in Figure 7.22.

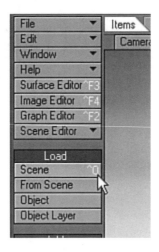

Figure 7.22   Load a basic scene into LightWave to set up some surfaces.

Tip

Here's a very handy tip! You can hide all the toolbars and menus in Layout and work with just the keyboard and mouse. Press o (not the number zero, the letter o) on the keyboard to access the General Options tab of the Preferences panel. Select Hide Toolbar (see Figure 7.23). Now when in Layout, you can access the Surface Editor (or any other panel) by holding the Ctrl and Shift keys together and then clicking either the left or right mouse button. Doing this pops up the list of commands and menus you've just hidden away (see Figure 7.24)! Press o again to access the General Options panel to unhide the toolbar. Now that you know where things are located, just use Alt+F2 to hide and unhide the toolbar. You can also open the Surface Editor quickly by pressing Ctrl+Alt+F3.

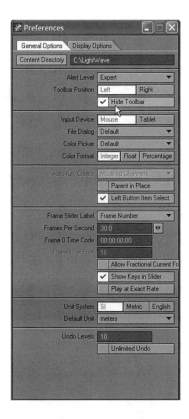

Figure 7.23 You can hide Layout's toolbars from the General Options tab.

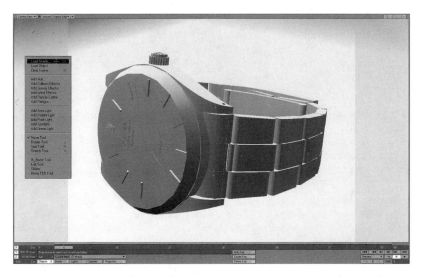

Figure 7.24 Find the Load Scene and other valuable commands by holding the Ctrl and Shift keys and then clicking in the Layout window with the left mouse button, as show in this example.

Tip

Remember that you should be using LightWave's default interface configuration for all tutorials in this book. To make sure you are, press Alt+F10 on the keyboard to call up the Configure Menus panel. Click the Default button from the Presets drop-down list at the top-right side of the panel's interface. If it is ghosted, you already have the default interface set. Select Done to close the panel.

3. After the scene has been loaded, click the Surface Editor button on the left side of the interface to open the Surface Editor panel.

You see that by default, the surface names of the object appear in the Surface Name list within the Surface Editor when using the Edit By Object mode.

4. Clicking the small triangle to the left of the Watch filename opens and closes the Surface Name list.

All the surfaces associated with the Watch object appear, as shown in Figure 7.25.

Figure 7.25 When an object is selected in Layout and the Surface Editor is opened, the selected object's surfaces are listed.

Tip

If you have more surfaces than you do space in the Surface Name list, a scroll bar appears. Simply click and drag to view the entire surface list.

5. LightWave enables you to resize the Surface Editor panel simply by clicking and dragging on the edge of the panel. Click and drag the bottom edge to stretch out the panel. Conversely, you can collapse the panel by clicking the small triangle centered at the top of the interface, and you can simply select your surfaces from the drop-down Surface list.

Tip

Naming your surfaces is half the battle when building 3D models. If you name your surfaces carefully, you'll save oodles of time when you have many surface settings to apply. Organization is key! You name your surfaces in Modeler, as explained in previous chapters. Here, you can see that the watch has a set of clearly named surfaces.

6. Make sure you're in the Camera view. You should be because the scene was saved this way before you loaded it. If not, switch to Camera view by selecting the drop-down list at the top-left side of the viewport title bar. Then, select the Backing surface from the list within the Surface Editor.

When a surface is selected, the name appears in the information window to the right of the surface preview. The number of polygons associated with that surface also appears. In this case, the selected surface, Backing, has 820 polygons, as shown in Figure 7.26. You'll also see a display at the very top of the surface panel that shows the number of objects and surfaces in the scene.

Figure 7.26   Selected surfaces have displayed information at the top right of the Surface Editor panel.

Because you got this watch from some dude on West Madison Avenue, it has no color, and the shiny metal surface is gone! Given that, you need to make the glass surface transparent and add metallic reflections.

7. First, you want the color of the glass to be a soft grayish blue color, so set the RGB value to 180, 180, 200.

There are a few ways to set a color to the glass surface of the watch. Under the Basic tab within the Surface Editor, you'll see the Color listing at the top. There is an RGB value indicator with a small color sample. This small area offers you a lot of control:

- Left-clicking on the small, colored square next to the RGB values makes the standard system color palette appear. Here, you can choose your color in RGB (red, green, blue), HSL (hue, saturation, luminance), or from custom colors you may have set up previously.

- Right-clicking and dragging on the small colored square next to the RGB values in the Surface Editor changes all three values at once. This is great for increasing or decreasing the color brightness.

- Clicking the left mouse button on either the red, green, or blue numeric value and dragging left or right increases or decreases the color value. You will instantly see the small color square next to the RGB values change. You'll also see the sample display update.

- If you're not keen on setting RGB values and prefer HSV values instead, rest easy. Clicking once on the RGB values with the right mouse button changes the selection to HSV. Figure 7.27 shows the change.

- Make sure you're using the display preview options as you like them. Right-clicking on the surface preview window shows more controls and options, as in Figure 7.28.

Figure 7.27   Right-clicking on the RGB value in the Surface Editor (Basic tab) changes the settings to HSV values.

 Important

HSV represents hue, saturation, and value. It describes colors directly by their overall color, unlike RGB values, which are three discrete subcolors. HSV is another way to change color values. However, you might have more flexibility using RGB values.

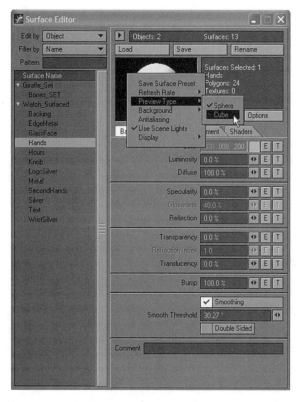

Figure 7.28   Right-clicking on the surface preview window in the Surface Editor offers more control over how the surface is displayed. Here, you can set a checkerboard background, which is great for dark surfaces.

With the Glass surface set to the soft gray color, you still need to see what's under it! You'll need to make the glass transparent and shiny. This next tutorial discusses surfacing the glass while introducing you to the rest of the Surface Editor. Remember that you will create many more surfaces throughout the chapters in this book, and that this is a brief introduction to just some of the features.

Exercise 7.3   Surfacing Glass

1. Make sure VIPER is opened and set off to the side of the Surface Editor so you can see your changes in real time.

With the GlassFace surface still selected as the current surface in the Surface Editor, go down the list of options and set each one accordingly.

2. Make sure that the value of Luminosity (the option just underneath Surface Color) is zero.

   Luminosity is great for objects that are self-illuminating, such as a light bulb, candle flame, or laser beam. Note though that this does not make your surface cast light unless radiosity is applied.

3. Set the value of Diffuse to roughly 60% to tell the glass surface to accept 60% of the light in the scene.

   The Diffuse value tells your surface what amount of light to pick up from the scene. For example, if you set this value to 0, your surface would be completely black. Although you want the glass to be black, you also want it to have some sheen and reflections. A zero Diffuse value renders a black hole—nothing appears at all.

4. Set the value of Specularity to 90%.

   Specularity, in simple terms, is a shiny reflection of the light source. 0% is not shiny at all, whereas 100% is completely shiny.

   When you set Specularity, you almost always adjust the glossiness as well. Glossiness, which becomes available only when the Specularity setting is above 0%, is the value that sets the amount of the "hot spot" on your shiny (or not so shiny) surface. Think of glossiness as how much of a spread the hotspot has. The lower the value, the wider the spread. For example, Figure 7.29 shows two spheres, one with a low Specularity setting of just 50% and Glossiness set to 16%. The result resembles a dull surface, like plastic.

   On the other hand, the sphere to the right has a Specularity setting of 100% and Glossiness of 40%. The result looks closer to a shiny glass surface with reflections turned on. A higher Glossiness setting gives the impression of polished metal, or glass in this case. There will be a lot of surfacing ahead in this book for you, such as glass, metal, human skin, and more.

5. Now, back to the watch surfacing. Set the value of the Glossiness for the GlassFace surface to 80%.

   This gives you a good, working glass surface for now.

6. Set the value of Reflection for the GlassFace surface to 40%.

   Most glass and clear plastic surfaces generally reflect their surroundings. In this case, the watch is placed on a simple set composed of just a few polygons. Three basic spotlights illuminate the scene, along with one set light.

Figure 7.29   The sphere on the left has a low Specularity and a low Glossiness setting, which results in a surface that looks dull. The sphere on the right with a high Specularity and high Glossiness setting looks more like glass.

   Tip

It's a good idea when setting reflections to balance the Reflection value and the Diffuse value to roughly 100%. The GlassFace surface has Diffuse at 60% and Reflection at 40% for a total 90%. This is not law, just a guideline. If your Diffuse setting is 100% and you add a reflection of 40% or more, you'd end up with an unnaturally bright surface.

7. To see the image underneath the glass face, it needs to be transparent. Set Transparency to 90%. There's one more option—Smoothing. You use this setting to apply Phong shading to smooth the surface.

    Phong is a shading method developed by Bui Tuong-Phong in 1975. Essentially, it interpolates the vertex normals of an object, rather than the intensity. The result is a smooth surface that is good for plastics, metals, or glass.

8. Because the GlassFace surface is smooth, the Smoothing option is necessary. With objects that are more round, this will take away any visible facets in the geometry. Turn Smoothing on and set the value to 30.

Tip

Often, flatter surfaces are simply "too" smooth, thereby creating odd renders. A lesser smoothing threshold fixes those problems.

9. Click the Environment tab within the Surface panel.

Figure 7.30 shows the Environment tab.

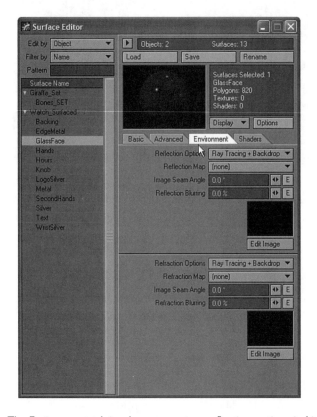

Figure 7.30 The Environment tab is where you set up reflection options in LightWave.

10. Set the Reflection Options to Ray Tracing and Backdrop, if it's not already.

This tells the surface to reflect what's around it (in this case, the basic set). If other objects were in the scene, they would be reflected too.

Because LightWave can calculate reflections, setting a reflecting image can often help create a more realistic surface. You'll do this for the metal portions of the watch. Glass, on the other hand, should reflect its surroundings, so Ray Tracing is used.

For LightWave to be able to calculate and draw the reflections for the glass surface, you need to tell the render engine that you want it to calculate reflections.

11. In Layout, click the Render menu tab at the top. On the left side of the interface, click the Render Options button to open the panel. Make sure Ray Traced Reflections is checked under the Rendering tab, as in Figure 7.31.

12. After you have this turned on, press F9 for a single frame render. While you're in the Render Options panel, make sure the Render Display is set to Image Viewer to see a pop up of your rendered image. Figure 7.32 shows the render.

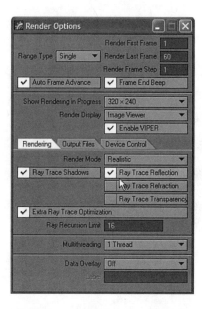

Figure 7.31   For Ray Trace Reflections to work for a surface, you must tell LightWave's renderer to calculate them.

What's that? You saw black or dark areas when rendering the watch? Figure 7.32 shows the render with the surface changes to the GlassFace surface, but for some reason, it renders almost black! If you look carefully, it's not really a black surface, but rather a shadow! Even though you have a transparent surface set for the glass, it is still casting a shadow onto the inner face of the watch.

13. Make sure the watch object is selected in Layout, and press the p key to open up the Object properties for it.

14. Under the Render tab in the panel, make sure Self Shadow is turned off, as in Figure 7.33. You'll see other similar options here as well that you can apply to your objects such as Unseen By Camera.

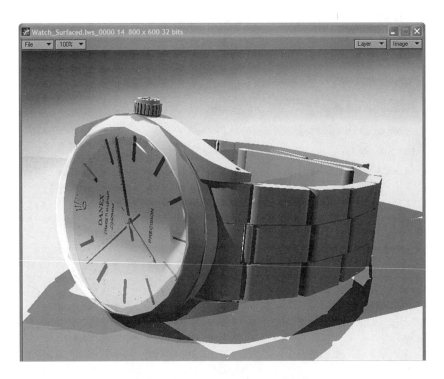

Figure 7.32 The basic glass surface applied to the face of the watch, with reflections. But there's a problem with the surface!

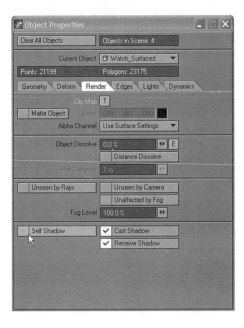

Figure 7.33 Sometimes, you'll need to tell objects not to cast shadows upon themselves.

15. Press F9 one more time after turning off Self Shadow. Figure 7.34 shows the rendering with the glass surface. Now, it's time for the metal!

Figure 7.34   With shadows fixed and glass surface applied, the watch is starting to look good.

Creating Metallic Surfaces

With an object such as a watch, you might think it would be difficult to match the real-world properties of metal. Believe it or not, this is easy to do within LightWave. The right amount of color, specularity, glossiness, and reflection helps create the visual effect. You've created the transparent glass surface, but if the surface is transparent, what's behind it? In this particular instance, a metal surface is needed for the backing behind the glass. This same metal can be applied to almost all the watch surfaces, with minor variations. This section takes you through the steps required to surface the rest of the watch.

Exercise 7.4   Surfacing the Watch with Metallic Backing

1. In the Surface Editor, select the backing surface. This is the metal plate behind the glass face of the watch. Set the color to a soft gray to simulate a silver metallic surface. Try an RGB value of 211, 211, 211.

2. Set Diffuse to 70%, Specularity to 50%, and Glossiness to 40%.

3. A reflection is needed, so make sure Reflection is set to 25%.

    At this point, the watch doesn't look much different than when you loaded it. Remember that other factors play a role in surfacing, such as surroundings and lighting, but you still need to apply the reflecting image.

4. With the backing surface still selected, click the Environment tab to the right of the Basic tab.

5. Set Reflection Options to Ray Tracing + Spherical Map, as in Figure 7.35. This tells the surface to reflect not only what's around it, but an image as well.

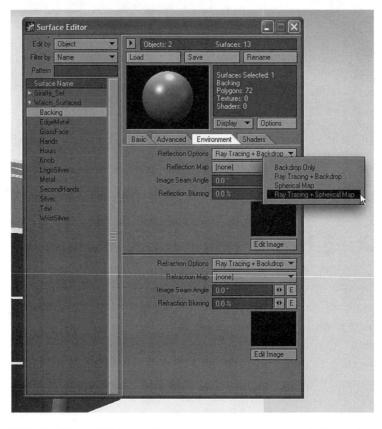

Figure 7.35   Ray Tracing + Spherical Map are a great way to make realistic metallic surfaces.

6. For the Reflection Map option, click the drop-down and select Load Image, as in Figure 7.36. Load the city lights image from this book's DVD.

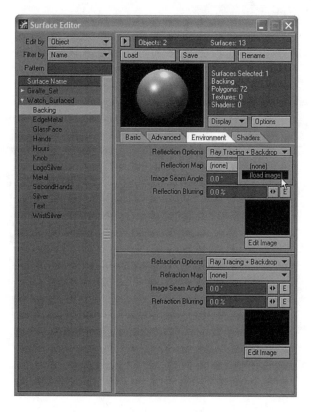

Figure 7.36   You can load an image directly from the Reflection Options in the Environment tab.

7. Guess what? That's about it for this surface! Press F9 to see how it looks. Figure 7.37 shows the new surface applied to the backing.

It's subtle, but effective. Now, you'll copy this surface to other more noticeable areas of the watch.

8. Click back to the Basic tab, right-click on the Backing surface (Mac people, Ctrl click!), and select Copy, as in Figure 7.38.

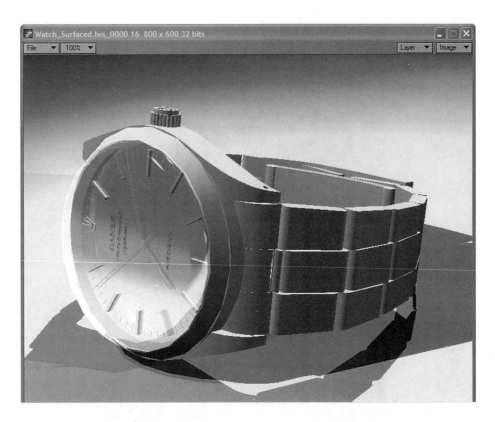

Figure 7.37   Adding ray traced reflections and a reflection image to a gray surface helps sell a metallic look for the area under the glass.

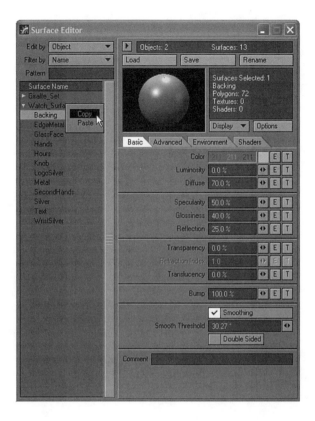

Figure 7.38 Right-clicking on a surface name in the surface list enables you to quickly copy all its settings.

You can also open the Presets from the Window drop-down in Layout and then double-click the preview display window in the Surface Editor to save this preset surface.

9. As you might have guessed, you can now select another surface and paste what you've copied. Select the EdgeMetal surface, right-click again (Mac people, you know what to do!), and paste the copied surface. Figure 7.39 shows the operation.

10. Also paste the backing surface copy to the WristSilver and Metal surface listings. Note that you do not have to right-click and copy the backing surface each time you want to paste it. Copy once, paste many! Just remember that if you accidentally copy something else, you need to go back and copy the desired surface again. Figure 7.40 shows the render with the new surfaces applied.

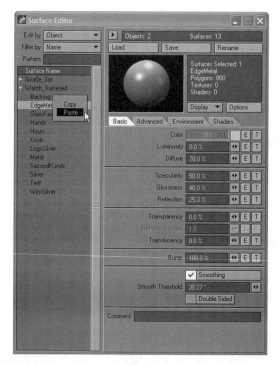

Figure 7.39 Right-clicking on a surface name in the surface list enables you to quickly paste what you've just copied.

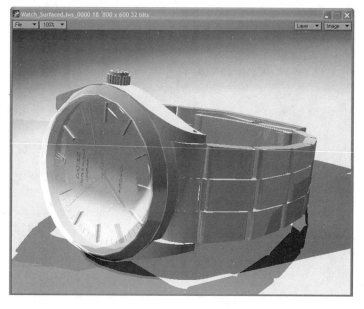

Figure 7.40 You can paste the metallic surface to other surfaces to quickly copy settings.

The render looks good, but perhaps it needs a bit more reflection? This is easy to do, and it can be done all at once.

11. While holding the Shift key on your keyboard, select the WristSilver, Metal, and EdgeMetal surfaces in the Surface Name list, as shown in Figure 7.41.

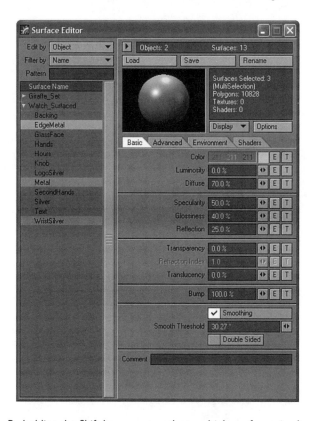

Figure 7.41   By holding the Shift key, you can select multiple surfaces simultaneously.

12. With three surfaces selected, change the Reflection amount to 50%. Remember to balance Diffusion and Reflection to about 100%. Therefore, if Reflection is 50%, change Diffuse to about 45%.

13. Press the F9 key and do a test render. Figure 7.42 shows the changes. The image looks nice, but perhaps the reflection image should have more contrast.

Figure 7.42   Changing the amount of reflection on three surfaces is easy to do.

14. From the top left of Layout, click the Image Editor button. This opens
    LightWave's image control panel, which enables you to edit, replace, and manip-
    ulate images. Figure 7.43 shows the selection.

15. You'll see the single city lights image you loaded in the Surface Editor. Make sure
    it's selected and then hit the Replace button in the Image Editor. Select the frac-
    tals image from this book's DVD.

    Anywhere you used the city lights image will now have the fractal image.
    LightWave didn't just load the image—it replaced it entirely.

    Before you render again, copy and paste the metal surface to the Silver surface
    listing as well.

16. Press F9 again to see the changes to your surfaces with a new reflection image.
    Figure 7.44 shows the render with a different reflection image.

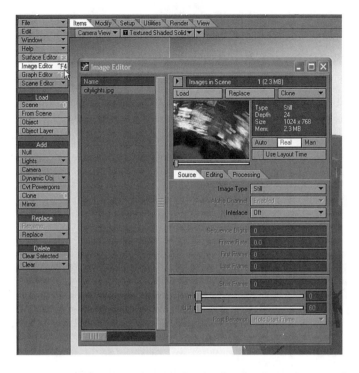

Figure 7.43   The Image Editor in Layout goes hand-in-hand with any images you're using in the Surface Editor.

Figure 7.44   Replacing an image is easy in the Image Editor, enabling you to quickly make a higher contrast reflection.

From this point, you can work with the other surfaces and apply a similar metal to the watch, text elements, and hands. You can even select all but the glass surface and change the basic gray color to a yellow-orange. Render again, and you've now made gold. All the other surface settings still apply.

A few final thoughts on surfacing with reflections. Many factors come into play, such as the glancing angle of the camera, light, and shadows. The angle of the camera in the previous steps could have been moved to reveal more of the reflection. At the current angle, the watch band reflected a lot of the ground. You can also try changing the metal reflections to just a Spherical Map in the Environment tab, rather than Ray Tracing and Spherical Map. This tells the surface to reflect only the image.

Important

Remember that simply saving a LightWave scene file does not save your surfaces. You must save your object in addition to saving your scene if you want to keep the surfaces applied.

You'll often come across a situation where you need to use the same surface settings on multiple surfaces, such as in the previous exercise. With so many variables being set within the Surface Editor, keeping track of identical surfaces could be a problem. Not to mention, you might want a quick reference to the changes you've made to the current surface. This is where the Preset Shelf comes in.

Working with the Preset Shelf

You may have noticed that the 3D watch you've been working with is composed of more than just one surface. The scene also includes a simple set that has its own surface. A few of the surfaces, such as WristSilver and EdgeMetal, are the same. Instead of redoing all the surface parameters, or constantly copying and pasting with the right mouse button as you did, you can use the Preset Shelf to save and apply the same surface and then simply make any necessary changes to the surface properties.

Tip

Loading and saving surfaces works as well, yet the Preset Shelf shows you a small thumbnail of the surface. Nice!

From the Window drop-down list in Layout, select Presets. The Preset Shelf defaults to a tall thin column that appears when you access the Surface Editor, but it can be resized as seen in Figure 7.45.

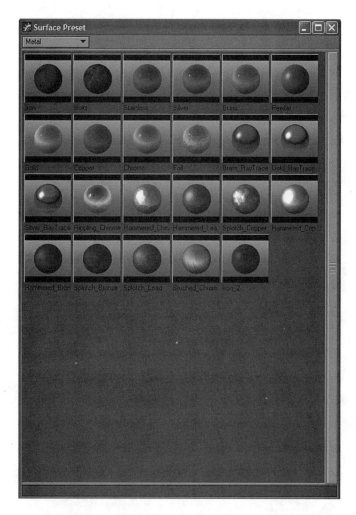

Figure 7.45   By default, the Preset Shelf opens as a tall window, but it can be resized to fit your screen.

If you don't care for the tall narrow look of the Preset Shelf, you can click and hold one of the corners of the panel and resize it to your liking. A good option is to stretch the shelf out across the interface from left to right and move it to the bottom of the screen. Because all of your Preset Shelf samples remain in the shelf, you also can open up the panel to fit your entire screen. The choice is yours.

Tip

> Using LightWave with a dual-monitor system is great when setting up surfaces. Simply set the Preset Shelf wide open on the additional monitor, maximizing preset visibility and workflow real estate.

Exercise 7.5   Saving a Surface

If you set up a surface you'd like to keep, you can simply save it in the Preset Shelf. To do this, follow these steps.

1. Open the Surface Editor and select the Metal surface. Double-click on the display preview at the top of the Surface Editor.

    You'll see that surface sample appear on the Preset Shelf (Figure 7.46).

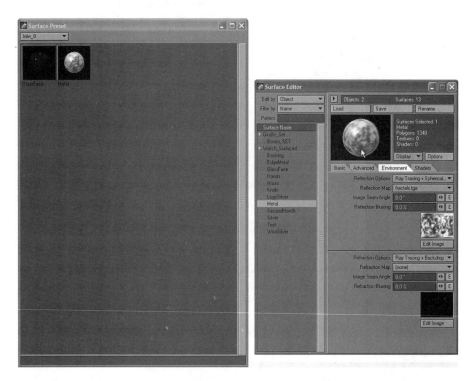

Figure 7.46   Double-clicking the display sample in the Surface Editor, shown on the right, instantly adds those surface settings to the Preset Shelf, shown on the left.

Tip

Although double-clicking the sample display is one way to add a surface to the Preset Shelf, you can also right-click on the preview window and select Save Surface Preset. You can also just press the s key while in the Surface Editor. Finally, you can click Add Preset from the VIPER window.

2. Select the second surface you need to apply surfacing to, such as the LogoSilver.

3. Go back to the Preset Shelf and double-click the sample you recently added.

   A small window appears, asking you to load the current settings. This is asking if you want the settings from the Preset Shelf sample to be applied to the currently selected surface in the Surface Editor. In this case, you do.

4. Click Yes, and all the surface settings are set for the LogoSilver surface. For any small changes, adjust as needed.

   By using a preset to copy and paste a surface, it's much easier to change one simple parameter, such as reflection, than it is to reset all the surface and reflection properties again.

As you can see from the previous examples, the watch is starting to look like a useable object. The next step is to continue surfacing it on your own, using the few simple parameters outlined in the previous pages. If you like, you can load the Watch scenes from the Projects/Scenes/Chapter7 folder on this book's DVD to study.

Color, diffuse, specularity, glossiness, and reflection are the base for just about all the surfaces you create. After you have a handle on setting up the basics, it's time for you to create surfaces that are a bit more advanced.

Making a 3D Surface from a 2D Image

Building 3D models requires more than just a keen insight into what you're sculpting within the computer. You also need to think ahead about your overall project and how much data is within your scene. Certain models might require massive amounts of detail that, if added up, can bring your renders to a screaming halt. This kind of detail can range from large terrains, ocean swells, or rocks, down to little things like carvings, bolts, or rivets. One way to avoid heavy geometry detail is to use LightWave's Surface Editor.

As you walk around your neighborhood, city, or school, look closely at the moldings, arches, or stonework. You might notice some detailed areas that would be too complex to model and too intricate to render reasonably.

Marble, granite, and stone are great surfaces for 3D animation. Terrific images for logo backgrounds, floors, sidewalks, and more, they are often easy to find on the Internet and in the world around you. Figure 7.47 shows a digital photograph of some stonework taken from a 50-story building in downtown Chicago.

Figure 7.47   This everyday earth-tone carving from the side of a building can be your start for a 3D render.

In this project, you'll start with this picture and use it to create bumps and specular highlights on a surface. Figure 7.48 shows the same image cropped to just the area you're going to use, with its contrast boosted in Adobe Photoshop.

Figure 7.48   A little work in Adobe Photoshop crops the image to just the area you'll use while boosting its contrast.

Exercise 7.6   Creating a 3D Surface with a Bump Map

To create a 3D surface, follow these steps.

1. Select Clear Scene in Layout from the File menu. Remember to save any work. Next, load the stonework object from the Chapter 7 folder of this book's DVD. This is a flat polygon in which you'll apply an image map. Select the Camera button at the bottom of Layout and then press 6 on the numeric keypad to switch to Camera View.

   Selecting Camera first tells LightWave that you want to work with cameras. Conversely, selecting Lights tells LightWave you want to work with lights, and so on.

2. Move the camera in toward the stonework object so that it fills the frame. Press the Enter key twice to create a keyframe at frame 0, which locks the camera in place (given that you have the Auto Key button off at the bottom of Layout).

3. Open the Surface Editor. You'll see that there is just one surface attached to this single polygon. Not enough geometry for cool carved stonework, but that's the beauty of bump mapping. First press the T key (to the right of Color, in the Basic tab) to open the Texture Editor. Figure 7.49 shows the Surface Editor with the Texture Editor opened.

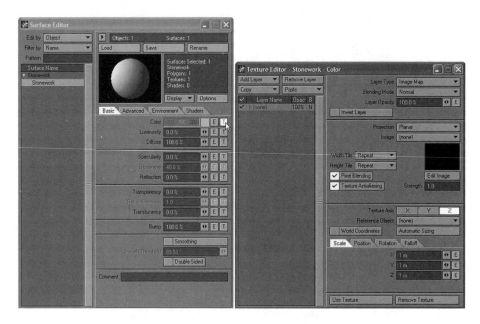

Figure 7.49 The Texture Editor for Color is your first step toward making a 3D image from a 2D object.

Important

Earlier in this chapter, you used the Texture Editor to apply an Image Map to Color. The Texture Editor for Diffuse looks identical, but because it's for Diffuse, not Color, its effect will be completely different. This is the same throughout LightWave. The panels look the same, but where you access them from is key to the results you achieve.

4. Starting at the top of the Texture Editor, make sure that the Layer Type is set to Image Map.

You're selecting an image map because you're using an image to enhance the surface. Image maps can be used on all types of surfaces as an alternative to procedural textures that are strictly computer-generated.

Here, you are mapping an image onto the flat object—think of image mapping like wallpapering. Another layer type you can set is Procedural, computer-generated surfaces that do not use image maps. You can also choose to set a Gradient layer type, which, on a small scale, enables you to use a spectrum of colors as a texture.

Tip

A gradient enables you to control an attribute based on an Input Parameter, like bump height, distances, weight maps, and so on. The real power of gradients is that you can control how the input parameter is applied using the gradient bar, which acts as a filter. Gradients in LightWave are complex and are used more throughout this book.

5. Set the Blending Mode to Normal from the drop-down list.

You can also select other blending modes: Additive uses the texture to its full extent for the selected surface. Subtractive subtracts the full extent of the image from the selected surface. Choosing Difference as the Blending Mode determines how a layer affects underlying layers, similar to Adobe Photoshop.

6. Experiment with Blending modes to see what results you can come up with.

Tip

Every surface layer can have a different blending mode.

7. Make sure that the Blending Mode is set to Normal, and keep the Layer Opacity set to 100% for now.

A setting of 100% tells LightWave to use this texture map completely. Because you are in the Texture Editor for Diffuse, you are using the brightness values of the image for the diffuse channel, and the Color data is disregarded.

8. Leave Invert Layer turned off.

In this instance of an image map, inverting the layer would reverse the image.

9. Set the Projection to Planar.

Remember, with an Image Map layer type, you are wallpapering. Planar tells LightWave to keep the wallpaper flat. You also can choose to set Projection to Cylindrical, Spherical, Cubic, Front, and UV. These additional values enable you to surface on tubes, balls, boxes, composited backgrounds, and organic surfaces.

Now, you need to tell LightWave what image you want to apply an image map to as a diffusion texture.

10. Next to the Image drop-down list, select Load Image, and from the book's DVD, select the stonework_color image file from Chapter 7's image directory.

   You see the image appear in the small thumbnail window.

11. Keep Pixel Blending checked (turned on) to smooth out the pixelization that can occur if the camera gets too close to the surface.

12. You don't need to set Width Tile and Height Tile to Reset because you are using Auto Sizing, so leave them alone. These settings enable you to repeat or mirror the image map.

   These two settings are used if you are tiling a floor, for example, and want a texture to repeat.

13. Uncheck Texture Antialiasing. Turning this off is important when applying textures. When you render animations, you will turn on Antialiasing in the Camera Properties panel. This setting smoothes out jagged edges throughout your scene. Setting Antialiasing within the Texture Editor smoothes your texture. However, when you add that to a final render that is antialiased, you end up with a blurry image. Too much antialiasing can sometimes be a bad thing.

   You told LightWave to set an image map and keep it flat (planar). Because this is a 3D animation program, you also need to identify the axis to which you want to apply this image.

14. Set the Texture Axis to Z, the axis that is in front (positive Z) and in back (negative Z) of you.

Important

You do not need to set a Reference Object for this surface. Setting up a Reference Object, such as a null object, enables you to interactively control the position and size of the image map in Layout. However, LightWave enables you to animate a texture's Position, Scale, and Rotation. The choice is yours.

15. Click the Automatic Sizing button.

   LightWave looks at the polygons of the selected surface and applies the currently selected image to them. The size parameters change under the Scale tab at the bottom of the Texture Editor interface. In most cases, Automatic Sizing works like a charm. When it doesn't, use a null object as a reference object to obtain precise image placement.

16. Leave World Coordinates unchecked.

When you tell LightWave to Image Map, you are wallpapering an image onto the surface of an object. If you move the object, the image should move with it. But imagine if you wallpapered a bumpy wall and decided to move the wall. When you did this, you wanted the wall to move, but not the wallpaper, making the bumpy wall move through the wallpaper. Clicking on World Coordinates does just that. Figure 7.50 shows the settings.

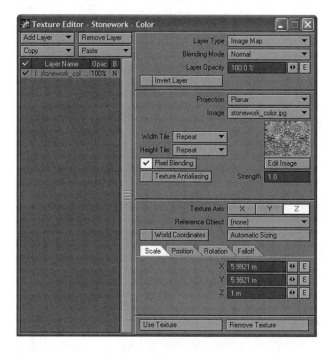

Figure 7.50   Applying image maps is like wallpapering in 3D.

Now, your texture surface is set up, but you have a few more things to do.

17. Go to the top of the Texture Editor interface and choose the Copy drop-down list. Select the Selected Layer choice, as in Figure 7.51. Then, click Use Texture to close the panel.

Copying the Current Layer enables you to apply all these settings to another aspect of the surface, such as a bump map.

18. Back in LightWave's Layout window, select the single light in the scene. Press 5 on the keyboard to switch to Light View. Position the light so that it shines across the stonework object.

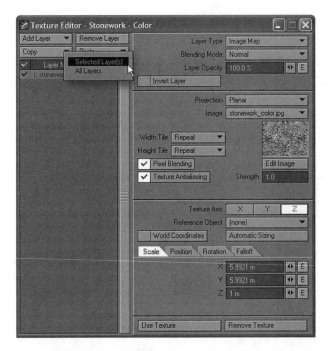

Figure 7.51 After you've laid out your Texture Editor parameters, you can copy the settings.

Change the light to a spotlight from the Lights properties panel. Also, move the light up and back slightly to fully illuminate the object. Press the Enter key twice to create a keyframe and lock the light in place at frame 0. Figure 7.52 shows the view from the light.

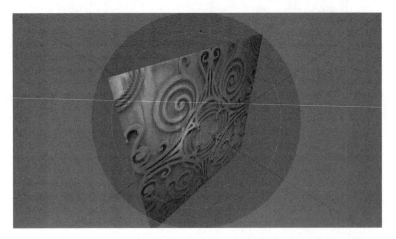

Figure 7.52 It's best to set your lights from the Light View to clearly see where you're pointing it. Here, the default light is made into a spotlight and moved up and pointed down across the object.

Important

If you can't see your texture applied in Layout, press the d key to call up the Display Options panel. Make sure that OpenGL Textures is turned on. Also, you can set the Texture Resolution in here, so that your image in Layout is not pixilated. Note that this has nothing to do with your surfacing or final render—it's a visual display option only.

19. Press F9 on your keyboard to see the stonework image with an image map applied. Figure 7.53 shows the render thus far.

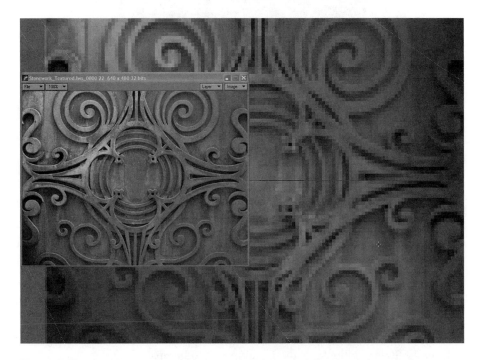

Figure 7.53   An image map applied to a single polygon with just one light applied.

Tip

Be sure that your Render Display is set to Image Viewer within the Render Options panel to see the F9 render. This makes the full frame appear after the render is complete.

20. Before you go any further, click the File drop-down list at the top of the Layout interface, select Save Object Copy, and save the object to your hard drive. From this point on, you can use Save All Objects from the Save drop-down list on the left side of the screen (see Figure 7.54). This saves the surface properties to your object thus far.

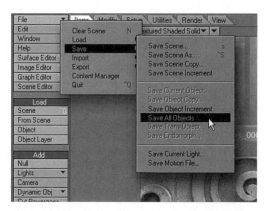

Figure 7.54   Make sure you select Save All Objects to keep the surface settings attached to the object for future use. If you don't do this, the next time you load the object, it will be blank, as it was when you started this section.

Applying Bump and Specularity to a Surface

The rendered result at this point doesn't look like much, does it? It looks like you just went through a lot of steps to create a rendered image that looks just like the original image. But in LightWave, you can apply as many textures as you'd like, and you can use the Texture Editor in other areas to do so.

Exercise 7.7   Using the Texture Editor

To use the Texture Editor for Bump mapping, follow these steps:

1. In the Surface Editor, click the T button next to Bump.

   The Texture Editor appears again. Although this is the same editor where you applied a Color texture, it has different results here. Instead of resetting all the same parameters, you only need to paste them. Remember the Copy Current Layer command you selected earlier? This copied all the Texture Editor settings for Color.

2. From the top of the Texture Editor interface, choose Paste and then Replace Current Layer.

   All the parameters are now aligned.

You'll see that the same stonework image has been loaded into the thumbnail window. Changes only need to be made to two areas, which is easier than changing all the settings. This is why you copied and pasted the settings.

3. For the Image in the Bump Texture Editor, click the drop-down and select Load Image. Load the stonework_bump file from the book's DVD. Figure 7.55 shows the change.

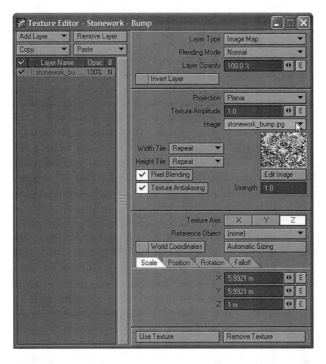

Figure 7.55   Load a new image for the bump map while using the same settings from the Color Texture.

Although you could very easily take the color out of the existing image in LightWave's Image Editor, this bump map has already been created for you with Adobe Photoshop. It's a high contrast black and white image, with the size and shape remaining the same.

By copying the color texture you created and pasting it as the bump, you're copying all the same settings. This is specifically important for the size of the image. If the size is slightly off when the bump map is applied, the image can look blurred, and the effect is lost.

The next step is to set the Texture Amplitude for the Bump Map.

About Bump Maps

Bump mapping is a way of creating surface detail. It is a shading function that perturbs the surface of an object, not the physical geometry, even though it appears to affect the physical geometry. Using a grayscale image interprets the incident light angles, the dark areas less and brighter areas more, although you can use color images because LightWave ignores the color data. However, if you're creating the bump map in an image-editing program, it's often easier to see the specific grayscale value.

You can also apply LightWave's Bump Displacement feature. This takes the bump map, which only changes the surface appearance, and applies a physical change to the surface, thereby enhancing the 3D effect even more. You can access this feature in the Deformations tab of the Object Properties panel. However, it's best to have at least a multisegmented object, or better, a SubPatched object for this feature. The object you've been using in this chapter is only one polygon and can't benefit from Bump Displacement. You'll learn about SubPatches in Chapter 9, "Simple Modeling and Animation." Right now, follow the next few steps to apply a Bump Map from the Surface Editor, which will help give depth to the appearance of the surface.

Exercise 7.8   Applying a Bump Map

1. In the Bump Map Texture Editor, set the Texture Amplitude to 6.0. Essentially, this is the amount of Bump the Texture Editor applies.

2. Now copy this surface as you did earlier from the top left of the panel and then click Use Texture at the bottom.

3. Be sure to select Save All Objects again and then press F9 to render a test frame.

   Figure 7.56 shows the surface with both Color and Bump maps applied.

Tip

It is not always necessary to use a grayscale image for bump mapping. If your color image has good variations in contrast, it will often work well as a bump map image.

4. With the bump texture copied, enter the Texture Editor (T) for Specularity.

   This is where you can take an average surface and make it exceptional. Because you copied the bump texture, simply paste it here. You are not trying to apply the bump map as a Specularity texture; that isn't how it works. By copying, you are taking the grayscale value of the image and its settings, such as size and position. Copying saves you the trouble of resetting all the values.

Figure 7.56   By adding a bump map to the surface, the surface starts to take on more depth.

5. Paste the copied surface to the current layer in the Specularity Texture Editor. This uses the same settings but makes the surface shinier where the image is brighter and less shiny where the image is darker. Click Use Texture to close the panel.

The last step you need to take to make this surface look great is to adjust the Specularity and Glossiness.

6. Move the light in a bit to create more of a streak across the object.

7. Leave the Specularity at 0% and set the Glossiness to roughly 15% or 20%.

Because the Specularity Texture Layer Opacity is set to 100%, the base (the 0% setting) is meaningless. This creates a nice wide gloss on the surface. However, you can play with the amounts to find a setting you might like more.

Figure 7.57 shows the three textures applied to the single surface, which is just one polygon. You can load this scene, stonework_textured, from this book's DVD. The bump map's amplitude might be a little high in the render, and it's something you can play around with for your own results. Changing specularity can instantly change the image from a wrought iron look to dull carving. Try it out!

Important

In the Camera panel, Antialiasing was set to Medium for Figure 7.57's render. This helps clean up any noise you might see in your render.

Figure 7.57 Adding a Specularity texture map helps bring this surface to life, all from a flat image. You've taken flat dull stone and made it look like wrought iron.

Specularity maps are useful any time you have bump maps. If you look at even the slight imperfections on your desktop or your computer monitor, you can see that there are bumps, but the light falls in and out of them. This is what a Specularity map does for your surface. Similarly to the bump map properties, it also bases its calculations on the grayscale image—the darker areas do not allow as much Specularity, where the lighter areas allow more.

The techniques are a foundation for your entire real-world surfacing projects. Anything from a plastic toy to a telephone to a dirt road can benefit from setting these three texture maps. As another example, read on to create a dirty metal surface with a few more involved steps.

Gradients for Added Aging

You also can use LightWave's gradients to apply specularity maps and help control contrasts. Surfacing the watch object earlier in the chapter was relatively simple. You used basic, everyday surfacing techniques and a couple of simple reflection images. This is great for logos and colored balls, but in today's marketplace, if you want to stay competitive, you need to make things look not so clean. In the early days of 3D animation, shine and reflection were big crowd pleasers, but now it's a different story, and you need to be aware of it. The trick is to use LightWave's Surface Editor to apply texture maps, bump maps, and procedurals to achieve the "not-so-perfect" surface.

What happens when you need to create a dirty and rusty piece of metal pipe? Fortunately, you can apply these surfacing techniques to anything you want, such as metal grates, steel, wood, fences, bricks, and much more. How? You can use image maps as you've seen, as well as procedurals for added dirt. But you can go even further with gradients. When you begin creating a 3D object, you most often work from some sort of reference, whether it's a physical model or a photograph.

The same idea applies to surfacing your model, but most people don't consider it. When you begin to surface an object, you will save yourself hours of frustration and many headaches by having a photograph or digital image of the surface you want to create. In this particular case, an image has been photographed and scanned into a computer at a high resolution. This single image is used as a reference to create an entire 3D surface. Essentially, you'll use the steps to create a 3D surface presented earlier, but you will take it further by adding noise and dirt.

There are a number of resources available to you for gathering image maps. One of the best resources is your own eye and a camera. Taking photographs of the world around you is the best way to get original and real textures into your 3D environment. Not to mention, they are your images, and they're royalty-free. You don't need an expensive digital camera; you can certainly use a traditional 35 mm film camera. Most digital cameras today produce excellent quality images. If you are using images in 3D for surfacing, you should always go for the highest quality. However, the quality of film sometimes has a much nicer look to it than digital images, especially when applied as image maps. Not to go unmentioned is the Kodak PhotoCD. You can have any of your photographs created on a PhotoCD that can be read in your computer's CD-ROM drive. Check your local photo shop for more information.

If you can't take your own photos, you can buy some wonderful sets of real-world textures. Marlin Studios (www.marlinstudios.com) has more than half a dozen CDs available with some of the best-looking rocks, foliage, wood, and more available today. A few sample images are provided for you on this book's DVD to experiment with.

To achieve a complex look from a base image, you can use LightWave's Layered surfaces in combination with your base image. Exercise 7.9 shows you the techniques to use LightWave's powerful texture layers to blend multiple textures on a single surface using a gradient.

LightWave's Texture Editor looks simple at first, but it actually offers extensive control. The next tutorial builds on the previous one.

Exercise 7.9   Blending Multiple Textures

1. Make sure you have the previous scene still loaded in Layout. If not, load the stonework_textured scene from this book's DVD. Also open VIPER from the Render menu tab in Layout. Do a quick F9 render to get the scene info into LightWave's internal buffers so VIPER can do its thing.

2. Open the Surface Editor, select the stonework surface, and click the T button next to Color.

    All the default values in the Texture Editor are settings you can use. The Layer Type is an Image Map, the Blending Mode is Normal, Layer Opacity is 100%, and because the object is flat in front of the camera, you want the Projection set to Planar. This is everything you've already set up.

3. From the Add Layer drop-down list at the top of the Texture Editor panel, select Gradient.

    A tall white bar appears, as in Figure 7.58.

4. Click in the middle of the gradient bar to create a key.

Important

Gradients are very powerful tools for LightWave surfacing. The tall bar you see works from the top down. That is to say, the top is the bottom of your surface (though this varies depending on what you set up). It's important to pay attention to where you apply your gradients—in other words, Color, Bump, and so on, as well as the Input Parameter you choose.

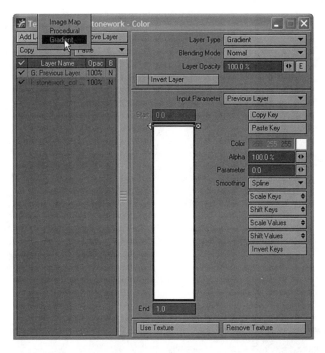

Figure 7.58   Adding a gradient offers additional control to your image mapped surface.

 Important

When you create a key in the gradient bar, you're able to make changes to the values you're applying. If you bring the Alpha value to 0%, you'll fade out the previous layer. Why previous layer? Take a look in the panel, and you'll see the Input Parameter setting defaults to Previous Layer, which is of course the image map you applied earlier. Figure 7.59 shows VIPER with the Gradient applied.

5. Take this further—keep the Alpha for the key at 0%. Select the key at the top of the gradient bar and change the color to a dull green.

6. Make sure the Input Parameter is set to Bump. This tells the gradient to use the bump map you've applied as its value for placement. This means the green color you're applying is added based on the highs and lows of the black and white bump map image.

7. Add one more key, but set its color to a greenish yellow. Figure 7.60 shows the setup with VIPER. You've now created an aged coloring underneath the bumped carvings.

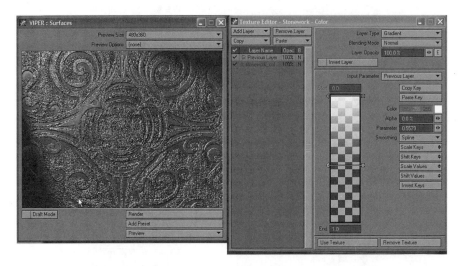

Figure 7.59 A gradient applied to the image map enables you to vary how the image map looks.

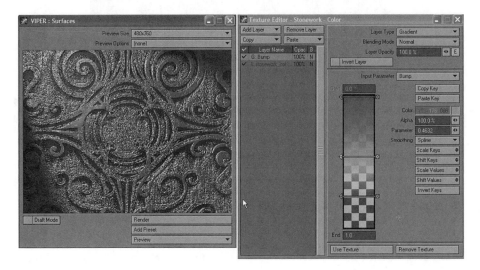

Figure 7.60 Changing the color of the top gradient key, along with the input parameter, creates a moss-like growth on the image.

Remember, this is still just a single polygon in Layout, with an image map applied from a digital camera. The rest is LightWave's Surface Editor. Now, you've only added a single image with one gradient. You can add more images, add more gradients, and apply procedurals until the cows come home. It's virtually limitless what you can do with these tools.

Tip

This will be the only mention of cows in this book.

You should know that LightWave's surface layers are stacked on top of each other. You can obscure lower layers if the upper layers show through, either by using Layer Opacity or setting certain procedural textures. All procedurals have some portion of the texture that is less than 100% (otherwise, it would be solid). Essentially, the darker parts are less than 100% and let the underlying layers show through. Gradients talk to other layers through the input parameter settings. You can quickly turn a texture layer on or off by clicking the check mark next to the listing within the panel.

The Next Step

From this point on, you can experiment on your own. Add more layers, play with gradients, and adjust procedurals. As a matter of fact, add as many as you like. Your only limitations are time and system memory! Try adding some of the other Procedural surfaces, such as Smokey, Turbulence, or Crust. Keep adding these to your rusty metal surface to see what you can come up with. Now if you remember the copy and paste commands you used earlier with the Bump mapped marble tutorial, you can repeat those same steps. Try selecting Copy All Layers from the Color Texture and applying them as Bump and Specularity textures. The results are endless. In addition, try applying LightWave's powerful surface shaders. For a complete list of the Shader plug-ins, refer to Appendix A, "Plug-in List," at the back of this book.

This chapter gave you a broad overview of the main features within LightWave's Surface Editor, including the Texture Editor. There are literally countless surfaces in the world around us, and it's up to you to create them digitally. As the book progresses, you will use the information and instructions in this chapter to create even more complex and original surfaces such as glass, skin, metal, and more. The next chapter takes you deeper into the power of LightWave—read on to discover the cinematic tools available to you.

Chapter 8

Cinematic Tools

One of the most overlooked features—not just in LightWave but in any 3D application—is the camera. When filmmakers create motion pictures, they block out their shots before shooting. Animators, on the other hand, often set up everything and then put the camera in. The camera should be an integral part of the animation process. Of course, you know better and want to read this chapter to learn all about the cameras in LightWave 8 so that you can plan your 3D camera shots, right?

Learning the art of 3D animation involves more than creating models, applying textures, and setting keyframes. 3D animation is an art form all its own, and it's still in its infancy. Part of learning this new and fascinating art form is understanding the digital camera. Not the kind of digital camera you pick up at the local electronics store, but the kind *inside* the computer software—it's your digital eye.

This chapter introduces you to everyday camera techniques that you can apply to your LightWave animations. The camera in LightWave is a significant part of every animation you create, from simple pans to dollies and zooms to dutch angles. If you have any experience in photography or videography, the transition to "shooting" in LightWave will be smooth. LightWave has always been a digital studio, and just like in a television studio or on a movie set, you can set up more than one camera in your scenes. This chapter instructs you on many topics, such as the following:

- Working with the 3D camera
- Exploring real-world camera settings
- Applying 3D cameras

Setting Up Cameras in LightWave

At this point, you're probably familiar with LightWave's workflow. As you work through Layout, you'll become familiar with the various Properties panels associated with objects and lights. The Camera Properties panel controls all the necessary camera settings, such as resolution, focal length, depth of field, masking, and more. You won't find render options in this panel. Those are located under the Render menu tab. Some programs, such as Adobe After Effects, contain all camera, resolution, and output information in the same panel. LightWave does not.

Look at the Camera Properties panel in Layout. Figure 8.1 shows the Camera Properties panel, accessed by first selecting the Cameras mode button at the bottom of the Layout interface and then clicking the Item Properties button (or pressing the p key).

Near the top of the Camera Properties panel, you'll see an item labeled Resolution. Figure 8.2 shows the selections that are available in the Resolution drop-down list.

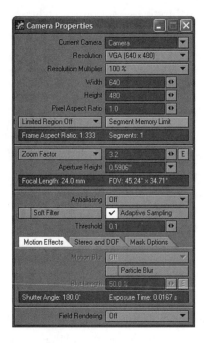

Figure 8.1   The LightWave 3D 8 Camera Properties panel.

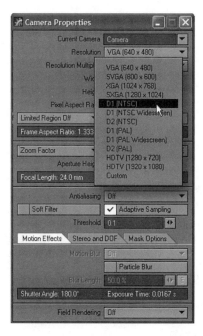

Figure 8.2   LightWave offers a wide range of camera resolutions for your animations.

Working with Cameras

Working with cameras in LightWave is easy. They are not only easy to use, but they are also easy to set up. Creative camera use can be very useful for any type of scene, moving or still. More specifically, you can use multiple cameras when you have a large scene that has action that needs to be covered from various angles, such as a stage play, virtual walk-through, or an accident re-creation. Multiple cameras can help you save time setting up animations that need to be viewed from different angles. Using the Camera Selector plug-in from the Master Plug-ins, you can switch between specific cameras during rendering. Also, you can render passes from any camera in the scene. Start here to begin working more specifically with cameras in LightWave.

Exercise 8.1   Working with Cameras

1. From the File menu in Layout at the upper left of the interface, select Clear Scene. Of course, save any work you might have done first!

2. Select the Items menu; under the Add category, click Camera, as shown in Figure 8.3.

You now have two cameras in the scene: the default camera that's always in a blank scene and the camera you just added.

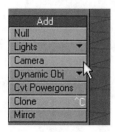

Figure 8.3 LightWave always has one camera in the scene, but you can add many more.

When you select Add Camera, a small panel comes up, asking you for a name. Clicking OK keeps the camera name as "Camera," which appears with a number next to it, such as "Camera (2)," for the second camera added, and so on.

You can choose whether to rename the cameras you add at that time, or you can always rename them later. Clicking OK sets the default name.

3. Click OK to add another camera to Layout.

You want to set up your cameras, but first you must select a specific camera.

With multiple cameras in a scene, you need to choose which camera you are currently using. Adding, selecting, or deleting cameras is the same as selecting any other scene item, such as objects or lights.

4. Select the camera by first clicking the Cameras button at the bottom of the interface.

5. From the Current Item selection, choose which camera you want to use.

6. To rename a camera, select the Replace command from the Replace category under the Items tab.

Whether you are working with one camera, two cameras, or ten, the settings are the same. Simply point and shoot! To get the most out of multiple cameras, set them up in a way that will be most beneficial to your animation. For example, suppose that you need to re-create a traffic accident and the client wants to see the accident from a bystander's viewpoint, an aerial viewpoint, and the driver's viewpoint. By adding three cameras to your scene and setting them in the desired positions, you can render the animation from any view. Try it!

Setting Camera Resolution

After you've chosen the current camera you want to work with, setting the Resolution is commonly the first setting you apply in the Camera Properties panel. This setting determines the width and height of your rendered images. LightWave also will set the appropriate pixel aspect of your rendered images when a specific resolution is set.

Tip

Rendering is a generic term for creating or drawing an image. This is done in LightWave by pressing the F9 key for single frames (Render Current Frame) and F10 for multiple frames (Render Scene).

The resolution you choose in the Camera Properties panel determines the final output size of your images and animations. The default resolution is VGA mode, which is 640 pixels wide by 480 pixels tall. This resolution is of a medium size, which is common for most computer work. You also can choose SVGA, which is 800 by 600 pixels, or XVGA, which is 1024 by 768 pixels. These are good resolutions to work with if your images or animations are being used in a computer environment, such as in QuickTime or AVI formats. Although these three resolutions might be too large for most QuickTime or AVI files, you can use the Resolution Multiplier to change the output size, which is discussed later in this chapter.

Tip

QuickTime is Apple Computer's basic multimedia application and format, now common on both Macintosh and Windows computers. Rendering an animation to a QuickTime movie creates a playable computer file. AVI (Audio Video Interleaved), developed by Microsoft, is another type of compressed audio/video format. Each has varying levels of compression, so check with your particular computer system for your ideal setting.

If you are creating animations that will end up on videotape, you'll want to use the D1 or D2 NTSC resolution settings (in the United States), or the D1 or D2 PAL resolution settings (in Europe).

Tip

In 1953, the National Television Standards Committee (NTSC) developed the North American television broadcast standard. This standard is 60 half frames, or fields, per second, with 525 lines of resolution. PAL stands for Phase Alternate Line. This standard, which most of Western Europe uses, is 625 lines of resolution at 50 fields per second.

Setting the Resolution Multiplier

A great time-saving feature in LightWave is the Resolution Multiplier. This feature is beneficial because it can help you more accurately set up animations in different sizes. It is handy in instances in which you've created an animation in low resolution (to work faster) but then you begin rendering in a higher resolution (for quality) and you do not achieve the same results. For example, suppose that you've created a scene that uses a lot of stars, made with small individual points. You set your resolution to a low setting to make sure that your test renders quickly. The individual points are modified and adjusted to look right. But when you choose a higher resolution, the stars are barely visible. This happens because the actual resolution of the image is changing. What looks large on a small image is not the same size on a larger image. This problem also occurs when setting up lens flares. LightWave's Resolution Multiplier, as shown in Figure 8.4, keeps the same resolution settings but multiplies the value by 25%, 50%, 100%, 200%, or 400%. 100% renders an image the exact size of the set width and height, whereas 50% renders an image half the size.

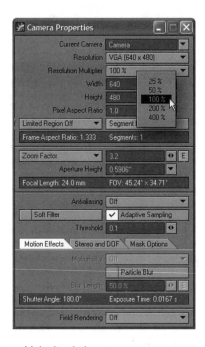

Figure 8.4 The Resolution Multiplier helps give you an accurate view of your render at smaller or larger sizes.

Understanding Pixel Aspect Ratio

Throughout most of your animations, setting the appropriate resolution automatically sets the proper pixel aspect ratio. By default, LightWave shows the Perspective view. The difference between VGA modes and D1 or D2 modes, aside from the resolution difference, is the pixel aspect ratio. The *pixel aspect ratio* is the shape of the individual pixels the computer draws. A *pixel* is a tiny picture element that is square or rectangular and is comprised of colored dots that make up the computer graphic image. Computer images use square pixels, which means a pixel aspect ratio of 1.0. Television images, generally 720 by 486, or 349,920 pixels, use rectangular pixels. NTSC D1 video is 0.9 pixels tall. Because the pixel aspect ratio is the ratio of the width to the height, a pixel aspect ratio of 0.9 yields a pixel that is narrower than it is tall.

To see the change in camera settings, you need to switch from Layout to Camera view. Pixel aspect ratio (PAR) is merely the shape of the pixel on the target display device. If the images will be viewed on a PC, you always want 1.0 because PCs use square pixels. If the images will be shown on a video device, such as television with a 4:3 screen ratio, you need a PAR that is .86 to .9.

For example, suppose that you have a perfect square in your image. If you use a PAR of 1.0, LightWave renders the square using the same number of pixels for its width and height. This looks cool on your PC monitor, but if you show the image on a TV, it looks tall. This is because televisions have tall pixels and although the same number of pixels make up the square's height and width, because they are "tall" they make the box tall. You need to compensate for this. If you use a PAR of .9, LightWave automatically scales the pixels it uses to make the image with the assumption of "tall" pixels. A television pixel aspect ratio might not always be exactly .9, but it won't be 1.0.

Exercise 8.2   Working with Aspect Ratios

To give you an idea of how the different aspect ratios work, open LightWave Layout and perform the following steps.

1. Select Camera View in the selection mode at the top of the Layout window, as shown in Figure 8.5.

   Remember that, although resolution settings can be seen directly in Layout, you won't see the stretching due to an incorrect PAR in Layout. Rather, it merely shows you what portions of the scene will be in the rendered image. It is the projection of this image on the display device that causes the stretching, if any.

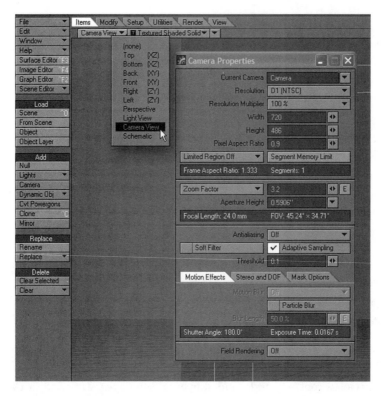

Figure 8.5 Resolution and the results of setting the pixel aspect ratios can be seen only through the Camera view in Layout.

> ⚠️ **Important**
>
> Safe areas are important to use as shot references. The outer line represents the video safe area—any animation elements outside this area will not be visible on a standard 4:3 ratio television monitor. The inner line represents the title safe area, and any text in your animations should not travel beyond this bounding region. Video has something called *overscan*, and the area you're not seeing is within this region. Broadcast monitors allow you to view overscan, but standard 4:3 televisions do not. Keeping within these guidelines will help your relationship with video editors as well.

2. To make sure that Show Safe Areas is selected, press the d key to enter the Display Options tab.

3. Select Show Safe Areas under the Camera View tab at the bottom of the interface, as shown in Figure 8.6.

Figure 8.6 Selecting Show Safe Areas from the Display Options tab turns on a visible outline through the Camera view in Layout.

4. Close the Display Options panel by pressing the d key again, or p (for panel).

Figure 8.7 shows the Camera view with the safe areas enabled, with a scene loaded from Chapter 6. This safe area represents the title safe and video safe areas of your view. You should set up animations with this feature enabled to ensure that your animation is viewed properly when recorded to videotape.

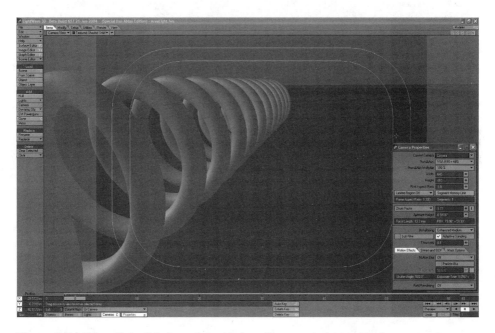

Figure 8.7 When Show Safe Areas is enabled, you'll see a television-style shape around your field of view through the camera.

Tip

You can change the color of the safe area outlines by changing the overlay color selection in the Display Options tab (press d) of the Preferences panel. Doing this also changes the color of any overlays seen in the Camera view, such as field chart.

5. Select Camera from the bottom of Layout, and then choose the Properties panel, or press the p key. Move the Camera Properties panel over to the far right of the screen, revealing more of your Layout window.

6. Go to the Resolution drop-down list and select D1 (NTSC Widescreen), as shown in Figure 8.8.

   This resolution changes the width to 720 and the height to 486, with a pixel aspect ratio of 1.2.

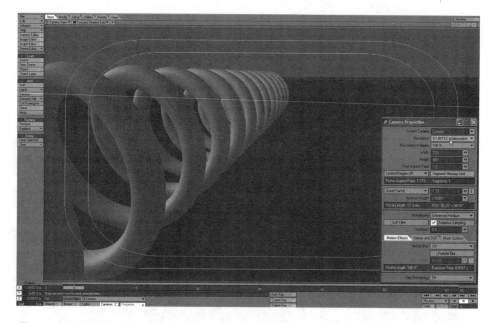

Figure 8.8 You have a number of choices when it comes to resolution, such as LightWave's widescreen settings. Setting a resolution to D1 NTSC Widescreen changes the pixel aspect ratio to 1.2, making the safe area viewed through the Camera panel appear stretched.

7. Press the p key to close the Camera Properties panel if it's cluttering your workspace. Otherwise, feel free to leave it open.

   You can see in Figure 8.8 that the safe areas now appear stretched with the widescreen resolution option.

8. Press p again to open the Camera Properties panel. Grab the slider button next to Pixel Aspect Ratio and drag it back and forth.

   Figure 8.9 shows the slider button. You should see the safe area field of view changing in Layout.

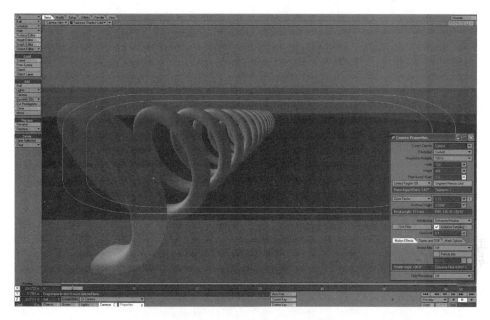

Figure 8.9   You can interactively control pixel aspect ratio by clicking and dragging the small slider buttons.

As an animator, you need to know that the pixel aspect ratio affects your renderings. Changing the resolution changes the size of the image, whereas changing the pixel aspect ratio changes the target pixel shape, which also can distort your final output if it is not set properly. Always remember what the target display device is, such as a video recorder, and set your resolution and aspect ratio accordingly. For example, if you are rendering an animation for video and accidentally set to D1 NTSC Widescreen resolution, your final animation when imported into an animation recorder or nonlinear editor will appear stretched. The computer will take the full image and squeeze it to fit the television-size frame your nonlinear editor or animation recorder uses. This happens because widescreen resolution is the incorrect resolution for the standard video recorder. Because setting resolution also sets the pixel aspect ratio, both are the wrong version for widescreen to video.

Setting Limited Region

Every now and then, there might be a situation in which the resolution settings are not the exact size you need for rendering. You sometimes might need to render just an area of an animation, saving valuable time rendering. For example, if you have an animation that has many objects, textures, reflections, and more, test-rendering the full image might take up too much of your time—especially if you want to see how one small area of the scene looks in the final render. Using the Limited Region setting helps you accomplish this. Figure 8.10 shows the selection in the Camera Properties panel. You can have a limited region with or without borders.

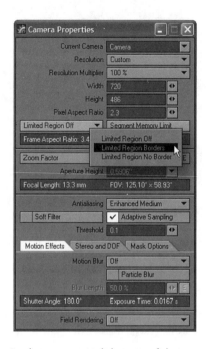

Figure 8.10   Limited Region lets you control the area of the screen to be rendered.

When using Limited Region, you can easily turn on a limited region directly in Layout by pressing the L key. A yellow dotted line appears, encompassing the entire Layout area. From here, you can click the edge of the region and resize it to any desired shape. Figure 8.11 shows a limited region for a small area of a scene. Figure 8.12 shows how the image renders would look in the Render Display window with this Limited Region setting.

Limited region settings are also useful for creating images for websites using LightWave. Perhaps you want to animate a small spinning globe or a rotating 3D head. Rendering in a standard resolution draws unwanted areas, creating images that are not only the correct size, but also larger. Setting up a limited region can decrease file size and create renders in the exact size you need, such as a perfect square. Limited Region essentially renders a portion of what normally would be a larger image. Try using a Web GIF animation program and render out a series of small GIF files, set up with a limited region. The GIF animation program imports the sequence of images to create one playable file. Limited Region works differently from a custom resolution. A limited region can be made to any size visually and set for any area on the screen. Setting a custom resolution sets only the specific size for the center of the screen. Also, Limited Region enables you to render limited regions of very high-resolution images. A custom resolution would not work this way.

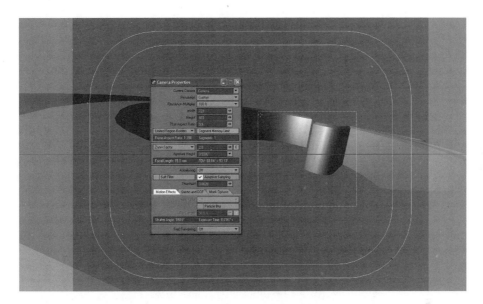

Figure 8.11   You can resize the limited region directly in Layout to render a selected area of the animation.

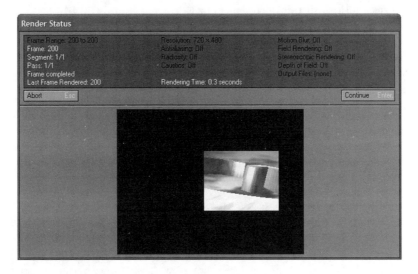

Figure 8.12   The Limited Region's rendered image is just the area assigned in Layout.

Tip

If you render an image or animation with the borders setting, the image will appear with a border that represents the rest of the un-rendered frame. Conversely, rendering with no borders displays only the limited region.

Segment Memory Limit

Too often, you'll run out of RAM while you are creating animations. RAM, or the memory in your computer, is used quickly by many images, large objects, and hefty render settings. The Segment Memory Limit feature lets you tell Layout the maximum amount of memory to use for rendering. Lower values allow you to render a frame in segments, which means the frames might take a bit longer to load and execute. The tradeoff is that you don't need as much memory.

For faster renders, you can increase the segment memory. Setting the segment memory to 20 megabytes, or 20MB of RAM, often enables you to render D1 NTSC resolution in one segment. Although this setting is only an example, LightWave's Segment Memory setting is a maximum setting. This means you can set this value to the same amount of RAM in your system, and LightWave will only use what it needs, often eliminating the need for your system to use virtual memory or a scratch disk.

Important

Remember that higher resolution settings require more memory.

When you click the Segment Memory button, a small panel pops up, asking you to enter a value. You can enter a value as large as you want, provided you have the memory in your system. When you click OK, LightWave asks whether you want to make this value the default. Click Yes, and you won't have to change this value when you start creating another animation scene. Figure 8.13 shows the Segment Memory selection in the Camera Properties panel.

Figure 8.13 Setting a segment memory limit tells LightWave how much memory is available for rendering. Setting a higher value allows LightWave to render animation frames in one pass.

Rename and Select Current Camera

Because LightWave allows you to add more than one camera to your scene, you need a way to select them to adjust each item's properties. The Current Camera selection list is at the top of the Camera Properties panel. If you have not added any cameras to your scene, you will see only the item "Camera." Like the Light Properties panel, you can select and rename this camera (or any you've added) directly in the Camera panel. If you have added multiple cameras, they will be listed here, displayed as Camera (1), Camera (2), and so on, if you have not set a name for them, as shown in Figure 8.14. Cameras added with names also appear in the list. Just click the drop-down next to the Current Camera listing to select the desired camera. These cameras listed are all available for selection in the Current Item selection list at the bottom of the Layout interface as well.

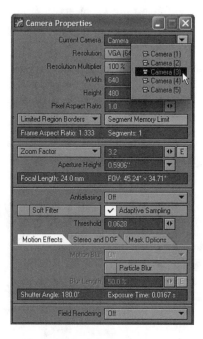

Figure 8.14 All of your scene's cameras can be selected within the Camera Properties panel, from the Current Camera selection list.

Zoom Factor

The Zoom Factor option is a misunderstood, and therefore overlooked, feature when it comes to working with cameras in LightWave. Essentially, the zoom factor is the camera's lens. Have you ever worked with a telephoto zoom lens on a real camera? This is the same thing, only in a virtual world. Pretend that you are videotaping a family party with your camcorder. You probably pan around and constantly zoom in and out to cover the action. In LightWave, you can do the same thing! Changing the zoom factor over time not only gives your animation a different look but also adds variation to your animations.

The default zoom factor is 3.2, as shown in Figure 8.15.

Figure 8.15   LightWave's default zoom factor is 3.2, or the equivalent of a 24mm focal length.

The 3.2 zoom factor setting is fine for most projects, but to make something come alive in 3D, you should lower this value. The 3.2 setting is equivalent to a focal length of 24mm, or an average camera lens. Figure 8.16 shows a scene with the default zoom factor setting. The image looks good, but the scene lacks depth. But take a look at Figure 8.17, where the same shot has a zoom factor of 1.5. Notice how wide the shot looks and how much depth is in the image. Now the image looks three-dimensional. This setting is only an example, and you should try different zoom factors on your own to see what works best for you. Note that in these two figures, the camera has not been moved; only the zoom factor has been adjusted.

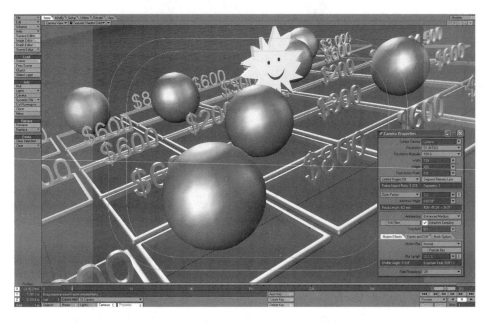

Figure 8.16   A scene set up with the default zoom factor of 3.2 looks fine but lacks depth.

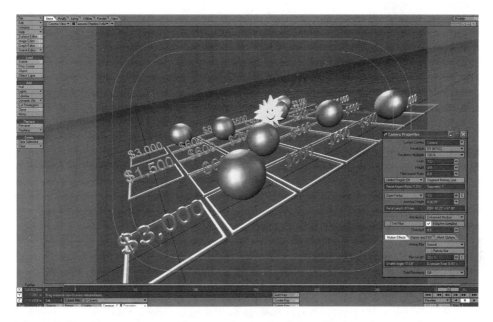

Figure 8.17   The same scene with a zoom factor of 1.5 gives the shot a lot more dimension-
ality and makes it much more interesting.

The cameras in LightWave are just as important as your objects. Don't overlook the possibilities of changing the zoom factor over time. Using LightWave's Graph Editor, you
can animate the zoom factor with stunning results.

Using Focal Length

The zoom factor in LightWave directly relates to lens focal lengths—the focal length itself
is measured in millimeters. The larger the focal length value, the longer the lens. For
example, a telephoto lens might be 180mm, and a wide-angle lens might be 12mm.
Because focal lengths represent everyday camera settings, just like your 35mm camera,
you may be more comfortable working with lens focal lengths instead of zoom factors.
You can do this by selecting the desired option from the Zoom Factor drop-down list.
Once chosen, you can see your setting in the camera panel, as shown in Figure 8.18.

Figure 8.18   You have the option to choose Lens Focal Length instead of Zoom Factor in
the Camera Properties panel.

Important

Each camera you add to Layout can have different zoom factors. For example, in the Camera Properties panel, you can select one camera and set the zoom factor so that it renders like a telephoto lens. Then, you can select another camera in the Camera Properties panel and make it render like a wide-angle lens. Each camera in LightWave can be set differently.

Field of View (FOV)

In addition to zoom factor and lens focal length, you can set up a camera's field of view (FOV) using the Horizontal FOV or Vertical FOV settings. Changing the values for zoom factor automatically adjusts the lens focal length, the horizontal FOV, and the vertical FOV. The horizontal and vertical fields of view give you precise control over the lens in LightWave. The two values listed next to FOV are the horizontal and vertical fields, horizontal being the first value. Working with FOV is useful when you are working in real-world situations and need to match camera focal lengths, especially when compositing.

Don't let all these settings confuse you, however. The Zoom Factor, Lens Focal Length, Horizontal FOV, and Vertical FOV settings all enable you to set the same thing. Simply use the one you're most familiar or most comfortable with—or choose whatever is called for to match a real-world camera. There is no inherent benefit in using one over the other.

Antialiasing

When you render an animation, it needs to look good. The edges need to be clean and smooth, and no matter how much quality you put into your models, surfaces, lighting, and camera technique, you won't have a perfect render until you set the antialiasing. Antialiasing cures the jagged edges between foreground and background elements. It is a smoothing process that creates cleaner-looking animations. Figure 8.19 shows a rendered image without antialiasing. Figure 8.20 shows the same image with a low antialiasing setting applied.

Figure 8.19   Without antialiasing, the rendered image can look jagged and unprofessional, especially when animated. Notice the bricks are hard to identify in the smaller areas. Lines along the roof are stair stepped.

Figure 8.20   After antialiasing is applied, even at a low setting, the image looks cleaner and more polished. You'll see that the bricks are clean and easy to make out. The lines along the walls and roof are sharp and clean.

Antialiasing can really make a difference in your final renders. Figure 8.21 shows the available Antialiasing settings.

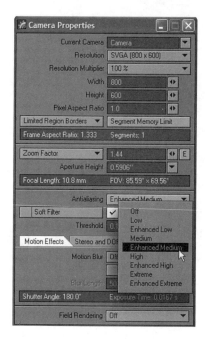

Figure 8.21 You can choose from a range of antialiasing settings, from none at all to Enhanced Extreme.

The higher the antialiasing setting, the more LightWave will clean and smooth your polygon edges. Of course, higher values mean added rendering time. Any of the Enhanced antialiasing settings smoothes your image at the sub-pixel level, which takes a bit more time to render, but it produces better results. In most cases, Medium to Enhanced Medium antialiasing produces great results.

Adaptive Sampling

Although you can set up an antialiasing routine for your renders, you still have to tell LightWave how it should be applied. Adaptive sampling is a flexible threshold that LightWave employs to evaluate the edges in your scene. Lower values evaluate more, enabling a more accurate antialiasing routine. Higher values evaluate less. A default setting of 0.1 is an average threshold value. Changing this to 0.01, for example, adds to your render times but helps to produce a cleaner render. A good way to work with adaptive sampling is to set a higher antialiasing setting, with a not-so-low threshold. For example, Enhanced Medium antialiasing, with a Threshold of 0.1, renders reasonably well (depending on your scene) and produces nice-looking images. For more details on adaptive sampling, refer to your LightWave manual.

Soft Filter

As an additional help to eliminate sharp, unwanted edges in a scene, you can turn on the Soft Filter option in the Camera Properties panel. As an alternative to setting higher antialiasing routines, you can set a lower antialiasing with Soft Filter applied. Soft Filter adds a small blur to your render, creating a soft look. Be careful using this as it may make your render appear too blurry. Its settings are either on or off. Sorry, no variable amounts!

Motion Effects

At the bottom of the Camera Properties panel, there are three tabs. Each tab offers even more control over your camera's settings. The first tab, Motion Effects, is home to some common, everyday functions like motion blur.

Motion Blur

When antialiasing is turned on (set to at least low), the Motion Blur option becomes available. From time to time, you may need to create motions that mimic real-world properties, such as a speeding car or a fast-moving camera. To give things a more realistic look, you can apply motion blur to your scene. Motion blur in LightWave combines several semi-dissolved images on each frame to give the effect of blurred motion. Motion blur mimics real-world actions. Remember that the multiple rendering passes used with antialiasing are needed to compute the dissolved images, which is why antialiasing needs to be set to low or higher. But, you can quickly see what your motion blur will look like right in Layout by pressing the MB Preview from the Render menu tab, or + and the F9 key together. You can see an example in Figure 8.22.

Motion blur should be used any time you have something fast-moving in your scene. Even if it's only a slight motion blur, the added effect will help "sell" the look. If your animation is perfectly clean, perfectly smooth, and always in focus, it won't look realistic. It will look better with some inconsistencies, such as motion blur.

Motion blur also is important to actions like a bee's wings flapping, an airplane's propellers, and so on. Many animated objects moving at this speed will require you to set Motion Blur. If you look at spinning propellers in the real world, all you see is a blur. To re-create that look in LightWave, turn on Motion Blur in the Camera Properties panel.

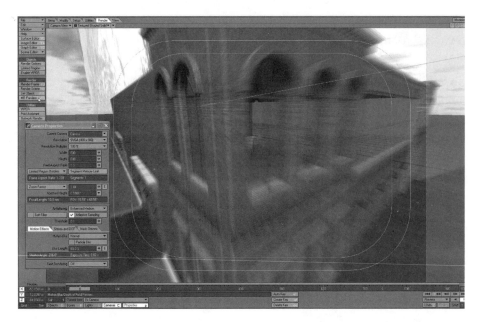

Figure 8.22 Motion blur is applied to a fast-zooming camera scene. Motion blur helps add the feeling of movement because in real-world cameras, the shutter speed is not fast enough to freeze the action.

Blur Length

Blur Length is the amount of motion blur you want to use. The default is set to 50%, which produces nice results. Depending on the animation, you may want to set this value slightly higher—for example, to 60% or 65%—for more blurring. When you apply the Blur Length setting, corresponding Shutter Angle and Exposure Time values appear beneath the Blur Length window. Most of your motion-blurred animations should have a 50% Blur Length set. This is because the blur length relates to the amount of time the theoretical film is actually exposed. Because of the physical mechanism, a film camera can't expose a frame for 1/24 of a second, even though film normally plays back at 24 frames per second. It turns out that this rotating shutter mechanism exposes the film for only 50% of the per-second rate; thus, 50% blur length is right on.

Particle Blur

Along the lines of Motion Blur is Particle Blur. Use this setting any time you have an animation whose particles need to blur, such as explosions, fast-moving stars, snow, rain, and so on. A blur length of 50% works well for particle blur.

Field Rendering

At the bottom of the Camera Properties panel is the Field Rendering selection. In NTSC video, there are 30 frames per second, or 60 fields per second. Applying field rendering to your animations is useful when your objects need to remain visible when moving swiftly and close to the camera. This setting is targeted for video, and it allows you to mimic the effect of video's interlaced fields. Motion will seem smoother on the video display. Field rendering makes the final output crisp and clean, especially when there are visible textures. Video draws half the frame first, or one field, and then the other half, or the second field. There are two fields per frame. You can set LightWave to render the even or odd fields first. Motion can occur between the time it takes to display these fields, just as it does from frame to frame, and applying field rendering accounts for this.

Stereo and Depth of Field (DOF)

Setting up additional camera properties can further enhance the final look of your animations. The second tab area at the bottom of the Camera Properties panel is the Stereo and DOF tab, as shown in Figure 8.23.

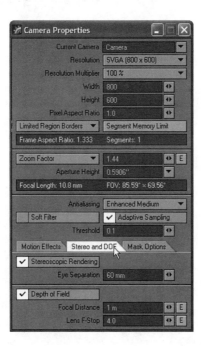

Figure 8.23   The Stereo and DOF tab offers stereoscopic rendering and depth of field functions to your cameras.

Stereoscopic Rendering

Within the Stereo and DOF tab in the Camera Properties panel, you can turn on Stereoscopic Rendering, which is yet another way for you to change the look of your animations. Applying this setting to your camera results in an image that looks separated, as though two images are blurred together. Simply put, this setting creates left and right stereoscopic image files. Changing the Eye Separation value tells LightWave how far apart to render the left and right stereo images. You can use this setting for various types of 3D imaging and even lintography.

Depth of Field

You see depth of field every time you look through a camera lens. It's used in movies, television, your own eyesight, and even animation. *Depth of field* (DOF) is defined as the range of distance in front of the camera that is in sharp focus. Depth of field is a fantastic way to add real depth to your animations. Without DOF, everything is in focus, as Figure 8.24 shows.

Figure 8.24 Without Depth of Field applied, everything in your scene is in focus.

By adding a DOF setting, you tell the camera where to focus. Anything before or after that focal point is out of focus. Figure 8.25 shows the same image with DOF applied. Notice how the building becomes out of focus farther away from the camera.

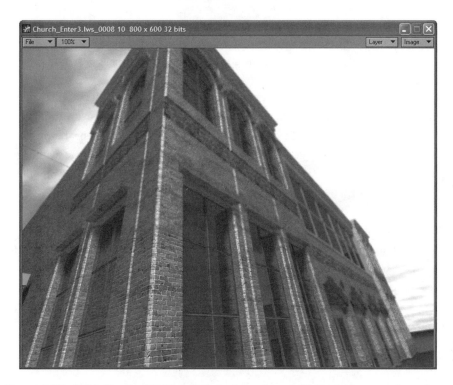

Figure 8.25   With Depth of Field applied, the image is out of focus farther away from the set focal point.

Depth of field can dramatically add to your LightWave renders because it enables you to set a focal distance for any of your LightWave cameras. The focal distance tells the camera in Layout where to focus when DOF is applied. The default setting is 1m. To use depth of field in your animations, you must have selected an Antialiasing setting of at least Medium quality.

Using LightWave's grid, which is the system of measurement in Layout, you can easily determine the focal distance from the camera to your objects in a scene. Figure 8.26 shows the information window in the bottom-left corner of the Layout interface. You'll see the grid measurement at the bottom. The default of 1m appears.

Figure 8.26 Using LightWave's grid measurement, you can easily determine where to set the focal distance from the camera to the objects in the scene.

The grid measurement relates to every square in the Layout grid. If the default grid size of 1m is present, each square of the grid in Layout equals 1m. Therefore, you can count the number of grids between the camera and the focal point in the scene. If you have a scene where the camera is 4 grid squares away from the front of the object, with a grid measurement of 1m, the focal distance setting should be 4m. This makes any object before or after the 4m mark out of focus.

Range Finder for DOF

You also can use a custom object to set depth of field. Simply add a Null object from the Items tab. Then, open the Object Properties for the Null (press p), and add a Custom Object called Range Finder (see Figure 8.27). Double-click the Range Finder plug-in when added, and in the numeric Range Finder pop-up that appears, you can set the Item to Camera, and then select Draw Link, as shown in Figure 8.28.

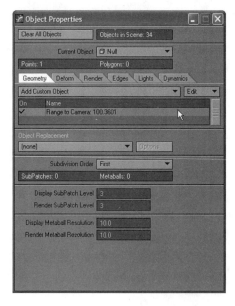

Figure 8.27 You can add a custom object to quickly measure distances in Layout from any item, such as the camera for setting depth of field measurements.

Figure 8.28   The Range Finder pop-up allows you to set the Camera as a link.

You'll see a line between the camera's pivot point and the Range Finder null. Make sure that Auto Key is enabled, and move the null. You'll see the measurement values change, as shown in Figure 8.29. This value is your distance from the camera that you can easily use to set depth of field. If you're specifically trying to set the focus on an object, simply put this range finder null on the object, and take the measurement. This is a really good way to calculate rack focuses for animated depth of field as well.

Figure 8.29   With the Range Finder custom object added, when Auto Key is on, you'll see a target line between the selected item (Camera) and the Range Finder. Cool stuff.

F-Stop

In addition to focal distance, you also can set an f-stop for any of your LightWave cameras. You do this through the Stereo and DOF tab.

The human eye automatically adjusts to brighter or darker lighting situations. Under low light, the human eye's iris and pupil open to allow in the maximum amount of light. Bright sunlight, on the other hand, makes the human eye close to protect the eye.

By the same token, cameras also have an iris and pupil that allow in more or less light. Although the human eye smoothly opens and closes to control incoming light, cameras need to have this control set. This is done through f-stops.

F-stops are numerical values that represent the amount of varying degrees of light transmission. A smaller f-stop allows more light into the camera, whereas higher values allow less light into the camera. Here are the common f-stop numerical values used in the real world:

- **1.4**—Softest focus, allowing a lot of light into the camera
- **2.0**
- **2.8**
- **4.0**
- **5.6**
- **8**
- **11**
- **16**
- **22**—Sharpest focus, allowing little light into the camera

Here's how it all comes together. When you have a higher f-stop number (which equates to a smaller iris opening), your depth-of-field value is greater. So, the depth of field on a LightWave camera set to an f-stop of 11 will be larger and less blurred than the default f-stop of 4.0, creating a flatter image. If you set an f-stop of 2.0, you have a smaller depth of field, making items behind and in front of the focal distance out of focus.

Mask Options

The final tab available for enhancing the LightWave camera is the Mask Options tab. Here, you can tell the camera in LightWave to render certain areas while masking out others. The remaining areas are defined by a color. This option is great for setting up pseudo widescreen renders, or a letterbox effect. You can set values for Left, Top, Width, and Height, as well as the Mask Color. Figure 8.30 shows the Mask Options tab. Figure 8.31 shows a rendered image with the mask option applied. You can use the Mask option for making letterboxed images, simulating a 16:9 or widescreen look on a 4:3 television.

Figure 8.30 The Mask Options tab within the Camera Properties panel enables you to mask areas of your Camera view for rendering.

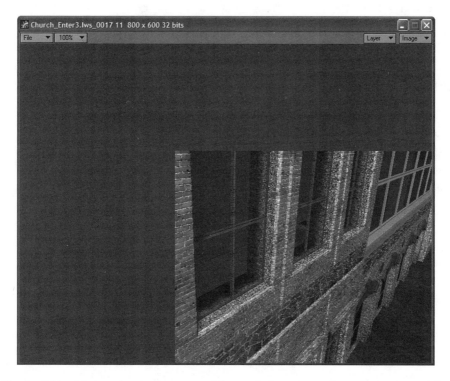

Figure 8.31 Mask options are great to use for rendering only portions of animations while setting a color for the unmasked area.

Important

Remember that masking covers up your rendered image based on the parameters you set. It does not resize your image.

You can see that the control available to you for LightWave's cameras can be a significant element in the animations you create. Too often, the camera is ignored and left in place. This is a crime—remember the camera when you animate! Animate it as well as your objects.

Camera Concepts

You want to incorporate the camera more into your animations but don't know where to begin? You may find yourself in situations where you don't know how to frame a shot or decide where to place the camera. This next section provides you with some basic instruction that you can use throughout any of your animations.

View in Thirds

To many animators, looking through a camera lens is like looking at a blank canvas. Where should you begin? How should you view a particular shot? Your first step in answering these questions is to get a book on basic photography and cinematography. References such as these can be invaluable to animators as well as a great source of ideas.

When you look through the camera in LightWave, try to picture the image in thirds. Figure 8.32 shows a sample scene as viewed through LightWave's default camera. However, lines have been painted in to demonstrate the concept of framing in thirds. If you visualize in thirds, you can see that the view in the image feels better; it is aesthetically pleasing. The shot takes into account not only the main focus, but also the surrounding areas of the frame. If you visualize the image in thirds, as in Figure 8.32, you can see that areas of the scene fit into place. Visually look for three vertical and three horizontal areas when viewing your shots.

By framing your shot in thirds in the vertical and horizontal views through the camera, you have areas to fill with action. Remember, you need to visualize this grid when setting up camera shots in LightWave. There is not an option to do this. By visualizing, you can begin to think more about your shot and framing. Figure 8.33 is an example of a bad camera shot. Figure 8.34 is the same scene with a decent camera angle.

When thinking of thirds while setting up a shot, don't be too literal. Your objects don't need to line up exactly into each third area. Visualizing your camera shot in thirds is a way to help frame the entire field of view. Don't be afraid to try different camera angles and different perspectives.

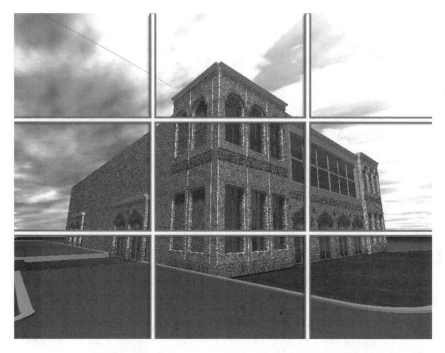

Figure 8.32   Framing your shot in thirds can help you to place the camera more accurately.

Figure 8.33   Here is a good scene gone bad because the camera is set up poorly. The car is not centered in view, a common mistake many animators make. This is bad because there is too much open or "dead" space on the top and right of the frame.

Figure 8.34   The same scene looks much better because the camera is set up properly, placing action within the frame. Notice that the dead areas at the top and right of the frame are now filled with subject matter.

Camera Angles

After you get the hang of framing a scene, the next thing you should think about is the camera angle. Consider what you are trying to portray in the render. Do you want the subject to look small, or should it be ominous and looming? What you do with the camera in LightWave helps sell the mood of your animations to the viewer. As good as your models and textures might be, your shot needs to work as part of the equation as well. Figure 8.35 shows the building from a bird's eye point of view.

Perhaps you need to convey that this building is more dominating. You want to convey a feeling that it is overpowering. Figure 8.36 shows how a different camera angle changes the feel of a shot.

Taking your scenes one step further, you can also employ dutch angles to your cameras. Adding a dutch angle conveys the feeling of uneasiness, or a creepy mood. Figure 8.37 shows a shot similar to Figure 8.36, with the camera rotated on its bank, or dutched.

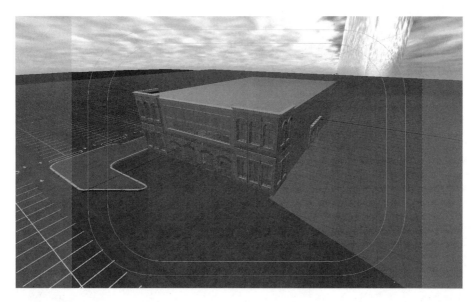

Figure 8.35 Setting your camera to a bird's eye point of view makes the shot unthreatening.

Figure 8.36 A wider camera angle, set low in front of the city, gives a grander look and feel to the shot.

Figure 8.37 Rotating the camera on its bank sets up a dutch angle that conveys the feeling of something being wrong, creepy, or uneasy.

The Next Step

The cameras in LightWave are as powerful as the software's modeling tools. When you model, you create shapes and animate them. When you animate, your motions create a mood, and without the proper camera angles, your work will not be as powerful. Practice setting up different types of shots. Load some of the scenes from your LightWave directory that installed when you loaded the program. Study the camera angles used there and try creating your own. Use reference books from real-world situations, mimic the cinematography in movies, and most importantly, experiment. Hopefully, this chapter got you thinking about the cameras in LightWave and the shots you can create and animate.

This chapter introduced you to the cameras in LightWave Layout. You learned how to add multiple cameras and set their parameters. Concepts were presented to you to change the way you look through the camera to make your animations more powerful and expressive. And, you read about navigating the interfaces, surfacing, cameras, and using the Graph Editor.

A large portion of what goes into a shot deals with lighting and environments. Be sure to use a generous combination of lighting, textures, motions, and, of course, cameras in your projects. Before you do that, you need to create some models! The next few chapters of this book discuss modeling using LightWave Modeler's powerful tools in a variety of ways. So, when you are ready and feel that you have a solid grasp on the concepts in this section, move ahead to the modeling chapters where you will put this information to the test with real-world projects.

Chapter 9

Simple Modeling and Animation

What is simple to some is complex to others. Often, one person's expertise is another's nightmare. The intent of this book is to provide a clear explanation of the tool set in LightWave so that you are excited about any project you tackle, whatever your skill level. The first eight chapters in this book provided a level playing field so you could quickly accomplish your goals for any project. With this chapter, we change our approach, focusing on complete projects. Here, you'll begin by creating some of the most basic 3D models you can—text. Although this basic 3D creation does not take an enormous amount of modeling skill, it will help you feel more comfortable with the program, and provide you with the knowledge you'll need to take care of your clients. The focus of this chapter is modeling; however, it's important to see a result, and therefore, you'll also create a full animation for the text. It will be a simple animation, with more complex motion. You can find this portion of the tutorial in Chapter 9 on this book's DVD.

The heyday of 3D animation has come and gone—that is, animated 3D logos were worth big bucks in the late 1980s and early 1990s. Television stations would spend more than $50,000 for "treatments" that included a main animated logo, weather graphics, sports pages, and so on. With the advent of increased computing power and increased software capabilities, television stations, post-production houses, and even corporations do most 3D art and animation in-house. Regardless, logo creations and animated text are still the meat and potatoes of 3D. Although you might wince at the mention of the term, flying-logo animations pay the bills in many animation studios around the globe. Perhaps your current job is with one of these television stations or post-production houses!

However, flying-logo animation is a generalized term. Even though the term is easily misconstrued as entry-level or non-professional work, you can rest assured that there are many companies and independent animators still making a very good living creating these types of animations. And not every job is for broadcast television; there is a significant market for logos in corporate and industrial video environments. This chapter focuses on modeling text in a variety of ways, which can then be animated into broadcast-style animations for television and corporate video. This chapter takes you full-speed ahead into a complete broadcast-style animation that goes beyond the typical chrome flying logo you might be familiar with. LightWave has a powerful rendering engine and excellent texture tools that will make your job easier, especially when creating logos. Figure 9.1 shows a still from the finished animation that you will create.

Figure 9.1   The final animation you'll create in this chapter.

In this chapter, you'll learn how to model text and elements that can give your animations depth and character—all in LightWave. No one cares to see a simple flying logo anymore, so it's your job to stay ahead of the proverbial motion curve. To do so, this chapter also instructs you on techniques used by professionals. You'll put things in constant motion, not just move one text object from point A to point B. This chapter gives you the knowledge to create stunning broadcast-style graphics and animations. Hopefully, it will also get you excited about doing it! It covers the following:

- Working with Modeler's Manage Fonts tool
- Modeling text

- Creating text from EPS files
- Importing background animations
- Creating continuous and multiple motions
- Using Follower for multitext movements

Modeling for 3D Graphics

Just about every television program and entertainment show has one thing in common—text graphics and animations. Such graphics and animations are bold, colorful, and downright cool to look at. Creating graphics and animations for video can be fun and even lucrative. Major television markets have high budgets for animation packages, which consist of a main title and bumpers—short versions of the main title that are used to go in and out of commercial breaks. These packages also can include variations on the main title theme for weather segments and news segments for television stations. Animation packages must represent the feeling and style the broadcaster is trying to convey. This could be serious and strong, classy and cute, or the best way, sharp!

These treatment styles also work very well for corporate or industrial video. You can even use these methods to enhance wedding videos, personal videos—the choice is yours.

What's more, LightWave is powerful enough to even make simple logo designs look cool. You'll see in this chapter how simple models put together with proper surfacing and lighting can create a cool and unique 3D look. You'll take it a step further using Follower, a LightWave motion plug-in, for enhanced movements.

Often, text and logo animation jobs are done in multiple passes and composited together in programs like Adobe's After Effects or Eyeon's Digital Fusion. But you know as well as the rest of us that those other tools are not always available. This chapter will show you how you can model text, import moving backgrounds, and then animate the text all in LightWave.

Backdrops in Modeler

For this project, you'll start by working with Modeler's text manager. One thing you should remember when working through these tutorials is that text modeling is not just for flying logos. You can use text to create shapes or various animation elements, as you'll see shortly. Text shapes in 3D are just additional three-dimensional shapes. Think in those terms and you'll have an easier time maximizing the toolset. Follow along to begin creating and surfacing text in Modeler.

Exercise 9.1 Setting Up Backdrop Images in Modeler

1. Open LightWave's Modeler.

   Start by first creating the background elements. This is a design that your client has initially created flat for a print piece. You've been hired to make it in 3D. Although it's quite boring at first glance, you know better. You know that you can use the LightWave camera to make the animation interesting and cool to look at.

2. Press the d key on your keyboard to call up the Display Options panel. Click to the Backdrop tab within the panel. For viewports, select BL, which stands for bottom left. Figure 9.2 shows the panel.

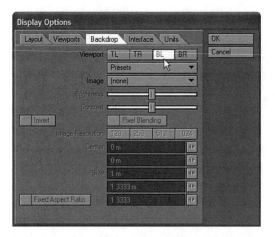

Figure 9.2   Your titling package begins by first loading a background image from the Display Options panel.

3. For the Image selection in the panel, click Load Image and load the LogoBlock.jpg from this book's projects folder on the DVD.

   Here, you can import various images as background references to build from.

Tip

You can use any image that LightWave accepts in the background, such as JPG, TIF, TGA, and so on.

4. After the image is loaded, you'll see it appear in the bottom-left viewport, as shown in Figure 9.3.

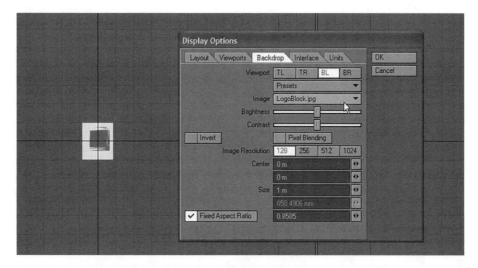

Figure 9.3   Loading a background image instantly shows it in the bottom-left viewport.

As you can see, the image is slightly small. Creating in 3D is relative, and building a tiny logo or a large logo really makes no difference when it comes to rendering. However, you'll have an easier time flying a camera through the logo's elements if you make it larger than this default size.

5. In the Backdrop tab of the Display Options panel, change the Size to 5m from the current 1m.

6. Change the Image Resolution to 1024. This will allow you to see the image clear and sharp in the background.

 Important

Changing the Image Resolution in the Display Options panel has nothing to do with the actual resolution of the image, or your 3D model. This is a display option only.

7. Bring the Brightness and Contrast down so that the backdrop image is not over-powering. When you create 3D models, the points and polygons might not be visible, or at least might be hard to see, with such a bright background image. Therefore, you want to dim it enough to just see it as a reference. Figure 9.4 shows the changes from the last three steps.

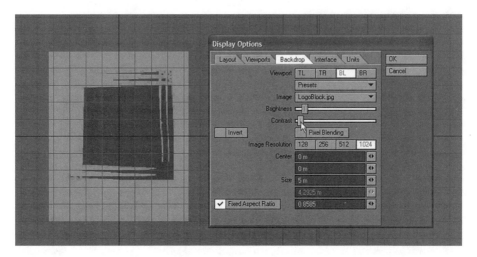

Figure 9.4 Increasing the size and resolution while decreasing the brightness and contrast gets the background image ready for modeling.

8. Just in case you want to use this backdrop later, go ahead and save it. Click the Presets selection in the Backdrop tab of the Display Options panel. Choose Save Current Backdrop and give it a name. Then, when you want to use this again, just click Presets and Load Backdrop. You'll use this feature later in Chapter 13, "Modeling Bipedal Characters," to model a character. Figure 9.5 shows the operation.

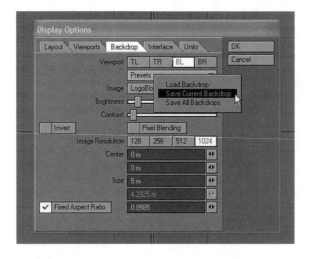

Figure 9.5 Save your backdrop to keep your settings for future use.

You're now ready to begin creating the background blocks that your camera will fly through. Read on to create these elements.

Building over Images

You'll use this technique often in Modeler for characters, automobiles, and, in this case, logos. That's right, logos. It seems that designers like to create cool print design elements, which often are a nightmare for animators. These painted backgrounds can sometimes be a real time waster when it comes to building logos and elements. However, by placing an image in the background as you've done in the previous steps, it's quick and easy to build 3D elements right over the image.

Exercise 9.2   Using Backdrop Images for Modeling

1. With the same backdrop image loaded into the bottom-left view, select the Pen tool from the Create tab. Then, click the Maximize Viewport button at the top-right corner of the bottom-left viewport. This expands your view to full screen. You can click it again to return to a Quad view. Figure 9.6 shows the button.

Figure 9.6
Use the Maximize Viewport button to make the bottom-left view full screen.

2. Press the period (.) key a few times to zoom into the view.

3. With the Pen tool, click with the left mouse button to create points, about 22 in all. Click the points around the bottom two slashes of the background image, as shown in Figure 9.7.

4. Using the Pen tool instantly creates polygons between the created points. Turn off the Pen tool and unmaximize your viewport (click the button in the top-right corner of the viewport) to return to Quad view. You should see a shape in the Perspective view similar to Figure 9.8.

Important

When you look at the Perspective view, you may not see your model. However, you may see the surface normal facing toward the negative Z-axis, away from you. If this happens, just press the f key to flip the normal forward. Remember to work with lowercase keys.

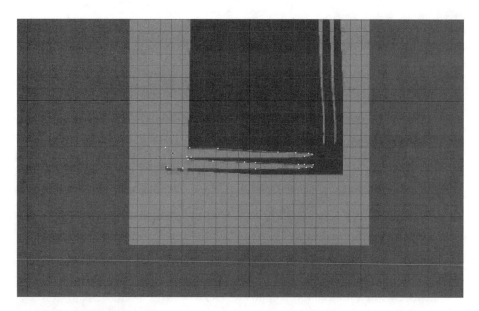

Figure 9.7   Click and create points around the bottom two slashes to create one object, using the Pen tool.

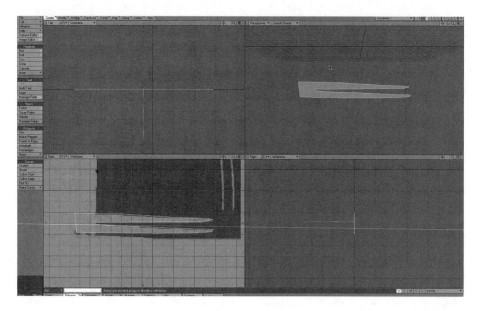

Figure 9.8   Going back to Quad view shows the polygon you've created with the Pen tool.

5. You have the first part of the logo block built, so save it! Press Ctrl+s to Save As, and save this as LogoBlock_1, or something similar.

Tip

A cool new feature in LightWave 8 is the capability to save in increments. Press Shift+s after the initial object has been saved, and you'll start saving incremental versions of your model. It is highly recommended that you always save with the Shift+s command for safety. You'll never have to worry about overriding your previously perfect model!

6. Create the other slashes at the top of the screen by mirroring the one you've created. Press Shift+V to select the Mirror tool from the Multiply tab. Mirror the object on the Y-axis. Then, turn off the tool. Figure 9.9 shows the Mirror operation.

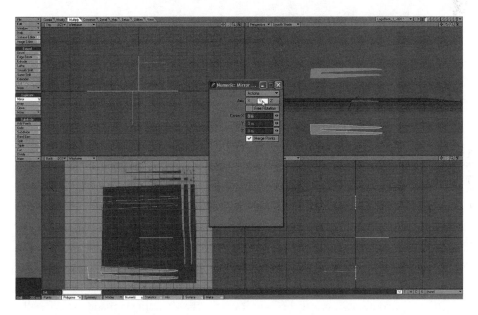

Figure 9.9   Mirror the first slash object to the top of the logo block.

7. Deselect the first object you created, and select the one you mirrored. Move it up into place based on the background image.

8. With the upper and lower slash objects now ready to go, you need to create the ones on the left and right. You have two options: either copy the ones you just created and shape them or build new ones. The time it would take to manipulate what you've already created would not be worth it. So, go to a new layer and select the Pen tool again.

9. Using the Pen tool from the Create tab, click and draw over the right side vertical slashes, as shown in Figure 9.10.

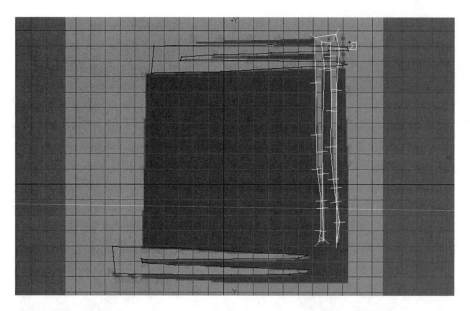

Figure 9.10   Build the right side vertical slash over the background image with the Pen tool.

10. After you have completed the slash, mirror the newly created polygon across the X-axis for the left side of the logo block. Select and move it into place as needed.

11. With the mirrored polygons still selected, move the mouse over the center of the object. Press the r key twice. Pressing r is a 90-degree Rotate operation! You'll use this to rotate the object so that it lines up with the logo block in the background image, as shown in Figure 9.11.

    The reason you're using the r key for a quick rotate is to show you the cool feature, of course, but mostly because it's easier than rotating by hand, or manually with the rotate command, and simply flipping it changes the direction of the surface normal.

12. Deselect the polygons. Press Ctrl+x to cut these two objects; go to layer 1 and press Ctrl+v to paste them down.

    Because these objects are just painted elements in print, it's okay if the polygons overlap when you extrude.

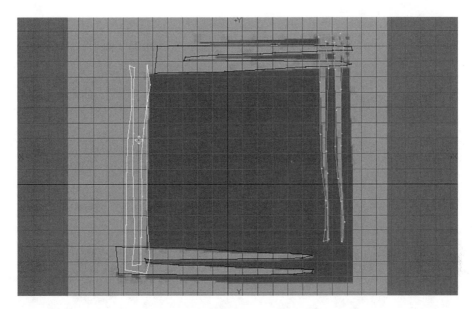

Figure 9.11   Use the r key for a quick 90-degree rotate. Do this twice!

13. With all four polygon objects in the same layer, select Extrude from the Multiply tab, or press Shift and the e key.

14. In the Top viewport, click and drag to the back to extrude the objects. Figure 9.12 shows the screen.

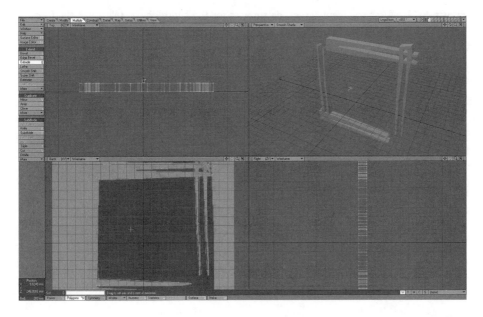

Figure 9.12   After the objects are cut and pasted into the same layer, extrude them slightly.

15. Press the q key to call up the Change Surface panel, or click the Surface button at the bottom of the Modeler interface. Here, identify the entire polygonal object as Slash_Sides.

16. Select just the front of the objects and identify their surface as Slash_Bevel, as shown in Figure 9.13.

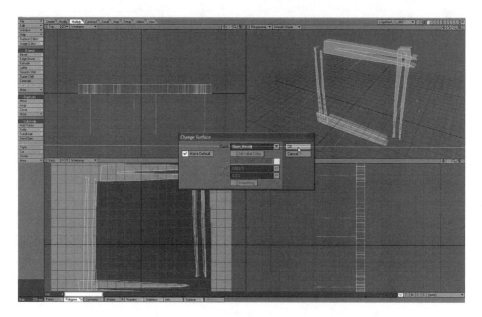

Figure 9.13 After you identify the side surfaces for the entire object, select just the front polygons and name them Bevel.

 Important

You don't need to set colors when identifying the surfaces in the Change Surface panel. This would help you make sure that you've set different surface names for selected polygons, but you'll apply all the final surfaces later in Layout.

17. After the surface has been identified, press b for Bevel and click and drag slightly.

If you've beveled before, you may have noticed that it's a little awkward. Here's the solution: Pay close attention to your movements. When beveling, concentrate on the forward and backward movements of the mouse. This is your *shift*. Then, concentrate on just the left and right movements of the mouse. This is the *inset*. When you randomly click and drag, it's difficult to bevel accurately. Concentrate on your movements, and you're good to go!

Be sure not to bevel too much so that the polygons cross over each other. You only want a slight bevel for added depth.

18. After you have a bevel you're happy with, press q again for the Change Surface panel and name these new polygons Slash_Face. Remember, you selected the front polygons and named them Bevel. Then, you beveled them. Beveling is a multiply function, and the named Bevel surface is left behind, with new polygons created. These new polygons are the Face surface. Figure 9.14 shows the operation.

19. Save your work!

20. Press the d key and in the Backdrop tab of the Display Options panel that opens, click to the BL viewport. Change the Image to None to remove it from the background of the viewports. The image is still loaded in Modeler, but it is not displayed. You may find that you will turn the background image on and off a few times while you are modeling, for visual reference.

Tip

If you would like to completely remove the image from Modeler, open the Image Editor, found on the top left of the Modeler interface. Select the image in the panel and press Delete on your keyboard.

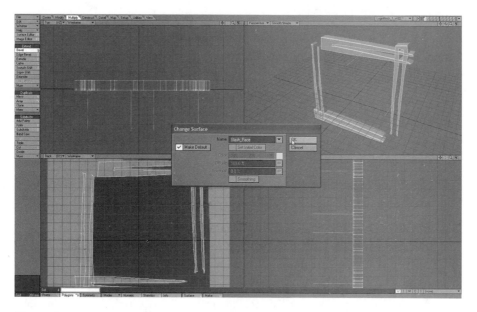

Figure 9.14   After beveling, name the newly created polygons Slash_Face.

If you read Chapter 3, "Modeler," you read about the various tools under the Create tab. In the previous pages, you used the Pen tool to create points, with attached polygons, and drew over a background image. This exact method can be used with points to make a curve, or with any of the other tools, even full primitives like box. Keep this in mind the next time you need to build over an image. In Chapter 13, you'll use this same technique with a Preset background provided for you, but instead of using just one backdrop, you'll use three! You'll also employ the Points tool to create spline curves. What you learn there can be used here for logo creation. It's all about control baby!

Duplication in Modeler

There are bad things and good things about a client coming to you with very little print elements to work with. The bad thing is that there's little to work with. The good thing is that there's little to work with! Confused? Don't be. This means that if you have little to work with in print, you have a lot to work with in 3D. Too many print elements can be nothing more than a nightmare in 3D. Think about it—a very complex logo design means more modeling time for you, more setup time in Layout, and often more rendering. When your client has little to work with, it's more challenging to you as an animator. This next section will quickly show you how to finish the logo block model you created previously, and how to lay out copies of it that you can animate. You'll see how fast this is done with LightWave 8.

Exercise 9.3   Creating Duplicate Elements

1. Back in Modeler, make sure the logo block you've created, extruded, and surfaced is loaded. Go to a new blank layer and make the existing model a background layer.

2. Draw a flat box in the center of the slash marks, slightly overlapping them, as shown in Figure 9.15.

3. Cut and paste the new flat box into the layer with the rest of the logo element. Also be sure to press the f key to flip the polygon forward as needed.

4. You should have just one layer with the complete object. Save it. Then, head on over to the Multiply tab. Under the Duplicate category's More drop-down menu, select Clone to Layer. In this panel, you can tell LightWave Modeler to make clones of your current layer into blank layers (or the same layer). You can set offsets, but for this project, you'll do that manually. Figure 9.16 shows the operation.

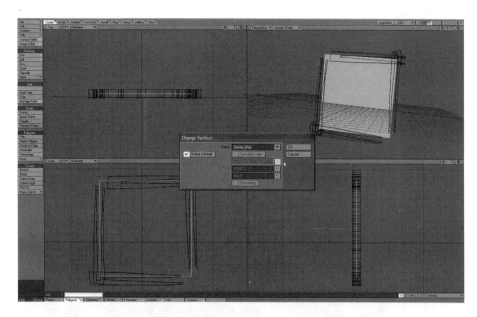

Figure 9.15   In a new layer, create a flat box centered in the slash marks.

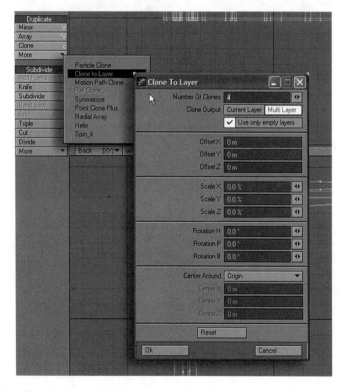

Figure 9.16   Clone to Layer makes creating animatable copies a cinch!

5. If you look closely at your layer buttons across the top of the interface, you'll see that the first five layers now have geometry in them. The first layer is your original, whereas the next four layers are your clones. Click to layer 2, and make layer 1 a background image. Move the logo block back and up a bit, as shown in Figure 9.17. You can hold the Shift key and select all of the layers to view them at once.

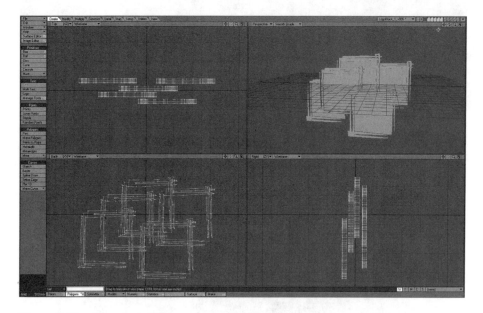

Figure 9.17   After cloning layers, you can move them around independently.

6. Move to layer 3 and do the same thing. Simply offset each logo block into a pattern you like. Overlapping is nice, but not on the Z-axis. You want to leave room for the camera to fly through.

7. One last thing: Select two of the four boxes and give them a different surface name, something like Center_Box_2. Figure 9.18 shows how it should look.

8. Save your work!

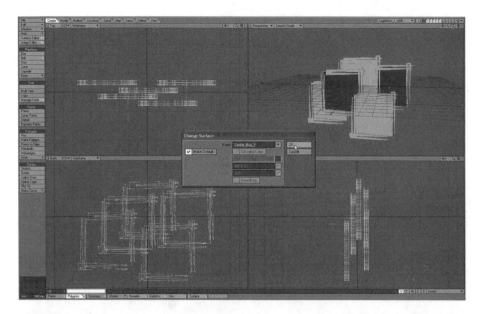

Figure 9.18 Give two of the inner box surfaces colors and a unique name for variation.

Now you have your individual elements created. You cloned each to its own layer, so that you can animate them separately later in Layout. If you were not going to animate them, you could leave them all on the same layer. However, another thing you need to do to animate each layer properly is set their individual pivots.

Pivot Points in Modeler

Pivots were discussed earlier in this book. Each object you create has an origin, or a center. This origin relates to the 0,0,0 axis, where the X-, Y-, and Z-axes all come together. If you do not specify an object's origin, it defaults to this 0,0,0 axis. This is okay for many things, but for precise animation, this could cause problems. Let's say you have a door on a building. The center of the building is at the 0,0,0 axis. If the door rests at the front of the house and you rotate it open, its origin at the 0,0,0 axis will make it swing too wide, inappropriately. Moving the pivot of the object, essentially changing its origin, will make it rotate properly. This section shows you how to change the pivots.

Exercise 9.4   Setting New Pivot Points in Modeler

1. Start by selecting layer 1 of your logo block model from the previous exercises. This model is probably not too far off the center 0,0,0 axis. However, it could be a little more precise, so click over to the View tab, and on the left under the Layers category, select the Pivot command.

2. When you activate the Pivot command, crosshairs appear in the viewports. Move the pivot to the center of the object. Be careful to pay attention to all views and move it on the Z-axis as well as the X-axis and Y-axis. Figure 9.19 shows the operation.

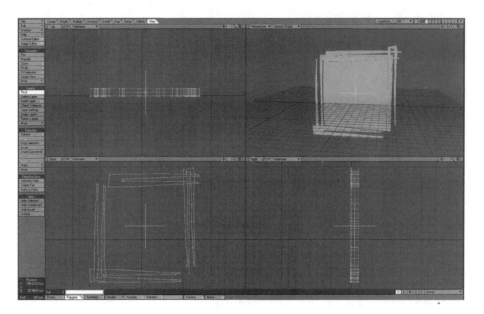

Figure 9.19   Manually move the pivot for layer 1's object.

3. With the Pivot tool still active, click over to layer 2. You can quickly move the pivot for this object. Again, center it out.

4. Set the pivots for the rest of the layers and save the object.

You've now created all the base animation elements for the logo treatment. The next steps are to build the main logo and the subtext that you'll animate as individual letters.

Importing EPS Files

LightWave also offers you the ability to import Adobe Illustrator files or EPS files. This is extremely handy for more complicated graphics designed out-of-house—that is, you'll often be hired to animate a logo but not design it. The capability to import EPS files not only saves enormous amounts of time, it also allows you to create a more accurate 3D version of the original piece.

Exercise 9.5   Creating Text and Elements from EPS

1. In Modeler, save any work you've done. Create a new object by pressing Shift and the n key, or select New Object from the File drop-down menu.

2. From the File drop-down menu, select Import, EPSF Loader. This enables you to load an EPS or AI file into Modeler. Figure 9.20 shows the panel that appears.

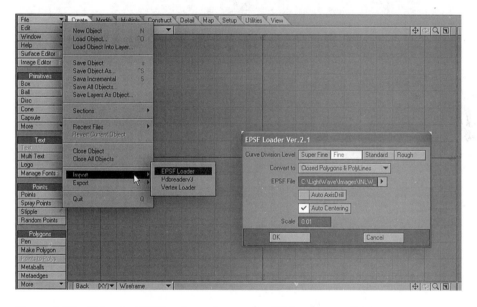

Figure 9.20   Using the EPSF Loader makes creating 3D from vector files a snap.

3. Be sure to set the Curve Division Level to Fine. Also, select Closed Polygons and PolyLines for the Convert to option. Click the right arrow next to the EPSF File and load the LW8.eps file from this book's DVD (see the Chapter 9 Images folder). Leave Auto Centering on and turn on Auto AxisDrill. If you don't turn this on, your object will have polygons where there should be holes, such as those shown in Figure 9.21.

Figure 9.21   Make sure the Auto AxisDrill option is checked within the EPSF Loader panel; otherwise, your imported object will have polygons instead of holes.

Tip

Sometimes, you might want to import your objects without the Auto AxisDrill on. Often, the centers of letters or fonts can be excellent animation elements. You can select them, cut and paste them to a new layer, and set them up for animation. While they're in this layer, you can use a Boolean subtract to have those centers of the letters cut holes from the main fonts.

4. After your object imports, extrude it about 300mm on the Z-axis to give it some thickness. Wham! Instant 3D object! Do you see the beauty of importing EPS files now?

5. Continue with this logo by first pressing q for the Change Surface panel, and name the entire object's surface LogoSides.

6. Select just the face polygons and name them LogoBevel.

7. Bevel the face polygons while they're selected.

8. Name the newly created polygons LogoFace.

Important

From time to time, when you bevel a surface, the corners fold over themselves. When this happens, you get what's called *non-planar polygons*. Essentially, the surface is all twisted up and doesn't display correctly, as in Figure 9.22. To fix this, bevel less or go to each corner and carefully select the points that are overlapping and press Ctrl+w to weld those points together. You'll see your surface correct itself.

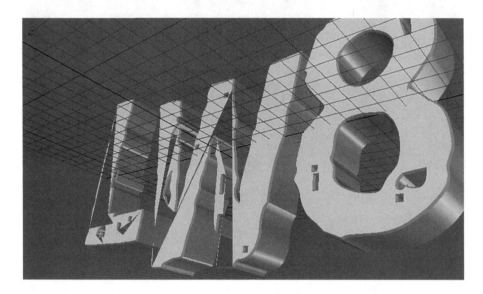

Figure 9.22   An example of non-planar polygons.

9. Save your work. Figure 9.23 shows the beveled, imported EPS file that took about three minutes to create.

10. Load the original logo block object you created earlier in the chapter. This will load as a new current object. Select the main LW8 logo object from the Current Object drop-down list at the top right of the screen next to the Modeler buttons. Here, you can see any objects loaded.

11. Be sure to press F2 to automatically center the object. With this function, your object is moved to the 0,0,0, axis. This saves you the trouble of using the Pivot tool to set the object's origin.

12. Save your new object and then go to a blank layer.

Figure 9.23   Using the EPSF Loader makes creating 3D from vector files a snap!

13. On the left side of the screen under the Create tab is a Text category. You might find that the Text tool is ghosted. This is because you've not loaded any fonts into LightWave Modeler. Do this by clicking the Manage Fonts button. In the panel that appears, load a few fonts from your system. Note that you can load as many as you like, but you'll need to load them one at a time.

14. After you have a few fonts loaded that you like, you'll see the Text tool active. Click it, and in the bottom-left view, click to begin creating text. You'll see the text cursor appear.

15. Enter the text **EIGHT** all in caps. Figure 9.24 shows the text created.

Important

Although you use many keyboard shortcuts as you're working through Modeler, these are disabled when you're using the Text tool. Otherwise, how would you type out your text? Often, however, you might require the use of a keyboard equivalent. Press the Esc key, and you'll be able to use your keyboard equivalent one time.

Figure 9.24 Use the Text tool to create the text EIGHT.

Another thing you can do with the Text tool is use your up and down arrows to cycle through any fonts you've created. Like creating a box, ball, or other primitive, after you turn off the tool, you've committed to it. So cycle through your fonts while you're in setup mode with the blue outline. You can also use the Numeric panel for additional control. What's more, you can kern your letters or resize them, either in the Numeric panel or by clicking and dragging the very top or bottom of the text cursor. When created, if your font is too large and goes offscreen, use the Numeric panel to change the size.

Tip

Try using the Multitext tool in Modeler to generate lines of text. This tool is also found under the Text category of the Create tab.

16. Extrude and surface this text as you have done with the previous exercises, creating a side, bevel, and face surface.

17. Move the logo over to the right so that the E of the EIGHT object is centered on the 0,0,0, axis.

18. Select and copy each letter and move it to its own layer. However, this time, don't change the pivot point. You want the pivots to remain the same; you'll see why later in Layout.

19. Save your completed new object and send it to Layout from the Send Object to Layout drop-down at the top right of the Modeler interface. This is found by clicking the small drop-down arrow.

You have created your objects. You've created elements using simple geometry and have created text with the Text tool. In addition, you've worked with importing EPS files. All three of these techniques can be used to build fonts, logos, and elements. Consider them the next time a project comes across your desk.

Text Scenes Setup

Now that you have your three objects in Layout (see Figure 9.25), you can begin setting things up. First, you'll set the placement, and then the lighting. After that's in place, you'll enhance the surfaces and set up camera moves. Are you ready?

Exercise 9.6   Text Setup in Layout

1. With the objects loaded into Layout, select the LW8 logo. Move it forward on the Z-axis in front of everything else. Create a keyframe at 0 to lock it in place.

Tip

Be sure you're working with the Auto Key option off for this project.

2. Add a null object to the scene from the Items tab. Name this null EIGHT_Master or something similar.

3. Open an instance of the Scene Editor. Select all five layers of the EIGHT object. You can do this by selecting the first layer, holding the Shift key, and then selecting the last layer. Then, drag these selected layers under the null object, so that they are indented and become parented to the null, as in Figure 9.26.

4. Be sure to save your scene. Press Ctrl+s to select Save As and give it a name. This saves the work you've done. From now on, you can press Shift+s to save incremental scenes.

5. Select and move the EIGHT_Master null object under the LW8 logo, and create a keyframe at 0 to lock it in place.

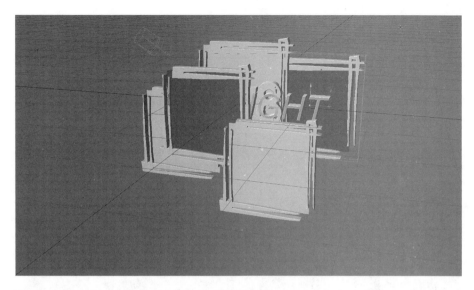

Figure 9.25   The three logo elements loaded into Layout.

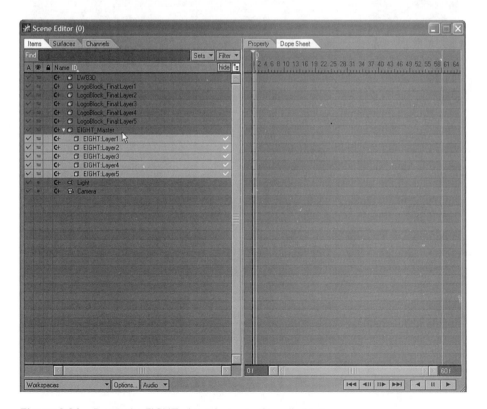

Figure 9.26   Parent the EIGHT object layers to the null object.

6. Rotate the Perspective view around and make sure that none of the objects is touching another. Then, save the scene and press 6 on your keyboard to jump to Camera view.

7. In the Camera view, push the camera in to fit the logos to frame. After the camera is in place, create a keyframe to lock it in place. Figure 9.27 shows the Camera view with the objects in place.

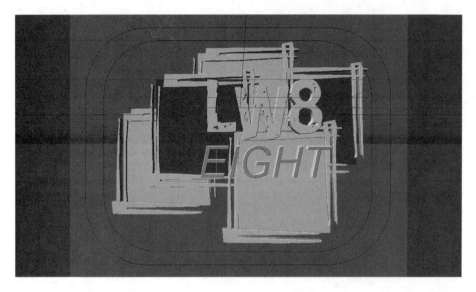

Figure 9.27   The EIGHT_Master null is moved and its children, the EIGHT object layers, go along with it.

Lighting and Motion

Until now, you've seen the basic setup before lighting. What you do next is totally up to you. Many people put everything in motion first, then light, then render. Others light first, then animate. Here, we'll do a little of everything!

Animated Multitext

This section shows you how to use Follower, a very cool motion plug-in that is great for animated logos. There are many variations, and this tutorial will set you up so you can experiment on your own.

Exercise 9.7   Lighting Text

1. Select the EIGHT:Layer1 object, which is the E portion of the EIGHT font.

2. The object is already in place because it's parented to the master null object, so just create a keyframe at 200 for the E.

   The reason you're creating a keyframe at 200 is because during the first 200 frames, you will have the camera pulling out from within the logo block elements. After it lands, the EIGHT letters will fly in. Rather than animating each one of these, you can use Follower to automate the process.

3. With the E letter keyframed at 200, move it back on the Z-axis behind the camera. Create a keyframe for it at 0 and at 180. This tells the letter object to stay put for the first 180 frames of the animation.

4. Make the length of your entire animation 300 frames by entering 300 in the end frame of the timeline, rather than the default 60. Save the scene.

5. Now, it gets a little more fun. If you drag the timeline, you can see the E letter object fly in. Feel free to add extra keyframes to make this spin, flip, or swoop in. For now, select the I letter object (EIGHT:Layer2).

6. Press the m key for Motion Options.

7. From the Add Modifier drop-down, select Follower. Double-click it to open the controls.

8. At the top, under Item to Follow, select the EIGHT:Layer1 object. For the Time Delay setting, enter 0.2, which means it will be 20% slower than the object it's following.

9. Click Continue and play the scene.

10. Do you see the I letter animate in right after the E? Now, repeat the process for the G, H, and T. But remember, each one of these also needs to follow the EIGHT:Layer1 object, because this is the object with keyframes. Figure 9.28 shows the panel.

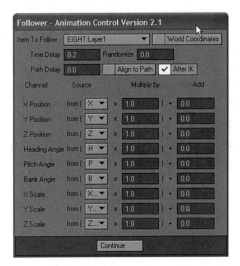

Figure 9.28   The Follower motion plug-in gives you cool animated control easily.

If the I is 0.2 offset from the E, G should be 0.4, H should be 0.6, and T 0.8. Set this up for each letter, save the scene, and test it out!

Your letters now evenly animate in one after the other. You can do amazing things like this—for example, you can add a tension to the first object so that it slows down as it lands. This will also apply to the objects being followed. Follower works really well on a fast moving set of letters—letters that enter in about three or four seconds, perhaps even faster! Try out some options.

Camera Motions for Logos

Although you want to avoid the stereotypical flying logos, Follower is cool. You can add more style to your animations by animating the camera.

Exercise 9.8   Creating Motions for Text

1. Select the camera and create a keyframe for it in its current position in front of the logo objects at frame 175.

2. Push the camera in on top of the logo. Create a new keyframe for it at frame 0. Figure 9.29 shows the view.

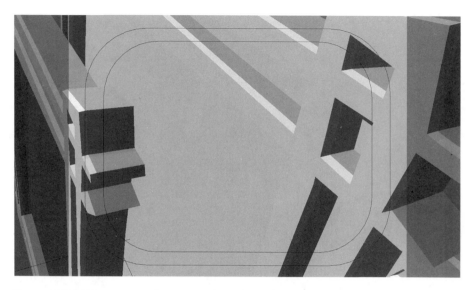

Figure 9.29   The camera will start out close, up inside the logo objects.

3. One thing you can do if you would like to enhance the shot is widen the camera angle by decreasing the Zoom Factor to about 2.2 from the Camera Properties panel.

4. If the frame you've created is at 0, and you've already created a camera position at frame 175, press the Play button and see how the animation looks.

5. You might find that the camera swings out too far as it pulls out. Because LightWave is interpolating frames, it's going from 0 position to 175 position. Drag the slider until the camera is halfway between keyframes, about 75 or so. Then, rotate the camera to face the logo objects and create a key at this frame. Press Play again.

6. You'll keep the logo in view throughout the course of the animation with this extra keyframe. But now, you need to tweak the motions. With the camera selected, open the Graph Editor at the top left of Layout.

7. In the Graph Editor, select all motion channels by first selecting the top channel, holding the Shift key, and selecting the last channel.

8. With the right mouse button (Mac people, hold down that Ctrl key), range select just the keyframes for the camera channels at 0, as shown in Figure 9.30.

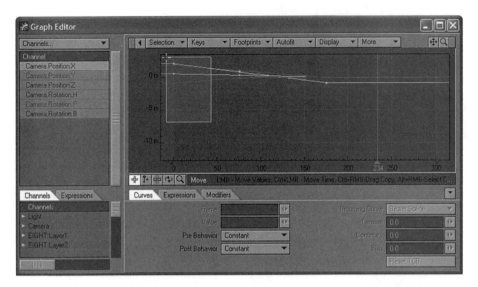

Figure 9.30 Select the keyframes at 0 for all camera channels in the Graph Editor to have them "ease out."

9. After the keyframes are selected, set the Tension to 1.0. Do the same for the keyframes of all channels at frame 175.

10. Close the Graph Editor and save the scene.

Tip

If it seems that your animation plays really fast, that's good! It means you have a great system. However, it's not entirely accurate, so press the o key for General Options. Make sure Play at Exact Rate is checked. This tells LightWave to slow down playback so that it matches the set frames per second. This also speeds things up by skipping frames to play back larger scenes as accurately as possible.

As you can see, it's not hard to set up cool-looking logo scenes. A simple camera move, a Follower plug-in, and you're on your way! The next section sets up some lighting and then textures. From there, you can practice and experiment on any of your own work or this chapter's files from this book's DVD.

Lighting for Logos

Lighting for logos is really no different than other lighting you might have already tried. What often works well is three-point lighting done with spotlights.

Exercise 9.9   Lighting Setup for Text

1. From the Items tab, under the Load category, select From Scene. Click this and select the 3PointLighting scene from the Chapter 9 folder of this book's DVD. This is a simple three-point lighting setup created in Chapter 6, "Lighting".

2. After you have selected this scene, you'll see a panel asking to also load lights from the scene. Because the scene is only lights, the correct answer is yes. Load lights!

3. These lights will not override the existing lights, and the default distant light will still remain. Delete this light and press F9. You should see the logo now rendered with shadows, as shown in Figure 9.31.

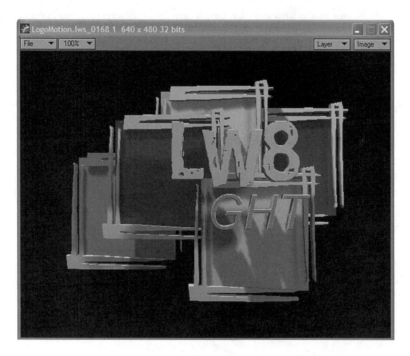

Figure 9.31   The pre-made lighting setup can work great for logos.

4. This is kind of boring to look at, so go to the Window drop-down list and select Backdrop Options. Set the default solid black background to a soft white. Test render again.

Your scene is now pretty much set up. You, of course, can take your own time and tweak, adjust, and perfect the motions, lighting, and so on. Add more light for different colors, and be more creative with the motions. However, you still need some surfaces.

The Next Step

The next step is to add some surfaces to these fonts. And tweak. Tweak, tweak, tweak! There's always more you can do with a scene, so take some time and do it! These little changes you make are what give your animations that extra something. Be sure to pop the DVD in and look at this chapter's video support tutorial. We'll take the logo you've created to a new level and recap what we've done here. Take your modeling and layout skills a step further in the next chapter. Learn how to model, texture, and render a cool, stylized giraffe!

Chapter 10

Modeling Quadrupedal Characters

Did you know that LightWave gives you all the tools you need to model anything you can imagine? There are many techniques you can use to accomplish your creation, and one of the most popular is the box modeling technique. The basic concept of box modeling is to start with a basic box primitive and, using subpatches or subdivision surfaces, transform it into a high polygon object while retaining the ease of manipulating a low polygon object.

Standard polygonal surfaces often need many polygons to approximate a smooth surface. Even so, a smooth surface made up of polygons will eventually reveal its inherently sharp-edged nature if it's examined closely enough. Although you can create such polygon-heavy objects, they are often difficult to manipulate and manage from the perspective of memory consumption and editing. In this chapter, you'll model a fun but useful giraffe. The techniques shown here can be used for any type of character you want to build, especially ones with more than two legs! You'll learn about the following:

- Creating complex shapes from primitives
- Working with subdivisions
- Using the Smooth Shift tool
- Adding detail with the BandSaw and Knife tools
- Controlling flow with the Spin Quads tool

Working with SubPatches

A SubPatch, an abbreviation for subdivision patch, is a bicubic patch. The idea behind SubPatching is to repeatedly refine the control mesh until you achieve a smooth surface, called the limit surface.

Get yourself comfortable and ready to learn one of the most valuable modeling techniques for creating organic objects quickly and with ease. Would you have ever guessed that you could create the objects shown in Figures 10.1 through 10.4 from a box?

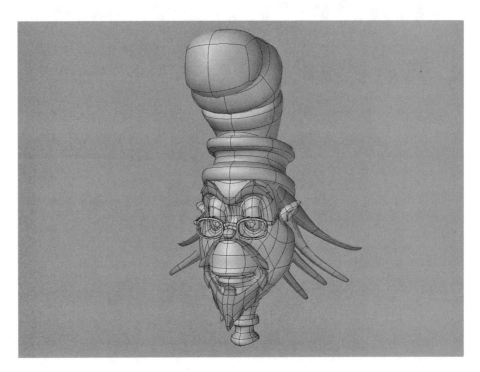

Figure 10.1 A fun character made with box modeling methods.

The goal in this chapter is to create a giraffe character using the very popular box modeling technique. Using just a handful of tools, we will take a box primitive and turn it into a full-grown organic giraffe model. These tools are used almost every time when creating characters or other organic models. Figure 10.5 shows the character you'll create.

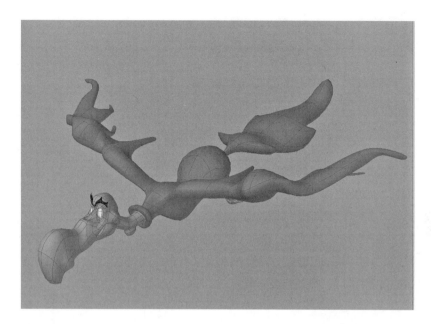

Figure 10.2   Techniques used in this chapter can help you create cool birds.

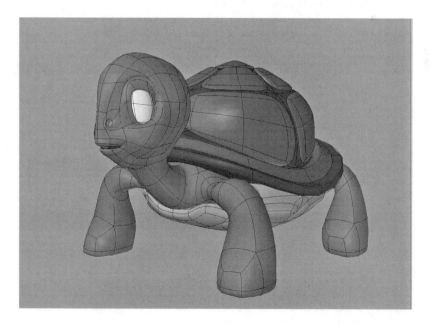

Figure 10.3   Quadruped characters are easy and fun to build with subpatches.

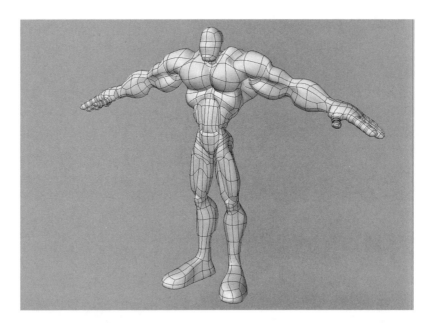

Figure 10.4   Although this chapter covers quadruped modeling, the techniques described work perfectly for biped characters.

Figure 10.5   Using box modeling methods, you'll create this cool giraffe.

Building the Head and Mouth

Organic modeling is very different from modeling a car or a building. In this project, you will be asked to manipulate the object using your own ideas of what looks right to you. The numeric window won't come into play that often and you will be asked to judge the placement of points and polygons by eye in some cases. That's what makes organic modeling so much fun—the freedom to explore and design as you go. Modeler's interface layout will be the default setup. Figure 10.6 shows Modeler at startup.

Figure 10.6   Be sure to use LightWave Modeler's default interface and settings for this project.

Exercise 10.1   Using Geometric Shapes to Build the Giraffe's Head and Mouth

1. Select Box from the Create tab and draw a box. First, drag out a two-dimensional shape and then add depth to your object by expanding it in a different viewport. The dimensions of the box are not important because we are modeling free form and can always scale the finished model to any scale easily with the Size tool. Figure 10.7 shows the box to start with.

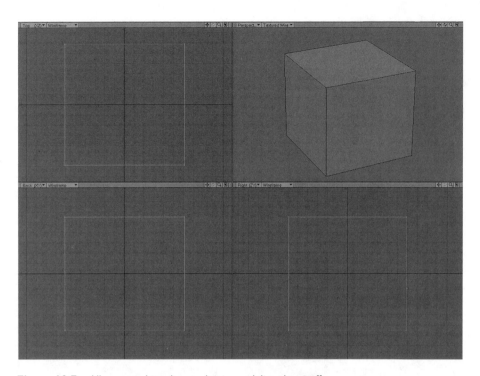

Figure 10.7   All you need is a box to begin modeling the giraffe.

2. You need to add a little more geometry to work with. Select the Subdivide tool located under the Multiply tab to subdivide the box. Choose Metaform as the Subdivision method and keep the rest of the settings as default settings, or press Shift+d.

   The box will be smoothed dramatically, with the original object acting as kind of a bounding box template for a slightly smaller, more rounded form. Metaform is very useful for creating smooth organic-looking objects out of simple geometric structures. Figure 10.8 shows the operation.

3. Using your right mouse button (Mac people, hold the Ctrl key), click and drag to lasso-select half of the object in the Back viewport, as in Figure 10.9.

4. Use Smooth Shift from the Multiply tab with an Offset of 0 and left-click in the viewport window once. You can press n on the keyboard (or click Numeric at the bottom of Layout) for Offset control. This will create new geometry to work with.

5. Move the polygons (which will still be selected) manually, using the Move tool found under the Modify tab, out to the side as shown in Figure 10.10. Be sure to do this while the polygons are still selected.

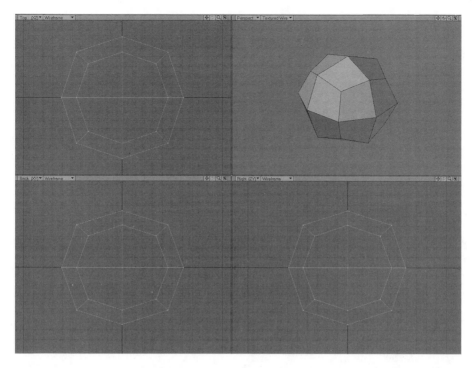

Figure 10.8   Metaform can help smooth out your beginning mesh for more control and added detail.

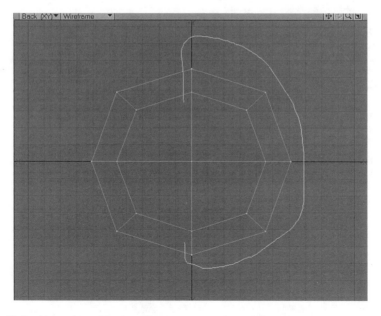

Figure 10.9   Using the right mouse button, you can lasso-select polygons.

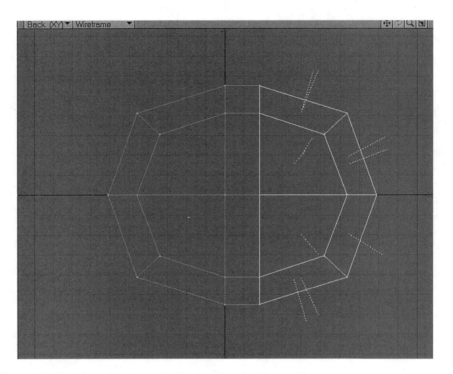

Figure 10.10   Move the selected polygons using the Move tool.

Tip

Holding down the Ctrl key while moving the object constrains it to the first axis the object is moved in.

6. Deselect the object by clicking in a blank area on the toolbar, or pressing / on the keyboard. Then, center the mesh to the 0,0,0, XYZ axis by using the center shortcut (pressing F2). Figure 10.11 shows the operation.

7. Using the Knife tool found under the Multiply tab, cut down the center of the object to create a center line on the mesh. Do this by clicking and dragging after the tool is selected. Figure 10.12 shows the deed.

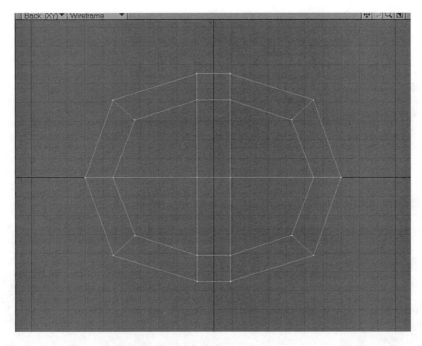

Figure 10.11   Deselect all polygons and then center the object by pressing F2.

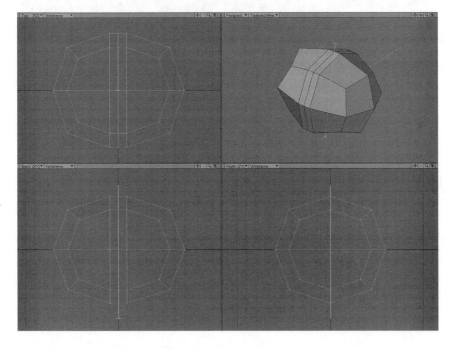

Figure 10.12   Use the Knife tool to slice the object.

8. The model is looking pretty basic at this point, but wait! Convert the model from polygonal mode to Subpatch mode using the Tab key. Figure 10.13 shows the change.

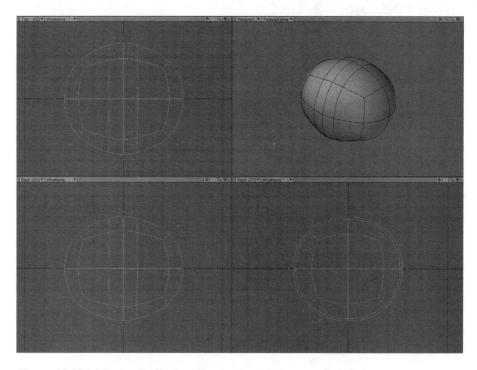

Figure 10.13   Pressing the Tab key converts the polygons to subpatches.

9. After the polygons are converted to subpatches, rotate the object about 40 degrees clockwise in the Right viewport using the Rotate tool (press y) found under the Modify tab. Figure 10.14 shows the rotation. You can calculate the rotation amount by watching the info area at the bottom left of Modeler.

10. Use the right mouse button to lasso-select the quarter of the object that is on the left side of the center line in the Right viewport. Figure 10.15 shows the selection.

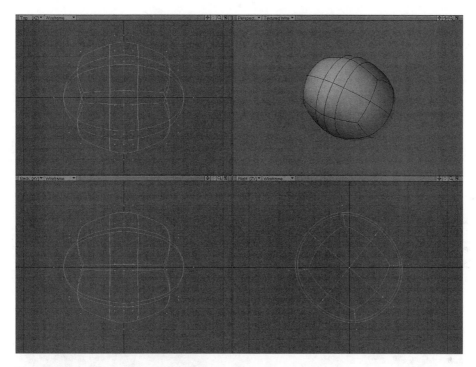

Figure 10.14   Rotate the object 40 degrees clockwise.

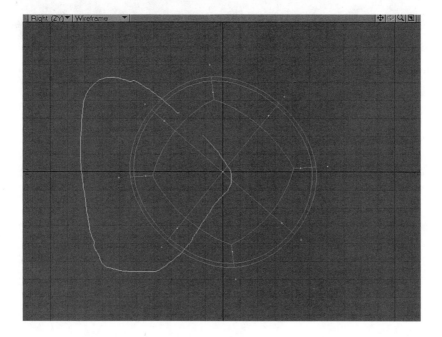

Figure 10.15   Lasso-select the left quarter polygons.

11. Use the Smooth Shift tool from under the Multiply tab or press Shift+F. Use the tool on the selection by clicking once with the left mouse button. Figure 10.16 shows the operation. Note that it might not look like anything has changed, but you've multiplied the number of polygons.

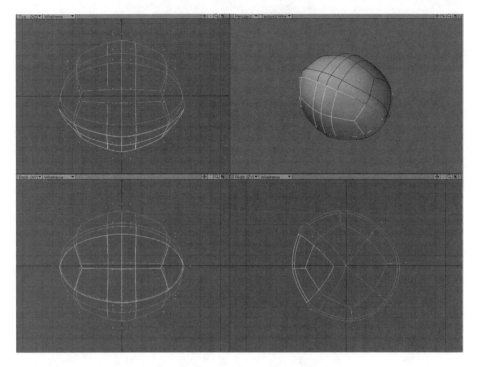

Figure 10.16   Click once on the selection with the Smooth Shift tool to multiply.

12. After the Smooth Shift operation has been performed, use the Move tool (on the Modify tab or press t) to move the selection away from the original geometry, as in Figure 10.17.

13. Select the eight polygons on the bottom of the object and use Smooth Shift to multiply, as shown in Figure 10.18.

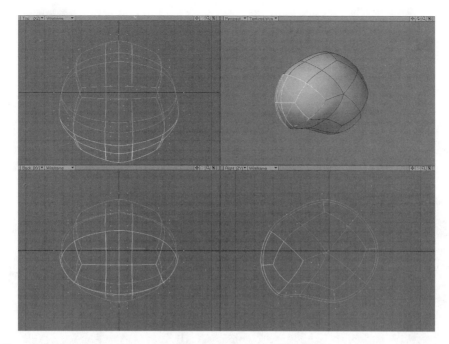

Figure 10.17   Using Move, you can move the newly created polygons away from the originals.

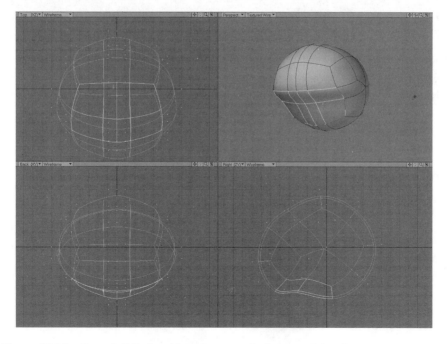

Figure 10.18   Smooth Shift the eight polygons at the bottom of the object.

14. Move the newly created polygons down and away from the original geometry, using the Move tool (on the Modify tab). As you can see from Figure 10.19, this is the start of the giraffe's snout.

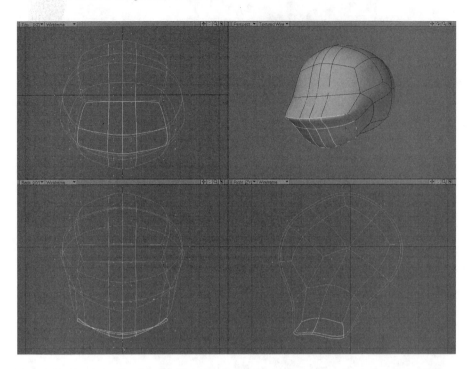

Figure 10.19 Move the Smooth Shifted polygons down and away from the original geometry.

15. Without dropping the selection, expand the number of polygons selected by one level by pressing Shift and the right bracket key (]). Then, stretch this new selection in the Back viewport using the Stretch tool (press h) located under the Modify tab. Figure 10.20 shows the operation.

16. Use the Stretch tool again to squeeze the selected geometry in the Right viewport as well, as shown in Figure 10.21.

 Tip

> Remember that the Stretch tool is nothing more than a sizing function. However, Stretch works independently on each axis. For example, if you click and move the mouse left to right, you'll stretch on one axis. Click and move forward and back, and you'll stretch on the other. Keep that in mind when using the tool.

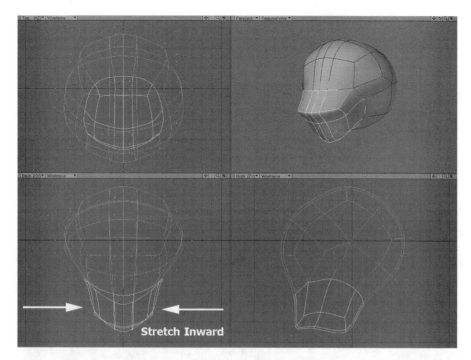

Figure 10.20 Stretch the new polygons in the Back viewport.

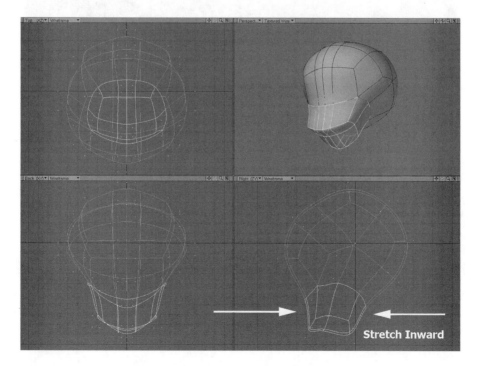

Figure 10.21 Smooth Shift the eight polygons at the bottom of the object.

17. Adjust the points on the start of the snout just a bit, as shown in Figure 10.22. You can try using various tools to do this from the Modify tab, but the Rotate and Move tools work well.

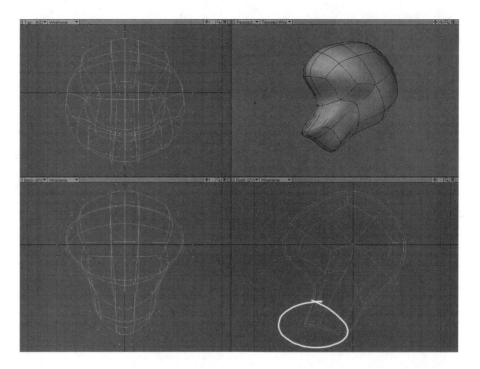

Figure 10.22 Adjust points of the giraffe's snout with the Move and Rotate tools.

18. Turn on Symmetry to help speed up the modeling process. The Symmetry toggle button is located on the bottom menu bar to the left of the Modes button.

Operations on the positive side of the X-axis also inversely affect the negative side of the X-axis. When this mode is active, your object is theoretically split in half at X=0.

 Important

Generally, you should perform all of your edits on the positive side of the X-axis when using Symmetry. Using the negative side may lead to unpredictable results.

19. Select the polygons on the side of the head—you'll need to consider the final model when selecting. These polygons will eventually make up the eyes, as you can see in Figure 10.23.

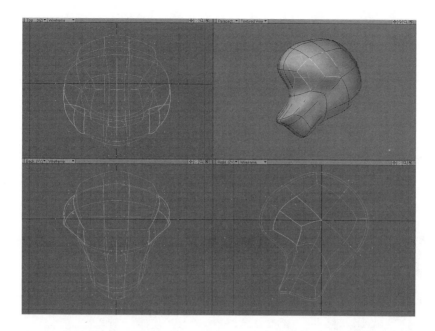

Figure 10.23   Select the polygons (with Symmetry mode on) that make up the eye area.

20. With the eye area polygons selected, perform a Smooth Shift operation to multiply them. Then, stretch the polygons slightly, as shown in Figure 10.24.

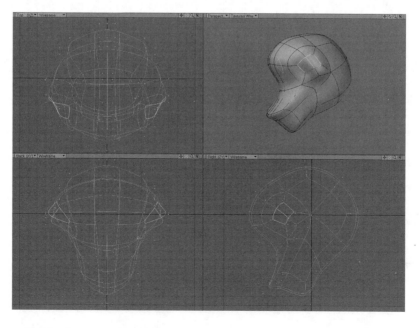

Figure 10.24   Smooth Shift the eye area polygons and then stretch them.

21. Using the Move tool (press t) from the Modify tab, move the polygons in toward the X-axis. Be sure to perform this operation in the Back viewport. Figure 10.25 shows the change.

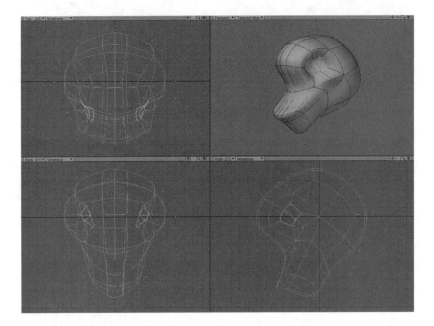

Figure 10.25   Move the polygons in on the X-axis.

Tip

You can perform any Smooth Shift step using LightWave 8's Super Shift, also found in the Multiply tab. Both have similar functionality, but each has a different "feel" when using it. It's great to have choices, isn't it?

22. Select the two polygons below the eye area and use Spin Quads from the Detail tab to smooth out the cheek area. The Spin Quads command can be applied to adjacent four-point polygons that share an edge. It merges the two polygons together and then splits them using a different set of opposing polygons. Figure 10.26 shows the selected polygons' problem area. Figure 10.27 shows the polygons' flow corrected after a Spin Quads operation.

Tip

If you apply Spin Quads three times, you'll be right back where you started.

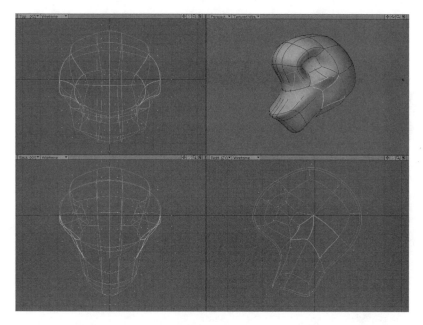

Figure 10.26   The flow of the selected polygons in the eye area is not very clean. Spin
Quads can fix this.

 Tip

> The "flow" of polygons is important when modeling organic models because
> SubPatched surfaces are built primarily from quad polygons (polygons made up of
> four points). These polygons tend to form grid-like structures. How these grids or
> patches align with the underlying form of the surface is important. Generally, you
> should have the grid follow the natural contours of the model. The advantage of this
> is that it leads to a more efficient use of geometry—the fewer polygons and vertices
> you can get away with using, the better! And, it makes the underlying surface much
> easier to follow, and therefore edit.

23. Spend a few minutes tweaking the points to refine the shape of the head a bit
     more, using various tools such as Drag and Move. Figure 10.28 shows the model
     at this point.

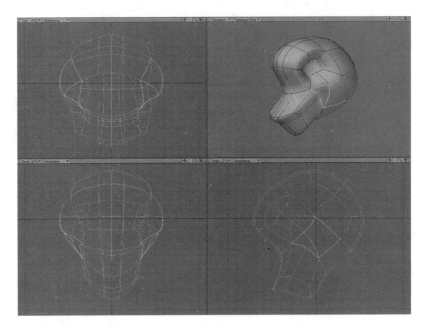

Figure 10.27   After Spin Quads is used on the selected polygons, the flow of the eye area is improved.

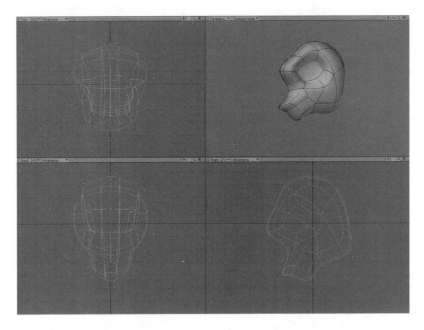

Figure 10.28   Some quality tweaking time gets the model into better shape.

24. Select the end of the snout and use the Smooth Shift tool from the Multiply tab to multiply the selected polygons. Next, move the newly created polygons down as shown in Figures 10.29 and 10.30.

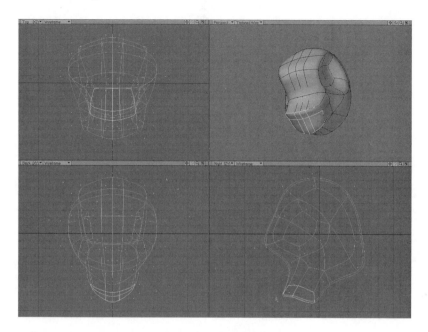

Figure 10.29   Smooth Shift again, but this time on the snout.

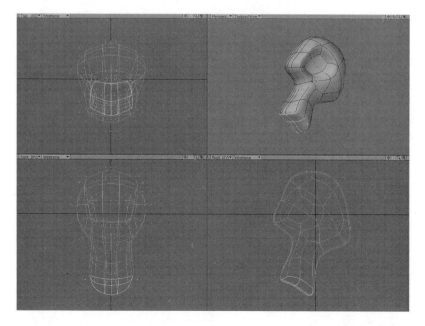

Figure 10.30   After the Smooth Shift operation, move the selected polygons downward.

25. Repeat the preceding steps (selecting polygons, Smooth Shifting them, and then moving them) twice and then tweak the points to start to shape the snout a bit. Figure 10.31 shows how the model should look.

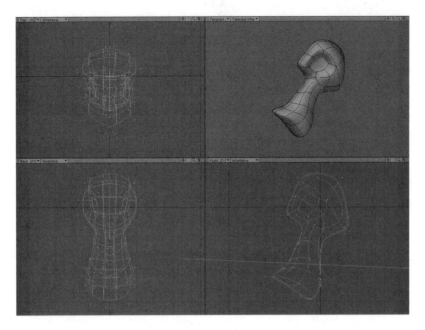

Figure 10.31   More Smooth Shift and Move operations help get the model's snout into shape!

26. Select the point in the middle of the brow area and move it in. This creates the two eyebrow areas of our character. You can use the Drag tool from the Modify tab. Figure 10.32 shows the operation.

Tip

> When modeling, it's often good to move around from place to place and sculpt the entire model. If you get buried in one area, it can really throw off the entire model's design and proportions.

27. The flow of geometry that is next to the eye isn't as good as it could be. To fix this, select the polygons and use Spin Quads to fix the flow and smooth out that area of the mesh. Figure 10.33 shows the selection, and Figure 10.34 shows the operation.

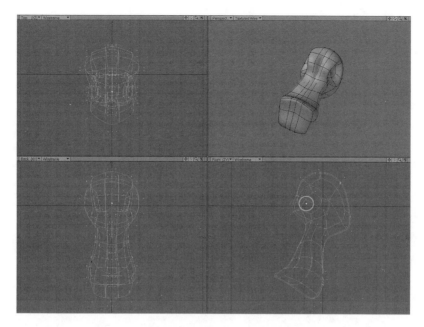

Figure 10.32   Drag the brow area point inward to separate the eyes.

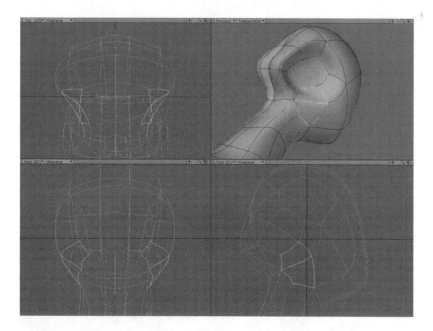

Figure 10.33   Select the polygons just underneath the eye area.

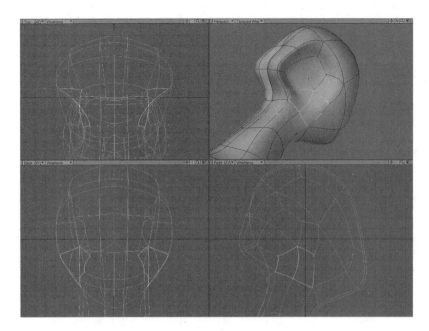

Figure 10.34 Using Spin Quads, the polygon flow is corrected.

28. Back to the giraffe's snout. Use Smooth Shift again by selecting and adjusting the polygons at the end of it, as shown in Figure 10.35.

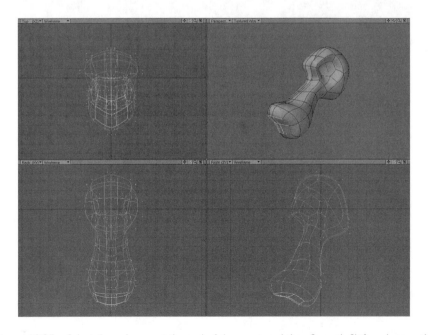

Figure 10.35 Select the polygons at the end of the snout, and then Smooth Shift and move them.

29. Smooth Shift again to inset the newly created geometry. Are you seeing the power of the Smooth Shift tool when box modeling yet? Figure 10.36 shows the move.

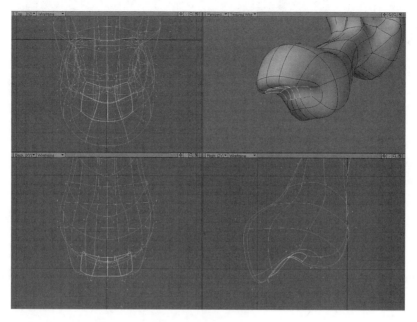

Figure 10.36   Smooth Shift the selected polygons again to inset the area of the snout to make up the mouth.

30. Guess what? Time to Smooth Shift again and start bringing the polygons back into the head to create the inside of the giraffe's mouth, as shown in Figure 10.37.

31. Spend a few minutes shaping the mouth without adding any new geometry. Just move points around till you have a shape you are happy with, perhaps using the Drag tool. Use Figure 10.38 as a reference.

32. After you have the snout adjusted and shaped, select the mouth polygons again and Smooth Shift them. Then, move them back into the mouth, as shown in Figures 10.39 and 10.40.

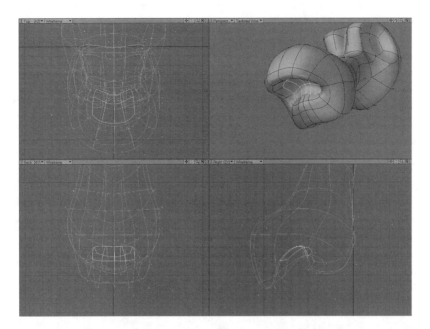

Figure 10.37   Using Smooth Shift, bring the polygons back inside the head to begin forming the mouth.

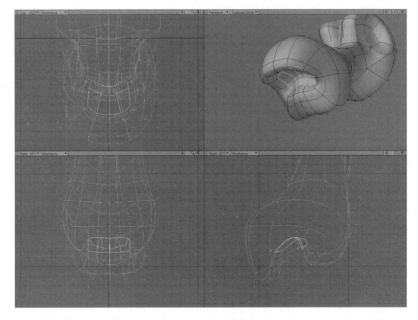

Figure 10.38   Using the Drag tool from the Modify tab, take a few minutes and shape the head to something like this.

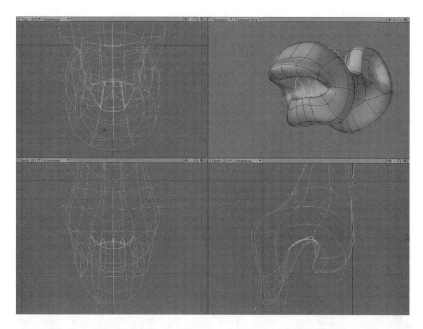

Figure 10.39   Select the mouth polygons again to begin shaping the inside of the mouth.

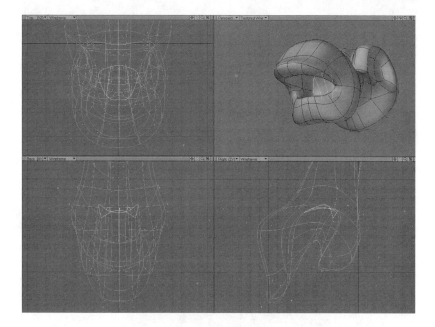

Figure 10.40   Smooth Shift the selection to bring the mouth inward even further.

33. Being able to think on your feet and see where things are headed is what makes a good Modeler. To get the nostrils and lower lip shapes to your liking, you need extra polygons. To create extra polygons, simply select a few polygons in the row around the mouth (see Figure 10.41) and use the BandSaw command (see Figure 10.42), located under the Multiply tab, to select the rest of the row of polygons and cut them.

34. Make sure Enable Divide is checked (in the BandSaw panel) and use the default settings for where the cut will be placed. Click OK. Figure 10.43 shows the result of the operations.

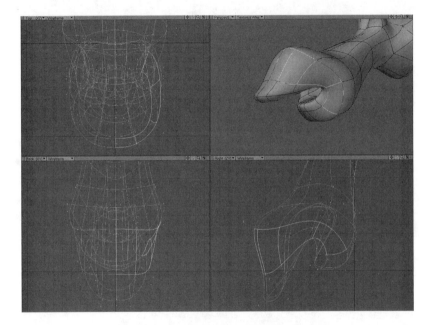

Figure 10.41   Select the polygons around the snout, near the mouth area.

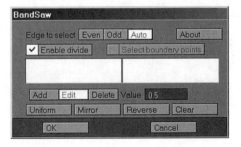

Figure 10.42   Use the BandSaw tool to slice up the geometry and create more polygons without disrupting the flow.

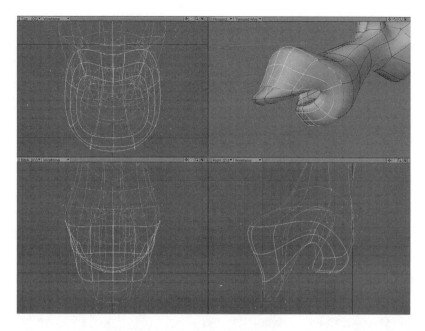

Figure 10.43   After the BandSaw settings have been applied, you'll have added geometry to work with around the mouth area of the snout.

35. With the new geometry you've created, you have more to work with. Adjust the points around the lower lip to emphasize it, as shown in Figure 10.44.

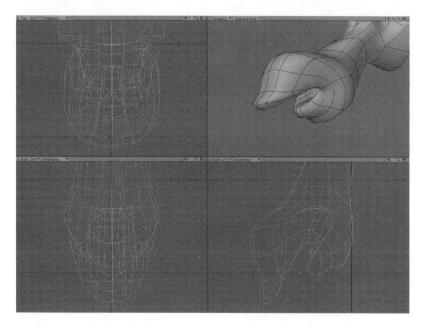

Figure 10.44   Adjust the points in the lower lip area to accentuate it.

Now you've come to a stage in the modeling phase that is a good spot at which to make sure the object is 100% symmetrical. Follow these steps to ensure that the model will continue to work properly in Symmetry mode. You need to do this because LightWave's symmetry tends to get off course every once in a while if you're not careful. These next steps will get you back on track.

Exercise 10.2   Mirroring Your Giraffe

1. Be sure that Symmetry is turned off at the bottom of the Modeler interface. Then, select just one half of the model, as shown in Figure 10.45.

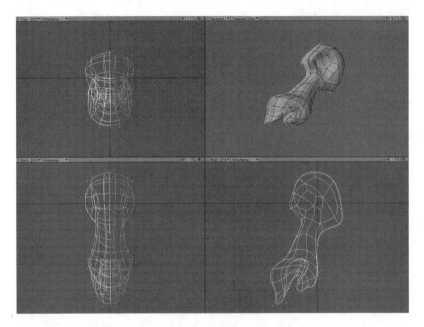

Figure 10.45   Select half of the model after Symmetry is turned off.

2. Using the Set Value command, give the X-axis a value of 0 and click OK, as shown in Figure 10.46.

3. After the polygons have been brought to the 0 X-axis, delete them. Figure 10.47 shows the polygons removed.

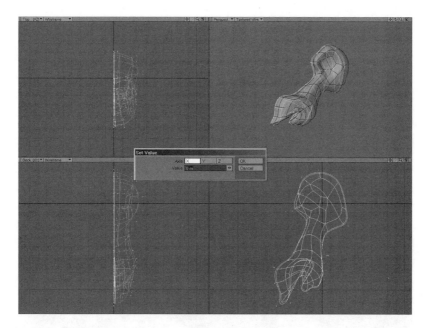

Figure 10.46   Use the Set Value command to move the selection to 0 on the X-axis.

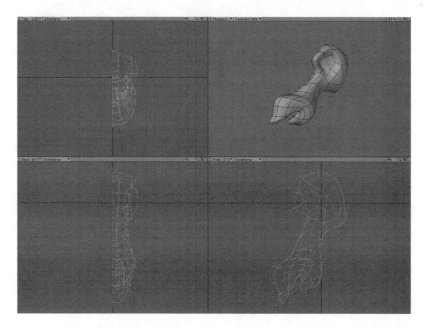

Figure 10.47   After the polygons are repositioned using the Set Value command, delete them.

4. Mirror the object on the X-axis and make sure that Merge Points is checked. The Mirror tool can be found under the Multiply tab. Your object will now be 100% symmetrical as shown in Figure 10.48.

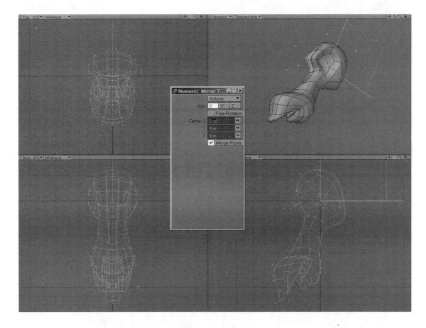

Figure 10.48   Mirror the remaining half of the model, making sure that Merge Points is checked.

 Tip

It's OK to repeat these steps a few times during the modeling process to ensure that you don't run into symmetry problems.

5. Time to make those nostrils! Turn Symmetry back on by clicking the button at the bottom of the Modeler interface, and select the two polygons that you would like to turn into nostrils, such as those shown in Figure 10.49.

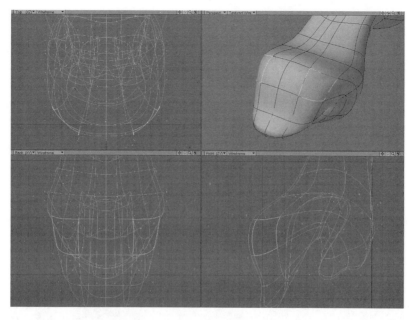

Figure 10.49   Select the polygons you want to create nostrils from.

6. Smooth Shift the selected polygons for the nostrils and stretch them in a bit. Bevel could work but you're on a Smooth Shift roll, so why stop now? Figure 10.50 shows the operation.

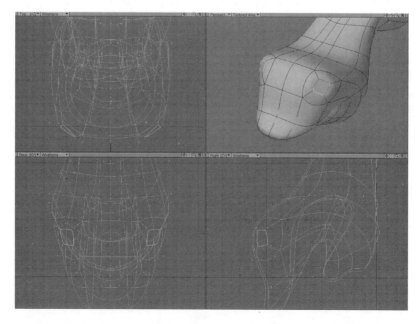

Figure 10.50   Smooth Shift the selected polygons inward to create the nostrils.

7. Use the Move tool to move the selected polygons into the snout, as shown in Figure 10.51.

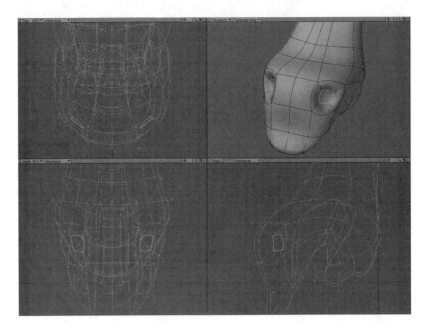

Figure 10.51   Move the selected polygons inward.

8. Smooth Shift again and adjust the newly created polygons to refine the shape of the nostrils, as shown in Figure 10.52.

 Tip

> At this stage, the model could be used to create a horse, dragon, sea horse, or various other characters. Be sure to save your steps and you can reuse your work. This is a big time saver used by many modelers in the industry.

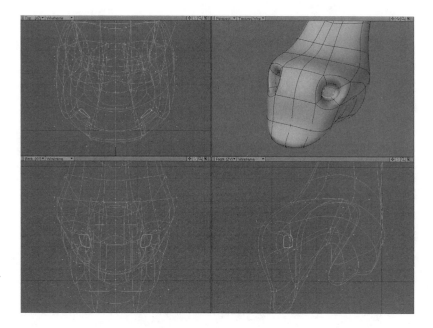

Figure 10.52   Smooth Shifting again helps refine the shape of the nostrils.

You've now created a model that can be used for just about any type of creature. The steps up to this point can carry you wherever you'd like to go in Modeler. This next section uses the same principles to create the eyes and ears of the giraffe.

Building the Eyes and Ears

The eyes are created exactly like the mouth but with fewer polygons. Smooth Shift, Move, and other Modify tools will be used along with Symmetry to create the next phase of the model.

Exercise 10.3   Building the Giraffe's Eyes and Ears

1. Select the two polygons that make up the eye socket, Smooth Shift them, and adjust the newly created geometry. Stretch it in and push the polygons back into the head, as shown in Figures 10.53 and 10.54.

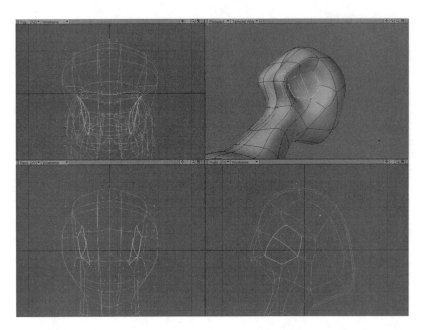

Figure 10.53   Select the polygons that make up the eyes and Smooth Shift to multiply them.

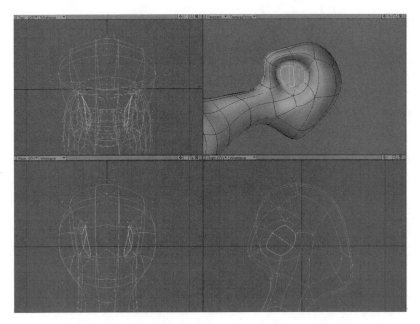

Figure 10.54   After the Smooth Shift tool has been applied, move the newly created
polygons inward.

2. Smooth Shift again and bring the polygons out away from head a bit, as shown
   in Figure 10.55.

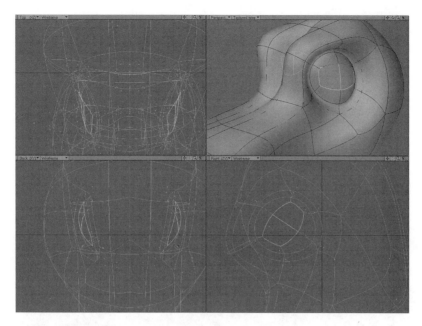

Figure 10.55   Smooth Shift again to multiply the selected polygons and begin moving them outward from the eye socket.

3. Smooth Shift the selected polygons again and stretch them in, as shown in Figure 10.56.

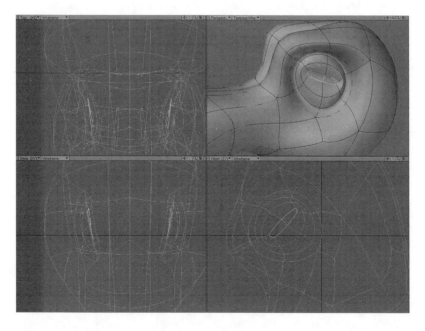

Figure 10.56   Stretch the polygons in after an additional Smooth Shift operation.

4. Another Smooth Shift operation is needed, and then push the selected geometry back into the head. Use Figure 10.57 as a reference.

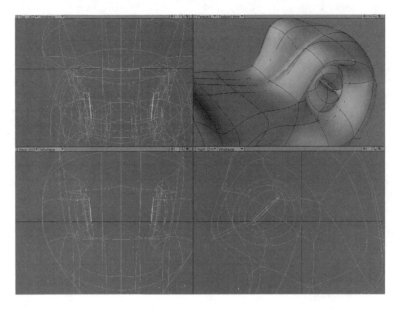

Figure 10.57   Multiply the selected polygons again with another Smooth Shift and push the geometry into the head.

5. Smooth Shift one more time and stretch out the geometry to create the eye socket, as shown in Figure 10.58.

6. Don't create any new geometry for this step. Just tweak points until you are happy with the shape of the eye and eyelid. This is where your own style will come into play, using tools like Drag, Move, or Rotate. Figure 10.59 shows the model.

7. Just like you did with the snout earlier, select the back of the head polygons, Smooth Shift them, and adjust them, as shown in Figures 10.60 and 10.61.

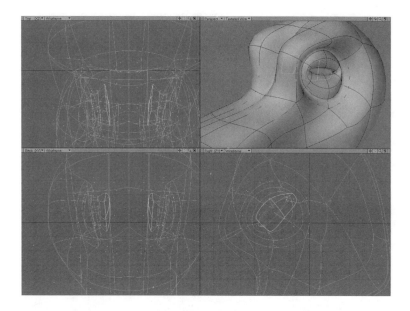

Figure 10.58   One more Smooth Shift operation and a Stretch operation helps create the eye socket.

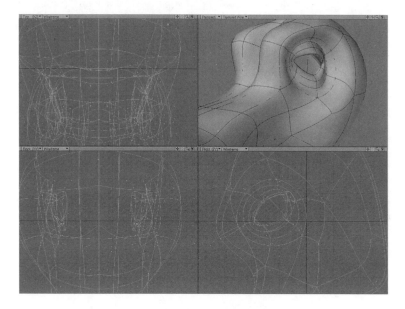

Figure 10.59   Spending time with your model and the Drag tool helps finesse the shape.

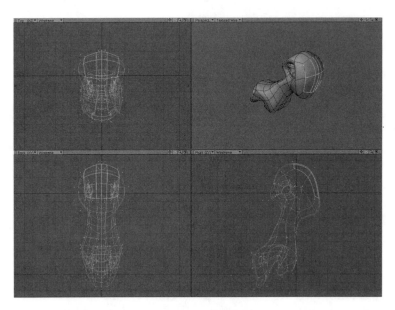

Figure 10.60 Select the polygons on the back of the head.

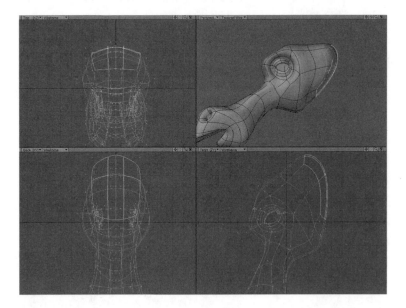

Figure 10.61 Smooth Shifting the polygons multiplies them to extend the head.

8. Extra geometry is needed for the top of the giraffe's head where the horns will be placed. To do this, select the eight polygons that make up the top of the head, as shown in Figure 10.62. Then, Smooth Shift and adjust them as shown in Figure 10.63.

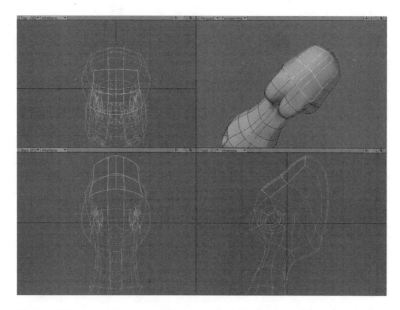

Figure 10.62 Select the eight polygons that make up the top of the giraffe's head.

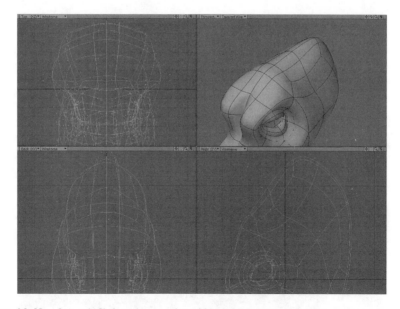

Figure 10.63 Smooth Shift and move the additional geometry to shape.

9. To build the horns, select the two base horn polygons and Smooth Shift them four times, adjusting as you build, as shown in Figures 10.64 and 10.65.

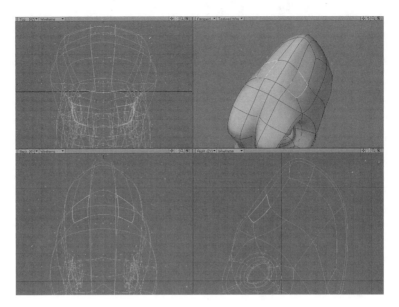

Figure 10.64   Select the two polygons on the top of the head that will be used to create the horns.

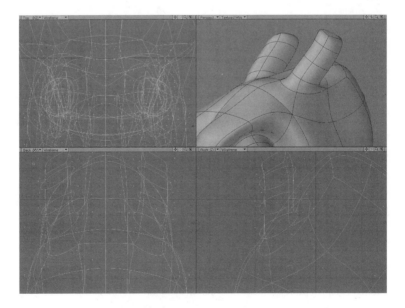

Figure 10.65   Smooth Shift the selection four times, adjust, and tweak to shape the horns.

10. For some finer details, select the polygons at the top of the horns, then Smooth Shift and squeeze the polygons in a small amount, as shown in Figure 10.66.

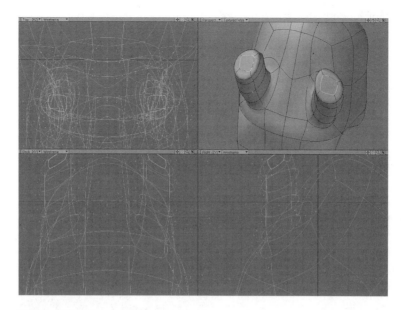

Figure 10.66   Select the top polygons of the horn to Smooth Shift and add finer detail.

11. Smooth Shift again, move the newly created polygons up, and stretch them out as well, as shown in Figure 10.67.

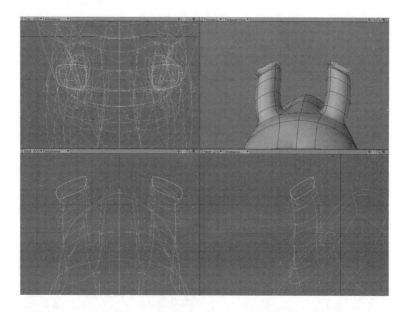

Figure 10.67   Smooth Shift the new polygons, but stretch them outward.

12. Again, Smooth Shift and move the polygons upward. Figure 10.68 shows the operation.

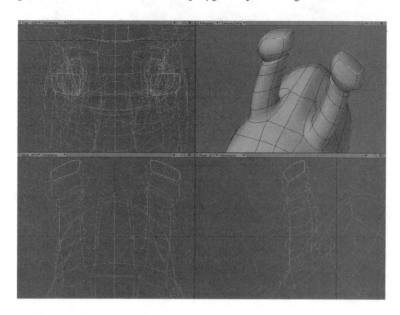

Figure 10.68 As before, Smooth Shift and shape so that your horns look similar to this image.

13. Time for some ears. Did you hear that? Select the ear base polygons that can be used to grow ears. Figure 10.69 shows the selection.

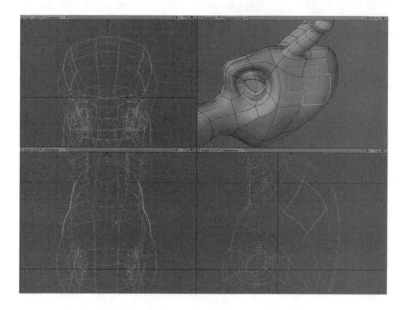

Figure 10.69 Select the base polygons to create the ears.

14. After you have selected the polygons, move them closer to the horns and size them down slightly, as shown in Figure 10.70.

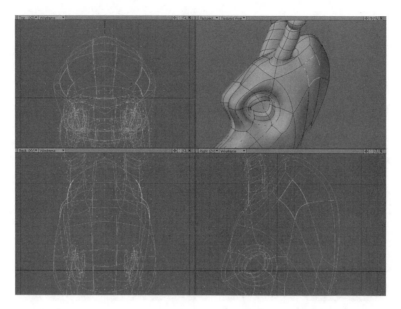

Figure 10.70   Move the selection up near the horns, before Smooth Shifting them.

15. As you might have guessed, it's time to Smooth Shift and move the newly created geometry in, as shown in Figure 10.71.

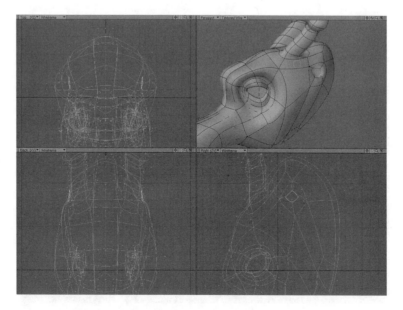

Figure 10.71   Smooth Shift and multiply the polygons; then move them in.

16. Smooth Shift the selection four times and adjust as you go to make the basic shape of the ear. Use Figure 10.72 as a reference.

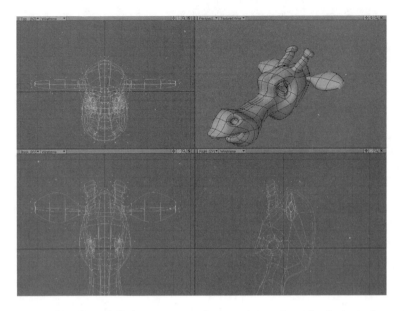

Figure 10.72   Four Smooth Shift operations and some adjustments make the basic shape of the ear.

17. Select all the polygons that make up the ear and rotate them counterclockwise until they face forward, as shown in Figure 10.73.

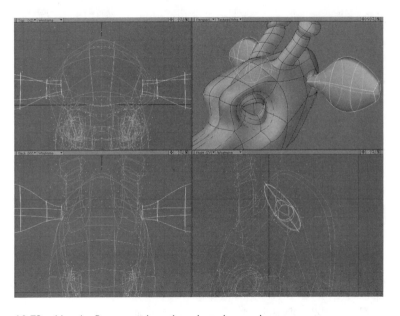

Figure 10.73   Use the Rotate tool on the selected ear polygons.

18. Select the six polygons that make up the front of the ear, Smooth Shift, and size them in. Figure 10.74 shows the selection, and Figure 10.75 shows the adjustment.

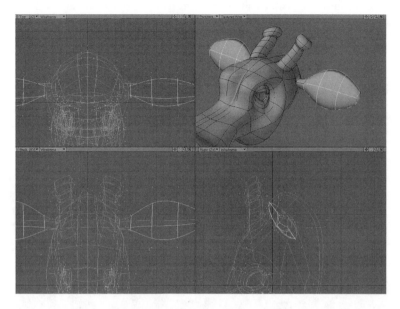

Figure 10.74   Select the polygons that make up the front of the ear.

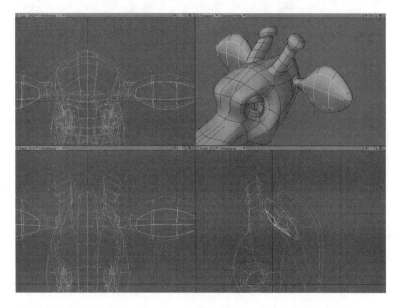

Figure 10.75   Smooth Shift them and apply Size to shape in added detail.

19. With the same polygons still selected, Smooth Shift again and push the polygons back into the ear. You'll keep the ears out straight so that if you decide to place bones for movement they will be easier to set up and control. Figure 10.76 shows the operation.

20. Save your work.

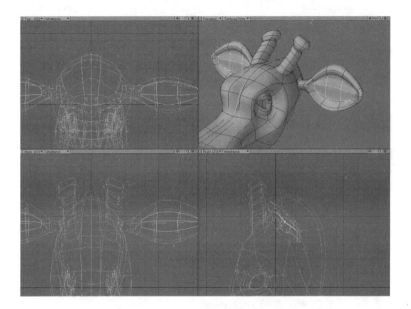

Figure 10.76   Smooth Shift again and move the selection inward.

By this point, you should have a great-looking giraffe head. It's not too important that you create one that looks just like what you're seeing within the figures, but rather, one that you like. You should be at a point where you understand the tools and how to go about creating geometry by making selections, multiplying polygons, and making adjustments with Drag, Move, Rotate, and other tools.

Creating the Neck and Body

This section builds out from where the previous section left off. You'll take your existing head model and continue building from it to create the neck and body of the giraffe. Stick your neck out and go!

Exercise 10.4   Building the Giraffe's Neck and Body

1. Start by first selecting the polygons that will be used to create the neck. Then, apply the Smooth Shift operation and adjust, as shown in Figures 10.77 and 10.78.

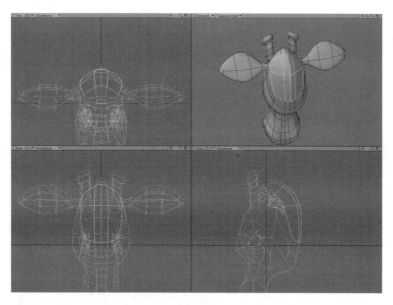

Figure 10.77   Select the polygons that will be used to create the neck.

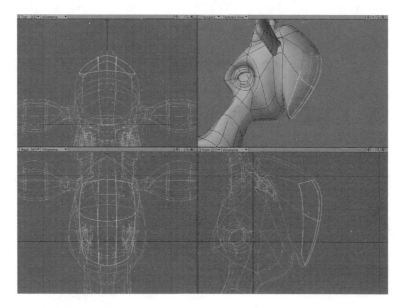

Figure 10.78   Smooth Shift to multiply the selection and adjust the polygons to begin building the neck.

2. As you will do with any model you create, take a few minutes and adjust the model, tweak it, and build it up to your liking. Figure 10.79 shows the model after a bit of adjustment.

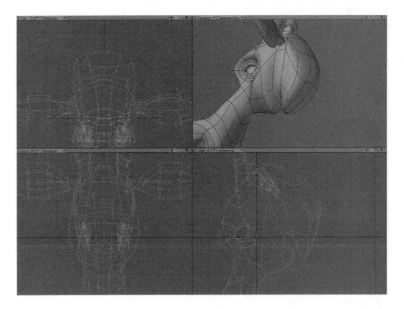

Figure 10.79   A little personal time with the model helps get its points and polygons in place.

3. It's time to clean up the flow of the polygons. The way the polygons in the cheek are aligning is not as good as it could be, so select the two cheek polygons and use Spin Quads one time. Figure 10.80 shows the selection, and Figure 10.81 shows the polygons after the Spin Quads operation.

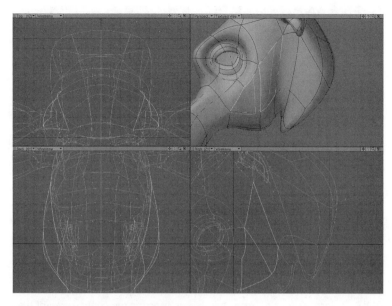

Figure 10.80   Select the polygons in the cheek area.

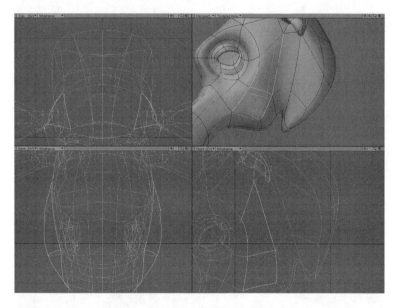

Figure 10.81   Perform a Spin Quads operation to control the flow.

4. At this point, you want to start reducing polygons on the way down the neck, so just select the four polygons that make up the base of the neck instead of eight, as shown in Figure 10.82.

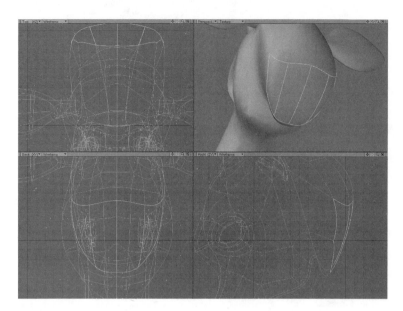

Figure 10.82   Select the four polygons that will be used for the continuation of the neck.

5. Smooth Shift, move, and adjust the newly created polygons. You have just successfully gone from eight polygons to four. Way to go! You're on the right path to streamlined models. Figure 10.83 shows your creation.

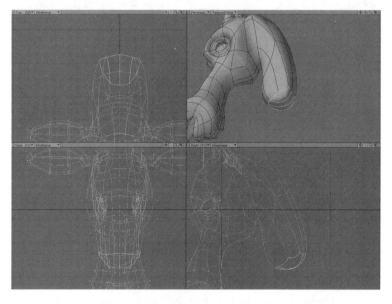

Figure 10.83   Smooth Shifting multiplies the selection, allowing for more detail.

6. Again, Smooth Shift the selection, use the Move tool to move the newly created polygons, and adjust twice more, as shown in Figure 10.84.

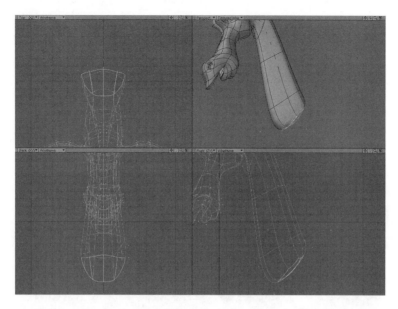

Figure 10.84   Smooth Shift some more and adjust to create the neck of the beast.

7. Spend some quality time with your creation, cleaning up the shape of the neck with the Drag tool, until you have something like Figure 10.85.

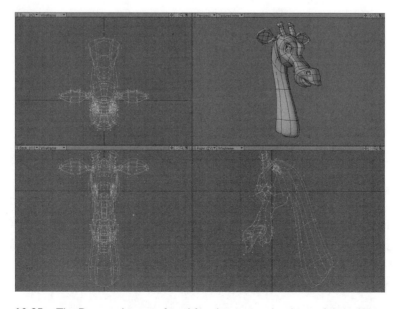

Figure 10.85   The Drag tool is your friend for cleaning up the shape of the neck.

8. You may look over your model from time to time and notice things you don't like—for example, in this model, the ear is too flat. To pull the back of the ear out, first select the points that make up the back of the ear and pull them out slightly. Figure 10.86 shows the selection, and Figure 10.87 shows the operation.

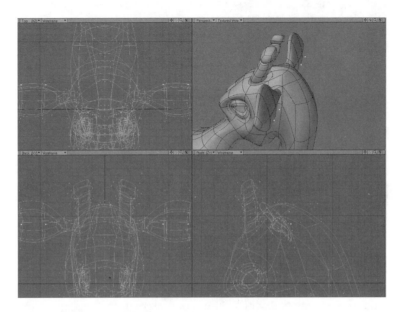

Figure 10.86 Points are selected at the back of the ear.

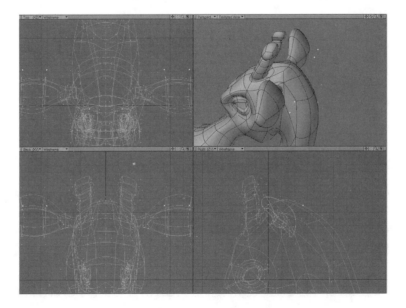

Figure 10.87 The selected points are moved out slightly to round out the ear.

Tip

With any 3D model, the little tweaks can really make your work look amazing.

9. You are halfway there! It's time to start on the body. Select the base of the neck, Smooth Shift, and adjust. Bet you didn't see that coming! Figure 10.88 shows the selection, and Figure 10.89 shows the operation.

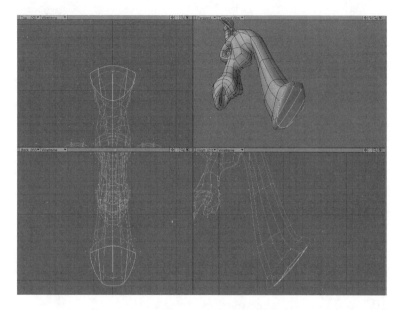

Figure 10.88   The base of the neck has a few polygons you can select to start making the body.

10. Do you remember what you just did to begin creating the body? Good. Repeat the previous step four times, so you end up with something like Figure 10.90.

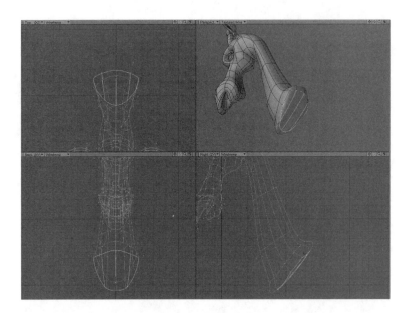

Figure 10.89   After selecting the polygons at the base of the neck, you can use Smooth Shift to build out the body.

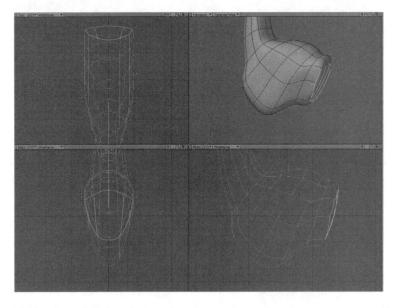

Figure 10.90   Smooth Shift and adjust the selection four times to create something like this.

11. Spend a moment tweaking out the newly created geometry. You'll want to bring the side of the chest out slightly and make a few other tweaks. Nothing major, just some small adjustments so you have something like Figure 10.91.

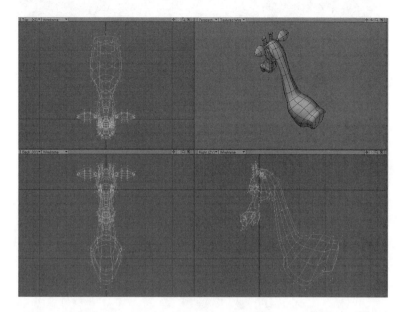

Figure 10.91   Adjustments make the model even better, using Drag, Move, or Rotate. Just simple tweaks to smooth out the mesh.

12. Break a leg…or just create one! You need to prepare the polygons from which you'll pull the front legs. Adjust the polygon on each side, as shown in Figure 10.92. You simply want to size up the area from which the leg will be pulled. Figure 10.93 shows adjusted polygons.

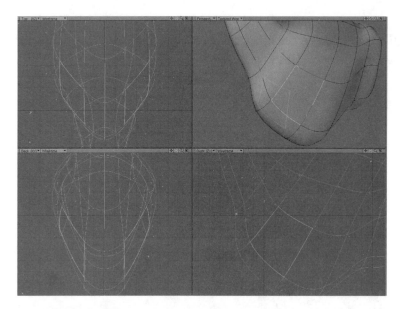

Figure 10.92 Select the first set of polygons to begin making the legs.

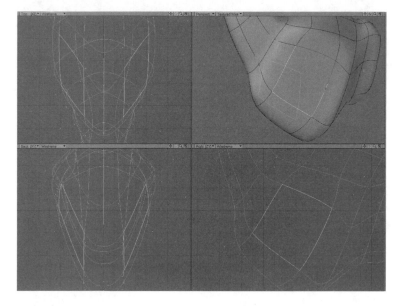

Figure 10.93 Size up the selection to begin creating the legs.

13. Smooth Shift away! Use the Smooth Shift tool to begin building out the leg, as shown in Figure 10.94.

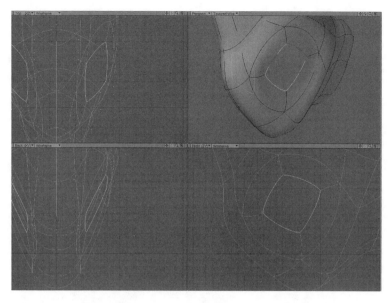

Figure 10.94   Use Smooth Shift to begin creating the leg of the giraffe.

14. As with the previous areas of the model, use Smooth Shift to multiply polygon selections and use Move to adjust them, as shown in Figure 10.95. Try using the Rotate tool on selections, and in the Back view, rotate the polygon so that it is facing the ground, as shown in Figure 10.96.

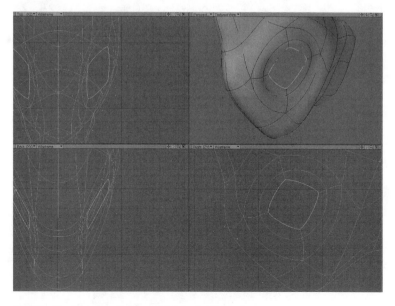

Figure 10.95   Use Smooth Shift to multiply the leg polygons.

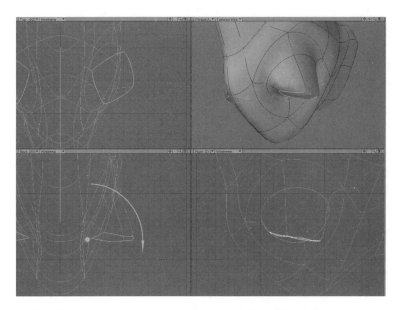

Figure 10.96   Rotate the polygon selection so that it's facing the ground.

15. Make sure the end of the leg's polygons are selected, as shown in Figure 10.97, and then use the Smooth Shift twice and adjust the selection, as shown in Figure 10.98.

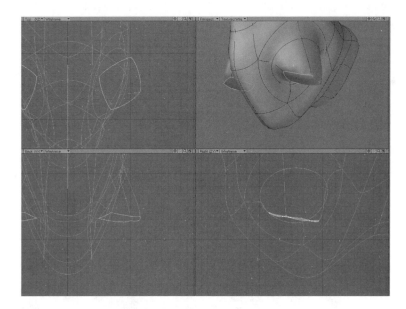

Figure 10.97   Select the polygons at the end of the legs.

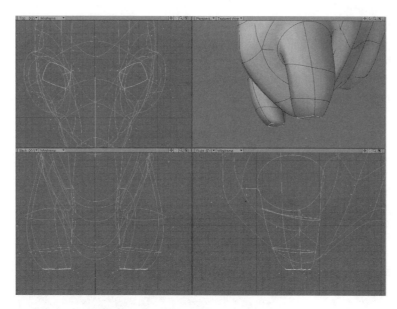

Figure 10.98   Smooth Shift twice and adjust the leg polygons.

16. Adjust the polygons around the chest where the legs connect, as shown in Figure
    10.99. What you're going for here is a nice rounded chest shape.

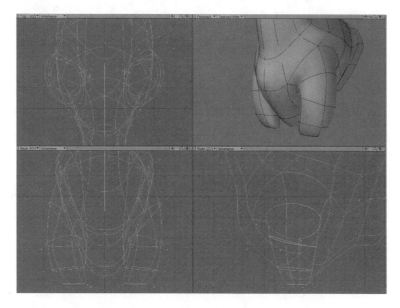

Figure 10.99   Adjust the leg polygons around the chest area.

17. Now is a good time to resync the two sides by removing half and mirroring. Do you remember the steps? Turn Symmetry off and select half of the model, as shown in Figure 10.100. Set the Value on the X-axis to 0, as in Figure 10.101, which will bring all selected polygons to the center axis, as shown in Figure 10.102. Then, delete the selection, as in Figure 10.103, and mirror the merged points, as in Figure 10.104.

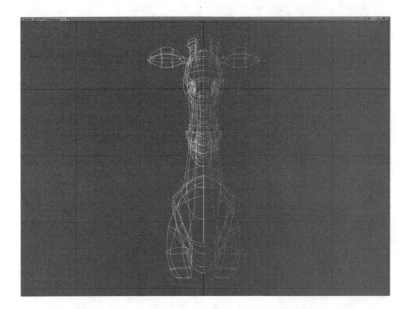

Figure 10.100   Turn off Symmetry and select one half of the model's polygons.

Figure 10.101   Set the value for the selection to 0 on the X-axis.

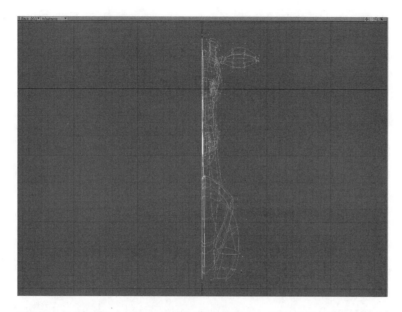

Figure 10.102   Setting the value to 0 on the X-axis brings all the selection to the same position value, essentially flattening the selection.

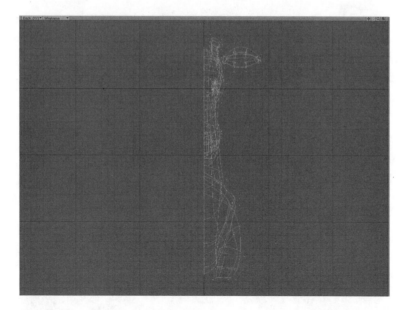

Figure 10.103   Delete the selected polygons.

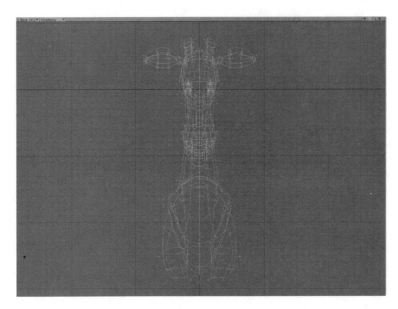

Figure 10.104   Mirror the remaining half of the giraffe with the Merge Points option active from the Mirror Numeric panel.

18. Continue with the creation of the legs. Turn Symmetry back on. Select the polygons on the base of the legs, as shown in Figure 10.105. Then, Smooth Shift eight times and adjust until your legs look similar to Figure 10.106.

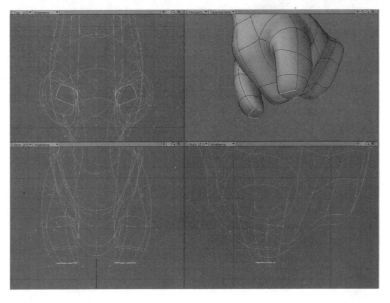

Figure 10.105   Select the polygons at the base of the legs.

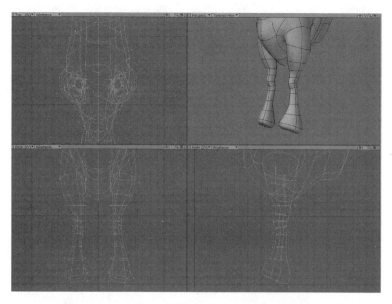

Figure 10.106   After you select the polygons, Smooth Shift to multiply the selection eight times, Move and adjust along the way to create the shape of the leg.

19. After you're happy with the shape of your legs, you're ready for the hooves. Select the base polygons of the legs, as shown in Figure 10.107, then Smooth Shift and shrink them in. Also, move them into the leg just a bit, as in Figure 10.108.

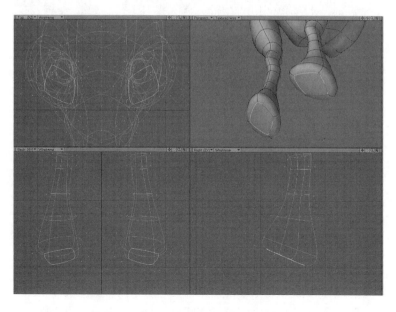

Figure 10.107   Make sure the bottoms of the legs are selected to begin creating the hooves.

Figure 10.108 Smooth Shift to multiply and move the polygons upward.

20. Smooth Shift the selection and pull them out and away from the leg, as shown in Figure 10.109.

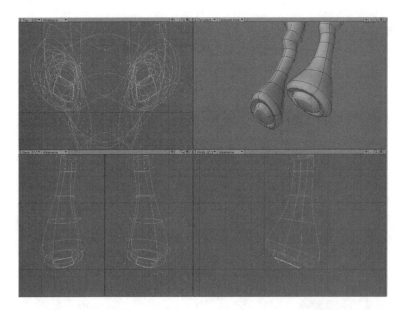

Figure 10.109 Smooth Shift the selection and move them out from the leg.

21. Stretch the polygons out slightly, as shown in Figure 10.110. Stretch works well for quickly shaping selections before you Smooth Shift and multiply again.

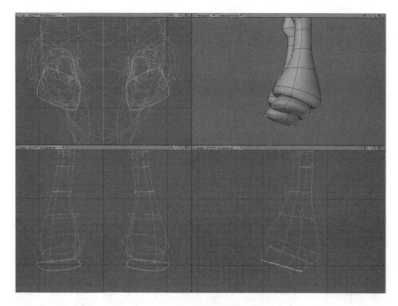

Figure 10.110 Stretch the selection to shape the hooves.

22. With the selection, Smooth Shift twice and move them to complete the hooves, as shown in Figure 10.111.

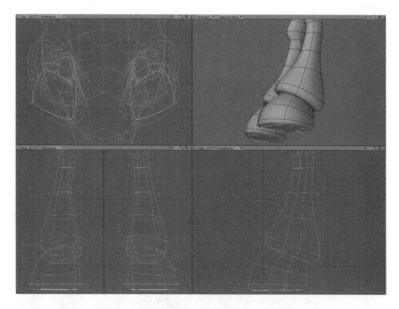

Figure 10.111 Smooth Shift twice and adjust to complete the hooves.

At this point, your model is almost complete, and you have a good idea of how it's looking. Figure 10.112 shows an overall look of where you should be with your model.

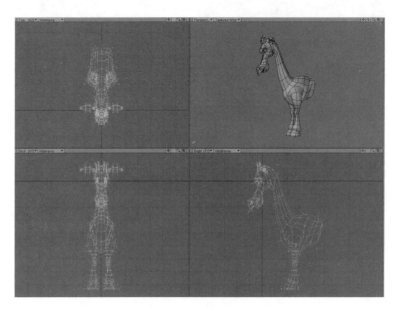

Figure 10.112 Your model should be looking something like this.

23. It's time to get this guy finished! Select the polygons at the end of the waist area, as shown in Figure 10.113, then Smooth Shift them and adjust twice, as in Figure 10.114.

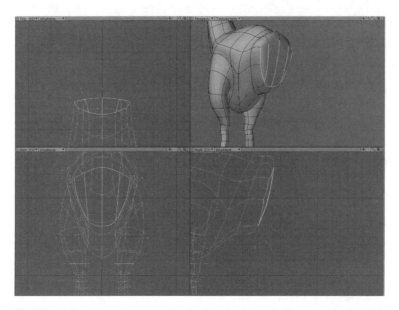

Figure 10.113 Select the polygons on the back end of the giraffe to create the back end.

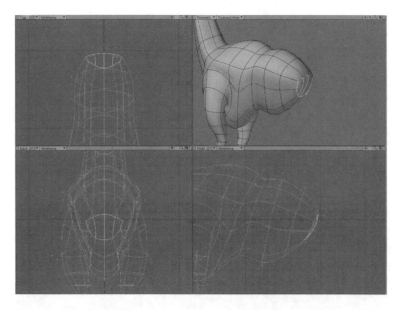

Figure 10.114   Smooth Shift to multiply the selection twice, and adjust the polygons to shape the back end.

24. You need to create the back legs the same way you did the front ones. It's pretty easy to do, so select and then size up the polygons from which you want to pull the legs, as shown in Figure 10.115.

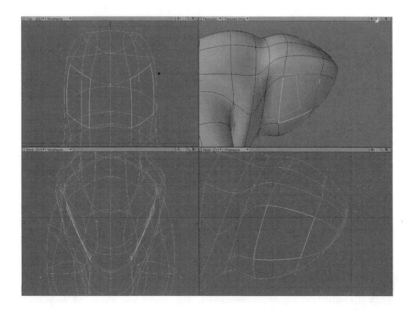

Figure 10.115   Select the back-end polygons and size them up to begin creating the back legs.

25. Smooth Shift the selected polygons and rotate them down to face the ground, as shown in Figure 10.116.

Figure 10.116 Smooth Shift the selected polygons and rotate them to begin creating the legs.

26. With the legs facing in the right direction now, Smooth Shift and pull them down to begin creating the legs, as shown in Figure 10.117.

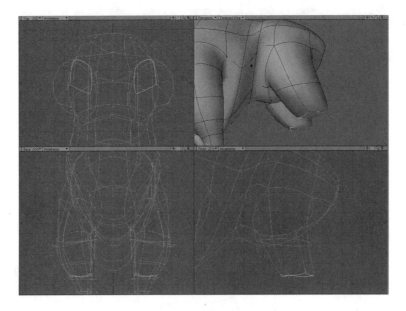

Figure 10.117 Smooth Shift the legs to build them out.

27. Spend some time cleaning up the points around the base leg. Use the Drag tool and work in the Perspective window to shape the leg, so you have something like Figure 10.118.

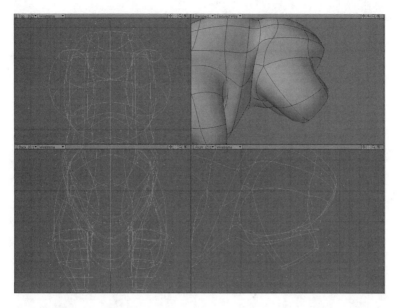

Figure 10.118   Use the Drag tool to shape the upper part of the legs.

28. With the base of the leg polygons still selected, use Smooth Shift eight times and then move and adjust the polygons to work your way down the back legs, as shown in Figure 10.119.

29. Using the same methods you used to create the hooves on the front legs, do the same for the back. Select the base polygon, Smooth Shift, stretch, move, and adjust to create the hooves, as shown in Figure 10.120. Remember, you're working in Symmetry mode.

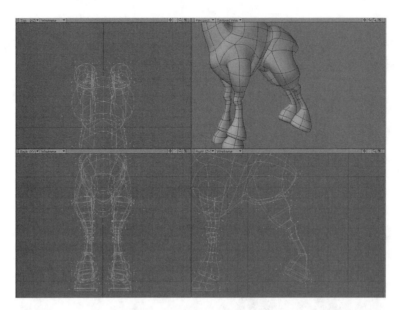

Figure 10.119   Smooth Shift about eight times and adjust the newly created polygons to build the legs.

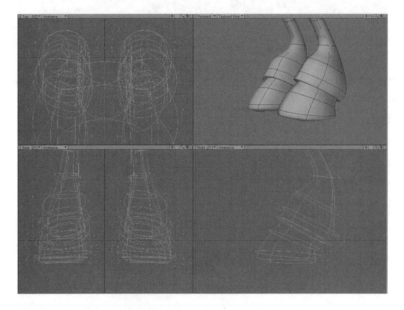

Figure 10.120   Use the same techniques as you did for the front hooves, by using Smooth Shift and making adjustments.

30. If you look closely at the polygon flow in the hips, they could be improved upon. Let's use Spin Quads to clean it up. Select the polygons in the hips, as shown in Figure 10.121. Then, use the Spin Quads tool to change their flow, so they look like Figure 10.122.

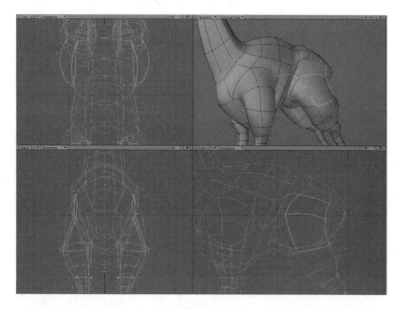

Figure 10.121   Select the polygons in the hips whose flow is not as smooth as they could be.

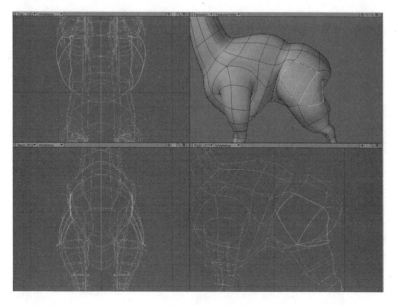

Figure 10.122   After the Spin Quads command is applied, the hip polygons flow correctly.

31. Go ahead and use Spin Quads twice on the polygons that make up the back of the upper thigh, as shown in Figure 10.123. This is the type of polygonal flow you should strive for in all of your modeling, as shown in Figure 10.124, and as mentioned earlier in the chapter.

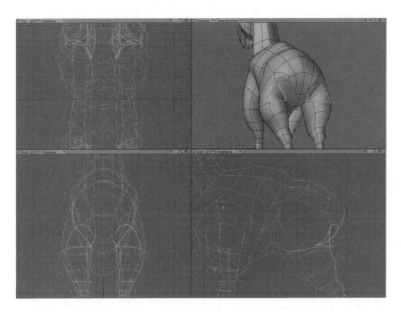

Figure 10.123 Select any other polygons whose flow is not so good.

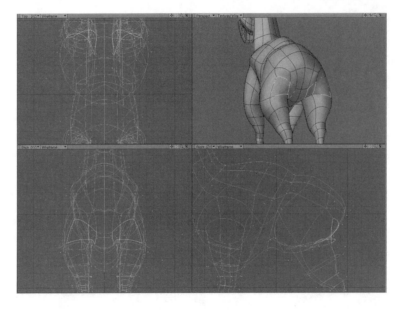

Figure 10.124 Apply Spin Quads to correct the flow of the polygons.

32. It's time to create the tail of the giraffe. Select the polygons where you would like to pull out the tail, as shown in Figure 10.125. Then, Smooth Shift and scale them down, as shown in Figure 10.126.

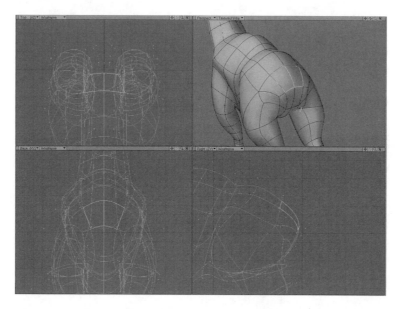

Figure 10.125   To begin creating the tail, select the polygons that make up the tail end of the giraffe.

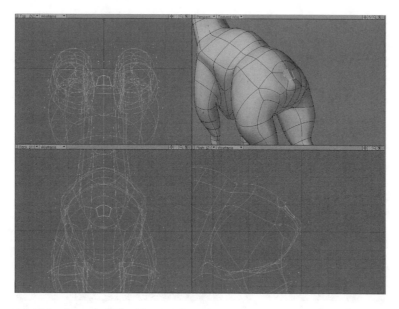

Figure 10.126   Smooth Shift and move the polygons to begin building the tail.

33. With the selection, Smooth Shift six times and adjust to create the shaft of the tail, as shown in Figure 10.127.

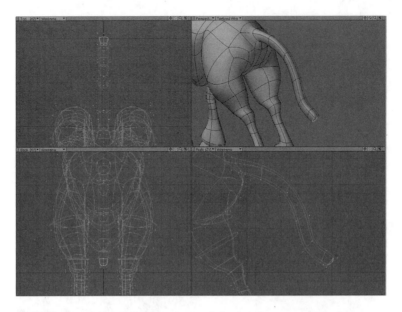

Figure 10.127 Use the Smooth Shift command six times to create the tail.

34. To make the bushy part of the tail at the end, you need to Smooth Shift five times, move the selection each time, and adjust to shape, as in Figure 10.128.

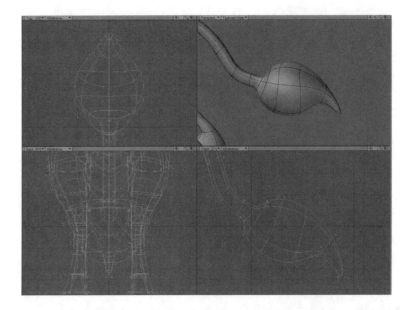

Figure 10.128 Smooth Shift the end of the tail and shape the polygons to create a fat end.

You're almost there! With just a few more details, your giraffe will be complete. Figure 10.129 shows the model at this point.

Figure 10.129   With the majority of the modeling complete, your giraffe resembles a quadruped character!

35. You need to add the hair that runs from the head down the neck. Select the neck polygons at the back, as shown in Figure 10.130. Then, Smooth Shift and squeeze using the Stretch tool, to bring the polygons inward, as shown in Figure 10.131.

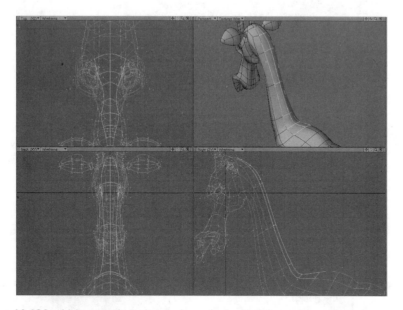

Figure 10.130   Make sure the polygons down the back of the neck are selected.

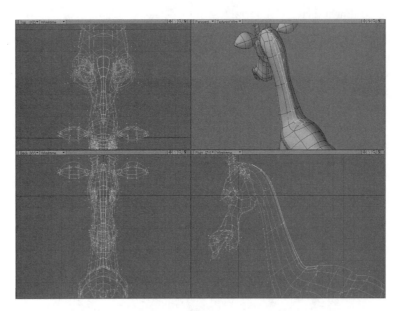

Figure 10.131 Smooth Shift the selection to multiply the polygons, and then use Stretch to squeeze them inward.

36. Smooth Shift the same selection again and pull the polygons away from the neck, as shown in Figure 10.132.

Figure 10.132 Use Smooth Shift again to multiply the polygons and move them away from the neck.

37. Adjust the shape of the hair until you are happy with it. You should go for something like Figure 10.133.

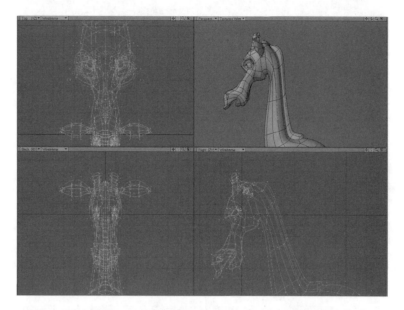

Figure 10.133   Use the Drag tool to shape the hair on the back of the neck to shape and adjust to your liking.

Now you have a giraffe with hooves, a tail, and polygons for hair down the back of the neck. The final touches are next, such as eyes and coloring.

Creating Eyeballs and Color

The giraffe is looking great and is almost complete. The last things you need to do are add the eyeballs and color the little guy! This section presents you with the steps to create the finishing touches.

Exercise 10.5   Creating the Giraffe's Eyeballs and Color

1. Time to make the eyes! Place your giraffe in the background layer and create a box where the eye goes. Figure 10.134 shows the operation.

2. Subdivide the box using Metaform (Shift+d) one time, and then press the Tab key to switch to Subpatch mode. Figure 10.135 shows the result.

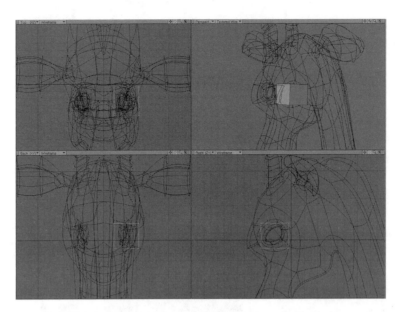

Figure 10.134   Make sure the giraffe is placed in a background layer and create a box in the area of the eye.

Figure 10.135   Subdivide the box using Metaform.

3. Use the Size tool to make the eye fit snugly into the eye socket and move it into place. Hold the Shift key to select both layers to see how the eye lines up, as shown in Figure 10.136.

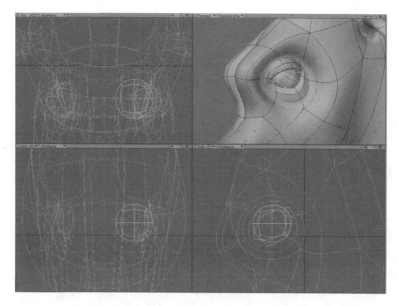

Figure 10.136   Size the eyeball so that it lines up with the head of the giraffe, and make both layers foreground layers to view.

4. With all the eye polygons selected, click the Change Surface button at the bottom of the Modeler interface (or press q), give the eye a unique name, such as G_Eye, and give it some basic surface attributes. You can choose black and give it some Specularity and turn on Smoothing. Figure 10.137 shows the operation.

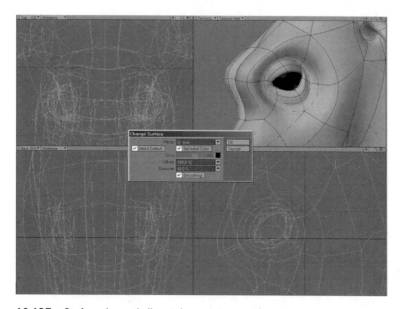

Figure 10.137   Surface the eyeball so it has a unique surface name.

5. You've created only one eyeball, so be sure to mirror the eye, as shown in Figure 10.138.

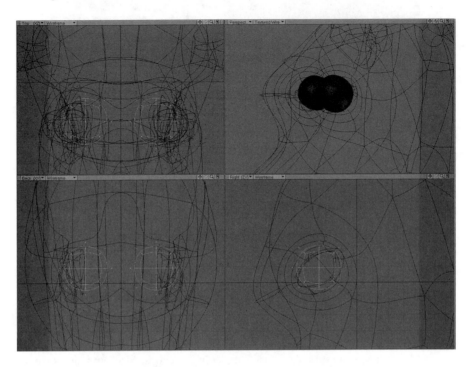

Figure 10.138 Mirror the eyeball so the giraffe has better eyesight.

6. A little more surfacing and your giraffe is ready to go! Go to the layer that contains the main object and surface the whole object with the name G_Base, or something similar. Figures 10.139 and 10.140 show the functions.

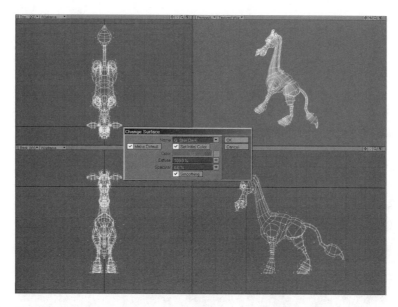

Figure 10.139   With the right polygons selected, you can call up the Change Surface panel to name the polygons. This is everything but the eyeballs.

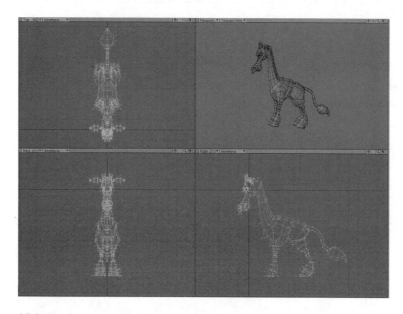

Figure 10.140   The giraffe has a fresh orange color applied.

7. Select the hooves on all four legs and give them a unique surface, such as G_Hoofs. Figure 10.141 shows the operation.

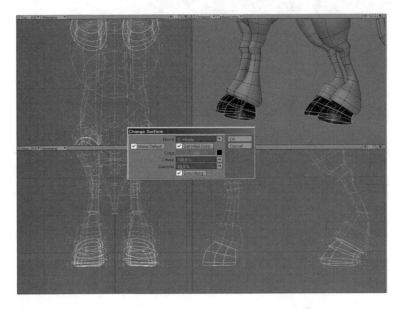

Figure 10.141   Surface the hooves of the giraffe with a unique surface name.

8. Don't forget to select the bushy part of the tail and the hair on the neck of the giraffe. You can give both of these surfaces the same name, such as G_Hair, as shown in Figure 10.142.

9. To add to the character's surfacing, select the polygons that make up the eye area and give them a surface name of G_ Eye Socket, as shown in Figure 10.143.

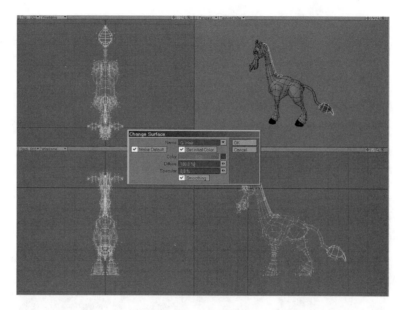

Figure 10.142   Give the hair polygons a surface name of something unique, like hair!

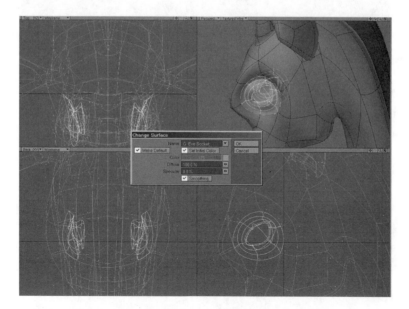

Figure 10.143   Give the area around the eye sockets a unique surface name as well.

10. Not to be outdone, the giraffe's nostrils need their own surface name as well. Select the nostril polygons and give them the surface name of G_Nostrils, as shown in Figure 10.144.

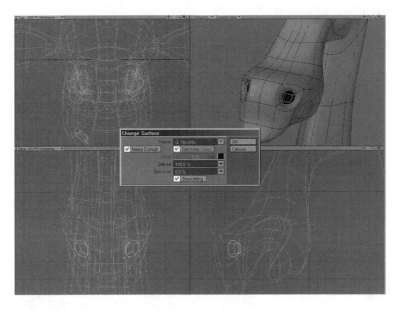

Figure 10.144 Don't forget to surface the nostrils.

11. Don't forget to give the mouth polygons a unique surface name. Select the inner mouth polygons and surface them as G_mouth. Figure 10.145 shows the surfacing.

12. Cut (Ctrl+x) the eyes from their current layer and paste (Ctrl+v) them into the same layer as the base model. Figure 10.146 shows the operation.

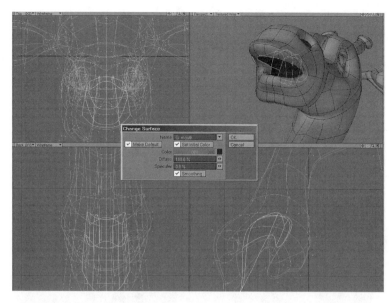

Figure 10.145   Give the inner mouth a unique surface name as you did with the nostrils.

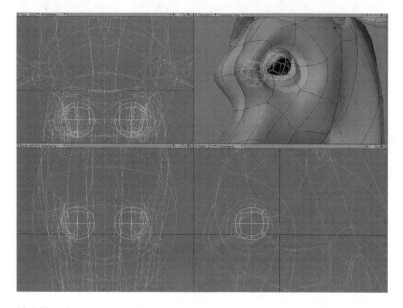

Figure 10.146   Cut and paste the eyes into the same layer as the giraffe model.

13. Select the polygons beneath the giraffe. Surface the strip that runs down the neck and belly as G_Skin Light, as shown in Figure 10.147.

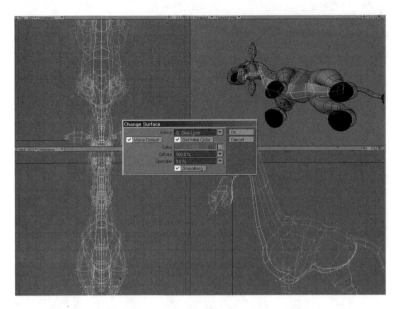

Figure 10.147   Surface the strip of polygons that runs down the neck and belly.

14. Add a unique surface name to the horns and inside ears as G_Horns and G_Inner Ear. Figures 10.148 and 10.149 show the operations.

Figure 10.148   Surface the giraffe's inner ears with a unique surface name.

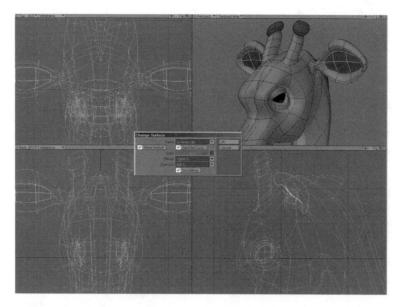

Figure 10.149 Give the inner ears a unique surface name as well.

Now that you're at the halfway point…just joking! You've completed the model and now it's time to break away from the computer long enough to grab a drink or take in a breath of fresh air. Congratulations! Figures 10.150 and 10.151 show the final giraffe model in wireframe and solid shaded modes in Modeler.

Figure 10.150 The final giraffe in Wireframe Shade mode.

Figure 10.151   The final giraffe in Texture Display mode.

The Next Step

What you've created in this chapter is a fun four-legged character. You can use these exact same techniques to create frogs, aliens, dogs, cats, bugs, or just about anything else you can imagine. If you need more detail, subdivide with additional Smooth Shift operations, use the BandSaw tool, tweak, adjust the points and polygons, and go! Don't forget to use photo references for models you want to create, but combine references with the techniques in this chapter and you'll create a great model every time.

To create an entirely different type of model, move on to Chapter 11, "Modeling Electronics." Have you ever wondered how to create a cool looking cell phone in 3D? Turn the page and learn how.

Chapter 11
Modeling Electronics

There's more to LightWave than making logos and characters. Many of you might not even have an interest in creating flying text or moving cartoons. Perhaps your job or your passion requires you to model real-world objects. If so, this chapter is for you! But this chapter is also good for anyone looking to do more in LightWave Modeler. You'll learn about:

- Creating real-world objects in Modeler
- Working with fine details in Modeler
- Surfacing for real-world looks
- Lighting for realistic product shots

Modeling Project Overview

Did you know that many of the print ads you see in newspapers and magazines for things such as cars, electronics, and furniture are often 100% 3D? That's right! Photography is often more expensive than 3D creation, and many ad agencies and production companies are turning to 3D for content.

This chapter walks you through creating a realistic cellular phone and setting up lighting and a render. The techniques used here can be applied to other types of electronics, food, or other inanimate objects. Figure 11.1 shows the model you'll create.

Figure 11.1   LightWave can be used for modeling real-world objects for print pieces, billboards, or television ads.

You can use the lighting and rendering methods in both print and animation. With that said, let's get started.

Modeling for Detail

The modeling you've done so far in this book has given you a really good working knowledge of Modeler. You've learned how to work with layers, set pivots, use primitives, and utilize a few other tools. This project takes you further, but as you'll see, it still starts out with the same simple methods. One thing that's cool about LightWave Modeler is that most projects start in a similar fashion—with points, simple polygons, or curves. When creating a 3D model for print, keep in mind that it will be rendered at a very high resolution, which means the viewer will see more detail in it because print is significantly higher resolution than video. Even so, for this project, you'll begin with nothing more than a box.

Exercise 11.1   Preparing for Detailed Modeling

1. Open Modeler and save any work you've been doing. Create a new object by pressing Shift and the n key.

2. For this project, you'll use the Numeric panel often, so press n on the keyboard or click the Numeric button at the bottom of Modeler.

3. Also, press F7 to open the Layers panel and press w for the Statistics panel. We'll refer to these throughout the project.

4. Move the three panels, Numeric, Layers, and Statistics, over to the right side of the Modeler interface, and grab the right side of the Modeler viewports and pull them in. Figure 11.2 shows the setup.

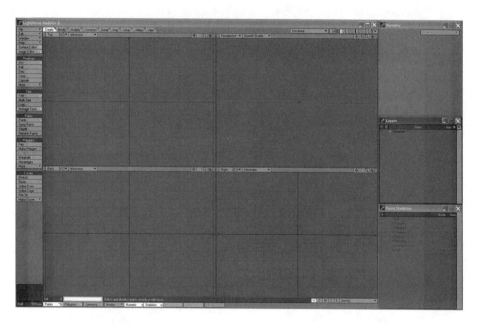

Figure 11.2   You can keep Modeler's Numeric, Layers, and Statistics panels open for easier access during your project.

5. Quit Modeler to save this configuration. Now when you restart Modeler, your panels will remain open.

6. Now that your Modeler interface is set up, remember to have these few things set as well:

   - Be sure you're working with the Caps lock key off on your keyboard. Keyboard equivalents are used in this chapter, and you'll end up with errors and strange results by working in Caps mode.

- Press the d key for Display Options. Under the Units tab, make sure Grid Snap is set to None. You don't want Modeler to guess where you're moving a point or polygon—you should do it!

- Also in the Units tab of the Display Options panel, be sure the Unit System is set to SI, for system international unit of measurement.

- The Default Unit should be set to Meters in this panel as well. That's it for the Display Options panel.

- In the General Options (press o), make sure Polygons is set to Quadrangles so that the geometry you create is built in quads (that is, four-sided).

- Also in this panel, Curve Divisions should remain at the default setting of Medium, and Patch Divisions should be set to 4. We're going to build a lot of detail in this model, and when you hit that Tab key to jump to SubPatch mode, a setting that is too high can really bring your system to a halt. 4 is a reasonable value to start with. We'll increase this as the tutorial progresses.

- Finally, make sure your Undo levels in the General Options panel is set to 128, LightWave's maximum value. Note that some people who work on extremely large models (you Hollywood people) might not want this set too high. Undoing a complex operation on a model of, say, 500,000 polygons can take up a lot of your system resources. For most things, this can remain at 128.

7. Press d one more time to open the Display Options panel. Click the Backdrop tab and select the TL button for top-left viewport.

8. From the Image selection, load the PhoneButtons.jpg image from the Chapter 11 folder of this book's DVD.

9. Bring the contrast and brightness down to the left so the image is just slightly visible in the Backdrop. This is done so that your points and polygons are more visible. Change Size to 6m.

10. Finally, set the Image Resolution to 1024 and click OK to close the panel.

11. From the Create tab, select Box and draw out a box with these values:

Width	3.2857m
Height	0m
Depth	5.9206m
Center X	7.9365mm
Center Y	-142.8571mm
Center Z	39.6825mm

Axis	Y
Radius	0m
Radius Segments	1
Segments X	7
Segments Y	2
Segments Z	3

Important

These values do not have to be precise for you to do this tutorial. The idea here is to draw a box with the right amount of segments over the background image in the Top viewport.

12. After you've created the box, press F2 to automatically center the box on the 0,0,0, axis. Then, press the Tab key to activate SubPatch mode.

13. At the bottom of Modeler, click the Symmetry button or press Shift+Y on your keyboard. Using the Drag tool from the Modify tab (Ctrl+t), pull the front points in slightly in the Top view to round out the box to match the background image. Figure 11.3 shows the look you're going for.

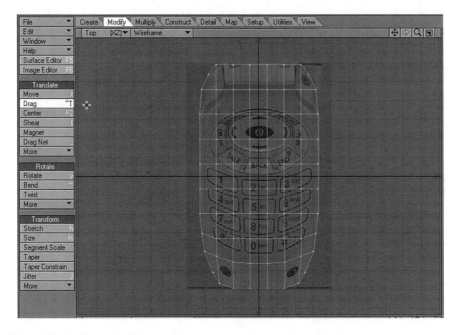

Figure 11.3   Using the Drag tool, round out the box you've created.

14. Using the Drag tool, shape the points to match the flow of the phone. Hold the Ctrl key down as you drag to constrain, and align the rows of points to follow the buttons, as in Figure 11.4.

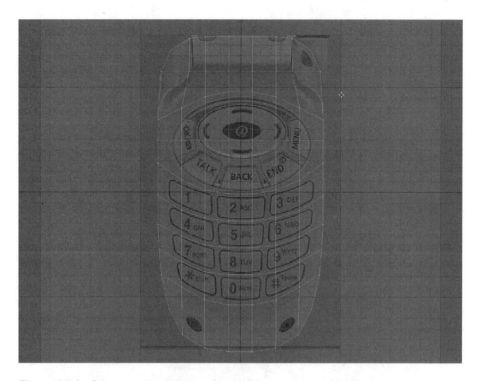

Figure 11.4   Points are dragged into a flow that begins to resemble the phone.

15. Select the third row of points from the right. Using the Move tool (t), move the selected points up toward the center of the phone image, just in front of the 3, 6, and 9 buttons. Use Rotate from the base to rotate the row. Refer to the selected points and their new position in Figure 11.5.

16. Deselect the points.

17. Using the Drag tool, in the same Top viewport, drag the second row of points over to the outside of the phone buttons. Yes, this is confusing, but your goal is to create a wireframe mesh over the phone buttons, as in Figure 11.6. Remember, Symmetry mode should be on, causing your movements on the right X-axis to be automatically mirrored on the left.

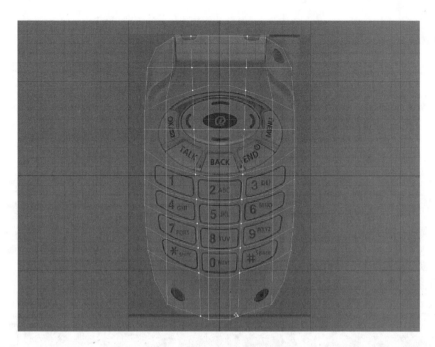

Figure 11.5   Move the selected points to the left and rotate them slightly to follow the contour of the phone buttons.

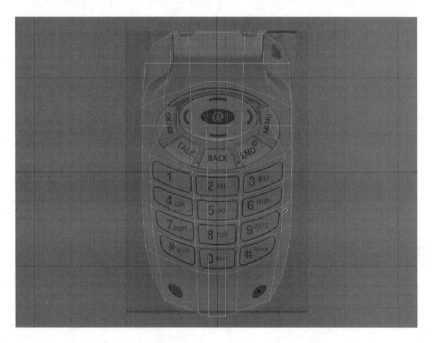

Figure 11.6   Using the Drag tool, move the points on the right side so that they frame the buttons.

18. At this point, go ahead and save your work! This is where LightWave 8's incremental save feature comes in very handy! With every save after this point, press Shift+s, and you'll save a new version. You'll always be able to step back to a previous version if you don't like something you've done.

19. Now, select just the top-center polygons, as in Figure 11.7. This should be a total selection of 9 polygons, which you can determine by looking at the bottom left of the Modeler interface, labeled Sel.

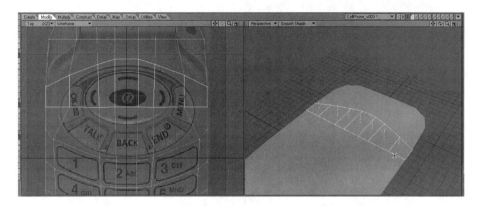

Figure 11.7   Select just the top-center polygons of the model.

20. From the Multiply tab, select BandSaw from the Subdivide category. In the panel that appears, choose Auto for the Edge To Select setting. Turn on Enable Divide and make sure Add is selected. Click OK. Your selected polygons now become subdivided for more control, as in Figure 11.8.

21. Deselect the polygons and select the bottom-center row of polygons. These are the polygons just beneath the row you just subdivided.

22. Again, run BandSaw from the Multiply tab to subdivide the selection.

    Anytime you perform an operation like BandSaw, always press the Tab key to see if your geometry is still made up of three or four polygons so that you can use SubPatch mode.

23. Save your work.

24. Deselect the polygons and then select the next row of polygons beneath the ones you just subdivided. Run BandSaw again, as in Figure 11.9.

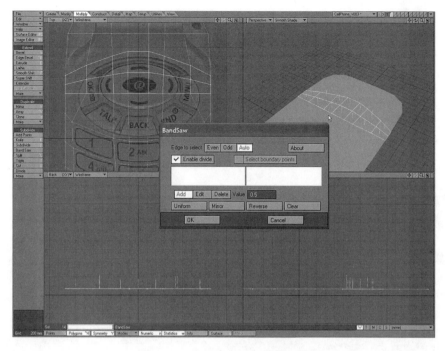

Figure 11.8 Using the BandSaw tool, you can subdivide a selection of polygons.

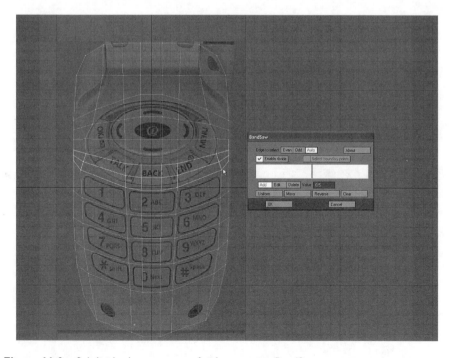

Figure 11.9 Subdivide the next row of polygons using BandSaw.

You're probably wondering, "Why so many BandSaw operations," right? Well, even if you're not curious, it's important to know that the method you're using in this chapter to model is adaptable to any type of model. Starting with a simple mesh, it's easy to add detail where you need it. You've created a simple flat box, and then you adjusted points, subdivided, and repeated the process. You'll do this a few more times, and then you'll give the phone some depth.

25. Deselect the newly created polygons, select the top row around the center, and run BandSaw. Figure 11.10 shows the operation.

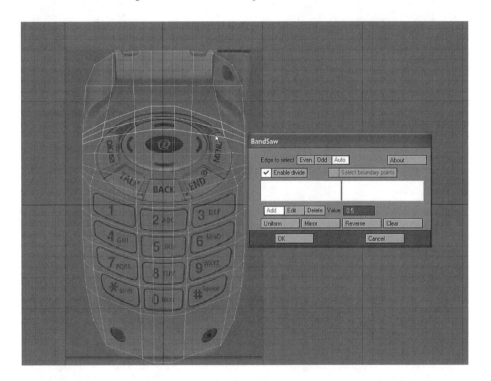

Figure 11.10   Run BandSaw again around the top area of the menu buttons on the phone.

26. Deselect the polygons and then select the entire second row of polygons on the right side. This is the row of polygons that covers the 3, 6, and 9 buttons. Run the BandSaw tool from the Multiply tab to subdivide this row. Figure 11.11 shows the finished operation.

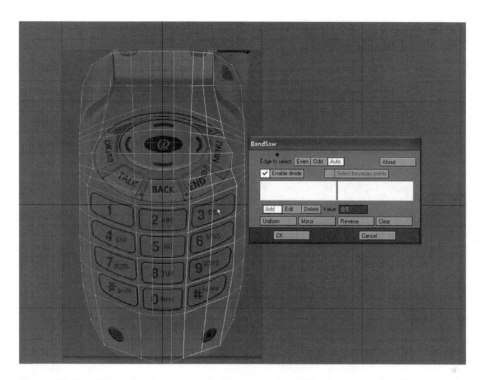

Figure 11.11   Select the entire row of polygons up the right side and run BandSaw.

27. Repeat this process for the same polygons on the left side of the phone.

    You've now created a simple yet powerful mesh around the image of the phone. From here, you'll subdivide more to create buttons with depth. Figure 11.12 shows the mesh around the buttons thus far.

28. OK! You're doing great. Save your work and perform some more BandSaw operations! Select the horizontal rows of polygons that cover each set of phone buttons and BandSaw them to subdivide them. You'll do this four times, once for the 0 row, then the 7 row, then the 4 row, and finally, the 1 row. Figure 11.13 shows the 1 row subdivision, with the other rows as well.

29. Deselect any polygons and then select each row of polygons that makes up just the bottom half of the number buttons. Figure 11.14 shows the selections. As you might have guessed, run BandSaw on each of these rows to subdivide even further.

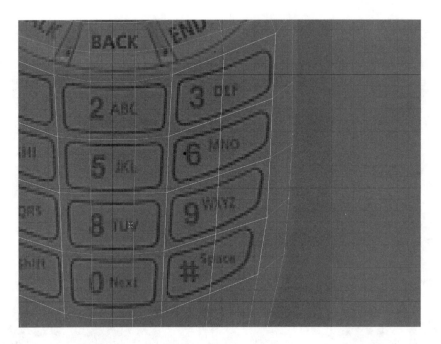

Figure 11.12 By using BandSaw and Drag, you're creating an even mesh around the buttons of the phone.

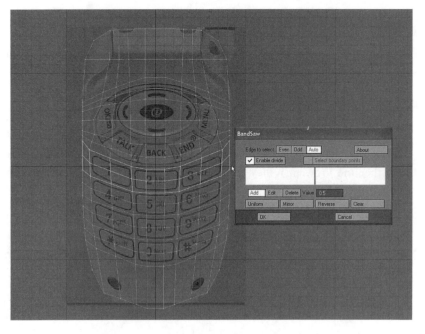

Figure 11.13 To subdivide the rows of polygons that cover each of the three buttons, select the horizontal rows covering the number buttons.

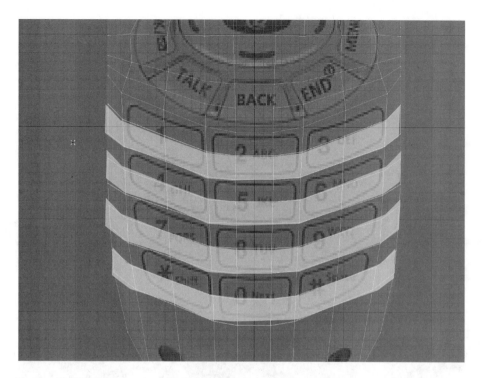

Figure 11.14   Select each of the horizontal rows of polygons that make up just the bottom half of the number buttons. Run BandSaw on each row to subdivide it.

30. Save your work! Now, move the points using the Drag tool to frame out the buttons, as in Figure 11.15. You can see that with these polygons selected, there are four polygons that make up the eight selected buttons, and they do not touch each other. This is important when you begin adding depth.

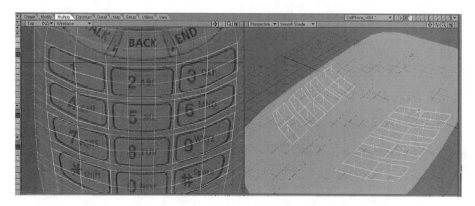

Figure 11.15   Points are dragged around to clearly define the polygons that make up the phone buttons.

However, if you select the center row of buttons (the 2, 5, 8, and 0), you'll see that they do touch the polygons next to them. You need to align the points with these buttons as you did with the rest.

31. Select the two center rows of points, as in Figure 11.16.

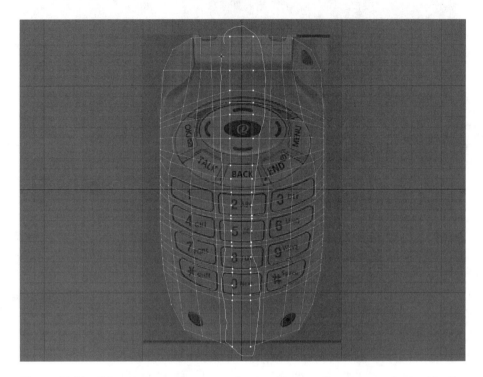

Figure 11.16   Select the two center rows of points. However, Symmetry mode should still be active, so if you select just the right center row, the left will also be selected.

32. Move the selected rows out so they line up with the edge of the center buttons, as in Figure 11.17. You can also rotate the row to help alignment.

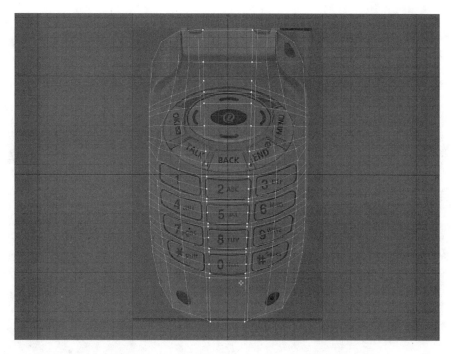

Figure 11.17 Move the selected rows of points outward to line up with the edge of the center buttons.

33. Once the points are aligned, select the polygons down the entire center of the phone. Subdivide them with BandSaw as you did earlier. Figure 11.18 shows the operation.

34. Now, use the Drag tool to clean up the points and shape them around the buttons of the phone. Each phone button should now be made up of four polygons, as shown in Figure 11.19.

35. Finally, go ahead and shape the polygons around the menu buttons at the top of the phone. Using the same techniques like BandSaw and Drag, shape the polygons to frame the additional buttons. You can take a look at CellPhone_v004 from this book's DVD for additional guidance.

36. This step is very important—save a copy of the flat version that you'll use later for the flip top of the phone. Save it as CellPhoneCover or something similar.

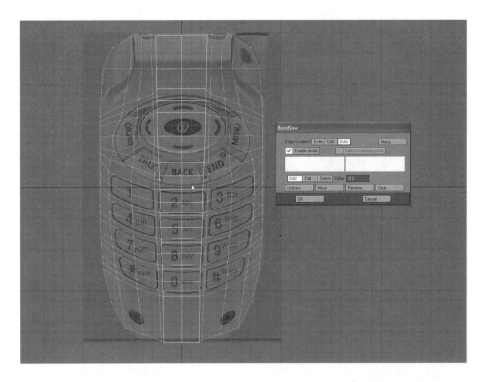

Figure 11.18 Select the center row of polygons and use BandSaw to subdivide them.

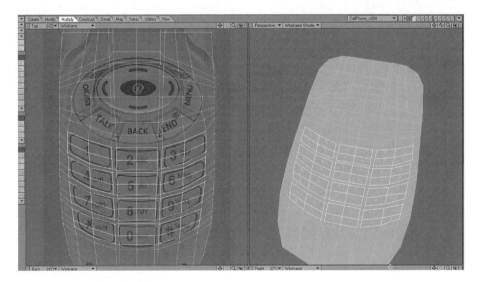

Figure 11.19 With the additional subdivisions, each telephone button is now made up of four polygons.

Up to this point, you've seen how far you can take LightWave's tools with just simple boxes, selection and deselection, and subdivisions. The next section takes you a step further, where you create the actual buttons of the phone, numbers, and textures.

Creating More Detail

Not all cellular phones are created equal, but generally, they're all about the same. You've created the mesh for the buttons, and so far they're still blank and flat. You'll add numbers shortly. But first, you need to create additional button details and thicken them up.

Exercise 11.2 Additional Details for Modeling

1. You're now going to use a handy process in LightWave—Smooth Shift. Take a look at Figure 11.20. You'll see the model with additional subdivisions created with BandSaw. At this point, we're about BandSawed out! So, select the polygons that make up the Menu button of the phone. Again, remember that Symmetry mode is still active from the bottom of the Modeler interface.

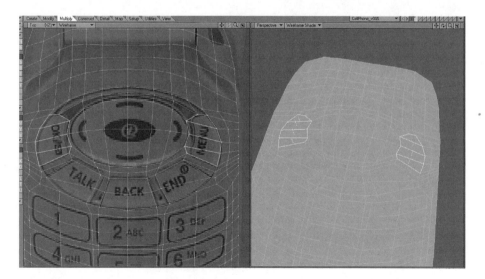

Figure 11.20 Select the polygons that surround the Menu button of the phone.

2. Press Shift+a to fit the selected polygons to view. Note that only the right-side polygons fit to view with Symmetry mode active, which is fine.

3. Press Shift+f to activate the Smooth Shift function. Click once on the polygons and do not drag.

4. Now, select Size from the Modify tab, or press Shift+h. Then, use the Size tool to size down the newly created polygons.

5. Smooth Shift works like Bevel, but it keeps selected polygons together as one. Applying Smooth Shift multiplies the selection, but be careful when using it because you won't see anything happen as you apply it. If, however, you click and drag, you might see the polygons separate. This is why you've clicked just once and used the Size tool to size down the newly created polygons. It's about control!

6. Figure 11.21 shows the polygons after the Smooth Shift and sizing.

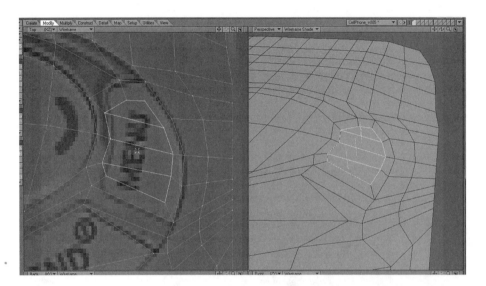

Figure 11.21 By using Smooth Shift to multiply the selected polygons and Size to shrink them, you create more geometry.

7. Using the Drag tool from the Modify tab, shape the polygons to better match the lines of the phone buttons, based on the image in the background.

8. Save your work (using Shift+s if you're saving incrementally). Then, press the Tab key to activate SubPatch mode. Can you see how the flow of the polygons works well as a blueprint for the phone object? Figure 11.22 shows the object with SubPatches applied.

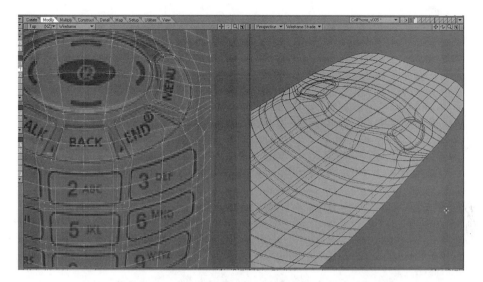

Figure 11.22   With SubPatch mode on (press the Tab key), you can see how the movement of points and various subdivisions has created a flat blueprint of the cell phone.

9. Make any final subdivisions to your model using either BandSaw or Smooth Shift and then save your work.

What you've done so far is tedious and not much fun at times, but it's crucial to the success of upcoming steps in this project. When we talk about polygonal flow, it's not just for characters! Too often, people think that flow is only important for modeling a character's head, body, and nothing more. But proper flow is important for any model you create—even a cell phone.

Creating Detailed Depth

Now that the base of the phone has been laid out, it's time to create the buttons. You'll notice that the cell phone is still flat, but this will be addressed shortly. If you're ready, load up the model you've been working on (or CellPhone_v005 from this book's DVD).

Exercise 11.3   Adding Depth to Models

1. What you'll do now is fun! This is where you'll see the model come to life with a very cool new tool in LightWave 8.

2. With the model open, set the top-right viewport to Perspective view if it's not already. Also, set this view to Wireframe Shade mode.

3. Press the Tab key to make sure SubPatch mode is active. Also, turn off Symmetry from the bottom of the Modeler interface.

4. Select all the polygons within the object and press the i key on your keyboard. This calls up the Info panel. At the bottom of the panel, you'll see a setting for Color. Change this to Black or whatever you want. This helps you see the wireframes better in the Perspective view. Figure 11.23 shows the panel.

Important

The Backdrop image has been removed, and the grid has been turned off at this point in the tutorial to make this book's screen capture images easier to view. You don't have to do this, but feel free if it makes your own viewport easier to work in.

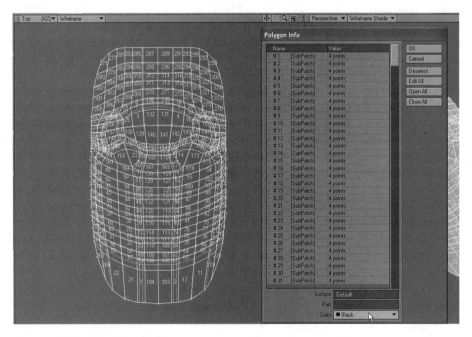

Figure 11.23   The Info panel allows you to see information about points and polygons, as well as set colors for wireframes.

Additionally, if you use the Hidden Line mode or Textured Wire mode in the viewports, this color appears. Blue works very well.

5. Close the Info panel by clicking OK. Deselect any polygons.

6. Now, select the four polygons of each of the number buttons on the phone object. This should total 48 polygons, as in Figure 11.24.

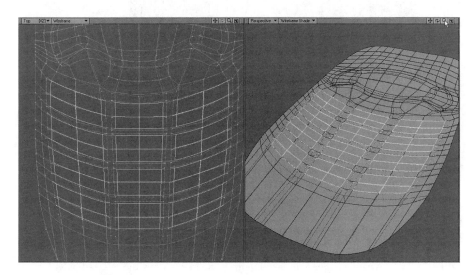

Figure 11.24   Select just the polygons that make up the phone buttons, totaling 48.

7. From the Multiply tab, select the Super Shift tool. Click in a viewport of your choice, such as the Perspective view. Drag to the left and right, and you'll see the selected polygons sizing equally. Move the mouse up and down, and watch them inset. Here, just size them up slightly, right-click once to multiply the selection, and then left-click and move them down, as in Figure 11.25.

Tip

To better see your bevels created with Super Shift, you can color the object, perhaps a soft metallic blue. Add some decent Specularity, and as you'll see in Figure 11.25, the bevel results are easier to identify.

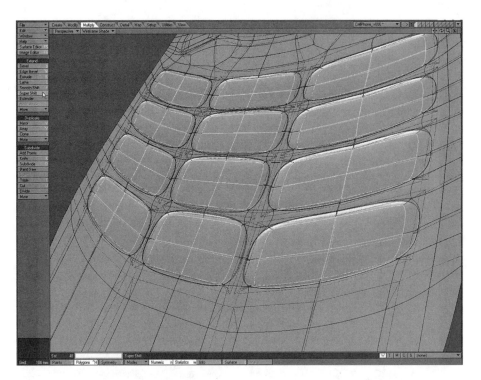

Figure 11.25 Using the Super Shift function from the Multiply tab, the selected polygons are, in essence, beveled.

What you're doing with this tool is beveling the selected polygons. Super Shift is cool because it retains the orientation of the selection and looks at the selected polygons as one, like Smooth Shift. This tool is better than Smooth Shift in that it understands both Shift and Inset and allows you to quickly bevel multiple selections easily.

8. Right-click again with the Super Shift tool active to multiply the selected polygons. Move the mouse to the left slightly to size them down.

Tip

At this point, it might be a good idea to go to the General Options panel (press o) and set the Patch Divisions to 8. This subdivides each subpatched area eight times, creating more detail in your mesh. Remember that in Layout, you can work with one subpatch level, perhaps 1, for very quick, simple object manipulations, but render higher, like at 8 or 12, for top detail.

9. Right-click again and move the polygons up to create the buttons. Figure 11.26 shows the result.

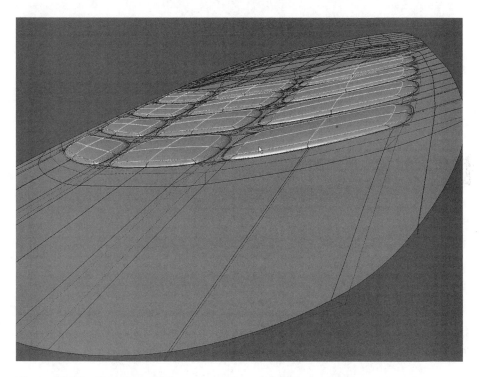

Figure 11.26   Using Super Shift two more times brings the buttons up.

10. Right-click one more time and move the mouse to the right to size the selection down slightly. This removes a bit of the roundness of the buttons, yet helps create a sharp beveled edge. Figure 11.27 shows the phone in Smooth Shade mode in the Perspective viewport.

11. Save your work! Now, select the buttons you've created around the menu area at the top of the phone. Figure 11.28 shows the selection.

12. User Super Shift on these buttons as you did with the number buttons.

13. Adjust, undo, and redo as needed! Save often, too. You'll soon see the power of SubPatch and Super Shift! Figure 11.29 shows the menu buttons after a few Super Shift operations.

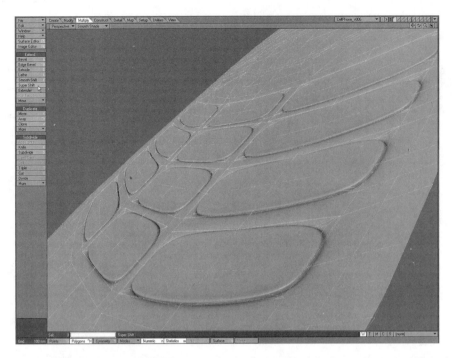

Figure 11.27 After a few Super Shift operations, the bevels of the buttons come to life and have depth with a nice, soft (but not too soft) edge.

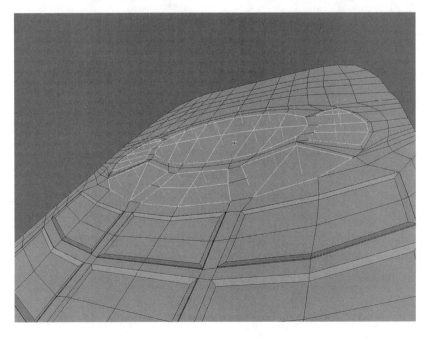

Figure 11.28 Select the polygons that make up the buttons around the menu area at the top of the phone.

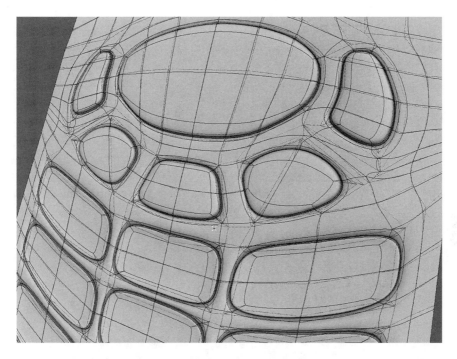

Figure 11.29   After a few Super Shift operations on the menu area buttons, the rest of the phone begins to take shape.

The next phase is to build the top areas of the phone that will hold the flip cover. From there, you'll go back and add final small details, then surface and render.

14. Make sure your object is saved, and then save a new incremental version by pressing Shift+s. This is a habit you should get used to. Next, turn Symmetry mode back on and select the five polygons in the upper-right corner. With Symmetry mode active, the left side should automatically be selected. Figure 11.30 shows the selection.

15. As you did with the buttons, use the Super Shift tool from the Multiply tab to perform four bevels—once to move the selection in and size it down slightly, another to shift the polygons up about 100 mm, another to shift them in, and one final one to flatten out the top. Figure 11.31 shows the result.

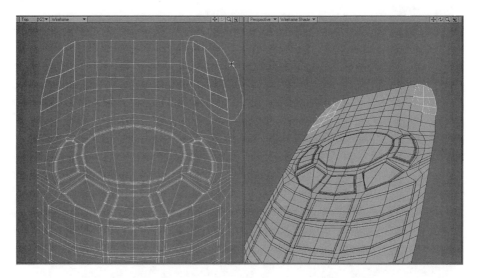

Figure 11.30 Five polygons in the upper-right corner are selected with Symmetry mode active.

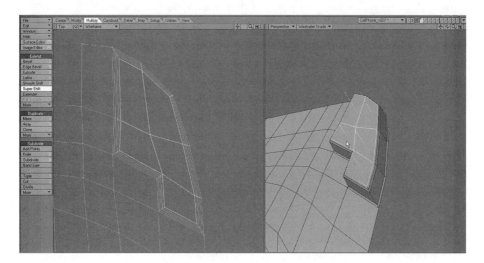

Figure 11.31 Use Super Shift on the selected polygons four times.

16. Deselect the polygons and press the Tab key to enter SubPatch mode (if it's not already active).

17. Using the Drag tool, drag the lower points of the newly created polygons down toward the phone buttons. You need to sort of slope these. Think of a ramp, rather than a lump! Figure 11.32 shows what you're going for. You might want to use the Drag tool (Ctrl+t) a few times to accomplish your goal.

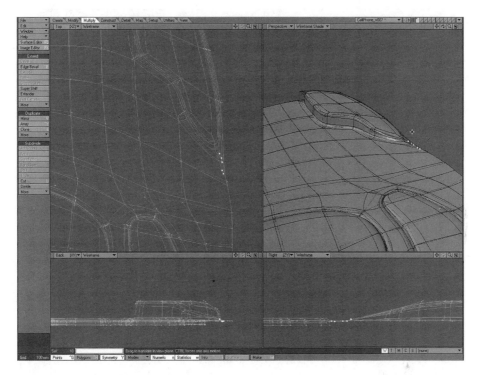

Figure 11.32   Using the Drag tool, you can shift the points of the newly created polygons to slope or ramp up the polygons.

18. You can also use Stretch, Move, or Rotate on points to shape them as you like. After you've moved the points to your liking, save the object.

19. Deselect any polygons and then select the top rows of polygons between the edge polygons that you just used Super Shift on. Figure 11.33 shows the selection.

20. With this selection, perform a Super Shift operation as you did with the previous to create the connection area for the flip lid of the phone. Use Super Shift once and then rotate the polygons from the base of the selection in the bottom-right viewport. Use Super Shift again and tweak as shown in Figure 11.34.

    The reason you didn't select all these polygons and Super Shift at once is because you want a separation between this center section and the edge sections. Refer to the original photo (Figure 11.1), and you'll see how this looks.

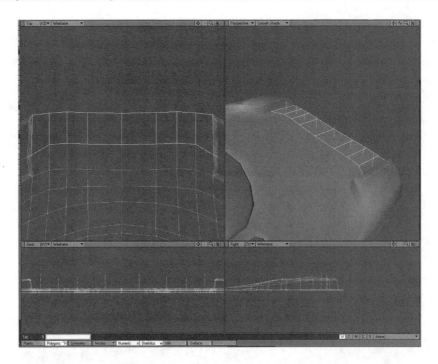

Figure 11.33 Select the polygons that make up the top area between the edges of the phone.

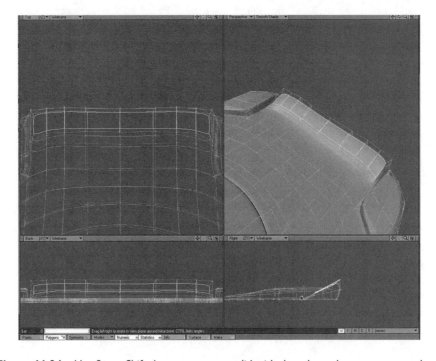

Figure 11.34 Use Super Shift the same way you did with the edge polygons to create the top-center area of the phone.

Creating the Flip Top of the Phone

When you begin creating any model, there are always areas that need to be built separately, even if they're part of the same final piece. In this particular case, the flip portion of the phone needs to be built in a similar fashion to the base, but with a bit less detail. Follow along with Exercise 11.4 to learn how to build it.

Exercise 11.4   Building Additional Phone Elements

1. When you first created the mesh for the base phone, before you used Super Shift for the buttons, you were asked to save a copy as something like CellPhoneCover. Load this object now.

2. With the object loaded, copy and paste it into a new blank layer of your existing phone model.

   When you load an object into Modeler, it does not load into a layer of your current model. Rather, it opens as a new object.

3. Put the original phone object in a background layer. Turn Symmetry mode on from the bottom of the Modeler interface. Now, select the five polygons that make up the top corner. Delete them. Figure 11.35 shows the model with deleted corners.

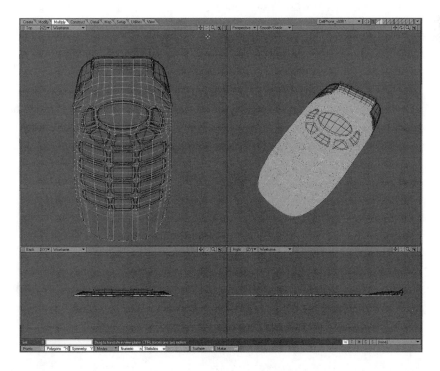

Figure 11.35   Select the top five corner polygons of the flat phone object and delete them.

Because the flip fits in between the corners that you've already beveled and thickened using the Super Shift tool, you don't need them on the flip cover.

4. Use the Drag tool to adjust the flip lid's points to match any edge or corner changes you've made. This is pretty easy to do in the Perspective view, as shown in Figure 11.36.

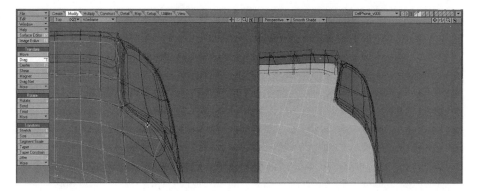

Figure 11.36 Use the Drag tool to tweak and adjust the points of the original cell-phone flip cover polygons to match the cell phone base you've created.

5. Save your work. Also, save a separate copy of this model as something like CellPhoneFlip to use later to create the back of the phone. Now, make sure your Action Center is set to Mouse. You can do this by clicking the Modes drop-down list at the bottom of the Modeler screen. This tells Modeler to base movements (such as Rotate) on your mouse position.

6. Select Rotate from the Modify tab or press y on the keyboard and from the Right viewport, rotate the flip top open. Place your mouse at the top of the phone, where the flip would normally pivot, as in Figure 11.37.

7. In the Front view, you'll need to align the points just in from the outer edge to create the trim of the display area. While the geometry was necessary for the buttons, you don't need so much for the flip cover. However, you want to keep the shape, and deleting polygons won't work for subpatching. So, select a row of polygons just beneath the center across the entire object (the flip cover of the phone). From the Construct tab under the Reduce category, click the More drop-down list and choose Bandglue. This tool essentially does the opposite of the BandSaw tool that you used earlier to subdivide.

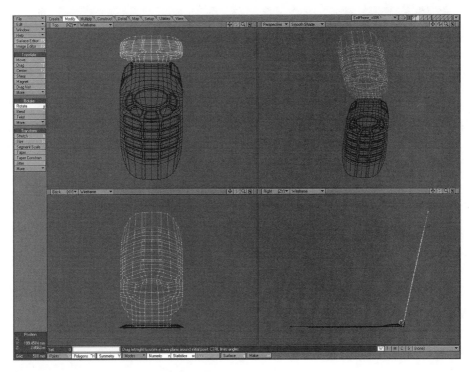

Figure 11.37   Rotate the flip lid open from the Right view.

8. Perform additional Bandglue operations, pressing the Tab key for the entire object periodically to make sure that you don't disrupt the quad mesh. Figure 11.38 shows the Bandglue operations performed on the object a few times. Basically, you're removing the tight areas you subdivided for the buttons with this operation.

9. In the Front view, using the Drag tool (Ctrl+t), shape the points to make what will be the cell phone display. Just even them out accordingly, as shown in Figure 11.38.

10. Now, select the polygons that make up the inside edge, as in Figure 11.39. Do this after you've shaped the points using the Drag tool.

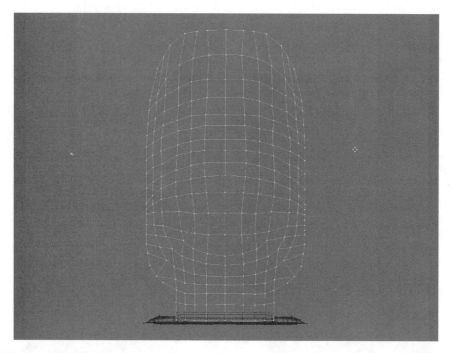

Figure 11.38 Bandglue is used a few times to tidy up the unneeded polygons of the flip of the phone.

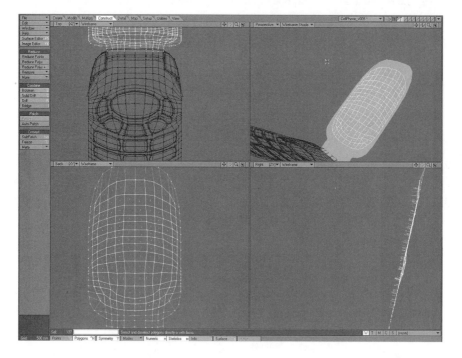

Figure 11.39 Select the polygons that make up the inside edge of the flip cover.

11. Using Super Shift from the Multiply tab, create about four bevels for this selection, once in, then down, then in a bit more, then out. Figure 11.40 shows the operation.

Tip

If the points of your flip-phone object are not perfectly aligned (they should be flat at this point), press Alt and the v key to call up the Set Value command. Set the value to, say, 0 on the Z-axis. The points will all move to the same exact value, essentially flattening out. Then, as a whole, move them back into place as needed. One more thing! Remember to try using the Spin Quads function from the Detail tab to control the flow of polygons, especially around the rounded corner selections.

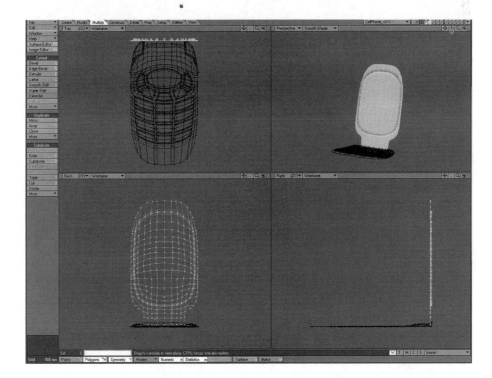

Figure 11.40   Using Super Shift, you can quickly create the edge trim for the center display area.

12. Now, create the display screen itself. Select the polygons in the center of the flip area, as shown in Figure 11.41. Be sure to square them off with the Drag tool.

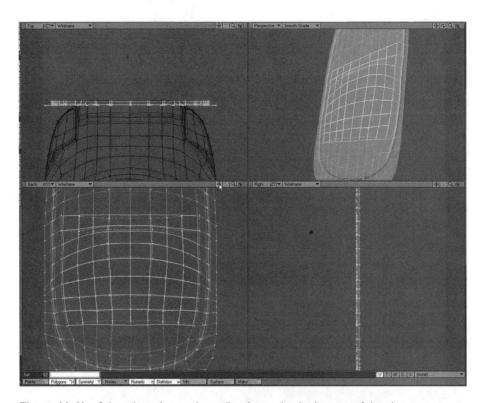

Figure 11.41 Select the polygons that will make up the display area of the phone.

13. Begin creating surfaces as you use Super Shift. With the selected polygons for the display area, press q (or click the Surface button at the bottom of Modeler) and name this selection Display_Trim.

14. Use Super Shift on these bad boys just as you did previously—once down, then in, then up, then in again. After you've done these four Super Shift operations, rename the still-selected polygons (press q) Display Screen, so that you end up with something like Figure 11.42.

15. Save your work!

At this point, the majority of the phone is built, and it's up to you to tweak any points to simply finesse the shape. This "massaging," as it's sometimes referred to, is performed using the Drag and Move tools on various points in the X, Y, and Z directions as needed to clean up the model.

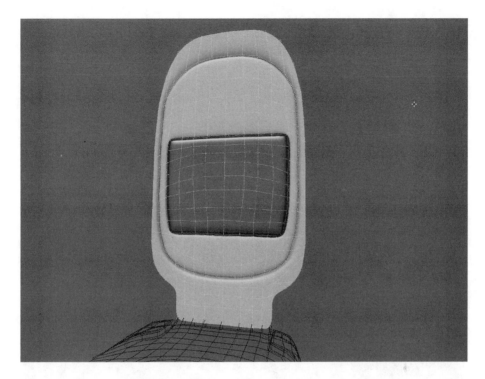

Figure 11.42   Super Shift these polygons to create the display of the phone.

Adding the Phone Backing and Antenna

There are two things left to do with this phone before you start applying textures. You need to build the antenna and then add depth to the base and flip cover.

Exercise 11.5   Adding Depth and Further Detail

1. With your phone object loaded, load that saved phone base from earlier in this chapter. It's the same object you used for the flip portion of the phone.

2. Copy and paste this into a new layer with your full phone object. From the Multiply tab, select Extrude and pull the polygons down on the Y-axis about 100mm or so.

Important

You could also have extruded earlier before you began creating the buttons. This chapter had you do it differently to keep the selection and editing of points less confusing. Also, using BandSaw could have really messed up your model if it had already been extruded. In addition, the procedure used in this chapter helps you practice working with multiple objects, saving copies, and using them later.

3. After the mesh is extruded, press the Tab key to activate SubPatch mode. Then, lasso select just the top polygons and delete them. Figure 11.43 shows what you should end up with.

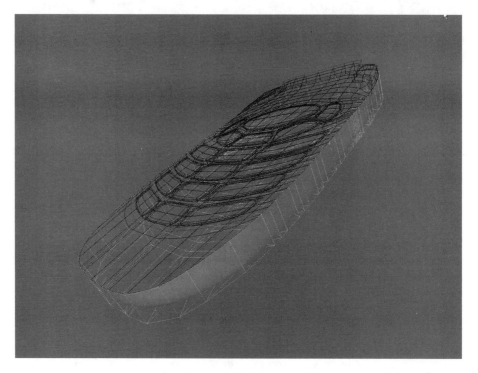

Figure 11.43   Extruding the flat phone object from earlier in the tutorial quickly creates the base of the cell phone. Deleting the top polygons is necessary because they're not needed when the base is attached to the rest of the cell phone.

4. Cut and paste the base into the first layer containing the original phone object.

5. Press m for Merge, and you should see the points that occupy the same space join together, smoothing out the edges of the phone, as in Figure 11.44.

Figure 11.44   Merge the points after you've cut and pasted the back of the phone into the first layer to smooth out the edges.

If you do not get a pop-up that says 65 points merged, or a similar amount, your points are not aligned. Somewhere along the way, you moved the edge points rather than the inside points. To correct, you can weld, or set the value of the points (the base and the button plate) to an equal position, then merge.

6. Go ahead and perform the same operation on the flip portion of the phone, loading the template you saved earlier while creating it. Extrude, cut and paste, and merge points. Figure 11.45 shows the model before the antenna is created.

   You should take into account the tiny details that are on the edges of the phone, such as the earpiece plug, power port, and so on. You can create these by selecting the polygons in those specific areas and using the Bevel tool, Smooth Shift, or the Super Shift tool to create the necessary holes.

7. To create the antenna, select the polygons in the upper-right corner of the phone. This selection should be about three polygons. Use Super Shift to extend them out. Figure 11.46 shows the movement.

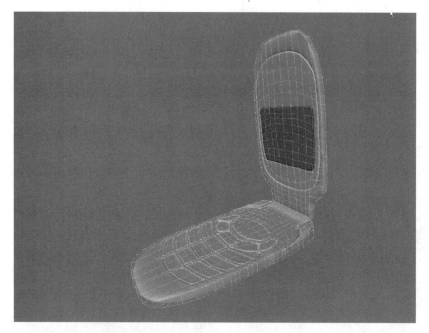

Figure 11.45 The flip portion of the phone is created also using Extrude.

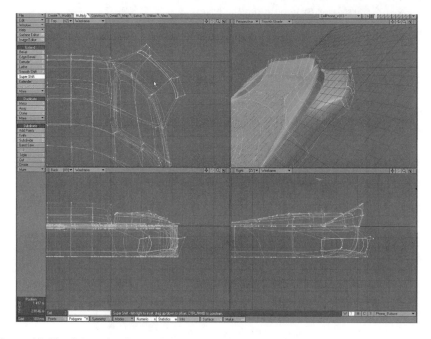

Figure 11.46 Select the three polygons in the upper-right corner and use Super Shift to move them out, thereby creating the antenna.

8. Now, use Rotate and straighten these selected polygons so they point up from the phone—you know, like an antenna would! But note that newer cell phones often don't have little wire antennas. Instead, they have a bulbous sort of fixed antenna.

9. User Super Shift one or two more times and scale the polygons as you create them. Then, use Super Shift a few more times to create a bit of cap on the antenna, as in Figure 11.47.

Tip

If Super Shift isn't working for you as the polygons get smaller, use Smooth Shift, change their size, and then move them.

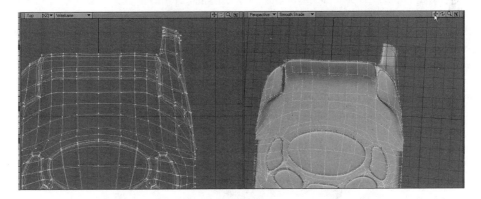

Figure 11.47   Use Super Shift on the antenna polygons to create the stem-like antenna found on newer cell phones.

10. Save your work!

11. One last thing to do before the textures—if you'd like to rotate the flip cover of the phone in Layout, you'll need to set its pivot! Go to the View tab and select Pivot. In the cell-phone flip layer, move the pivot to the bottom center of the object, the point around which it would rotate. Save the object.

Surfacing the Phone

You have a few options when it comes to surfacing this object. Although the focus of this chapter is modeling practices, it's important to follow through and see how to surface and render your work. In many instances, you could freeze the subpatch, creating just a highly detailed polygonal model, and then stencil in letters and numbers. This would work like a branding iron. However, this makes a model that is overbuilt and slow to work with in Layout. It's also not very adjustable for future revisions.

The subpatch model you've created in this chapter is still very adaptable for future changes, and you can modify it at any time. Therefore, a better choice for surfacing is an image map. Now, you need to apply the basic cell-phone metallic color, and you need to add numbers on the buttons and information on the display. Rather than giving each button a surface name and making multiple image maps, you can do it all at once with a UV map.

Exercise 11.6   Adding Surfaces for the Phone

1. From the bottom of the Modeler interface, select the T button. Then, to the right, click the dropdown and select New. In the Create UV Texture Map panel that appears, type a name for the UV Map, such as Phone_Buttons. Select Planar, as you'll apply the image down flat as opposed to wrapping it, and select Y for the Axis. Click on Automatic and click OK. Figure 11.48 shows the panel.

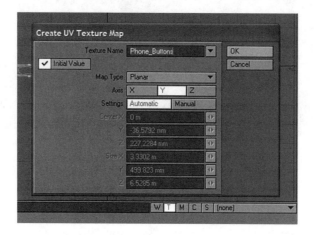

Figure 11.48   Create a flat UV map texture on the Y-axis for the phone.

2. When you first create the UV map, it appears as if nothing has happened. But go to one of the viewports, such as the Back (bottom-left) viewport. Change the view to UV Texture, and you'll see a wireframe of your phone, as in Figure 11.49.

3. You can use the Stretch tool to squeeze the UV map in to match the shape of the phone. Then, from the File menu, select Export and then Encapsulated Post-script. You'll be able to export a viewport that you can paint over in Adobe Photoshop or your favorite image-editing program. Figure 11.50 shows the panel.

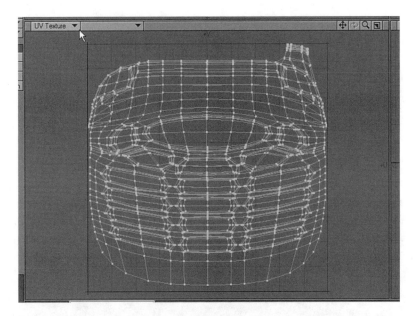

Figure 11.49   You can view the UV map you've created from any viewport.

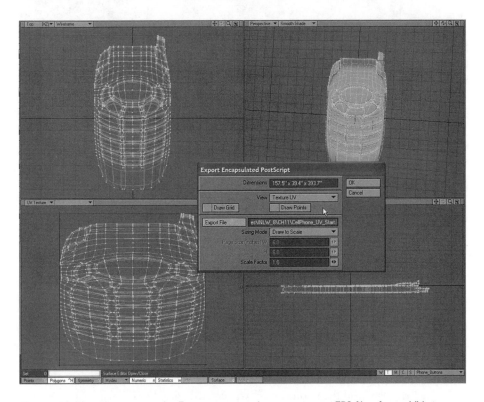

Figure 11.50   You can use the Export command to save out an EPS file of your UV view.

After you've exported, you can load the EPS file in an image-editing program and paint your letters and numbers over it. Create any letters or markings in their own image layers and save the image as a 32-bit TGA or TIF file without the wireframe EPS background.

4. We've created an image for you to use, so back in Modeler, go to the UV Texture view, and at the top of the viewport, click the drop-down button (normally reserved for Viewport Style) and select Load Image. Choose the Phone_UV image from this book's DVD.

5. Figure 11.51 shows how the image, created in Adobe Photoshop, loads perfectly aligned with the buttons of the phone. You can adjust the UV map if needed with Modeler's tools. However, this is a 32-bit TGA image, and it won't display in Modeler's Texture view modes. So, save the object and then head over to Layout.

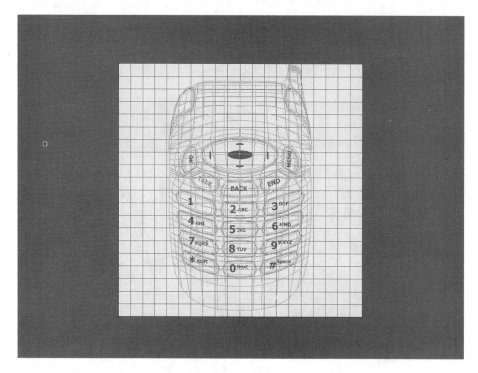

Figure 11.51   In Modeler, you can load an image in the UV map view to see how your image
aligns.

6. Load the Set.lws scene from the Chapter 11 folder of this book's DVD.

7. This is a basic set with no lighting. You'll handle that in a moment. First, from the Items tab, load the phone object you created with the UV map.

8. The phone might load in the set instead of on it. So, first select layer 2, the flip part of the phone. Press m for motion options and at the top of the panel, parent it to layer 1, the phone buttons.

9. Select layer 1 and move it up so that it's resting on the set. Move it back into view as well. The Set.lws scene you loaded had the Camera view selected, so remember that the render will look like what you're seeing.

10. Select the camera, move it up, and push it in for a better view of the phone object. Remember to create a keyframe at 0 to lock the new camera position in place. Figure 11.52 shows the view.

Figure 11.52   Move the camera into a better position to view the phone object.

11. Now, open the Surface Editor from the top left of the Layout view. In the Surface Editor, select the Phone Metal surface (or whatever you called the base surface). Click the T button next to Color.

12. In the Texture Editor window, create a planar image map, but select the UV image and apply it. Figure 11.53 shows the panel.

13. You'll see the map applied in Layout, as in Figure 11.54, but you'll notice that all the white around it is visible as well. This, of course, would cover up the blue metallic surface that needs to be applied. However, it's important to remember that this is a 32-bit image! Press F9 and you won't see the white, but rather just the numbers perfectly aligned with the buttons. Figure 11.54 shows the comparison.

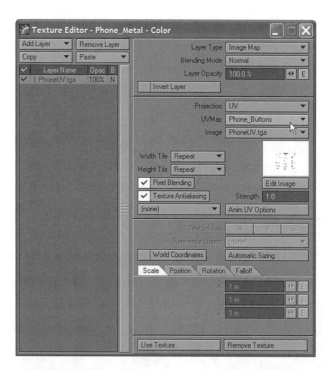

Figure 11.53 Apply the UV map you created (or the one from this book's DVD) in the Texture Editor for the phone.

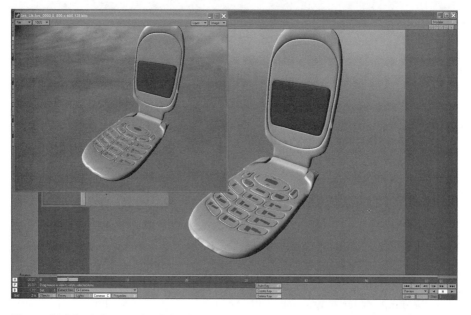

Figure 11.54 In Layout, the alpha channel is not omitted, but it is nowhere in sight in the render.

14. Select the camera and move it in nice and close on the buttons. The image you loaded was a 300 dpi image, so you can get close to it without it being pixilated. However, the model might have jagged edges—or will it? Because this is a sub-patched object, you can tell LightWave to increase the render resolution.

15. Select layer 1 of the object and press the p key to open the Object Properties panel. In the Geometry tab, change Display SubPatch Level to 2 and Render SubPatch Level to 10. This creates a simple working version of the object in Layout but a high-quality render. The tight curves and corners will be nice and clean. Figure 11.55 shows the new Camera view with the Object Properties panel open.

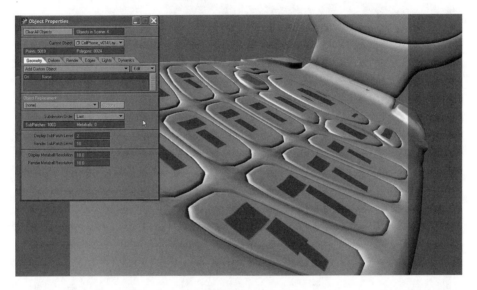

Figure 11.55 Use LightWave's variable SubPatch in the Object Properties panel to set different render and display subpatch levels.

16. Press F9 and take a look at the render—looking pretty good, eh? Well, let's take it further. Back in the Surface Editor, select the same phone surface to which you applied the UV map. Change the Diffuse value to about 70% and Reflection to 30%.

17. Make the Specularity about 30% and set the Glossiness to 30% as well. You can change these as you like, based on the quality of your render tests.

18. In the Environment tab, set the Reflection Options to Spherical Map. Set the Reflection Map to fractal reflections, found on this book's DVD. Then, set a 20% value for Reflection Blurring.

The trick to creating a soft-brushed metal or aluminum-type surface is to create a generic reflection, but blur it so that it softens the look. Figure 11.56 shows the render.

Important

Setting a higher Render SubPatch level and Reflection Blurring adds to your render times, so be patient! You've done nothing wrong, other than utilize some processor-heavy features of LightWave.

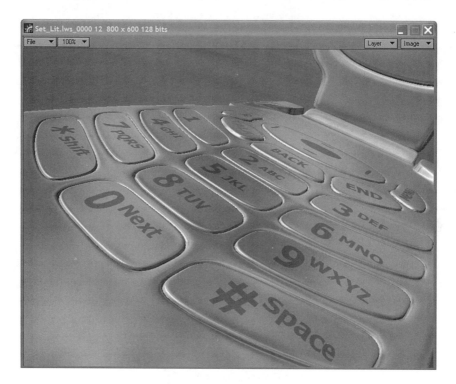

Figure 11.56   A slight reflection on the metal surface along with reflection blurring adds to the image.

Now, there are a few other surfaces to take care of, such as the display panel. What should go on there? You'll also need to set the lighting for shadows and color, which will help bring out the details in the object.

19. Select the Display surface and load the PhoneDisplay image from this book's DVD or your own image.

20. Apply this image as a planar image map on the Z-axis for the Display. Increase the Specularity to about 80% and the Glossiness to 80%. This helps create a glassier feel.

21. For the Display Trim, you can use a dull gray to make it look like a sort of rubber seal.

22. From here, simply tweak and adjust the surfaces as you like. Perhaps add a leopard skin surface to the entire phone, and so on. Move the camera out to see the display, and set a keyframe to lock it in place. Figure 11.57 shows the render thus far.

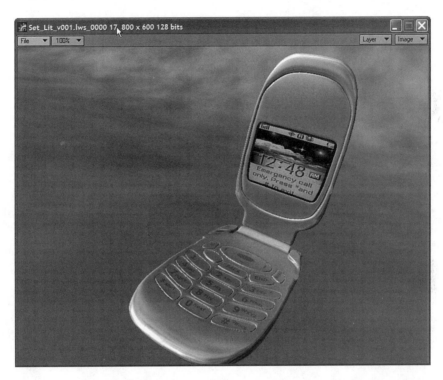

Figure 11.57   With the metal surfaces applied and a display image inserted, the phone is coming along nicely!

Lighting the Scene

One of the last things you need to do is light this puppy. Lighting, as you might have read earlier in this book, is crucial to making your images and animations pop out at the viewer. For this particular case, shadows and properly placed lights are very important because of the small details in the buttons. Follow along to set up lighting for this model.

Exercise 11.7   Lighting for Electronics

1. The default light in the scene is a distant light. Open the Light Properties panel and change this to an Area light. Bring its intensity down to about 60%. Set the color to an off white, and turn on Ray Traced Shadows for it.

2. In Layout, press 5 on your keyboard to jump to Light view. Move the light so that it rests above the phone, as in Figure 11.58. Don't forget to set a keyframe for the light to lock it in place.

3. Go back to the Surface Editor, and for the phone metal surface, change the Reflection Options in the Environment tab to Ray Tracing and Spherical Map. This takes your blurred reflections one step further by reflecting not only the image, but the surroundings as well.

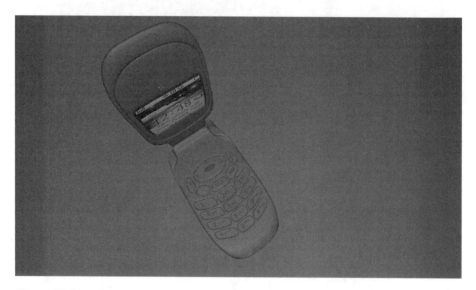

Figure 11.58   Move the light up above the phone, looking through the Light view.

4. In Layout, go to the Render tab and open the Render Options panel. There, click on Ray Trace Shadows and Ray Trace Reflection. Press F9 to render a frame. Figure 11.59 show the render with one area light and shadows applied.

5. Now, add a Spotlight to the scene. Remember that you can quickly do this from the Items tab in Layout. Make this light's intensity about 130% and orange in color.

6. Place the Spotlight to the back right of the phone. Use the Light view to set it up, and don't forget to create a keyframe to lock it in place. Also, change the Spotlight Soft Edge Angle to equal the Spotlight Cone Angle.

Figure 11.59   A render of the phone with one area light and shadows applied.

7. Make sure Shadow Maps are enabled for Shadows.

8. Copy this spotlight by pressing Ctrl+c in Layout. Choose 1 for the number of copies and move this light to the left side of the phone. Change the intensity to about 80% and keyframe it in place at frame 0. Also, in the Lights Properties panel, click Global Illumination and set the ambient intensity to about 3.

9. Save your scene, and don't forget to select Save All Objects from the File drop-down menu to save the surfaces you've applied to the phone.

10. A few other tweaks you can make are to add about a 15% reflection to the set to make it reflect the phone resting on it.

11. Additionally, you can employ depth of field to the render when the camera is close up for added depth.

Figure 11.60 shows the final render.

Figure 11.60 With two additional lights added, the cell phone render has a good amount of depth. You can also see how the blurred reflections mixed with ray-traced reflections to add realism to the surfacing.

The lighting for this setup is an excellent way to render images for print, but it can also work for movies, television, or corporate video. What's more important for rendering for print in this project is the amount of detail in the geometry. The larger you render the image, the more detail the viewer will see. This is why it was important to model this cell phone entirely as a subpatched object—doing so gives you the flexibility to increase the render detail, as you did earlier. This process also allows you to get the camera in very close to the buttons without seeing any jagged edges.

The Next Step

This project gave you a strong working knowledge of how to build objects from images in Modeler, specifically real-world objects. Your next step is to experiment with added detail on the cell phone, such as holes for headphones, connections, or power cords. Add in the holes that make up the earpiece and tweak as you see fit. To do this, you can use the exact same techniques described throughout the chapter, such as Super Shift, Smooth Shift, and Bevel.

But there's more to modeling than just Super Shift! Turn the page and learn how to use a combination of spline modeling and polygonal modeling to create the fun character from the cover of this book.

Chapter 12

Modeling Vehicles

Whether you're interested in characters, electronics, or logos, don't overlook this area of modeling. Modeling vehicles isn't just about cars; it's about motorcycles, spaceships, or perhaps your own creation. Add to that the modeling techniques as applied to weapons, and you can build your own science fiction fantasy! This chapter will instruct you on the following:

- Modeling a corvette
- Working with fine details in Modeler
- Surfacing for real-world looks
- Lighting for photorealistic renders

Modeling Project Overview

For years, advertising agencies, production studios, and producers relied on photography for car ads. Expensive shoots lasting days not only were taxing on the body, but the wallet as well. Those days, however, are fleeting, as many agencies are now looking to 3D imaging for print and television advertising. This first project will guide you through the steps to model a Chevrolet Corvette. From there, you'll surface it, and you'll learn how to create that metallic car paint surface often only seen in actual studio photographs. What creates this awesome look is a combination of surfacing, reflection, and lighting—all of which you'll set up for yourself in this chapter. Figure 12.1 shows the car you'll build, texture, and render in this chapter.

Tip

Check out the bonus tutorial on this book's DVD! Learn how to use LightWave 8 to model weapons!

Figure 12.1   Make your own custom Chevrolet Corvette entirely in LightWave.

Modeling a vehicle isn't just about pretty renders for ad agencies. Your job might require you to create models for video games. The techniques in this chapter can be applied there as well.

Modeling for Shape

In the previous chapter, you began modeling the cell phone with attention to detail right from the start. You needed to pay close attention to where you were going with the model from the moment you created the first polygon. It was important to do that because the small buttons and necessary details required precise polygons. That's not to say you can be sloppy with your planning in this project or others, but this model is approached differently. Proper polygonal flow is important no matter what model you're creating. Although you started with a square box when modeling the giraffe in Chapter

10, "Modeling Quadrupedal Characters," and a segmented box with a pre-defined shape when modeling the cell phone in Chapter 11, "Modeling Electronics," this time, you'll start with points.

Exercise 12.1   Point-by-Point Modeling

1. Open LightWave 8 Modeler and press the d key for display options.

2. Select the Backdrop tab, and with the Viewport set to TL for Top Left, select Load Image from the Image drop-down list.

3. Load the Vette_TL image from this book's DVD. Set the Resolution to 1024 for best quality and the Size to 8m, so the image fills the viewport.

4. Load the Vette_BL and Vette_BR_back images for their appropriate viewports. Figure 12.2 shows the images loaded in all views in Modeler.

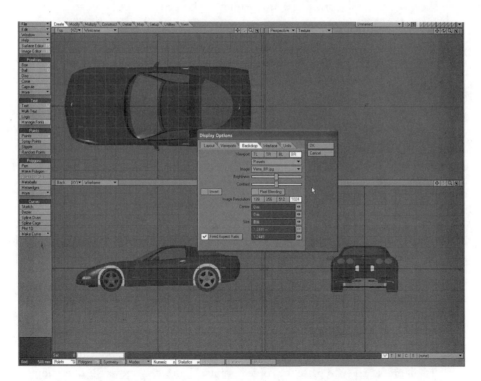

Figure 12.2   Load the images of the corvette in all viewports from the Backdrop tab of the Display Options panel.

Tip

You should save your backdrops for future use. Saving just the object does not save the backdrop images. In the Backdrop tab of the Display Options panel, click the Presets drop-down list, and choose Save All Backdrops. Then, the next time you want to load the backdrop images, simply use the Load Backdrop option from this selection.

You'll begin by creating the Corvette in just one view, while using the other views as reference. Additionally, you only need to model half of the car; later, you'll mirror it to complete the other half. Cars are symmetrical, and even though you can use the Symmetry option, it's easier to model half and then mirror it.

5. Start in the bottom-left view labeled Back (XY). To make things easier, make this viewport a full frame by clicking the maximize button in the top-right corner of the viewport, or by pressing 0 on the numeric keypad of your keyboard.

6. Zoom in from the driver's-side wheel, either by using the Zoom command button at the top-right of the viewport (click and drag on the button) or by pressing the period key a few times.

7. Select the Points tool from the Create tab, under the Points Category. Start by building points around the front wheel well to shape the fender. Remember that the left mouse button aligns the points, and the right mouse button lays the points down. Mac users, hold the Command key to simulate right mouse button functions. Create about 13 points around the outside of the wheel well, as shown in Figure 12.3.

Important

The upcoming backdrop images have had their contrast and brightness lowered to make the points more visible. In addition, the grid has been turned off in the Display Options panel for better visibility.

8. You can start anywhere you like, but you'd use this same method. The points will be automatically selected after they are created. Do not deselect them. Press Ctrl+c on the keyboard to copy them, and then size them up about 100 mm. Then, press Ctrl+v to paste the copied points. Figure 12.4 shows the operation.

Figure 12.3   Begin building your car with simple points around the front left fender.

Figure 12.4   Copy the points and size them up, then paste down the points you copied.

9. After the points are pasted down, deselect all of them. Then, in a clockwise manner, select the first four points on the front left of the wheel well, and then press the p key on your keyboard to make a polygon, as in Figure 12.5.

Figure 12.5 Select the first four points to create a polygon.

10. Select the next four points and press p to make a polygon, as in Figure 12.6.

11. Continue creating polygons, selecting four points in a clockwise order, pressing p after four points to make a polygon. Continue all the way around the fender until you've created 12 polygons.

12. Save your work!

This process might seem tedious at first, but it's not. It allows you to precisely create the points you need, where you need them. Unlike the electronics modeling in Chapter 11, where you made a highly segmented box and shaped its points, you're now building from points. The next section will introduce you to new tools in LightWave 8 that make this point-by-point method even easier.

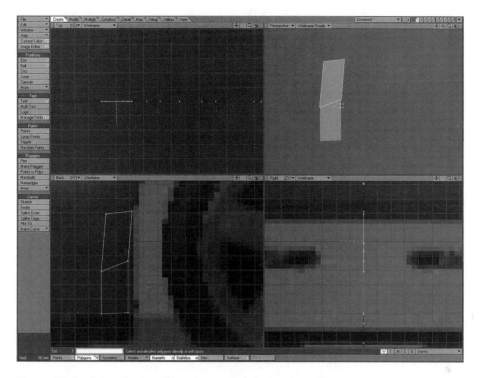

Figure 12.6   Select the next four points and make another polygon.

Extend Points

If you're familiar with LightWave's previous versions, you might have used the cool Extender tool. Extender is like extruding for points. However, in the past, when Extender was used, it left behind an extra polygon. This meant you needed to stop what you were doing and delete the unwanted polygon. At first, this seemed like no big deal, but as your model progressed and became more complicated, the extra polygon deletion was not just a pain, but it was also difficult. The more geometry you had, the harder it was to select the polygon to delete. And it was possible to accidentally delete polygons you wanted to keep!

The Extender tool remains in LightWave 8. If you look under the Extend category of the Multiply tab, you'll see the More drop-down list. Click this and you'll find the Extender Plus tool, as shown in Figure 12.7.

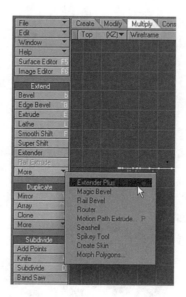

Figure 12.7 Extender Plus is found under the Extend category in the Multiply tab.

Extender Plus is also accessed by pressing the e key. Let's try it.

Exercise 12.2 Multiply Polygons with Extender Plus

1. Position the polygons you've created so they line up properly with the wheel well, based on the backdrop image in the Top viewport. This is why you loaded images in all views, rather than just one. Figure 12.8 shows the new position.

2. Select the top row of points in the fender polygons you've created. Press the e key once. It will appear that nothing has happened, but wait! Press the t key for move, and click and drag up in the Back view. You'll see a row of points connected with new polygons, as in Figure 12.9.

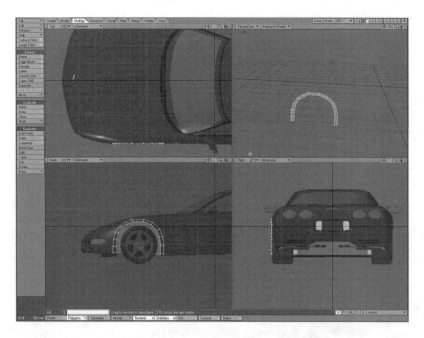

Figure 12.8 Move the created polygons so they line up with the backdrop image in the Top viewport.

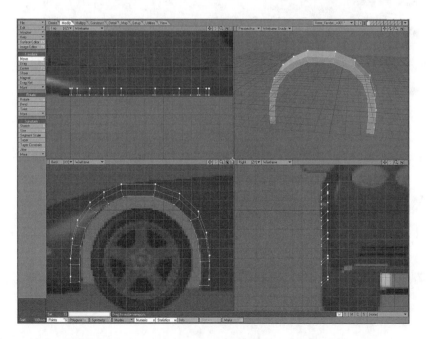

Figure 12.9 Select the top row of points, use Extender Plus to multiply the selected points, and move them.

3. In the Right viewport, move the points over and up so they line up with the car image in the backdrop.

4. Stretch (from the Transform category of the Modify tab) the newly created points that Extender Plus created so they are properly spaced with the rest of the polygons, as shown in Figure 12.10.

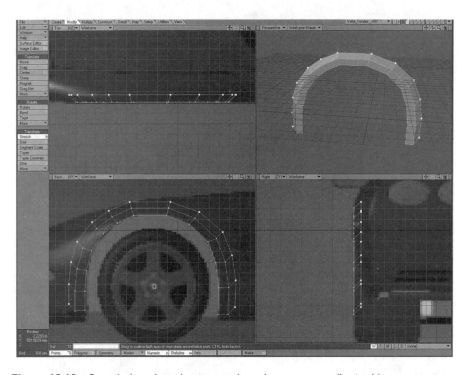

Figure 12.10 Stretch the selected points so the polygons are equally sized between points.

5. Run Extender Plus again on the third row of points, and move them out and up from the original row.

6. You can open the Display Options panel (press d) and change the Right viewport backdrop image to Vette_BR_front.jpg. Load this image from this book's DVD. Both front and back images of the car are provided so you can model the entire beast!

7. After these points are created, use the Drag tool (press Ctrl+t) from the Modify tab to begin positioning the points to match the backdrop images. Figure 12.11 shows the progress.

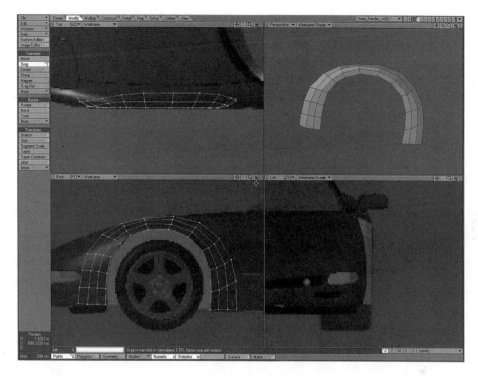

Figure 12.11   Use Extender Plus again, and then position the points using the Drag tool.

8. Press the Tab key to activate SubPatch mode. You can see the nice curvature of the fender starting to form. Press Tab again when ready to return to Polygon mode. SubPatch mode might confuse things at this point.

9. Select the top row of points, run Extender Plus, and move and drag to continue shaping the hood of the Corvette. Go for something like what is shown in Figure 12.12.

10. Guess what's next? Right! Coffee break! When ready, use Extender Plus another time, but you'll need to take more time to shape the points of the hood and fender, as shown in Figure 12.13.

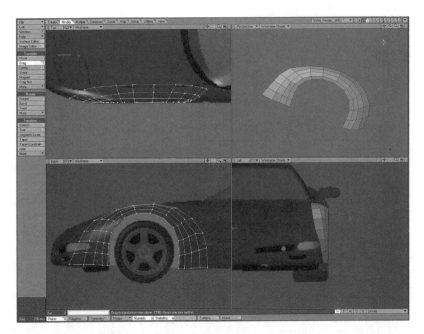

Figure 12.12   Continue using Extender, Move, Stretch, and Drag to shape the hood of the Corvette.

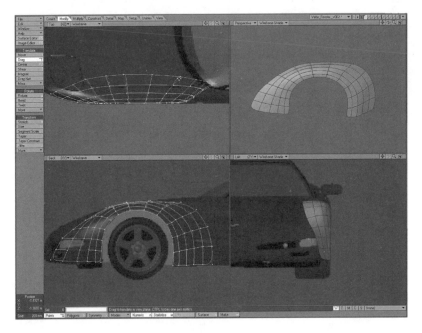

Figure 12.13   Use Extender Plus again to shape the hood and fender of the Corvette. Here, the Tab key has been pressed to see the model in SubPatch mode.

11. For the next use of Extender Plus, you don't need to select the entire row of points. You should be at the point where extending the entire row will be hard to manipulate, due to the side of the car and the hood being two different axes! So, select the last row of points you just created, but do not select the four points on the right side, as in Figure 12.14.

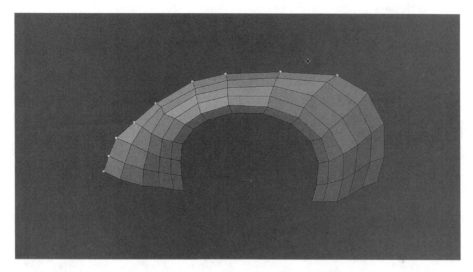

Figure 12.14   Select all but four points on the last row of points.

12. Use Extender Plus again and continue to shape out the hood of the car.

 Important

It's important to not become obsessed with matching the background images perfectly. There is always going to be a good amount of your own interpretation—that is, use the backdrop images as a guide, paying attention to a shaded Perspective view to guide the shape of your model. You'll find this technique highly efficient!

13. Select the last row of points for the hood of the car, use Extender Plus, and move and shape. We'll come back to the sides of the car in a moment.

    At this point, you might find that you don't really have to shape the rows that much. This is what's great about using an Extender tool. When one row of points is shaped and aligned, you can quickly extend them to build your model.

14. Use Extender Plus one more time and move the points roughly to the 0 Z-axis.

15. Press q, or click the Surface button at the bottom of the Modeler interface, and name this object Vette_Body or something similar. Give it a nice burgundy color, or whatever you like. Press the Tab key to see how the SubPatched version of your model is coming along.

16. Save your work! Remember to use Shift and the s key together to save incremental versions. Figure 12.15 shows the progress.

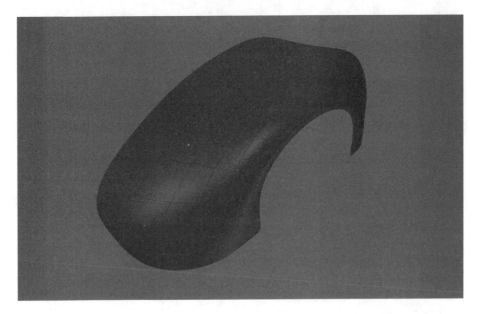

Figure 12.15   A little tweaking, some color, and you have your own Chicago chop shop! A fender is created. It's a boy!

17. There is one last thing to create before moving on to the doors. Select the row of points that you first created in the wheel well. Use Extender Plus on this row and move the newly created points down slightly and in to create the underside of the hood, around the wheel.

18. Use Extender Plus again and bring the points in to create the deeper part of the wheel well. Size them up a little to create a well, and extend again pulling the points in, as shown in Figure 12.16. This is similar to the beveling, smooth shifting, and super shifting you have done in previous chapters, except now you are using points. You bevel down, in, up, and back to create the wheel well.

19. Save often, and remember that Ctrl+z is Undo, and z is Redo. Practice this Extend, Move, Extend operation a few times and you'll get the hang of it. Remember to use Stretch, Drag, Move, and even Rotate on the selected points to shape them.

Tip

As with any model you create, flow is important. Rather than always moving every single point, consider moving entire rows of points, or multiple points at the same time, to shape the model. Doing this helps to keep the flow of the shape, making a smoother model.

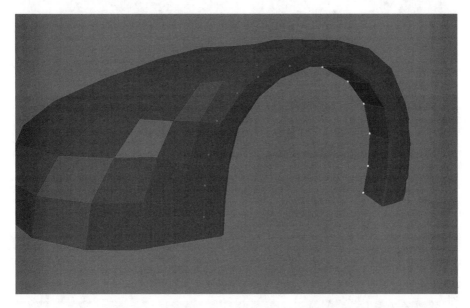

Figure 12.16   Use Extender Plus again to pull the points inward to create the wheel well.

Your hood is coming along nicely. Now, you'll move forward to create the side panels of the Corvette, and then the windshield and side windows, and then the back. You'll create the top part of the hood when you create the windshield.

20. In the Back viewport, select the four rightmost points of the existing model, as shown in Figure 12.17.

21. Use Extender Plus and move the newly created polygons to the right, about 100 mm. Then, use the Drag tool to shape the points to the front edge of the door, based on the background image as in Figure 12.18.

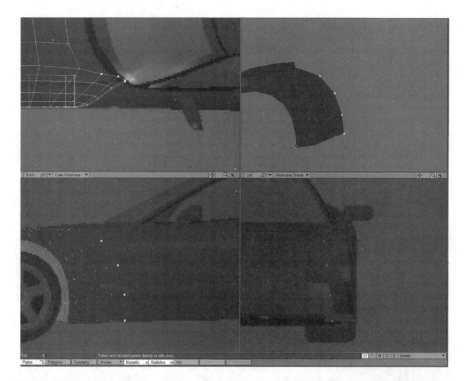

Figure 12.17 Select the four rightmost points and use Extender Plus to multiply them.

Figure 12.18 Move the points to the right and use the Drag tool to shape them to the door of the car.

22. Use Extender Plus about six more times, and use Drag to shape the points to the door of the car. Figure 12.19 shows the progress.

Figure 12.19   Use Extender Plus by pressing the e key and moving the newly created points. Do this about six times to create the panel of the door.

Tip

> Extender Plus is very quick and easy to use. When creating the extra points for the door area of the car, for example, press the e key to multiply the selected points and activate Extender Plus. For instance, press the t key for Move, and then drag the points. Now, press e, and move, then e again, and move, and so on. The Move tool stays on, and pressing the e key quickly creates one activation of the Extender Plus tool. Neat!

23. Take the last points you've created around the wheel well and move them to the backside of the wheel rim; press Ctrl+c to copy; Ctrl+z to undo the move; then Ctrl+v to paste. You now have four points in the same plane that you can quickly position around the wheel area. Doing this helps keep the flow of the polygons after they are connected.

24. Move and copy the new points, about 100 mm. Then, connect them as you did earlier in the chapter, in order, selecting four points and then pressing p to make a polygon. Connect all polygons, as in Figure 12.20.

Figure 12.20   Create the polygons on the back end of the wheel well.

25. Use Extender Plus to create the back quarter panel of the car, as in Figure 21.21.

Figure 12.21   Use Extender Plus to create the back quarter panel, and shape it using the Drag tool.

26. Select the top row of polygons across the entire side of the car, and extend them up to create the upper portion of the door and quarter panel, as in Figure 12.22.

Figure 12.22   Select the points across the top of the door and quarter panel and extend them up to continue building.

27. Align and shape the points to fit the side of the car. Then, take some time and use the Drag tool to evenly space out the polygons. Then, for the area on top of the back wheel well, select the four points in order on top of the rim, and press p to make a polygon. Figure 12.23 shows the creation.

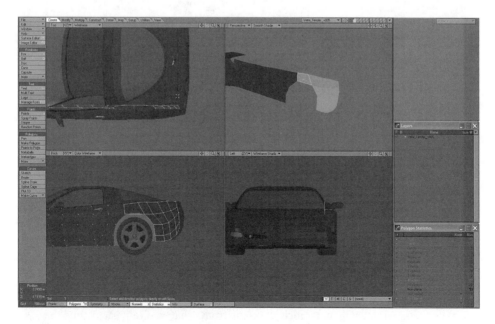

Figure 12.23   Connect the points at the top of the wheel well to join the door panel and the back quarter panel.

You've created this side of the car in just the Back viewport. Now, you need to shape the points using the images in the Left (side) view. Remember to use both front and back images of the car in the backdrop to properly line up your polygons. Also, use your keen sense of style and judgment in the Perspective view to tweak the shape. Figure 12.24 shows the model this far.

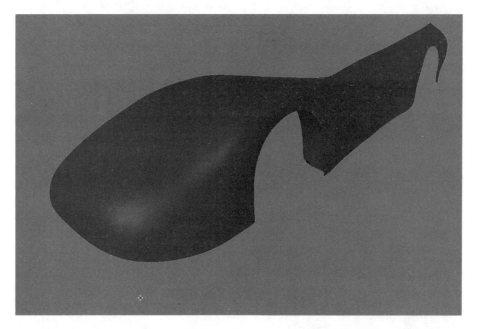

Figure 12.24   After points on the door and back quarter panel have been moved and shaped, the car is coming together.

Spending 20 minutes or so pulling points, or as some would say, "massaging" them, is necessary in almost any model that you create. Using the Perspective view, hold the Alt key and then click and drag to rotate the view. Using the Drag tool (Ctrl+t), move points so they're in line and equally spaced, keeping your object made up of a quad mesh as much as you can. Remember that you can move polygons and groups of points as well.

28. Save the work you've done as an incremental version (press Shift and the s key).

Creating Windows

Creating the windows is not much different from what you've created thus far. It is important to name the surfaces you create as you go. This will make your job surfacing much easier later in Layout.

Exercise 12.3   Creating Car Windows

1. Select the row of points at the top of the hood. Extend them with Extender Plus. Figure 12.25 shows the model.

    Pay close attention to the placement of these points in the Top view. Move them to the edge of the hood and, if needed, use Drag to position them. Watch the points in the Back view as well, because you'll need to move them up on the Y-axis to form the slope in the hood. You'll connect these to the side points next.

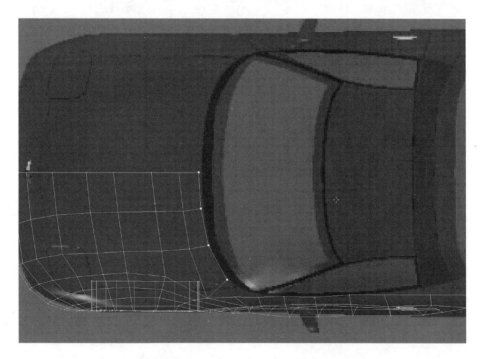

Figure 12.25   Extend the points at the top of the hood to begin creating the windshield.

2. Look at all four views; you can clearly see the corner of the hood and the side panel you need to connect. Select the four points, in order, and press the p key to make a polygon. Figure 12.26 shows the new polygon.

3. Select the points at the top of the hood, with a slight wrap around the side that makes up the edge of the hood. Extend them with Extender Plus and move them out slightly, and then down to create a nice beveled edge to the hood, as shown in Figure 12.27.

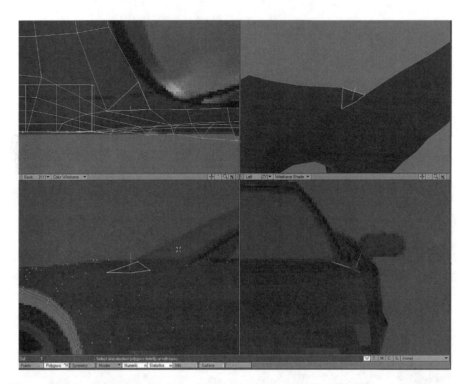

Figure 12.26   Connect the hood to the side panels by connecting the four points and creating a polygon.

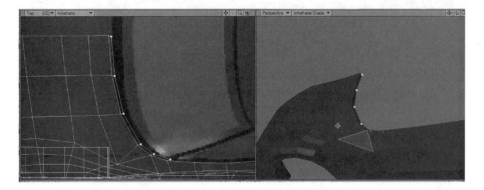

Figure 12.27   Extend the points at the top of the hood to bevel the edge.

4. Extend the newly created points again, move them out slightly, extend again, and move them up. Apply one more use of Extender Plus, and move the points up to begin creating the windshield.

5. After you've created and shaped the new polygons, select the first row in front of the hood, and give it the surface name of Vette_Rubber_Trim, or something similar. Then, surface the base of the windshield with its own unique name, such as Windshield_Base. Figure 12.28 shows the progress.

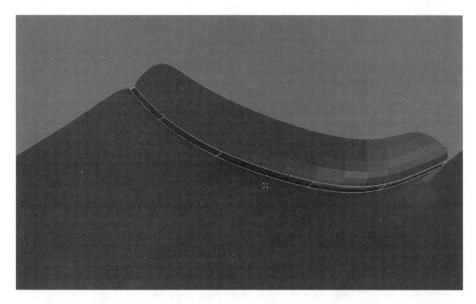

Figure 12.28 Extend the points three times to finish the lip of the hood and the beginning of the windshield, and apply surface names. Here, a windshield is not yet built, but by adding to the polygons, your surface will be created.

6. Extend the points up the windshield a few times, keeping a smooth flow to the quad mesh. Figure 12.29 shows a Wireframe and Smooth Shade SubPatch view of the model.

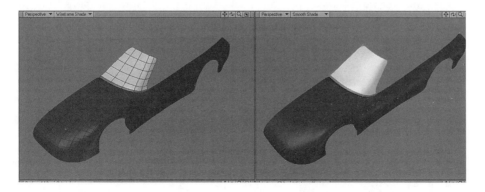

Figure 12.29 Extend the points up the windshield, using Drag to shape and smooth the mesh.

7. Save your work, and then build up the side window of the car. First, create a polygon to form the upper corner of the door, the area where the rear-view mirror will reside. Figure 12.30 shows the created polygon.

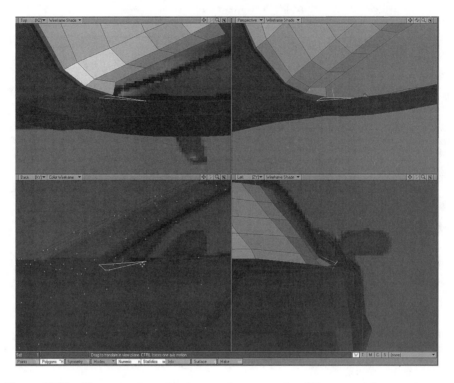

Figure 12.30 Create a polygon for the area that eventually will be around the rear-view mirror.

8. Select the points on the edge of the windshield, use Extender Plus, and pull them around the side of the car to create the doorframe. Color these polygons with the color of the car surface.

9. Continue creating points with Extender Plus to build the side window, and name the polygons appropriately. Figure 12.31 shows the progress.

10. Create the roof in the same fashion that you created the windows, connecting any polygons as needed.

11. Select the polygons on the corner of the car's windshield, the frame of the door. Use Super Shift from the Multiply tab on these to bevel them out and thicken them up slightly. You can do this procedure twice, as in Figure 12.32.

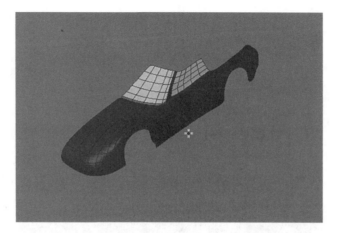

Figure 12.31   Continue creating points with Extender Plus to finish the side window.

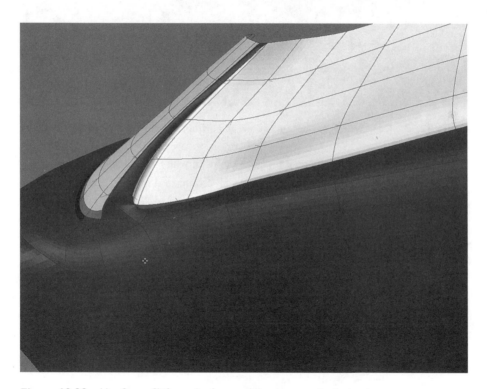

Figure 12.32   Use Super Shift on the frame of the door to give it depth.

12. You might have a situation where the curves just don't work for you, as in Figure 12.33.

Figure 12.33 Certain polygons become askew and disrupt the flow of the model.

13. This example illustrates precisely what we mean when we talk about polygon flow. Select the two polygons that are troublesome, and from the Detail tab, use Spin Quads to change the flow of this connection, as in Figure 12.34.

    Use the Spin Quads function where there needs to be better flow.

14. Continue using Extender Plus around the back end of the car. For the back itself, create multiple sets of polygons, because you'll need them to create the taillights. Also, have the curvature of the car follow the shape to match the license plate area in the background image. Then, create new polygons beneath the plate, and connect them. Figure 12.35 shows the partial back end with four points.

Figure 12.34   Spin Quads quickly and easily changes the flow of the polygons to create a cleaner body.

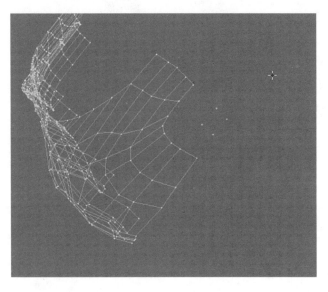

Figure 12.35   Create the necessary points in the back end that wrap around the license plate area.

15. After the model is tweaked to your liking, select the row of points on the open end. Press Alt+v to activate the Set Value command. This takes all the selected points and moves them to a specific location. In the Set Value panel that opens, set 0m for the Z-axis, as shown in Figure 12.36.

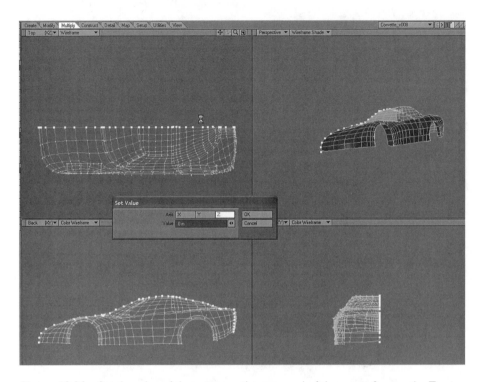

Figure 12.36   Set the value of the points on the open end of the car to 0 m on the Z-axis.

Doing this makes mirroring the car clean and easy. The Mirror tool automatically merges points (if chosen) and you don't have a seam. You still have some modeling to do before the final mirror, but go ahead and press Shift+v for Mirror, and then press the n key for Numeric, which activates the tool. In the Numeric panel, select the Z-axis, and you'll see a solid car, as shown in Figure 12.37.

Using the information in this tutorial, create the rest of the car's initial shape, including the back window and trunk. Using the same techniques that you used to create the hood and the windshield, create the back half of the car. Don't forget to create the small trim on the underside of the back wheel well, just as you did with the front wheel.

The next section will guide you through creating the smaller, finer details such as lamps, rear-view mirrors, and vents in the doors.

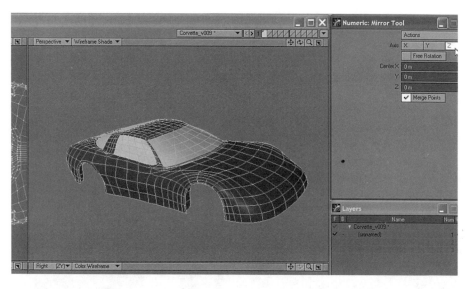

Figure 12.37 Mirroring the car polygons on the 0 Z-axis shows how the full car is looking.

Creating Necessary Detail

At this point, you should have a good idea of how to build a car based on a background image. Whether you're creating the model to match the image or simply need a reference for scale, the techniques presented thus far are the same no matter what type of vehicle you're building. However, each vehicle has a good amount of fine detail. These details, such as vents in the doors, edges, and so on, are the necessary minutiae that each vehicle needs to look real.

Exercise 12.4   Modeling Fine Details

1. Using the model you've created this far, or version 8 of the Corvette from this book's DVD, make sure you're set up in a quad view in Modeler. If you're using your model, undo the Mirror tool from the previous exercise, just so you have only one half of the car for these next steps.

2. Select the five points on the side edge of the door. Figure 12.38 shows the selection.

3. From the Multiply tab's Extend category, select the Edge Bevel tool. This handy little feature allows you to add the right amount of detail, while keeping a nice quad mesh for SubPatching.

4. You'll see a duplicate set of points appear, as well as some additional polygons. Use the Stretch tool from the Modify tab to bring the points closer together.

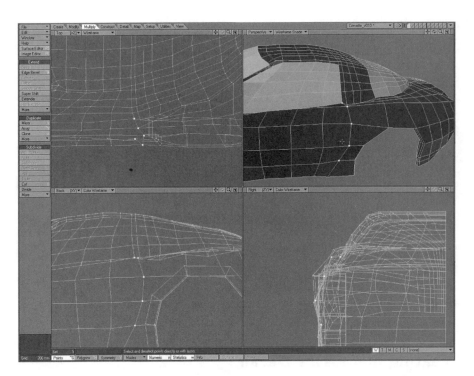

Figure 12.38 Select just the points on the edge of the car door.

5. Carefully select the polygons (three of them) that make up the edge of the door between the new points you just squeezed together. After they are selected, use the Super Shift command from the Multiply tab to bevel these in slightly. Do this about three times.

6. Move the polygons back into the body of the car to create the door separation. Figure 12.39 shows the operation. Note that your spacing should be a little tighter—the image here has the polygons spaced more to demonstrate.

7. Select the points around the edge of the rest of the door, as in Figure 12.40. Repeat the Edge Bevel operation.

8. Go to Polygon mode and press the Tab key. You might see a warning that you cannot fully SubPatch the model. If you go to your Statistics panel by pressing w on the keyboard, and look for the more than (>) four polygons selection. Click the small plus to the left of it. The polygons in question will be selected in Modeler's viewports.

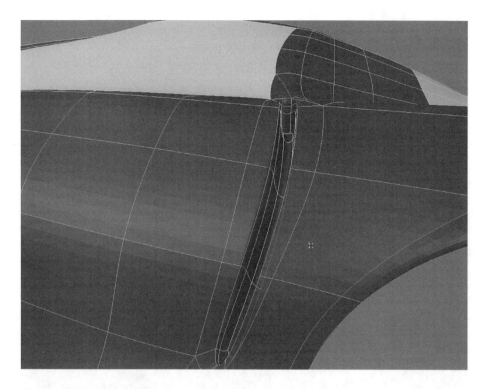

Figure 12.39   Use Super Shift to create the beveled edge of the door.

Figure 12.40   Select the points around the edge of the door to bevel.

9. Of course, you could have run the Edge Bevel on the entire door from the beginning, but doing so wouldn't allow us to show you this new tool. With the bad polygon selected, choose the Add Edges tool from the Detail tab.

10. You'll see small, light blue circles appear around the edges of the selected polygon.

11. Click one and then click the other. You'll have sliced the geometry! Figure 12.41 shows the operation.

Figure 12.41   Use the Add Edges tool to fix any polygons that are made up of more than four polygons.

12. Add another edge as needed to fix the polygon so that it is made up of four vertices. This tool allows you to add necessary detail to individual polygons. Be sure to press the Spacebar to turn off the tool and keep your operation. Turning off the tool directly, or clicking a blank area, removes edges you might have added.

Tip

When using the Add Edges command, you can click and drag a light blue circle so that it lines up with an existing polygon edge. From there, connect that blue circle to another blue circle by clicking it.

13. Repeat the Edge Bevel steps for the hood. When the hood is complete, save your work.

14. Select the polygons in the middle of the door and use Super Shift two or three times to create the stylized edging on the side of the car. Then, drag the points out to angle the inset, or simply rotate the polygons from the Top view to shape. Figure 12.42 shows the operation.

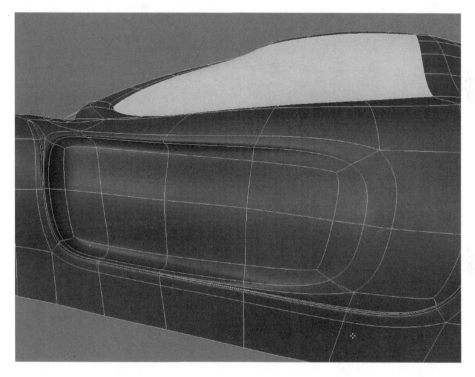

Figure 12.42   Use Super Shift on the side of the door two or three times to create the stylized insets.

15. Select the front corner of the hood—the four polygons that make up the general area of the turn signal lights. Use Super Shift to multiply the selection. Then, use the Drag tool to tighten up the area into more of a square.

16. Run Super Shift two more times; set the polygon surface name to Side Lights or something similar; and run Super Shift again. Give the lights a unique color. Figure 12.43 shows the new front lights.

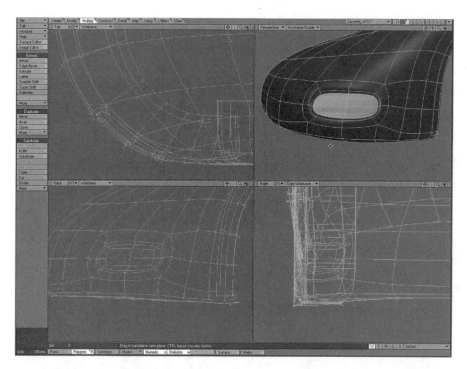

Figure 12.43 Use Super Shift on the four polygons in the front corner of the car to create the front lights.

17. Repeat this process for door handles and rear taillights. Remember that you can undo whatever operation you did, so set the Undo levels to the max of 128 in the General Options panel (press o).

18. After you add the taillights and make any final tweaks, make sure that the open edge of the model's points lie exactly on the 0 Z-axis. You can select all of them and press Alt+v to use Set Value as you did earlier. Even though you've done this already, it's a possibility that you've moved some of those points with any additional changes.

19. After the points are lined up on the 0 Z-axis, mirror the model (Shift+v) over the same 0 Z-axis. Press the Tab key and check out your new ride! Save an incremental version!

Creating Tires

Of course, your new Corvette is useless without tires. This section will show you a quick way to create tires for your Vette.

Exercise 12.5   Building Tires for Your Vette

1. Go to a new blank layer and place the car in the background layer.

2. Select the disc tool and, holding the Ctrl key, draw out a disc to represent the front wheel, as shown in Figure 12.44.

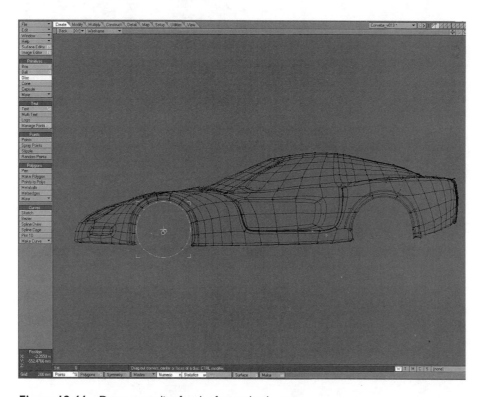

Figure 12.44 Draw out a disc for the front wheel.

3. Give the wheel some depth, and then turn off the tool. Move it into position based on the background car layer. Next, select the outer edge polygon of the disc and, using the Bevel tool (b), bevel four times: once down and out slightly; down; down and in slightly; and then back into the wheel, as in Figure 12.45.

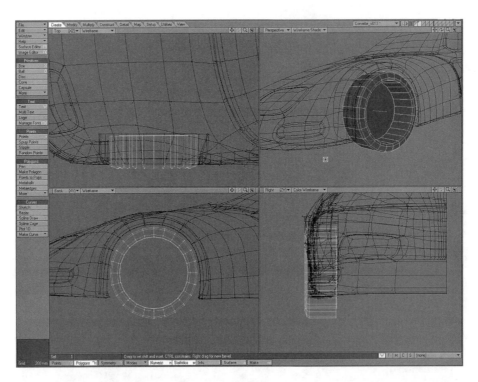

Figure 12.45 Use the Bevel tool to create the tire.

4. After you've beveled to the back of the tire, delete the polygon, leaving only the tire itself, as in Figure 12.46.

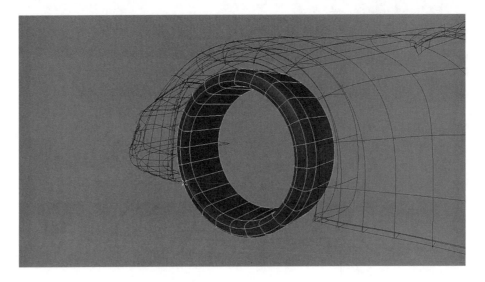

Figure 12.46 Delete the polygon you used to bevel, making a hole in the tire.

Deleting this polygon also allows you to apply SubPatches to the tire for smoother renders.

5. Give these polygons the name Vette_Tire, or something similar, by pressing q and entering the name.

6. Carefully select the points on the inner edge of the tire, as in Figure 12.47. Copy (Ctrl+c) and paste (Ctrl+v) them into a new layer.

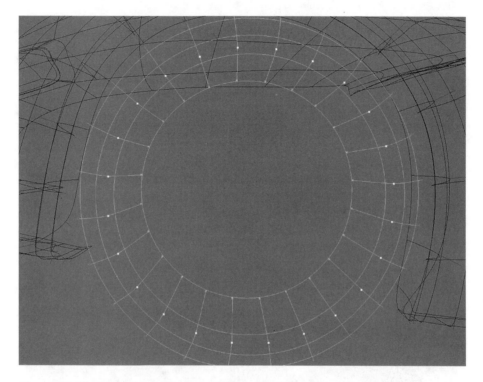

Figure 12.47   Select the points on the inside edge of the tire to begin creating the rim.

7. Select the points and press p to make a polygon. Bevel the disc four times, similar to the tire. However, you should bevel it to create a nice edge rim, and then bevel down towards the center. Bevel a little more to create the center of the rim.

Be creative here. To bevel, press the b key, and click and drag with the left mouse.

Then, click the right mouse button once to bevel again, use the left mouse button to move and position, and repeat. Mac users: Remember to use the Command button to simulate right mouse button functions. Pay attention to all views to keep the polygons in line.

8. When your rim gets down to the very center, bevel the points down as small as you can, and delete them. You can put your own logo in the wheel if you like, or a flatten object, or even just a 3D letter. Figure 12.48 shows the progress.

Important

When beveling or working with discs, it's helpful to have the Action Center set to Selection. From the Modes drop-down list at the bottom of Modeler, choose Selection. Your mouse movements, such as Size or Bevel, will be based on the selected polygons, not your mouse position.

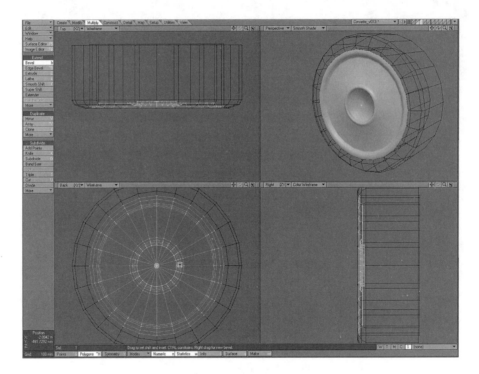

Figure 12.48   Bevel the rim to make a shape you're happy with.

9. Starting with the second polygon to the right of center on the rim, select two polygons, then skip two, hold down the Shift key, select two more, and so on. You should end up with a selection of 12 polygons, as in Figure 12.49.

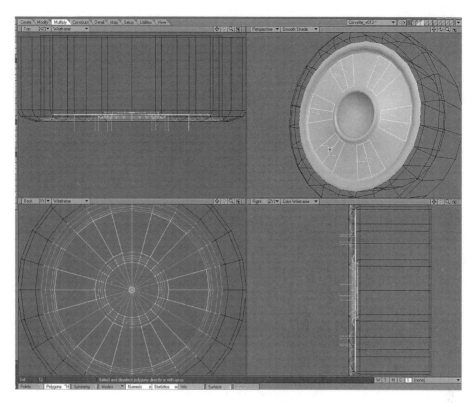

Figure 12.49 Select every other two polygons, totaling 12.

10. After you have selected the 12 polygons, press the Tab key and you'll see the beginnings of your rims.

11. Press the Tab key again to turn off SubPatch mode, and then use Super Shift to bevel the selected polygons down and inward. Right-click to apply another Super Shift, and then left-click and move the selection in. Then, delete the selected polygons to make the spokes of the rims.

12. Don't forget to give this rim a surface name such as Vette_Chrome.

13. You may feel the need to select the points in the center of the rim and size them down to your liking. Figure 12.50 shows the finished rim. When you're ready, cut and paste the rim into the tire layer.

14. Save your work!

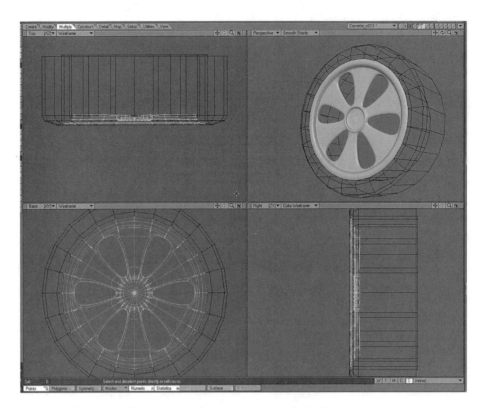

Figure 12.50 Super Shift and size points to create the finished rim.

15. After the entire wheel is created with the rim, go to the Multiply tab. Under the Duplicate category, click the More drop-down list. Select Clone to Layer, and in the panel that appears, enter 3 for the Number of Clones, and Multi Layer for Clone Output. At the bottom of the panel, select User Defined for Center Around, and leave everything else at their defaults. Click OK. Figure 12.51 shows the panel.

16. Go to the first new layer and place the car in a background layer. Move the cloned wheel to line up with the back of the car.

17. When the tire is lined up, go to the next layer and line up the wheel. Then, do the same for the fourth wheel.

18. Take the last two wheels and select both layers, then press Shift+v to mirror them over the 0 Z-axis. After you have mirrored, delete the originals. You now have four tires, on four layers, in their proper positions.

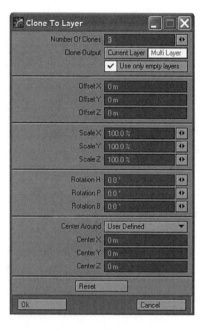

Figure 12.51   Using Clone to Layer, you can quickly place the tire on different layers for animation.

19. But wait! There's more! Go to the first wheel's layer, and from the View tab, select the Pivot tool under the Layers category. Set the pivot crosshair that appears directly in the center of the wheel.

20. Repeat setting this pivot for each wheel. Doing this ensures that your wheels rotate properly in Layout.

21. Save your work!

You may find creating tires and rims easy with this method. However, you can spend more time with them using backdrop images (such as the original image) or use splines and a lathe to create more complex shapes. It all depends on the project and how much detail you're looking for.

With the information presented in this tutorial, you now have the power to create any vehicle you can imagine. You can model exactly to an image, as mentioned, or create something completely unique. Here are a few tips to consider when building vehicles:

- Keep polygon count to a minimum. You can always add more, but it's harder to take away.

- Remember to use Edge Bevel and Add Edges to add necessary details and fix polygons that are more than four vertices.

- Use the Spin Quads tool to keep the flow of your polygons smooth and clean.

- Pay attention to all views and modify point position using Drag or Move.

- Remember that you can use Rotate, Stretch, Size, and more on groups of points. It's not always needed to move just one point at a time. Moving groups of points helps keep polygonal flow.

Rendering Vehicles

This next section discusses how you can render great looking scenes for your vehicles, be it a car, a motorcycle, or your own invention. The techniques presented here can also be used on things like electronics and product shots. The project begins in Modeler.

Exercise 12.6   Building 3D Reflectors for Rendering

1. Create a new object and build out a flat box in the Top viewport.

2. Move it off the X- and Z-axes about 1m. Mirror it across the X-axis. Then, mirror the two polygons across the Z-axis. Figure 12.52 shows the creation.

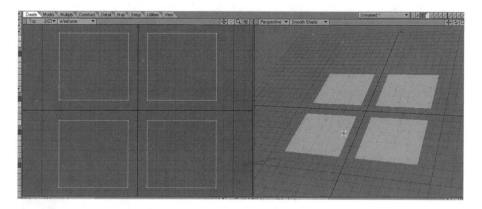

Figure 12.52   Create four polygons to be used as a reflector.

3. Press the f key to flip these polygons downward. Give them a surface name of reflector, or something similar.

4. Save your work and head into Layout.

5. In Layout, load the final Corvette model you created. Then, load the reflector object you just created. Also, load the Vette_Set object from this book's DVD. This is nothing more than a box with its front and top removed and SubPatched.

6. Move the camera in close to view your car. Create a keyframe to lock it in place. Feel free to widen the camera angle a bit by decreasing the Zoom Factor from the Camera Properties panel.

7. Move the reflector up over the hood and windshield of the car, and size it down slightly. Create a keyframe to lock it in place. Figure 12.53 shows the view.

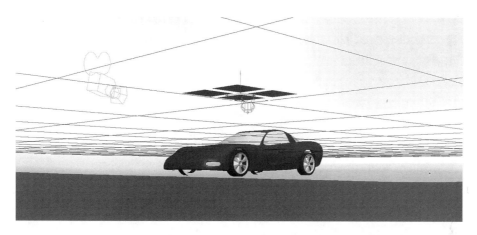

Figure 12.53 The polygon reflector is moved above the hood of the car.

8. To surface the car, first make the reflector object surface a bright white in color. Set the Luminosity in the Surface Editor to 100% and bring diffusion to 0%. Then, in the Surface Editor, choose your first surface: the body paint of the car.

9. Make the paint a deep color, such as a rich burgundy color, because it will pick up the reflections better.

Also set the following in the Basic tab:

Color	145, 053, 043
Luminosity	0%
Diffuse	70%
Specularity	100%
Glossiness	80%
Reflection	30%
Transparency	0%

Translucency	0%
Bump	100%
Smoothing	On
Smoothing Angle	50°
Double Sided	On

In the Environment tab, apply these settings:

Reflection Options	Ray Tracing & Spherical Map
Reflection Image	none

10. Select Save All Objects from the File drop down list. You can also save this surface to your preset shelf. Remember to open the presets from the Window drop down button at the top of Layout.

11. Set the glass surface with the following settings in the Basic tab of the Surface Editor:

Color	213, 217, 244
Luminosity	0%
Diffuse	50%
Specularity	100%
Glossiness	100%
Reflection	50%
Transparency	0%

12. Click the T button for Transparency. You'll use a gradient here to surface the windows. In the Texture Editor for the Transparency panel, make the Layer Type a Gradient. Set the Input Parameter to Incidence Angle. This changes the amount of transparency (either more or less) depending on the camera angle and reflection. Without this, the transparency will just be there, no matter the angle it's viewed from, which is not how the real world works.

13. Create two keys in the gradient bar—one in the center with a value of about 150%and another at the bottom with a value of 0%. Figure 12.54 shows the gradient.

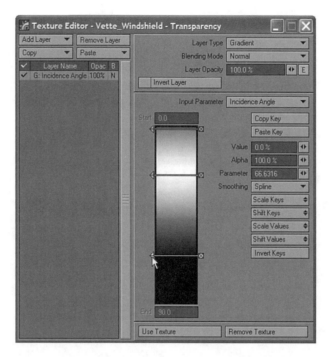

Figure 12.54   Set up a Gradient texture for the transparency for the glass of the car.

14. Click Use Texture to close the Texture panel. In the Surface Editor, set the following:

Refraction Index	1
Translucency	0%
Bump	100%
Smoothing	On
Smoothing Angle	60°
Double Sided	On

In the Environment tab, apply these settings:

Reflection Options	Ray Tracing & Spherical Map
Reflection Image	none

15. Save your object to keep your surfaces attached to the car permanently! Now let's see how this is looking. First, click the Render tab in Layout, and then click Render Options. In the Render Options panel, click Ray Trace Reflection.

16. Save the scene. Always save the scene before you render. Press F9 to render the current frame.

17. The render looks good, but what about the lighting? Take the default distant light that's in the scene, and move it to the back right of the car. In the Lights Properties panel, change the light to an area light, as in Figure 12.55.

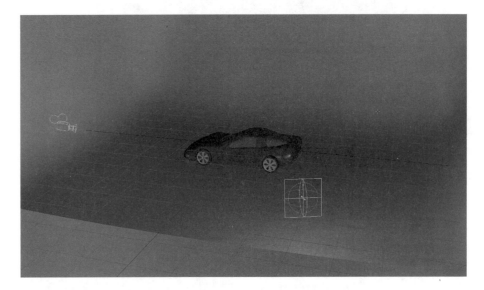

Figure 12.55   The view of the scene with just one area light applied.

18. Change the Light Intensity to 70%. Make sure Ray Trace is set for Shadows.

19. Set the Ambient Intensity to 5% from the Global Illumination panel, accessed from the Lights Properties panel.

20. Back in Layout, select the reflector object, and press the p key to open the Object Properties panel. In the Render tab of the panel, click Unseen by Camera so the object doesn't render. Then, turn off Self Shadow, Cast Shadow, and Receive Shadow. Be sure that you do *not* turn on Unseen by Rays. Clicking this removes the reflection's purpose in Layout!

21. Save the scene, and press F9 to render. Figure 12.56 shows the image.

22. In the Surface Editor, select the glass surface of the car. Increase the Reflection to about 75% and bring Diffusion down to 25%. Additionally, you can adjust the value of the gradient to add more or less transparency to the glass.

23. Lastly, add surfacing, such as simple chrome or silver to the wheels and perhaps another light in the scene for a more dramatic appearance.

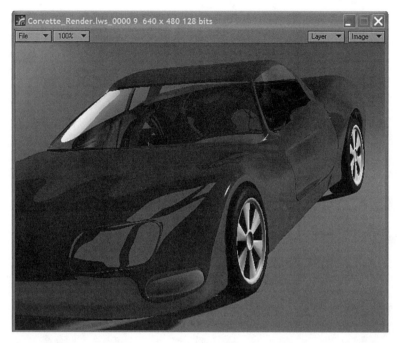

Figure 12.56   With the lighting in place and shadows applied, the image is coming along nicely. The reflections in the glass need to be enhanced.

The goal of this chapter was to teach you how to model vehicles while maintaining polygonal flow throughout. You can create just about anything with this point-by-point method, but it works especially well for vehicles.

The Next Step

The next step is for you to take this tutorial and branch out on your own. Use the modeling techniques to create your own cool creations, like cars, bikes, toys, or spaceships. Using the technique of a reflection board as you saw here, you can create that wet, glossy look that is so popular in magazine and television ads. Imagine how that surface would look with the camera moving across the hood of the car. Pretty cool! This is why building your model for use with SubPatch is powerful, because from the Object Properties panel, you can tell LightWave to render at a SubPatch level of 10, making for a much smoother, cleaner render.

Learning how to model and render like this is exciting, because now the only thing limiting you is your imagination.

Chapter 13

More Character Modeling

No matter what type of 3D business you're involved in, at some point, someone will ask you to create a 3D character. This may or may not be something you're interested in, but it's certainly something you should try. Building characters can be extremely fun if you know the proper methods. Every modeling project is approached differently, and the same goes for character modeling. You basically have three options:

- There is box modeling, where you begin with a box and build upon it, like the fun giraffe model in Chapter 10, "Modeling Quadrupedal Characters."
- You can begin with a more complex mesh and shape it, using SubPatches and various multiplication tools like Super Shift and Bevel, as you did in Chapter 11, "Modeling Electronics," modeling the telephone.
- The third method begins with points, outlining and then building upon those as you did in Chapter 12, "Modeling Vehicles," modeling the car.

What method is best? The choice is really up to you. No one method is better or worse. What is important are the amount of geometry and the control of the flow of polygons. You should strive for making all of your LightWave models as quads—polygons with four vertices. What method will you use in this chapter? Surprisingly, there's one more way you can begin building models; you can incorporate multiple methods in one model. This chapter will teach you how to begin modeling a character head with spline curves, and then use tools you've already learned about, such as Edge Bevel, Super Shift, and more, to create the details.

In this chapter, you'll learn about the following:

- Creating a character from a real sculpture
- Working with splines to outline the shape
- Patching splines to create surfaces
- Converting to SubPatches to build detail

Modeling characters is very subjective. Everyone has his or her methods and reasons for doing what he or she does and why he or she does it. Don't let that cloud your judgment, and more so, do not let images you may find on the Internet persuade you to quit. That is to say, building the perfect character takes time and patience. When you see images from artists, be encouraged about what's possible, not discouraged about what you haven't created. Building that ultimate 3D character takes more time than you can imagine—certainly more time than afforded by an afternoon. Sure, you can sit down with LightWave and in a matter of minutes have a decent-looking character—the tools are that powerful! But for the really perfect-looking character that you want to show the world—those characters take practice and time. The tools shown to you in this chapter are the resources you can rely on to build any type of character, from a realistic human, to a cartoon character, or something of your own.

Modeling Project Overview

In the year 2000, Axis Animation's Stuart Aitken created a beautiful-looking model for the cover of *Inside LightWave 6*. The tutorial he wrote was updated and edited by me (Dan Ablan) in 2001 for *Inside LightWave 7*. Since then, those publications, the Internet, graphic magazines, and training videos have been flooded with steps to create 3D female heads. Some people have taken it a step further and modeled the male form. Others have completely gone the opposite direction and modeled stylized cartoon characters. To step things up a notch with *Inside LightWave 8*, I decided to go a different route altogether. The cover image created for this book is completely 3D, and it is the focus of this chapter. It is based on a sculpture created by a talented artist named David O'Keefe. You can see all of his amazing work at `www.davidokeefe.com`. I contacted David after seeing some of his sculptures in person in Tampa, Florida.

I had been thinking about what to do for the cover of this book for months, probably longer. Of course, we could update Stuart's female head model, and the original idea was to show more of her body while teaching you how to build it. But you know what? That's getting a bit tired. After all, aren't there enough female and male 3D modeling tutorials out there? After talking with Mr. O'Keefe, he thought it was best to create a character exclusively for this book! Figure 13.1 shows the original sculpture made from clay.

Figure 13.1   The clay sculpture created for this book by artist David O'Keefe.

Too often, it's easy to follow a trend. We've broken barriers with the *Inside* series of books, so to get going with LightWave 8, you're going to model this sculpture for yourself. Overall, it's truly not that different than modeling a realistic human or a cartoon character. What is different, though, is that this model is not perfectly symmetrical. Each side of its head is different. So how would you approach this? What is the best way to begin creating the structure? Point by point method (as shown for the car modeling in Chapter 12) could work very well. Box modeling probably would not, as it's sometimes hard to define a specific shape. This is where spline modeling comes in handy because you can determine an "outline," if you will, of the shape of the character. From there, you can patch (create polygons) the splines together, and then use LightWave 8's powerful modeling tools to build the head's detail. Each side of the head should be built separately, but this chapter will show how to model one side, then mirror the model and modify it to match the original sculpture.

Creating Splines for Characters

You'll start this project like many other modeling projects, using backdrop images. At this point, you should know how to place images in LightWave Modeler's backdrop. You've done this for the car in Chapter 12, and earlier in Chapter 3, "Modeler," when discussing Modeler's features. For this chapter, a complete backdrop image setup has been saved for you on this book's DVD.

Exercise 13.1 Building a Character's Head with Splines

1. Start LightWave 8 Modeler and press the d key for Display Options. Click over to the Backdrop tab.

2. From the Preset drop-down button, select Load Backdrops; and from the Images folder of this chapter on this book's DVD, select the 8_dude_bkds file. This loads up three photos of the character, each placed in the appropriate viewport, as shown in Figure 13.2.

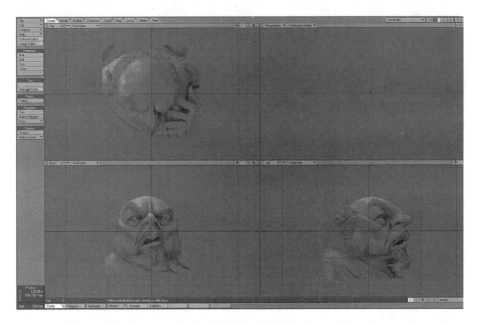

Figure 13.2 Loading the pre-made backdrops in Modeler places three photographs in the backdrop of three viewports.

These backdrop images have been cropped from original photos in Photoshop, and are aligned in the Backdrop tab. These images are found on this book's DVD in the Chapter 13 images folder.

3. To start, expand the Left view (the side of the character) to full screen by clicking the expand button in the top-right of the panel. Or, place your mouse in the Left view and press 0 on your numeric keypad. Make sure this viewport is set to Left (ZY) view as shown in Figure 13.2. Then, press the period key a few times to zoom into the backdrop image.

4. Click the Create tab at the top of Modeler and select the Points tool.

5. With the right mouse button, click down 19 evenly spaced points outlining the head of the character, as in Figure 13.3. Mac people, remember to hold down the Command button to perform right mouse button functions. Don't worry about creating points around the hair on the chin; you can add that later.

Important

Pay close attention to the shape of this character's head. It's a complex shape and is not symmetrical. When you create the points, consider the shape of the center of the character's head, not just the image outline.

Figure 13.3   Using the Points tool, create 19 points around the outline of the character.

6. When the points are created, press Ctrl+p to make a spline curve. Conversely, you can also choose Make Open Curve from the Curves category, under the Make Curves drop down, in the Create tab. Figure 13.4 shows the curve in all four views.

7. Use the Drag tool (Ctrl+t) to adjust any points and help align the curve to the backdrop image.

8. Save the curve as Caeser_Spline_v001. From now on, every time you save, remember to save incrementally by pressing Shift+s.

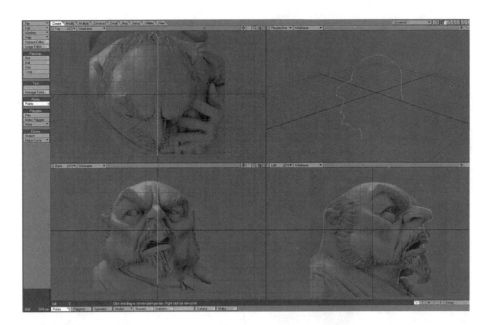

Figure 13.4 An open curve, a spline curve, is created from the points.

9. Start creating the cross sections. Create about ten points following the curvature on the left side of the character, from the bottom-left viewport (the Back (XY) view), as you're looking straight at his face. Then, deselect the points you've created, and select from the top of the head on the original curve, the first point. Select the rest of the points in order down the side, and press Ctrl+p to make a spline curve, as in Figure 13.5.

Tip

Creating points in the Back (XY) view aligns them on the X-axis, but possibly not the Z-axis. Be sure to move all the points to the center of the head, so that they line up with a point at the top of the head, similar to Figure 13.5.

10. In the Back view, create eight points around the character's right eye. Then, from the Create tab under the Curves category, select the Make Curve drop-down and choose Make Closed Curve, as in Figure 13.6.

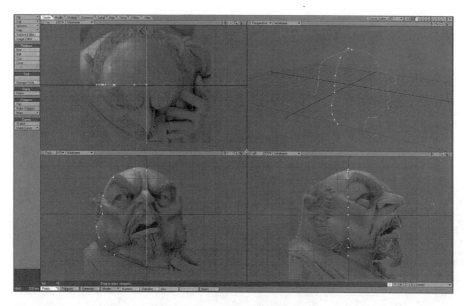

Figure 13.5   Create a spline curve down the middle side of the head.

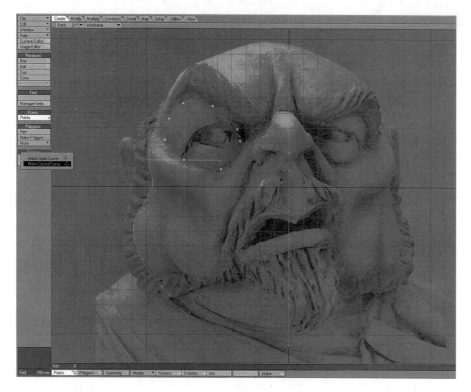

Figure 13.6   Eight points around the right eye and a closed curve make a connected spline
curve, which you'll soon attach to the rest of the head.

11. Using the Drag tool (Ctrl+t), adjust the points to fit the eye area, based on the backdrop images. Figure 13.7 shows the curve.

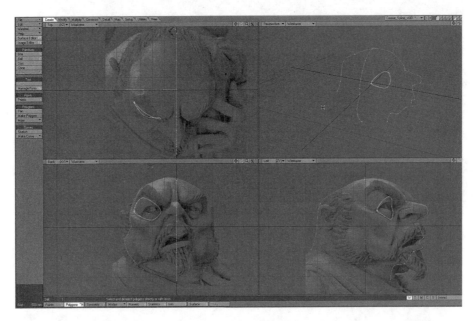

Figure 13.7   Using the Drag tool, you can shape the spline curve to match the shape of the eye area to follow the form of the head in the backdrop layer.

You're first setting up key area splines, from which you'll build upon. So, you have the main outline created first, and then the side of the head. Just looking at these two curves already shows the shape of the character. From there, you've start creating the cross sections, and then you'll add and delete various points to even out the curves. After that is done, you'll start adding smaller curves for detail.

12. Just as you did with the eye area, create seven points around the inner mouth. Deselect them and then select them in order starting with the corresponding point on the spline making up the center of the head. Use the Drag tool as you did with the eye area to shape the curve, as in Figure 13.8. Remember, select one point, then the next, then the next, and then press Ctrl+p to make a curve.

13. Press Shift+s to save your work. Then, make another curve by selecting a point at the corner of the mouth, then a corresponding point on the curve at the side of the head. Press Ctrl+p to make a spline. Figure 13.9 shows the curve, but because it's only two points at this stage, it's a straight line.

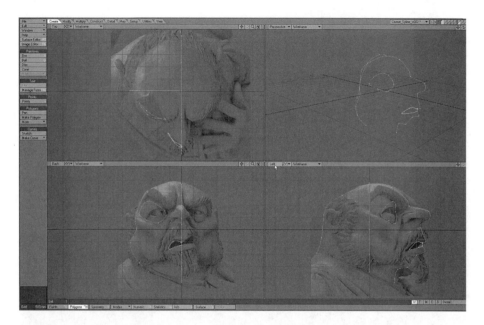

Figure 13.8   Create a spline curve with seven points to make up the mouth area.

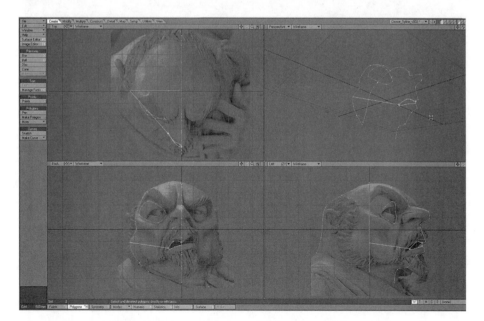

Figure 13.9   Create another spline for the mid-section of the head from the corner of the mouth.

14. You might notice that this curve you just created on the side of the head does not follow the shape of the character's head. Therefore, you need to add a few points to the curves. Go to Polygons mode at the bottom of Modeler. Select the curve that rests on the side of the head you just created.

15. Switch back to Points mode, and from the Multiply tab, select Add Points from the Subdivide category. Click directly on the curve on the side of the head. Doing this adds a point to the curve. Create three points, and then use the Drag tool on those newly created points to shape the curve to match the backdrop image. Figure 13.10 shows the additional points.

Figure 13.10 Add points to the newly created curve with the Add Points tool under the Multiply tab. Use Drag on the points to shape the curve to match the backdrop image.

16. Begin filling out the shape of the head with curves. Remember that you're just creating an outline, not the full polygonal mesh. Select the point under the eye spline, close to the nose, and then select the point in the middle of the cheek spline, and press Ctrl+p to make the curve, as shown in Figure 13.11.

17. Deselect the two points used to create the new curve. Then, select this new spline by first pressing the spacebar to switch to Polygons mode and then selecting the curve (if it's not already selected). Go to the Multiply tab, select Add Points from the Subdivide category, and add two points to the selected curve.

18. Use the Drag tool on these newly created points to follow the contour of the character's cheek based on the backdrop images, as shown in Figure 13.12.

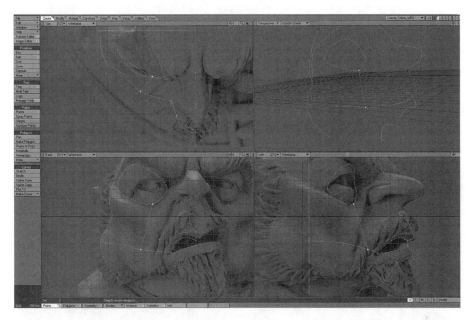

Figure 13.11   Begin connecting the eye spline to the rest of the head, starting with the cheek.

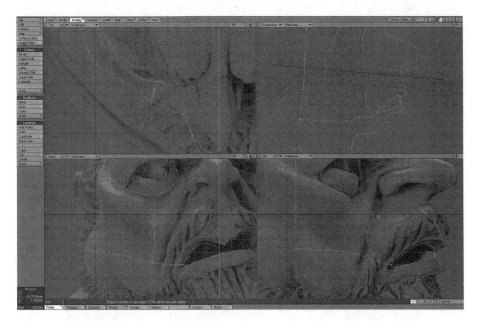

Figure 13.12   Use the Drag tool (Ctrl+t) to shape the curve to match the backdrop images.

Important

As you begin building a character—this character or any other—it's important to pay attention to the overall flow of the curves using the Perspective view. Although the images in your backdrop are excellent references, they do not shape the curves—you do. Use your own instincts and judgment to properly position points and curves.

19. Connect the corner of the eye to the spline at the side of the head, and then add a point to it. Drag the point out to create a curve to match the cheek, as shown in Figure 13.13.

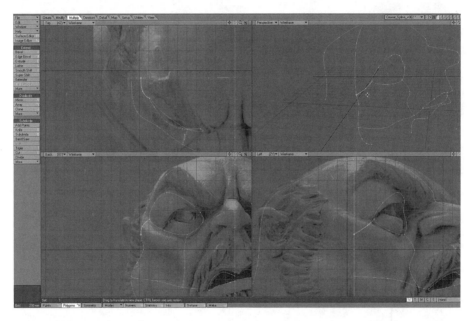

Figure 13.13   Connect the corner of the eye to the curve on the side of the head. Add a point and shape it to match the cheek of the character.

20. Take some time and outline the shape of the character on your own. You'll want to create spline curves from two points and then add points to the curves while shaping with the Drag tool from the Modify tab. Figure 13.14 shows a continuation of the spline patching thus far.

21. Add a little more control to the eye area by connecting one additional spline. Be sure to make this a closed curve as you did earlier for the outer portion of the eye. Select the Points tool from the Create tab, use the right mouse button to create the points (about five of them), and then under the Create tab, select Closed Curve from the Make Curve option under the Curves category. Figure 13.15 shows the addition.

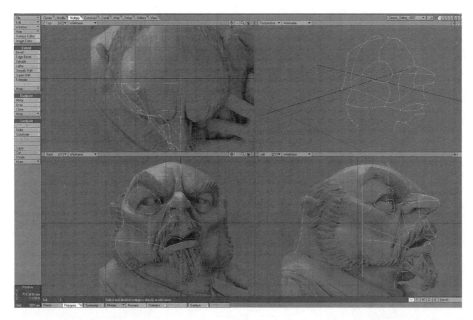

Figure 13.14   Continue on your own and add more curves to outline the shape of the character. Remember to add a point or two to the curves and use the Drag tool to shape.

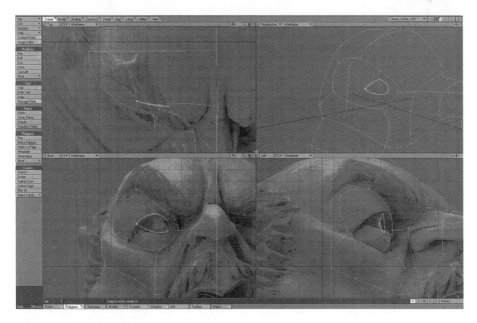

Figure 13.15   Add another spline curve in the eye area for additional control.

22. Connect this curve to the existing curves of the outer eye. Then, add a point to each curve and create another spline curve to add to the eye area, looping around the one you just created. Use the Drag tool (Ctrl+t) to shape the curves by adjusting the points. Figure 13.16 shows the patching.

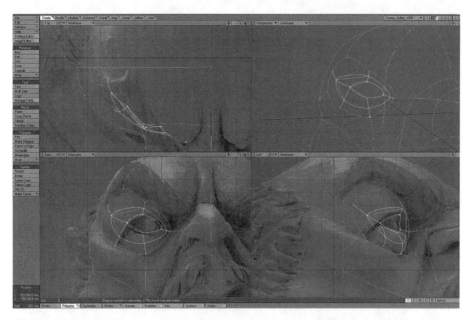

Figure 13.16   Creating an additional looping spline curve to the eye area will help create the necessary detail for the eyes.

23. When you start connecting these curves into polygons, you'll want to keep a uniform mesh across the entire model. If you look at Figure 13.17, you'll find that the nose does not patch evenly (you'll be patching soon). Select the curve that makes up the side of the nose and add a point to it, as shown in Figure 13.18.

24. After the point is added to the curve, make sure you're in Polygons mode, and with just the same curve selected, press the k key to "kill" the curve, leaving just the points.

25. Select the three points around the bulb of the nose and create a curve (Ctrl+p), as in Figure 13.19. Note that these points start with the bottom point, then move to the point that is floating, and then the top point.

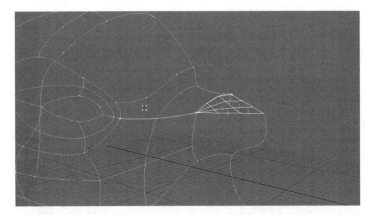

Figure 13.17   When the curves at the front of the nose are patched, they do not patch correctly, as there are three curves, rather than four.

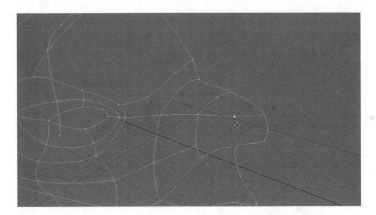

Figure 13.18   Select the curve at the side of the nose and add a point to it in the front of the nose.

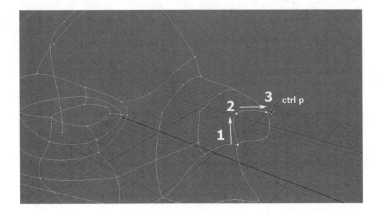

Figure 13.19   Select the points in the bulb of the nose and create a curve.

26. Reconnect the curve at the side of the nose, as shown in Figure 13.20.

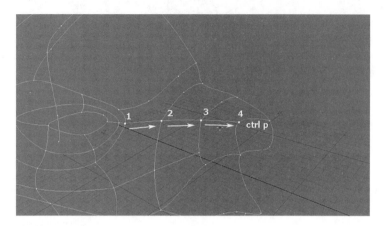

Figure 13.20 Reconnect the points along side of the nose, creating a curve.

27. Take some time and add points and curves on your own to shape the rest of the face. Figure 13.21 shows the spline patch for the character's face.

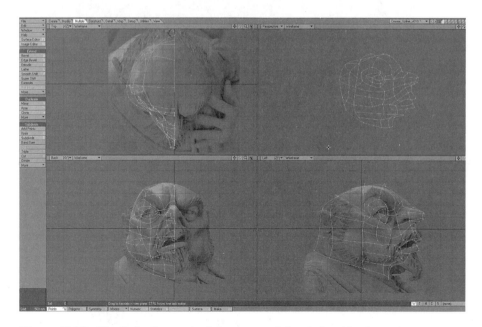

Figure 13.21 The final spline patch of the character's face before it's mirrored.

From this point, the process is just like what you've already done, adding points to curves to create the necessary cross sections, as well as adding more spline curves to control the shape of the face, such as around the mouth. Take some time and continue creating spline curves so that you have something like the object in Figure 13.20. Remember to use the Drag tool to grab points and shape the curve to match the backdrop images. Feel free to load up the object shown in this image from this book's DVD. This is the Caesar_Spline_v010.

Your goal is not to build the entire model out of curves, creating every detail and each wrinkle. Rather, you're trying to achieve a carefully placed outline of your character. For example, around the eyes, you don't need to create every fold of the eyelid with curves. Instead, go for framing the eye with curves, one on the top, and one on the bottom. From there, you'll patch the curves and create the polygons.

Controlling Spline Cross Sections

You're getting close to patching the spline curves. This process is a matter of selecting curves, four to be exact, and running the LightWave Make Patch command. Before you do that, you need to make the curves cross each section correctly. Because of the way you created the curves, some of them, such as the main outline of the head, run together as one. You need to split this up to create the patches.

When you created the initial curve around the characters head, it was one continuous curve with multiple points. Connecting additional curves to it began the mesh that eventually shapes the face. To "patch" the curves, or "skin" them so that they have a surface, you need to make sure that each curve can be selected according to the area you want to patch. Certainly, this sounds confusing, but follow along with this next tutorial to get the hang of controlling your spline curves.

Exercise 13.2   Controlling Splines and Cross Sections

1. Make sure your current spline patch is loaded, or load the Caesar_Spline_v010 from this book's DVD.

2. Maximize the Perspective view and set it to a Wireframe Shade mode.

3. Let's start patching around the nose. If you select the curves on the bulb of the nose, first the left side and then the center, you'll see that you only have two curves, as in Figure 13.22. You need to separate these to create four curves.

Figure 13.22   Selecting the curves around the nose yields just two curves, not four. Because of this, you won't be able to patch the nose correctly.

4. Leaving these curves selected, press the spacebar on your keyboard to switch to Points mode. Select the point at the tip of the nose, shown in Figure 13.23, and then use Split (Ctrl+l) from the Subdivide category of the Multiply tab. This splits the curve at the selected point.

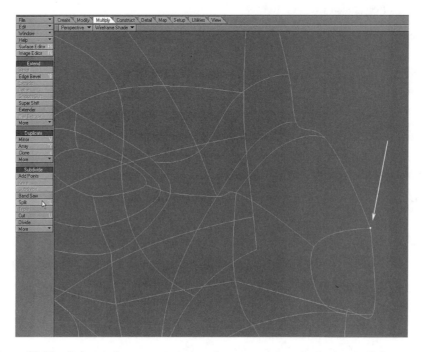

Figure 13.23   Separate the curves to isolate the area to be patched using the Split command on the selected point.

5. Select the next point at the bulb of the nose and split it.

6. One at a time, split the remaining two points that make up the bulb of the nose. Take a close look at the shape of the curve after the split, as shown in Figure 13.24. The curve is now more like straight lines. Remember, the point of using spline curves to build this head is to keep a smooth flow.

Figure 13.24   Splitting the curves tends to straighten the curves.

7. To fix the problem that occurs with using Split, go back to Polygons mode and select the curves that make up the bulb of the nose. Then, from the Detail tab, select Smooth from the Curves category. Figure 13.25 shows the smoothed curves.

Important

You don't always need to use the Smooth command after you've split curves. In this particular case, the split left the curve with just two points. Two points on a curve simply makes a straight line. Other curves that are made up of multiple points after a split may not need to be smoothed. As the parents in *Risky Business* would say, "Just use your best judgment."

8. With the curves of the bulb of the nose still selected, choose the Patch command from the Patch category of the Construct tab. Set the Perpendicular and Parallel to 3, and choose Length, as in Figure 13.26.

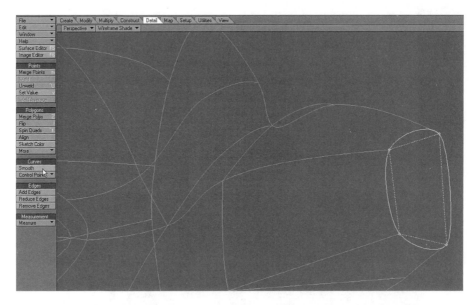

Figure 13.25 Using the Smooth command from the Detail tab, you can smooth out the split curves.

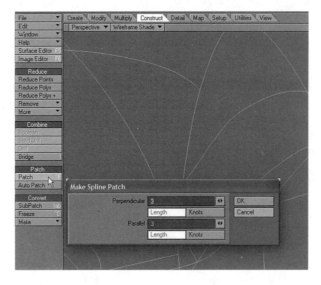

Figure 13.26 The Patch command from the Construct tab patches the selected curves based on your settings.

These settings represent each cross section of the selected curves. There are times, depending on your model, that you might want to use different values. Choosing Lengths or Knots tells LightWave Modeler to create the spline patch based on the curves, or the points. In this particular case, you want the patch to follow the curves, so Length is chosen. As you patch through your model, you'll change these values for the polygons to line up.

9. After you've entered these values, click OK, and you'll see a patched surface! Figure 13.27 shows the polygons created from running the Patch command from the Construct tab. Note that the viewport has been changed to Smooth Shade mode.

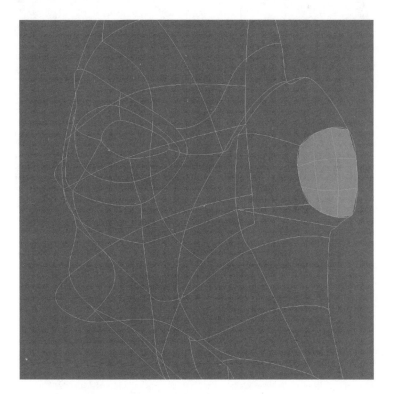

Figure 13.27   After the Patch command has been used, polygons are created between the selected curves.

10. Save your work. Move up the nose, and just as you did with the bulb of the nose, select the curves you're going to patch next. If the selection moves beyond the area you're going to patch, which it will, select the points of the patching area and split (Ctrl+l) them. Then, smooth out the curves using the Smooth tool.

11. After you've split and smoothed the curves, select them in order, making sure you have four selected, as in Figure 13.28.

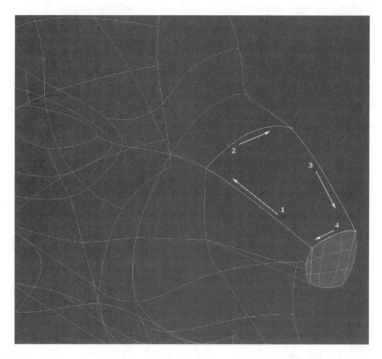

Figure 13.28   Select the curves on the top of the nose in order.

12. After you have selected the four curves, run the Patch command again with the same settings as earlier and click OK. You'll see three polygons created for the perpendicular and parallel lengths. Figure 13.29 shows the patch.

Tip

After you've patched your polygons, it might appear that they're not there! Often, the polygons will be facing the wrong way. Be sure to patch with at least one viewport set to Wireframe mode so that you can see the geometry when created. After you've created the polygons with the Patch command, flip them forward by making sure they're selected and pressing the f key.

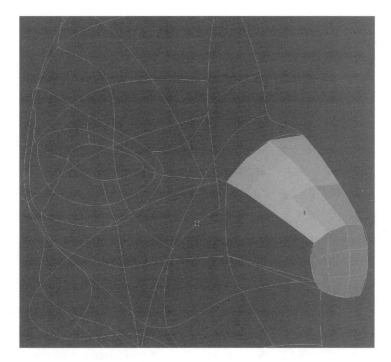

Figure 13.29   Patch the curves to create polygons.

Guess what? You now know how to create splines and patch them! That's all there is to it. The trick is to pay attention to the flow of the curves and to be sure that your curves cross correctly, using the Split command and Smooth command to control your patching. On your own, work on the rest of the head as you did with the nose in the previous steps. If you like, load up the Caesar_Spline_v010 object from this book's DVD and practice patching with it.

Joining Spline Curves

There are times when creating spline patches when an area just has too many curves— that is, a perfect patch could be made to selected curves, except that there are five curves instead of four. For example, Figure 13.30 shows an area of the nose near the eye of the character where there are five curves. The two selected in the image can be joined to create one curve. Simply select them, and from the Polygons category of the Detail tab, use the Merge Polys command. This joins the selected curves, making them one. Now, you can select the three remaining and make your patch.

After you've used Merge Polys on certain curves, the adjoining points might not line up. Patching could result in gaps, as shown in Figure 13.31. To fix this, simply select the point of the curve that lines up with the nearby point of the adjoining curve, and use Weld from the Points category of the Detail tab (Ctrl+w) to combine them.

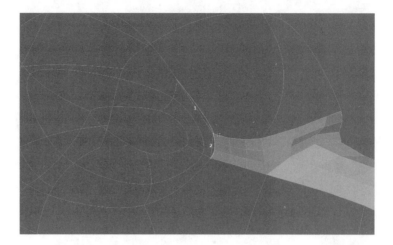

Figure 13.30 Selecting two adjoining curves and using the Merge Polys command from the Detail tab turns them into one curve.

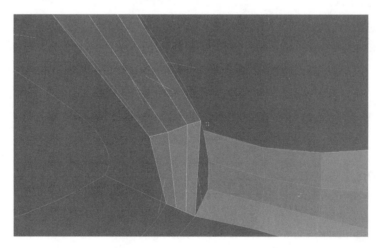

Figure 13.31 When polygons do not line up after patching, you can merge two selected points.

Patching splines is a valuable option for modeling, especially around areas of a model such as the mouth. It's great for adding the necessary detail because you can precisely tell an area to have one, two, or more polygons.

Continue patching, splitting, and smoothing curves as needed. Don't forget that if your perpendicular and parallel lengths do not line up properly, undo (Ctrl+z) and redo, setting the appropriate values. If you need to weld a couple of points together, do so to keep the flow of the polygons connected.

One more additional step is to merge the points of the newly created polygons. After you've patched a few areas together, press m for Merge on your keyboard. You should see a message pop up that says how many points are merged. However, if you have Expert mode set from the Modeler Options panel (press o), the Merge message will appear at the bottom of the interface. After you've merged points, go ahead and press the Tab key to activate SubPatch mode. Figure 13.32 shows a partially SubPatched character.

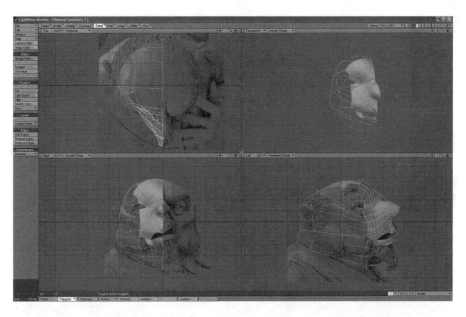

Figure 13.32   After patching a portion of the character head and then merging points by pressing m on the keyboard, using the Tab key to activate SubPatch mode shows the beginning of the character.

Tip

Splitting curves does not change the eventual flow of the polygons for SubPatch mode. In fact, you will find that after splitting some curves, you can delete areas, such as the center of the mouth.

Continue patching and be sure to save your work. From here, you'll use additional modeling tools to shape and build the rest of the character head.

Adding Detail to Patched Polygons

By now, you should have the hang of modeling with splines. It might seem tedious at first, but after you understand the process, it doesn't take long to create a full character. First, you'll separate the original curves from the newly created polygons.

Exercise 13.3   Creating Necessary Details to Patched Polygons

1. With your patched model loaded, you should have a complete half of the character head. If not, load the Caesar_Patch_v001 object from this book's DVD.

2. Open the Statistics panel, if it's not already, by pressing w or clicking the button at the bottom of the Modeler interface.

3. Make sure you're in Polygons selection mode (spacebar). In the Statistics panel, press the small plus mark on the left of the listing called Curves. All the spline curves you've created become selected. Figure 13.33 shows the selection.

4. Cut (Ctrl+x) and paste (Ctrl+v) the curves to their own layers.

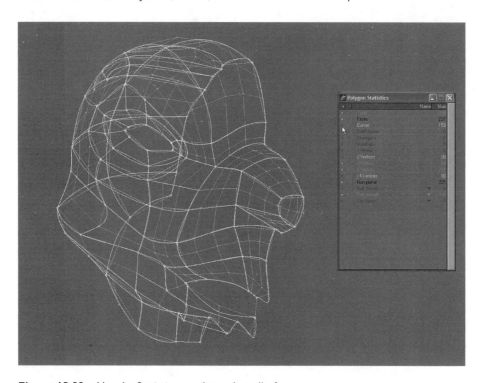

Figure 13.33   Use the Statistics panel to select all of your curves.

Tip

Don't delete the curves at this point. You can use them again later to re-create your object if you like, or even better, build a new object from these. You may even want to create a new object layer set (Shift+n) and paste the curves there, saving it as its own object.

5. In the Back view, change the view to a Wireframe Shade. You'll start adding detail around the eye.

6. Select the points that make up the inner eyelid, around the opening for the eyeball. Extend these using Extender Plus, or just press the e key once. Then, use Size (Shift+h) to size the points down. Figure 13.34 shows the addition.

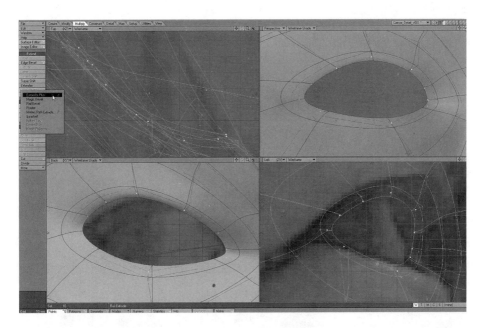

Figure 13.34   To begin creating details with the model, start by extending the points of the eyelids.

7. Press the e key once to apply Extender Plus again, and move the newly created points into the head. Then, use Extender Plus again, and size them up slightly to make the fold of the eyelid. Figure 13.35 shows the operation.

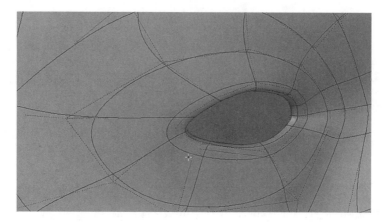

Figure 13.35   Use Extender Plus twice more to create the folds of the inner eyelid.

8. Deselect any points and save your work. Remember, you can use Shift+s to save an incremental version.

9. Select the two rows of polygons that make up the eyelid and lower brow area. Move them forward, as in Figure 13.36.

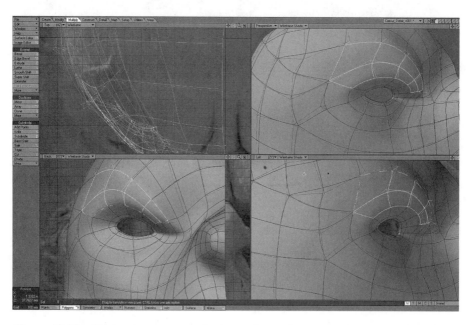

Figure 13.36   Moving the two rows of polygons forward starts to add more depth to the character's eyes.

10. Press the spacebar to switch to Points mode, and select the row of points between the two rows of polygons you just moved. After they are selected, move them back into the head and up a little, and you'll have created the deep-set eyelids, as in Figure 13.37.

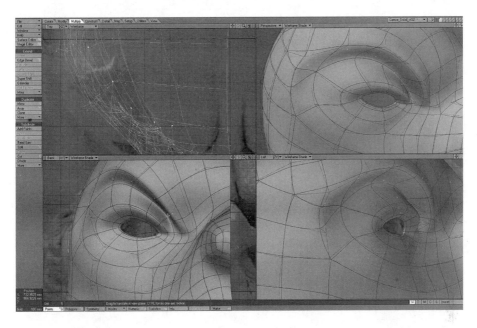

Figure 13.37   Moving the middle row of points back into the head helps shape the deep-set eyelids.

11. Select the row of points on the lip of the upper eyelid and move in and down slightly to sharpen the crease of the eyelid. Also, use Drag on the corner point of the eye to create the fold of the lid, as in Figure 13.38.

12. Perform the same steps on the bottom of the eye as you did for the top, first moving two rows of polygons forward, and then dragging the row of points back into the eye area. Figure 13.39 shows the operation.

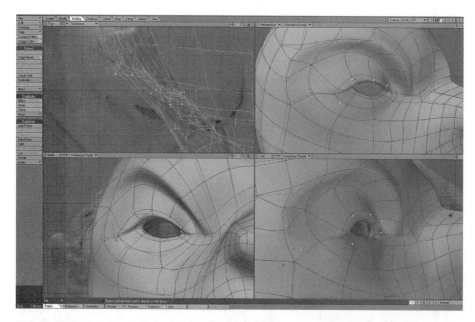

Figure 13.38 Adjust points on the edge of the eyelid to sharpen the edge of the lid.

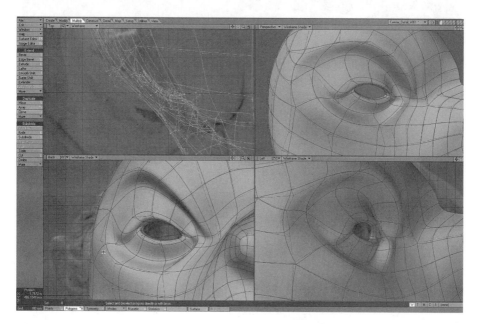

Figure 13.39 Perform the same operations on the bottom of the eye as you did for the top. Adjust with the Drag tool as needed.

13. At this point, you can take some time and use the Drag tool on areas of the eye and compare your work with the backdrop images. However, it's also fun to use a full screen Perspective view and, with SubPatch mode active (Tab key), move points and polygons to shape the face.

14. If you want to make a stronger bag under the eye, you can also take a row of points near the eyelid and move the points down. This creates a sharper curve near the cheek. Pull those points forward slightly, and a bag is created under the eye, as in Figure 13.40.

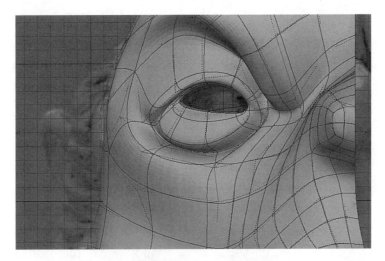

Figure 13.40   Select the row of points for the eyelid opening (near the eye socket) and pull the points down to create a bag under the eye.

15. For the furrowed brow of the character, pull the points of the brow forward using the Drag tool (Ctrl+t).

16. Add a little more to the eyebrow area, for which you'll eventually create hair. Do this by selecting the polygons of the eyebrow and using a multiply tool like Smooth Shift to multiply them. Then, use the Drag and Move tools to shape them down so that they round out the eyebrow. Figure 13.41 shows the addition.

17. To create the dent in the forehead to enhance the furrowed brow, select the two points that are above the bridge of the nose and use Edge Bevel from the Extend category of the Multiply tab. Then, pull the points in to create the "dent" that's in the furrowed brow. Use the Drag tool to shape. Figure 13.42 shows the change.

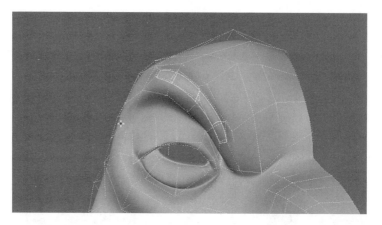

Figure 13.41   Smooth Shift the eyebrow area and then size down; Move and Drag the points to round out the eyebrow area.

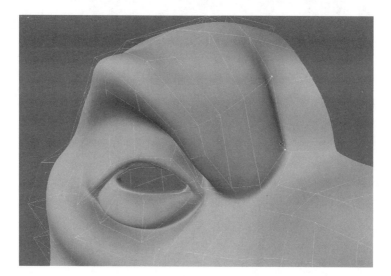

Figure 13.42   Using the Drag tool, you can shape the brow of the character.

18. When you've built the shape to your liking, select all the points on the open edge of the character and select Alt+v for Set Value. Set the value of these points to 0 on the X-axis. Then, mirror the character over. Be sure that Merge Points is selected from the Numeric panel to remove the duplicate points.

19. After it is mirrored, select the mirrored polygons and then shape the head to match the backdrop image with tools such as Taper or Stretch. From there, select groups of points and adjust them to match the backdrop image, making your character asymmetrical. Note that you do not work with Symmetry on for this.

Do you have it yet? Do you get it? Can you see how this all comes together? If you've read the previous two chapters, you can see that just a handful of tools enable you to create anything you want, from cartoon characters to electronics to cars, and more. In this tutorial so far, you've outlined a shape with spline curves, and then patched them together. From there, you use modeling tools like you have in other tutorials, such as Extender Plus, Drag, Move, and so on, to adjust the shape.

Here are some key things to keep in mind when building characters:

- Always pay attention to the flow of the polygons. Make sure that they roll cleanly into each other.
- Less is more. You can always add more geometry, and even though you can take away if needed, your model will be cleaner. What's more, you'll have better control over the shape, especially when using SubPatches.
- Even if your character is asymmetrical, as demonstrated in this chapter, you can still model half, then mirror it over and adjust the shape.
- Take your time. Practice. Don't give up. Building characters is a never-ending process.
- Think forward to your goal and use visual references whenever possible. Of course, you may be a visionary and not need them; if so, congratulations!

The Next Step

From here, create the lip of the character just as you did when creating the eyelid of the character. Select the points around the area and use Extender Plus to multiply them, and then shape and continue. For curves in the cheeks, you can use Edge Bevel on selected points, just as you did with the furrowed brow.

This kind of modeling takes a good amount of time—and of course, patience. Although this chapter uses splines to outline the character and create the polygons with patching, you can also use point-by-point as you did with the car modeling chapter. Additionally, you can use the box method as shown with the giraffe in Chapter 10 to model this character. It's totally up to you!

There's still so much of LightWave 8 to cover! Read on now to learn more about texturing, and follow that up with rigging characters, animating characters, and more. But don't think we're leaving you high and dry with our cover's character! Head on over to this book's DVD for a video tutorial of the surfacing of this character, along with lighting and rendering.

Chapter 14

Enhanced Textures and Environments

One of the best ways to determine how to texture an object in 3D is to get away from the computer and look at real-world objects that are similar to what you are working on. By examining such objects, you will find that a variety of factors determine how they should be textured. What is the object made of? Are there stains on it that change the way the base material looks? Factors such as weathering, as well as normal wear and tear, will also change the appearance. All of these should be considered when building up your textures. When you look at a render of an object, there may be something that isn't right about it. Usually, the smallest details escape most of us. Continue to study the everyday items around you and ask yourself why something looks the way it does.

To avoid the exercise and sunlight that come with going out and looking at these things in real life, you can fire up your web browser of choice and find images of related objects. There are also plenty of sites on the Internet that are repositories of reference images you can dig through and find almost anything you want. Chances are, however, that you will not find an image that you can just slap onto a surface; you will likely have to make your own.

You can ask many people the best way to texture in LightWave, and you may get a variety of answers based on what style each person prefers. LightWave's render engine is known for its capability to render out images that range from cartoon shading to photo realistic. Just like the rest of the chapters here, entire books can be written on this topic.

The information in this chapter is meant as a guide to give you an idea as to what can be done with LightWave's texturing system. Learning how LightWave's texturing system works is the focus, so feel free to experiment with the settings.

Procedural Textures

As you may have seen before, procedural textures are created through algorithms defined by the program. This doesn't mean that they are inflexible and limiting. For example, they do not have resolution limits and will not become blocky as you zoom in on them. They also do not take up space in memory while you are working on your scene.

They are not without their drawbacks, though. You cannot see them directly in your OpenGL view because they are calculated at render time. Because they are calculated at render time, they will slow down the render. Computers have gotten faster, but with every speed increase, we place bigger loads on the CPUs. One procedural texture will render pretty fast. As your scene gets larger with many texture layers per surface, and dozens of surfaces, your machine may slow down more than you want.

This is not to say that procedural textures are bad—far from it. Procedural textures can add randomness to any surface and can prevent an object from looking like a person has painted the textures onto the surface.

Many of the procedural textures built into LightWave are noise functions. The complex math in these noise functions has the capability to emulate many things, such as clouds, shorelines, rocky surfaces, and other natural phenomena. In addition to the noise functions, you will also have other structured patterns such as Bricks, Dots, Honeycomb, and more. All procedural textures have different settings based on the texture itself. Quite a few are similar and others are unique, as seen in Figure 14.1.

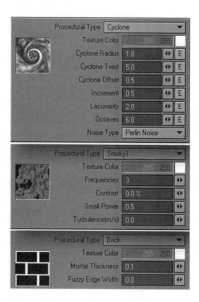

Figure 14.1
Each procedural texture can have settings unique to itself.

Gradients

Gradients come in handy when you need to create variations in a surface based on other attributes on the surface or in the scene. Depending on where you find the gradient setting, you will have different options for the Input Parameter. Because gradients change a value based on these inputs, they are typically used to enhance existing layers in the texture. Using Bump as an Input Parameter, you can set gradient keys very close to each other and create the look of a painted surface with holes showing another color underneath. Many of the available options for gradient Input Parameters deal with distance to an object. Nulls are perfect for controlling these particular parameters.

Tip

> To help visualize distances for gradients set to the Distance To parameter, you can add the Item Shape plug-in in the Custom Item window in the Items panel. Set the Item Shape to Ball and the Ball Scale at the distances in your gradient. You can apply more than one of these plug-ins and see where your important keys are.

Image Maps

Using an image will give you the greatest control over determining how your surface looks because you are defining exactly what it looks like at the pixel level. The problem with using image maps is that you will need to create this image yourself with an understanding of how it will be applied. This is not as bad as it sounds. We will go over a few different ways to create this image map and have LightWave help you do it in the process.

Figure 14.2
Projection choices for placing images onto a surface.

Although the projection methods shown in Figure 14.2 work in quite a few circumstances, not all objects will conform to a plane, cylinder, sphere, or cube. When you use these, you may notice that textures will not only project onto a surface but also through it.

UV Mapping

Along with the normal projection mapping options, you have a more complex method available. UV mapping is a way to tell LightWave how to place an image on the surface based on how you assign the UVs, not just the direction the surface is facing. We will have to assign these UV coordinates in Modeler ourselves.

Figure 14.3 shows a curved surface that would have problems using normal projections, so we use UV mapping. Instead of using the X-, Y-, and Z-axes to apply textures, we are going to use two directions that actually exist on the object itself—U and V. Adding two new directions isn't as bad as it sounds. A good way to relate to a real object is the paper models where you insert tab A into slot B. Instead of building a model, however, we will be taking them apart. Setting UVs allows you to tell LightWave how textures see the model. Depending on what kind of model you are working with, your UV layout may change. If you need to texture a person's head, many prefer a cylindrical-based UV map. Why would you need to go through the trouble of setting up UVs if you are just going to go with a cylindrical projection to make it? Using a UV map allows you to adjust areas that you need to tweak. If you think about a head, you will get areas that overlap, like ears. The texture running out to the chin will likely stretch as it turns perpendicular to the cylinder's axis. By using a UV map, you can spread out the face to avoid overlap. As you might have guessed, UV layout can be an art unto itself.

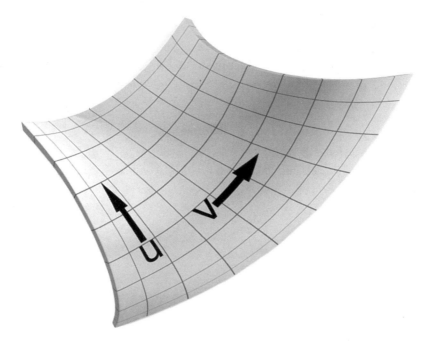

Figure 14.3 UV coordinates follow surfaces around twists and turns.

Just as one hundred modelers can take a concept sketch and develop as many models with their own variations, UV maps can come in a variety of variations as well. Each modeler has his own style when it comes to creating UV layouts. Although there *is* a wrong way to create a UV layout, the list of wrong ways is very short. One of the things that will create a UV setup that LightWave does not like is by projecting it from the side of a polygon. In the UV Texture window, this would show up as a line. Other than that, you can't really go wrong. This does not mean that you can't create an inefficient UV layout. Inefficiency in a UV map would be taking up space on polygons that aren't seen by the camera very well or just creating a general mess on the layout that is impossible to texture. Figure 14.4 shows two different UV layouts of the same object. Which one would you want to texture?

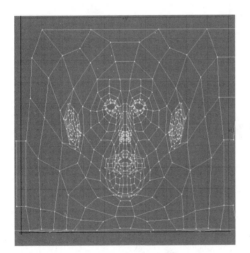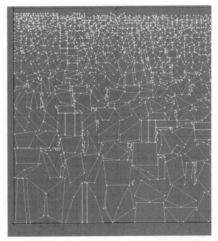

Figure 14.4   Easy-to-follow UVs versus a polygon explosion.

Laying Out UVs

When you perform your texturing using UV maps, you need to begin in Modeler. There are a few ways to assign UVs to your model. Some of these are as simple as a few clicks; others may take days of work. For this next tutorial, we are going for the "few clicks" option.

Tip

You can also use the new UVEdit plug-in in LightWave 8 Modeler for more control.

Exercise 14.1 Assigning UVs with a Few Clicks

1. In Modeler, load the Support_Clean.lwo object from this chapter's folder on the accompanying DVD.

   This is a fairly simple object that we will be using later as a support to floor plating.

2. To see what is going on with the UV map, change your Perspective viewport to the UV Texture view.

   This view is different from the others in that it isn't a view looking down an axis without a vanishing point. This window is strictly a 2D view representing how your object's surface will receive an image map.

3. Having LightWave generate the UV coordinates for you can be done in two places. You can use the Make UVs button from the Map tab or you can go to the Vmap buttons in the bottom-right corner of the Modeler window. Select the T button to tell Modeler you are going to be working with a Texture Vmap.

4. Next to all the Vmap buttons, you will see another gray button that is set to (none). Click the button to change it to a drop-down and select (New). This pops open a new window for your choices for the new UV map.

5. The Create UV Texture Map panel has only a few options. Usually, most of the defaults work. For this UV map, we are only going to make two changes. The top input is the map name. Change this to Floor_Support.

6. The next important setting is the Map Type. Click the Type button and you will notice the options. The first three options will look familiar (just like the normal image mapping options). You can select any of these three to see what they do, but none will work with the model we are using.

   Because the object is a non-organic model, there are some straight edges, and it will benefit from the fourth mapping type. Select Atlas and watch how it takes the model apart in the UV Texture viewport. This is a low polygon count object with an easily identifiable profile. As you work with more complex objects, it may become difficult to figure out where the different sections are.

Congratulations—you have just created a UV map for your object. There are other methods for creating the maps. One important thing to keep in mind is that when LightWave creates a map for you, it has to use a somewhat generic approach. Modeler needs to use a method that will work for most objects, so it cannot always generate the optimal placement of the UVs.

To see other ways to set up UVs, load the Support_UV.lwo object from this chapter's folder. You will have to set the Texture Vmap to Floor_Support to see this layout. This is more of an unfolded view of the support object. Select some of the polygons in the UV view to see where they are in the actual model in one of the other views.

This version of the model was unwrapped by hand, which takes a little longer. One of the best ways to generate these is to create a new endomorph, unfold your geometry, and then create a planar UV map from that to take a snapshot of the unfolded version. Figure 14.5 shows some of the polygons being unfolded. This gives you the advantage of being able to rotate polygons into a third dimension that the UV Texture panel doesn't give you.

This process becomes more difficult depending on the complexity of the model being worked on. Mechanical models, such as the one we are looking at, have many straight edges and angles that are easy to align. Organic models, such as people or animals, can be layed out in a similar style. Some people refer to this as *pelting*. One advantage organic models have is that they usually don't have many straight lines in their textures. At the same time, you may notice distortions because they are usually done as one piece.

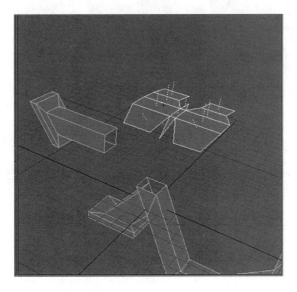

Figure 14.5   Unfolding your object by hand takes a while, but gives you greater control.

Important

While editing your UV map, you may find it necessary to use the Unweld command, which disconnects all the polygons on the current layer from each other. You may be wondering the reason for this. When you have discontinuous UVs on your object, a single point may appear to have multiple UV coordinates. If you select and then move a polygon that shares a point with other polygons, you may inadvertently distort them. Because of the way discontinuous UVs are handled, you are usually required to use the Unweld command before performing major UV editing so that you move only the points you intend to move. This may seem an annoying extra step, but having the user perform the Unweld command allows you to use all the normal Modeler tools for adjusting UV maps.

Looking at the UV layout in Figure 14.6, you can see that the object was created with each side of the box sitting next to each other. This is an example of discontinuous texture coordinates. This type of mapping may work great for a simple object, but when you get into complex objects, it is better for the user to create the UV layout rather than LightWave.

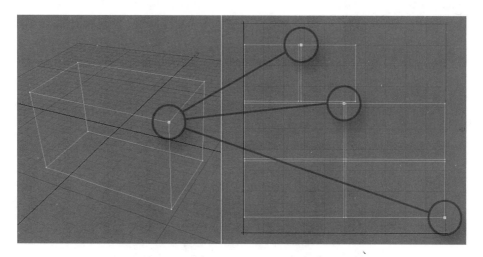

Figure 14.6 One point at three different UV coordinates.

To reduce texture stretching and non-uniform UVs when unfolding an object, you can create a box around what you intend to create the UVs for (see Figures 14.7). Make sure the box is 1:1 constrained by holding down the Ctrl key when you create it. It is also a good idea to leave a little room for the box so you don't have to worry about LightWave antialiasing into the edge of the image.

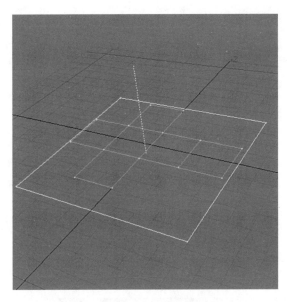

Figure 14.7 Creating a box around your unfolded endomorph ensures you will not get textures stretching in one direction over the other.

Baking

While setting up your scene, you may notice that the render process can be very slow. You may have a large scene with layers and layers of complex procedural textures. Your scene might look fantastic with radiosity and caustics adding that extra touch of realism. Sometimes, a shadow mapped spotlight doesn't give you the soft shadows that you want so you use an area or linear light. If you have a lot of frames to render, you could be in for the long haul with all of those features turned on. What if you could bake as much of that info into a texture and only have to sit through a long render once instead of for every frame?

Aside from the speed increase, baking textures has other benefits. Although it is possible to tweak a procedural texture to death, it is ultimately going to play by its own rules. Turning that texture into an image map enables you to paint onto it all you want.

The Bakeoff Begins

In this exercise, you bake some color into an image map. You will be using a model, from this book's DVD, that already has UV coordinates assigned.

Exercise 14.2   Baking Color into an Image Map

1. In Layout, load the Support_Color.lwo object from this chapter's folder on the accompanying DVD.

   This is the same object we used earlier so you should be familiar with the UV.

2. To begin texturing, open the Surface Editor. You can see that this object has only two surfaces associated with it: Support_Metal and Support_Stripes.

Tip

If you use surface names with prefixes like those on this object, you can find related surfaces easily when you have a large scene. This keeps you from wondering if the surface named "black leather thing" belongs to a car seat or a character's jacket. This also allows you to use the pattern-matching filter in the Surface Editor, shown in Figure 14.8, to temporarily reduce the list to specific objects and find surfaces when the list gets too big.

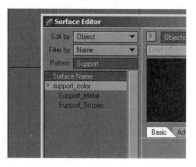

Figure 14.8   The Pattern filter allows you to show surface names based on what you type into the Pattern field.

3. Let's start with the easy surface first. Select the Support_Stripes surface in the Surface Name list. With that surface selected, press the T button to open the Texture panel for the Color channel.

4. We will add some cool black and yellow caution stripes to this surface. The default for an empty surface will be set to a planar image map with an empty image slot. Click and hold down the image button. You will see the (None) expand to show a (Load Image) option. That is a nice shortcut, isn't it? Load in the Caution_Stripe.png image.

5. Leave the Texture Axis to project down the Z-axis and click the Automatic Sizing button. This gives black and yellow zebra stripes on part of the support object. That isn't quite what we want, so go into the Rotation tab at the bottom of the

panel, and set the texture's pitch to 30 degrees. Click Use Texture at the bottom to close the panel.

Important

Be careful when closing the Texture panel; you can choose to Use Texture and Remove Texture. As a habit from other programs, you may be familiar with having the positive choice (like OK or Yes) in the bottom-right corner. Many texture artists have lost hard work to Remove Texture when they press the wrong button. It may be best to develop the habit of closing this panel with the close window box (X) in the top-right corner.

6. Because we don't want that new showroom look, we need to grunge this surface up a little. Open the Texture panel for the Diffuse channel. Switch the layer type from Image to Procedural Texture. Turbulence is a great starting point for noise; this will come up as the default procedural texture.

Because we are adding a layer of grime, we need to set the diffuse lower to darken the surface. Crank the Texture value down to about 10%. Set Frequency to 6, Contrast to 20%, and Small Power to 1.0.

7. Before you close this panel, click the Copy button in the top left of the panel and select Current Layer. We have plans for this layer.

Tip

At first, many people don't understand why you would want to adjust the Diffuse channel instead of darkening the Color channel. For example, if you create a model of some big nasty monster and want him to have dark red markings, you could set these markings to an RGB value of 10,0,0. However, when you start lighting that monster, it could boost that surface to render as a medium gray with a slight red tint, or as the rest of the world would call it...pink. So much for that big nasty monster.

8. Jump to the Support_Metal surface and open the Diffuse channel's Texture panel. Next to the Copy button is the Paste button. From there, select Replace Current Layer. After that, change the Texture Value to about 50% and close the Texture panel.

9. Now that we have some variation to the surface, you are going to add the Surface_Baker shader. Switch to the Shader tab and use the Add Shader drop-down list. Find Surface Baker in the list of available shaders and add it to the surface by selecting it.

You will see the shader listed in the Shader panel with a check in the On column. This comes in handy when you want to do a test render, but don't want to bake during the render. You won't lose your settings by turning this check off instead of removing it.

10. Open the interface to the baker shader by double-clicking the name. Bake Entire Object is at the top of the list of options , and it is set as the default. This is why it wasn't important which surface we applied. This takes care of both the Support_Metal and the Support_Stripes.

Important

As long as everything you want to bake is on one layer, this setting bakes to that object. If you want to bake something that exists on another layer or another file, you need to find a surface that is used on the other object.

11. Because we changed the Color and Diffuse channels, we will leave them on but shut off the Bake Illumination button.

This bakes both channels to one image. If you want to end up with two separate images for greater control, one for color and one for diffuse, you can run one pass with just Color turned on and one with just Diffuse. To reduce steps and simplify things, we are going to go with the one image here.

12. At the bottom section of the panel, you will see a UV Map button. From this, select Floor_supports; it will be the only available map for this object.

13. Image Resolution is set for 512. The larger the image, the better result you will have, but the longer it takes to bake off the image. An image size of 512 should be enough for our baking needs.

Although you could enter almost any value, it is best to stick with powers of 2 such as 128, 256, 512, 1024, and so on. This will help when LightWave needs to antialias the texture later.

14. From the next drop-down list, select an image type you want to save to. This list will be the same as the choices you have in the Save Image list from the Render panel. The format is up to you for this baking session, so pick your favorite flavor here.

15. The Image Base Name button brings up a standard File panel. Find a good home for your image and give it a name. Let's call it Support_Color so we can find it later.

Tip

The Surface Baker shader bakes high dynamic range images, so if you are doing anything to get your color above the 255 range—such as overdriving your diffuse settings to get a super bright surface-like reflective tape—you need to choose a format that supports extended range values, such as Radiance, TIFF LogLUV, or NewTek's Flexible format.

16. Given the fact that the one surface has those angled stripes, a little antialiasing is good. Depending on the content of your surfaces, you may want to have antialiasing on or off. The best way to decide is to bake an image and look at it.

17. That's all you need to change. Close the window and press F9 to start the render. You will see another window pop up for the Surface Baker, as shown in Figure 14.9.

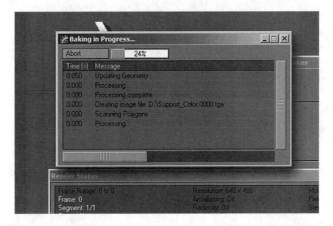

Figure 14.9   The Baking in Progress window keeps you updated while LightWave creates the image.

Important

Sometimes, you might see an error show up while baking. It may tell you, "Only faces with three or four vertices can be baked. Other faces will be ignored." If you get this error, you need to triple your object. You can triple by bringing the object into Modeler, and pressing Shift + t. Or, go to the Multiply tab and select Triple. If you save two versions, you can bake the tripled version and apply the result to the untripled one because the coordinates will be the same.

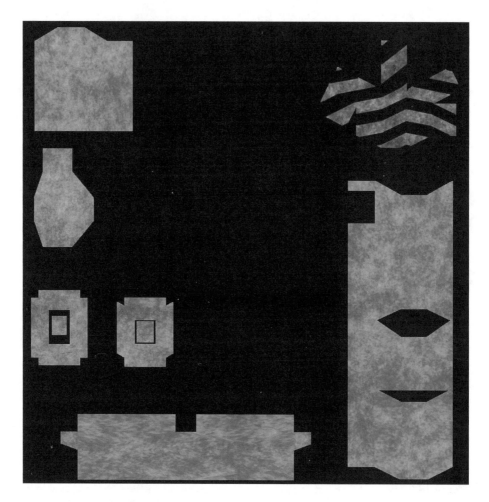

Figure 14.10   The resulting color image from Surface Baker, complete with procedural
texture converted to an image.

When baking to an image, the render engine is called up a second time during the normal
render process. The image rendered will be only for the surfaces and does not have an
actual camera that it is rendering from. Not rendering from a camera prevents view depen-
dant effects, such as specularity, reflections, or refractions, from being baked off. Baking is
another render process, as stated earlier. This means that you may be waiting for some time
depending on what you are asking LightWave to bake for you. Very high radiosity settings
or many area lights can take a long time to render. When baking, you are not just rendering what the camera sees, but possibly every polygon on an object. This can send your render time through the roof; it's a good thing you have something to read handy.

Examining Textured Objects

Instead of overwhelming you with a few hundred steps to get to a finished textured scene, we are going to take a completed scene and dissect it so we can learn how and why certain texturing methods are used. We will also look at some atmosphere added to the environment. Figure 14.11 shows a render of our example. This is by no means the perfect example of how to texture every object. This was written for you to see how textures work. Texturing can go far beyond what is presented here; we have only a chapter to work with. Be sure to check out Owen Demer's *Digital Texturing and Painting* from New Riders Publishing.

Figure 14.11   We will be tearing this scene apart to look at the texturing.

Load the Corridor.lws scene from the scene folder in this chapter's folder on the DVD. This scene was created with a relatively low polygon count in mind; this way, you don't need a high-end system to look at the scene.

To begin our examination, let's start with the walls of our scene. They consist of very simple geometry with the intent to use textures to add detail. The panels could have been modeled in, but they were drawn in and have matching values for Color, Diffuse, and Bump channels. The walls for this scene are basically symmetrical columns. The

UVs were set up on one of the columns first. After the UVs were established, the geometry was mirrored to produce walls for an intersection. Because the UVs were set up first, the UVs started the same and allowed all the texture maps to use the same exact maps. Instead of taking up space for three separate wall sections, the maps were mirrored with the geometry. This was used in much of the geometry in this scene.

The drawback to using this is the viewer may notice the mirrored textures or a repeating image. To cover a repeating pattern from the mirrored geometry sharing the same UVs, a procedural layer can be applied over the top of the images. This breaks up the image on one section differently than the rest.

To get the UV layout into a paint program, a simple base color was baked off into an image. When in the paint program, color layers were added instead of changing the color of the base layer. This way, different color schemes could be tried without having to change too much. Figure 14.12 shows the various texture channels.

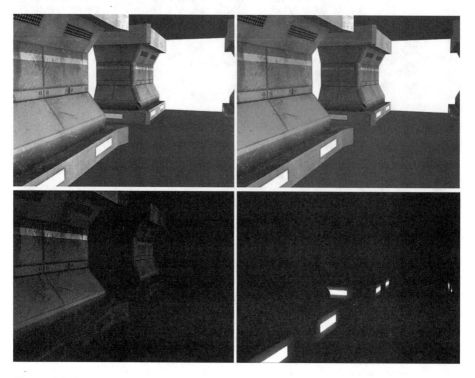

Figure 14.12   Wall texture channels clockwise: Color, Diffuse, Luminosity, shading from Bump and Specular channels.

Important

While building up textures, be sure to save the layered images, because you will likely want to go back and tweak something that could be buried in the middle of a map. If you included text on an image, you may not want to start the texture over because you reduced it to one layer. If you are concerned with memory consumption, save off a flattened version of the image, but keep the layered file to work on.

A trick used to build these maps was an accessibility map to find areas where dirt would have built up. These maps are made by baking off radiosity from a white background lighting your scene instead of lights. Any areas that are blocked from seeing the background will bake out as darker than a part of the surface out in the open. This emulates where people or other objects would come in contact and rub off dirt so that cracks and grooves would collect gunk.

Tip

To set a scene to bake accessibility maps, you need to have UVs assigned to the object; baking to vertex maps will not have enough resolution. Here are some key things to remember:

- Set all of your objects to a white surface with 100% diffuse.

- Lights need to be set to 0 intensity or to not affect diffuse shading, including Ambient Intensity.

- Background Radiosity must be set to on.

- The Backdrop Color should be set to White.

To speed up this sort of baking, you can set the camera resolution to the smallest it can render, a 16×16 pixel image. Because the camera's render doesn't matter for the baking process, it is a waste of time to wait for a large render of the scene with Radiosity turned on.

The diffuse mapping for the wall texture relied heavily on this map for both its value level and as a mask for the grunge layers that were hand painted. Just sticking in the baked radiosity on the model will not look completely real, so smudging the map will add to the effect. Look for outcropping areas where water will drip down and carry the dirt.

Given that there is so much flat area on the walls, the surface needs to be broken up with the specular reflections across it. Instead of just creating a separate image for the Specularity channel, this surface is using the color image with a gradient remapping the values. By using a gradient with the Input Parameter set to Previous Layer, as shown in Figure 14.13, we are compressing the range from the other layer. This gives the surface a greater contrasting image for the specular level.

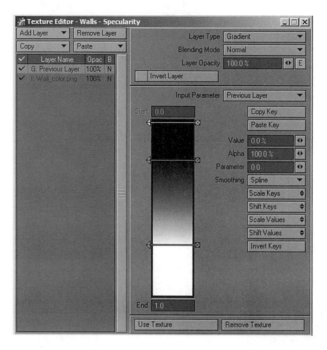

Figure 14.13   Using a gradient to remap another layer.

Lastly, for the walls, we have a luminosity map. This covers the areas that are representing light panels under the flooring. To fake lighting from the panel, a slight blur was added to the map to give the appearance of the panel doing the lighting. Just as we did with the Specularity channel, we have used another gradient to remap the image to adjust it for what the scene calls for. Instead of adjusting it in a paint program and losing something from the existing image, a gradient allows you to change it non-destructively and even use VIPER to see these changes.

The scene actually contains two different types of supports. The geometry at the corners that are on 45-degree angles is longer than the rest. During the texture creation for the supports, the longer support was the texture worked on. The UV coordinates are shared between the two sizes with the larger geometry spilling into unused areas on the map, as shown in Figure 14.14. The smaller supports will never see this extra texture information. You can also see that there was extra space added to this map for the inclusion of notes. When a model is split like this, it can be easy to forget what set of polygons belongs to what part of the object. This isn't always something that can be done, because usually, texture space is at a premium.

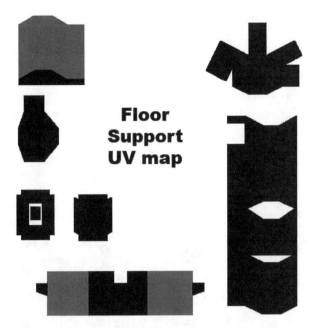

Figure 14.14   Similar geometry—sharing UVs. Black areas show shared space. Gray indicates the space taken up by the longer supports.

Aside from the cool UV trick, there is nothing spectacular about the supports. They are using a dirty color map, along with a diffuse map, that have some similarities. There are smudges on the map in other areas to show grease or other discolorations. A bump map with the dented procedural texture is used to break up the repeating pattern used here. On a side note, the use of micro bevels in the geometry would help pick up highlights. These are edges that do not meet up at 90 degrees. In real life, you would not get perfect edges like that. Figure 14.15 shows the textures.

Figure 14.15   Left to right: Color, Diffuse, Render.

This scene has some geometry that is barely visible, because it uses different techniques than what is included in the examination. The door object is being used to cap the end of one hallway. Because it is not part of the focus, some corners have been cut in the texturing. The door object uses standard diffuse/color textures for the most part, but it also pushes some of the cheats used on the walls. Figure 14.16 shows that the object is very low resolution. The supports that angle down to the opening are completely drawn in, as is the appearance of the separation of the two doors. Originally, this was intended to be off in the distance, so the shading was mostly added in a paint program. Depending on lighting, this trick may not work. Moving lighting may dispel the illusion.

Figure 14.16   Left to right: Actual Geometry, Diffuse, Color.

To break up the ceiling area, we have some pipes running along the corridor. They stay near the top of the scene, but you can still see every aspect used to texture them. The first step to texturing the pipe object was the Bump channel. Inside the Bump channel are two procedural layers—Dented and Turbulence. These set up the kind of look we wanted for the rusted metal, as shown in Figure 14.17.

Accenting the bump was the use of gradients on this surface; it used gradients more than any other surface in the scene. Going to the top of the Surface panel, we can see that the Color channel uses a gradient that runs from black to brown. Two keys in the middle of the gradient keep the color from being a linear interpretation as the bump map changes. By changing to a non-linear gradient, we have a mostly brown color that quickly ramps to black in the deepest pits.

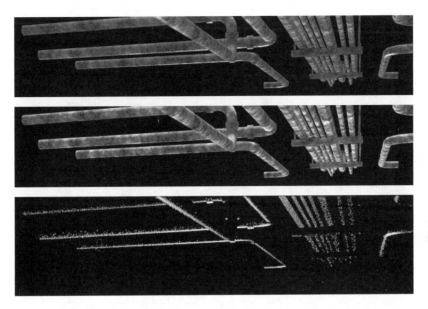

Figure 14.17   Pipes: Color, Diffuse, Bump and Specular Shading.

Because dust in the air would settle on the tops of objects, another gradient was added to the base noise in the Diffuse channel. The Slope input falls off as a surface changes angle from facing upward to rolling off on the side. Dust would absorb moisture; therefore, the slope gradient was set to an Additive mode. This pushed the diffuse component higher where the surface faced upwards. The rough surface would collect more dust than a smooth one, so the gradient has multiple keys to make this gradient non-linear also.

Most rust in the world is usually rust colored, so in the Advanced tab, of this and other rusty surfaces we used, Colored Highlights have been set to 50%. This partially changes the specular highlights to the textures color. If the color of the highlights stayed white, it would have the appearance of a rusty pipe with a nice, clear-coat finish. Usually, these finishes would prevent rust, so we would have to pick rusty or brand new. In this scene, anything new and shiny would look strange.

In this scene, the floor textures took the longest to set up. As you can see in Figure 14.18, there isn't actual geometry that has slots cut into it. There is a small amount of modeled detail to pick up shading, but most of the flooring is texture. The hard part about this feature was that the access maps couldn't be generated by the normal means. To have the shading pick up the smaller changes in the mesh, a gradient background was used instead of a solid white one. The gradient ran from medium gray to white in the middle and back to gray.

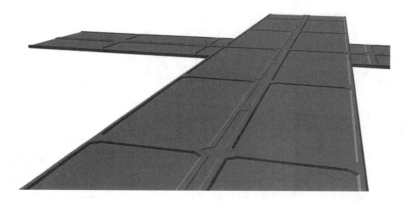

Figure 14.18   Geometry for the floor plating. This is not as complex as it looked in the render.

To get the cutouts, a series of shapes were created in a paint program and then used as a clip map, because shadow mapping cannot see through transparent surfaces. Even though clip mapping is part of the object Properties panel, it allows us to use shadow-mapped lights. Because there are no holes in the geometry, the object can look very thin. To avoid this, the floor surface was turned to a double-sided surface in the Texture panel.

Back in the paint program, the clip map was used in various ways to adjust the amount of dirt and rust that were built up in layers. This map remained an important part of the texture.

Like the object before it, the floor object had the UVs built in one section first. The floor was made from three unique parts: a main section and two smaller plates for where an intersection is formed. New sections can be added in Modeler and they will automatically retain the textures assigned to them because the UVs will stay with them.

This does not complete the rendered image shown at the beginning of this section. There was more than just this little section of a corridor. To find out what the rest of the image holds, we will look at little finishing touches to the rest of the scene environment. We cannot have the corridor drop off—that would bring all kinds of safety violations. The truth is that the rest of the corridor doesn't exist; through the magic of the Compositing tab, we were able to set a background image in to be a digital matte painting. This extended our set off into the distance into another length of our intersection and continues into another room with some sort of machinery in it.

Another aspect of the scene that blended the parts into a whole was volumetric lighting. Because our set extends off into the distance, we could have run into trouble matching up the foreground and the background. To avoid this, with a foggy effect, a volumetric spotlight (named Smoke_Light) was aimed in from the side. A warmer colored light was placed across the way. The lower panels on the left side under the floor were added to make it look like the light panels on the walls were actual lights. To tie them all together, they were all given the same texture for the volumetric light parameters and set for world coordinates. This way, the texture didn't clash when the lighting overlapped.

The Next Step

A wide variety of texturing options is available that we haven't touched on, such as animated textures. One of the features new to LightWave 8 is Animation UV Cycler. By creating an image map that can repeat, you can have a texture flow over your object based on how you set up your UVs. This is as simple as setting the U or the V rate. For example, this could be used for creating the surface of a river, turbulence flowing along with the shape of the river, or even as a transparency map to make it look like there is debris floating on top of the river.

Covering every single feature in LightWave's texture arsenal would be a daunting task for the writer and the reader. Hopefully, this chapter started you along the path to further understanding the texturing process.

Chapter 15

Bones and Rigging

Learning to model characters is only one aspect of 3D character creation. Believe it or not, there are entire jobs created around the art of rigging. Yes, that's right, art. Rigging is an art. You might find that hard to believe because rigging a character often seems like a chore to many animators. Rigging involves properly setting up a skeletal structure so that your character can be animated. Without a decent rig, you're bound for trouble during the animation process.

If you're the sort of person to jump right into character animation, then this is clearly the chapter for you. Or perhaps you think you might never use the character animation tools in this software. But the reality is that the tools available in LightWave 8 to create movable characters can be used for projects beyond character animation. You should know that these tools are different from those in previous versions of LightWave. Understanding how they work when applied to 3D characters can help spark ideas for any project you may encounter. Whatever your situation might be, you should read this chapter, because it provides you with a solid understanding of these new tools and how to use them in your animations.

The focus of this chapter is bones, Skelegons, and proper character setup for animation. As with the previous Inside LightWave books, we won't bore you with technical babble about theory and muscle structures; rather, this chapter discusses the following:

- Understanding bones
- Working with Skelegons for character rigs in Modeler
- Weighting characters for precise control
- Rigging characters directly in LightWave Layout
- Creating inverse kinematics with the IK Boost tools

Understanding Bones

Before you begin the first exercise, take a quick look at the following examples to help you better understand the concept of bones. Bones are a deformation tool; that is, they are controls that deform your objects. Represented by a tie-shaped outline in Layout, a bone changes the position of the points of an object rotationally, transitionally, or by scale, and because points make up polygons, the polygons are then manipulated. The purpose of bones is to create a skeletal deformation of a solid object to give it movement and life. Without the use of bones, objects would need to be built of separate parts or limbs; that is, they would have to be built of individual objects that move independently of each other. A human, for example, does not have any visible joints at the elbows, wrists, knees, and so on—a human appears to be a seamless whole, not something made up individual objects or pieces. For the arms and legs of a human character to bend, a bone structure must be set up to deform the polygonal mesh. In contrast, a character such as a robot would be made up of individual objects including separate forearms, upper arms, a neck, a head, and so on, so bones would not be needed. With that said, keep the idea of bones in the back of your mind for other uses such as shaping curtains or animating a beating heart. Figure 15.1 shows a bone in Layout.

Bones are easier to work with than you might think. However, you must follow some rules to make them work properly. First, and most importantly, bones must be associated with an object. That is, you can't just add a bone to Layout. You need to attach a bone to an object, even if it's just a null object. The following exercise provides the steps to do just that.

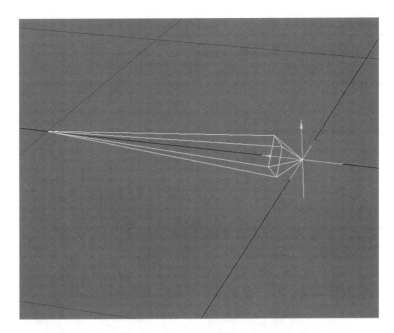

Figure 15.1 A bone in Layout looks like a necktie. It does not render, but it is a powerful control item.

Exercise 15.1   Creating Bones in Layout

As mentioned, bones must be attached to an object. The purpose of a bone is to deform an object, right? Well, if you think about it, bones have no purpose by themselves other than as a representation in Layout. Even then, an object needs to be present to create bones.

1. Start Layout, or if it's already running, choose Clear Layout from the File drop-down menu at the top left of the interface. Then click over to the Setup tab. This is where all of Layout's bone controls are located. If you look to the Add category on the left, you'll see that all the commands are ghosted! You have no objects loaded, so LightWave can't put a bone into the scene. Select the Items tab at the top of Layout and, from the Add category, add a null object to the scene. Rename the null object if you like, but the default name "Null" is fine.

   This null object is your base or root object. Even though bones need to be associated with an object, the object can be just a null object.

Tip

Instead of clicking away from the Setup tab to the Items tab to add a null object, you can always just press Ctrl+n on your keyboard to quickly add a null object.

2. With the Null object selected (it should be by default), click back over to the Setup tab. Then from the Add category, select Bone, Add Bone. LightWave asks you to rename the bone. Just click OK for now.

   You'll see a 1 m bone, like the one in Figure 15.1, but sticking out the Z-axis from the null object at the 0, 0, 0 axis. Figure 15.2 shows the example.

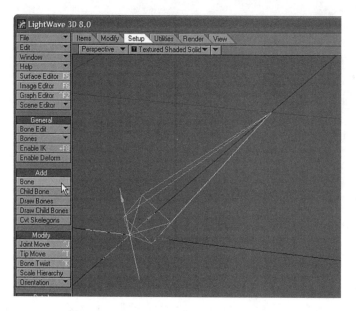

Figure 15.2   Adding a bone to a null object creates a 1m bone heading down the Z-axis.

   Next, you set up a chain of bones using child bones.

3. With the first bone selected, click the Child Bone button. Click OK because you don't need to set a name when the requester asks you to.

   You'll see a bone attached to the end of the previous bone. Figure 15.3 shows the additional bone.

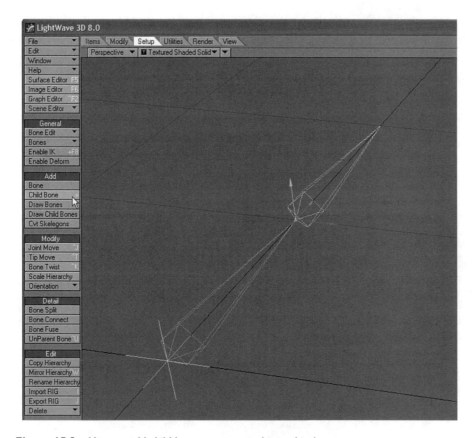

Figure 15.3   You can add child bones to create a hierarchical structure.

4. Add one more child bone as you did in Step 3. After it is added, select the first bone and rotate it.

   You'll see the child bones rotate as well. If you select and rotate the second bone, the child of that bone rotates.

This hierarchical structure is explained in detail later in the section "Creating Hierarchies." For now, you can think of this structure as similar to your own arm. The shoulder is connected to the upper arm, which is connected to the forearm, which is connected to the hand, and so on. If you move the shoulder, the other parts of your arm move, too.

Tip

Using the LightWave 8 Scene Editor, you can recolor the bones for easier visibility and better organization in Layout. The color change does not affect the bone's influence, only its visibility.

This quick and dirty example showed you how to create bones in Layout. The null object that you assigned bones to does not have to be null! The base object can be anything you want, from a character to a snake to a piece of paper. Anything you want to deform can have bones added to it. Granted, this wasn't very exciting, was it? No, probably not. But it was necessary. Read on to see bones in action!

Important

For bones to deform an object, the object must be made up of multiple polygons. A solid object, such as a box that has a minimum of six sides, will not deform well with bones. If the box were subpatched or subdivided into multiple segments, it would be more malleable and therefore could be deformed by bones.

Exercise 15.2   Adding a Bone to an Object

If you're like most people, you want to see this feature work, right? This exercise shows how to put bones into an object, taking you a step further than the previous tutorial. From there, you'll see how bones can be used to manipulate the shape of an inanimate object.

1. First, make sure that Auto Key is enabled from the bottom of the Layout interface. When working with bones, it's good to use this feature. Then select Clear Scene from the File drop-down list in Layout. Load the TVGuy object from this book's DVD-ROM. Bones need to be added to move the character.

2. Figure 15.4 shows the object loaded in Layout from the Perspective view. Press 3 on your keyboard to switch to the side view (Right).

3. Change your viewport render style to Wireframe from the top of the interface. This will help you see the placement of bones. Figure 15.5 shows the operation.

4. With the object selected, click over to the Setup menu tab and then click Bone from the Add category. Enter the name Upper Leg for this bone in the panel that appears and click OK. You'll see a bone added to the object at the base of the foot, as in Figure 15.6.

   The bone is not actually added to the bottom of the foot; rather, it's added to the object facing down the Z-axis. It's your job to position the bone.

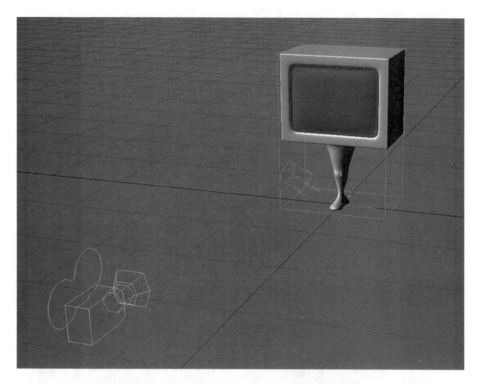

Figure 15.4   The TVGuy object is loaded into an empty layout, ready for some bones!

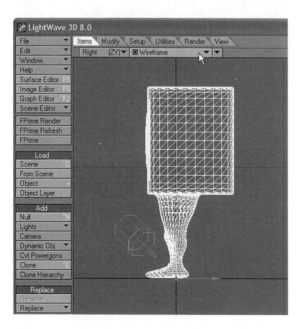

Figure 15.5   Change your view to look at the Right side and switch to a Wireframe style.

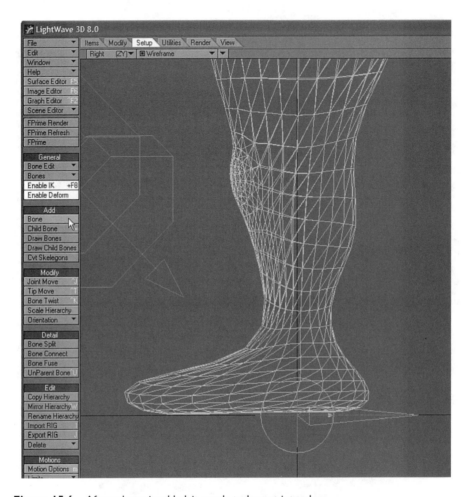

Figure 15.6 After a bone is added, it needs to be put into place.

5. The bone position now needs to be set so that it can properly control the object. Select Move from the Modify tab (or press t) and move the bone up to the top of the leg.

6. Use Rotate from the Modify tab (or press y) and rotate the bone so that the pointy edge is facing down, as in Figure 15.7.

Tip

The TVGuy object is a subpatched object. For visual clarity, its Display SubPatch Level has been set to 0 in the Object Properties panel. Its Render SubPatch Level is set to 6. When the object is rendered, it will be smooth and subdivided.

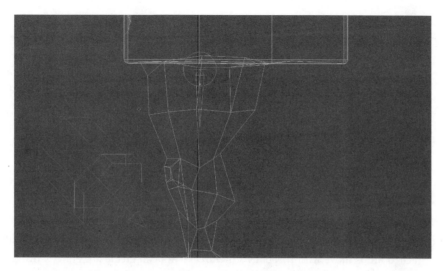

Figure 15.7   Move and rotate the bone so that it rests in position at the top of the leg.

7. With the single bone selected, press the p key on your keyboard to open the bone's Properties panel. In the middle of the panel, change the Rest Length to about 1.9 m, as shown in Figure 15.8. Changing the Rest Length tells LightWave to give this bone a larger range of influence.

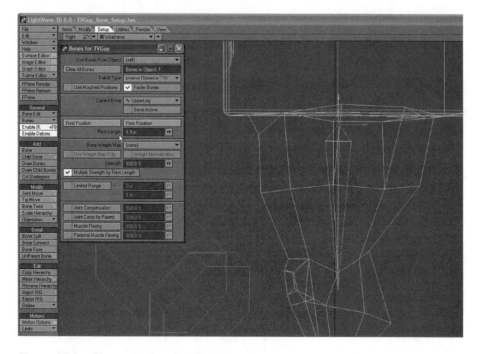

Figure 15.8   Change the Rest Length of the bone so that it will deform a larger area. Do this from the bone's Properties panel.

Important

> To adjust the bone to the proper length, you must change the Rest Length, not the size. This can't be stressed enough. The Rest Length is the final length of the bone before it is made active—in other words, its resting position. The number-one mistake LightWave animators make with bones is changing the size to set up a bone instead of the rest length. If you change the size of the bone now, after it is activated, it will change the size of the object with which it is associated.

Creating Hierarchies

What exactly is a hierarchy? Your fingers are attached to your hand, your hand is attached to your wrist, your wrist is attached to your forearm, and so on. Move the shoulder, and its attached limbs move with it. That's a hierarchy! You can create a hierarchy of bones in LightWave (and objects) so that if you move an Upper Leg bone, the rest of the bones in the leg move with it. This is also called forward kinematics. You may have heard the term inverse kinematics. Say you move the foot bone of your leg; what should happen? The leg should bend accordingly, right? This is inverse kinematics. This section demonstrates how to build bones into a hierarchical structure.

Setting Child Bones

Setting up that first bone is the hardest part. Now that it is in place, you can set child bones. And because they will be "children" of the base bone, their scale will match the hand better when added, unlike the first bone.

Exercise 15.3   Creating Child Bones

1. This Upper Leg bone will begin the hierarchy of the leg, meaning that it is the parent bone. Each bone that extends from this one is a child bone. If the parent bone moves, the children move with it. Make sure the Upper Leg bone is selected, and from the Setup menu tab in Layout, click Child Bone from the Add category. Note that you can also use the (=) key. You can name this new bone Lower Leg.

2. You can see that an exact duplicate of the Upper Leg bone is attached right beneath it. Change this new bone's Rest Length to about 1.33 m so that its tip meets the ankle area of the leg, as in Figure 15.9. If you rotate the Upper Leg bone, the new child bone moves with it.

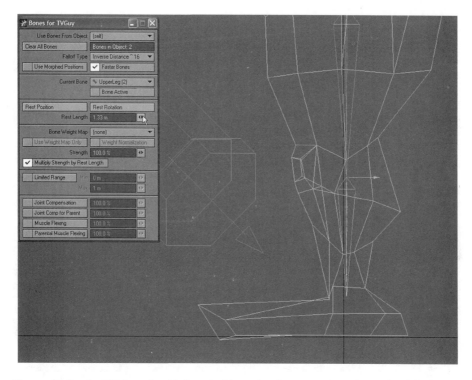

Figure 15.9 A child bone is added to the Upper Leg bone, creating a hierarchical duplicate.

3. Now add another child bone, naming it Ankle. Set its Rest Length to about 210 mm.

4. Add another child bone, naming it Foot. For this bone, rotate it 90 degrees on its pitch. You can do this by first pressing y on the keyboard and then grabbing the green handle and dragging. Or you can click in the Numeric panel at the bottom left of the Layout interface and directly enter the value. Set this bone's Rest Length to 1.3 m so that it encompasses the foot.

The bones are now in place, but they are not yet influencing the model. This is because they are not active. If you rotate say, the lower leg bone, the ankle and foot bone should follow. However, as you can see in Figure 15.10, the leg of the object does not move.

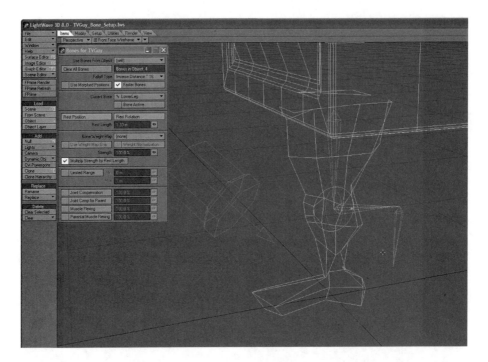

Figure 15.10   After the child bones are added, rotating the lower leg bone moves the foot bones accordingly. However, the object itself is not deformed.

Now you need to activate the bones. Activating tells LightWave where you want the bones to rest and begin working. But here's the thing—people often set their bones to rest, and suddenly, their object disappears or becomes grossly deformed. Try it out and see.

5. First, rotate the Lower Leg bone back to its original position in the shape of the leg. Then, with the Foot bone selected, press the r key. Your object changes positions, essentially falling over, as in Figure 15.11.

Do you see what happened? The object seems to be messed up, and many animators stop here and freak out, usually emailing the author of this book! But wait! Read on. You did nothing wrong.

What's happening at this point is that the bone you've set into position is now active and influencing the model. However, it is the only bone influencing it, so the model is deforming based on the position of this bone only. When you activate the other bones, the model returns to its proper shape and position. Start activating the bones, beginning from the base bone, and your object will not distort this way.

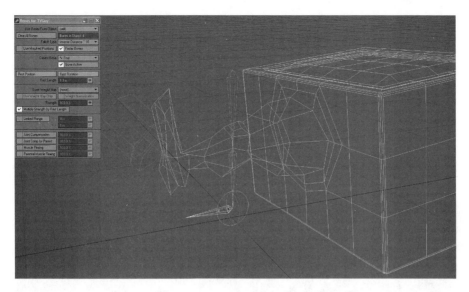

Figure 15.11   Activating a bone by pressing the r key tells the bone to influence the model. When only one bone is influencing the model, the model responds accordingly.

Tip

Pressing Ctrl+r deactivates a bone. Press r again to activate it again.

6. Use the up arrow to select the next bone, press r, and repeat the bone activation by pressing r for each bone.

When you activate all the bones, the model returns to its original shape. This is because all bones are now active and properly influencing the deformation of the model. When only one bone was active, such as the last bone for the object, the entire TVGuy was being influenced by only one bone.

Important

You can differentiate between an inactive bone and an active bone based on visibility. Dashed lines represent an inactive bone, and solid lines represent an active one. And remember, you can change the color of these lines with the Visibility commands in the Scene Editor.

7. Go back to the Perspective view and change the Maximum Render Level in the scene to Shaded Solid. Select the Lower Leg bone and press the y key to rotate the bone. You'll see the object deform, as in Figure 15.12.

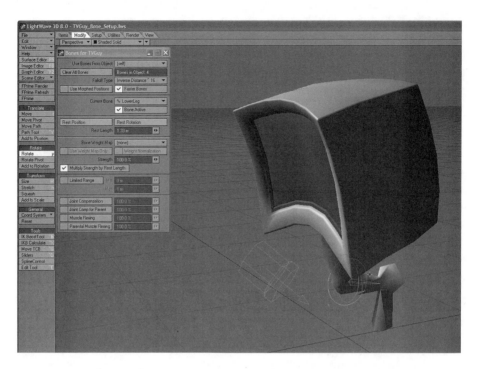

Figure 15.12 When the bones are in place and active, rotating deforms the object.

8. Make your bones completely visible in your solid shaded object by choosing the Bone X-Ray mode from the top of Layout, as in Figure 15.13.

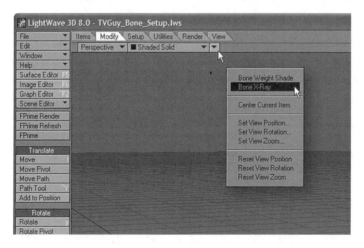

Figure 15.13 Turn on Bone X-Ray mode from the top of Layout to see all the bones in your object.

You might have noticed that when moving the Lower Leg bone, the upper part of the object deforms. This is normal. Because the upper part of the TVGuy object doesn't have any bones associated with it, the bones in the lower area affect the entire object. You have two options to correct this: You can either add more bones to the object or set up weights in Modeler. Often, you'll do both! First, you add more bones to the upper part of the TVGuy object, and then the next exercise shows you where to begin using bone weights.

Creating Multiple Hierarchies

The leg bones you've added work very nicely to bend and animate the leg of this object. It has a nicely placed hierarchy and is an object that is not too difficult to work with, unlike a hand with multiple fingers and multiple bones. You might think that because you've already created a hierarchy of bones, you don't need to build onto this existing chain. However, you can create an entirely different hierarchy elsewhere within the object. Remember, bones are attached to the object with which they are created.

Tip

Although bones are attached to the objects they are created with, you can tell any object to "Use Bones From" another object. You do this in the Bones Properties panel. You would use this feature if your bones were created initially as Skelegons in Modeler and live on a different layer. You might also use this for objects that need influencing from another object's bones.

You created the first hierarchy starting with the Upper Leg bone. You rotated it downward so that the rotational pivot point of the bone was at the top of the leg, similar to a hip. Next you create a similar hierarchy pointing upward into the body of the TVGuy.

Exercise 15.4   Setting Up Multiple Hierarchies

1. From the Setup tab, click Bone from the Add category. Move and rotate this bone so it rests just above the Upper Leg bone, essentially mirroring it. As you did earlier, increase the Rest Length in the Bones Properties panel so that it reaches to the middle of the TV screen, as in Figure 15.14.

2. Now add a child bone to the bone you just created.

3. Go ahead and activate (rest) these two bones by pressing the r key, as you did for the leg bones.

4. Select the Lower Leg bone and rotate it. You'll notice that the upper portion of the TVGuy object still bends but not as severely as it did without the upper bones. Figure 15.15 shows the deformation.

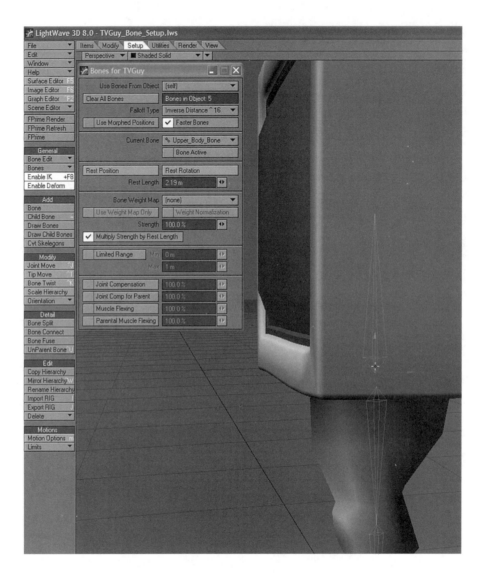

Figure 15.14 Add a bone to the TVGuy object, move it up, and rotate it so that it points up into the character.

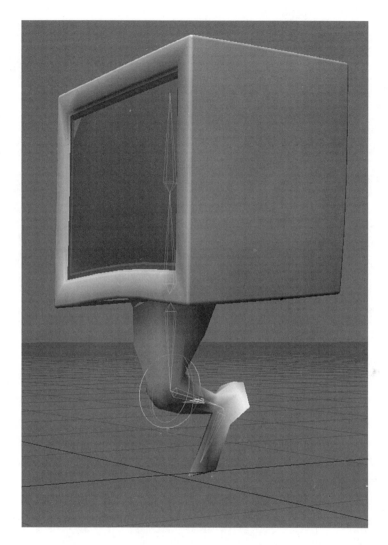

Figure 15.15   Moving the Lower Leg bone with bones added to the upper portion of the body show less deformation.

5. Select the first bone of the upper body you added. Add another child bone to it and then rotate the bone 90 degrees on the heading (the red handle), as in Figure 15.16.

Figure 15.16   Create a child bone from the first bone in the upper body to act like an arm.

The reason you're creating a child bone from the first bone in this hierarchy is to create a human-like structure. This new child bone will be like an arm within the TVGuy.

6. Select the first bone of the upper hierarchy again and create another child bone. This time, however, rotate the bone -90 degrees on the heading to create the other arm.

7. After both arm bones are in place, activate (rest) them by selecting each and pressing the r key.

8. Again, select the first, or as it's often called, the base or parent, bone of the upper hierarchy and rotate it. You'll see that its three child bones rotate with it! Figure 15.17 shows the operation.

9. Now select the Lower Leg bone and rotate it. You'll see that, as in Figure 15.18, the upper body doesn't really move or deform. This is because the bone structure you've created is holding the geometry in place. The leg bones don't really have much influence on the upper part of the TVGuy object.

Figure 15.17   With two child bones in place, rotating the first bone, often called the base or parent bone, rotates the child bones.

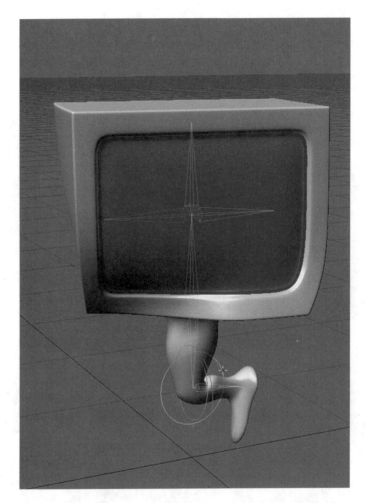

Figure 15.18 Rotating the Lower Leg bone does not deform the upper body of the TVGuy object now that it has bones holding the geometry in place.

Tip

For Figure 15.18, the Display SubPatch Level has been set to 6 in the Object Properties panel for the TVGuy object.

Even though you've added bones to the upper body, and the leg bones aren't deforming it much, you can add even more control through the use of Bone Weights.

Bone Weights

When we discuss Bone Weights, we're talking about a Modeler tool that is used for setting up limited ranges of influence by bones. The Bone Weights feature automates the process of creating weight maps that approximate what the normal bone influence would be. However, you must have Skelegons already in place. Discussion of Skelegons is coming up shortly. A weight map, on the other hand, is applied directly to points or polygons rather than bones. weight maps can be used not only with bones but also with other Layout tools as well.

After a weight map is created, you can adjust the maps to suit your needs through the Bone Weights feature. It basically gives you a starting point when creating weight maps for your bones. Figure 15.19 shows the Make Bone Weight Map panel in Modeler, found under the Map menu tab list of tools.

The reason this is mentioned here is so that you are aware of the tools available to you when setting up bones for object deformation. Bone weights are just one option of weighting in LightWave. This section discusses using Bone Weights; however, you can also create weights for bones without bone weights or Skelegons. As you work through the rest of this chapter and other Modeler functions in the book, you'll see how useful and versatile weights really are.

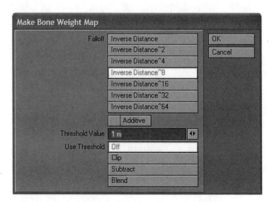

Figure 15.19   The Make Bone Weight Map panel in Modeler.

Weight Maps in Modeler

The first step in understanding the use of Bone Weights is to explore LightWave's weighting features in Modeler. Weight maps enable you to scale the falloff of various tools in LightWave. With a weight map, a bone affects points according to the weight you set. The result is a controlled influence that eliminates the problem you saw in Exercise 15.3 and in Figure 15.12, when the lower leg movement deformed the entire body of the TVGuy object.

Falloff

The Falloff selections within the Bone Weights panel determine how the influences of bones fade with distance. The settings work mathematically, and the default is Inverse Distance^4. This exponential value of ^{4} sets a fair amount of falloff for a bone, whereas a higher value of ^{16} will have a greater (or faster) falloff effect. Layout's Bones Falloff Type ranges from ^{2} to ^{128}.

Additive

The Additive selection within the Bone Weights panel tells LightWave to add weight to any existing value. If you create multiple Skelegons for an object using the same name, LightWave adds the weight values to each. Using Additive quickly sets up Bone Weights without requiring you to rename every bone.

Threshold Value

The Threshold Value is similar to Limited Region for bones in Layout. It is an encapsulated region around a bone, and the value set (such as 1 m) determines the size of the region.

Use Threshold

This setting takes the weight value of the set threshold distance as Off, Clip, Subtract, or Blend. Off ignores the Threshold Value set. Clip simply cuts the weight when outside the threshold to 0. Subtract subtracts the weight from all values, making the weights run smoothly at 0 and negative at the threshold. Finally, Blend subtracts the Threshold Value and then clips the negative weights to 0. This setting often is the most useful.

Applying Weight Maps

This next exercise instructs you on the method of weighting. This process is done in Modeler and enables you to tell a bone to control a specific area rather than the entire object. For example, with weighting, moving the lower leg would not affect the upper area of the TVGuy, as it did in Figure 15.12.

Bone Weights enable you to specify regions of influence. Much of the time when creating character animation you'll be building your model from the ground up, and you can assign weight maps as you go. However, you can also use existing models from a previous project, from another artist, or perhaps from this book's DVD-ROM.

Exercise 15.5   Creating Weights

1. Open Modeler and load the TVGuy_Weight object from this book's DVD-ROM. You can also just load the object directly from Layout by selecting it from the drop-down object list at the top of the Modeler interface next to the Layers buttons. This loads the object by using LightWave's HUB. This is a copy of the same simple object you used in the previous exercises. Figure 15.20 shows the model loaded. Press the a key to fit the model to the view to match the figure.

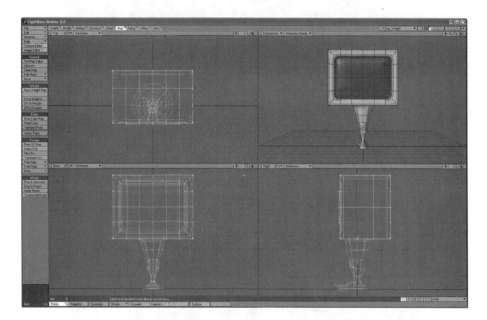

Figure 15.20   An existing model is loaded into Modeler and ready to have weights assigned to it.

In Exercise 15.3, you created four bones: one for the top of the leg, one for the lower leg, one for the ankle, and one for the foot. Now you only need to set up some weight maps for these areas, and your model will deform properly in Layout.

2. Choose Polygons Selection mode by clicking the Polygons button at the bottom of the Modeler interface.

3. In the Right view (bottom right quadrant), lasso select the thigh area of the leg. Remember, hold the right mouse button down and drag around the area you want to select in order to "lasso" it. Mac users, hold that Command key for right mouse button functions. Figure 15.21 shows the lasso selection.

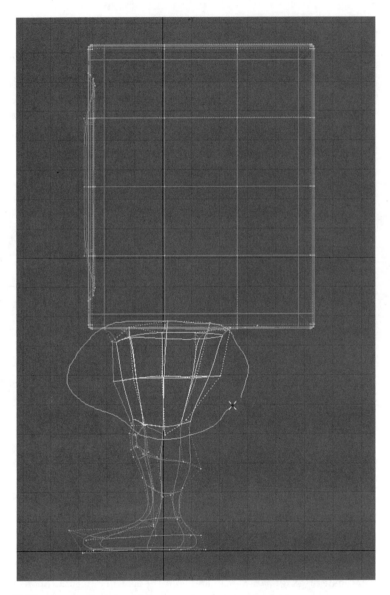

Figure 15.21 Lasso select the thigh area polygons to apply weights.

You could have also just held the mouse button down and dragged it across the areas you wanted to select. The choice is yours!

4. With the polygons of the top of the leg selected, select the W at the bottom of the Modeler interface (next to T, M, C, S) to choose Weight mode. In the drop-down list next to these choices where it reads (none), select [new]. Figure 15.22 shows the selection.

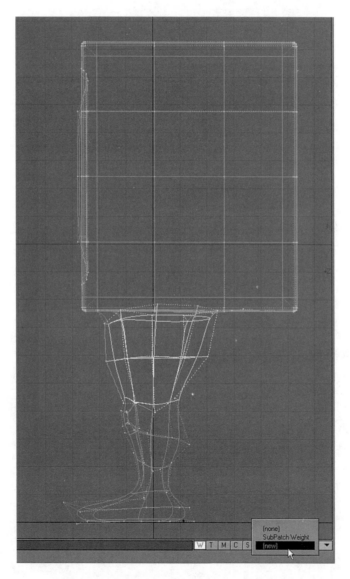

Figure 15.22   You assign a weight map to selected polygons by selecting [new] from the W drop-down list.

The Create Weight Map panel comes up. You can now assign a weight map to the selected polygons. Remember, the selected polygons are for the TVGuy.

5. Change the Name to TVGuy_Thigh. You don't need to call it "weight," but it helps to keep things clear when many weights and surfaces are similarly named. Keep Initial Value checked and leave 100% applied, as shown in Figure 15.23.

Figure 15.23   When you assign a weight map, you can also set the name of the weight. This is a good habit to get into for organization.

You've now set a weight map for the upper leg of the TVGuy object, but if you remember, there are four bones in the entire leg. This is a good time to change your Perspective view (or any view) to Weight Shade render view mode. When you view your model in Weight Shade mode (selected from the top of each viewport), you can see the weight applied as bright red.

6. Deselect the upper leg polygons, and select the polygons that make up the lower leg. Select [new] again from the W command to create a weight map for this selection. Name the new weight map TVGuy_LowerLeg, as shown in Figure 15.24.

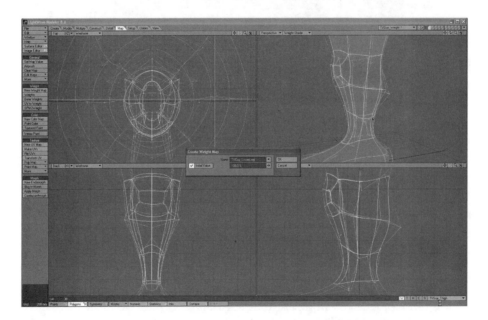

Figure 15.24   Another weight map is added to the lower leg of the TVGuy object.

You can assign weight maps to selected polygons or points, but if you apply a weight map to selected polygons, you are really applying the weight to the points of the selected polygons.

7. Switch over to Points mode by selecting the Points button at the bottom of the Modeler interface or by pressing Ctrl+g. This tells Modeler you're now working with points.

8. With the right mouse button in the Right view, lasso the points of the foot from the middle ankle down. Figure 15.25 shows the selection.

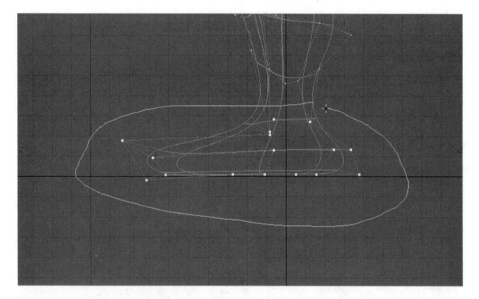

Figure 15.25 You can assign weight maps to points as well as polygons. Here, the points of the foot base are selected for a weight map to be applied.

 Tip

Selecting polygons over points or vice versa for setting weight maps is your choice. You've been shown both here to understand how it all works. However, polygons are sometimes a better choice for weight map selection because it is much easier to see what is and (more importantly) what is not selected.

9. From the same drop-down list next to the W, choose [new] and Create Weight Map for the foot. Set the name to TVGuy_Foot in the Create Weight Map panel when it appears.

10. Save your object! Saving the object saves the weights you've applied.

That's all there is to it! You've identified a range of polygons that is controlled by a bone in Layout. Remember, you use LightWave Modeler to create weight maps. You can adjust them in both Modeler and Layout, but creation is always done in Modeler.

This next exercise instructs you on the method of assigning a particular bone of your model to the weights you've just created in Layout. As a result, the bone will only influence the weighted area.

Exercise 15.6 Assigning Weights

1. Hop on into LightWave Layout. From this book's DVD, load the TVGuy_Bone_Weight scene. You'll find it in the Chapter 15 Scenes folder of the Projects directory.

2. Make sure Bone X-Ray mode is on from the top of Layout to see the bones in the object. Then select the upper leg bone of the TVGuy object and press the p key.

3. In the Bone Properties panel, select TVGuy_Thigh as the weight map for the Bone Weight Map option, as shown in Figure 15.26.

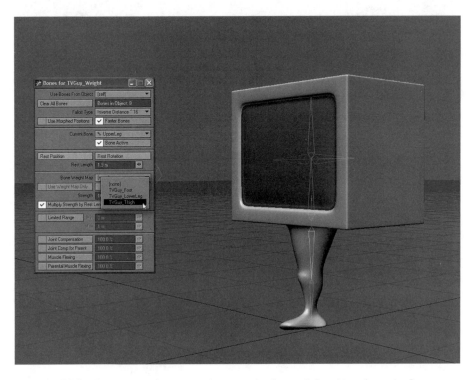

Figure 15.26   Assign a weight map to the upper leg bone of the object from the Bones Properties panel.

4. Press the down arrow on your keyboard to select the Lower Leg bone and then assign the appropriate weight map to it.

5. Press the down arrow again, select the ankle bone, and assign the foot weight map to it as well as the foot bone.

6. Close the Bones Properties panel and select the Upper Leg bone. Press y to rotate the bone around. You'll see, as in Figure 15.27, that only the leg reacts! The upper portion of the TVGuy is not affected at all.

Figure 15.27 Assigning weight maps to bones alleviates any problems of bone movements influencing areas of the model they shouldn't.

Important

When working with the Auto Key feature, remember that movements, rotations, and the like, are recorded. If you happen to rotate a bone and deform the object when you didn't intend to, you can always undo! LightWave 8 has multiple undo's in Layout for actions such as moving or rotating a bone. Just press Ctrl+z, and you're all set. Pressing just z is redo. You can set the undo levels in the General Options panel by pressing o.

You might have noticed that some other selections were available in the Bones Properties panel, such as Use Weight Map Only and Weight Normalization. If you want your weight maps to be the only control over influence, you can activate Use Weight Map Only. When you do, the Weight Normalization simply "normalizes" the weight values, which is useful for bone weighting. Otherwise, you have to be very careful with what the weight values are.

Tip

There's a little trick in LightWave you can try when setting up additional bones and weights. If the weight map created in Modeler is named exactly (capitalization included) as the bone, the weight map in Layout will be automatically applied.

The subtlety of using weight maps with bones is that you can define the falloff influence of a bone. This exercise created all weight maps with 100% initial value, which tells the models to rely on the bone falloff with this value only. You can have even more power over your models with weight maps because you can absolutely control the bone influence. For example, you can use one of the weight tools to drop off the weighted influence from 100% to 0% toward the top of an object. Try experimenting with the scenes on this book's DVD-ROM and change the influences to see what sort of results you can come up with.

Skelegons

As you worked through the setup of just four bones for the leg of the TVGuy earlier in this chapter, you probably realized that applying bones can be a tedious process. And it can! However, Skelegons are often a much better method for setting up bone structures. You do this in Modeler.

You'll grow fond of the term Skelegons as you work through this next section because Skelegons are polygons that resemble bones. In Modeler, you can create and modify

Skelegons as if they were polygons and then convert them to bones in Layout. The benefit of this is the ability to set up bones for a character in a Perspective view with modeling tools such as Drag and Rotate. Furthermore, the skeletal structure you create for a character is saved with the object! This means you can set up full bone structures for characters and load them individually into a single scene.

When you create a character with Skelegons, you can change the model at any time and adjust its skeletal structure. In addition, you can create one base skeletal structure and use it over and over again for future characters. The next exercise gets you right into it by setting up Skelegons for a full figure.

Important

Be sure to always save a copy of your model with Skelegons. When you convert Skelegons to bones, they can't be changed back to Skelegons.

Creating Skelegons in Modeler

There are a couple of ways to create Skelegons in Modeler. You can build them point-by-point and convert single-line polygons to Skelegons, such as two points connected with a line polygon or a curve. This is useful for creating Skelegons from existing models. There is also the Draw Skelegons feature, which is fast and easy and is the focus of this next exercise.

Exercise 15.7   Creating Skelegons

This exercise uses an existing model to demonstrate how quick and easy it is to set up a full hierarchy for a quadruped character. Using the Bone Weight information from the previous exercises and the Skelegons information provided here, you'll be animating a fully articulated character in no time. However, you're going to use an automatic feature in LightWave to automatically apply weights to the character. The trick is keeping the Skelegons in the same layer as the geometry. However, for the purpose of providing visual examples, this tutorial shows you the Skelegons in a separate layer. However, you should build the Skelegons in the same layer as the geometry.

1. In LightWave 8 Modeler, save any work you might have been doing and create a new object by pressing Shift+n.

2. From this book's DVD, load the Giraffe_Basic object.

3. Select a new layer, making the giraffe a background layer. Bring the bottom right viewport to a full screen and, from the Setup menu tab, select Skelegons, as shown in Figure 15.28.

Figure 15.28   To create Skelegons, start with a blank layer but put your model in a background layer for alignment.

Tip

The hierarchy you'll create can be used for any type of four-legged creature, as well
as two-legged ones. You'll soon see how easy it is to create a setup like this using
Skelegons. However, do not miss the video portion of this chapter on this book's
DVD. The DVD video takes you even further into bones and rigging by showing you
how to set up a full skeletal structure for a human character, all within Layout.
LightWave 8 has more tools than we can write about in this chapter alone!

The small circles around the ends of the Skelegons are the controls for that bone.
If you are in Draw Skelegons mode (which is activated by clicking the Create
Skelegons button), clicking outside this circle draws a Skelegon attached to the
one before it. If you need to adjust the Skelegon, be sure to click within the circles.

4. You start building the skeletal structure for the giraffe's upper body first. Click
and drag from the middle of the giraffe up to about his chest, as in Figure 15.29.

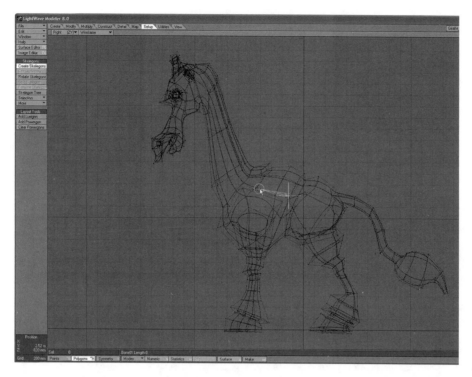

Figure 15.29 Create the first Skelegon, which will be the parent bone of the upper body hierarchy.

⚠️ **Important**

Be careful to click and drag just once. It's very common for people to click, let go of the mouse, and then click and drag again. Although you can't see it, doing that creates a tiny little bone that will haunt you later in Layout.

5. With the initial Skelegon still selected, simply click in front of it to create an additional Skelegon reaching to the base of the neck. This Skelegon will become a child bone later in Layout. Figure 15.30 shows the creation.

6. Now create another Skelegon up the neck, as in Figure 15.31.

7. Create six more Skelegons, as in Figure 15.32, that travel up the neck, through the head, and down to the jaw and lower mouth.

Figure 15.30   Create a second Skelegon that leads to the base of the neck.

Figure 15.31   Create a Skelegon for the lower portion of the neck.

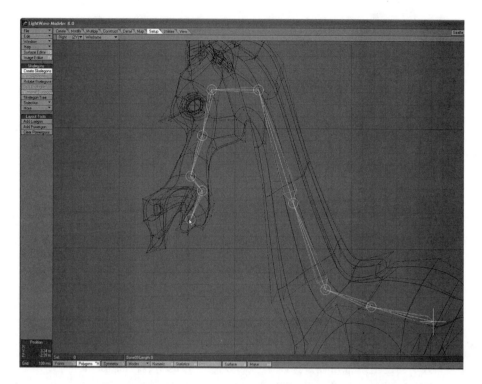

Figure 15.32 Continue creating Skelegons up the neck and around through the head and jaw.

Each Skelegon should start and end at a joint within the character. For example, the Skelegon for the head begins at the base of the head. When the Skelegon becomes a bone in LightWave Layout and is activated, it will rotate from its base, which will then rotate the head. If it were placed, say, in the middle of the head, rotating it would deform the head in an uncomfortable way, to say the least.

Tip

> With the Numeric panel open (n), you can set a name for the Skelegon and create a weight map assignment all at once. To do this, you must draw your Skelegons into the same layer as the geometry. Figure 15.33 shows the panel. However, this can be very tricky and hard to do because of lack of visibility. Instead, you'll add the weights after you create the Skelegons. The Digits selection in the Numeric panel for Skelegons tells Modeler to sequentially name the Skelegons as you create them. Sometimes, you might not set a name for each Skelegon, so Modeler names them Bone.00, Bone.01, Bone.02, and so on. In addition, these settings determine how the weight map is applied to the geometry based on the Skelegon in the same layer. If you are using this auto-weight map feature, you need to draw Skelegons in the same layer as the geometry. This is a real-time implementation of the Bone Weights function.

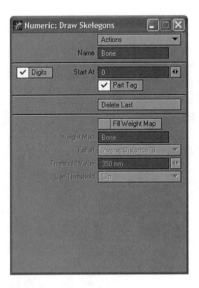

Figure 15.33 The Numeric panel for Draw Skelegons.

Tip

Now if you screw up while creating Skelegons by accidentally creating too many for
example, don't worry! It's a common mistake. Just press the Spacebar to turn off the
Skelegons command and then press the Delete key to get rid of them. Select
Skelegons and create them again, remembering to name them and set the weights in
the Numeric panel if you want. You can also select one Skelegon as you would a polygon and then simply delete it. Then select the last polygon in the chain, choose Draw
Skelegons, and continue. The next Skelegon you create will be properly added into
the hierarchy.

8. Press the Spacebar to turn off the Create Skelegons command. Then select the
   Skelegon in the middle of the snout and click the Create Skelegons tool again.
   Doing this tells Modeler to begin creating child Skelegons from the selected
   Skelegon. The result is that if you move the snout Skelegon, the attached
   Skelegons (those of the upper and lower mouth) move with it.

9. Create two more Skelegons for the upper mouth, as shown in Figure 15.34.

10. From the Setup menu tab, select Skelegon Tree. When the panel comes up, drag
    the corner to expand the size of the panel slightly if you need to.

    You'll see a hierarchy of Skelegons named Bone01 (the first Skelegon you drew),
    Bone02, and so on. Figure 15.35 shows the Skelegon Tree.

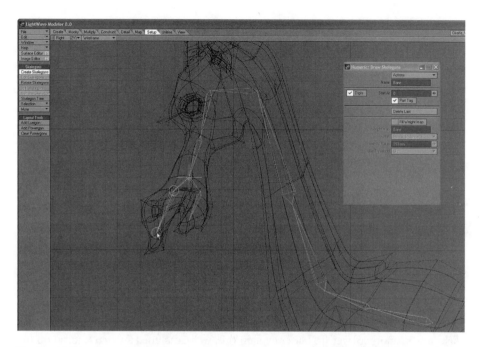

Figure 15.34   Create two more Skelegons starting from the snout of the giraffe.

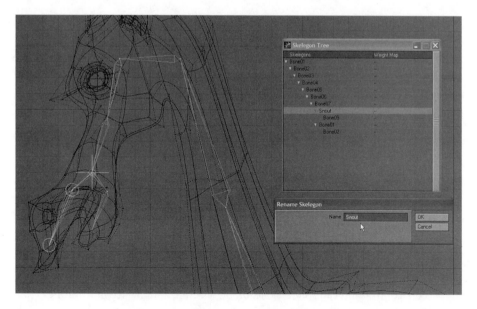

Figure 15.35   The Skelegon Tree helps you manage your Skelegon structures. Because no name was applied for the first Skelegon, it simply reads Bone01. Every Skelegon thereafter uses the same name. Remember that you can name each Skelegon as you create it in the Numeric panel. After you name a Skelegon, each one you create from that point takes on that name as well.

11. Double-click the fourth bone listing up from the bottom under the Skelegon heading. Double-clicking calls up the Rename Skelegon command. Rename this bone "Snout," as it was created in the snout area of the object.

You can continue naming Skelegons in this panel. Note however that it can't stay open, so finish your business and close it to move on.

12. Save your object. Saving the object also saves the bone structure.

From here, you can create the Skelegons for the legs. However, you need to build these Skelegons from the original mid-section Skelegon. This is the first Skelegon you created, which is the parent of the upper body structure.

Tip

If you name the Skelegon and the weight map identically, the weight maps are automatically applied in Layout when the Skelegons are converted to bones. Note that this is case-sensitive.

Creating Skelegons for the legs can be slightly tricky because you need to now build the Skelegons in another layer. To better explain this, we've included a video tutorial on this book's DVD. Open up the Skelegons tutorial video and continue rigging this beast!

Completing the Skelegon Rig

The process you've just completed puts you on your way to successfully creating a bone structure for a four-legged character. You still would need to build the leg structure of the character for all four legs. However, the advantage of Skelegons is that you can quickly and easily mirror the structure for the opposite side of the object. You don't have to draw Skelegons again because Skelegons are a polygon type. In the video exercise, you can apply Modeler tools to them and adjust their position, size, and so on.

Here area few extra tips about Skelegons:

- You can use them like polygons, adjusting the points and varying the size.
- After an object has a Skelegon structure, it can be loaded back into Modeler and adjusted or added on to at anytime without affecting the model.
- If you have created a full structure for a creature but realize later that you need more control, you can split a Skelegon by selecting Split Skelegon from the Construct tab.
- You can define a weight map for a Skelegon (Detail tab).

- If you need to separate a hierarchy, you can use the UnWeld command (Detail tab).

- You can instantly create Skelegons for points of an object by choosing the Convert Skelegon command from the More drop-down menu, found under the Skelegons category in the Setup tab in Modeler.

Using Skelegons in Layout

The final part of this chapter takes you back into Layout, where you convert these Skelegons to actual bones and make them control your model. You assign the weight maps created to each Skelegon as well. It's not necessary to move the Skelegons to the Modeler layer that contains the object that will be influenced. The Skelegons can keep their own layer. However, for a full body character with full weight maps, it's good to take advantage of the automatic weight map feature. After your Skelegons are created and in place, you can cut and paste them into the object layer. If your weights are named identically to your Skelegons, when you convert the Skelegons to bones in Layout, the weights will automatically be applied.

Important

> There is so much to LightWave 8's bone tools that we couldn't fit into one chapter. So be sure to check out all the cool video tutorials for this chapter (and others) on this book's DVD. Learn about new bone tools for LightWave 8 and the new IK Boost Tool.

After your model is loaded into Layout with Skelegons, you can simply select the Cvt Skelegons command from the Setup Menu tab. An information display or popup window tells you how many Skelegons were converted to bones. From there, your bones will be visible and useable in Layout.

Tip

> If Layout has Expert mode set from the General Options tab in the Preferences panel, you don't see a Skelegons to Bones conversion message. Instead, it is highlighted in the status bar underneath the timeline at the bottom of the interface.

Beyond this exercise, you can select portions of the model to assign weight maps just as you did with the TVGuy object earlier in this chapter and then apply the bones in Layout. You can go further and select the regions of points on the full giraffe object, assign a weight map, and apply the bone weights. If you remember, applying weights to the leg of the TVGuy object enabled you to control the influence of bones—you can do the same throughout the body, for the tail, the neck, the legs, and so on. You'll see all of this done on the Skelegons video on this book's DVD. Remember that the Skelegon Tree in Modeler shows the name of the weight map that will be used if you've created one. If you've assigned weights in the Numeric panel along with a bone name, your weights should automatically be assigned to the appropriate bone in Layout.

The exercises here are basic and straightforward. However, much of your character work does not need to be more complex than this. You can go further by adding Skelegons for the giraffe in the ears and perhaps in the toes as well. At any time, LightWave enables you to bring this model back to Modeler, make adjustments, and add more Skelegons or weight maps.

The Next Step

To give you the most complete coverage of bones, the DVD includes a bunch of video tutorials for this chapter alone. It takes the TVGuy character further and shows you how to edit its existing bone structure directly in Layout for additional control using LightWave 8's new bone tools. You'll be able to view the Skelegons video to further rig the Giraffe and apply weight maps. You'll also find the Human Rig video, which guides you through a complete setup of bones for a human object. You can view videos on applying weights to a fun character and a video showing how to attach bones to the weights in Layout. You'll also find a video showing how to use LightWave 8's IK Boost tool, a fast, easy way to create inverse kinematics. Lastly, you'll find a tutorial video called Layout Bones, which takes you through more of LightWave 8's bone features, including exporting hierarchies, mirroring, and more.

This chapter introduced you to bones and Skelegons and how to create both. You saw how to set bone weights to control the influences of bones. The weighting applies to many areas of LightWave, especially character animation.

With the basic knowledge presented here, you can practice setting up full characters, whether they're full humans, simple characters, or even inanimate objects such as a chrome toaster—the bone and Skelegon information here still applies. Position bones using the Drag tool and use the Mirror tool to copy the Skelegons. See what other kinds of uses you can apply these tools to, such as animals, aliens, or your own fascinating creatures.

Skelegons and Bones are powerful animation tools in LightWave. Of course, one chapter can't present all the different possible uses of these tools. With the right project and a little time, however, you'll be setting up skeletal structures faster than you could have imagined. But where can you go beyond this? You can turn to Chapter 16, "Animating Characters," and make your characters not only move with bones but also talk with Endomorphs.

Chapter 16
Animating Characters

When it comes to 3D animation, most people think about character animation in films like Pixar's *Toy Story* or *Finding Nemo*. Even though you know very well that 3D animation is made up of much more than character animation, everyone at some point wants to take a stab at creating moving characters. Many animators, of course, dream about becoming a full-time character animator at the top Hollywood studios. This chapter introduces you to the concepts of character animation and demonstrates the techniques used in LightWave 8 to get a 3D character in motion.

Project Overview

Character animation is an art form that is difficult to master. It takes a lot of study of motion and timing. Young animators spend years at school studying fine art, drawing, and various classes on theory and movement in order to become the best character animators they can be. That said, this chapter isn't enough to replace that learning. However, you *will* learn what it takes to create moving characters. You'll learn enough so that you can "get it" and practice on your own. When you think about it, this is sometimes one of the best ways to learn! In this chapter, you'll learn:

- Character animation basics
- How to put characters in motion, using pose-to-pose animation techniques
- Keyframing and motion for timing
- How to use the Dope Sheet to edit keyframes and timing

Proper Character Setup

When building a house, there are a number of factors that come into play. You start with a blueprint to plan out what's going to happen. You gather the right materials and the right contractors and begin working. It's not much different when it comes to character animation, except that in many circumstances, you play all the roles. Creating animated characters also begins with a blueprint—a storyboard. You work out what your character will do and over what timeframe. From there, you need a proper character setup, created in Modeler with Skelegons or in Layout with bones. Whichever the case, the bone setup (the rig) in Layout, combined with inverse kinematics and sometimes forward kinematics, gives you the controls to build motions. Be sure to read through Chapter 15, "Bones and Rigging," to learn how to set up a full character bone structure. There is also a video tutorial on this book's DVD showing how you can set up a character rig directly in Layout.

A proper character setup makes all the difference when animating characters. There is nothing worse than trying to properly time your character's motions with a bad bone structure. It is truly a nightmare. On the flipside, when you have a really good bone setup (a good "rig"), it is fun to create motions and see your character come to life. Again, be sure to read Chapter 15 and view the associated videos from 3D Garage.com on this book's DVD. You'll find four videos for Chapter 15 demonstrating more bone and Skelegon tools.

Inbetweening

After your character is set up with a bone rig, either directly in Layout or with Skelegons in Modeler, the next step is to get it in motion! Many animators work out their character animation with a blank scene and just the character. After the character's moves are in place, that scene is saved, and using LightWave's Load From Scene command, you can load the moving character scene into a large scene with other characters, props, buildings, and so on.

The advantage computer animators have over traditional animators is that a computer automatically creates the inbetween frames. Commonly known as inbetweening, traditional animators without computers must draw every single frame. Computer animators, on the other hand, can create "key" frames, and the computer interpolates the rest. This is a good thing and a bad thing. It's a good thing because it saves enormous amounts of time. It's a bad thing because this automated process can tend to remove subtle nuances that make your character have a life of its own.

Auto Key or Manual Key

When it comes to character animation and the proper working methods, the type of keyframing you use is up to you. Manual keyframing requires you to move an arm, leg, or other body part and specifically create a keyframe, telling that item to stay put at a particular frame. You've done this throughout the course of this book. Auto keyframing, on the other hand, in many cases can cause problems in your scene setup. However, for character animation, Auto Key is a welcomed addition to your setup. When working with Auto Key (found at the bottom of the LightWave Layout interface), your item movements are recorded for you. When creating character animation, you can move the timeline, pose the character, move the timeline again, and pose the character again. When you scrub the timeline back and forth, you see your character in motion. Because LightWave Layout now has undo for motions, you can very easily press Ctrl+z to undo a movement you don't like. This chapter employs the Auto Key feature, and you'll see how it helps your workflow.

Tip

Using Auto Key for character animation is a plus because it's fast and provides you with instant feedback. When you use Auto Key, it is like having a posable puppet on your computer screen.

Using Auto Key with Pose-to-Pose Animation

There are two development phases you need to be aware of before you move into character animation. You probably are already aware of them at this point, but it can't hurt to review them. First, there is the creation of the rig. This is done either with a Skelegon setup in Modeler or by directly creating bones in Layout. Skelegons are converted to bones in Layout. After a bone structure has been set up, you need to assign inverse kinematics to the rig. This is done either manually, one bone at a time, or through LightWave 8's new IK Boost tool. All this information is covered in Chapter 15 and in the associated videos on this book's DVD. After you have that taken care of, you can begin the second phase: posing your character.

Exercise 16.1   Posing a Character

1. From this book's DVD, load the Character Surprise scene from the Chapter 16 folder.

   This is a simple character with a bone rig and weight map setup (described in Chapter 15). This character also uses inverse kinematics applied through the IK Boost tool.

2. With the scene loaded, resave it with a different name to a location on your hard drive. After that's done, you can press Shift+s to save incremental versions. This is a good practice to get into for character animating.

3. Click to the Modify tab and select the IK Boost Tool button at the bottom left of the interface. This activates the IK Boost setup. Then, carefully click with the right mouse button directly on the pivot of the character. This is the small dot located between the character's feet at the 0 axis.

4. Turn Auto Key on at the bottom of the interface. Press o on the keyboard (that's o as in OH! Not zero) and make sure Auto Key Create is set to Modified Channels. This tells LightWave to create keyframes automatically as you work your way through the timeline.

5. Click to select the tip of the right hand. The setup is shown in Figure 16.1.

   When setting up a pose-to-pose type animation, you're creating key poses and allowing LightWave to interpolate. The result is often a more expressive form of animation than that achieved with other methods. In this particular scene, you're going to relax the character, then have him suddenly surprised.

6. Drag the right hand down to the side of the character as in Figure 16.2.

7. Do the same for the left arm, making it droop just a bit. It doesn't need to match the right arm. Figure 16.3 shows the change.

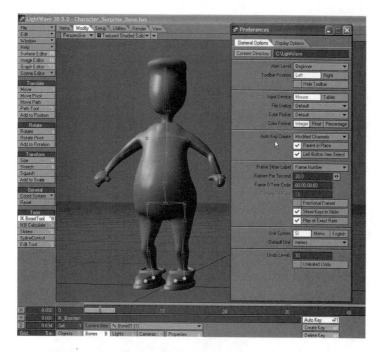

Figure 16.1   With Auto Key enabled and IK Boost active, you're ready to pose the character.

Figure 16.2   Bring the character's right arm down to his side by dragging the hand.

Figure 16.3 Drop the character's left arm down by pulling his hand and elbow if needed.

8. Next, how about making him slouch a bit? Grab and drag the IK control right in the middle of his belly, as shown in Figure 16.4. Just drag it down on the Y-axis slightly to squish the character down a bit.

Figure 16.4 Drag the IK handle in the center of the character at his belly so that he slouches a bit.

9. At the top of the character's head, click and drag to droop his cranium. Also try pulling one of the arms forward slightly as well. Figure 16.5 shows the change.

Figure 16.5   Drop the character's head down and perhaps move an arm forward slightly.

Tip

Remember to always watch your changes from all views. When you make a change to a character's position in a side view, such as the Left or Right view, be sure to check it in the front. Often, one change leads to problems in other areas, so keep an eye out.

10. Last, for frame 0, reposition the character's legs so they're not so even. Figure 16.6 shows the setup.

Because Auto Key was on, all your position changes have been recorded. And while it didn't take you very long to set them up, wouldn't it be a pain to find out you forgot to keyframe? Here, using the Auto Key is a must. It enables you to concentrate on your work without the hassle of remembering to create a key-frame. Everything you've done is now a new position for the selected items at frame 0.

11. Here's a cool trick. With Auto Key still on and IK Boost enabled (it should be unless you turned it off) move the timeline to frame 4. Press the Enter key or click Create Key at the bottom of Layout. You'll see a small mark appear in the timeline at frame 4, and your bone change should highlight. You just created a keyframe for the bones in their current position (from frame 0) at frame 4. Figure 16.7 shows the view.

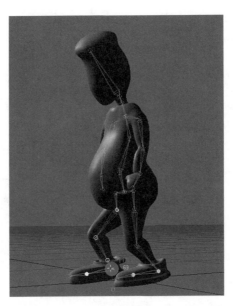

Figure 16.6 A slight change to the character's leg position completes the first frame setup.

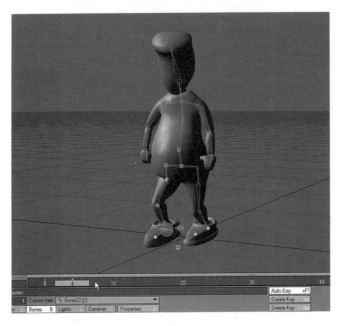

Figure 16.7 Creating a keyframe at frame 4 with IK Boost and Auto Key enabled automatically creates keyframes for the selected IK chain.

12. Creating a keyframe for the IK chains at frame 4 simply lets the character sit for four frames before moving to his next pose. Go to frame 8 and pull the head back, as in Figure 16.8.

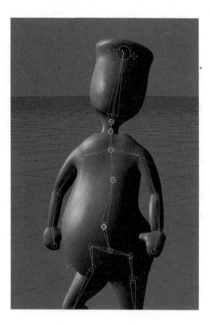

Figure 16.8 At frame 8, move the character's head back.

Tip

Take a close look at the area in front of the head when you move it back at frame 8. You'll see a string of dots! This is a new feature in LightWave 8 that shows your inbetweens from previous keyframes, similar to an onion skinning effect that traditional animators rely on. This can really help you keep track of your motions and timing.

13. Open the arms wide. Don't make them perfectly even, but rather have one higher than the other and one back slightly more, as in Figure 16.9. Picture the character being surprised and pose him accordingly.

Tip

Many animators have a mirror at their desk. No, it's not to see how lovely they look, but rather to mimic motions. Stand up in front of a mirror and slouch a bit. Find yourself in a relaxed pose, and then be surprised! How do you react? What do your arms do? Another idea is to videotape yourself as reference and then re-create those positions on your characters in LightWave.

Figure 16.9   Open the character's arms, but don't make them perfectly even. Picture the character being surprised!

14. Pull the character's body up and back a bit so that he stands straighter. You might even want to bend him backward as well, but just a little bit. Figure 16.10 shows the position.

Figure 16.10   Bend the character back slightly and stand him up more to add to his surprise.

15. Save the scene. Now, drag the timeline slider back and forth to see how your motions look. You might notice that the character itself, as a whole, moves. Select the character and delete the keyframes for it at frame 4 and 8. The character right now should have only one keyframe at 0. Only the bones should have multiple keyframes because they are the items moving the character.

Tip

If you seem to be clicking Create Key or Delete Key at times and nothing happens, there's a reason. Make sure that you have some sort of translate mode active, such as Move. Often, when you have other tools active in Layout such as the IK Boost Tool, Delete Key does not work, obviously. The IK Boost Tool is not something you set or delete keys with, so LightWave responds accordingly. This is just something to keep in mind when character animating or really when doing anything else in Layout.

16. If the character's feet slide after removing the keyframes of the full object, simply select the IK control of the heel of each foot and reposition the keyframes at the necessary points in time.

17. At frame 11, move the left hand carefully up to the mouth. It's OK to select the individual bone of the hand and rotate it. You can do this directly on the IK Boost values. (Be sure to view the IK Boost video from Chapter 15 on this book's DVD.) Move the left hand up to the character's mouth as if he were gasping. Bring the right arm in slightly, as in Figure 16.11.

Figure 16.11   The next pose you should create is the gasp. This is where the character brings his hand up and covers his mouth.

18. Go a few frames further in the timeline to frame 15. Now, pull the right arm in a bit, as if the character is frightened. Figure 16.12 shows the change.

Figure 16.12 Bring the character's right arm in to show that the character is frightened.

19. Drag through the timeline again, and you'll see the character in motion. Feel free to hit the play button in Layout as well.

As you can see, after a full IK setup and bone rig has been applied to the character, you can really have a lot of fun posing it. This is one reason pose-to-pose animation works so well. It's clean, neat, and easy yet still enables you to change inbetween keyframes for added variation to your animation. This exercise shows you that with Auto Key enabled, you can quickly set up character animation.

But what if you wanted to edit these frames? What's the best way? How do you prevent the frames from appearing identical? That is, how would you add a little more impact and variation to each keyframe? Sure, you could go to the Graph Editor and vary each bone channel value, but with 28 bones in this character and already a few keyframes, that might take just a little bit too long. Enter the Dope Sheet.

Exercise 16.2 Editing in the Dope Sheet

The Dope Sheet is a fantastic tool that LightWave has desperately needed for years. LightWave 8 finally saw the inclusion of not just the Dope Sheet, but the powerful Scene Editor as well. This next exercise guides you through the new Scene Editor, showing how to apply one setting to multiple bones at once and how to change your keyframes.

1. Continuing on from the previous exercise, go to the Scene Editor drop-down list at the top left of LightWave Layout. Click Open to open a single instance of the new Scene Editor.

Tip

LightWave 8 enables you to have multiple instances of the new Scene Editor open. To do so, just click open from the Scene Editor drop-down list each time you want to create a new instance. Or, if you close the Scene Editor and want to get back to it, you'll find it in the list as well.

When you look at the Scene Editor, you can see the keyframes for your items on the right side under the Dope Sheet tab, as shown in Figure 16.13.

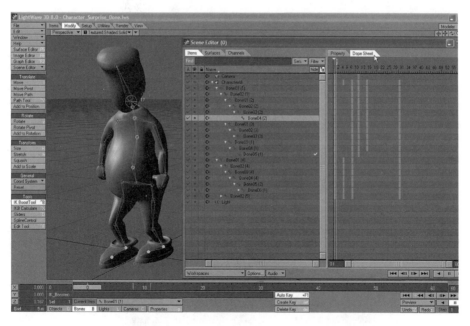

Figure 16.13 The Dope Sheet in LightWave 8 enables you to control the keyframes for all your motions.

2. You can quickly adjust the timing of all your keyframes in the Dope Sheet. From the bottom-right corner in the Dope Sheet window, click and drag up and over all the keyframes. This selects all of them, as in Figure 16.14.

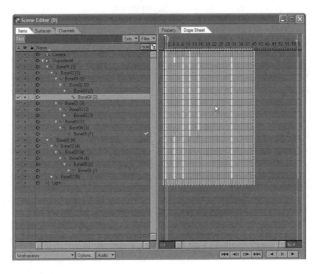

Figure 16.14 You can click and drag a region in the Dope Sheet to select the keyframes you want to edit.

3. Click and drag to the right. You'll see all your keyframes moved over! You've just retimed your animation. Figure 16.15 shows the change.

Figure 16.15 When a range of keyframes is selected, you can drag them to change the timing of your character.

In most cases, you'll edit more specific motions, perhaps on an arm or hand. The animation you set up in Exercise 16.1 worked well by creating general keyframes every three or four frames. This is great in most cases, but sometimes, you'll want a couple of frames to be delayed, perhaps for a head or eye or arm. You can easily change that item's timing in the Dope Sheet.

4. Using the Dope Sheet, you can easily view all your bones' motions, which is good to do because you can compare one keyframe to another and make any changes you like. Open the Scene Editor up wide and make sure you have the Items tab selected on the left and the Property tab selected on the right. Figure 16.16 shows the view.

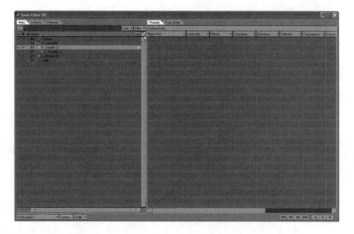

Figure 16.16 Open up the Scene Editor to be able to see all your object's bones.

5. You might think to start expanding the object's hierarchy by clicking the small white triangle for it at the left side of the Scene Editor. Although that works for simple two-boned objects, a character with 28 bones could take you some time. At the top middle of the panel, there is a tiny square button (atop the center divider). Click this, and your object's hierarchy expands automatically, as in Figure 16.17.

6. When you select a bone within the character, a small check mark appears in the Scene Editor. Unless you've specifically named objects, this is how you can identify the appropriate bone you want to edit. On the right side under the Property tab, you can click the top header bar to reveal just about all aspects of your settings, such as Bone Weight Map. Figure 16.18 shows all the bones in the character with all the associated weight maps.

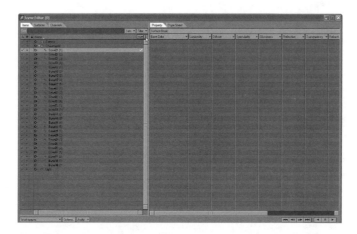

Figure 16.17   It's easy to expand the hierarchy of a character in the Scene Editor by clicking the tiny button that lives at the top of the center divider.

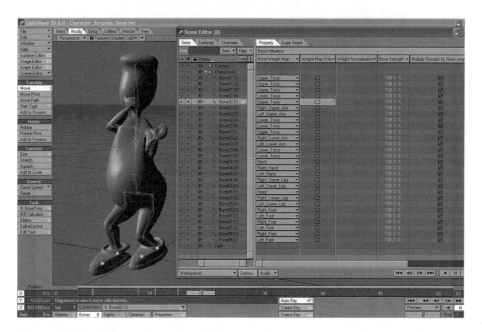

Figure 16.18   Using the Scene Editor's Property options, you can see all aspects of your character's bones, such as weight maps.

7. Click the Dope Sheet tab at the top of the Scene Editor, and for the selected chest bone, click and drag over the keyframes. Then, click and drag to the right just one frame. Figure 16.19 shows the change.

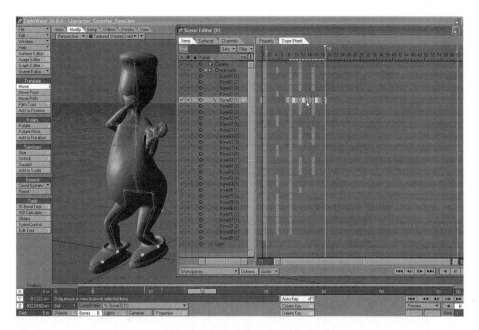

Figure 16.19   You can quickly edit and change motions for bones for your characters with the Scene Editor's Dope Sheet.

What you've just done is quickly and easily change three keyframes by one frame. Doing this in Layout directly would require you to select the bone, go to the first keyframe you want to change, re-create the keyframe one frame up, and then delete the previous keyframe. From there, you'd have to do this two more times. It would take six steps in all to do in Layout. In the Dope Sheet, it was a quick two-step process. What's more, you got a visual blueprint of your keyframes and how they relate to the keyframes of the other bones. This added frame gives more variation to the movement of the character's upper body. You can click the play button directly in the Dope Sheet at the bottom right to see the playback in Layout.

From here, go ahead and adjust keyframes and see how they look. Experiment and play around with the Dope Sheet to see how useful it can be for character animation.

Next, move on to create one more move with the character created earlier in this book.

More Animation Practice

At this point, you've modeled, and set up bones, Skelegons, weight maps, and inverse kinematics. You've applied all these tools to a character and have even created a quick pose-to-pose animation. The pose-to-pose animation you created was simple but effective. At one frame, the character is in one position, a few frames later, he's at another, and so on. But sometimes, pose-to-pose animation doesn't always fit. Sometimes, you need to just create the motions a few frames at a time. This exercise takes the TV Guy character from Chapter 15 and makes him move across the screen. Later, on your own, you can add a rendered animation to his screen or video that you've made. Why? Well, why not?!

Exercise 16.3   An Animated Television

1. Open the TVGuy_IKBoost scene from the Chapter 15 folder on this book's DVD. Figure 16.20 shows the scene loaded.

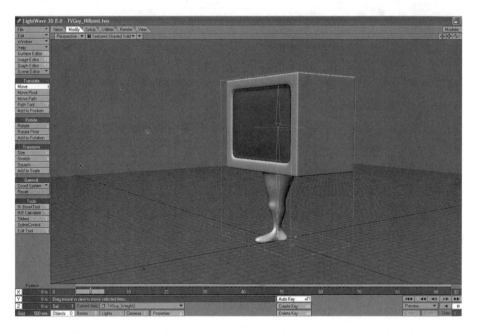

Figure 16.20   The TVGuy_IKBoost scene loaded into Layout. Here, you can have hours of fun and fool your friends! OK, maybe not—but it's a fun little scene to get you working with animated characters.

2. Go to a side view such as Left or Right, and move the character back about 20 m on the Z-axis for frame 0, as shown in Figure 16.21. Note that Auto Key is active.

Figure 16.21 Position the character about 20 m back on the Z-axis for its starting frame.

3. Drag the timeline slider to frame 90 and move the character about -20 m on the Z-axis, opposite of its starting point. This will be the character's ending point. Figure 16.22 shows the position.

Figure 16.22 Move the character to -20 m or so on the Z-axis at frame 90 for the ending frame.

4. Go to frame 45 and move the character to the center at the 0 point on the Z-axis.

5. Create a keyframe at frame 45. It will look as if the character moved to a keyframe there already, but really it's just the point between frame 0 and 90.

6. Halfway between frame 0 and 45 is roughly 22. Drag the timeline slider to 22 and create a character there for it.

7. Go to frame 11 and create a keyframe for the TVGuy. Move him up on the Y-Axis about 3 m, as shown in Figure 16.23.

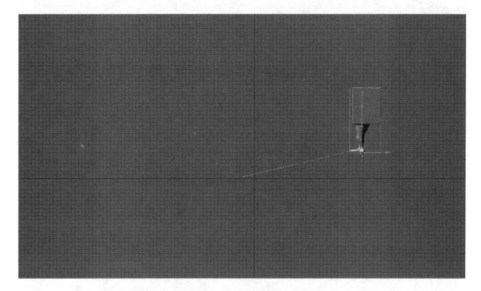

Figure 16.23   The character has evenly placed keyframes at 11 and 22, between frames 0 and 45. At frame 11, however, the character is 3 m up on the Y-axis.

8. Also at frame 45, move the character up on the Y-axis 3 m.

9. Go to frame 67 and bring the character back down to 0 on the Y-axis.

10. At frame 80, bring him back up 3 m on the Y-axis.

11. Save the scene.

By creating the initial keyframes at the beginning and end, you've created a linear motion path for the character on the Z-axis. Creating the inbetween frames was easy because all you really needed to do was change the position of the character on the Y-axis. The computer's "inbetweening" power helped do the rest.

If it's not already obvious at this point, you're making the TV Guy hop across the view. You've now set up the basic motions, so it's just a matter of adjusting the bones for deformation.

12. Go to frame 0. From the Modify tab, make sure the IK Boost Tool is on. Then, click the base of the top bone of the character (make sure Bone X-Ray mode is on from the viewport styles at the top of the interface) and drag it forward to tip the head. Also, grab the knee of the character and bend it, as in Figure 16.24.

Figure 16.24   Bend the head and knee of the TV Guy to get him ready to jump!

13. Go to frame 11 and arch the character back. Straighten out his leg and bend the TV screen back, as in Figure 16.25.

Figure 16.25   At frame 11, when the character is at his jumping high point, arch the object back and straighten the leg.

14. You want him to hold this position slightly until just before he hits the ground, so go to frame 19 and, making sure the IK Boost Tool is still active, create a keyframe. This creates a keyframe for the object's hierarchy.

15. Frame 22 is where the character lands, which is the keyframe you set up earlier. Bend the TV Guy's head forward and bend his leg. Level out the foot and play the animation. Figure 16.26 shows the landing.

Figure 16.26 At frame 22, the character lands hard.

16. At frame 45, when the character is up in the air again, he'll arch and stretch as he did at frame 11. Figure 16.27 shows the frame.

Figure 16.27 At frame 45, the character jumps and arches as it did at frame 11.

17. At this point, you can repeat the process for the remainder of the keyframes. Remember to save the scene.

This exercise shows how a combination of moving the character and its IK chains can result in an animated, moving character. The point of these steps was not to produce the ultimate jumping one-legged television, but rather to show you how keyframing, motion, and inbetweening come into play with an object and inverse kinematics. Now there are many ways this animation can be perfected, specifically before the take off and landing. Here are a few pointers to try on your own:

- Before a character jumps, it needs anticipation. Have the character bend forward and "wind up" before it takes off.

- Just before the character leaps from the ground, it should arch its back to gain momentum. Then, it should spring forward over a couple of frames as it leaps into the air.

- As you saw for frame 11 in the previous exercise, when the character is in the air, it should be arching its back.

- Setting a keyframe for a landing position should include having the character bend forward and crunch down upon impact, similarly to the starting frame. However, setting this frame and only the mid-air frame doesn't produce the best results. The computer interpolates between the mid-air arch and the crouch of the landing position. So, you need to create a keyframe just one or two frames before the character lands that holds a variation of the arched position. Then, at the landing frame, the character will have a stronger impact.

- After landing, the character should stay there for a few frames to steady himself before he leaps again. In the exercise, he continually jumps, which is fine. But for more realism, about two more frames should be added.

- When the character is in mid-air, it's a good idea to move his bones to bend the TV screen. This adds more variation to the animation.

Character animation is something that you can work at day in and day out. It requires much time and patience. There is so much to it that we can only skim the surface within these pages and give you the basics. However, thanks to the DVD included with this book, you'll find a video tutorial showing another character animation. Additionally, you'll learn about making characters talk. Both of these videos can be found in the Chapter 16 folder on this book's DVD, under the 3DGarageVideos folder.

Talking Characters

Moving characters should always be your main focus when it comes to character animation. The movement, the timing, and the subtle changes in weight all result in bringing a character to life, be it a simple tin can or a monstrous dragon. Yet, as you know, there is more to many characters, such as talking.

LightWave gives you the ability to make your characters talk through a feature called Endomorphs and Morph Mixer. To best demonstrate this technique, a complete video has been provided for you on this book's DVD. Here's a rundown of what you'll learn:

- Endomorphs are created in Modeler. They are recorded sets of data of an object's selected points. For example, you can select the points of the lips of character, move them into the shape of an A sound, and tell LightWave to save that position—creating an Endomorph. You do this for the necessary vowel sounds or phonetic shapes you need.

- Endomorphs are saved with an object. The data is recorded when you save your object and can be edited later, anytime you need.

- LightWave Layout enables you to bring in sound, which appears in the timeline. You can scrub through the timeline to hear the audio, which gives you a much better sense of timing to animate your character's speaking and facial expressions.

- To animate a character talking or facial expressions, you use LightWave 8's Morph Mixer, as pictured in Figure 16.28. The Morph Mixer is a displacement plug-in. It reads the Endomorph data you create in Modeler, and over time, you can set keyframes for these values. The Morph Mixer provides sliders for each Endomorph you create, making it very easy to animate. You get real-time feedback directly from Layout.

Figure 16.28   The Morph Mixer in Layout is where you can animate your character's facial expressions and more.

Be sure to view the Endomorph video and Morph Mixer video on the book's DVD for tutorials on using these features.

The Next Step

The next step for you is to practice. Sure, we've said it before, but it's truer with character animation than anything else. This chapter has shown you the power LightWave provides when it comes to animated characters. Even though you only animated a television and simple blobby character, the principles and techniques shown here apply to anything you can think of, from flying bats to animals, animated credit cards, and of course, 3D humans. The style of the animation you want to create is totally up to you. The pose-to-pose method works well for many types of animations, while good old-fashioned manual frame-by-frame creation works well, too. There is no set rule for what constitutes a proper working method. This is completely up to you, and the bottom line you need to remember is that it's the end product that matters.

Sure, there are ways to speed up your workflow and ways to enhance your user experience. No one wants to work in a program with poor tools and slow feedback. The point is that the final output is what matters most. You have the power to create anything you want. And when it comes to character animation, you can evoke emotions from nothing! Think about it. You can take some polygons, add some color and texture, and in a matter of hours, you can create fear, sadness, or excitement!

Hopefully, this chapter piqued your interest in character animation and answered your questions about it. Be sure to view the videos on rigging, weighting, and animation on this book's DVD—there's a lot more there to help you refine your learning. Now, turn the page and learn about LightWave's killer particle system.

Chapter 17

Particle Dynamics

People often confuse the term particle with animations involving small dots or dust. Although you can create animated dust with particles in LightWave, you can do much more! Particle animation is a very cool aspect of LightWave 8. Particles (in Layout only) can be used for many types of animations, from simple sparks to wisps of smoke, fire, falling snowflakes, or even swarming bees. Add to the particle effects the dynamic power available in this release, and these two features alone are worth the price of your software. But more than their value, these tools give you control and flexibility over the types of images and animations you can create. That, my friends, is what makes LightWave great!

This chapter takes you into the world of particle animation in LightWave. You start with the basics so that you can familiarize yourself with how the PFX controls integrate directly in Layout. From there, you apply surfacing to particles using HyperVoxels to create wispy smoke, fire, and water. Then you go further to learn how you can apply dynamics to the particles, such as wind and collisions. In this chapter, you learn how to:

- Work with particles in LightWave 8
- Create surfaces to particles using HyperVoxels
- Use dynamics to change particle motions

Particles In LightWave

Animators at one point or another want to create smoke or fire. You've probably heard the term "particles" a lot when watching "behind the scenes" or "making of" shows. Animators have been using particles for years to set up a wide range of dynamic animations, from water to smoke to swarming objects and more. Read on to quickly create your own particles in LightWave. It's easier than you think!

Creating a Basic Motion Particle Scene

For some reason, people tend to think you need to run out and buy the expensive standalone particle creation tools to get decent particle animation. Although those tools have their benefits, you'll see from this project that you can achieve exceptional particle animation directly in Layout. The particle engine in LightWave 8 is robust and fast, as you'll see shortly.

In this project, you don't create anything with the particles; you merely apply them to a scene to see how you can interactively adjust parameters for instant feedback.

Using Emitters

The first thing you should know about particles is that for particles to "live" in a scene, they need an emitter. Think of the emitter as a faucet where your particles spill out. The various controls within the particle control panel enable you to adjust how the particles come out, how many, how quickly, and so on. An emitter can also be an object, though, such as a ghostly figure drifting through the air, emitting particles that have HyperVoxels applied as a smoke trail. No strict rule exists to using an object as an emitter instead of a standard particle emitter—the task at hand usually determines your choice.

Important

HyperVoxels are a volumetric rendering tool within LightWave 8. They enable you to add smoke-like surfaces to particles, as well as more solid forms for things like water and fluids. HyperVoxels apply to points of an object or particles.

Exercise 17.1   Creating a Particle Emitter

1. Open LightWave Layout.

   For this scene, you need nothing more than Layout.

2. From the Items tab under the Add category, click the Dynamic Obj button and choose Particle, as in Figure 17.1. When the Add Particle Emitter panel appears, you can change the name or simply leave the default name, "Emitter" (See Figure 17.2).

Important

When the Add Particle Emitter panel appears, you can change the name. You can also tell LightWave to change the Emitter Type. It defaults to HV Emitter for HyperVoxels, but you can change the Emitter Type to Partigon. A HV Emitter looks and acts the same way in Layout as a Partigon Emitter. So what's the difference? Good question! A HV Emitter generates points only. This means they don't appear in the render unless HyperVoxels is applied—hence, the name HV Emitter. A Partigon Emitter, on the other hand, generates single point polygons. These particles will render without HyperVoxels. You would use them to create, say, a fine mist spray, stars, or perhaps added particle debris from an explosion.

Figure 17.1   You add a particle emitter from the Add category of the Items tab, just as you would with an object, light, or camera.

Figure 17.2   After an emitter is added, you can apply a name to it and tell LightWave to make it an HV Emitter or a Partigon Emitter.

3. After the emitter is added, you'll see an outlined box in the Layout view, and the FX_Emitter panel pops up, as in Figure 17.3. In the timeline at the lower right of the interface, set the last frame of the animation to 200.

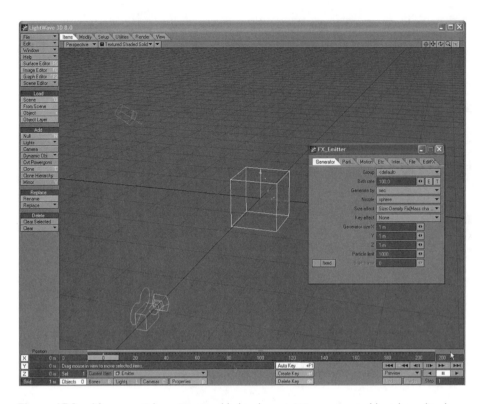

Figure 17.3 After a particle emitter is added to Layout, it is represented by a bounding box, and the FX_Emitter panel appears.

4. Make sure Auto Key is enabled; click on the button beneath the timeline if it's not.

Before you move on, press the o key to open the General Options tab within the Preferences panel. Make sure that for the next Auto Key Create, the selector is set to Modified Channels. The Auto Key button directly on the Layout interface acts as a remote control to turn Auto Key Create Modified Channels on or off. Close the options panel.

5. Back in Layout, make sure the emitter is selected. Press t for Move.

6. Press the play button and move the emitter around in Layout. Look at that—instant particles (Figure 17.4)!

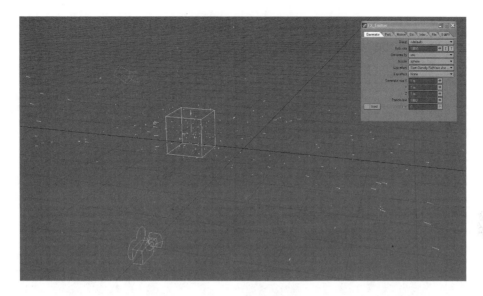

Figure 17.4   By using Auto Key with Auto Key Create set to Modified Channels, your motions can be recorded in real time in Layout. Moving the particle emitter around shows the spray of particles.

You can see that just by moving an emitter around, the particles spray out. This is great for sparks, sprays from wet hair, dust, and more, but it lacks control. The particles fall out of the emitter without any rhyme or reason. In most cases, you'll want to specifically control the particles for something like a stream of smoke or a running faucet, so move on to the next exercise to learn more.

Controlling Particles

It isn't necessary to always move the particle emitter to see moving particles. The particles can move on their own in a variety of ways. This next section shows you how to create a particle stream to simulate a running faucet, which is also good for water fountains, molten lava, gooey chocolate, smoke, and more.

Exercise 17.2   Controlling Particle Flow

1. Select Clear Scene from the File menu in Layout. Then load the Faucet scene from this book's DVD. This scene is premade for you without particles. It's your job to add the streaming water.

Tip

Do you want to learn how to texture and light this faucet scene? Be sure to view the Faucet video on this book's DVD!

2. From the Items tab, add Particle Emitter as you did in the previous exercise. Name it "water" when the Add Particle Emitter panel appears.

3. You'll notice that the particle emitter (named "water") is quite large! You need to scale it down to fit the faucet. You'll do this almost every time you create an emitter to match an object. Figure 17.5 shows the scene from Perspective view where you can see the extra-large emitter. It is large because its default size is 1 m, and the objects in the scene are smaller than that.

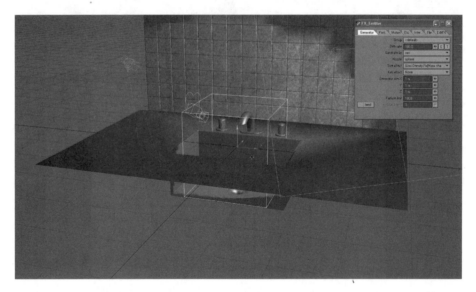

Figure 17.5   Adding a particle emitter to the scene gets you started, but first, you'll need to scale it down to fit the faucet.

4. The FX_Emitter panel is the control center for your particle emitter. Move it off to one side of the Layout interface to see the actual emitter in the scene (as in Figure 17.5). Also, set the last frame of the animation to 300.

5. In the Generator tab of the FX_Emitter panel, change Generator size to 35 mm for the X, Y, and Z. Then move it into position under the faucet nozzle, as shown in Figure 17.6. Note that Auto Key should be on, and you should be working at frame 0.

Figure 17.6   Scale the emitter to match the size of the faucet, and position it in place under the nozzle.

Tip

Changing the Generator Size in the FX_Emitter panel tells the emitter to be larger or smaller at the point where particles emerge. Changing the actual size of the emitter in Layout scales the emitter itself, not the area of particle generation.

Tip

Should you accidentally close the FX_Emitter panel, don't worry! There's a great new location for it in LightWave 8. Select the emitter item in Layout and press the p key for Object Properties. In the panel that appears, you'll see a tab labeled Dynamics. Click that, and in the list in the middle of the panel, you'll see the FX_Emitter listing. Select this listing, and you'll see all the controls, as in Figure 17.7.

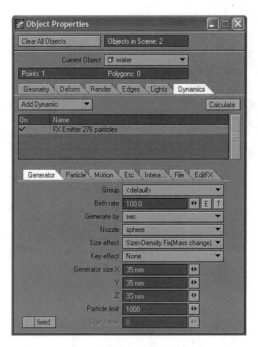

Figure 17.7 In case you accidentally (or on purpose) close the FX_Emitter control panel, you can find the panel again under the Dynamics tab within the Object Properties panel.

6. In the FX_Emitter panel, click the Motion tab and bring the Vector Y value to negative 1, as in Figure 17.8. Press the play button in Layout, and you'll see the particles pour out of the faucet.

   You can see that by simply adjusting the value, the particles update in Layout. Note that you can click and drag the arrow buttons to the right of a value for true interactivity. Play around with the Vector values for X and Z to see how the particles are affected.

7. Now that the particles are streaming out of the faucet, move the camera around for a better view of the bottom of the sink. Right now, the particles are going through the bottom of the sink. Make sure you can see them—shortly, you'll make them splash.

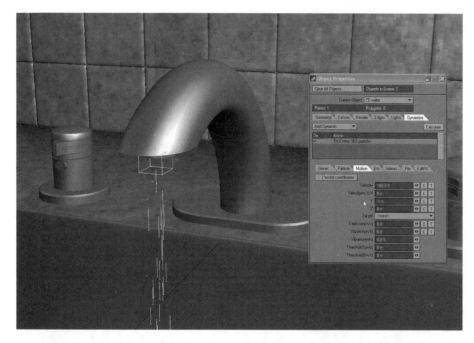

Figure 17.8   Changing the Vector value for the Y-axis dumps the particles out of the faucet.

8. Bring the Explosion value to .3, and you'll see the particles spray outward, as in Figure 17.9.

9. Now try adding a little Vibration. Set the value to .3 or .5 and watch the particles freak out. They sort of scatter. Note that this is the first Vibration setting in meters per second (m/s) under the Explosion setting.

Important

Remember that you can play the animation and make value changes to your particles at the same time. This is the best way to set up particle animations because you can see exactly what your changes are affecting.

The second Vibration setting is a minimum percentage that you can apply as well.

Figure 17.9 Changing the Explosion value makes your particles spray outward.

10. Up at the top of the Motion tab, set the Velocity to 65%. This causes the particles move a little slower, like water flowing out of a faucet! Figure 17.10 shows the settings.

If you watch the particles flow, they seem to be moving evenly at first, but by only setting a Velocity on the Y-axis, you're sort of pushing the particles out of the faucet. Look closely at the particles after they've come out; they seem to slow down. This is because there's nothing pulling them, like gravity.

11. Click over to the Etc tab. Set the Y value for Gravity to -3. You're using a negative value because you want the particles to be pulled downward on the Y-axis after they are emitted.

Tip

True gravity is -9.8 meters per second squared.

Figure 17.10   Changing the Velocity setting can speed up or slow down your particle stream.

12. Click over to the Particle tab and set the Life time value to 0. If you left this at 60, the particles would only last 60 frames (2 seconds). But by setting it to 0, you're telling the particles to flow infinitely.

If you were to set a value for the Life time to something like 60 or 90, the particles would die out exactly at that frame. You can set a variation by entering, say, 20 in the + - field.

13. Finally, save your scene.

Your LightWave 3D manual gives a good description of the numerous settings and values available to you in the Particle FX_Emitter panel. You should reference this as you work through the tools. For now, these first two exercises introduced you to particle emitters and the controls available to them. However, you can do much more with this system, so read on.

Introducing Particle Collisions

Now that your particles are in place and flowing nicely, you might have noticed that they just fall right through the sink. Either you've got some serious plumbing problems, or you haven't told the particles to have collisions. And, if you're like most 3D artists, you want to see exactly how something is done with visual effects. Sure, it's good to know the theory and value settings for various mathematical properties, but often the best learning method is by experience. This next exercise takes the basic emitter example discussed in the previous exercise and expands on it by changing its particle flow with collisions.

Exercise 17.3   Interactive Particles

1. Use the same scene from the previous exercise or load the Flowing Particles scene from this book's DVD.

2. Select the faucets object and press the p key to open the Object Properties panel. Then click over to the Dynamics tab.

3. From the Add Dynamic drop-down list, choose Collision, as in Figure 17.11. You can add dynamics to any object this way.

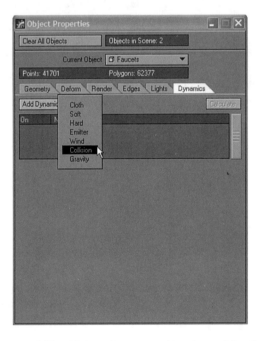

Figure 17.11   You can quickly add dynamics to any object by applying them from the Object Properties panel.

4. From the Dynamics tab within the Object Properties panel, select the Collision dynamic after it's been added. You'll see the appropriate controls appear within the panel.

5. Change your viewport to a Right (side) view by pressing 3 on your keyboard. Also, change the viewport render style to Wireframe so you can see the particles in the sink. Move the Properties panel over to one side of the interface and adjust the view to see the particles coming out of the faucet, as in Figure 17.12.

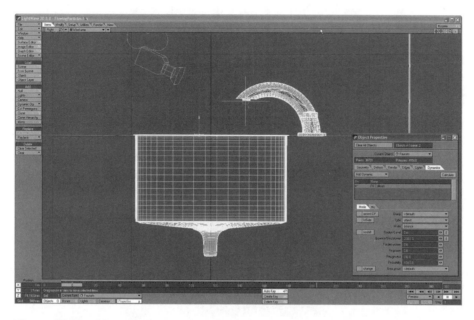

Figure 17.12   After your faucets object has had a collision dynamic added, change your view to a Right (side) view and switch to wireframe mode.

6. Press the play button beneath the timeline, and you'll see the particles flow. You might also notice that they flow right down through the sink object! Even though you have added a collision dynamic to the faucets object (which includes the sink), you still need to set up some parameters.

7. Make sure that in the FX_Collision dynamic properties you set the Type to Object. This tells LightWave to look at the object for collision, rather than a box or sphere. If you had, say, a flat ground surface, you could choose Plane for the object type.

8. Switch to the Water emitter object. Do this by changing the Current Object at the top of the Object Properties panel. You should then see the FX_Emitter dynamic listing. Select it, and the controls appear.

9. Click to the Interaction tab and make sure the Interaction setting is set to Bounce. Then click the Calculate button within the panel. This might take a few seconds, so be patient.

10. You should see your particles flow out of the faucet, hit the sink, and bounce. However, you might notice that some of the particles are bouncing and some are going right through, as in Figure 17.13.

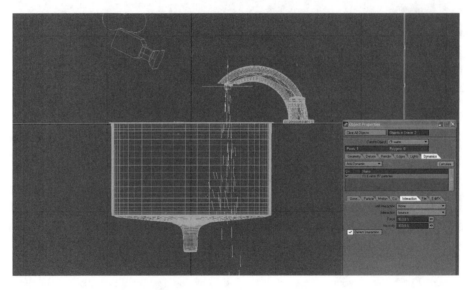

Figure 17.13 Some of the flowing, interacting particles bounce, but some particles don't react as they should.

11. Click over to the Etc tab for the water particle emitter. Change the Gravity setting from -3.0 to -1.0. Calculate again, and you'll see all your particles contained within the sink, as in Figure 17.14.

12. Now that the particles are contained, they are bouncing a bit too much. Is that water coming out of the faucet, or rubber? Select the faucets object and select the Collision dynamic to access its controls. Then change the Bounce/Bind Power from 200% to about 90%. Press the calculate button again and see what happens. The particles should hit the sink without bouncing around like a flea circus!

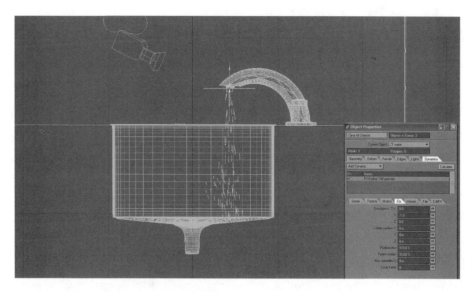

Figure 17.14   Lessening the Gravity applied to the particle emitter helps keep the particles in the sink, where they should be.

13. Switch back to a Perspective view and change your viewport render style to Front Face Wireframe mode. Play the animation and watch the particles. Not only do they not bounce around in a crazy way, they also drop and move down to the drain! Figure 17.15 shows the action.

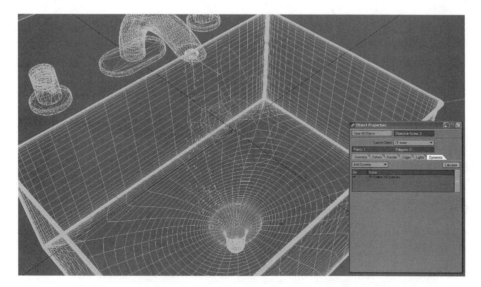

Figure 17.15   After the amount of bounce is decreased, the particles hit the collision surface (the sink) and slide down the drain.

> **Tip**
>
> Particles can be hard to see in Layout. So when playing back an animation in Layout, select the particles first because they'll be easier to see. Also be sure to set the Life time to 0 in the Particle tab of the FX_Emitter controls. This will make your particles run infinitely.

As you've seen in these first three exercises, making particles interact and applying dynamics is not very difficult. You've easily added an emitter, positioned it to an object, scaled it, and made particles flow. You then made those particles interact with an object by adding a collision dynamic. You're on your way to making a complete scene, except there's one thing missing—surfacing the particles!

Surfacing the Particles

As you can see, you can exert a ton of control over your particles using things like gravity and collision dynamics. You can take the water particles a step further by setting up a hand object as an additional collision object and sticking it under the particles! You can interactively change the parameters of the particle emitter with more vibration and faster velocity for cooler effects. For now, these particles are cool, but what good are they?! If you render a frame, you'll see nothing but the sink and faucet. That's because you created an HV Emitter earlier in the chapter, meaning you must apply HyperVoxels to them to be visible.

Another type of emitter you could add is a Partigon emitter. It works similarly to an HV Emitter, except that it generates single point polygons that will show during a render. These are great for tiny sparks, water sprays, or even stars.

Three surfacing options are available for HyperVoxels: Surface mode, for solid blobby objects, Volume mode, for 3D clouds and smoke, and Sprite mode. A sprite is a "slice" of a volume HyperVoxel. It's just a portion of it that renders much faster than volume-type HyperVoxels. These are fast, great for smoke effects, easy to set up, and always visible in Layout!

Exercise 17.4   Surfacing Particles for Water

1. With the scene loaded from the previous exercise (or the Flowing Particles scene from this book's DVD), select the Volumetrics and Fog Options from the Window drop-down menu at the top left of the Layout interface. You can also press Ctrl+F6. This takes you to the Volumetrics tab of the Effects panel, as shown in Figure 17.16.

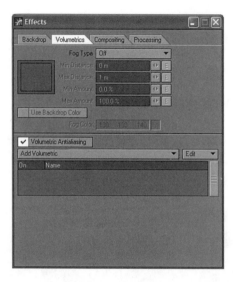

Figure 17.16   Pressing Ctrl+F6 takes you to the Volumetrics tab of the Effects panel, where you can access the HyperVoxels volumetric control.

  2. From the Add Volumetric drop-down list, select HyperVoxels. Double-click the name in the listing when loaded. The HyperVoxels panel opens.

  3. You'll see the name HV_Emitter (named "water") ghosted in the Object Name list, as in Figure 17.17.

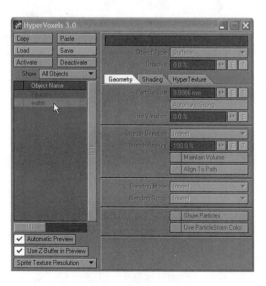

Figure 17.17   As soon as you load up HyperVoxels, your particle emitter is visible in the Object Name list but inactive.

4. Either double-click the water listing in the Object Name list or select it once and click Activate. These both do the same thing—they activate HyperVoxels for the particle emitter.

5. The panel becomes active, and an automatic particle size is already in place. Now, the best way to begin setting up smoke for these particles is to use VIPER. So, go to the Render menu tab at the top of Layout and then click the VIPER button on the left of the interface. Because you're in HyperVoxels, VIPER shows your particles with the effect applied, as in Figure 17.18. You might need to press the Render button directly in the VIPER window to see your particles.

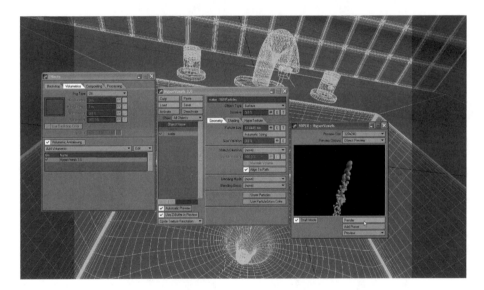

Figure 17.18   VIPER is the only way to go for setting up HyperVoxels interactively on your particles.

 Important

Be sure to move your timeline in Layout so that some particles have been emitted; otherwise, you won't see them at all in the VIPER window!

6. In the VIPER window, you'll see some white blobs. By default, HyperVoxels uses Surface as the Object Type. This is great for lava, blood, shaving cream, and things of that nature. It's also great for water. If you change the Object Type to Sprite, you can make great-looking smoke. If you change it to Volume, you can produce puffy clouds. For now, keep the Object Type set to Surface.

Tip

Learn how to use LightWave 8 Particles to make smoke by watching the video included on this book's DVD.

Tip

When using VIPER, you'll see your particles from the Camera view, not the current view, which is Perspective. You can set your Camera view up to match the Perspective view if you like for a full VIPER display.

7. Now all you need to do is tweak the settings. In the HyperVoxels panel, click the Show Particles button found at the bottom of the panel within the Geometry tab. Move the HyperVoxels panel and VIPER aside to see the Layout. Your Hypervoxel sprites are now visible in Layout (see Figure 17.19).

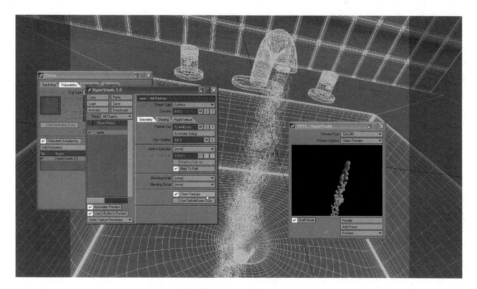

Figure 17.19   Turning on Show Particles in the HyperVoxels panel shows your HyperVoxel surface representation in Layout.

8. Back in the HyperVoxels panel, click and drag the arrow for Particle Size. Set the particles to 35 mm.

9. Set Size Variation to 180% to randomize the size of the Sprite particles a bit. Note that although the slider for Size Variation stops at 500%, you can manually enter a value much higher than this for added control.

10. Set Stretch Direction to Velocity so that the particles stretch slightly based on their movement and set Stretch Amount to 185%. Make sure Align to Path is checked.

Tip

If you want to see how this setting looks, go ahead and make a preview of your particle animation directly in the VIPER window! From the Preview drop-down menu, click Make Preview. After the preview is generated, play buttons will appear. You can stop the preview generation at any time by pressing the Esc key on your keyboard.

11. Click over to the Shading tab. Set the particle color to a cool blue, about 150, 165, 220 RGB.

Just as you set up textures throughout the book using LightWave's Surface Editor, you can do the same here in the HyperVoxels panel. You can apply a texture to the Hypervoxel particles just as you would for an object's surface.

12. Set the Specularity to 90% for the wet look. Set the Glossiness to about 45%.

13. Change the Reflection to 75% and then the Diffuse to 25%. This tells the water to be mostly reflective, while only taking 25% of the scene's light. What you're doing here is relying on the reflection to surface the water.

14. Set the Transparency to 90% and Refraction to 1.33. Refraction makes the water appear thicker and distorts what you might see when looking through it, like a glass.

15. Hop on out to the Render Options panel in Layout by clicking the Render menu tab and then the Render Options button. Turn on Ray Trace Refraction. Figure 17.20 shows the panels.

16. Finally, back in the HyperVoxels panel, go to the Environment tab and make sure that Ray Tracing + Backdrop is selected for the Reflection Options. This tells the particle surface to reflect the surroundings of the scene when rendered. Also be sure to turn on Ray Trace Reflection in the Render Options panel, just as you did with Ray Trace Refraction.

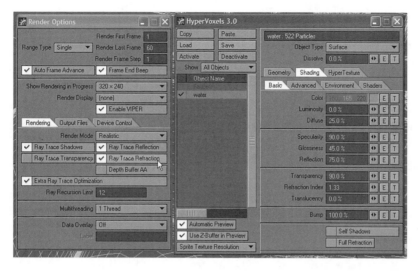

Figure 17.20   Setting the surface properties for particles using HyperVoxels is not too different from surfacing objects in the Surface Editor. Settings in this panel, such
as Refraction, are controlled globally in the Render Options panel.

What you've done here is basic, but it can also be about as complex as it gets for many types
of particle animations. Figure 17.21 shows a render from LightWave on the particle scene
you just set up. Although that sounds contradictory, with the power of LightWave's particles, in combination with Hypervoxel surfaces, added textures, and even gradients, the possibilities are endless. Endless how? Read on for another variation on these particles!

Figure 17.21   After the settings are in place, you can press F9 in Layout to render the scene
and see how the particles look.

> **Tip**
>
> You can speed up render times slightly by turning off the Volumetric Antialiasing option in the Volumetrics area of the Effects panel.

Using Images on Particles

Yes, you read that heading correctly—using images on particles. Although it sounds odd, it's actually a very cool feature for all sorts of animations—falling snow, falling leaves, bubbles, pictures of your dog—whatever!

Check this out.

Exercise 17.5   Using Images on Particles

1. With the same scene loaded from the previous exercise, open the Image Editor. Load the Coin.tga image from this book's DVD, as shown in Figure 17.22.

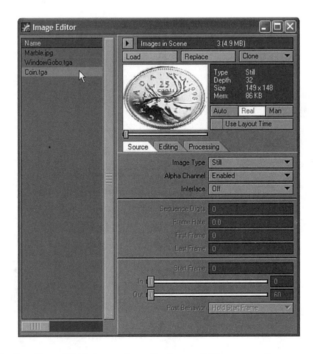

Figure 17.22   Loading a 32-bit image from the Image Editor can make your particles flow with pictures!

2. Back in the HyperVoxels panel, with the same scene loaded from the previous exercise, change Object Type to Sprite.

3. Next, click over to the Shading tab. From there, click the Clips tab.

4. Select the Coin image from the Add Clip drop-down list. Watch what happens in Layout! You'll see the bubble image applied to the particles, but they grossly overlap each other and probably are misshaped too.

5. Go back to the Geometry tab and set the Particle Size to about 16mm, the Size Variation to 0%, and the Stretch Direction to none. Figure 17.23 shows Layout with the bubbles in place.

Tip

You can also set the Sprite Texture Resolution from the bottom left of the HyperVoxels panel. Also, at the bottom of the Clips tab where you applied the clip, you can tell LightWave how to use the Alpha, set a threshold, and choose a Frame Offset.

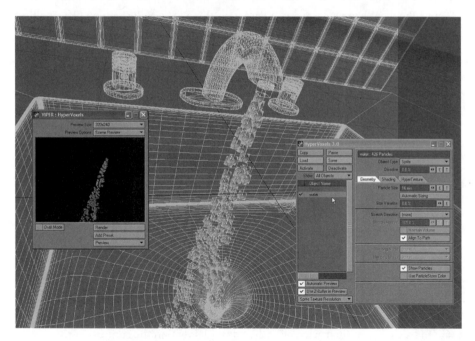

Figure 17.23   A small image is replicated and applied to every particle in the emitter using a HyperVoxel sprite and clips.

That's it! You now have a faucet that pours money! Hypervoxel sprites with clips are very cool and quite useful. As we just saw, one of the reasons they're so useful is because you can take tiny images and animate them quickly based on particles. You can see them directly in Layout, so you know what's happening with their size and color, and they always face the camera.

Of course, you can adjust the motion of the particles, perhaps by adding another wind effector at the top of the path to make the particles spread out as they reach their end. You can also change the emitter to a large, long, flat shape to emit sprite clips such as coins, bubbles, puffs of smoke, and so on. The examples here should get you started with your own particle animations. All you need to do is create a 32-bit TGA image.

Editing Particles

You can do a lot to particles within LightWave 8. As you've seen, you can push them, pull them, make them collide with other objects, and so on. They can look like water, smoke, or coins! But what happens when you have everything looking just as you like, and then some pesky particle takes on a life of its own? Read on to learn how to edit particles.

Exercise 17.6   Editing Particles

1. Load the Flowing Particles scene from this book's DVD (Chapter 17 Scenes folder).

2. Go to a Side view and make sure your view in Layout is in Wireframe mode for better visibility.

3. Select the particle emitter named "water" and press the p key to open the Properties panel.

4. Click over to the Dynamics tab within the Properties panel and select the FX_Emitter listing. Press the Calculate button in the middle of the panel.

5. After the calculation is complete, drag the timeline slider, and at about frame 80, you'll see a couple of stubborn particles escape beneath the sink, as in Figure 17.24.

6. To fix these crazy particles, click the EditFX tab within the controls of the FX_Emitter.

7. Click the edittool button, and then select one of the erroneous particles directly in Layout, as shown in Figure 17.25. When the particle is selected, you'll see a line appear—that's its motion path. You'll also see a number, which is its ID, if you will.

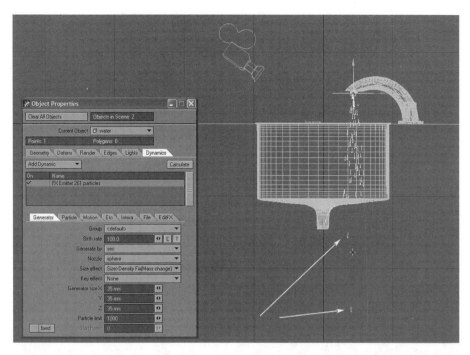

Figure 17.24 Even though the particles are calculated to collide with the sink, a few at times have a mind of their own.

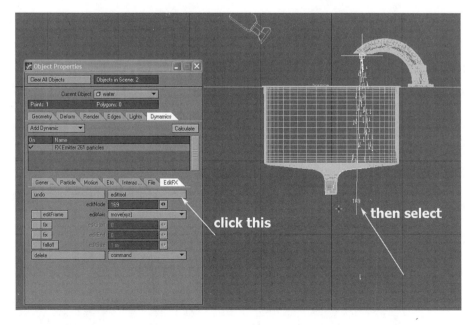

Figure 17.25 Using the edittool button in the FX_Emitter panel, you can delete isolated, single particles from the emitter.

8. When the particle is selected, click the delete button in the FX_Emitter controls. The selected particle is deleted!

9. Perform steps 7 and 8 again to remove any other particles that do not remain in the sink or ones you just don't like. Figure 17.26 shows the particles removed.

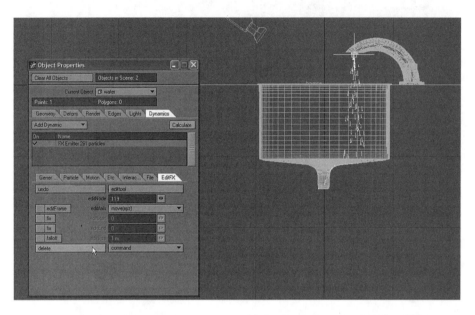

Figure 17.26   It's easy to remove two bad particles from the particle emitter within the EditFX tab.

Other things you can do within the EditFX tab include cloning a particle, copying its motion path, rotating its path, and more.

The Next Step

This chapter introduced you to some of the cooler additions to LightWave 8's arsenal. The information in these exercises can easily be applied to projects of your own and ones for your client. You'll find that particles are so fun to use, you'll be looking for projects to use them in. Be careful though—don't let your client know how easy it is! On this book's DVD, you'll find an additional tutorial showing how to use particles to create a fireball using HyperVoxels. This is great for explosions! You'll also see how to create smoke. Check out the videos when you can. For now, turn the page and learn about more cool dynamic effects you can create in LightWave 8 beyond particles. Take a look at the 3D Garage Videos folder on this book's DVD, and under the Chapter 17 folder, you'll find videos on how to surface and light the sink and faucet used in the tutorial, as well as a video on how to use particles to create smoke.

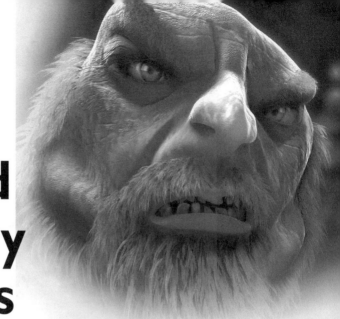

Chapter 18

Hard and Soft Body Dynamics

In the previous chapter, you were introduced to LightWave 8's particles and dynamics. This chapter will take you even further by showing how to create various dynamic type effects for creative animations. The added dynamic effects in LightWave 8 will allow you to make objects collide with other objects, have gravity, create soft-body dynamics, and much more. Tools like these will help take your animations to the next level.

This chapter takes you into the world of dynamic effects. You will work through various projects so that you can quickly and easily learn how to apply these powerful tools to just about any animation. In this chapter, you'll learn about the following:

- The dynamics panel and tools
- Applying hard body dynamics
- Applying soft body dynamics
- Making objects collide and react

Dynamics in LightWave

Just what exactly is a dynamic? It's promoted, it's talked about, but what does the term really mean? The word *dynamic* is an adjective that means of or relating to energy or to objects in motion. What puts these objects in motion in LightWave are clever commands that you control. To use any of the dynamics in LightWave, you just need to think about what you want an object to do.

Let's say you have created a fun character with a big, uh, animator's belly. As your character walks, you want his girth to shake a bit. Although you could use bones with a weight map and apply bone dynamics, a simpler and more effective method is to use a "soft" dynamic. Or, perhaps you're an avid bowler, or want to be. Instead of wearing those silly shoes to go bowling, just create some 3D bowling balls and pins and create an animation with "hard" dynamics and "collisions." No matter the kind of dynamics, after you've learned the buttons and process, it's really only a matter of making your scene come to life. Now, take a quick tour of the dynamics panel to familiarize yourself with it.

Understanding Dynamic Controls

Dynamics in LightWave are easy to set up after you understand how the panels work—or better, what the controls mean. Figure 18.1 shows the dynamics for the SoftFX. This panel is accessed through the Dynamics tab within the Object Properties panel. You can see from the image that there are six tabbed areas within the dynamic controls.

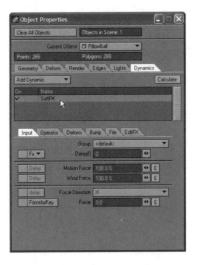

Figure 18.1   When a dynamic is applied, the controls are found within the Object Properties panel.

Depending on which dynamic you apply, you'll see various amounts of differently named tabbed areas. As the tutorials progress in this chapter, you'll see how the different areas are used.

The types of dynamics you can apply to objects are as follows:

- Cloth
- Soft
- Hard
- Emitter (for particles)
- Wind
- Collision
- Gravity

Each of these dynamic types has its own set of commands and controls that work similarly to its counterparts. When you apply a dynamic to an object, you need to think about your process, just as you do when modeling or animating. Think about where you are going with the animation and what you want to do with it. After you understand that, you can choose the appropriate dynamic for your object and know what tabbed area to access within the controls.

Hard Body Dynamics

Hard body dynamics have been around for a while, but not so much on a user level. Complex scripting and heavy calculations often made this top-notch feature available only to an elusive few. Now, thanks to some clever programmers at NewTek, this feature is available interactively in LightWave 8. Hard body dynamics is a term used for objects that essentially see each other in the form of a solid. That is in comparison to soft body dynamics, which will be discussed shortly. Hard body dynamics allow objects to run into each other, have gravity, weight, collide, and more.

Exercise 18.1 Creating Hard Body Dynamics

Instead of making cloth drop on a ball or a waving flag, this tutorial will take a few basic objects and show you how to make them interact. From there, you'll change variables to see the how the dynamic toolsets work.

1. Open LightWave Layout. For this scene, you need nothing more than Layout to do the work.

2. Load the Slide object from this book's DVD. Figure 18.2 shows the object loaded. This object has two layers: a slide made from the letter c, which was then lathed with an offset, and a simple red ball.

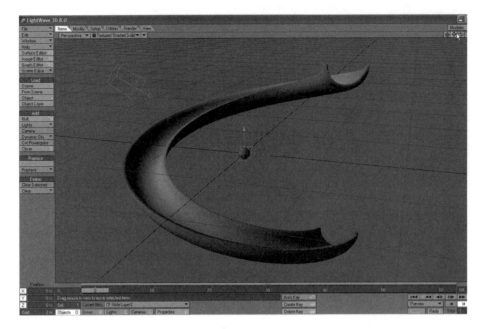

Figure 18.2   The slide object has two layers, a slide and a red ball. Exciting, isn't it?

3. Select the ball and move it up on the Y-axis so that it's positioned at the top of the slide. Create a keyframe at 0 to lock it in place, as in Figure 18.3. Rather than keyframing motions, as you would have had to do before LightWave 8's dynamic features, you're going to let LightWave do the work for you.

4. With the ball still selected, press the p key to open the Object Properties panel. Although this tutorial is simple, you'll see how cool the dynamic effects can be.

5. Click the Dynamics tab, and from the Add Dynamic drop-down list, select Hard to add a HardFX dynamic for the ball. Position your view to see the slide, ball, and Properties panel, similar to Figure 18.4.

6. Now that you've come this far, it's a good idea to save the scene. Save this scene as Slide Setup and then save it again as Slide Working, or something similar. The idea behind this is that at any point, you can call up the setup scene and start again.

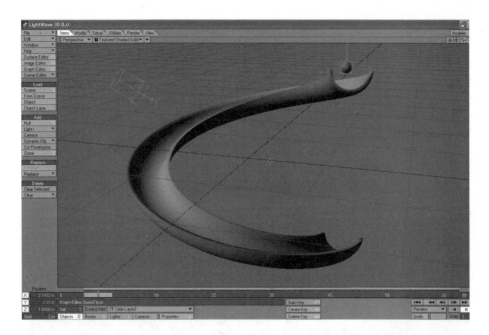

Figure 18.3   Position the ball at the top of the slide.

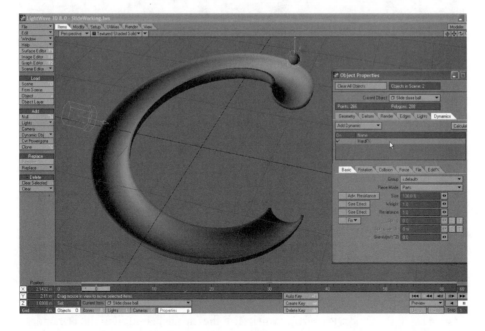

Figure 18.4   Add a hard dynamic to the ball and position the view to see everything.

Tip

Don't forget that you can also use the Shift+s command to save incremental versions of your scenes.

7. Choose the slide object and add a collision dynamic to it from the drop down list, as in Figure 18.5.

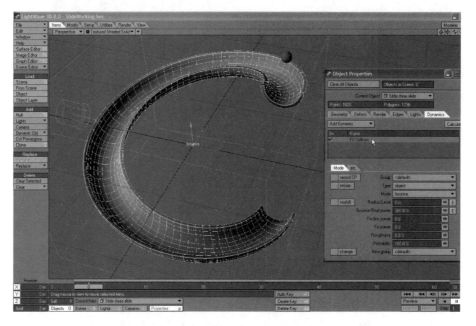

Figure 18.5   Through the Object Properties panel, add a collision dynamic to the slide object.

8. If you click the Calculate button in the Dynamics tab, nothing happens. You've not yet given the dynamics any properties. So, go back to the ball object and select the HardFX listing to access its controls. You only need to click it once for the controls to appear in the Dynamics tab.

9. The first thing you want to do is give the ball some gravity. In the Basic tab of the HardFX controls, set Gravity to -9.8. It's the last setting, at the bottom.

10. In Layout, set the last frame of the animation to 300.

11. Back in the Object Properties panel, click the Calculate button in the Dynamics tab. Whoa! The ball falls and bounces down the slide! Figure 18.6 shows the movement.

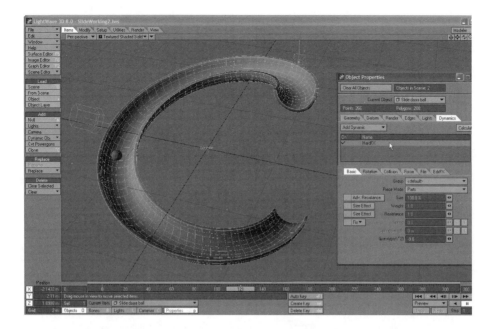

Figure 18.6   With two dynamics applied, your animation works as it should!

Believe it or not, that's all there is to it! You've just created hard body dynamics. However, there are many more controls to play with, so save the scene and move on to experiment a little.

12. After the calculation is complete, you can click the Play button at the bottom of the Layout interface to loop the playback. Notice that the ball bounces around a little too much. This might be fine if you're animating a rubber ball, but what if it's a marble? It would not bounce as much, and the way to control this is through the collision dynamic.

13. Select the slide object and go to the Dynamics tab of the Object Properties panel. Select the FX Collision dynamic to access the controls. You'll see that there are just two tabs: Mode and Etc. The Etc tab is where you can load, save, copy, and paste collision effects. Given that, all the collision dynamic controls for this object are located in the Mode tab.

14. At the top of the control listings, you'll see the Group selection. Right now, this reads <default>. Figure 18.7 shows the panel. The following list presents a rundown of the controls and settings.

Figure 18.7 The collision controls are located mainly within one tab, the Mode tab.

- Setting a group through the Group option is useful for times when you are working with larger scenes and multiple objects. For instance, let's say you have three slides going in this scene. You could create a group so that the collision and hard dynamic objects are tied together and don't react to other objects with dynamics applied. It's a way of separating and isolating dynamics, while maintaining control.

- The Type listing (second from the top) within the controls tells the object how to calculate the collision—that is, should the collision be based on a sphere, a box, a plane, or in this case, an object. If your object was SubPatched, set the Type to object-subdiv.

- The Mode listing is where you can change how the collision reacts. Right now, it's set to bounce. You can also set this to stick, erase, event, scatter, or attract. This means that when a collision happens, the colliding object will bounce off the collision object. Stick means the colliding object will stick to it. Erase means it will be erased. Event can be used to create a collision based on a specific event, such as a wind gust or other type of dynamic. You'll also see scatter and attract, which change the dynamic accordingly.

- The Radius/Level setting can change the collision position. For example, if you change this value from 0 m to 400 mm and then press the Calculate button again, the ball would not fall and drop down the slide like it did before. It would sort of collide with an invisible object. This object, of course, is the slide, but it now has a larger radius. Keep this setting at 0 for this project.

- Bounce/Bind Power is where you can change how the ball reacts with the slide. Right now, the ball sort of bounces its way down the slide. Change this value to 50% and click the Calculate button. The ball now glides down the slide.

Tip

When setting a Radius/Level or Bounce/Bind Power, you can click the E buttons to the right of the values to change these settings over time! Make your ball bounce hard, and then suddenly stick!

- You can set Friction Power to 20.0 rather than the present 0 value. This makes the ball roll less down the slide, adding friction. The ball moves down the slide at a slower rate with the added friction. You can play with this value to see how the dynamics react, but for this project, keep the setting at 0.

- You can increase the Fix Power and Roughness to change how the collision reacts throughout the animation. Let's say you increase the Fix Power to 20. The ball will not bounce as much on the collision. It will not slow down, but rather stay attached to the collision object more, throughout the calculation. Roughness on the other hand, will make the ball bounce around, sort of like rough terrain. Set the value to say, 40%, and you'll see the ball bounce down the slide. Change these values to add variations to see how the ball movement changes as it moves down the slide.

- Finally, you can set the Probability, telling LightWave the percentage of probability that the collision should happen. Right now, it's set to 100%, meaning there's a 100% probability of a collision. Lower this value, calculate again, and see the difference.

15. There's one more thing you should notice with this hard dynamic animation. Select the ball object, and then from the top of Layout, change the Render view style to Textured Shaded Solid Wireframe, as in Figure 18.8. This way, you can see the wireframe of the ball. Click the Calculate button again from the Dynamics tab and closely watch the ball. It slides down the slide (no pun intended). Ideally, it should roll.

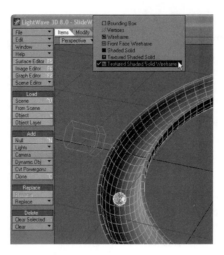

Figure 18.8   Set the Layout to Textured Shaded Solid Wireframe to see the makeup of the objects.

16. Click over to the HardFX controls for the ball within the Dynamics tab of the Object Properties panel. Click over to the Rotation tab, as shown in Figure 18.9.

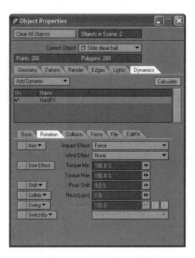

Figure 18.9   The Rotation tab of the HardFX dynamic controls.

17. Notice that the Impact Effect setting at the top of the controls is set to Force. Change this to Roll. Click the Calculate button again, and the ball now rolls down the slide. Voilá!

18. To the left of the Impact Effect setting, you can tell the ball to roll on a specific axis only. Click the Axis drop-down list and you can see that currently, it's set to Free, but you can change this to the Y-axis, or X-axis, and other variations.

19. You can also change some of the other values, such as Wind Effect or Torque. If you increase the Torque Max value to 300%, for example, the ball will roll faster than it is moving. A good example of this is a children's ball thrown into water, which has a lot of torque coming out of the child's hand. It spins faster than it is moving (or sliding) on the water.

20. Additionally, you can give the ball a Resist (Spin) setting to have it hold back on its spin amount.

21. You may have noticed that the calculations were not the fastest. Click the Collision tab of the HardFX controls for the ball. Notice the Collision by setting reads Node. This tells LightWave to look at the object's points. In many cases, this is great. However, because this object is a round ball, you can set this to Sphere, as in Figure 18.10. You can also set this to Box. Set this value to Sphere, and then click the Calculate button. You'll see the ball zip down the slide.

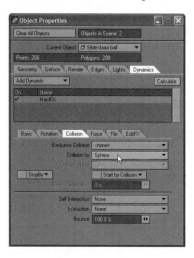

Figure 18.10   You can tell the HardFX object to have its collisions based on points (node) or sphere, as pictured here.

In the middle of the Collision tab controls, you can tell the ball to start by collision— that is, the dynamics will begin upon collision detection. This saves processing time. Conversely, you can set a StopBy collision event.

As you can see, setting up hard body dynamics is not too complicated. You need to just slow down and think about the process. Think about what you're going for, and it'll come together. In this previous exercise, you had a ball, which you told LightWave was a "hard" object. If you calculated after setting this, you might see an error. That's because LightWave doesn't have anything to work with, and you need to set something for this object to interact with. So, you told the ball to collide with the slide. The slide object had a "collision" applied.

Let's take this scene a step further. How about making it blow apart? That would be cool, wouldn't it?

Exercise 18.2   Making Objects Blow Up

First of all, this exercise does not include pyrotechnics and is safe for all ages! Actually, what will benefit this exercise is incorporating the Fireball video tutorial on this book's DVD (Chapter 18 folder). The video will show you how to create a cool explosion using HyperVoxels. This exercise will show you how you can blow apart the ball object rolling down the slide. This is also a hard body dynamic effect.

1. Load the SlideBlowUpSetup scene from this book's DVD. This is the same scene from Exercise 18.1, except for one very important thing.

   For the dynamic collisions to happen in this exercise, the object you want to blow up needs to have separate parts. That's not to say it needs objects on separate layers. However, the slide from Exercise 18.1 was one solid unit. The slide in this exercise has various polygons existing on their own—that is, they are not merged with neighboring polygons. This was created simply by taking a selection of various polygons in Modeler, cutting them, and then pasting them back down.

Figure 18.11
Add a dynamic object straight into Layout from the Items tab.

   The dynamic collision you'll apply would have still hit the slide object, but the slide would then just be pushed as one, not blown apart.

2. From the Add category of the Items tab, select the Dynamic Obj drop-down list, and add a Collision. Figure 18.11 shows the selection.

   How is this different than the collision you added in Exercise 18.1? In the previous exercise, you added an object, the slide, and then instructed LightWave to make this a collision object. In this exercise, you simply want a collision effector, something to blow apart the slide object. Instead of building another object, you can just apply a dynamic object directly. You can then add a HyperVoxel explosion for a fiery finish.

3. When you add the collision, a panel appears for you to enter a name. You can call this BlowUp_Collision, or something similar. Or, you can just leave it alone and click OK. Its name is not important. After you add the name, the FX_Collision panel appears, and you'll see a wireframe ball representing the collision dynamic in Layout, as in Figure 18.12.

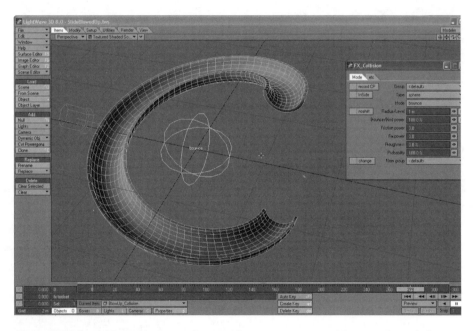

Figure 18.12   Adding a dynamic collision to Layout is represented by a wireframe ball. Because the collisions default mode is Bounce, you see the name bounce with the wireframe object in Layout.

4. In the FX_Collision control panel, you'll notice the same controls as in the Dynamics tab you saw throughout Exercise 18.1. LightWave often has multiple locations for the same file types. Here, increase the Radius/Level to 2.35m, as in Figure 18.13.

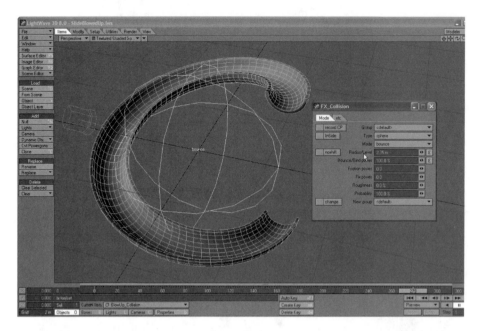

Figure 18.13 Increase the collision dynamic from the FX_Collision control panel.

5. Click into Layout and press t for Move. Move the collision object down beneath the slide and create a keyframe at 0 to lock it in place.

6. Move the collision object up above the slide and create a keyframe at 60. Figure 18.14 shows frame 60 and the motion path of the collision object.

7. Open the Object Properties panel. Go to the Dynamics tab and click the Calculate button. Nothing will happen except for the ball rolling down the slide.

8. If you think about it, you only told the slide object to be a collision object. For it to break apart, you need to apply a hard dynamic to it. Select the slide object, and from the Dynamics tab in the Object Properties panel, select Hard from the Add Dynamic drop-down list, as shown in Figure 18.15.

9. Select the HardFX listing to access the controls, and you'll see that the Piece Mode is set to Parts. Change this to 1Piece and click the Calculate button. The collision dynamic in Layout hits the object and it pushes away. This control is important to how your object breaks apart.

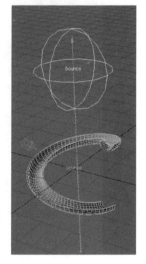

Figure 18.14
You can move and keyframe the dynamic collision object directly in Layout. Here, it's set to move up through the slide object.

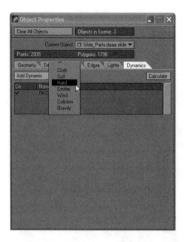

Figure 18.15   Add a hard dynamic to the slide object.

10. Change the Piece Mode back to Parts and click calculate. Ahh! There it is; the object breaks apart as the collision dynamic hits it. Figure 18.16 shows the break up.

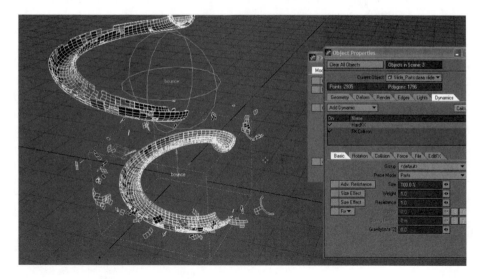

Figure 18.16   Setting the Piece Mode.

11. You're probably noticing that the pieces of the slide break apart, but sort of drift off and do not really explode. In the HardFX controls for the slide, set the Gravity to -9.8. Click Calculate, and you'll see them start to drop before and after the collision. That's okay, but you want the gravity to not apply until the collision happens.

12. Click the Collision tab of the HardFX controls and turn on Start by Collision, as shown in Figure 18.17. Then calculate again. The slide sits still, and as the collision dynamic runs through it, the pieces expand and drop.

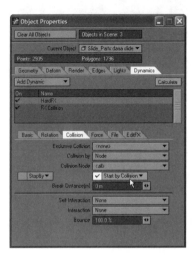

Figure 18.17   Changing the event to Start by Collision will make the slide sit still until it breaks apart.

Tip

If you want to make sure that the exploding pieces do not collide with each other, you could also set Self Interaction to Box within the Collision tab.

13. From this point, it's a matter of tweaking the settings and seeing the effects until you find something you like. Head back to the Basic tab of the HardFX controls and increase the Weight to 5.0. This increases the weight of the pieces when they break up.

14. Click into Layout and select the dynamic collision object. Change its keyframe at 60 to 20 and calculate again. The exploding parts' reactions are more intense, because the colliding object is hitting them at a faster rate.

15. Add one more thing to this animation and then get ready to learn about soft body dynamics. From the Add category of the Items tab, add another collision dynamic object. Name this Ground.

16. In the FX_Collision controls panels for the ground collision, set the Type to Plane. This makes a flat collision plane.

17. Change the Radius/Level to 0m. This tells the collision to happen at the 0 axis. Click the Calculate button and you'll see the exploding parts now fall and hit a ground surface (granted, there is not a visible surface).

18. The parts should bounce a little more when they hit the ground, don't you think? So, change the Bounce/Bind Power to 175% in the FX_Collision for the ground plane. Calculate again, and you'll see the pieces fall and bounce randomly, as in Figure 18.18.

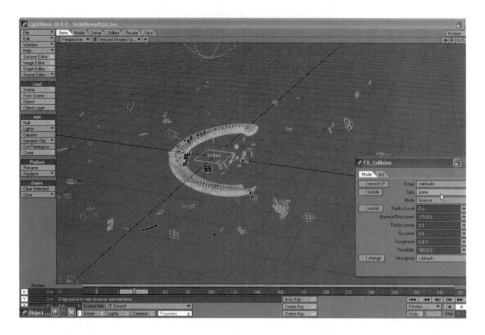

Figure 18.18   A Plane type collision object makes the parts fall and bounce on the ground.

19. Change one more thing. You might have noticed that the slide started to react to the ground plane collision after it was added. Select the slide object and go to the HardFX controls for the dynamic.

20. Click the Collision tab within the controls and change Exclusive Collision to the BlowUp_Collision dynamic. This is the first dynamic you added and kept as a sphere. Calculate again, and you'll see the object hold until the collision hits. Figure 18.19 shows the settings.

Tip

On this book's DVD, take a look at the Break Apart video, which uses a plug-in (also included on the DVD) allowing you to break up objects into dozens of pieces. The video will show how you can shatter the object with dynamics.

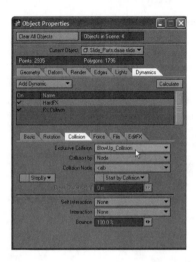

Figure 18.19   Using Exclusive Collision, you can tell an object to exclusively collide with other objects.

There you have it: some cool hard body dynamics. Although the examples here are simple, they work well for demonstration purposes. Everything you did in these two exercises will apply to any other type of object, more complex or less. Characters that need to react to a brick wall will work the same way. A five-year old dropping a bag of marbles will be set up the same way. Anything you can think of for hard collisions can be created with these methods. Here are a few more tips you can try when working with hard body dynamics:

- Under the Rotation tab in the HardFX panel, change the Wind Effect to Roll. When your parts are exploded after the collision, they'll roll, as if blown out. This adds a nice touch to exploding objects.

- In the Rotation tab of the HardFX panel, change the Torque Min and Torque Max values to balance the amount of initial and ending spin and motion on the exploding parts.

- Try changing the Pivot Shift value so that the exploding pieces rotate differently. At 0%, the parts rotate upon themselves. Change this value to 100%, and the parts rotate from a much larger axis, as if you've moved their individual pivots! You can also set this to just an X Shift, Y Shift, or Z Shift from the drop-down control to the left of the value.

- Increase the Resistance setting under the Basic tab of the HardFX panel to slow down the exploding parts.

- If your exploding parts sort of hop like little bugs after they land, you need to bring down the Bounce/Bind Power for the collision plane.

- Use the EditFX panel (as you did in Chapter 17, "Particle Dynamics") to select and remove or reposition any exploding parts of the collision.

- Experiment with one setting at a time! Have fun!

What about soft things, like blankets or pillows? How does soft body dynamics differ from cloth dynamics? When should you use one over the other? Read on to learn about more cool features of the dynamics in LightWave 8.

Soft Body Dynamics

What is a soft body dynamic? Is it just for making plump characters move naturally? Well, sure, you can do that. But soft body dynamics can do much more. A soft body dynamic is anything that is well, soft! More specifically, it's anything that is soft yet holds its shape. Consider a water balloon, or even pants on a character walking, or couch cushions. Cloth, on the other hand, can be blown around and does not hold its shape. Consider the difference here when trying to decide which dynamic to apply to your object.

Exercise 18.3   Working with Soft Body Dynamics

1. In LightWave Layout, save any work you've done and clear the scene.

2. Load the Pillow object from this book's DVD. Set up the view to a comfortable Perspective view and open the Object Properties panel for the object. Figure 18.20 shows the scene.

3. From the Dynamics tab, add a soft dynamic from the drop down list, for the pillow object.

4. Back in Layout, add a collision dynamic from the Dynamic Obj selection under the Add category under the Items tab.

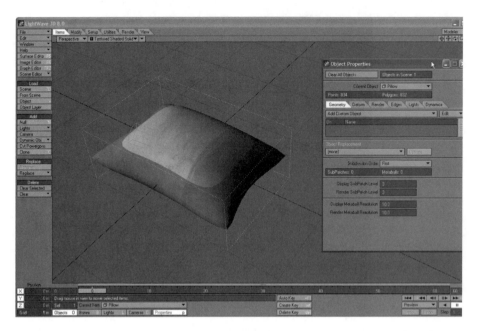

Figure 18.20 Load the pillow object into Layout and view the scene from a Perspective view.

5. For this collision dynamic, set the Type to Plane and Radius/Level to 0 m.

6. Select the pillow object in Layout and create a keyframe at 15 for it in its current position.

7. Move it up on the Y-axis about 3 m. Create a keyframe at 0 to lock it in place. Figure 18.21 shows the scene.

8. Click the Calculate button in the Dynamics tab and you see the pillow fall and sort of bounce like Jell-o on the collision object.

   Although this bounce looks okay for Jell-o or perhaps a marshmallow, it's not effective for a pillow.

9. Check this out: Click the Deform tab within the SoftFX controls. Make sure Collision Detect is set to All. Exclusive Collision should be set to None. Increase the Collision Size to about 5.55 m, as in Figure 18.22.

10. Click the Calculate button. The pillow drops and actually looks like a pillow!

   As you can see from this exercise, setting up objects with soft body dynamics is easy. However, as you might have guessed, there is much more you can do with these dynamic settings, so read on!

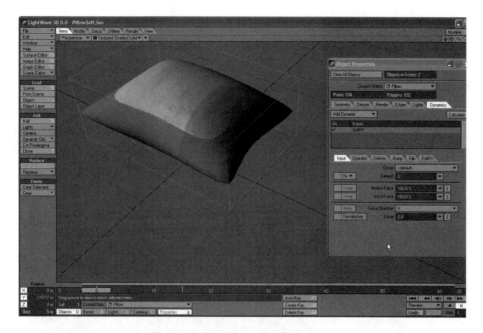

Figure 18.21   Two keyframes are set for the pillow object.

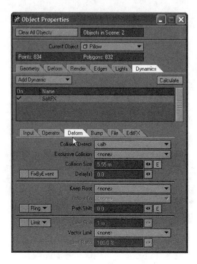

Figure 18.22   Changing the values in the Deform tab tells the pillow how to react to the collision.

Exercise 18.4 Creating a Bouncing Belly

What other things can you think of to create with soft body dynamics? Aside from things like tires hitting the ground, or animating Jell-o, soft body dynamics can also be used for characters. Follow along with this exercise to apply soft body dynamics to a fun character.

1. In Layout, save any work you've done. Then, load the LittleDudeSetup scene from this book's DVD. This scene has a character that rotates and jumps.

   This is a fun character that you can use for practicing character rigs, animating, or anything else you can think of. Hey, maybe you can blow it up with a collision, as in Exercise 18.2!

2. Open the Object Properties panel for the character and select the Dynamics tab. Add a soft dynamic to the character, as shown in Figure 18.23.

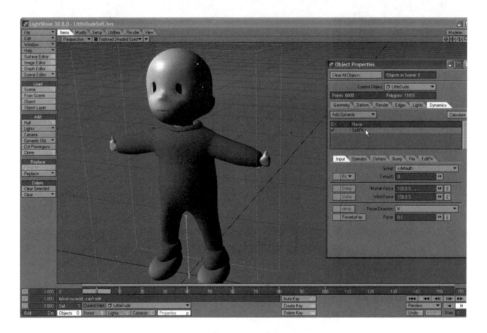

Figure 18.23 You can even add soft body dynamics to characters.

3. In the Operator tab of the SoftFX panel, set Operator1 Map to BellyPoints/ pointset. This pointset is created in Modeler by selecting a particular group of points (or single point) and applying a point selection set. Figure 18.24 shows the operation.

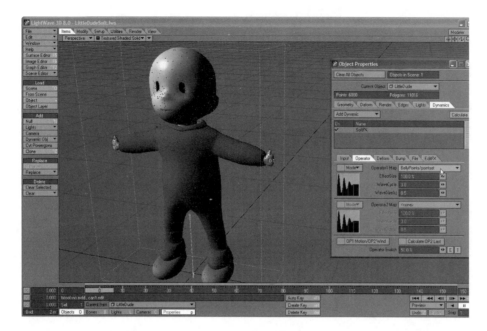

Figure 18.24 Set the Operator1 Map to BellyPoints/pointset.

4. Go ahead and click the Calculate button. You'll see the little dude rotate and jump, but watch his belly—it jiggles!

   The operator map you've applied is a unique way to quickly add a setting for soft body dynamics. You can easily vary the size of the effect, the wave cycle, and the wave size. What's cool about the operator maps is that you visually can see what's happening in the thumbnail display. By changing the wave cycle, you'll instantly see the change in the display. Go ahead, make some changes to these values, and calculate again to see the effects.

5. Now try something even crazier. Select the Bump tab and set the Compress Bump setting to 750. Look at the character's belly as you do this. Because you've set up the pointset already to work with the BellyPoints, this setting knows where to be applied. Figure 18.25 shows the newly sized belly.

Like many of the other variables you've seen used with hard dynamics, the soft dynamics also can be adjusted. Also, remember that you can use the EditFX tools to change the shape of various points, as described in Exercise 18.5.

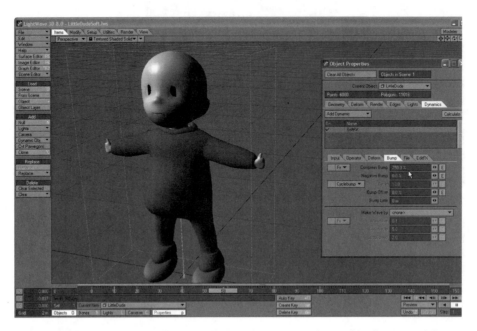

Figure 18.25   Increasing the Compress Bump value, you can change the effect size of the BellyPoints/pointset.

Exercise 18.5   Adjusting Points with EditFX

The EditFX tab is found within many dynamic properties panels, and you can even use it on particles. This exercise will quickly show you how you can edit any point on your character.

1. With the scene loaded from the previous exercise, go to the SoftFX panel.

2. Select the EditFX tab.

3. Click the Edittool to activate. When you do this, you'll see the points of the object highlight, as in Figure 18.26.

4. Click and drag on any point of the character, perhaps the chest or belly. You'll see the object deform, as in Figure 18.27.

5. If you click and drag through the Edit Node variable setting, you'll see the points of the object highlight with their individual node, or point number.

This tool is very useful for editing and working with stubborn points of an object. You can access this tool any time you want to change a point's position during a calculation. Although this might not be used often, it's a great addition to your dynamic toolset.

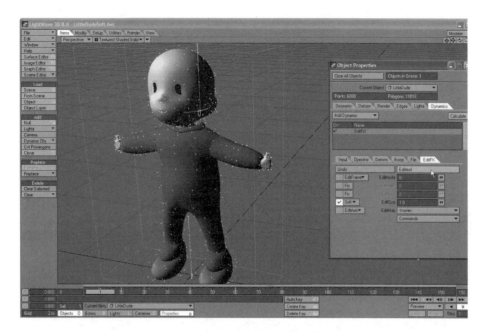

Figure 18.26   When the Edit tool is activated, the points of the object highlight in Layout.

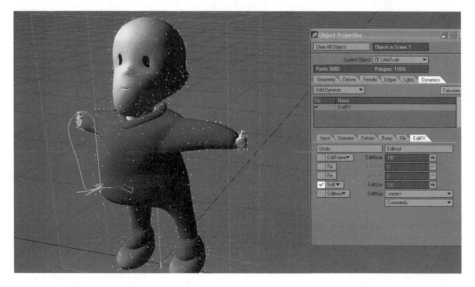

Figure 18.27   Using the Edit tool, you can edit the position of points of an object directly in Layout.

The Next Step

This chapter introduced you to hard and soft body dynamics. Even though the tutorials were simple, their methods, practices, and results are the same whether you're building New York City in 3D or just a ball and box. The only difference is speed. Working with simple objects while setting up dynamics will help your workflow. Regardless of object detail, the process described in this chapter is the same no matter what project you tackle.

It's been mentioned before and it'll be mentioned again—practice and experiment! Change a value; see the results. Work with one value at a time, and as always, consult your LightWave 3D manual for any specific technical questions. Now, turn the page and learn about cloth dynamics!

Chapter 19

Cloth Dynamics

If you're a long-time user of LightWave, you may be familiar with the former cloth system LightWave 3D used called Motion Designer. It did its job of animating cloth well, even though the name didn't fit! This same technology has been updated and improved in LightWave 8, and is now integrated into the Dynamics tab within the Object Properties panel. The previous chapter discussed the different types of dynamics available to you. This chapter will focus specifically on cloth. No one would have guessed during the mid-1990s that a program on your desktop computer would have the power that LightWave does today.

In the upcoming pages, you'll see just how easy it is to create animated cloth by following the exercises. The exercises here will illustrate the tool's interactivity as well as demonstrate its functionality. The goal for this chapter is that you gain the knowledge you need to build even greater creations on your own. This chapter will show you how to do the following:

- Set up animated cloth from basic motion
- Apply dynamic collisions with cloth
- Use cloth in a large complex scene

Cloth Dynamics Versus Soft Dynamics

The interface controls for many of the tools within LightWave often are misleading, and this includes dynamics. You might have asked yourself when using the dynamics available in LightWave, when to apply a "soft" dynamic over a "cloth" dynamic. Cloth is soft, right? Yes, but to make things clear, think of it like this. Let's say you're animating a person lying down on a bed. When that person puts his head down on a pillow, the pillow should be a soft dynamic. A soft dynamic is when the object generally holds its shape when being deformed, like a tire hitting the road, or a racquetball squashing when it smacks a wall. When the person is covered by a blanket or sheet, that object should be a cloth dynamic. The blanket is soft, yes, but in this case, the object does not generally hold its shape. Wind, gravity, and even perhaps a person that it is covering significantly deform it. Make sense? Here are a few more ideas to think about:

- JELL-O: soft dynamic
- Flowers: soft dynamic
- Sofa Cushions: soft dynamic
- Curtains: cloth dynamic
- Jacket or Shirt: soft dynamic
- Bathrobe: cloth dynamic
- Flesh: soft dynamic

Get the idea? You just need to think about what it is you're trying to create, and you'll have a better time finding the right dynamic to use.

Creating a Basic Cloth Scene

In the first exercise, you will take a basic look at cloth dynamics and set up a very simple blowing cloth. From there, you'll make an object collide with it. It's nothing fancy, and not a whole lot different from Motion Designer in previous versions of LightWave. However, there are better controls and more flexibility in LightWave 8.

Exercise 19.1   Modeling Cloth Objects

You need to ask yourself, "Self, what sort of cloth should I animate?" The answer should be, "Any kind you want!" In all seriousness, you can animate any kind of cloth, such as cotton T-shirts, theatre drapes, skirts, or anything else you'd like. It doesn't matter what you build, as long as you build it properly. In particular, building properly means don't overbuild it. Because you can use SubPatched objects in Layout, the cloth dynamic will understand this geometry. The result: highly subdivided objects that bend and animate smoothly and cleanly.

1. Open LightWave's Modeler.

   The object you'll create is nothing more than a large rectangle.

2. From the Create tab, under the Primitives category, click the Box button. In the Top view, click and draw out a large rectangle. Press the up arrow on your keyboard two times, and press the right arrow two times to create multiple segments. Be sure that your mouse is in the Top view when making the segments. Figure 19.1 shows the creation.

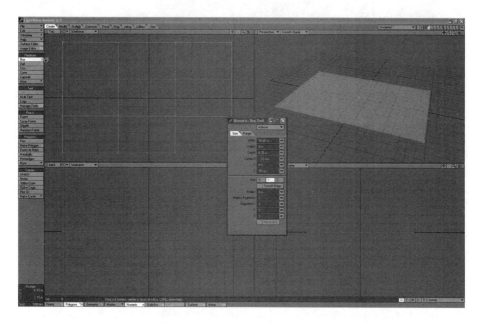

Figure 19.1   You can begin creating cloth objects from simple shapes like a flat, segmented box.

3. Press the Spacebar once to turn off the Box tool (or just click once on the Box tool), and your object is created.

Tip

If your created box object does not appear in the Perspective view, press the f key to flip the polygons forward.

This next step is very important. To control the cloth, you need to identify a few key points. These points act as anchors on the cloth. Think about this: When cloth dynamics are applied, such as wind or gravity, if nothing is controlling the cloth, it will just blow away.

4. Be sure you're working in Points selection mode at the bottom of the Modeler interface. Then, select the four points on the outer edges of the polygon, as shown in Figure 19.2.

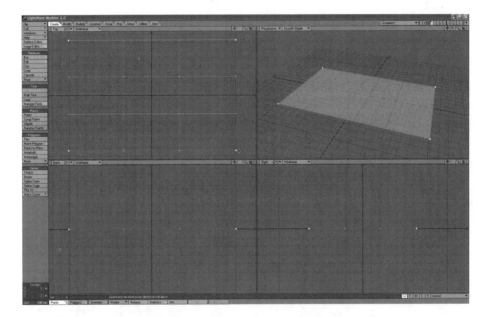

Figure 19.2 Select the points (four total) on the outside corners of the polygon.

5. With the points selected, click the S button at the bottom right of the Modeler interface. To the right of that button, click the drop-down list and select New, as shown in Figure 19.3.

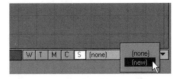

Figure 19.3 Create a selection set for the four selected points.

6. When you select New for selected points, you are giving these points a name, which you can access later in Layout. Name the points Cloth_Anchors, as shown in Figure 19.4. Click OK to close the panel.

Figure 19.4 Name the selected points Cloth_Anchors to identify the selection set.

7. Deselect the points and then click the Surface button (or press q) and give the polygons a surface name, like cloth. (You know, because naming your cloth "cloth" is pretty darn original!)

8. After you have named the surface, press the Tab key on your keyboard to activate SubPatch mode for the object.

9. Save your object and send it to Layout. You can do this by selecting the tiny drop-down triangle at the top right of the Modeler interface and selecting Send Object to Layout. This sends the object directly to Layout without you needing to load it from disc—the operation is automatic. (If your HUB is not activated, you'll see these controls ghosted. So, either activate your HUB or simply load the object directly from Layout.)

10. Alt+Tab over to Layout and press 4 on your keyboard to make sure you're in Perspective view mode. Change the total length of the animation to 400 in the timeline.

11. Move and rotate the Perspective view (using the viewport controls at the top-right corner of Layout) to see the object in full frame.

12. With the cloth object selected, press the p key to open the Object Properties panel.

You're now ready to begin animating this cloth. It's really, really difficult to do—so get ready.

Exercise 19.2   Creating Moving Cloth

You now have everything in place to see moving cloth. It's going to be a bit taxing, but if you hang with it, you'll see the cool results. Okay, if you haven't noticed the sarcasm, this next exercise is not difficult at all. In fact, it's so easy you're probably going to be finding ways to include cloth into your next job.

1. Picking up where the last exercise left off, make sure your object is selected and the Object Properties panel is open.

2. Click over to the Dynamics tab and add a Cloth dynamic from the Add Dynamic drop-down list.

3. After the ClothFX listing appears, select it, and you'll see the necessary controls, as in Figure 19.5.

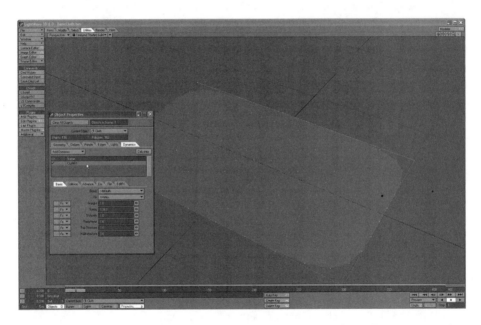

Figure 19.5   Adding a cloth dynamic is easy to do directly in the Object Properties panel.

4. Just because you've added a cloth dynamic does not mean anything is going to happen at first. If you click the Calculate button in the Object Properties panel, you'll see LightWave run through the timeline, but the object won't move.

5. Click over to the Etc tab within the ClothFX controls, and you'll see a Preset already set to Cotton[thin]. Click the listing and change it to the Silk preset.

6. In the same Etc tab, change the Gravity setting to -9.8 for the Y-axis. This is the setting for real-world gravity.

7. Click the Calculate button. What happens? The cloth object drops out of sight!

Earlier, you created a selection set for some points in Modeler. You named them Cloth_Anchors, which is exactly what you need here—something to hold this cloth!

8. Click the Basic tab within the ClothFX settings, and from the Fix listing, choose the Cloth_Anchors/Pointset, as shown in Figure 19.6. This is the point selection set you created in Modeler with the four selected points.

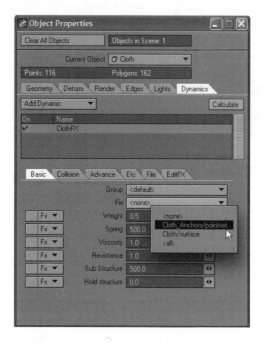

Figure 19.6   Set the Fix settings to Cloth_Anchors/Pointset, which is the point selection set you created in Modeler.

9. Click the Calculate button. Ah! Better! The cloth drops and swoops like a hammock, anchored by the four points, as shown in Figure 19.7.

You've just animated cloth. Easy, isn't it? This method works very well for draperies, cloths, flags, and more. All you need to do is anchor some points using a point selection set in Modeler, apply a little gravity to the cloth in Layout, and you're on your way. However, there's so much more you can do, so read on.

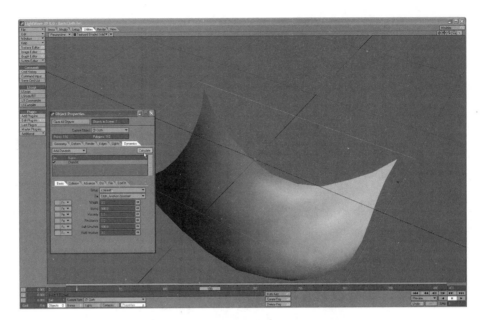

Figure 19.7 Calculating the cloth dynamic shows that the anchor points are doing their job holding the cloth in place!

 Important

Your object is a SubPatched object. The cloth dynamic applied is a deformation tool. So, you need to tell your object when to be subdivided. In Layout, select the cloth object and press the p key to open the Object Properties panel. In the Geometry tab, set the Subdivision Order to Last, as in Figure 19.8.

 Tip

When setting up cloth dynamic scenes, your Bounding Box Threshold for your object needs to be equal to or greater than the points or polygons of your object. For example, the cloth object in this exercise contains 162 polygons, with 116 points, at a SubPatch level of 3. Therefore, the Bounding Box Threshold Level (see Figure 19.9) should be 540 or higher. Whatever value you add will be saved when you quit LightWave. So, set this to at least 10,000 in the Display Options tab (press d). Keeping a value this high (or higher) helps with other scenes that contain objects with higher point and polygon counts. You won't have to constantly change this value by setting it to a higher value just one time.

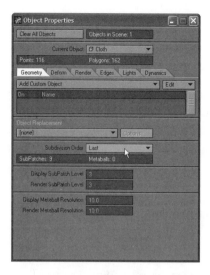

Figure 19.8   Remember that when using SubPatched objects, you need to tell LightWave when to subdivide. Do this from the Geometry tab of the Object Properties panel for the selected object.

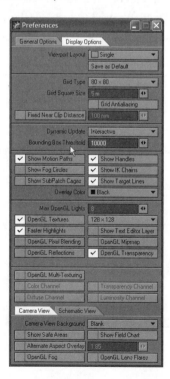

Figure 19.9   To make life easier when working in LightWave, especially with SubPatched objects, set the Bounding Box Threshold in the Display Options panel to 10,000 or higher. Most systems with a 64 MB graphics card or higher work well with a value of 40,000.

Adding More Dynamics

Creating 3D animations with cloth is just one way to animate with dynamics. You can also apply other dynamics for added effects.

You've set up a motion for a piece of cloth—the concepts covered in the previous two exercises are the same basic principles you'll use for just about any cloth creation. After the gravity took a hold of this cloth, it moved nicely, dropped, and hung from the anchored points. But after a short time, the cloth sort of drooped there, didn't it? You can easily add wind and turbulence to this cloth for added coolness.

Exercise 19.3   Adding Environment Variables to Cloth

1. With the cloth scene still loaded, make sure the Object Properties panel is open for the cloth object. Then, select the Items menu in Layout, and from the Dynamic Obj drop-down list, select Wind to add a wind dynamic to the scene.

2. The FX_Wind panel should appear. Make sure that the Wind Mode is set to Direction. Blend Mode should be Add, Size Effect should be Wind, and Falloff Mode should be OFF. You don't need to use any falloff now because the cloth is the only object in the scene. Figure 19.10 shows the settings.

Tip

Any time after you've pressed the Start button, you can cancel the calculations by pressing the Ctrl key.

Figure 19.10   A few simple settings within the FX_Wind panel and you're almost ready to see the effects.

3. Click over to the Vector tab and set the Wind Y value to 10 m; the X and Z values should be 0 m.

4. Back in Layout, select the wind dynamic, move it down (press the t key) beneath the cloth, and create a keyframe to lock it in place.

5. In the Object Properties panel, click Calculate. Wham! You have a parachute! Figure 19.11 shows the effect.

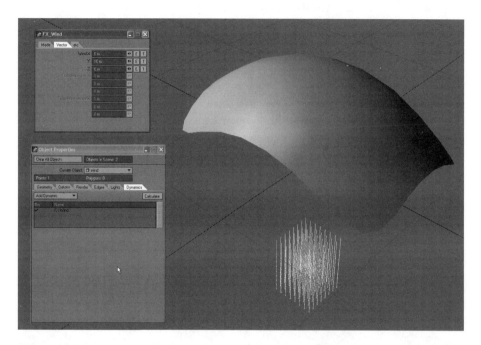

Figure 19.11 While gravity is applied to the cloth to make it drop and fall, a wind dynamic pushes up from underneath, creating a parachute-like effect.

What you've done here is basic, but powerful. Even on slower systems, the dynamic operations calculate fast, making it easy to experiment and make changes. Play with different Wind modes to see effects like Vortex, Rotation, and more. You can find these settings under the Mode tab, in the Wind Mode drop-down selector, all within the FX Wind panel.

Tip

Play around with the various settings, adding one value at a time and clicking the Calculate button in the Dynamics tab of the Object Properties panel to see the change and effect.

This exercise has guided you through some of the necessary requirements for using Motion Designer. The next exercise will show you how you can set up collision objects with cloth.

Exercise 19.4   Adding Collision to Cloth

Now that you've put some cloth into motion, and added a little wind to it, you've seen that the dynamics in LightWave 8 are pretty easy to set up. Let's take things a step further by adding collision to the cloth. This next exercise will show you how to take a 3D object and drop it into the cloth, as if the cloth were catching it like a baseball glove.

1. Save any work you've been doing and load the Basic_Cloth scene off this book's DVD. This is a version of the cloth scene you created earlier in this chapter. After it is loaded, resave the scene onto your hard drive as Cloth_Collision.

2. Load the red ball object from this book's DVD.

3. When the object is loaded, move the ball up so it's resting just above the cloth object, as shown in Figure 19.12. Create a keyframe to lock it in place at frame 0.

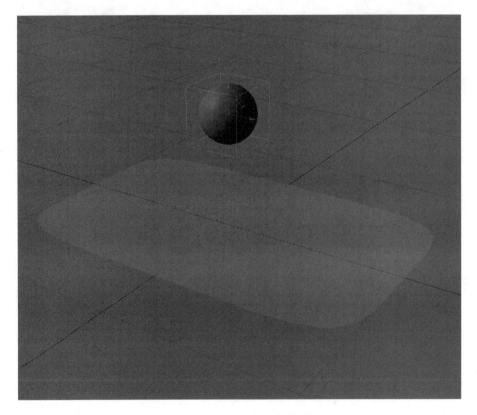

Figure 19.12   Load the red ball object from the book's DVD and position it above the cloth.

4. Press the p key to open the Object Properties panel for the red ball. Click over to the Dynamics tab, and from the Add Dynamics drop-down list, add a hard dynamic to the red ball. After it is loaded, select the dynamic to view the controls. Figure 19.13 shows the addition.

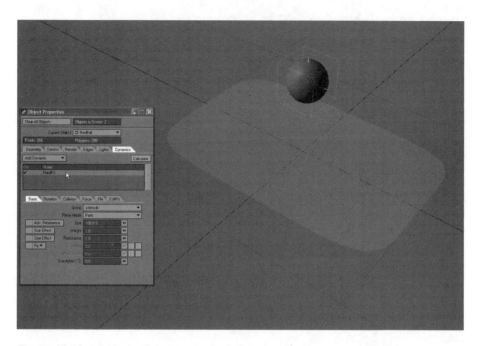

Figure 19.13   Add a hard dynamic to the ball.

5. Set the Gravity to -9.8 in the Basic tab of the HardFX controls. Then, click the Calculate button and you'll see the cloth drop as it did in the previous tutorials. The red ball will also fall because you applied gravity to it. However, it passes right through the cloth! Figure 19.14 shows the scene.

6. In the Object Properties panel, make the current object the Cloth.

7. Add a new dynamic to the cloth from the Add Dynamic drop-down list. Choose Collision, and after it is loaded, select the FX_Collision listing to access the controls.

8. Under the Mode tab, select Object as the Type, and again click Calculate. You'll see the red ball fall and collide with the cloth, as shown in Figure 19.15.

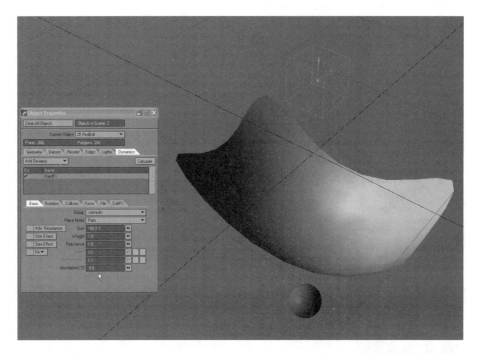

Figure 19.14   With gravity applied to the red ball, it falls, but does not collide with the cloth.

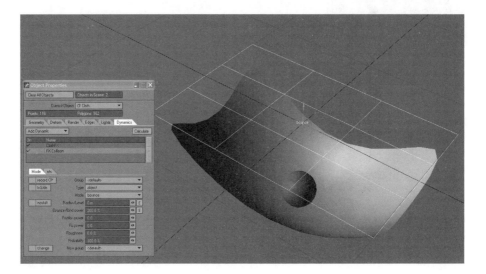

Figure 19.15   With a collision set to the cloth object, the ball now falls and collides with it.

9. The red ball sort of falls and lands like a bowling ball—fast, hard, and heavy. How about softening that up a bit? Under the Mode tab for the FX_Collision, change the Mode to Stick.

10. Bring the Bounce/Bind Power to 50%. Also, make sure Friction Power is set to 100. Click the Calculate button again and the ball falls and gently lands. If you should change the Mode back to Bounce, the lower Bounce/Bind Power will also help decrease the hard landing of the red ball.

Important

Dynamic calculations are not saved with a scene just by saving a scene. If you reload a scene, you need to calculate again by clicking the Calculate button in the Dynamics tab of the Object Properties panel. However, you can record and save the calculation files. For the collision on the cloth object, click over to the Etc tab and you'll find Save, Load, Copy, and Paste commands. All dynamics in LightWave 8 have these features available to you.

11. Select the cloth object and create a keyframe at frame 120. Then, move it up about 4 m and rotate it about −36 degrees on the bank.

12. Return the cloth object to its position at 120 and create a keyframe for it there at 140, unless you have Auto Key enabled, which creates this key automatically.

13. Select the red ball object and in the HardFX settings for it, change the Impact Effect to Roll. Click the Calculate button again, and the red ball falls and is pushed around by the moving cloth. Figure 19.16 shows the action.

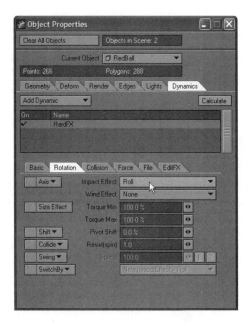

Figure 19.16   Changing the ball's Impact Effect allows it to be pushed around by the collision object (the cloth).

To the left of the Impact Effect, you'll see an Axis control drop-down list. Here, you can tell the Impact Effect to be controlled freely: either by the X, Y, Z axis or by the XZ, XY, or YZ axis. Additionally, you can select Fix and lock the roll all together. Within each of the dynamic panels, as explained in the previous dynamics chapter, you'll find these effect controls throughout and be able to fix a certain effect on a specific axis, randomly, or otherwise. Check them out when you get a chance, and as mentioned, test one setting at a time! Make a change, click the Calculate button to see the effect, and keep going.

Cloth and Characters

You've made it this far. You've seen basic cloth move and worked with multiple objects for dynamic interaction. Now, take what you've learned and go a step further. Although not every button and value has been highlighted, the tools you're using in these tutorials can help you set up enough elements to physically see changes of any parameters you might choose to adjust. Adding cloth to a character is a little more work than the previous exercises, and more calculation time is needed. Honestly, that's the worst part. Setup is not difficult, but calculation times can increase greatly. Because of this, simple objects are used in this exercise to get you going.

Exercise 19.5   Adding Movement to Clothing

1. Load the skirt object from this book's DVD into Layout. This is a very out-of-style skirt that no one would wear; however, it works well for demonstration purposes.

2. Position the Perspective view to get a good view of the skirt. With the skirt selected, press the p key on your keyboard to open the Object Properties panel. Click over to the Dynamics tab.

3. In the Dynamics tab of the Object Properties panel, add a cloth dynamic to the skirt. Then, select the ClothFX listing to access the controls. Figure 19.17 shows the setup.

4. Rotate the skirt 360 degrees on the heading over 60 frames. Create a keyframe at frame 60 for the rotation.

5. Set the end frame to 200 in the Layout timeline.

6. Back in the ClothFX controls under the Dynamics tab, click over to the Etc tab, and choose the Cotton[thick] Preset, as shown in Figure 19.18.

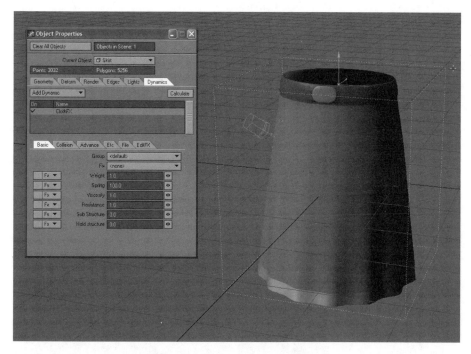

Figure 19.17 Creating more advanced cloth dynamic setups begins in the same manner as creating simple ones.

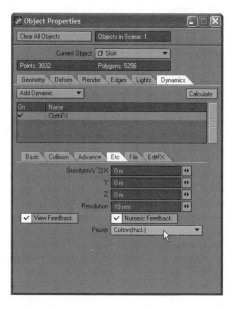

Figure 19.18 The best way to set up any cloth—from flags to curtains to clothing—is to first use a preset.

7. Click the Calculate button. The skirt twists and flows, as shown in Figure 19.19.

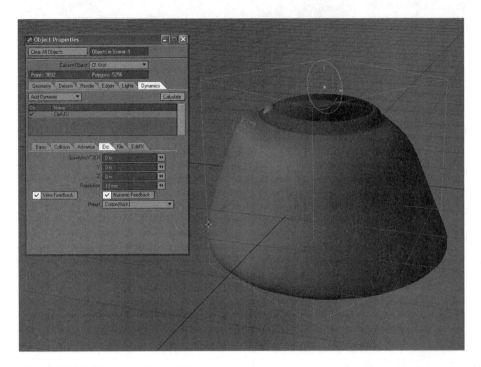

Figure 19.19   Changing the skirt's Impact Effect allows it to be pushed around by the collision object (the cloth). However, without a few key settings, the skirt loses all shape.

8. If your calculation is still working, press the Ctrl key to stop. Then, click over to the Basic tab, and select Waist/Pointset for the Fix listing. The points in the waist have had a selection set created in Modeler.

9. Click the Calculate button again, and you see the skirt rotate and keep its shape; however, it has suddenly decided to blow up in the air. This is because you've not told it to have any gravity. The momentum of the spin makes it swing up on the Y-axis, as shown in Figure 19.20.

10. In the Etc tab, set a Y Gravity value of -9.8m. Calculate again and you'll see the skirt flow more appropriately. However, it folds over itself, as in Figure 19.21.

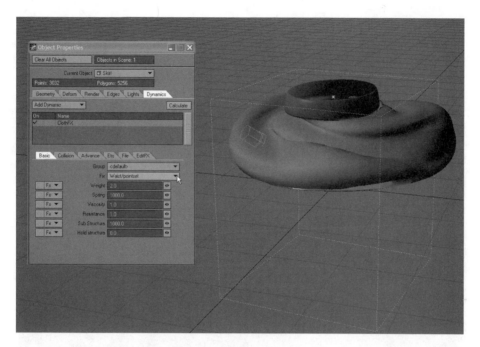

Figure 19.20   Fixing the waist of the skirt holds it in place during the rotation, but without gravity, the skirt floats into the air.

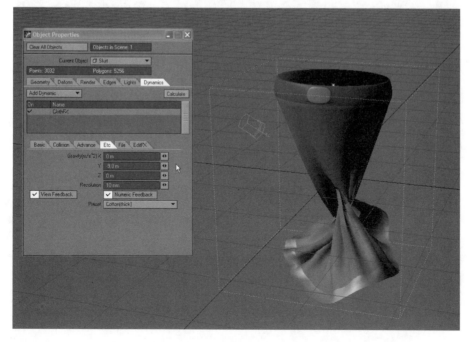

Figure 19.21   With gravity applied, the skirt flows more naturally; however, it collides with itself.

11. In the Collision tab, make sure Collision Detect is set to All. At the bottom of the Collision tab, make sure Self Collision also is set to All.

12. In the Geometry tab of the Object Properties panel, make sure that the Subdivision Order for the skirt object is set to Last. This tells LightWave to subdivide and make the object smooth after the dynamics have been applied.

13. Click the Calculate button in the Dynamics tab and you should see the skirt flow nicely, as shown in Figure 19.22.

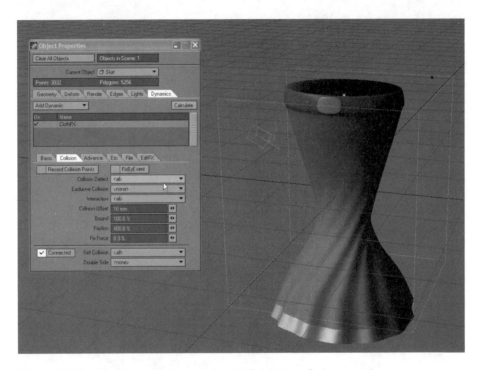

Figure 19.22 The skirt now flows nicely with Subdivision Order set to Last.

14. You might notice that the skirt stretches slightly upon rotation. This is easy to fix. In the Advance tab of the ClothFX controls, set the Stretch Limit from 30% to 1%. Calculate again, and you'll see a less stretched skirt, as in Figure 19.23.

15. After the skirt swings around, it's a little too flippy—it swings too much. To give the skirt more control and less swing, click over to the Basic tab. Bring the Hold Structure to 3.0. If you set this value higher, you get a sort of spongy, or JELL-O effect.

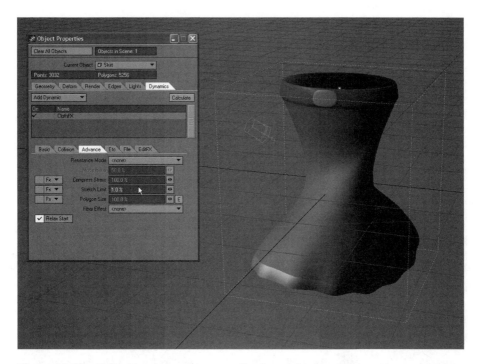

Figure 19.23 Telling the cloth to have a smaller Stretch Limit makes it—you guessed it—
stretch less!

Tip

If your skirt (or other cloth) folds over itself even with Self Collision applied, try
increasing the Resistance slightly, about .5 or so in the Basic tab of the ClothFX
controls.

16. Change the Sub Structure to 500. It was set to 1000 with the thick cotton preset
you applied earlier in the exercise. This value lessens the hold of the underlying
structure of the polygons. You need to experiment to find a good balance
between Sub Structure and Hold Structure in your projects. But as mentioned,
start with a preset, make a single change, calculate to see its effects, and then
continue on. Figure 19.24 shows the change.

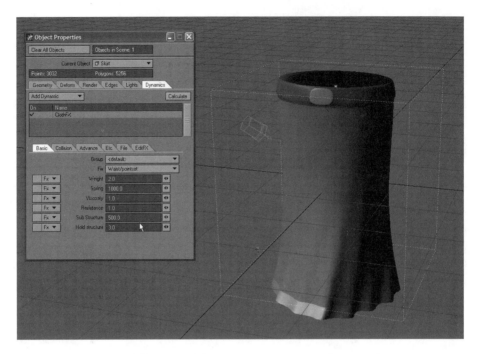

Figure 19.24 With a stronger Hold Structure setting, the skirt flips less after its rotation.

A few other things you can try include the following:

- Increase the Viscosity in the Basic tab to give the cloth a slow, sort of underwater effect.

- Increase Resistance to give the effect of resistance. The motion you create will be applied, but the motion from the cloth dynamic will be delayed.

- Change the Polygon Size in the Advance tab to increase or decrease the affected polygons during calculation. You can make cloth shrink with this setting! There is an E for setting an envelope here. For example, you could increase the polygon size over time, as the skirt spins, to make it billow out.

- Increase the Resolution under the Etc tab for calculations that are more accurate. If you have a very high resolution model, decrease this for speedier calculations.

- Turn off View Feedback in the Etc tab if your cloth dynamics require heavy-duty calculations. This helps speed up calculation times because LightWave won't display the effects until the calculation is complete.

- If your cloth object has multiple surfaces, you can apply various Weight, Spring, Viscosity, and other settings to those specific surfaces in the Basic tab. Simply click the FX setting to the left of the chosen value.

There are many variables available with the cloth you create. Here, you've seen some of the most common. Go ahead and take this skirt animation one step further by adding some legs!

Exercise 19.6   Clothing Characters

Everything you do in the cloth dynamic settings is similar, no matter how big or small the job. Earlier in the chapter, you created a soft cloth and dropped a ball on it. Now, you're going to use the animated skirt from the previous exercise and put some legs underneath it.

1. Load the Skirt_Swing scene from this book's DVD. This is the scene from the previous exercise, so if you've followed along and would like to use your own scene, please do so.

2. Load the legs object from the DVD also.

3. Open the Object Properties panel for the legs and add a collision dynamic. Select the FX_Collision listing to access the controls.

4. Because this is the only object in the scene, you don't need to set a Group. You can see in the Mode tab of the FX_Collision controls that you have the ability to group dynamics. Let's say you have a much larger scene with multiple characters; grouping certain objects gives you a level of control through the scene with other dynamic controls.

5. Keep the Type to Object. Here, you can set this to Object Subdiv for calculations that are more accurate. Because the legs are subdivided, this setting can help you, but in many cases, it's not necessary and only adds to calculation time.

6. Set Mode to Bounce. Your skirt is not really needing to "bounce" off of the legs; rather, this setting tells the skirt to collide and mind its own business—that is, it's acting opposite of another Mode setting called Stick. You don't want the skirt to stick (unless you're looking for static cling).

7. Change the Radius/Level to 400 mm. This setting is key and the value here is arrived at by trial and error. By changing the increments by 100 mm and calculating each time, you can see the effect. This increases the area of collision. For example, if your colliding object (the skirt) is falling into the object, you can increase the Radius/Level until the dynamic is correct.

8. Set Bounce/Bind Power to 50%. The default of 200% can often make the collision pop or jump around. Lowering this value smoothes out the collision effect.

9. Leave all other settings alone and click the Calculate button. The skirt spins and flows nicely around the legs, as in Figure 19.25.

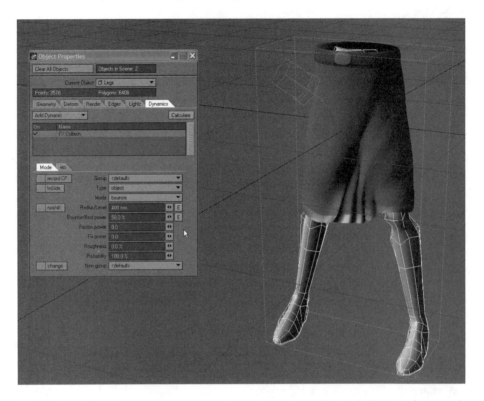

Figure 19.25   With just a few settings to the collision object (the legs), the skirt flows nicely around the object.

From this point, you can parent the skirt to the legs and then move the legs around to see how the collision reacts. Depending on the speed and movement of your objects, you can increase the Radius/Level setting and vary the Bounce/Bind Power. Load up the Skirt_Legs2 scene from this book's DVD to see a slight change in the previous exercise.

With the information presented here, you can tweak the settings and recalculate the motions for varying results. While you do, here are a few very important tips to keep in mind when working with cloth dynamics:

- Make sure the Bounding Box Threshold in Layout is set to (or higher than) the point or polygon count of your object, whichever is greater.
- Balance Radius/Level and Bound/Bind Power for collision objects.

- Set Viscosity for thicker, less fluid objects such as JELL-O.

- If your object has sharp movements, you should up the Resolution setting accessed from the Etc tab within the ClothFX controls.

The Next Step

Experiment! Like HyperVoxels, there are only a few key settings for cloth dynamics that you'll use all the time. Get those down, understand them, and create a working scene. Start with a preset, see how it looks (by clicking the Calculate button) and make changes to the settings. From there, change some of the other values one at a time and see the results. There's no better way to see what changing those values can do! Be sure to check out the reference manual that came with your software for a listing of the other less used dynamic controls. Combine that knowledge with the practical examples in this chapter and you'll be on your way.

Without becoming too technical, this chapter has provided a clear set of examples of working with cloth. Although the interface and values seem odd at first, they can be used for a great number of cloth animations. Don't think of it as a physics simulator but more as a cloth designer. With the information provided here, you can create just about anything from bedding to drapes to flowing hair to flags, and more.

Chapter 20

Compositing and Match Moving

Some of the coolest 3D animation you see is work you don't even notice. That's right, animators and compositors spend months in front of a computer creating visual effects that you don't even notice. For example, in the movie *Hart's War* starring Bruce Willis, animators used LightWave to add snow outside a moving train. If you saw the movie, you wouldn't even think twice that the snow wasn't real. Or how about the movie *A Beautiful Mind* starring Russell Crow? There's a scene where a little girl is running around a park, surrounded by pigeons. If you've ever run toward a pigeon or other flying rodent, you'd know that as soon as you get close enough, it runs or flies away. But in *A Beautiful Mind*, director Ron Howard needed the girl to be a figment of the main character's imagination. Because she's not real, the birds do not notice her and don't fly away. All this is done in 3D, be it LightWave or something else. But the process to get there is more than modeling, texturing, and animation—it's compositing and match moving.

Match moving is the process of making your 3D camera match that of the real world camera. For example, if you took a photograph of a street and then brought it into LightWave, you could easily place a 3D object, such as a car, into the shot. But what if you brought in a moving clip rather than a still image? Think about it—the video would be moving, but just placing a car in the shot wouldn't match the moving footage. Therefore, you need LightWave's camera to move in unison with the camera that took the footage. This match moving process is usually done by using very expensive third-party software that exports camera data to LightWave or another program. From there,

3D objects can be placed in the scene, lit, and rendered. However, it is possible to track camera motions directly within LightWave. You'll learn how in this chapter. If you've ever worked with a match moving program, you might even find the method discussed here an easier way to go.

After you've tracked your camera to match moving footage and set up your 3D objects, you need to composite them to match, to look as if they're integrated into the footage. This, my friends, is an art all its own. Do it correctly, and no one will notice your work. That is the mark of a good composite—it's seamless! First, read on to learn more about compositing with a simple image and then move up to the big guns!

In this chapter, you examine several different compositing techniques and learn how to track moving footage. You use LightWave's compositing tools to do the following:

- Place a 3D object against a still background
- Place and move a 3D object in front of and behind a photograph
- Import moving footage and track LightWave's camera
- Attach a 3D object to footage of a moving vehicle
- Examine the basic techniques for doing two-pass compositing
- Learn about LightWave's render engine and output options

Understanding Compositing

When we talk about compositing, we're talking about seamlessly blending 3D computer-generated images either with other 3D computer-generated images or with 2D images, such as photographs of real settings or people. Most of the visual effects created for film and video consist of 3D animation and digital effects composited over, or more accurately into, live-action. This can include photography, video, and film, as well as AVI or QuickTime movies. Using compositing, you can make it seem as though a 3D object is there when it actually isn't.

An important aspect of compositing with LightWave is that it enables you to do more, especially if your system is not as fast as you'd like it to be. Compositing in this sense enables you to blend multiple images together. Of course, before you can complete a composite in LightWave, you'll need to render! Later in this chapter, you'll learn about the steps needed to render your composite animations for many types of applications.

Production houses often have entire departments devoted to the task and thousands of dollars invested in the software. From the optically composited spaceships of *Star Wars* to the digital people of *The Matrix*, compositing has come a long way. Over the years, compositing technology has evolved from purely optical techniques, such as matte paintings and frame-by-frame painting, to completely digital methods, but compositing will always be an important part of animation and visual effects. It is its own unique art. That is the core of success for most Hollywood production studios.

Indeed, the enormous importance of compositing has led to the development of many high-powered, complex, and *expensive* programs dedicated to the task. But LightWave comes with its own rather extensive set of tools both for compositing within the program and for exporting images to be composited in other software packages.

Compositing Basics: Background and Foreground Images

Compositing can be an extraordinarily complicated process, combining hundreds of separate 2D and 3D elements into one final image. However, many times, it's just as simple as placing a 3D object against a background image. You did this in Chapter 1, "Quick-Start," in the Quick-Start tutorial.

A background image, or *background plate*, as it is commonly called, is a 2D image. It is usually a digitized photograph or sequence of film, though not necessarily; sometimes, other rendered 3D footage is used as the background image. A 3D object is placed against the background image to make it appear as though the 3D object was always a part of the background. An example of this is the creatures in *Jurassic Park III*. Real settings were filmed with a regular camera, the footage was digitized, and then the 3D dinosaurs were composited into the footage to make them appear to be part of the picture.

Of course, compositing can be more complex than the preceding simple explanation. But regardless of how complex the composite, the background image is the beginning of every composited scene, either still or moving. You'll use both in this chapter.

In LightWave, the background image or movie has its place in the Effects panel under the Compositing tab (see Figure 20.1). This is where you begin the first exercise.

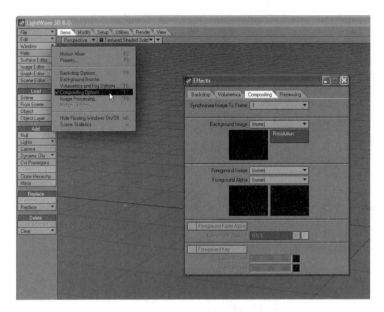

Figure 20.1   The Compositing tab is located under the Effects panel. Most everything
needed for compositing in LightWave can be found here. You can open this
directly from the Window drop-down menu at the top left of Layout or by
pressing Ctrl+F7.

Exercise 20.1   Adding a 3D Object to a Still Image

In this first exercise, you learn the basics for setting up just about any composited scene.
You learn how to load a background plate, as well as a 3D object, and marry the two
seamlessly. Study this process because it will be the same for any composite you do in
LightWave, including video footage.

1. From Layout, press Ctrl+F7 to open the Compositing tab of the Effects panel.

2. Click the drop-down menu for Background Image and select Load Image.

3. Load the Vegas_Street image from this book's DVD, as shown in Figure 20.2.

Tip

In addition to loading images directly from the Compositing tab, you also can go
directly to the Image Editor (F6) and select Load Image. This enables you to load
your image or sequence while having access to image-editing features.

Figure 20.2   A shot of a typical day in Las Vegas—outside of the casinos!

4. Render a frame by pressing the F9 key. You'll see the Vegas_Street image and nothing else. Exciting, isn't it?

Only the street image is displayed in the render because nothing else has been added to the scene. There are a few important things to note at this point that apply to both still and moving images:

• When using a background image, this image overrides any backdrop color or gradient backdrop.

• The background image is not affected by fog, though it can be used as the fog color instead of a solid color.

• By default, the background image is not refracted by transparent objects. However, you can set this option for each surface in the Surface Editor.

• The background image is always centered and stretches itself to fill the camera's entire field of view. This also is true of the foreground image, which you'll get to shortly.

• The background image can be seen directly in Layout through Camera view if the Camera View Background is set to Background Image in the Display Options tab (d).

The next step involves adding a 3D object into the scene.

5. Load the Porsche object from this book's DVD.

6. Select the Porsche object and press 6 on the numeric keypad to switch to Camera view. Make sure that Camera View Background is set to Background Image in the Display Options tab (d).

7. Move the camera so that the LightWave grid is roughly in line with the Vegas_Street background image, as in Figure 20.3. Start by moving the camera up and then rotating it.

Figure 20.3 To make your compositing job easier, first move the camera into a position that more closely matches the position of the real world camera that took the original photograph. You can align the camera easily by using LightWave Layout's grid as a guideline.

8. Move the Porsche object back into the frame and rotate it so that it is behind the cab in the middle of the street. Create a keyframe at 0 for the car to lock it into its new position, as shown in Figure 20.4.

Figure 20.4 To composite the car, move and rotate it into position so that it rests behind the cab in the middle of the street.

Now, the 3D object is composited against the background image, the most basic of all compositing situations. By moving the camera into a similar position as the camera that took the photograph, positioning the car was not too difficult. The LightWave grid helps you align to the background image.

This technique works for any situation in which a 3D object does not need to go behind a 2D image. You can also render, say, a logo background as its own animation. That rendered animation then can be applied back into LightWave as a background image. The 3D letters would then be animated on top. The benefit of this is control—not only do you have control over what you deliver your client, but you also have control over shadows, reflections, lights, shaders, and more. Rendering in passes is vital to proper compositing, and it is covered more fully later in this chapter.

Many times, however, you need to use a foreground image for situations in which a 3D object *does* need to go behind a 2D image. For example, suppose that a 3D car driving down the street needs to pull up behind other cars that are in the footage. Using a combination of foreground images (the cars) and a background image (the other parts of the footage), you can literally put a 3D element "into" your still or moving imagery.

The foreground image behaves in most ways like the background image. The main difference is that whereas the background image appears *behind* the 3D objects in the scene, the foreground image is applied *on top of* the 3D objects.

Exercise 20.2   Applying Foreground Images

You've seen how easy it is to place a 3D object in front of a photograph. The look is convincing, and you can go further with moving images. But what if you need to make the Porsche blend more with the photograph? What if it needs to come out from behind the other cars? This exercise shows you how to do just that.

1. Continue in Layout from the previous exercise.

2. In the Compositing tab of the Effects panel, make sure the Vegas_Street is still set as the background image.

3. Be sure you're in Camera view so that you can see the backdrop image (press d for Display Options to view backdrop images). You should see the background image pop up into the Layout screen when you select Camera view.

4. In the position the car rests in now, it only needs a shadow and lighting, which you'll create shortly. But for now, you want to make the car object appear behind other objects. Move the car to the other side of the street behind the palm trees, as in Figure 20.5.

Figure 20.5   Position the car on the other side of the street so that it's behind the trees, or at least it will be shortly!

5. Press F9 to render a frame.

You'll see that as in Exercise 20.1, the 3D object is pasted over the background image. But in this case, it needs to be *behind* the trees! You might think that's a problem. Most compositing programs show you how to composite behind a solid object, like a rock or building, but what about something with various see-through areas, like trees? LightWave makes it easy.

Now you add the foreground image and see how that changes your final output. You just need to create a mask for the trees in Modeler.

6. Jump into LightWave Modeler and press the d key for Display Options. Go to the Backdrop tab and load the same Vegas_Street image as a background image for the bottom left view. Increase the size to 5 m. Figure 20.6 shows the Modeler setup.

Tip

You can make the Image Resolution 1024 for better display in your backdrop images.

7. Expand the bottom left view and then zoom in to the image, focusing on the trees in the middle of the road, as shown in Figure 20.7.

Figure 20.6 Place the Vegas_Street image in the background display in Modeler to create mask objects.

Figure 20.7 Zoom into the background image to get a better view of the trees, the area you'll create a mask for.

8. Using the Pen tool, create a polygon in the shape of the bushes and trees, as shown in Figure 20.8. Just click to create points around a specific area of the image.

Important

When building this mask (or any mask), you only need to create enough of an object to meet your needs. For example, in the current exercise, you do not need to create a mask for the tops of the trees. You're building a mask so that a car on the street can pass behind them. Therefore, you only need to create a polygonal mask for the trees that is big enough to make the car object appear to be behind them. If, however, you had a flying object that needed to move behind the trees, you would then need to build a larger mask.

Figure 20.8 Using the Pen tool, you can quickly create a mask for any area of an image.

9. After you've laid down the necessary points with the Pen tool, press the Spacebar to turn the Pen tool off. Then, using the Drag tool (Ctrl+t), shape the points to better fit the image, if needed.

10. Press q (or the Surface button at the bottom of the Modeler interface) and name this new polygon Vegas_Street_Mask. Then save the object.

11. After the object is saved, send it to Layout from the drop-down arrow at the very top right of the Modeler interface, as shown in Figure 20.9.

Figure 20.9 Use the Send Object to Layout command at the top right of the Modeler interface.

12. After the object has been sent to Layout, move and position it so that it rests on the trees in the image. You'll need to do this from the Camera view, as that is the only way to see the image in Layout. Note that a bit of sizing might be needed to properly place the mask.

13. When the object is in place, create a keyframe at frame 0 to lock it down. Figure 20.10 shows the mask in place.

Figure 20.10 A little bit of Size and Move in Layout puts the mask object in place.

14. Be sure to save the scene at this point. Don't forget that pressing Shift+s saves incremental versions.

15. Press the F9 key to see how the scene looks. You should see something like Figure 20.11. The mask you made for the trees does indeed block the car object behind it, but the object is just gray.

Figure 20.11   Rendering a frame shows the mask in place blocking the car but not really looking like part of the scene.

16. Open the Surface Editor and select the Vegas_Street_Mask surface. Press the T button to the right of Color to open the Texture Editor. You're going to apply an image map to the mask.

17. With the Texture Editor open, make sure you have the Layer Type set to Image Map. Blending Mode should be set to Normal, while Opacity should be 100%. These values are usually the default values when you start up the Texture Editor.

18. For Image, select the Vegas_Street image. It's already loaded into Layout, and even though it's applied as a background image, you can apply it to the Vegas_Street_Mask as well. When selected, you'll see a thumbnail of the image appear.

19. Right above the Image listing is Projection. Instead of the default Planar type of projection, choose Front. This tells LightWave to use a Front Projection map on the surface, which essentially uses the same data applied in the background for the selected surface. Figure 20.12 shows the Texture Editor with these settings.

Front Projection Image Mapping is one of the most powerful compositing tools LightWave has to offer. It enables your 3D objects to interact with your 2D images in almost every way that they can interact with other 3D objects.

Front Projection Image Mapping works by—you guessed it—projecting an image onto an object. The image is "projected" from the camera's point of view such that it would appear exactly as though it were a background or foreground image.

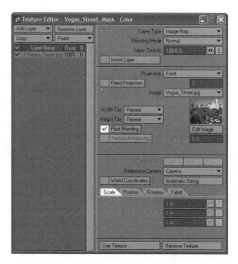

Figure 20.12   The Texture Editor with a Front Projection map applied.

20. Click Use Texture at the bottom of the panel and, back in Layout, press F9 again to render a frame. You should see that the trees now have a surface on them that matches the background plate. Figure 12.13 shows the render and the car object now behind the trees.

Figure 20.13   With a Front Projection Map applied to the mask, the car now really looks like it's behind the trees.

In most cases, you'll need to adjust the Luminosity and Diffuse values for the front projection mapped surface. Because of the lighting in the scene, you need to carefully balance these two values so that the polygons that make up the mask perfectly blend and match the background image. In this particular tutorial, the mask is small, just a few trees, and overall is fine.

Tip

Remember to move, rotate, size, and stretch the mask object. Render a frame. It will always show a portion of the image, no matter where you place it or what its angle is. Remember that using OpenGL Textured Shaded Solid view, you'll be able to see your textures applied in real time, directly in Layout. Rendering an image gives you a more accurate idea of the setup with surface values.

21. To make the mask blend a bit better, in the Surface Editor, set Luminosity to 40% and Diffuse to 70%. Render a frame again (F9), and you'll see that it's hard to see where the Front Projection mask ends and the background image begins.

22. Oh, and did you save? Yep, gotta save all objects to save the surface changes, and be sure of course to save the scene.

However, the car itself still looks like it's floating. This is because all the real cars in the background image have shadows—your 3D car does not. Shortly, you'll learn how to create matching shadows to finish off your composite. The next section takes the compositing scene a step further using foreground images.

Foreground Key and Foreground Alpha

In the next exercise, you'll learn about the Foreground Key. The Foreground Key is nothing more than a color-keying system such as the blue- and greenscreen systems used by TV weathermen and in visual effects throughout the industry. It works by *keying out*—removing—a range of colors that you specify. LightWave gives you two colors: a Low Clip Color and a High Clip Color.

The Low Clip Color is generally the darkest, most saturated color you would want to remove from your foreground image. The High Clip Color is the brightest, least saturated color you'd want to take out. Any colors between these two colors are removed from the foreground image before it's pasted over the rendering. For the current exercise, the Vegas_Street image can be used, specifically to make an airplane appear behind the strip of buildings. There's no Photoshop involved—it's all done directly within LightWave.

Exercise 20.3   Setting Up a Foreground Key

In this exercise, you key out the sky and leave the buildings of the Vegas strip. To do this, you want to pick the darkest, most saturated color in the sky and set this to be the Low Clip Color, and you'll set the brightest, least saturated color for the High Clip Color.

1. Starting where you left off in Exercise 20.2, in the Compositing tab of the Effects panel, check Foreground Key to On. Set the Foreground Image to Vegas_Street.

2. Set the Low Clip Color to R:94 G:146 B:204. Set the High Clip Color to R:140 G:175 B:197.

   Now, you're probably wondering where these values come from. Although you can use another image-editing program to determine the color value of the Low Clip (the sky in the street image), you can do it directly in LightWave.

3. From the Rendering drop-down list at the top left of Layout, select Render Options. In the Render Options panel, set the Render Display to Image Viewer. You'll see two options there: Image Viewer and Image Viewer FP, or "floating point." The FP version is useful for determining values for HDR, or High Dynamic Range imagery.

   For this project, you want to use just the Image Viewer for RGB images (not Image Viewer FP). You can simply select a color based on your own eye. Remember, this is a range of color, high and low—it's not specific.

4. Press F9 to render a frame. After the frame is rendered, the Image Viewer opens. Move the mouse over to the sky. Click and hold the mouse and look at the title bar of the Image Viewer panel. Figure 20.14 shows the Image Viewer.

   Values appear there! Those are the RGB values of the image where the mouse is. You'll see four values—Red, Green, Blue, and Alpha. The first two sets of numbers before the dashed line are the pixel number of the image.

   The 140, 180, 240 RGB value for the Low Clip Color setting was determined using the Image Viewer. Cool, huh?

Tip

You can set color values quickly by dragging with the right mouse button directly over the color square.

5. Back in Layout, load the 747 object from this book's DVD. This is a simple generic plane that you can use for compositing in this exercise. Move the plane back into the frame and position it so that it's rising up from behind the buildings, as in Figure 20.15.

Figure 20.14 Using LightWave's Image Viewer from the Render Options panel, you can easily find RGB color values of your background image.

Figure 20.15 Load the 747 object and position it behind the buildings.

6. Press F9 to render a frame and watch as it renders. You'll see the background render, the mask you created for the trees, and the Porsche behind the trees. But where's the 747? Figure 20.16 shows the scene rendered, but the 747 object is obscured by the sky.

Figure 20.16 Even though you've set the high and low clip colors, the range is too small for LightWave to key out the sky, so the 747 is obscured.

7. Often, the color values you set for the low and high clip values aren't enough. So, set the high clip color to R:221 G:230 B:236 in the Compositing tab of the Effects panel.

8. After you've set the new clip color, press F9 again. Figure 20.17 shows the 747 now rising up from behind the buildings.

Figure 20.17 With a slight change in the High Clip Color, the 747 now appears to be rising out from behind the buildings.

This is a good technique to use when your foreground image can support it. In this case, the image was a good candidate for this technique because the area you needed to key out was a large bright area with very little variation in color, and it was significantly different in color than the rest of the picture. You might think that this method would have been much simpler for the trees to block the car instead of making a mask. Yet the trees and the area behind it (the road) are simply too close in color to create an easy keying effect; therefore, a mask was made. For the sky, this image was perfect to use because there is a clear distinction between the buildings and the sky. There is little haze and a strong variation in brightness and color.

Foreground Keying

However, not all images are this easy to use for keying and compositing. For images that are more complex, or for those times when you want more control, LightWave offers you the Foreground Alpha.

An *alpha* is a grayscale image that is used to tell a program where certain things should happen. In the case of a surface texture, an alpha image tells the surface where to apply a texture map. It could, for example, tell a surface where to be transparent and where to be opaque. And in the case of a foreground image, the alpha image determines where the image appears and where it doesn't.

Exercise 20.4   Using Foreground Alpha

This exercise uses a feature available in LightWave that enables you to key out portions of an image for foreground compositing. This technique uses the Foreground key features to remove parts of an image.

1. Using the Image Editor, continue from the previous exercise and load the image Vegas_Street_Alpha image from this book's DVD. Turn off Foreground Key in the Compositing tab if it's still active.

2. In the Compositing tab of the Effects panel, beside the Foreground Alpha image, click the selector and choose the Vegas_Street_Alpha image. If you want, you can load an image from here as well.

3. Click the check box beside Foreground Fader Alpha.

    This tells LightWave to ignore the areas of the foreground image that the Foreground Alpha has marked pure black. Otherwise, those areas would be added to the image, making that part of the image much too bright.

4. Move the 747 in front of the large building to the right of the image. Angle it so that it appears to be jetting out from roof of the lower building in front.

5. Press F9 to render a frame. Figure 20.18 shows the rendered image.

Figure 20.18   Using a Foreground Alpha image gives you precise control over where the composited foreground image will be clipped.

Obviously, the 747 doesn't belong in the image like this; however, other objects could, and that's the point. Using a foreground alpha image provides the control you might need for specific keying purposes.

The alpha image you used was created in Adobe Photoshop from the original Vegas_Street image. It has had its sky and the large building on the right painted black, while everything else is painted white. The white areas block the objects from rendering, enabling the foreground image to show, thereby making it look as if the plane is jetting out from the roof of the building.

Tip

> Using the techniques here, you can very easily create the street of your dreams. Build a 3D sign, and yes, you can finally see your name in lights!

Now you can see that the rendered image appears much as it did with the Foreground Key but this time using an alpha image. Using an alpha image gives you much more flexibility in determining where your foreground image appears. It is also more accurate than using a range of colors to clip the image. However, both methods are suitable depending on the project and the images at hand.

Using alpha images when compositing gives you the most control over your scene because the alpha image can be used to shape the foreground image into any shape you desire.

The situation outlined in the previous exercise would be fine if your 3D object needed only to be placed behind the buildings and in front of the sky. But if your object needed to start out behind the trees, rise up above them, and then swoop down in front of them, it wouldn't work. The foreground image would be pasted on top, no matter what.

Another, more common situation is that of having a 3D object cast shadows and otherwise interact with your 2D images. Earlier in this chapter you put the Porsche 3D car object on the street and created a mask so that the car appeared to be behind the trees. It now needs some shadows. This kind of seamless compositing is the mainstay of the visual effects industry. Without it, the movies and television shows you watch every day would be tremendously different.

As you might have guessed, LightWave has the answer to compositing and casting shadows.

Shadows

Without question, compositing is cool. But what makes it cooler is when the user can't tell the difference between what's real and what's not. Adding shadows to your 3D objects helps you move one step closer to creating a perfect composite.

Exercise 20.5   Creating Shadows for Compositing

Front projection image mapping is unique in the way it maps the texture image, but in every other way it's just a normal surface texture. It can receive shadows, reflect other objects, and be transparent. By using these characteristics, you can make the objects appear to interact with the scene.

1. Load your scene created from Exercise 20.2 or load the Compositing_Shadows scene from this book's DVD. This is the background image, with the tree mask and Porsche object loaded.

2. Back in LightWave Modeler, create a large flat polygon about 160m in size, as shown in Figure 20.19.

3. When created, press q to name the new polygon street_shadow or something similar. Save the object and send it to Layout.

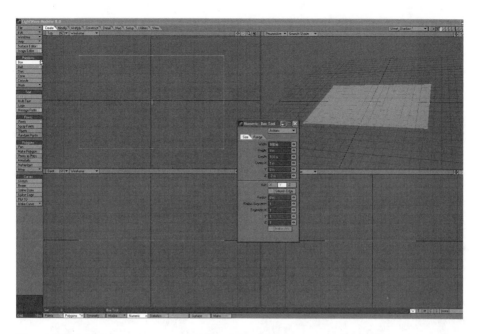

Figure 20.19   You can create a simple large flat polygon to catch the shadows of the car in Layout.

4. In Layout, move and position this new object to the street area where it will be used to catch a shadow from the Porsche. Be sure to check a side view to make sure that the Porsche object is resting directly on this polygon, as in Figure 20.20.

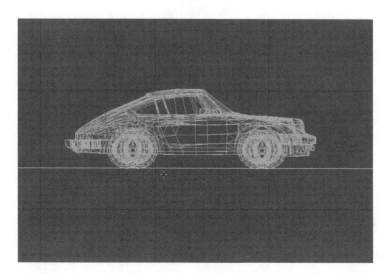

Figure 20.20   Position the large flat polygon so that the Porsche object rests right on top of it.

5. Just as you did with the trees, apply a Front type projection image onto the large polygon representing the street.

6. Increase the Luminosity to about 40% for the street surface, as shown in Figure 20.21.

Figure 20.21   Be sure to make the front projection map blend with the background image by increasing the luminosity of the surface.

At this point, you need to set up the lighting so that you can match the real world lighting and cast shadows.

7. Select the light in the scene. While still in Camera view, press y to rotate the light so that it casts light onto the car matching the other cars. Looking from the Camera view, this light's position is to the upper left. Figure 20.22 shows the light from three angles.

8. Be sure to create a keyframe for the light at frame 0 to lock it in place. Then, from the Render Options panel under the Render menu tab, turn on Ray Trace Shadows. Press F9. Figure 20.23 shows the car on the street with shadows closely matching those of the real cars!

As you can see, it's not very difficult to cast shadows in composited images. There are a few more things that will help integrate the Porsche into the background image.

9. Add another distant light to the scene. Name it fill light or something similar.

Figure 20.22   A single distant light is used to light the composited scene. Its position is not important—but its rotation is. However, moving it into a key location helps you visualize its effect on the scene.

Figure 20.23   After the light is in place and shadows are turned on, the Porsche object is now more closely integrated into the background image.

10. Make sure the new light is selected, and press the p key to call up the Light Properties panel. Set the Light Intensity to 90%. Change the Light Color to a soft blue, something along the lines of the sky.

11. Finally, position the light so that it casts on the top and backside of the car, as in Figure 20.24. Be sure to create a keyframe for the light to lock it in place. Also, turn off Affect Specular. You do not want this light creating hotspots on the car—it's just a general fill light.

Figure 20.24   Add a new light to the scene and position it so that it casts a light on the back and top of the car.

12. You might have noticed that adding light to the scene also brightens the ground polygon that you made to catch the shadow. So, in the Light Properties panel, select the Objects tab. You'll see a list that reads Exclude. Click the space to the left of the Street_Shadow, and you'll see a check mark. What you've done here is told the light to exclude (don't light) the selected object. Figure 20.25 shows the operation.

13. Save the scene.

14. Select the tree mask object you made earlier in the chapter. Press the p key to open the Object Properties panel (if it's not already open). Selecting an object after a light with a properties panel open simply makes the panel change over.

15. In the Object Properties panel for the tree mask object, select the Render tab. At the bottom of the panel, turn off Self Shadow, Cast Shadow, and Receive Shadow. This object needs none of these, and if you noticed in the earlier renders, the mask object also casts a shadow on the street, as did the car. You only want the car to cast a shadow. Figure 20.26 shows the panel.

16. Press F9 again to render a frame. Now, you should see only the car casting a shadow, and its back is lit more.

17. Save the scene!

Figure 20.25
The new light added helps create an ambient fill light for the top and back of the car; however, it needs to not light the street shadow object, so it's told to exclude it.

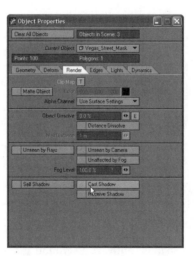

Figure 20.26 Make sure that only the objects that are supposed to be casting shadows should. Here, the shadows are turned off for the tree mask object in the Object Properties panel.

Many times, animators are looking for a magic variable to set up composite shots. In actuality, nothing is better than your own eye and sense of judgment. Does the 3D object look too big for its environment? If so, make it smaller. Does the object look out of perspective? If it does, rotate and reposition it. The same goes for lighting.

The shadow cast from the car has a pretty nice value, closely matching the shadows the other cars in the image are casting. This is as far as you're going to take this project, but you could do a lot more with it to flesh it out, such as adding in your own street signs, adding more cars, or even taking all the cars out! You can make a front projection map in the shape of the road, paint out the cars in Adobe Photoshop (or similar paint program) so that the road is empty, and then use that image in Lightwave. Add your cars and shadows, and you've manipulated reality! A few other tips to think about are:

- Set other objects, such as curbs or buildings, in place to receive shadows or even model an entire stand-in of the other buildings on the street.

- Model the cars' windows to receive not just shadows but also reflections!

- Add more lights to more fully simulate the light in the scene, such as a light on the front side of the car.

- Add a bit of fog or some blur to help blend the Porsche into the background.

- Add post-processing filters such as film grain. A bit of film grain usually helps to really set in the objects. Right now, the object is too clean for the image.

This was a simple example with a single frame, but everything in it applies properly to image sequences and movies as well. Situations like you've just seen—casting shadows on flat surfaces—are fairly common. But what's even more likely is what you'll examine next: how to composite something into moving footage!

Match Moving

Compositing is fun, and at this point, your imagination should be on a roll. Hmm, what's next, spaceships over a city? Dinosaurs in your backyard? The possibilities are endless. But what about putting a 3D object into moving footage? It's easier than you think with LightWave! The best way to demonstrate this technique is visually. We've included the match moving tutorial on this book's DVD.

Having a 3D object cast a shadow onto "real" ground is probably the most common compositing situation you'll have to deal with. By *ground shadow*, we're referring to flat shadows on the Y-axis. It's hard for people to comprehend at times how you can have a shadow beneath an object when the image is behind it. However, it's a lot easier than it sounds, as you saw. But what happens when you need to composite a 3D object into moving footage? Match moving is best explained visually so that you can see the moving video. Therefore, the tutorial for match moving is on this book's DVD. You'll find a match moving video tutorial visually showing you the following:

- Loading an image sequence into LightWave Layout

- Creating reference points for 3D tracking

- Tracking the moving footage

- Adjust the lighting

- Adding and attaching a 3D object to a moving vehicle

In the exercise, you're going to place a 3D logo on a "real" moving truck and make it fit right in. Figure 20.27 shows the footage you'll use for match moving, provided for you on this book's DVD.

Figure 20.27   Using a sequence of real video, you'll learn how to composite into this footage and learn to track it.

When we talk about "tracking" the footage, we're talking about matching the LightWave camera to the real world camera that shot the footage. Doing so enables you to put 3D objects in real images.

The Next Step

This chapter gave you a good working knowledge of using images and 3D objects together. You can see that the possibilities are endless, using a combination of backdrop images, front projection mapping, and 3D objects. It is very possible for you to make your own robots, monsters, or characters come to life in photographs and moving footage. LightWave's compositing tools are all you need for working with moving footage as well. Be sure to try out some ideas on your own, and don't forget to watch the video portion of this chapter from the book's DVD. You'll see just how easy it is to track a moving shot and build your 3D objects into it. After you've done that, turn the page and learn about LightWave's render engine and networking rendering options.

Chapter 21

Rendering and ScreamerNet

Rendering was mentioned in Chapter 1's Quick-Start tutorial, and throughout this book, you've rendered test frames to see how lights, textures, and various effects look in their final form. But at some point, you'll need to set up a serious render. That is, one that needs to be saved properly, in both the right pixel size and the right format. After you set up your animations, you must ask yourself at some point, "Now what?" This chapter shows you the methods and options available for rendering and outputting your animations. It demonstrates rendering on a single computer and on multiple machines by using Lightwave's built-in network rendering engine, ScreamerNet. Specifically, this chapter provides information on the following:

- The LightWave rendering engine
- Camera settings for rendering
- Rendering options
- Setting up a network render

LightWave provides you with a variety of rendering methods that are easy to set up and use. Figure 21.1 shows the LightWave Render Options panel in Layout. You can find this panel by first going to the Render menu tab at the top of Layout and then clicking the Render Options command on the left side of the interface.

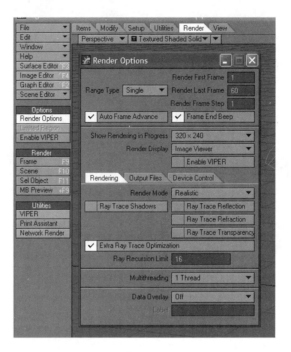

Figure 21.1 The Render Options panel in Layout.

The LightWave Render Engine

You will find that the LightWave render engine is one of the best in its class. It's fast, efficient, and, most importantly, good at what it does. As you can see from the images throughout this book, on the enclosed DVD, and on NewTek's web site, LightWave produces the highest quality renders in its class. Through the software's radiosity rendering, area lighting, and shadow options, the LightWave rendering engine can deliver beautifully rendered images and animations. But before you can get to this level of rendering, it's good for you to know the process of setting up an animation to render.

Setting Up an Animation to Render

Before you can move into rendering an animation (on one machine or across a network), the animation must be set up properly. There are a few details you need to run through first to properly set up an animation for rendering.

Camera Settings for Rendering

Without even knowing it, the steps involved in rendering an animation will become second nature. You'll be jumping easily between the Render Options panel and the Camera Properties panel, making sure that you have all your settings in place. Figure 21.2 shows the Camera Properties panel. This panel is mentioned in this chapter because the settings here are directly related to the output of your animation. Access this panel by selecting the Camera button at the bottom of Layout and pressing the Properties button to the right (or press the p key).

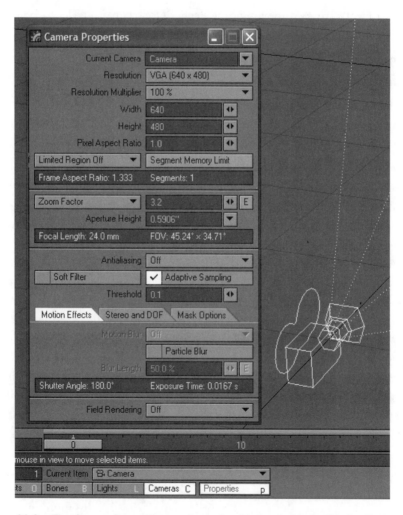

Figure 21.2   The Camera Properties panel goes hand-in-hand with the Render Options panel. Here, you define the current camera's resolution for rendering, antialiasing settings, and the aspect ratio.

Using the Camera Properties panel, you can check out your settings for rendering. For proper camera placement, these values should be set up before you begin animating, and it's always a good idea to double-check them before you render. In addition, you set up any motion blur, field rendering, or antialiasing here.

Range Type Rendering

Normally you wouldn't find too much information in this chapter about single-frame rendering. Press F9, and you've rendered a single current frame. But there's more to this feature in LightWave 8. At the top of the Render Options panel (refer to Figure 21.1) you'll see a selection named Range Type. Here, you have three options for rendering:

- **Single**. Setting Range Type to Single tells LightWave to render one frame at a time. Pretty easy, huh?

- **Arbitrary**. This cool setting enables you render a range of frames. Let's say you wanted to render frames 1 through 10, as well as 12, 13, and 20. Set these frames in the panel, and away you go! LightWave renders the specific frames.

- **Keyframe**. Here, you can tell LightWave to render just a specific object on a specific axis. Say you wanted to render the giraffe from Chapter 10, "Modeling Quadrupedal Characters," on just the Z-axis. Set those values next to Range Type and render your animation. The Keyframe option renders the frames on an object's channel that has keyframes. For example, if you had a keyframe on the X channel for a light at 0, 15, 30, 45, and 60, those frames would be rendered with this setting.

General Purpose Rendering

After you've chosen which range type of rendering you'll use, you'll need to set up the rest of the render options. Most often, to render a full animation, you'll choose Single as the Range Type. This exercise guides you through the kind of rendering most commonly used by LightWave animators: rendering that generates animations for video or computer work. If, however, you are using LightWave for rendering anything other than video or computer work, such as film or print, the information here still applies, and the differences are noted.

Exercise 21.1   Creating a Basic Render

1. In Layout, load the RenderThis scene from this book's DVD.

This scene is from an earlier chapter in the book, with lights and ray trace options applied. Figure 21.3 shows the scene when loaded.

Figure 21.3   For rendering purposes, use the RenderThis scene from this book's DVD.

Now generally, you would have set up your camera when you set up the animation in Layout. You'd do this because a different camera setting can change how your Layout setup looks. The first thing to do when you're ready to render is display the Camera Properties panel. You are ready to render when you have all your lighting, textures, and motions in place. This scene has all these in place.

2. Select the camera (if it's not already selected) and press the p key to enter the Camera Properties panel.

The Current Camera at the top of the panel should read Camera because only one camera is in the current scene.

3. Set the Resolution to D1 (NTSC) for video resolution. Change the Resolution Multiplier to 100% for equal size. You'll see the Width and Height values change when you do so.

Figure 21.4 shows the information area in the Camera Properties panel that displays the Frame Aspect Ratio and Segments.

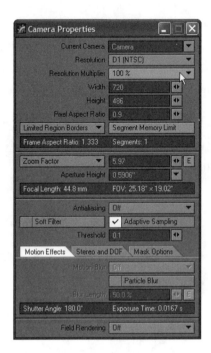

Figure 21.4   The information area within the Camera Properties panel shows how many segments LightWave is currently using to render each frame.

4. Make sure that Segments shows a value of 1 by increasing the Segment Memory Limit to that value.

   If the Segments value is higher than 1, your render times could increase. Don't worry, though. If you are short on system memory, you can use less RAM for rendering. In that case, the Segments value can be greater than 1—say, 3 or 4.

   At this point, you want to tell LightWave to use more RAM for rendering.

5. Click the Segment Memory Limit button and change the value to 20 or higher.

   LightWave now has more memory with which to work and will render your frames in single segments.

6. When asked if you want this value set to the default, click Yes. LightWave won't use this RAM until it needs it, so you can set it fairly high.

   The Zoom Factor should have been set up before you began creating your animation. If you change it now, you might have to change your shots and reset the keyframes.

7. Leave the Zoom Factor set to 5.97. The Aperture Height should be left at the original setting as well.

Important

While you're working, it's not necessary to have Antialiasing on, but you definitely want this on for your final renders. Although you have the choice of Low to Extreme settings, it's recommended that you render all your animations for video in at least Enhanced Low Antialiasing. Medium or Enhanced Medium Antialiasing can provide you with a cleaner render. High Antialiasing is overkill and a waste of render time for video. It might actually make your images look blurry.

8. Click Adaptive Sampling.

Activating this setting tells LightWave to look for the edges to antialias in your scene. The Threshold value compares two neighboring pixels, and a value of 0 sees the entire scene. A good working value is .12. You can set the value higher, which lowers rendering time. For this scene, you do not need any motion blur.

9. Do not change the Stereo and DOF setting or the Mask Options setting. This scene will not use these. You can read more on these settings in Chapter 8, "Cinematic Tools."

10. Go back to the Motion Effects tab and select Odd First for Field Rendering.

Field Rendering renders two fields of video for every frame rendered, with the odd field first. Figure 21.5 shows the selection.

Figure 21.5   Field Rendering is selected and set to Odd First in the Camera Properties panel. This tells LightWave to render the odd fields of each frame first.

11. Close the Camera Properties panel and save your scene. All your settings are saved along with it.

You should visit the Camera Properties panel at least twice during an animation, if not more—once to set up the camera and zoom factors before beginning animation setup, and once before you are ready to render to set up antialiasing, motion blur, field rendering, and proper resolution size. From here, you can set up the Render Options panel.

Basic Rendering

The Camera and Render Options panels go hand in hand. This exercise continues where the Exercise 21.1 left off.

Exercise 21.2   Creating a Render with LightWave

1. With the RenderThis scene from this book's DVD still loaded, go to the Render Options panel.

   Figure 21.6 shows the Render Options panel. This is where you tell LightWave what to render and where to save it. You'll see Render First Frame, Render Last Frame, and Render Frame Step values. If your LightWave animation in Layout has a first frame of -30 and a last frame of 300, it will not render those frames unless they are entered here.

   The frame numbers you assign to your timeline in Layout do not automatically apply in the Render Options panel.

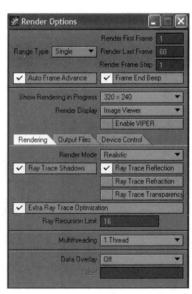

2. Leave Render First Frame set to 1 and set Render Last Frame to 300 (10 seconds). Render Frame Step should be at 1 to render every frame. A Render Frame Step of 2 would render every two frames, for example.

3. Turn on Automatic Frame Advance.

   This tells LightWave to advance to the next frame and continue rendering, which is very important for full animations!

Tip

> Frame End Beep is useful for monitoring the completion of your rendered frames but is not necessary. It's kind of annoying after a while.

Figure 21.6
The Render Options panel is home to all the controls you need for setting up renders.

4. Uncheck Show Rendering in Progress to turn it off.

   Although it is useful for monitoring your rendering, Show Rendering in Progress slows down the rendering process if left on for longer animations.

5. Turn off the Render Display.

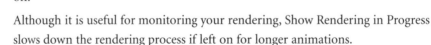

Important

The Image Viewer and Image Viewer FP render display remembers your rendered frames. Turn this on while performing test renders on individual frames (F9) and leave it open. You can select any of your previously rendered images from its Layer list. You also can view the alpha channel in this viewer and save an image.

6. Turn off Enable VIPER from the Render menu tab if it's on.

   VIPER is needed when setting up surfaces and other VIPER-ready features in Layout, but for final rendering, this should not be applied. Leaving VIPER on while rendering multiple frames increases render times and memory usage.

   The Rendering tab is where you tell LightWave what parameters to use for rendering, such as ray tracing. Here, you can tell LightWave to calculate Ray Traced Shadows, Ray Traced Reflections, and Ray Traced Refraction.

7. Make sure Ray Trace Shadows are on, as well as Ray Trace Reflection, but turn off Ray Trace Refraction. This option is not needed in this particular case. No refraction is used in this scene, so keeping this option on increases render times.

   You also can add Ray Trace Transparency for objects that need to have a transparent surface reflect a certain way, such as a car window.

8. The Render Mode is usually set to Realistic and is not often changed. However, you do have the option to render Wireframe or Quickshade versions of your animations here.

9. Click Extra Ray Trace Optimization. Set the Ray Recursion Limit to 6. The higher the value, the longer LightWave takes to render, but the more accurate your Ray Tracing is.

   The Ray Recursion Limit, which doesn't often change, determines the number of times LightWave calculates the bounced rays in your scene. In the real world, this is infinite, but in LightWave, you can set a Ray Recursion Limit up to 24. Changing this setting increases render times. A good working value is 12. However, setting a lower value of 6 or 8 can be a real timesaver when using the Ray Trace Reflection option. For best results, try not to set this value lower than 6. If you find render errors, such as black dots, bring this value back up to 12 or so.

Important

Setting a Ray Recursion limit too low for scenes that have transparent surfaces may result in a black opaque surface instead of a see-through surface! If this happens, just up the Ray Recursion limit a bit.

10. If your computer has more than one processor, select 2, 4, or 8 for Multiprocessing. If you have only one processor, set the Multiprocessing to 1. If you have multiple processors and have applied pixel filter plug-ins, such as HyperVoxels, make your processors work for you by clicking Multithread Pixel Filters. Some plug-ins, however, might not be compatible with multithreading, so remember to check this setting if you find errors in your render.

11. Set Data Overlay to display the Frame Number, SMPTE Time Code, Film Key Code, or Time in Seconds in the bottom-right corner of your animation.

    This is good for reference test renders. In addition, when one of these values is set, you can add a note in the Label area. This is good to do for test renders for clients that have a history of not paying and/or stealing your work. You can put a copyright notice in the upper corner, for example.

12. After you've set all the render options, be sure to save your scene. Saving regularly before any render (even a single-frame render) is a good habit to get into.

Those are the main parameters you must set up to render an animation. However, you still need to tell LightWave where to save the files and what type of files to save. The next section discusses the various file formats and procedures for saving your animations.

Saving Renders

Within the Render Options panel is another tabbed area, titled Output Files. This area is where you tell LightWave what type of file you want to save and in which format it should be saved. Figure 21.7 shows the Output Files tab within the Render Options panel.

The first area within the Output Files tab is the Save Animation selection. This confuses many people. You are creating an animation in LightWave, right? Save Animation! Makes sense—but it means something a little different. Clicking Save Animation enables you to save your rendered frames as one animation file, in a format such as .AVI, QuickTime, or .RTV (Video Toaster). It saves one complete file. You select different types of animations to save by using the Type selection option. Note that you'll need a Video Toaster board from NewTek for the RTV option.

Using Save Animation is great for previewing QuickTime movies or for using Aura and Video Toaster, but you also can save individual frames—and do so at the same time. If you select the Save RGB button, you're telling LightWave to save the individual frames as they are rendered. Similarly to Save Animation Type, you select from a variety of RGB formats in which to save your animations by selecting the one you want from the Type drop-down list, as pictured in Figure 21.8.

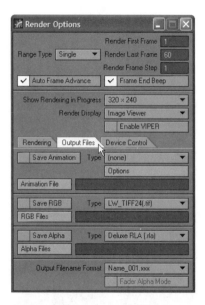

Figure 21.7   The Output Files tab within the Render Options panel is where you tell LightWave what type of file to save and where to save it.

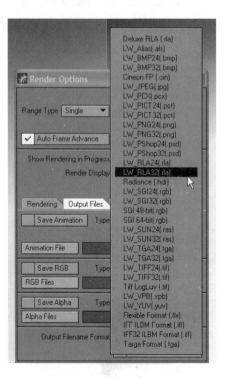

Figure 21.8   LightWave gives you a slew of formats for saving your RGB frames. This is the best way to render your animations if you do not use Video Toaster NT. The individual frames can later be imported into a variety of programs.

Finally, in the Output Files tab, you also can save the alpha channels of individual frames. Figure 21.9 shows the alpha channel setting in the Render Options panel.

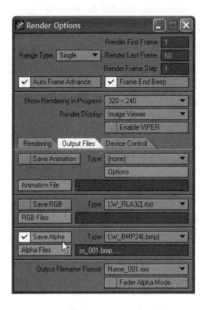

Figure 21.9   You can save the alpha channel information of individual frames in the Output Files tab.

This is great for later compositing in a post-production environment. Remember that all these file types can be saved with one rendering. You can save a QuickTime or .AVI file, plus the RGB and alpha files all at once. Pretty cool, huh?

When all this is set—the camera resolutions, the rendering information, and the output file information—you're finally ready to render your animation. Pressing the F10 key renders your animation. Congratulations!

Tip

You might have a high-resolution frame that needs to render over a long period of time. You can tell LightWave to automatically save this frame by setting up the Render Options as though you were rendering a full-length animation. Set the RGB format, output filename, and location for saving, and then click Automatic Frame Advance. Make the First Frame and the Last Frame the same frame you want to render—say, frame 10. LightWave renders that frame and saves the RGB, and because it's also the Last Frame, rendering then stops.

Render Selected Objects

If you click the Render drop-down list in Layout, you'll see the Render Selected Objects selection. Because LightWave enables you to select multiple objects, you can save significant amounts of rendering time with this option. In the Scene Editor or in Layout, you can select all objects at once by holding the Shift key and clicking the objects. Rendering selected objects has two useful functions:

- It saves render time by rendering only the objects you're interested in at the moment.

- It enables you to render multiple passes of the same animation with or without certain objects. This is great for special effects or compositing, or even for rendering before-and-after sorts of animations.

Thoughts on Rendering

You can refer to this section of the book often when it's time to render your animations and images. But then you have to answer the question that arises: "What's next?" When your animations are complete, the next step is to bring them into a digital animation recorder and lay them off to tape or edit your final animations with audio and effects in a non-linear editor.

The exercises in this chapter have not only introduced you to the compositing tools in LightWave but have also given you the knowledge to create your own composited images and animations. From here, you can build your own 3D objects, such as cars, spaceships (don't overdue it with these), insects, or people, and experiment with compositing them into real-world images. You can use the color photographs on this book's DVD for your projects. Take a look in the Extras folder, and you'll find royalty-free images that you can use in the same manner as the images from the exercises in this chapter. Try using some of the city photographs to fly objects in front of and behind buildings while casting shadows. Use other images to make a 3D character walk down a long sidewalk or a flight of stairs. Try photographing or videotaping your living room and rendering 3D objects on the table! From here, experiment and practice whenever you can. If you have a digital camera, keep it with you at all times to create your own images for compositing.

Rendering your animations must be done. Someday, you might not need to render, as processors and video cards become increasingly powerful. For now, though, LightWave still has to render, just like any other 3D application. But you'll find that the rendering engine inside LightWave is one of the best around. It's strong and stable, and most importantly, it produces beautifully rendered images.

NewTek has added many OpenGL enhancements. These speed up your workflow and give the poor F9 (Render Current Frame) key a break. Work through the exercises in this book and make your own animations anytime you can. You can't be in front of your computer 24 hours a day—well, maybe you can, but you shouldn't. Try getting on the treadmill, too! When you get ready to take a break, set up a render. Don't just wait until the animation is "perfect." Render often and see how your animation looks. You might find new ways to enhance it and make it even better. Or you might just find that it's per-fect the way it is. Now, if they only had a way to do LightWave in the bathtub...

Network Rendering

LightWave enables you to render over a network of computers, not just the individual machine on which you're working. Whether you have a few computers or hundreds of computers at your location, you can use all of them for rendering the same animation.

LightWave ships with some important network rendering software called ScreamerNet. ScreamerNet has been a part of LightWave for years. With ScreamerNet, LightWave needs to be installed on only a single machine. This distributive rendering can send your animations to other networked machines that have a ScreamerNet process running. You don't have to use this feature, because it is used more in larger animation studios that want to maximize time by using multiple computer environments. Please refer to your LightWave manuals for proper instruction.

ScreamerNet also is useful on a single machine for batch-processing your animations. Think about setting up four versions of your animated logo to render one right after the other. Because LightWave saves the Render Options information within a scene file, ScreamerNet knows where and what to save from your specific animations. You even can run ScreamerNet without running LightWave. Use ScreamerNet to batch-render animations without loading your scenes. The distributed rendering section of your LightWave manual can instruct you further on the proper command lines needed to set up this process. The following sections provide a complete tutorial on how to set up your own network render farm.

Overview of Rendering in LightWave Utilizing ScreamerNet

The ScreamerNet software has two parts to it; the first resides in the LightWave layout program, found under the Rendering, Network Rendering popup menu. This is the "controller" part of ScreamerNet. The second can be found in the Programs folder, found in the main LightWave install directory. It's a separate program called LWSN.exe; this is the program that is run on the machines that are "controlled."

What Is ScreamerNet and How Does It Work?

The concept is relatively simple. One of the computers on the network is designated the "master" computer. This is usually the computer with the full LightWave installation on it. The master controls the other computers, or "nodes," by passing "render commands" to them. These commands tell the node which scene to load and which frame to render.

When a node has finished rendering a frame, it passes a command back to the master saying it has finished and is ready for the next frame; the process is repeated until all the frames have been rendered.

The Command Folder

These render commands are not actually passed directly from computer to computer— the LightWave program on the master computer isn't talking directly to the LWSN.exe program on each node. Instead, they are talking to each other through a special folder: the command folder.

This is an important folder that the master and all nodes must be able to see somewhere on the network. This is because the render commands are actually text files with the command inside. The text files are saved into the command folder with a unique name to separate one node's commands from another. These commands are better known as "job" files. Each job file has a number corresponding to the node it is designed for, so node 1 is passed job1, node 2 is passed job2, and so on.

Likewise, for the nodes to talk back to the master, they too need to save files with unique names so that the master knows which node is talking back to it. These returned commands, or acknowledgments, are known as "ack" files, and like the job files, the ack files have a number to say which node sent it; thus, node 1 returns commands to the ack1 file, node 2 returns commands to the ack2 file, and so on. Figure 21.10 presents a diagram of the process.

We know that the master and nodes need to be able to find the command folder in order to "talk" to each other, but the command folder only stores instructions on which scenes and frames to render; it doesn't actually pass any scene data to the nodes. So like the command folder, the render nodes also need to know the location of the scene's content.

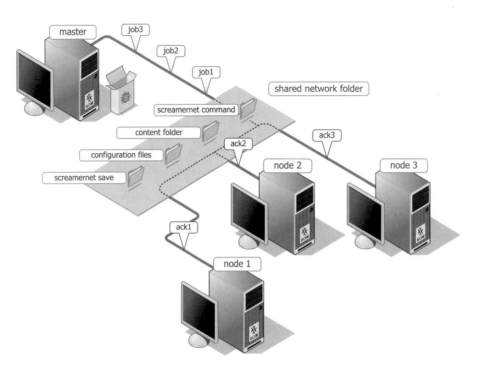

Figure 21.10 Diagram of ScreamerNet command passing technique.

The Content Folder

This is where the content folder comes into play. It stores all the objects and images used to make up the scene, as well as the scene file itself. Like the command folder, all the nodes must be able to see this folder so that when told to render a frame from a certain scene, they know where on the network to look for it.

Good Content Organization

Good organization of content is essential if you want to make your life easier in LightWave. Storing files all over your hard drive to make up one scene will just give you headaches, so instead try to organize your LightWave projects in a logical manner. Good content organization is especially important when using ScreamerNet. Before I go into this, you must first understand how LightWave finds content. Bear with me on this; it's long-winded but worth a read!

Ignoring ScreamerNet for a second, start up LightWave Layout and bring up the Options panel (use the o key or go to the popup menu Layout, Options, General Options). The first setting you'll see is the Content Directory input. This is where you tell LightWave where to look for any content files when it first tries to load anything. This location, along with other settings, is saved inside the LightWave preference file (LW8.cfg) when you quit the program.

If you load the LW3.cfg preference file into a text editor (it's just a text file, really), among many other entries, you will find these:

```
DirectoryType Scenes C:\LightWave\Scenes
DirectoryType Objects C:\LightWave\Objects
DirectoryType Surfaces C:\LightWave\Surfaces
DirectoryType Images C:\LightWave\Images
DirectoryType Previews C:\LightWave\Previews
DirectoryType Motions C:\LightWave\Motions
```

These are additional search locations added by LightWave that are scanned when you try to load anything. For example, if you tried to load an object, LightWave looks in C:\LightWave\Objects first. It looks in C:\LightWave because that is where the content directory has been set. If you were to set your content folder in your preferences to D:\Somewhere\on\my\harddrive, LightWave would automatically change the entries in this list:

```
DirectoryType Scenes D:\Somewhere\on\my\harddrive\Scenes
DirectoryType Objects D:\Somewhere\on\my\harddrive\Objects
DirectoryType Surfaces D:\Somewhere\on\my\harddrive\Surfaces
DirectoryType Images D:\Somewhere\on\my\harddrive\Images
DirectoryType Previews D:\Somewhere\on\my\harddrive\Previews
DirectoryType Motions D:\Somewhere\on\my\harddrive\Motions
```

LightWave takes the content directory setting and adds those subdirectories. If they don't exist, LightWave uses only the content directory you set, in this case D:\Somewhere\on\my\harddrive.

The point is, LightWave expects to find these subdirectories within the content directory. Taking this into account, when you save a scene (which is also a text file you can read), LightWave saves the location of any items in the scene file without the content directory part of the location. For example, if your content folder was set to C:\Program Files\LightWave\Content, and in your scene you had loaded an object called final_object.lwo that was stored in a folder called My Objects and then a subfolder called "Final Versions," the scene file would have an entry that loads the object from disk like this:

```
LoadObjectLayer 1 My Objects/Final Versions/final_object.lwo
```

The LightWave program knows the top-level location of the content directory (taken from the LW8.cfg file), and the scene file knows the rest (see Figure 21.11).

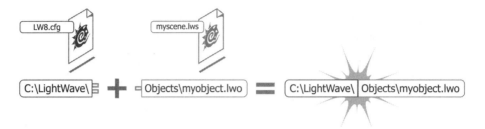

Figure 21.11   This diagram shows how the path works when a scene file is saved.

There is a reason for this, and it's important! Let's imagine LightWave didn't have a content directory preference, and instead it saved the full location of any objects, images, and so on with the scene file. Thus, it would be C:\Program Files\LightWave3D 7.5\Content\My Objects\Final Versions\final_object.lwo. If you were to give that scene to someone else to work on, or if you wanted to work on a different computer, unless you copied the files into exactly the same directory structure, LightWave would complain about missing files.

This is because LightWave tries to load the files using the locations from the original computer, which might not match the current computer. Hard-coding file locations isn't a good idea, which is why LightWave doesn't work this way.

So what is the best way to organize content files? Well, that depends on how you work with your files. The favored method is to have a folder with the project name, and inside that are the objects, scenes, and images folders. You would then set your content directory to the top-level folder before trying to load anything. This method is great if you constantly work on a project in various places, or if several people are working on it and it needs to be passed around because everything needed for the scene is in a self-contained set of folders.

However, if you are the sole user and you work from one machine, this method can be a pain when working on several projects because you must keep setting your content directory to each project before loading. This is shown more clearly in Figure 21.12.

Personally, it's easier to organize your content files as shown in the figure. The benefit of doing it this way is that you must point your content directory to one folder only once. This is essentially a reworked version of the first method. It is still portable because you just have to collect items for a scene in several places, and if you don't move your content around much, I find this a better way of organizing content files.

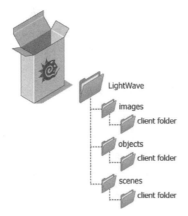

images
  client folder
objects
  client folder
scenes
  client folder

Figure 21.12   A good working content directory within LightWave could work something like this.

If none of that made any sense, don't worry. As far as ScreamerNet is concerned, it doesn't matter how you store your files as long as it can find them, but it is good practice to organize your files logically.

Another very important fact to remember when saving scenes, objects, and textures is that spaces in file and folder names can sometimes cause problems with ScreamerNet. Instead, use the underscore symbol (_) or a hyphen (-).

Back to ScreamerNet; let's recap. We've learned so far that for the master computer to "talk" to the nodes, they all must be able to see the command folder because they use this to pass messages to each other. The nodes must also be able to see the content folder because it stores all the files needed for rendering. Thus, the content folder holds the files for rendering, while the command folder stores the instructions on what to render.

Configuration Files

In addition to the content and command folders, a third item must also be accessible to the nodes: plug-ins. Any plug-ins you've used to create effects in your scene must also be found on the network. For example, if you've used Sasquatch to create hair on a character or a motion plug-in to move an object (LightWave itself uses plug-ins to load and save files), even if you haven't used any FX plug-ins, ScreamerNet still needs to know where they are to save files after it has rendered them. All these plug-ins are separate files that need to be loaded by the LWSN.exe program, just as LightWave did when you created your scene.

When you think about it, if the ScreamerNet program needs to know the location of all the plug-ins you have installed, you would need to type the location of every single one! That would be a lot of typing! The way LightWave deals with this is by storing the location of all the plug-ins in a configuration file. When you scan your plug-ins, LightWave is "writing down" where they all are; it then saves them to a configuration file. This file is called LWEXT8.cfg (LightWave EXTensions). So to tell ScreamerNet where all your plug-ins are, all you need do is tell it where the LWEXT8.cfg file is on the network.

There is another config file ScreamerNet needs to find in order to work: LW8.cfg. As we mentioned earlier, this is the LightWave Layout configuration file. It stores a whole bunch of settings, but most importantly, it stores the location of the content folder we mentioned earlier.

Let's recap. Table 21.1 presents a breakdown of what ScreamerNet needs to be able to find on a network in order to run.

Table 21.1   ScreamerNet Needs

Needs to Find	Needed For	Information Stored In
Command Folder	Master computer to "talk" to render nodes	Nodes told at initialization time
Plug-ins	Plug-ins used in the scene and for file saving	LWEXT8.cfg
Scene Content	All objects, images, and scene files	LW8.cfg Nodes told at initialization time

Technically, these items don't need to be in one place; they don't need to be in the same building or even the same country! As long as ScreamerNet can find them, they could be anywhere. However, for the sake of simplicity, it makes sense to group these items in one place: a shared network folder (see Figure 21.13).

There are many methods of physically networking Windows machines together, but because there are so many variables to consider—too many for this book—I'm going to assume that you already have a Windows network up and running. If not, the Internet is your best resource, or your computer administrator if you have access to one.

Sharing files across a network obviously means you are going to refer to locations using pathnames. As far as ScreamerNet is concerned, there are two main methods for doing this. The first is using Universal Naming Convention (UNC), while the other is using Drive Mapping. They ultimately do the same thing but differ very slightly.

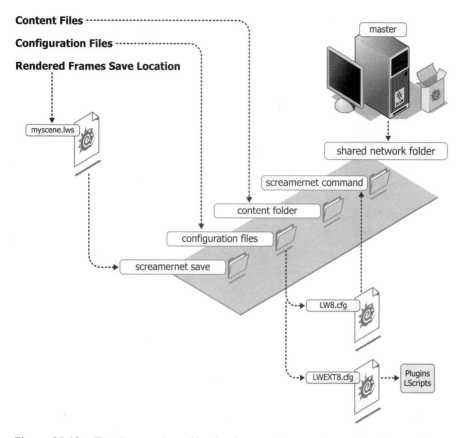

Figure 21.13   This diagram shows files that ScreamerNet needs on a shared network.

UNC Naming

This is the simpler method of the two. UNC naming is exactly as it sounds—it's a standard naming convention for finding drives or folders on a network.

Whenever you browse through folders using Windows, the address or network path can be seen in the address bar (the screenshot shown in Figure 21.14 might differ depending on your Windows version).

 Tip

In the Windows 2000 and Windows XP versions of Explorer, you might need to set the address bar to display the path by going to Tools, Folder Options, View and turn on Display the full path in the address bar.

Figure 21.14   An address path in Windows.

In the example shown in Figure 21.14, the address path tells us that the computer name on the network is dansboxx, and on that computer is a folder (which has to be shared to be seen) called screamernet. Inside that folder is another called screamernet_command.

That is essentially it! Locating folders and files for ScreamerNet using this method requires us to type the location of the shared network folder, kind of like the address for your house. So as long as you can see the computers, drives, and folders you are trying to access on the network, it's very easy to work out the network path by simply looking at it in the address bar as shown in Figure 21.14.

Drive Mapping

This technique was favored by a lot of the ScreamerNet tutorials I read, but I could never understand why, because it takes more time to set up and can be confusing.

Drive mapping is the process of replacing a network path to a folder with a letter. Imagine we had a folder on a computer on a network, and its pathname was something like \\my_computer\documents\excel\timesheets\2003. You could substitute all that with a letter, T: for example. Then whenever you accessed the T: drive, it would take you straight to the folder 2003.

Sounds great, doesn't it! Well, not quite. If we were to use this method for ScreamerNet, we would have to map the path to the shared ScreamerNet folder to a letter on each computer. The problem arises when a node computer tries to access a mapped drive on a computer that is switched off or unavailable; it complains that the path can no longer be found.

This can be a problem if you are setting up ScreamerNet in an office using your colleagues' computers, especially if they don't know what the error message means! They will soon tell you about it!

However, if you are intent on using this method for resolving pathnames, here's how to map a letter to a pathname. I won't be using this method for this tutorial because it offers no benefits over UNC naming that I'm aware of.

Right-click on the My Network Places icon (again this will differ depending on the version of Windows you are using; if in doubt as to where the option is, do a search in Windows Help). See Figure 21.15.

Figure 21.15   Right-click on My Network Places and select Map Network Drive.

There will be an option called Map Network Drive. Clicking the option invokes another window, as shown in Figure 21.16.

Figure 21.16   The Map Network Drive dialog box is where you can configure drives from your network.

The Map Network Drive dialog box is where you set which letter you want to assign; in our ScreamerNet example, S: seems to makes sense. After a letter is selected, you can then set the path to map the letter to in the Folder pull-down menu. Alternatively, you can click the Browse button and browse the network for the folder (see Figure 21.17).

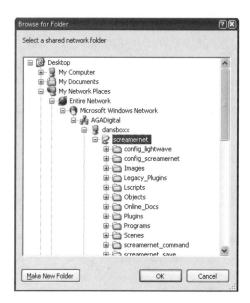

Figure 21.17 The Browse for Folder panel lets you point to a specific folder.

When done, click the Finish button. If you now look in My Computer, you see a new drive called S:, which points to the folder you specified. Any reference to the S: drive goes straight to that folder, as shown in Figure 21.18.

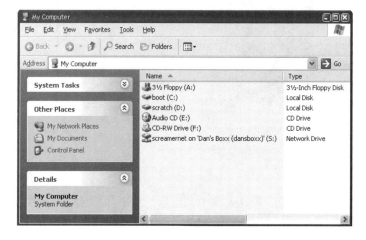

Figure 21.18 A newly mapped drive from your network.

Setting Up Sharing

Okay, back to ScreamerNet and sharing the files it needs.

We know what ScreamerNet needs to be able to find. Now is the time to figure out where to put these files. By default, LightWave stores most of its files in one folder, usually found on the main hard drive in a folder called LightWave. If yours is different from this, don't worry.

When we say "most files," this is because Windows steps in here and interferes a little! If a program is written to conform with Windows protocol, it stores its preference files in user-specific folders. The idea is that many people using one machine can have their own preferences and setups, and technically this is a good idea, but it can cause problems with ScreamerNet if you're not sure which preference files LightWave is using. To avoid confusion, either use one set of preference files or "point" LightWave to the right files when it starts up—more on this later.

The location of these preferences depends on which version of Windows you are using, but it is either in C:\WinNT\Profiles\WhichUser or C:\Documents & Settings\ WhichUser. If in doubt, do a search for LW8.cfg and see where they are.

The content files are also usually stored within the main LightWave folder, but again these can moved anywhere you like as long as you tell LightWave and ScreamerNet where the new location is.

To make this tutorial the same for all users, I'm going to suggest that the LightWave content, config files, and command folder all be stored in the main LightWave folder (on the master computer). If you don't want to do this, just make sure you replace all pathnames to these items with the new location you've decided on.

Before we start sharing these files, you must create some new folders in your LightWave directory. Figure 21.19 shows the folder structure for a typical LightWave installation and the new folders you need to create.

The new folders are screamernet_command, screamernet_save, config_lightwave, and config_screamernet. These are in the command folder, a folder to which to save the rendered frames, the regular LightWave config folder, and a config folder specifically for ScreamerNet use.

Okay, we now have placeholder locations for all the items ScreamerNet needs. They are all in one place, and all we need to do now is share the folder across the network so all the computers can see it.

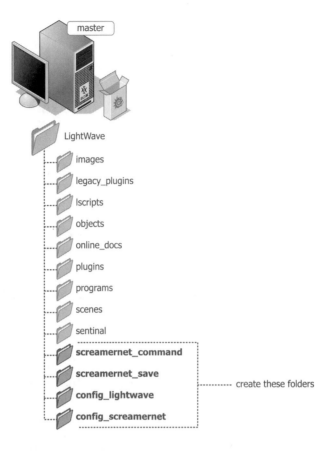

master

LightWave

images

legacy_plugins

lscripts

objects

online_docs

plugins

programs

scenes

sentinal

screamernet_command

screamernet_save

config_lightwave

config_screamernet

create these folders

Figure 21.19   Here is a typical LightWave directory showing the folders created during installation and the new ones you must create.

The process for this might differ slightly depending on which version of Windows you are using. I'm writing this on Windows XP Professional, but the principles are the same for nearly all versions of Windows.

Locate your main LightWave folder on the master computer and right-click it to bring up the context-sensitive menu. In the list, there should be a Sharing and Security option (see Figure 21.20); if not, select the Properties option and find the Sharing tab.

You should now be presented with another window. Under the Sharing tab, there should be an option to turn on sharing for that folder. When activated, you can enter a name in the Share name box. You can call this anything you like, but something succinct like "screamernet" is all that is needed, and just to be safe, make sure it's all lowercase with no spaces, as in Figure 21.21.

Figure 21.20   Right-click your LightWave folder to view the Sharing and Security options.

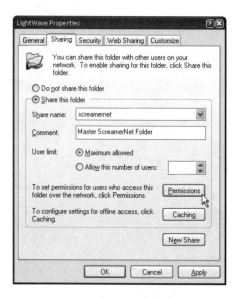

Figure 21.21   The Sharing option for the LightWave folder.

While you're in there, make sure you set the Permissions for the folder to Full Control so that any computer (or render node) can read from and write to the LightWave folder. See Figure 21.22.

Now if you browse your Windows network, you should be able to see the folder you've just shared (see Figure 21.23).

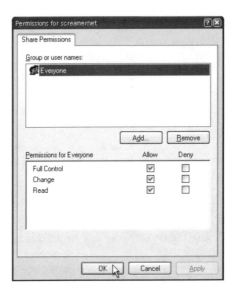

Figure 21.22   When accessed, you'll find the Share Permissions dialog box.

Figure 21.23   After you set up the folders for sharing, you can view them.

Setting Up the Master Computer

Now that all the folders are in place and are accessible across the network, we can begin to set up the computers.

Setting up the master is a little more involved than setting up render nodes because this computer has the main LightWave installation on it, which means it's the computer that is normally used for editing scenes, creating objects and texture maps, and so on.

As mentioned earlier, LightWave uses config files to determine where certain things are. The pathnames to these items are local to the computer they reside on. This causes problems for ScreamerNet because it needs the pathnames to be "network-aware."

What this means is that we will need two sets of config files: one set for when we are working with LightWave as normal and another set for when we are using ScreamerNet.

This is why we created the two folders (config_lightwave and config_screamernet) earlier.

By default, LightWave won't know anything about these folders because we created them, so we need to tell LightWave to use them. The easiest way to do this in Windows is to "point" LightWave to the correct set of config files when it loads.

Fortunately, this is easy to do in Windows using shortcuts. Windows shortcuts can pass information to a program as it loads by typing commands into the Target box. To locate this box, you'll need to find the existing shortcut to LightWave Layout in your Start Menu or create some new ones from scratch in the usual manner.

You'll need to create two shortcuts to the LightWave Layout program, one for regular LightWave use and one for ScreamerNet use (see Figure 21.24).

Figure 21.24   Create two shortcuts to LightWave Layout, one for everyday LightWave use and the other just for ScreamerNet.

After you've created the two shortcuts, right-click them and bring up the Properties dialog box for each one (see Figure 21.25).

Find the box called Target.

For normal LightWave use, enter the following:

```
C:\LightWave\Programs\lightwav.exe  -cc:\LightWave\config_lightwave
```

For ScreamerNet use, enter the following:

```
C:\LightWave\Programs\lightwav.exe  -cc:\LightWave\config_screamernet
```

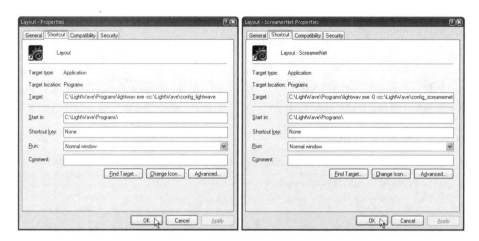

Figure 21.25   Right-click on the shortcuts you've created to bring up the Properties dialog box.

The first part, C:\LightWave\Programs\lightwav.exe, has to do with the shortcut, and it's simply a path to the LightWave Layout program. The second part is the bit we're interested in, -cc:\LightWave\config_screamernet, where the -c switch tells LightWave you are providing the location of the config files, and c:\LightWave\config_screamernet is the path to where the config files are located. Note there is NO space between the -c and c:\LightWave\config_screamernet.

We don't need these paths to be "network-aware" because they are not used by ScreamerNet; they simply point LightWave to the files that do contain the information ScreamerNet needs.

Now that we have the shortcuts for LightWave pointing to the correct config files, you need to actually copy your existing config files to both the config_lightwave and config_screamernet folders so that any custom menus, color settings, plug-ins you've added, and so on are loaded when you run LightWave. As mentioned earlier, these config files might be located in different places depending on your version of Windows, so simply do a search for LW8.cfg. When found, copy the files LW8.cfg and LWEXT8.cfg into the two config folders you've created.

Okay, now everything is in place to run the version of LightWave Layout that will be using the ScreamerNet config files.

We need to set up a few things in this version of LightWave so that the settings are saved to the ScreamerNet version of the config files when you quit the program.

The first item is where the command folder is located on the network. This option is found under the Rendering, Network Rendering menu (see Figure 21.26) in the Network Rendering dialog box (see Figure 21.27).

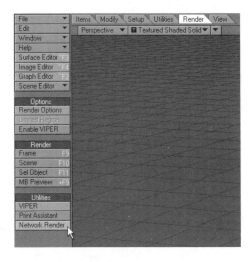

Figure 21.26   LightWave's Network Rendering panel is found under the Render tab in Layout.

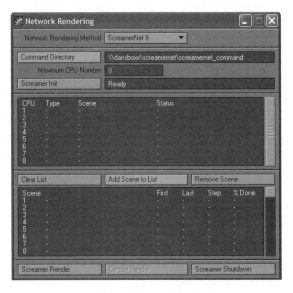

Figure 21.27   LightWave's Network Rendering panel, where you can set up multiple renders and network rendering.

Clicking the Command Directory button opens another window in which you can locate the shared network folder on the master machine. If you are using the names suggested in this tutorial, it the folder is called screamernet_command and is inside the screamernet shared folder. Figure 21.28 shows the dialog.

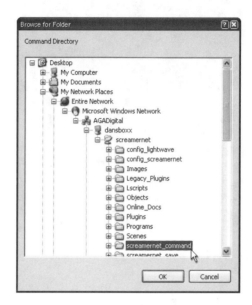

Figure 21.28   The Browse for Folder panel, shown accessing the screamernet_command and other folders.

Whenever you browse for anything in the screamernet shared folder like this, make sure you browse from Entire Network. If you added screamernet as a Network Place shortcut and used that, it seems Windows resolves to a local pathname, which causes problems because the path is no longer "network-aware." I learned the hard way!

The next item to set is the content directory. This is found under the General Options panel (press the o key), as shown in Figure 21.29. Click the Content Directory button and locate the screamernet shared network folder again. Select the top-level screamernet folder and click OK (see Figure 21.30).

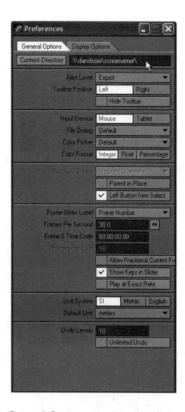

Figure 21.29   LightWave's General Options panel, accessible by pressing o on the keyboard.

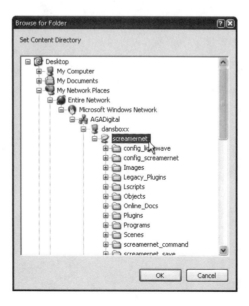

Figure 21.30   The Browse for Folder panel used again.

Almost done! The last thing we need to set up is the location of the plug-ins on the network. Some tutorials tell you to open the LWEXT8.cfg file and perform a search and replace on the pathnames. You could do it that way, but it's easier (and less error-prone) to rescan your plug-ins using the shared network path location.

The option to scan your plug-ins can be found under Layout, Plugins, Edit Plug-ins menu (or Alt+F11), as shown in Figure 21.31.

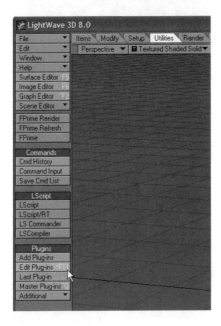

Figure 21.31   LightWave's Edit Plug-ins panel is found under the Utilities tab in Layout and Modeler.

This opens the Edit Plug-ins window, where you will find the option to Scan Directory (see Figure 21.32).

Click the Scan Directory button, locate the Plugins folder on the shared network, and click OK to scan the folder (see Figure 21.33).

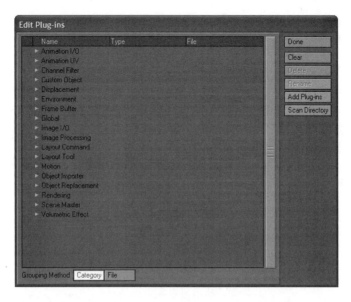

Figure 21.32   The Edit Plug-ins panel enables you to scan for multiple plug-ins or to simply add one at a time.

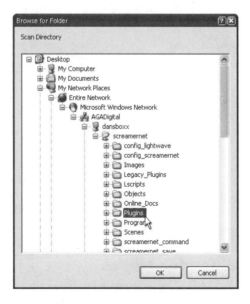

Figure 21.33   When scanning for plug-ins, you can also scan across your network.

Repeat this process and locate the Lscripts folder. That's the master computer setup (see Figure 21.34)!

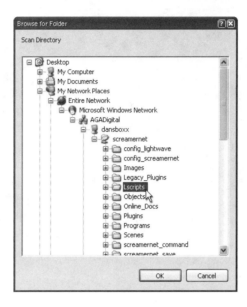

Figure 21.34   The Browse for Folder panel again, used for adding plug-ins.

To recap, you created two shortcuts to the LightWave Layout program. Each shortcut pointed to a different set of config files, one for normal LightWave usage and the other for ScreamerNet use.

You then copied the existing config files into the config_lightwave and config_screamernet folders. When done, you loaded the version of LightWave pointing to the ScreamerNet config files.

Next, you set up the content folder and the command folder, and rescanned the plug-in list. This saved the "network-aware" pathnames for each item into the ScreamerNet config files.

Setting Up the Render Nodes

Setting up the nodes is relatively simple compared to the master computer because you can set up one node and then simply copy the same set of files to the other nodes, changing only a few bits of information.

At this point, you need to decide whether your master computer itself is a render node. When ScreamerNet is up and running, the master computer isn't doing anything more than passing commands around, and it's certainly not doing any rendering. So unless you plan to do some work while the other computers are rendering, you could make the master a render node, too.

Whether you decide to use your master computer as node 1 is up to you, but the process of setting up the master as a node is exactly the same as if it were a totally different computer. You simply run both LightWave and the LWSN.exe program.

Before you start with the detailed stuff, the first thing you'll need to do is copy some files from the master computer onto the hard drive of each computer that will be a render node.

Create a folder called LightWave on the main hard drive (usually the C: drive) of each node computer (obviously, you don't need to do this on the master because it should already have LightWave installed). Now copy the entire folder called Programs from the master computer into the "LightWave" folder you've just created on each node (see Figure 21.35).

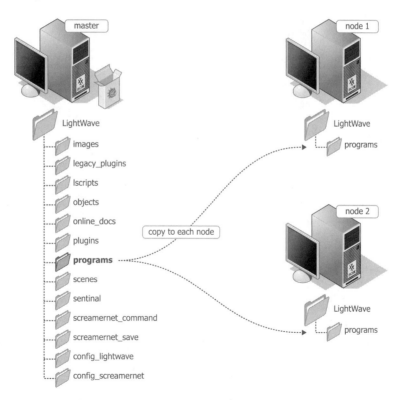

Figure 21.35   Copy the LightWave programs folder to each node, as shown here.

The last part of setting up a node requires a little explanation. If you are unfortunate enough to remember computers in the days of MS-DOS, you'll be familiar with running programs through a command line. MS-DOS didn't have a lovely GUI with icons for programs, so you had to type the name of the program to run it, along with any "commands" the program needed after its name.

Well, nostalgia is back! Despite the lovely Windows XP interface, some programs still require you to run them through the command line, and LWSN.exe is one of them!

The LWSN.exe program needs to know a few things at runtime: where the config files are stored, where the content directory is located, and which job and ack number it is going to be in order to distinguish itself from the other render nodes.

Having to type all this information for each node every time you needed to run ScreamerNet would be a pain. Fortunately, Windows enables you to create a text file that acts as a stored command line. This text file has a special name—a batch file. It has the file extension .bat, but really it's just a plain text file.

To create a render batch file, open up a text editor. (Notepad is fine.) Type the following text, replacing any reference to \\Mattxp\screamernet with the network path to your own shared folder we set up earlier.

```
echo "LightWave ScreamerNet Node 1 Initialisation . . ."
cd c:\lightwave\programs\
LWSN -2 -c\\Mattxp\screamernet\config_screamernet -
➡d\\Mattxp\screamernet\ \\Mattxp\screamernet\screamer_command\job1
➡\\Mattxp\screamernet\screamer_command\ack1
```

Now save the file (as a text file) with the extension .bat and place it inside the LightWave folder of the computer that will be node 1. You can call the batch file sn_init_1.bat, for example, although you can call it anything you like.

The render batch file script might look complicated to users unfamiliar with MS-DOS, but it's pretty straightforward when broken down, so let's do it.

```
echo "LightWave ScreamerNet Node 1 Initialisation . . ."
```

This line has nothing to do with ScreamerNet whatsoever; it's just a little text that is echoed to the screen to tell you to which node number the batch file has been assigned. You can leave this out if you want.

```
cd c:\lightwave\programs\
```

This line changes the current directory to the Programs directory on the main hard drive so that the next line knows where to find the LWSN.exe program. If you installed LightWave somewhere else, then change this line to reflect where you put it.

```
LWSN -2
```

This runs the LightWave ScreamerNet program. The `-2` sets up which mode ScreamerNet will run in. The `-2` basically says you're accepting commands from the master computer on which scene or frame to render. There is a `-3` mode, which enables you to specify the scene and the start/end frames, but this mode defeats the point of using several computers to render a scene because `-3` mode only enables you to pass it one scene. Basically, you'll never need to use `-3` mode!

```
-c\\Mattxp\screamernet\config_screamernet
```

This command tells LWSN.exe where the config files are kept on the network. The `-c` is the switch that says the following text is the path to the config files. If you have your config files elsewhere, now is the time to tell ScreamerNet where they are. Remember, LWSN.exe needs to know the location of the config files in order to find the location of the plug-ins, the paths to which are stored in the LWEXT8.cfg file. Note that it's important that there is no space between `-c` and the pathname after it.

```
-d\\Mattxp\screamernet\
```

This command tells LWSN.exe where the content directory is on the network. The `-d` is the switch that says the following text is the path to the content directory. I've never quite understood why you need to tell ScreamerNet this because it should be stored in the LW8.cfg. I guess it's just in case you want to store them somewhere else. Again if your content directory is not in the shared network folder, replace `\\Mattxp\screamernet\` with the path to where you put the shared network folder containing these items.

```
\\Mattxp\screamernet\screamer_command\job1
```

No switch this time, but this is where you tell LWSN.exe where to look for job commands and which job number it is to be allocated.

```
\\Mattxp\screamernet\screamer_command\ack1
```

This is almost the same as the previous line, but instead of a job number, an ACKnowledgement number is provided. The number must be the same as the job number.

The diagram in Figure 21.36 shows how this all links up with our shared network folder we set up earlier.

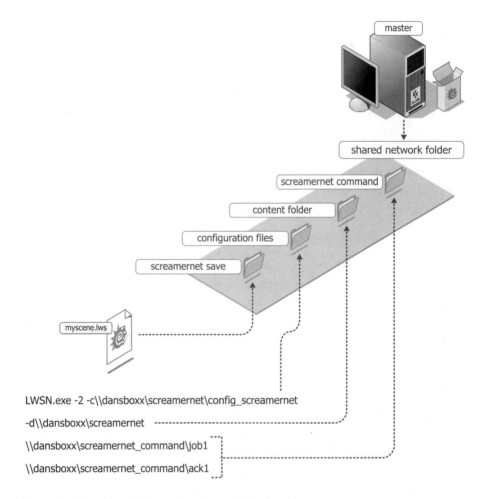

Figure 21.36   A batch file matches shared folder locations.

That's the node 1 setup. To set up the other nodes, simply copy the sn_init_1.bat file (or whatever you named it) to the LightWave folder on all the other nodes.

After copying, you need to rename the file to reflect the render node it is going to be. You also need to edit the job and ack numbers to reflect the node number. Depending on how many nodes you have, you should have something like what is shown in Figure 21.37.

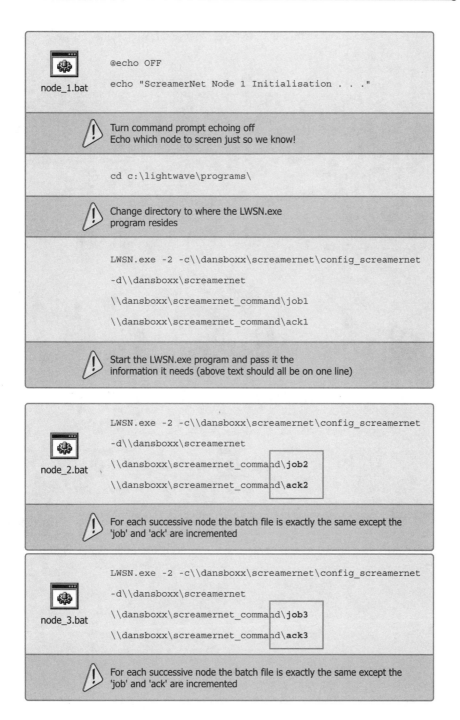

Figure 21.37   Successive nodes are set up as shown here.

Before we run ScreamerNet through its paces, Figure 21.38 presents an overview of what's been set up.

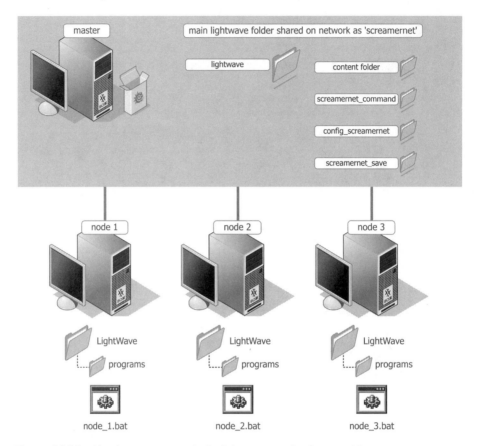

Figure 21.38 Here's an overview of what's been set up for ScreamerNet.

If you decided to set up the master computer as a node, it should look like Figure 21.39.

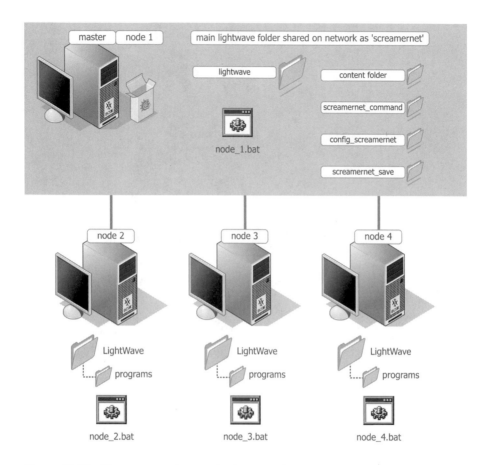

Figure 21.39   The master node setup for ScreamerNet.

Setting the Save Location

You need to do one last thing before you run ScreamerNet, and that is set the save location for the rendered frames. You could have all the render nodes save their frames locally; the only downside to this is that you have to go hunting for them across the network before you can build them into the final animation.

It makes sense then to use the shared folder that all the machines can see because all the frames can be saved in one place, making them nice and easy to find. As I'm sure you guessed already, this is why we created the screamernet_save folder earlier.

The only place you can set the save location for the rendered frames is within the scene file itself. So run the version of LightWave using the normal config files, open up the scene you want to render, and bring up the Render Options panel (found under the Rendering, Render Options menu), as shown in Figure 21.40.

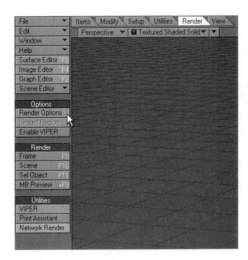

Figure 21.40 LightWave's Render Options panel is found under the Render tab in Layout.

In the Render Options panel under the Output Files tab, there is an option to Save RGB. Clicking the check box invokes a file save window; here you need to set the location for the rendered frames. This should ideally point to the screamernet_save folder in the shared network folder, although this can be anywhere you like, as long as ALL render nodes can see it on the network. With that done, save the scene, and you're ready to render it using ScreamerNet (see Figure 21.41).

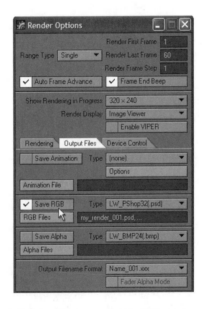

Figure 21.41 LightWave's Render Options panel enables you to set a save path for renders.

Rendering Using ScreamerNet

You're almost there, but first let's run through a quick checklist:

- Master Computer
  - ❑ Created new folders in main LightWave folder: config_lightwave, config_screamernet, screamernet_command, screamernet_save
  - ❑ Copied existing config files to new config_lightwave and config_screamernet folders
  - ❑ Set main LightWave folder to share across network using the name screamernet
  - ❑ Created two shortcuts to LightWave Layout
  - ❑ Pointed one shortcut to the config files in the folder config_lightwave, the other shortcut to config_screamernet
  - ❑ Ran LightWave Layout using the config_screamernet config files
  - ❑ Set the command directory to the folder screamernet_command in the shared network folder
  - ❑ Set the content directory to the shared network folder screamernet
  - ❑ Rescanned the plug-in list from the shared network folder screamernet location
- Render Nodes
  - ❑ Created folder called LightWave on main hard drive
  - ❑ Copied programs folder from LightWave folder on main computer to LightWave folder on render node
  - ❑ Set up render batch file using config_screamernet as config folder, shared network folder as content directory and each with unique job/ack numbers
- Scene Files
  - ❑ Set save folder to screamernet_save in the shared network folder

Okay? Let's go!!!

If you can remember that far back, I mentioned that ScreamerNet had two "parts" to it; the first is the controller part that is the Network Rendering panel in LightWave, while the second part is the LWSN.exe program sitting on each node.

When a node is activated, it looks for its first job file. However, there won't be any there until you initialize ScreamerNet in the Network Rendering panel, but it's pointless initializing it until you've activated all the nodes!

When you run ScreamerNet, a node does two things: It looks for job files and sticks its hand in the air, saying "I'm here, I'm over here!" Well, not quite, but it's waiting to be found by the controller part of ScreamerNet. This is where some confusion lies with ScreamerNet. Nodes complain they can't find job files when they're first run. This is perfectly normal. Bearing this in mind, double-click each render batch file to activate it. You'll see output like that shown in Figure 21.42.

Figure 21.42   The current directory is identified.

The first thing the node should tell you is where it's looking for the content files. If this is wrong or if it comes up with an error, close it down and check the script for errors in the path names.

The next thing you should see is the node complaining that it can't open a job file (see Figure 21.43). This is perfectly normal because there isn't one to open, but the important thing to note is that the node is running. If the render nodes still repeat the line "Can't open job file" after you have initialized ScreamerNet, then they can't find the command folder. Close them down and check the path in the script to the command folder. Make sure it's visible on the network.

Returning to the master machine, run the version of LightWave that uses the configuration files in config_screamernet and bring up the Network Rendering panel (see Figure 21.44).

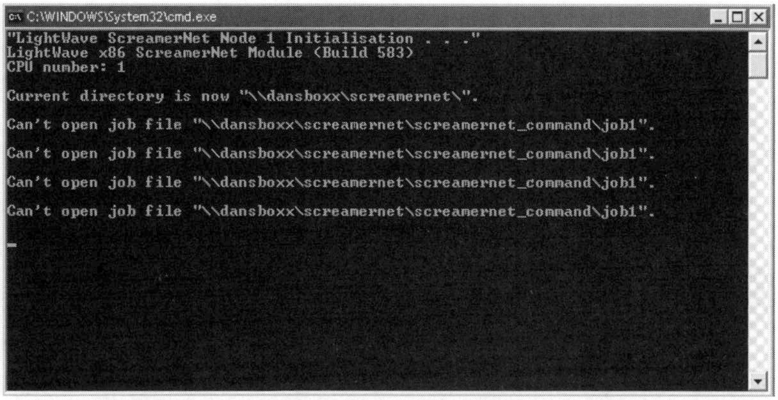

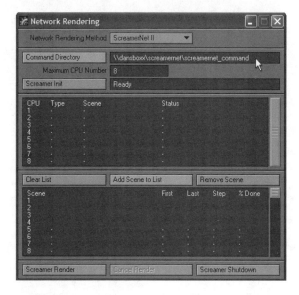

Figure 21.43   The node complains that it can't open a job file.

Figure 21.44   LightWave's Network Rendering panel.

The box called Maximum CPU Number requires you to enter the number of the highest numbered node you have set up on your network. Here, there are 8 nodes, numbered 1 through 8, but you should put in the highest number of nodes you might have, such as 3. Nodes can be numbered from 1 to 1000; they don't even have to be in sequence. You could have nodes 1, 7, and 68 running, but if you do this, you would have to put 68 as your maximum CPU number, not 3 as you might think.

Now click the Screamer Init button. ScreamerNet checks for nodes that are sitting there complaining about job files! If successful, you are told how many CPUs (or render nodes) it has found. If the number isn't correct, then check the job/ack numbering in the render script files and try again. If no CPUs are found, check that the nodes and Network Rendering panel are both looking for the same command folder, which should be visible on the network. Also check that all machines have access rights to read/write to that folder.

If everything has gone well, the nodes should now be happily repeating, as in Figure 21.45.

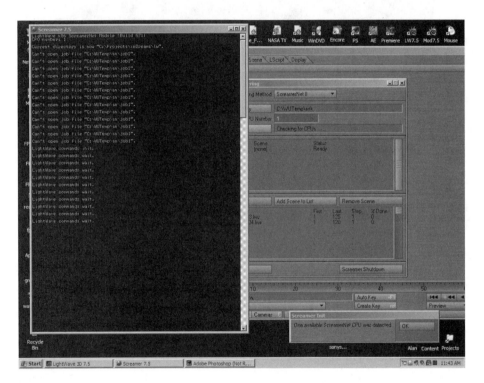

Figure 21.45 Here is what the LWSN.exe output looks like if all goes well.

This means they have successfully found a job file with a command inside saying "wait there and do nothing!"

All that's left to do now is to fill the Network Rendering panel with scenes, click render, and watch it fly! So click the Add Scenes button and browse to the projects you want to render. After you've added them all, you can click the button you have been waiting to click for awhile now—Screamer Render (see Figure 21.46)!

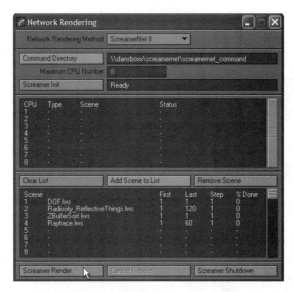

Figure 21.46   When rendering, LightWave's Network Rendering panel displays the current status.

The panel tells you what's going on as it goes, such as which node is rendering which frame and how far through the rendering it is.

When all the frames have rendered, the render nodes sit there repeating the "LightWave command: wait" line. At this point, you can click the Screamer Shutdown button. This closes all the node windows. You should now have lots of frames in the save folder you specified earlier, ready for building into an animation.

Batch Rendering on One Machine

As mentioned in the early pages of this tutorial, ScreamerNet is also useful for batch rendering on one machine. You may find this to be more valuable than networking multiple computers. This is for users who don't have a network but who need to render multiple scenes. This is extremely helpful for, say, rendering multiple camera angles or rendering multiple scenes over a long weekend. Maximize that time!

The good news is the process is no different from rendering with 1,000 computers. There is no bad news!

The overview of the folder structure for a batch render would look like that shown in Figure 21.47.

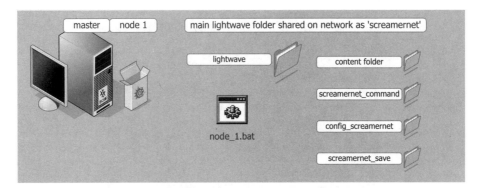

Figure 21.47   For batch rendering on a single machine, the node setup should look like this.

This setup assumes that all your content files are located in the main LightWave folder, that you copied all your config files to the new folder config_lightwave, and that you set the LightWave shortcut to point to that folder.

The only difference between batch rendering on one machine and network rendering is that all the pathnames to the config, content, and command folders can be local. You don't need to rescan your plug-ins, either, because they are already set up for normal LightWave use.

Setting Up Batch Rendering on One Machine

Before attempting this, it is probably a good idea to read all the previous material in this chapter (if you haven't already) so that you are familiar with the terminology and concepts. We're mentioning this just in case you've nipped straight to this section!

 Important

> When batch rendering on a single machine, be sure that each scene file knows where the objects are located and that the objects know where the texture maps are located. This is one area where a proper content directory is crucial. Another important issue is to set up so that your scenes will save files. Do this from the Render Options panel and then save the scene. When ScreamerNet calls up the scene to render, it will know where to save the rendered images.

If you haven't already created the folders screamer_command and screamer_save, do so now. Then create a batch file (node1) with the following text (replacing *c:\lightwave\ programs* with the path to your LightWave installation):

```
@echo OFF
echo "LightWave ScreamerNet Node 1 Initialisation . . ."

cd c:\lightwave\programs\

LWSN -2 -cc:\lightwave\programs\config_lightwave -dc:\lightwave
c:\lightwave\screamer_command\job1 c:\lightwave\screamer_command\ack1
```

Load the scene files you want to render, set the Save RGB path to screamer_save (assuming you want to save them there), and then save the scene.

Now go through the process described in the section "Rendering Using ScreamerNet," which is essentially starting the render batch file. Then, in the Network Rendering panel in LightWave Layout, set the Max CPU Number to 1, press the Screamer Init button, add the scenes for rendering, and click the Screamer Render button.

Setting Up Multi-Processor Machines

If you have multiprocessor machines available on your network or if you want to batch render on one multiprocessor machine, the process is the same and very simple!

All you have to do is treat each processor as a separate render node. We know that each render node has a batch script file that is run to identify that it is render node "X." So if a machine has more than one processor, it simply has more than one batch script but with different job/ack numbers. An overview of the setup for a batch render on a multiprocessor machine would look like what is shown in Figure 21.48.

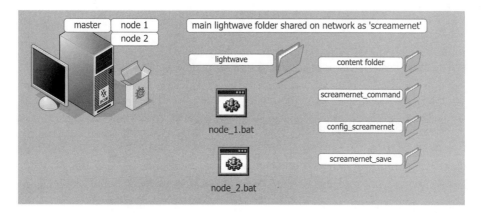

Figure 21.48   A batch render for dual processors would look something like this.

Figure 21.49 shows what the setup for a network render involving multiprocessor machines would look like.

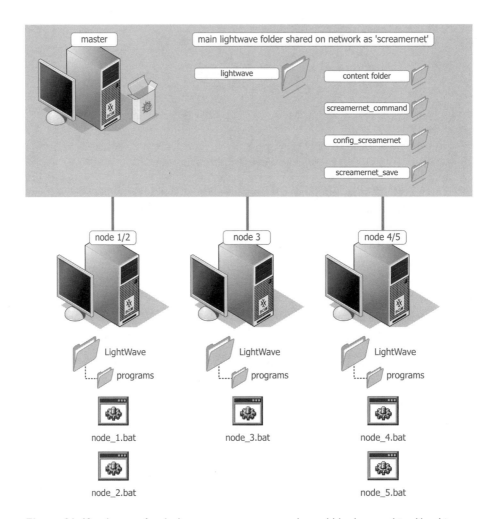

Figure 21.49   A setup for dual processors on a network would look something like this.

Troubleshooting and Limitations

Hopefully everything is running smoothly (if not, reread sections that don't click until they do; it's the only way!), but problems can occur, usually because something is set up incorrectly. Some of the main problems that might arise are listed in this section along with possible remedies.

Plug-In Problems and Limitations

The biggest limitation of ScreamerNet is that of plug-ins that are not written to take advantage of it. To date, there is no definitive list of all the ones that do and don't work. If in doubt, read the documentation that came with the plug-in; it should say whether it has problems. If it doesn't say, but the plug-in still does not seem to be working, rescan your plug-ins to update the LWEXT8.cfg file. If it still doesn't work, then chances are it's not compatible with ScreamerNet.

If your scene uses procedural textures (fractal noise and so on), you might experience differences in the pattern if you render on machines with different processors. Mixing old and new processors or different brands, such as AMD and Intel, could lead to problems. This is really only a problem with animations because textures can suddenly change from frame to frame. If in doubt, run a test or use only computers with the same processor type.

Another known problem with ScreamerNet (corrected as of v7.5c of LightWave) is its dislike for scenes that have had Spreadsheet used on them. Plug-ins like Spreadsheet save data to the scene file, which causes ScreamerNet to hang. The only way around this is to remove the entry in the scene file made by Spreadsheet.

Scene files are just text files; if you force-load a scene file into a plain text editor, you can read it!

Near the top, you will find an entry that says:

```
Plugin MasterHandler 1 .SpreadsheetStandardBanks
```

followed by:

```
EndPlugin
```

There will be another entry right after that entry that starts with:

```
Plugin MasterHandler 2 SpreadsheetSceneManager
```

If you scroll down, there will be another:

```
EndPlugin
```

Highlight all the text between the first `Plugin MasterHandler` and the last `EndPlugin`, delete it, and then save the file. It should now render without problems.

Other Common Problems

This section covers other problems that you might run into and offers solutions for each.

Problem:

"My nodes can't find the job files."

Possible solution:

The nodes can't find the job files because they can't see the command folder. The command folder holds the job files, so open up the batch file and check the script lines that end in "job" and "ack." Make sure that the pathname before these words points to your command folder. Also check that all the render node computers have access to read and write to the folder.

Problem:

"My nodes seem fine, but when I press Screamer Init, it can't find any CPUs."

Possible solution:

Again this is a command folder problem; check that the Network Rendering panel has the same command directory path set that the nodes are pointing to. Also check that the master computer has access to read and write to the folder.

Problem:

"Rendering seems to be working, but no files are saved."

Possible solution:

First, make sure your scene file is saving RGB files and not an animation (.MOV, .AVI and so on) in the Output tab of the Render Options panel. ScreamerNet can only save RGB image sequences.

Next, check that your plug-ins file (LWEXT8.cfg) is up-to-date by rescanning your plug-ins using the pathname all the nodes use to find them on the network.

Finally, check that the render batch files are looking in the correct place for the config files and that they can access the folder on the network.

Problem:

"Rendering seems to work okay, but all my saved files are in .FLX format."

Possible solution:

There are two possible reasons. The first is that ScreamerNet can't find the plug-in to save in the format you've specified, so check that your plug-ins file (LWEXT8.cfg) is up-to-date by rescanning your plug-ins using the pathname all the nodes use to find them on the network. Also, check that the render batch files are looking in the correct place for the config files and that they can access the folder on the network.

The second reason is that the render node that saved the file ran out of memory to load the saver plug-in, so ScreamerNet used the last-resort, built-in FLX saver.

To convert them, you can use LightWave as a converter; load the FLX images into LightWave using the Images panel, highlight the image in question, and double-click the preview to open it up in the image view. Now you can save in the format you need.

Problem:

"My particles aren't working."

Possible solution:

ScreamerNet can have problems with particle FX. The best way to address this is to save the particle FX calculation to disk (as a .PFX file) in the folder with the scene file.

Problem:

"Dynamics aren't working."

Possible solution:

ScreamerNet might have problems with certain dynamics. The best way to address this is to save the dynamics calculation to disk from the File tab within the Dynamics tab under the Object Properties folder. Save this in the folder with the scene file.

The Next Step

As you've seen, LightWave has plenty of rendering power. These examples can help you maximize your use of your computer and network, as well as your time. There's not much more to it, other than using moving images rather than stills. Use programs like NewTek's VT3, Eyeon's Digital Fusion, or Adobe's After Effects for compositing final rendered images, and make your work really stand out!

Plug-Ins and Technical Reference

LightWave 8's architecture is built around plug-ins. It would be cool if there was a book covering just the plug-ins, because there are so many. Add to that the crazy amount of third-party plug-ins available to you—some for purchase, many for free—and you can be in plug-in heaven. You've used LightWave plug-ins throughout the book already! Many of the tools and commands used, such as Super Script in Modeler or IK Boost Tool in Layout, are plug-ins! This appendix will give you a better understanding of where the plug-ins are located and how to work with them.

Plug-in Categories

You'll find plug-ins throughout LightWave Modeler and Layout. These plug-ins are necessary and have various purposes. They are divided into the following categories:

- **Animation I/O.** Plug-ins used for input and output.

- **Animation UV.** Plug-ins used for animated UV maps.

- **Channel Filter.** Plug-ins that perform direct control over channels, such as expressions and Motion Mixer.

- **Custom Object.** Plug-ins that are used for object control, such as particle effects.

- **Displacement.** Plug-ins that can shape and deform objects, be it points or polygons.

- **Environment.** Plug-ins that add functionality to Layout environment variables such as SkyTracer2.

- **Frame Buffer.** Plug-ins used for certain types of render display, such as the new DV View, found within the Render Options.

- **Global.** Plug-ins that look at the entire scene, such as the Spreadsheet Scene Manager.

- **Image I/O.** Plug-ins for loading and saving images. Generally, you won't access these plug-ins directly, but you'll use their functions when loading or saving in both Layout and Modeler.

- **Image Processing.** Plug-ins that control the various image-related functions, such as pixel calculations for SasLite for fur and Image Filters for things like Bloom and Corona.

- **Modeling.** Plug-ins and tools used throughout LightWave Modeler.

- **Layout Command.** Plug-ins that are used in Layout to control the interaction of other plug-ins that use representation in Layout.

- **Layout Tool.** Plug-ins used for specific Layout tools, such as Bone Twist, Bone Scale Hierarchy, IK Boost Tool, Sliders, and more.

- **Motion.** Plug-ins for various motion operations, such as Jolt! or Gravity.

- **Object Importer.** Plug-ins for importing object formats other than just LightWave.

- **Object Replacement.** Plug-ins used to replace objects during the course of an animation.

- **Rendering.** Plug-ins used for textures and shaders.

- **Scene Master.** Plug-ins for various scene-related functions, like Proxy Pic for item selection.

- **Volumetric Effect.** Plug-ins that are good for things like ground fog.

Where to Find LightWave's Plug-Ins

In Layout, finding the various plug-ins is easier than it is in Modeler. Modeler's plug-ins are accessible usually via a button added within the interface, or a selection in a list. In Layout, most plug-ins can be accessed from the various areas throughout the program. Those areas are as follows:

- Object Properties panel, for Custom Object plug-ins and Displacement Map plug-ins.

- Motion Options panel, for a selected item's motion plug-ins.

- Effects panel, which is home to the plug-ins for the Environment (Backdrop tab), Volumetrics (Volumetrics tab), and Pixel Filter and Image Filter plug-ins (Processing tab).

- Graph Editor, under the Modifiers tab for plug-ins like Oscillator.

- Master plug-in list, found under the Utilities tab.

- Additional, which is a drop-down list found within the Utilities tab. These plug-ins range from basic system tools to key functions to third-party plug-ins.

Loading Plug-Ins

When you install LightWave, your plug-ins are already loaded for you. However, there may come a time when you might want to reload certain plug-ins or add third-party plug-ins. You can do this through LightWave or Modeler, regardless of the plug-in. The information within the plug-in file is read by LightWave, and it is installed in the proper place to one of the areas in the preceding list.

Loading plug-ins is very easy, and only needs to be done one time. LightWave writes the information to a configuration file when you close the programs. In Layout, you can click to the Utilities tab, and you'll find a Plugins category. There, you can access various plug-in commands such as Add Plug-ins, Edit Plug-ins, Flush Plug-ins, Last Plug-in, Master Plug-in, or select from the Additional list. Figure A.1 shows the Plugins category within the Utilities tab in Layout. Figure A.2 shows the Plug-ins category within the Utilities tab in Modeler.

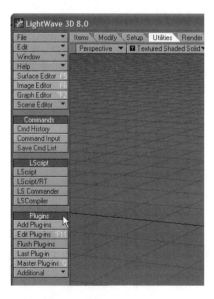

Figure A.1   Plug-in options and controls in Layout are accessible from within the Utilities tab.

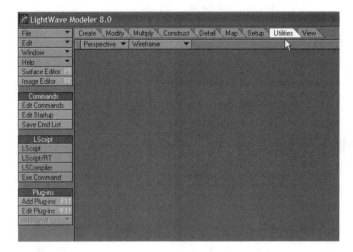

Figure A.2   Plug-in options and controls in Modeler are also accessible from within the Utilities tab.

The easiest way to add plug-ins in LightWave is to use the Edit Plug-ins panel and select Scan Directory. Click this, and point your system to the Plug-Ins folder. Select OK, and in a moment, a small dialog box appears telling you how many plug-ins were added, as in Figure A.3.

Figure A.3   The Scan Directory option in the Edit Plug-ins panel allows you to load all plug-ins in one click for both Layout and Modeler.

Clicking OK displays the plug-ins loaded, as in Figure A.4.

To add more than one plug-in, you can use the Scan Directory option. To add just a single plug-in file, click Add Plug-ins, point your system to the plug-in, and click OK. You can also delete or rename plug-ins in the Edit Plug-in panel. Image Filters are available in the Effects panel, as well as the Image Editor, and so on. Other plug-ins, however, are only available in specific locations, such as Pixel Filter, or Modeler plug-ins. You'll also notice that plug-ins vary in name, based on their usage, such as a modifier, tool, command, or generic plug-in.

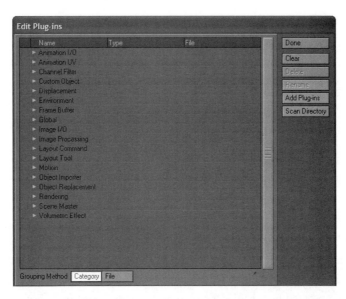

Figure A.4   When loaded, the plug-ins are displayed within their appropriate groupings.
Notice that Modeler is not listed here, as these are all Layout or Global plug-ins.

LScripts

LScripts, LightWave's custom scripting language, are also loaded as plug-ins, although they are slightly different. If you have an LScript you've written or have one compiled from a third-party source, you can load it the same way you do a regular plug-in. Select Add Plug-in, and then select the LScript. Certain plug-ins such as LScript are available in more than one location.

Learn Your Tools

LightWave's Layout and Modeler are extremely powerful creation tools. The tools within LightWave require a lot of time and experimentation. Hopefully, the information in this book has given you a good indication of what can be accomplished. There's nothing better than knowing the tools you have available to you. To expand even further on the powerful plug-ins throughout LightWave, here are a few more references for you when creating surfaces and rendering.

Technical Reference

This section of the appendix consists of various charts and tables that come in handy when you're trying to find that particular property or specification that you swore you knew but just can't seem to remember. It consists of the following:

- RGB color values
- Reflection properties
- Refraction properties
- Color temperatures of light
- Film output resolutions
- Video output resolutions

It can't be stressed enough that the following information should be used as a guideline only! The scientific world routinely deals in absolutes. However, animators do not. The information presented here should be used as a starting point only. Feel free to adjust anything as necessary to achieve the look you are going for. Don't worry that your diamond doesn't have the exact refraction value of a real diamond. If it looks better tweaked higher or lower, do it! If your banana looks kind of funky with the "proper" banana color, change it! There are no hard and fast rules, and in the end, the only thing that really matters is that you and your client are happy with the end result.

RGB Color Values

In Table A.1, we provide a good mix of various RGB color values. The diffusion value and lighting scheme you use in a particular scene can have a pronounced effect on the visible color of an object, so keep that in mind. Also, there are very few things in this world that have a 100% diffusion value. For most objects, except metals, 70% to 80% is a good starting point if you don't know an object's diffusion value.

Table A.1   RGB Color Values for Common Colors

Base Color	R	G	B
Black, True	0	0	0
Base Color: Blue			
Blue, Cobalt	61	90	170
Blue, Dodger	30	144	255
Blue, Indigo	8	46	84
Blue, Manganese	3	168	158
Blue, Midnight	25	25	112

Base Color	R	G	B
Blue, Navy	0	0	128
Blue, Pastel	131	147	202
Blue, Peacock	50	160	200
Blue, Powder	176	224	230
Blue, Royal	65	105	225
Blue, Slate	106	90	205
Blue, Sky	135	206	235
Blue, Steel	70	130	180
Blue, True	0	0	255
Blue, Turquoise	0	200	140
Blue, Ultramarine	20	10	143
Base Color: Brown			
Brown, Beige	163	148	128
Brown, Burnt Sienna	138	54	15
Brown, Burnt Umber	138	51	36
Brown, Chocolate	210	105	30
Brown, Flesh	255	125	64
Brown, Khaki	240	230	140
Brown, Raw Sienna	199	97	20
Brown, Raw Umber	115	74	18
Brown, Rosy	188	143	143
Brown, Saddle	139	69	19
Brown, Sandy	244	164	96
Brown, Sepia	94	38	18
Brown, Sienna	160	82	45
Brown, Tan	210	180	140
Brown, True	128	42	42
Base Color: Cyan			
Cyan, Aquamarine	127	255	212
Cyan, Pastel	109	207	246
Cyan, True	0	255	255
Cyan, Turquoise	64	224	208
Base Color: Green			
Green, Chartreuse	127	255	0
Green, Cobalt	61	145	64
Green, Emerald	0	201	87
Green, Forest	34	139	34
Green, Lawn	124	252	0
Green, Lime	50	205	50

continues ▶

Table A.1   Continued

Base Color	R	G	B
Green, Mint	189	252	200
Green, Olive Drab	107	142	35
Green, Pastel	130	202	156
Green, Sap	48	128	20
Green, Sea	45	140	87
Green, Spring	0	255	127
Green, Terre Verde	56	94	15
Green, True	0	255	0
Base Color: Grey			
Grey, Cold	128	138	135
Grey, Slate	112	128	144
Grey, True, Medium	128	128	128
Grey, Warm	128	128	105
Base Color: Magenta			
Magenta, Blue	138	43	226
Magenta, Orchid	218	112	214
Magenta, Pastel	244	154	193
Magenta, Plum	221	160	221
Magenta, Purple	160	32	240
Magenta, True	255	0	255
Magenta, Violet	143	94	153
Base Color: Orange			
Orange, Cadmium	255	97	3
Orange, Carrot	237	145	33
Orange, Red	255	69	0
Orange, True	255	128	0
Base Color: Red			
Red, Brick	156	102	31
Red, Cadmium	227	23	13
Red, Coral	255	127	80
Red, Firebrick	178	34	34
Red, Indian	176	23	31
Red, Maroon	176	48	96
Red, Pastel	246	150	121
Red, Pink	255	192	203
Red, Raspberry	135	38	87
Red, Salmon	250	128	114
Red, Tomato	255	99	71
Red, True	255	0	0

Base Color	R	G	B
Base Color: White			
White, Antique	250	235	215
White, Azure	240	255	255
White, Bisque	255	228	196
White, Blanch	255	235	205
White, Corn silk	255	248	220
White, Eggshell	252	230	201
White, Floral	255	250	240
White, Gainesboro	220	220	220
White, Ghost	248	248	255
White, Honeydew	240	255	240
White, Ivory	255	255	240
White, Linen	250	240	230
White, Navajo	255	222	173
White, Old lace	253	245	230
White, Seashell	255	245	238
White, Smoke	245	245	245
White, Snow	255	250	250
White, True (White is all colors combined!)	255	255	255
White, Wheat	245	222	179
Base Color: Yellow			
Yellow, Banana	227	207	87
Yellow, Cadmium	255	153	18
Yellow, Gold	255	215	0
Yellow, Goldenrod	218	165	32
Yellow, Melon	227	255	0
Yellow, Pastel	255	247	153
Yellow, Orange	247	148	29
Yellow, True	255	255	0
Metals			
Aluminum	220	223	227
Brass	191	173	111
Copper	186	110	64
Gold	218	178	115
Graphite	87	33	77
Iron	115	115	120
Silver	230	230	215
Stainless Steel	125	125	120

Reflection Properties

Table A.2 presents a good mix of materials and their basic reflective properties. There are many factors that affect an item's reflectivity, so use these values as a starting point.

Table A.2   Percentage of Incident Light Reflected by Various Materials

Material	%
Aluminum	45
Aluminum Foil	65
Asphalt	14
Brass	40
Brick	30
Bronze	10
Chrome	70
Copper	71
Earth, Moist	08
Gold	84
Graphite	20
Green Leaf	21
Iron	15
Linen	81
Marble, White	53
Mercury	69
Paper, Newsprint	61
Paper, White	71
Pewter	20
Platinum	64
Porcelain, White	72
Quartz	81
Rubber	02
Silicon	28
Silver	90
Slate	06
Stainless Steel	37
Steel	55
Tin Can	40
Vinyl	15
Wood, Pine	40

Refraction Properties

Table A.3 provides a rather extensive list of items. Chances are you won't need most of them until someone comes along from a scientific institution wanting work done that has to be scientifically accurate. You'll be glad you have it then!

Indices of refraction for various elements, materials, liquids, and gases at STP (Standard Temperature and Pressure) in visible light are listed.

Table A.3   Indices of Refraction

Material	Index
Vacuum	1.000 (Exactly)
Acetone	1.360
Actinolite	1.618
Agalmatoite	1.550
Agate	1.544
Agate, Moss	1.540
Air	1.000
Alcohol	1.329
Alexandrite	1.745
Aluminum	1.440
Amber	1.546
Amblygonite	1.611
Amethyst	1.544
Amorphous Selenium	2.920
Anatase	2.490
Andalusite	1.641
Anhydrite	1.571
Apatite	1.632
Apophyllite	1.536
Aquamarine	1.577
Aragonite	1.530
Argon	1.000
Asphalt	1.635
Augelite	1.574
Axinite	1.675
Azurite	1.730
Barite	1.636
Barytocalcite	1.684
Benitoite	1.757
Benzene	1.501
Beryl	1.577

continues ▶

Table A.3 Continued

Material	Index
Beryllonite	1.553
Brazilianite	1.603
Bromine (liquid)	1.661
Bronze	1.180
Brownite	1.567
Calcite	1.486
Calspar1	1.660
Calspar2	1.486
Cancrinite	1.491
Carbon Dioxide (gas)	1.000
Carbon Dioxide (liquid)	1.200
Carbon Disulfide	1.628
Carbon Tetrachloride	1.460
Cassiterite	1.997
Celestite	1.622
Cerussite	1.804
Ceylanite	1.770
Chalcedony	1.530
Chalk	1.510
Chalybite	1.630
Chlorine (gas)	1.000
Chlorine (liquid)	1.385
Chrome Green	2.400
Chrome Red	2.420
Chrome Yellow	2.310
Chromium	2.970
Chromium Oxide	2.705
Chrysoberyl	1.745
Chrysocolla	1.500
Chrysoprase	1.534
Citrine	1.550
Clinozoisite	1.724
Cobalt Blue	1.740
Cobalt Green	1.970
Cobalt Violet	1.710
Colemanite	1.586
Copper	1.100
Copper Oxide	2.705
Coral	1.486

Material	Index
Cordierite	1.540
Corundum	1.766
Crocoite	2.310
Crown Glass	1.520
Crystal	2.000
Cuprite	2.850
Danburite	1.633
Diamond	2.417
Diopside	1.680
Dolomite	1.503
Dumortierite	1.686
Ebonite	1.660
Ekanite	1.600
Elaeolite	1.532
Emerald	1.576
Emerald, Synth flux	1.561
Emerald, Synth hydro	1.568
Enstatite	1.663
Epidote	1.733
Ethyl Alcohol (Ethanol)	1.360
Euclase	1.652
Fabulite	2.409
Feldspar, Adventurine	1.532
Feldspar, Albite	1.525
Feldspar, Amazonite	1.525
Feldspar, Labradorite	1.565
Feldspar, Microcline	1.525
Feldspar, Oligoclase	1.539
Feldspar, Orthoclase	1.525
Fluoride	1.560
Fluorite	1.434
Formica	1.470
Garnet, Almandine	1.760
Garnet, Almandite	1.790
Garnet, Andradite	1.820
Garnet, Demantoid	1.880
Garnet, Grossular	1.738
Garnet, Hessonite	1.745
Garnet, Rhodolite	1.760
Garnet, Spessartite	1.810
Gaylussite	1.517

continues ▶

Table A.3   Continued

Material	Index
Glass	1.517
Glass, Albite	1.489
Glass, Crown	1.520
Glass, Crown, Zinc	1.517
Glass, Flint, Dense	1.660
Glass, Flint, Heaviest	1.890
Glass, Flint, Heavy	1.655
Glass, Flint, Lanthanum	1.800
Glass, Flint, Light	1.580
Glass, Flint, Medium	1.627
Glycerine	1.473
Gold	0.470
Hambergite	1.559
Hauynite	1.502
Helium	1.000
Hematite	2.940
Hemimorphite	1.614
Hiddenite	1.655
Howlite	1.586
Hydrogen (gas)	1.000
Hydrogen (liquid)	1.097
Hypersthene	1.670
Ice	1.309
Idocrase	1.713
Iodine Crystal	3.340
Iolite	1.548
Iron	1.510
Ivory	1.540
Jade, Nephrite	1.610
Jadeite	1.665
Jasper	1.540
Jet	1.660
Kornerupine	1.665
Kunzite	1.655
Kyanite	1.715
Lapis Gem	1.500
Lapis Lazuli	1.610
Lazulite	1.615
Lead	2.010
Leucite	1.509

Material	Index
Magnesite	1.515
Malachite	1.655
Meerschaum	1.530
Mercury (liquid)	1.620
Methanol	1.329
Moldavite	1.500
Moonstone, Adularia	1.525
Moonstone, Albite	1.535
Natrolite	1.480
Nephrite	1.600
Nitrogen (gas)	1.000
Nitrogen (liquid)	1.205
Nylon	1.530
Obsidian	1.489
Olivine	1.670
Onyx	1.486
Opal	1.450
Oxygen (gas)	1.000
Oxygen (liquid)	1.221
Painite	1.787
Pearl	1.530
Periclase	1.740
Peridot	1.654
Peristerite	1.525
Petalite	1.502
Phenakite	1.650
Phosgenite	2.117
Plastic	1.460
Plexiglass	1.500
Polystyrene	1.550
Prase	1.540
Prasiolite	1.540
Prehnite	1.610
Proustite	2.790
Purpurite	1.840
Pyrite	1.810
Pyrope	1.740
Quartz	1.544
Quartz, Fused	1.458
Rhodizite	1.690
Rhodochrisite	1.600

continues ▶

Table A.3   Continued

Material	Index
Rhodonite	1.735
Rock Salt	1.544
Rubber, Natural	1.519
Ruby	1.760
Rutile	2.610
Sanidine	1.522
Sapphire	1.760
Scapolite	1.540
Scapolite, Yellow	1.555
Scheelite	1.920
Selenium, Amorphous	2.920
Serpentine	1.560
Shell	1.530
Silicon	4.240
Sillimanite	1.658
Silver	0.180
Sinhalite	1.699
Smaragdite	1.608
Smithsonite	1.621
Sodalite	1.483
Sodium Chloride	1.544
Sphalerite	2.368
Sphene	1.885
Spinel	1.712
Spodumene	1.650
Staurolite	1.739
Steatite	1.539
Steel	2.500
Stichtite	1.520
Strontium Titanate	2.410
Styrofoam	1.595
Sugar Solution (30%)	1.380
Sugar Solution (80%)	1.490
Sulphur	1.960
Synthetic Spinel	1.730
Taaffeite	1.720
Tantalite	2.240
Tanzanite	1.691
Teflon	1.350

Material	Index
Thomsonite	1.530
Tiger eye	1.544
Topaz	1.620
Topaz, Blue	1.610
Topaz, Pink	1.620
Topaz, White	1.630
Topaz, Yellow	1.620
Tourmaline	1.624
Tremolite	1.600
Tugtupite	1.496
Turpentine	1.472
Turquoise	1.610
Ulexite	1.490
Uvarovite	1.870
Variscite	1.550
Vivianite	1.580
Wardite	1.590
Water (gas)	1.000
Water 100°C	1.318
Water 20°C	1.333
Water 35°C (room temperature)	1.331
Willemite	1.690
Witherite	1.532
Wulfenite	2.300
Zinc Crown Glass	1.517
Zincite	2.010
Zircon, High	1.960
Zircon, Low	1.800
Zirconia, Cubic	2.170

Color Temperatures of Light

The color temperature of light is the temperature to which you would have to heat an object (a black body) to produce light of similar spectral characteristics. Low color temperatures produce warmer (yellow/red) light, whereas higher temperatures produce colder (bluer) light.

The color of light is measured in Kelvins. LightWave has a handy Kelvin scale on its color picker, which makes it easy to plug in these values when you want an accurate starting point. For example, if you want to light your gunfight scene from High Noon, you would select a starting temperature of 6000 to 6500 degrees Kelvin (noontime) for your skylight and adjust from there. Table A.4 presents various temperatures and the type of light they represent.

Table A.4   Kelvin Temperatures for Various Light Sources

Temperature	Light Source
1400-1930	Candlelight
2000-2500	Sunrise
2680	40W incandescent lamp
2800-2850	100W household (tungsten) bulb
2950	500W tungsten lamp
2960-3200	Tungsten studio lamp
3000	Fluorescent light (warm white)
	200W incandescent lamp
	1000W tungsten lamp
3200	Halogen bulb, Nitraphot B
3400	Photoflood (floodlamp)
	Halogen bulb, Nitraphot A
3800-4000	Clear flashbulb
4000	Moonlight
4400	Sun two hours after rising
5000	Fluorescent light
5000-6000	Daylight sun at midday to noon
5500	Daylight (for photography)
	Electronic flash tube
5500-6000	Blue flashbulb
6000-7000	Electronic flash
6500	Daylight (sun and sky averaged)
7000	Overcast sky
8000	Cloudy sky, light shade
9000	Hazy sky, light shade
11000	Sky light without direct sun
13000	Blue sky, thin white clouds
16000	Average blue sky, medium shade
18000-19000	Clear blue sky, deep shade

Film Output Resolutions

Table A.5 represents the most common resolutions you are likely to run into when working with film. These numbers are not absolute, however. There are many factors that could change the final output resolution. The second rows under some of the formats represent alternate resolutions asked for by some postproduction facilities. Some facilities may also ask for rendered output resolutions not on this chart. It all depends on the particular needs of the project.

Video Output Resolutions

Table A.6 represents the most common video and computer resolutions for working with video. Although NTSC and PAL are interlaced formats, it is a common practice today to render final output as frames rather than fields. It should also be noted that HDTV formats are still far from being standardized across various industries. Always find out from your clients which format they are using.

Table A.5 Common Film Resolutions

Film Resolutions	Image Aspect	Pixel Aspect	<1K	1K	1.5K	2K	4K
35mm Full Aperture	1.33	1.00	768×576 1024×778	1024×768 1556×1182	1536×1152 2048×1556	2048×1536 4096×3112	4096×3072
35mm Academy	1.37	1.00 914×666		1024×747 1536×1119	1556×1134 1828×1332	2048×1494 3656×2664	4096×2987
35mm Academy Projection	1.66	1.00	512×307 914×551	1024×614	1536×921 1556×938	2048×1229 1828×1102	4096×2458 3656×2202
35mm 1.75:1	1.75	1.00	560×320	1120×640	1575×900	2048×1170	4096×2340
35mm 1.85:1	1.85	1.00	512×277	1024×554 914×494	1536×830 1556×841	2048×1107 1828×988	4096×2214 3656×1976
35mm 2.35:1	2.35	1.00	512×218	1024×436	1536×654	2048×871	4096×1743
35mm Anamorphic 2.35:1	2.35	2.00	512×436	1024×871	1536×1307	2048×1743	4096×3486
70mm Panavision	2.20	1.00	880×400	1024×465	1536×698	2048×931	4096×1862
Panavision	2.35	1.00			1536×653	2048×871 1828×777	4096×1742 3656×1555
70mm IMAX	1.36	1.00	512×375	1024×751	1536×1126	2048×1501	4096×3003
VistaVision	1.50	1.00	512×341	1024×683	1536×1024	2048×1365 1828×1219	4096×2731 3072×2048
Cinemascope	1.17	1.00		1024×872	1536×1307	2048×1743 1828×1556	4096×3487 3656×3112
Cinemascope	2.35	1.00			1536×653	2048×871 1828×777	4096×1742 3656×1555
35mm (24mm×36mm) slide	1.50	1.00	512×341	1024×683	1536×1024	2048×1365	4096×2731
6cm×6cm slide	1.00	1.00	512×512	1024×1024	1536×1536	2048×2048	4096×4096
4"×5" or 8"×10" slide	1.33	1.00	768×576	1024×768	1536×1152	2048×1536	4096×3072

Table A.6 Common Video and Computer Resolutions

Video Resolutions	Image Aspect	Pixel Aspect	Resolution	Frames/Sec.
D1 NTSC	1.33	0.90	720×486	30i
D1 NTSC Widescreen	1.78 (16:9)	1.20	720×486	30i
D2 NTSC	1.35	0.86	752×480	30i
D2 NTSC Widescreen	1.87	1.15	752×480	30i
D1 PAL	1.33	1.07	720×576	25i
D1 PAL Widescreen	1.78 (16:9)	1.42	720×576	25i
D2 PAL	1.33	1.02	752×576	25i
HDTV	16:9	1.00	1920×1080	60i;30p,24p
	16:9	1.00	1280×720	60p,30p,24p
	16:9 (4:3)	1.00	704×480	60p,60i,30p,24p
	4:3	1.00	640×480	60p,60i,30p,24p
VGA	1.33	1.00	640×480	
SVGA	1.33	1.00	800×600	
XGA	1.33	1.00	1024×768	
SXGA*	1.25	1.00	1280×1024	
SXGA	1.33	1.00	1280×960	
UXGA	1.33	1.00	1600×1200	

*Note: 1280X1024 should be avoided, as it is not the correct aspect ratio for video or computer monitors.

More References You Can Use

The tables listed here are tremendous assets when creating the various surfaces and resolutions available to you in LightWave. What makes them even better is they're already created for you! Be sure to head on over to www.3dgarage.com and get a free set of color value presets. Installation instructions are located with the presets file. These presets are ready to go, and after they are placed within your Preset folder in LightWave, you can instantly apply them to your object surfaces.

Create, practice, and enjoy!

Learning Resources and Web Links

OK, sure—we wanted to be the be-all end-all to LightWave learning, but that's not fair. Not fair to you, that is! There are so many resources out there, it'll make your head spin. Because of that, we've included a comprehensive list of other LightWave learning resources, as well as books and videos related to the art of 3D modeling and animation.

Reading References

Some might say that books are becoming a thing of the past, because of the Internet and various learning videos on the market. Not so! In fact, book production is higher than it ever has been! So here are some great books that you can use to help learn the art of 3D. There are so many out there, so search online, at your library, and at your local bookstore:

- Birn, Jeremy. *Digital Lighting & Rendering.* New Riders Publishing, 2000.

- Maestri, George. *Digital Character Animation.* New Riders Publishing, 1996.

- Ablan, Dan. *Digital Cinematography & Directing.* New Riders Publishing, 2003.

- Kerlow, Isaac V. *The Art of 3D: Computer Animation and Imaging,* Second Edition. John Wiley and Sons, 2000.

- White, Tony. *The Animators Workbook.* Watson-Guptill Publications, 1988.

- Lord, Peter. *Creating 3D Animation.* Harry N. Abrams Publisher, 1998.

- Thomas, Frank and Ollie Johnson. *The Illusion of Life: Disney Animation.* Hyperion Press, 1995.

- Culhane, Shamus. *Animation: From Script to Screen.* St. Martin's Press, 1990.

These are just a few books of interest, and there are more emerging every day. Browse online, read reviews, and check around to see who's used a book you're interested in. Get feedback and see if it's right for you. Often, one simple tip or idea is worth the price of a book alone, especially during a project! What's better, head on down to your local bookseller and browse the shelves yourself. Often getting your hands on a book before you buy it gives you the opportunity to review it and see if the info you need is in there.

Audio/Visual References

Like most people, you enjoy a good thick LightWave book. You can read it on the train, in bed, even while in the bathroom! But sometimes, you want to see something being done. You want to hear the click of the mouse. If that's the case, there are plenty of visual reference materials out there to help you learn LightWave, as well as many other applications. Below is a list of great learning resources:

- **3D Garage** (www.3dgarage.com) has become the number one site for visual LightWave learning. This CD-ROM based LightWave learning course comes direct from this book's author, Dan Ablan. It is a course that Dan has taught for years and updated for CD. It is a very high-quality, high-impact learning course. If you're a student or teacher looking to learn LightWave from the ground up, the Signature Courseware is for you. If you're looking to go further, to take that next step, the Advanced Courseware is for you. Additionally, module-based training is now available to learn the art of LightWave 8 Character Animation. Learn at your own pace and create it all. Visit the site for free downloads and examples.

- **Class On Demand** (www.classondemand.net) sells not only LightWave training videos and DVDs, but also Video Toaster, Speed Razor, and many others. If you're not looking for a course but rather an inexpensive spot tutorial, you've come to the right place. Visit the site to check out the full list of topics and check with your local reseller for pricing.

- **Desktop Images** (www.desktopimages.com) has been around for years, teaching cool LightWave techniques to students around the globe. Visit the site for updates and information on products.

- **Motion Blur Artwork** (www.mba-studios.de) sells LightWave training DVDs of excellent quality through Carnera 3D Seminars. Clear and concise, the tutorials are very complete.

Web Resources

Often the best place for information is right on your computer! The Internet is a terrific place where you'll find not only information on the latest version of LightWave but tutorials as well. While many tutorials need a little figuring out on your part, there are a ton of freebies that can help you pick up a quick tip or technique. Here is a list of just a few LightWave-related websites you can check out:

- **The History of LightWave** (http://personal.southern.edu/~dascott/ lwhistory/index.html#10). Have you ever wondered where LightWave came from? What it looked like in the beginning? It has come a long way. Check out this site for some great history lessons!

- **NewTek, Inc**. (www.newtek.com). Makers of LightWave, this is a great place to begin learning with many online tutorials, free of charge.

- **Scott Cameron's Website** (http://members.shaw.ca/lightwavetutorials/ Main_Menu.htm). Plenty of resources here.

- **Flay** (www.flay.com). Hands down, the single best online reference for LightWave, be it tutorials, plug-ins, and more.

- **3D Links** (www.3dlinks.com/tutorials_lightwave.cfm). Another user-based site that is a great resource.

- **LW HUB** (www.lwhub.com) is another terrific resource for LightWave tutorials and reference.

- **LightWave Oz** (www.lightwaveoz.org). Our friends from down under set up this killer LightWave resource page.

- **3D Palace** (www.3d-palace.com). This site includes information for LightWave and other applications.

- **3D Buzz** (www.3dbuzz.com) A leader in free 3D training, 3D Buzz offers LightWave tutorials, links, and references.

- **MD Arts** (www.md-arts.com). Simply a great LightWave tutorial page.
- **Creative Cow** (www.creativecow.net). The cow has forums set up where you can discuss LightWave and many other related applications. Find links to more information there.
- **LWG3D** (www.lwg3d.org). The LightWave Group is a cool site for forums, links, and tutorials.
- **Simply LightWave** (www.simplylightwave.com). What more can you say? Simply LightWave! Check it out for some great tutorials.
- **Dan Ablan** (www.danablan.com). The author's site for more links to LightWave information and training.

These are just a few sites, but a search on Google.com, Lycos.com, or Yahoo.com yields a plethora of wonderful resources. Some may or may not be helpful in your situation or project, but it doesn't hurt to check them out. You never know what you can pick up!

Be sure to also cruise the forums, which are great places to view, discuss, and critique 3D work. Try these:

- **NewTek Forums** (www.newtek.com)
- **CG Talk** (www.cgtalk.com)
- **3D World** (www.3dworld.com)
- **Safe Harbor** (www.toasternt.com)
- **The LightWave Group** (www.lwg3d.com)

And there is much more out there. Search, and you shall find. Happy learning!

Appendix C
What's on the DVD

The accompanying DVD is full of resources. It contains all the exercise files to help you work with this book and with LightWave 8. The following sections contain descriptions of the DVD's contents and how to use the content included for the tutorials in this book. In addition, exclusive video tutorials have been included just for this book direct from 3D Garage (www.3dgarage.com). These quick-start tutorials help you get up to speed quickly and easily with LightWave 8.

For specific information about the use of this DVD, please review the ReadMe.txt file in the DVD's root directory. This file includes important disclaimer information as well as information about installation, system requirements, troubleshooting, and technical support.

Technical Support Issues

If you have any difficulties with this DVD, please check out our tech support website at www.peachpit.com. Go to Customer Support and choose Contact Us then select Defective Products Support under Select Your Type of Question.

DVD Contents

We've literally packed the DVD with hours of video and cool resources to enhance your learning. On the DVD, you'll find:

- Hours of additional video tutorials to complement the chapters, exclusively from 3D Garage.com.

- High-quality color JPEGs of the book's screen grabs

- A bonus set of new and fantastic textures from Tom Marlin of Marlin Studios, makers of the popular Seamless Textures series

- A full working demo of Mimic2 for LightWave

- All the scene files for the book's projects and tutorials

- Over 1 gigabyte of textures and example HDR images from Industry Graphics, makers of realtexture.com.

- A full working demo of Wondertouch's Particle Illusion

- Demo products from TechSmith Corporation, allowing you to create your own screen grabs and video captures

- Royalty-free textures and backgrounds from 3D Garage.com.

Using the Video Files

In order to play the 3D Garage video tutorials supplied on the book's DVD, you'll need to install the proper codec. The videos have been recorded using TechSmith's Camtasia (http://techsmith.com/) and work on both PC and Mac. To play the video files on a PC, you'll need to install the TSCC codec. After you've installed the codec, be sure to restart your system. We recommend using the included Camtasia Player for optimal quality during playback. For Mac users, you'll need to install the EnSharpen decoder. This will allow you to play the same files back through QuickTime. And like the PC users, restart your system after installing the video files.

The video tutorials are supplements to the chapters, some of which coincide with the tutorials in the book and some that stand on their own. Be sure to check out all of them for additional tips and tricks.

For more video training and LightWave courseware, visit www.3dgarage.com.

System Requirements

This DVD was configured for use on systems running Windows NT Workstation, Windows 98, Windows 2000, Windows XP, and Macintosh OSX or OS9.

Loading the DVD Files

To load the files from the DVD, insert the disc into your DVD/CD-ROM drive. If auto-play is enabled on your machine, the DVD setup program starts automatically the first time you insert the disc. You can copy the files to your hard drive or use them right off the disc.

Important

This DVD uses long and mixed-case filenames, requiring the use of a protected mode CD-ROM driver.

Project Files

This DVD contains all the files you need to complete the exercises in *Inside LightWave 8*. These files can be found in the root directory's Projects folder. To properly access the project files, do the following:

1. In LightWave's Layout, press the O key to call up the General Options panel.

2. At the top of the panel, select the Content Directory button.

3. A system file dialog box titled Set Content Directory opens. Select your DVD/CD-ROM drive, go to the Projects folder, and click Open.

   If you'd like to use the files directly from your own hard drive, simply copy the Projects folder from the book's DVD to your drive.

4. Your Content Directory is now set for working through the exercises. The Content Directory path should look something like \X:\Projects\, where X is your DVD/CD-ROM drive.

When you select Load Scene, LightWave opens the Projects folder. There, you'll see folders named Scene, Objects, and Images. Within these folders are the individual chapter folders. Selecting Load Object within LightWave points to the Objects folder within the Projects folder.

Third-Party Programs

This DVD also contains several third-party files and demos from leading industry artists and companies. These programs have been carefully selected to help you strengthen your professional LightWave skills.

Please note that some of the programs included on this DVD are only demo versions. Please support these independent vendors by purchasing or registering any shareware software you use for more than 30 days. Check the documentation provided with the software on where and how to register the product.

Please view the Read-Me text file on the DVD for complete information on the free DVD third-party content.

We've worked hard to make sure the contents on this DVD are just as useful as this book. The combination of the two makes this a tremendous resource. Enjoy!

Index